Special Places to Stay

Fifth edition
Copyright © 2008 Alastair Sawday
Publishing Co. Ltd
Published in May 2008
ISBN-13: 978-1-906136-04-8

Alastair Sawday Publishing Co. Ltd,
The Old Farmyard, Yanley Lane,
Long Ashton, Bristol BS41 9LR, UK
Tel: +44 (0)1275 395430
Email: info@sawdays.co.uk
Web: www.sawdays.co.uk

The Globe Pequot Press,
P. O. Box 480, Guilford,
Connecticut 06437, USA
Tel: +1 203 458 4500
Email: info@globepequot.com
Web: www.globepequot.com

Series Editor Alastair Sawday
Editor David Hancock
Editorial Director Annie Shillito
Writing David Hancock, David Ashby,
Jo Boissevain, Nicola Crosse,
Alison Davison, Mark Taylor,
Glyn Williams, Mandy Wragg
Inspections David Hancock, David Ashby,
Colin Cheyne, Alison Davison,
Sarah Fergusson, Rebecca Harris,
Charles Edmondson-Jones, Mark Taylor,
Jenny White, Glyn Williams, Mandy Wragg
Accounts Bridget Bishop,
Rebecca Bebbington, Christine Buxton,
Sally Ranahan
Editorial Sue Bourner,
Rebecca Thomas, Jo Boissevain,
Nicola Crosse
Production Julia Richardson,
Rachel Coe, Tom Germain,
Anny Mortada
Sales & Marketing & PR
Rob Richardson,
Sarah Bolton, Thomas Caldwell,
Toby Sawday
Web & IT Joe Green,
Russell Wilkinson

Alastair Sawday has asserted his right to be
identified as the author of this work.

Responsible business: we are committed to being a green and socially responsible
business. Here are a few things we already do: our pool cars run on recycled cooking oil
and low-emission LPG; our award-winning eco-offices are equipped with solar-heated
water, wood-pellet heating, and rainwater-fed loos and showers; and we were the world's
first carbon-neutral publishing company. Find out more at www.sawdays.co.uk

Paper and print: we have sought the lowest possible ecological 'footprint' from the
production of this book. Whenever possible, we use paper that is either recycled (with a
high proportion of post-consumer waste) or FSC-certified, and give preference to local
companies in order to foster our local economy and reduce our carbon footprint. Our
printer is ISO 14001-registered.

*We have made every effort to ensure the accuracy of the information in this book at the time of going
to press. However, we cannot accept any responsibility for any loss, injury or inconvenience resulting
from the use of information contained therein.*

Alastair
Sawday's

Special Places

Pubs & Inns
of England & Wales

4 Contents

We are a small company, born in 1994 and growing slowly but surely every year – in 2007 we sold our millionth book. We have always published beautiful and immensely useful guide books, and we now also have a very successful website.

There are about 35 of us in the company, producing the website, about 20 guide books and a growing series of environmental books under the Fragile Earth imprint. We think a lot about how we do it, how we behave, what our 'culture' is, and we are trying to be a little more than 'just a publishing company'.

Environmental & ethical policies

We have always had strong environmental policies. Our books are printed by a British company that is ISO 14001 accredited, on recycled and/or FSC-certified paper, and we have been offsetting our carbon emissions since 2001. We now do so

through an Indian NGO, which means that our money goes a long way. However, we are under no illusions about carbon-offsetting: it is part of a strong package of green measures including running company cars on gas or recycled cooking oil; composting or recycling waste; encouraging cycling and car-sharing; only buying organic or local food; not accepting web links with companies we consider unethical; and banking with the ethical Triodos Bank.

In 2005 we won a Business Commitment to the Environment Award and in 2006 a Queen's Award for Enterprise in the Sustainable Development category. All this has boosted our resolve to promote our green policies.

Eco offices

In January 2006 we moved into our new eco offices. With super-insulation, under-floor heating, a wood-pellet boiler, solar panels and a rainwater tank, we have a working space kind to ourselves and to the environment. Lighting is low-energy, dark corners are lit by sun-pipes, materials are natural and one building is of green oak. The building is a delight to work in.

Ethics

We think that our role as a company is not much different from the role of those within it: to play our part in the community, to reduce our ecological footprint, to be a benign influence, to foster good human relationships and to make a positive difference to the world around us.

Another phrase for the simple intentions above is Corporate Responsibility. It is a much-used buzz phrase, but many of those adopting it as a policy are getting serious. A world-wide report by the think tank Tomorrow's Company has revealed quite how convinced the world's major companies are: convinced that if they do not take on full responsibility for their impact, social and environmental, they will not survive.

The books – and a dilemma

So, we have created popular books and a handsome website that do good work. We promote authenticity, individuality and good local and organic food – a far cry from corporate culture. Rural economies, pubs, small farms, villages and hamlets all benefit. However, people use fossil fuel to reach our special places. Should we aim to get our readers to offset their own carbon emissions, and the B&B and hotel owners too?

We are gradually introducing green ideas into the books: celebrating those who make an extra environmental effort; gently encouraging the use of public transport, cycling and walking.

In 2006 we published the very successful *Green Places to Stay*, focusing on responsible travel and eco-properties around the globe. Our aim is to be a pioneering green publisher, and to be known as one. We hope one day to offer energy audits to our owners, to provide real help to those who want to 'go green'. And we will continue to champion the small-scale. We will also continue to oppose policies that encourage the growth of air traffic – however contradictory that might seem.

Our Fragile Earth series

The 'hard' side of our environmental publishing is the Fragile Earth series: *The Little Earth Book*, *The Little Food Book* and *The Little Money Book*. We have also published *One Planet Living* with WWF. A flagship project is the *The Big Earth Book*; it is packed with information and a stimulating and provocative read.

Lastly – what is special?

The notion of 'special' is at the heart of what we do, and highly subjective. We discuss this at the front of every book. We take huge pleasure in finding people and places that do their own thing – brilliantly; places that are unusual and follow no trends; places of peace and beauty; people who are kind and interesting – and genuine.

We seem to have touched a nerve with hundreds of thousands of readers; they obviously long for the independence that our books provide, for the warm human contact of Special Places, and to be able to avoid the banality and ugliness of so many other places.

A night in a Special Place can be a transforming experience.

Alastair Sawday

Welcome to Edition 5 and another great Sawday selection. Nearly 900 of the best pubs in England and Wales, chosen because we believe them to be special and hope you will too.

What makes this collection stand out from the rest? Alastair Sawday's guides are about individuality, and our quest is to seek out the quirky, the unusual and the little-known. We look for that special something that draws you back time and again: it could be the short menu of earthy, rustic dishes, the real ales and the chalked-up wines, the welcoming

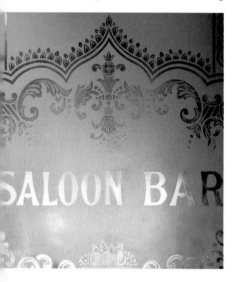

bedrooms, the cushioned settles, the riverside setting, the real fires. Certainly our inspectors appreciate a genuine welcome from hands-on publicans, a respect for local, seasonal or organic food, an enthusiastic staff, character and

charm. The result is 651 pubs and inns, nearly a quarter of which have rooms (and a full-page entry), and a further 234 pubs in our Worth a Visit sections.

What's new in this edition

Keeping pace with the fascinating and ever-evolving pub scene continues to be a challenge, with landlords changing, chefs moving on and the powerful pub companies swallowing up small (often excellent) freeholds. Some pubs have disappeared from the guide, others have been moved sideways to the Worth a Visit sections and await re-inspection, and 132 great new places have made it into the guide for the very first time.

Key to the survival of Britain's rural ale houses is the provision of good food — and, increasingly, bedrooms. Pubs are now seen as places to eat, drink and sleep. This growing trend is reflected in the increased number of pubs and inns wishing to include bedroom details in their entry — we now have 143 pubs with rooms. All have been inspected and found special, all have full-page entries.

In the Worth a Visit sections you will find top-flight pubs that have recently changed hands, pubs that we believe are on the up, and great little locals that didn't make a full entry but are still worth seeking out. Having been placed at the back of the guide in previous editions, the Worth a Visit pubs are now listed after each county. We look forward to your comments and feedback.

Photo left: Shepherd Neame
Photo right: The Pear Tree Inn, entry 726

The smoking ban

The single most important challenge that faced pubs in 2007 was the smoking ban. A good number of the foodie pubs listed in this guide went smoke-free well before the ban was imposed (in Wales, 2 April; in England, 1 July) and trade increased significantly because of it, with people choosing to eat in the (often livelier) bars rather than in the more formal dining areas. Pubs that are primarily drinking pubs are still adjusting to the change and some have suffered a drop in trade. However, many are upgrading their outdoor areas, providing heated awnings and shelters for dedicated smokers.

Pub or restaurant – a fine line

Too many pubs are losing sight of their pubby roots as cash tills tot up meals rather than pints of beer. If 90% of the tables are prepared for dining and covered in 'reserved' signs, if you are greeted with a menu and a "have you booked a table, sir", and if the bar is virtually devoid of ale handpumps, then your once-treasured boozer has morphed into a restaurant.

Choice and price of food is another determining factor. Some pubs now offer little in the way of bar snacks, with both lunch and dinner menus listing expensive main courses or set two- and three-course affairs. Prices are beginning to rise at an alarming pace, especially in the smarter dining pubs, where main courses often exceed £15 and side vegetables may be added as an extra. Yes, cooking standards in pubs have risen in recent years and a growing number of pubs are sourcing the best ingredients from the best producers, but this is no excuse for pubs to charge restaurant prices.

A pub is a pub when you find three or more (often local) real ales, a welcome for those popping in just for a pint, a menu that includes ploughman's or other old-fashioned pub classics, and an easy-going, convivial atmosphere.

'British rustic' cooking

From adventurous gastropubs to village locals, the liveliest pub kitchens are placing an emphasis on British tradition. So goodbye to Mediterranean and oriental cooking, hello to classic British dishes of low or 'rustic' origin (Lancashire hot-pot, ginger parkin).

SANDWICHES #
BAR SNACK
SANDWICHES AVAILABLE
MON - SAT
BACON, TOMATO
E4
STEAK b

SMO
CRE
5.50
MASH £
£10.95
QUAIL
£1.50

Photo: Hind's Head, entry 21

Regionality, authenticity and seasonal bounty are gaining momentum: 'slow food', so deep-rooted in Italy, France and Spain, is gathering pace in Britain. Lamb is not just lamb, it's Lancastrian and heather-reared. Asparagus is English and served in season. Pork is Tamworth and free-range, and individual farms are sometimes named on the menu. These British-rustic delicacies tend to have simple, strong flavours and go down rather well with a pint.

A common complaint in the restaurant world is that service is slow. It is worth noting that slow food may indeed be slow to arrive; after all, it is freshly prepared, freshly cooked and hasn't seen a microwave. So, given that you don't have to wait more than twenty (thirty?) minutes between courses, settle back, enjoy the company and relax into your meal.

Sunday lunch

Pubs are becoming more flexible as far as Sunday lunch goes: the trend to go out for a traditional roast is on the up. Pubs are mirroring a laid-back approach to Sundays: a lie-in and a late breakfast, a walk and then lunch. Many now serve roasts up to 4pm or even 5pm. Another trend is to bring the joint to the table.

David Hancock

Photo: The Hoste Arms, entry 453

The notion of 'special' is at the heart of what we do, and is highly subjective. We also recognise that one person's idea of special is not necessarily another's so there is a big variety of places in this book, from dog-walker friendly to contemporary chic. Those who are familiar with our Special Places series know that we look for originality and authenticity, and disregard the anonymous and the banal. We also place great emphasis on the hosts' welcome – as important to us as the setting, the architecture, the atmosphere and the food.

Inspections and subscriptions

We visit every entry in this guide. We pick up those details that cannot be gleaned over the internet or the phone, and we write the descriptions ourselves, doing our best to avoid misinterpretation. If a pub is in, we think it's special, and the write-up should tell you if it's your sort of special.

Owners pay for their bedrooms to be mentioned but it is not possible for anyone to buy their way in; their fee goes towards the cost of the inspection process and includes a presence on our website.

Feedback

Things evolve at an astonishing pace in the pub world, so between inspections we rely on feedback from our readers as well as our staff, who are encouraged to visit properties across the series. Feedback is invaluable to us and we always follow up on comments.

Photo: Masons Arms, entry 191

Do tell us if your visit has been a joy or not, if the atmosphere was great or stuffy, or whether the staff were cheery or bored. The accuracy of the book depends on what you tell us. Occasionally misunderstandings occur, even with the best of intentions; if something is awry, please say so at the time! The landlord or owner will be keen to put things right, if they can.

We look for originality and authenticity in the places we choose

A lot of the new entries in each edition are recommended by our readers, so keep telling us about new places you've discovered. You can use the forms on our website (www.sawdays.co.uk) or at the end of this book.

Disclaimer

We make no claims to pure objectivity in choosing these places. They are here simply because we like them. Our opinions and tastes are ours alone and we hope you will share them. We have done our utmost to get our facts right but apologise unreservedly for any mistakes that may have crept in.

You should know that we don't check such things as fire alarms, kitchen hygiene or any other regulation with which owners of properties receiving paying guests should comply. This is the responsibility of the owners.

Finding the right place for you

Drink, eat, sleep A growing number of pubs and inns combine atmosphere with good food and bedrooms to match – and at lower prices than many hotels. It's true that some pubs are virtually indistinguishable from some small hotels, but a lively bar serving real beer should put them into the classic inn category. Some pubs with rooms are more modest village affairs where the enthusiasm to get things right in the bar extends upstairs. (If you are worried about noise at weekends, you can ask for a room at the back or a room across the way.) So the next time you take a weekend or business break, dismiss those roadside lodges and impersonal hotels in favour of a friendly country inn.

Gastropubs and country dining pubs

Our best pubs are luring foodies away from pricier restaurants as a wave of

casual dining enfolds the nation. Many backstreet boozers have been transformed, the fruit machines and beer-stained carpet being replaced by chalked-up menus and chunky tables. In the countryside, too, old-fashioned locals are being rejuvenated by landlords and chefs who believe that gastronomy is rooted in the soil and that food should be fresh, seasonal and sourced from the best local suppliers.

Our favourite food pubs in England and Wales are described within these pages; all strike a happy balance between restaurant and pub. (Note that booking is not always a given and you may have to take your chance with a table.)

Old boys and ale Expect few frills and modern-day intrusions, just real ale tapped from the cask, a game of shove ha'penny and a packet of pork scratchings. Some of these town or country gems are simple in the extreme, others offer more in the way of food and facilities (newspapers, piano, real fire) but remain genuine examples of the British boozer. We have unearthed a much-loved crop.

Pub as hub The reality is that pubs are closing at a rate of twenty-six a month across Britain, due to high rents and falling sales. However, put the right landlord at the helm and a pub can thrive. With a big welcome, a roaring fire, tasty food and fine beer such a pub can draw a community together,

Photo: Devonshire Arms, entry 150

spawning darts, pool, football and cricket teams, raffles and comedy and quiz nights. A growing number are taking on a wider community role, becoming part-time post offices, shops and delicatessens as village stores close, even venues for farmers' markets, polling stations, theatre performances and exhibitions of art.

Old boys and ale: real ale tapped from the cask, a game of shove ha'penny and a packet of pork scratchings

Maps and directions

The maps at the front of the book show the position, via a series of coloured flags, of each of our pubs and inns. Mauve flags indicate pubs with rooms, gold flags the award winners, blue flags the Worth a Visits. The maps are for guidance only; use a detailed road map or you could lose yourself down a tangle of lanes. The entry and map numbers are given at the foot of the separate guide entries; our directions are for guidance only.

Symbols

Below each entry you will see a line of symbols, which are explained at the very back of the book. They are based on the information given to us by the owners but things change, so use the symbols as a guide rather than an absolute statement of fact. Please note that the symbols do not necessarily apply to the bedrooms. Double-check anything that is important to you. A fuller explanation of some symbols is given below.

Children – The symbol is given to places that accept children of any age. That doesn't mean that they can go everywhere in the pub, or that highchairs and special menus or small portions are provided. Nor does it mean that children should be anything less than well-behaved! Call to check details such as separate family rooms, whether children are allowed in the dining room and whether there is play equipment in the garden.

Dogs – The symbol is given to places where your dog can go into some part of the pub, generally the bar and garden. It is unlikely to include eating areas.

Wheelchairs – We use the symbol where we have been told that those in wheelchairs can access both the bar and the wc. The symbol does not apply to accommodation.

Pub awards

Every year we choose those pubs that we think deserve a special mention. Our categories are: pubs serving local, seasonal and organic produce; authentic pubs; community pubs; and pubs with rooms. More details are given on page 18, and all the award winners have been tinted green and stamped so you can spot them easily.

Opening times

We list the hours pubs are closed during the afternoon and whether or not they are closed during particular lunchtimes and evenings. We do advise that you check before setting out, especially in winter.

Meals and meal prices

We give the times meals are served and the approximate cost of main courses in the bar and/or restaurant. Note that some pubs charge extra for side dishes, which significantly increases the main course price. Where set menus are mentioned, assume these are for three courses unless stated. Note that many pubs do fixed-price Sunday lunches, and that prices in general may change. Check when booking.

Bedrooms, bathrooms and breakfasts

If you're thinking of staying the night in a simple pub or inn, bear in mind that an early night may not be possible if folk are carousing below. A few bedrooms do not have en suite bathrooms – please ask on booking – and pub room check-ins are often late, eg. from 6.30pm. Breakfasts are generally included in the room price, and most places serve breakfast between 8am and 10am.

Bedroom prices

Prices are per room for two people sharing. If a price range is given, then the lowest price is for the least expensive room in low season and the highest for the most expensive room in high season. The single room rate (or the single

occupancy of a double room) generally follows. Occasionally prices are for half board, ie. they include dinner, bed and breakfast. Do check.

Bookings and cancellations

Tables – At weekends, food pubs are often full and it is best to book a table well in advance; at other times, only tables in the dining rooms may be reserved. Tables in the bar may operate on a first-come, first-served basis. Some of the best gastropubs do not take reservations at all, wanting to hold on to their pubby origins – so arrive early! Always phone to double-check meal times.

Rooms – Most pubs and inns will ask for a credit card number and a contact phone number when you telephone to book a room for the night. They may take a deposit at the time of booking, either by cheque or credit/debit card. If you cancel – depending on how much notice you give – you can lose all or part of this deposit unless your room is re-let. Ask the pub to explain their cancellation policy clearly before booking so you understand exactly where you stand; it may avoid a nasty surprise.

Payment

Those places that accept credit or debit cards are marked with a credit card symbol.

Tipping

It is not obligatory but it is appreciated, particularly in pubs with restaurants.

Local, Seasonal & Organic Produce Award

Hearts soar when our inspectors find chalkboard menus promoting regional, seasonal produce: farm meats, village-baked bread, locally shot game, fish from local catches, organic wines and local brewery ale. A passion for actively sourcing seasonal foods from high-quality local suppliers now extends to deli counters by the bar, farmers' markets in pub car parks and poly-tunnels and vegetable plots bursting with home-grown produce. Our champions of local, seasonal and organic produce are:

The Highwayman
Lancashire
entry 377

The Kingham Plough
Oxfordshire
entry 530

The Talbot
Worcestershire
entry 757

Authentic Pub Award

We have visited scores of simple, authentic, unadulterated pubs and they are a diminishing breed. Those that we found particularly special are:

The Five Mile House
Gloucestershire
entry 251

The King's Head
Suffolk
entry 613

The Sair Inn
Yorkshire
entry 766

Pubs with Rooms Award

With an increasing number of pubs wishing to promote their rooms above the bar – or in the converted barn, coach-house or stables across the way – our inspectors have visited more bedrooms than ever for this edition. Our eclectic bunch of inns-with-rooms get full-page entries and include bedrooms that range from swish suites with plasma TVs to simple but good rooms overlooking the sea. Our winners are good 'all-rounders', too, serving excellent food, beers and wines.

Devonshire Arms
Derbyshire
entry 150

The Peat Spade
Hampshire
entry 282

The Trout at Tadpole Bridge Oxfordshire
entry 514

Community Pub Award

Within these pages you will find some great little locals run by enterprising, hard-working landlords who have succeeded in making their pub the hub of the community. Our shining examples are:

The Lamb Inn
Devon
entry 181

Fighting Cocks
Shropshire
entry 564

Ye Old Sun Inn
Yorkshire
entry 816

The Great British Pub

For centuries, the pub has been one of Britain's quintessential institutions.

Public houses can be found right in the heart of distinct and thriving communities and form part of the rich fabric of British life.

They're a great place to relax and they offer a unique combination of quality beer and locally sourced food in an informal setting to rival many a top restaurant.

Heritage and provenance

Alastair Sawday Publishing is delighted to be associated with Britain's oldest brewer, Shepherd Neame.

Shepherd Neame is the guardian of the largest number of listed buildings in Kent with stories to tell about the county's remarkable heritage. The Kent landscape and its many landmarks have been the inspiration for such literary and artistic heroes as Charles Dickens, Geoffrey Chaucer and J M W Turner.

Known as the Garden of England, Kent also has some of the finest produce in Britain and Shepherd Neame works closely with local producers and farmers to bring the flavours of Kent to the company's pubs.

Recycled malt from the brewing process finds its way back to the county's farms as cattle feed

Sourcing all the food served in its pubs locally wherever possible goes hand-in-hand with brewing a traditional portfolio of celebrated Kentish ales. Ingredients are sourced as near as possible to the brewery and its pubs, significantly reducing road miles and transport costs.

Recycled malt from the brewing process finds its way back to the county's farms as cattle feed, and recycled cooking oil from the pubs is used as bio-diesel to fuel the brewery's drays in a 'virtuous circle' for the environment.

More than half the beer made at Faversham is traditional bitter, maintaining a brewing tradition that goes back centuries. It is the commitment of independent brewers like Shepherd Neame that is preserving this tradition for the future.

Two of Shepherd Neame's core products, Spitfire Premium Kentish Ale and Bishops Finger Strong Kentish Ale, have achieved PGI (Protected Geographical Indication) status from the European Union – meaning that their provenance and use of local products cannot be imitated anywhere else.

The brewery's speciality ale portfolio includes both a 'bottle conditioned' and an organic variety. The 1698 Bottle Conditioned Ale is an award-winning, thrice-hopped ale which includes some yeast in the bottle, allowing secondary fermentation and resulting in more complex flavours. In contrast, Whitstable Bay Organic Ale is a clean refreshing ale served in stemmed glassware, named after the East Kent coastal town renowned for seafood, particularly oysters.

Shepherd Neame also brews beers under licence to suit three Asian cuisines – Asahi Super Dry with Japanese food, Sun Lik with Chinese, and Kingfisher with Indian – and a trio of continental lagers – Dutch pilsener Oranjeboom, German Holsten Export and Swiss Hurlimann Sternbrau.

More than half the beer made at Faversham is traditional bitter

Beer and food – a great match

It's not surprising that the combination of a fresh local Dover sole washed down with a light golden ale such as Whitstable Bay Organic Ale or a rack of Romney Lamb with a deep amber pint of Spitfire Premium Kentish Ale works so beautifully. To follow, a beer such as the 1698 Bottle

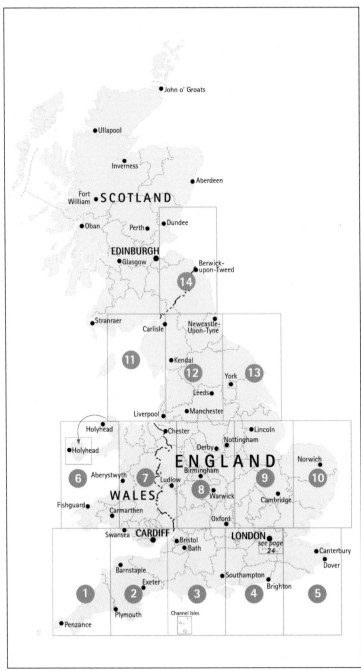

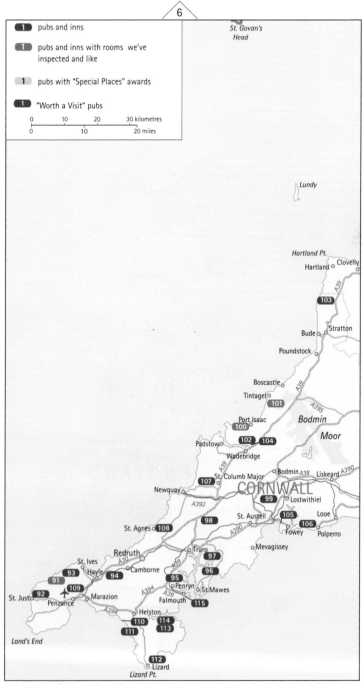

6

pubs and inns

pubs and inns with rooms we've inspected and like

pubs with "Special Places" awards

"Worth a Visit" pubs

| 0 | 10 | 20 | 30 kilometres |
| 0 | | 10 | 20 miles |

St. Govan's Head

Lundy

Hartland Pt.
Hartland   Clovelly

103

Bude   Stratton
Poundstock

Boscastle
Tintagel
101
Port Isaac   Bodmin
100   Moor
Padstow   102   104
Wadebridge

St Columb Major   Bodmin A38 Liskeard A390
107
Newquay   CORNWALL
A392   99   Lostwithiel
98   St. Austell   105   Looe
St. Agnes 108   106
Fowey   Polperro
Mevagissey
Redruth
St. Ives   97
93   Hayle   94   Camborne
91   95   96
St Just 92 109   Penryn St.Mawes
Penzance Marazion   Falmouth 115
Helston
110   114
111   113

Land's End

112 Lizard
Lizard Pt.

Map 2

27

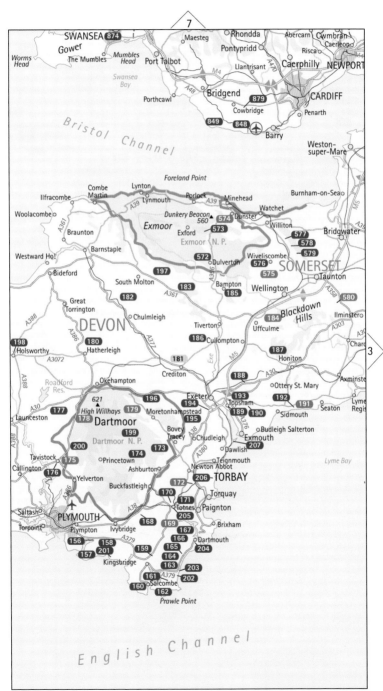

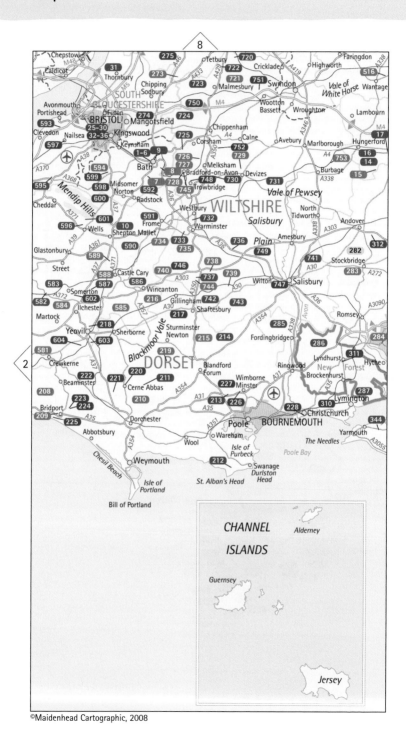

Map 4   29

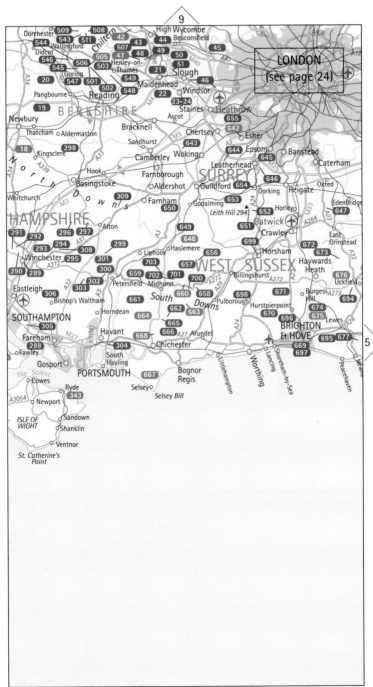

LONDON
(see page 24)

©Maidenhead Cartographic, 2008

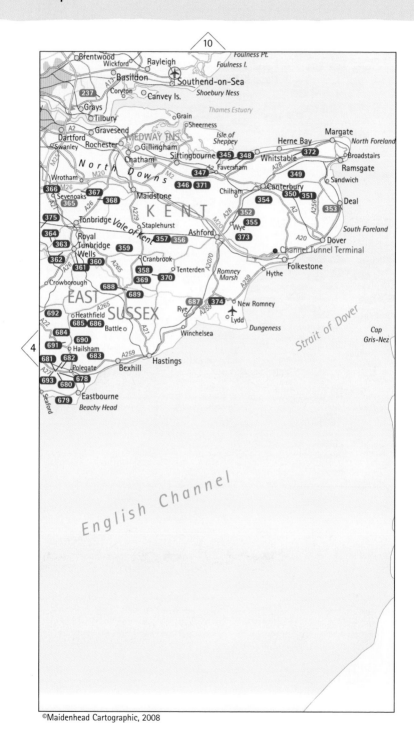

Map 6   31

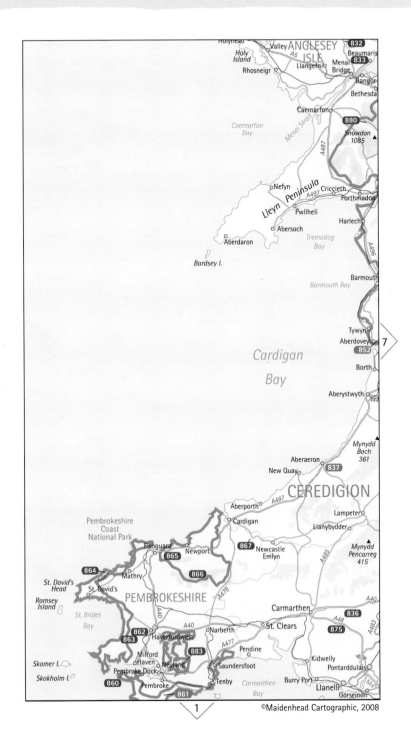

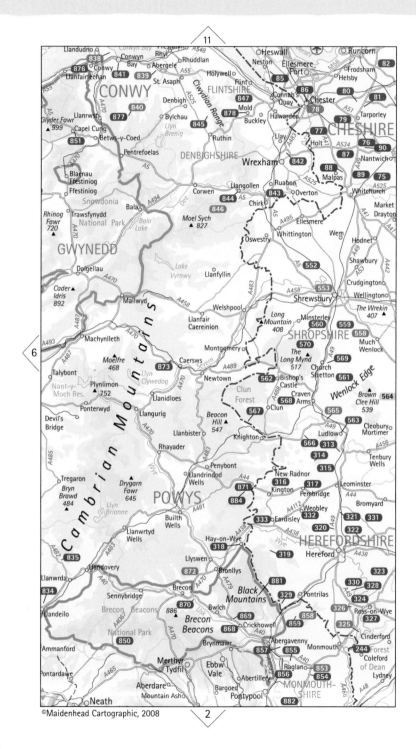

©Maidenhead Cartographic, 2008

Map 8

33

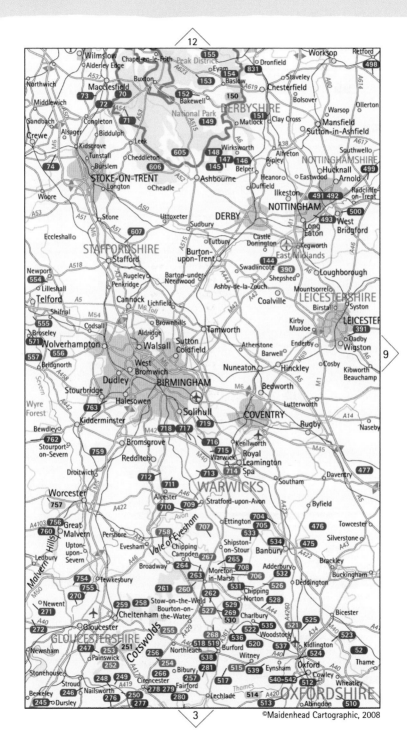

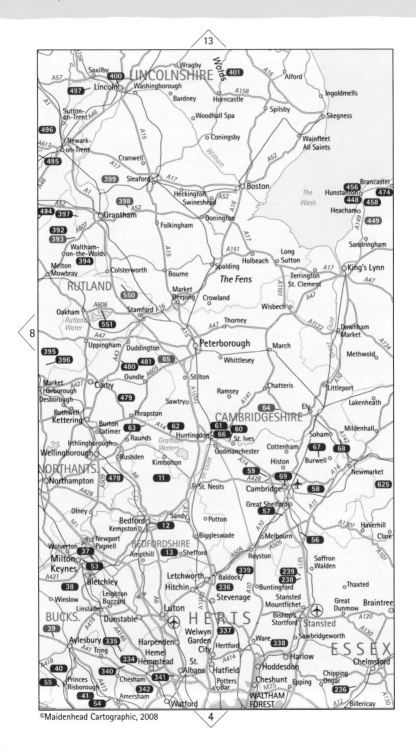

Map 10

35

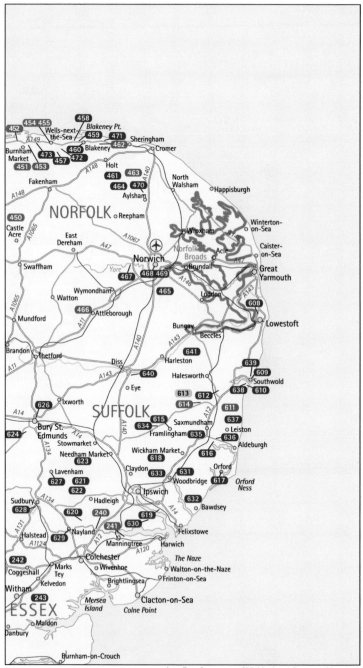

©Maidenhead Cartographic, 2008

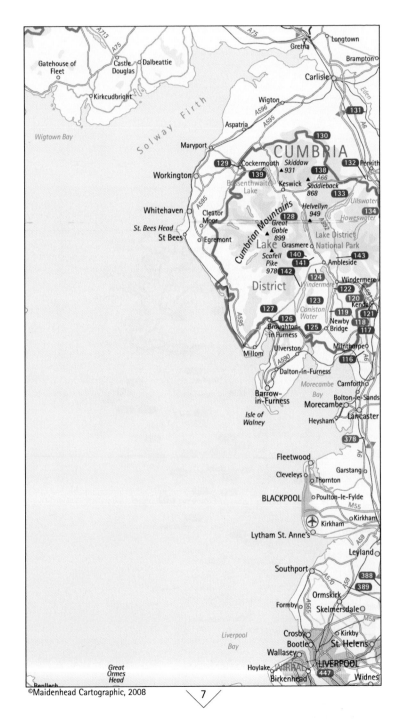

Map 12   37

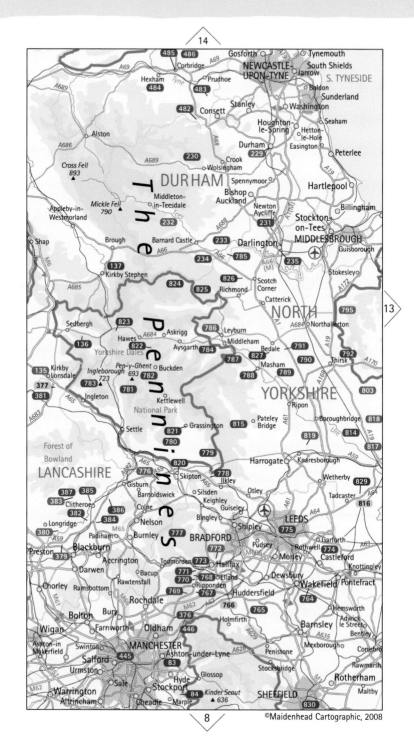

©Maidenhead Cartographic, 2008

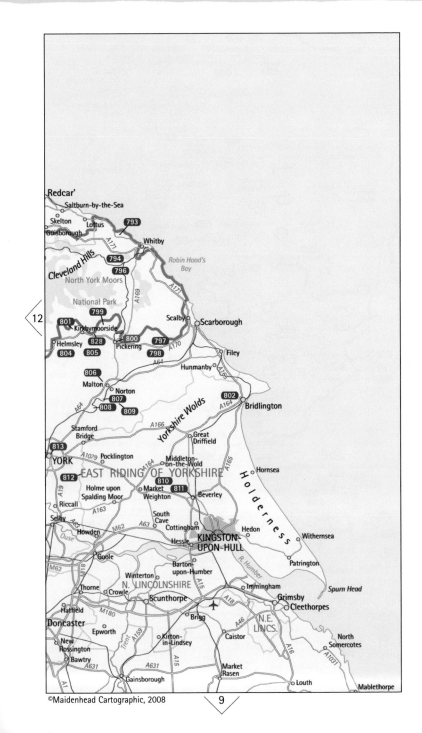

Map 14

39

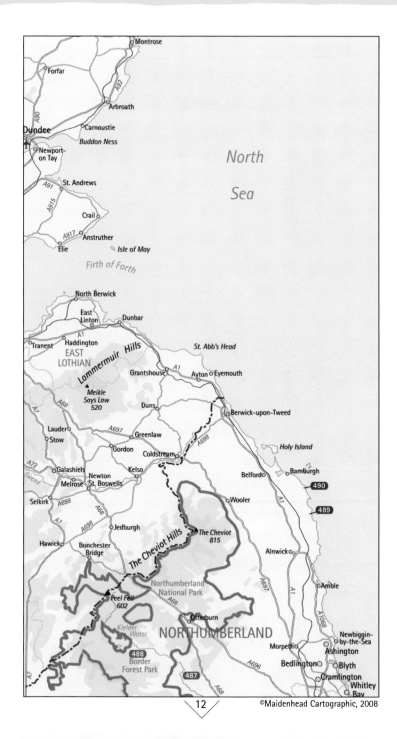

©Maidenhead Cartographic, 2008

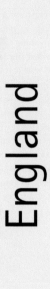

England

Garricks Head
Bath

The famous pub by the Theatre Royal, a refuge for actors and a theatre since 1720, has become a second success story for the proprietors of the King William. Enter a lovely lazy sofa'd bar, with a chic utilitarian dining room to the side. The drinking side of things is important still but the food is something special. Chef Charlie used to work at the Anchor & Hope in Waterloo so the style is robust English. Top produce and seasonality are paramount and the dishes pay a debt to Clerkenwell's celebrated St John's: in one critic's words, "a paragon of everything British eating is heading towards." Just try the snails with braised oxtail and mash, and the rib of beef with goose fat chips. The beers change all the time with the emphasis on small breweries and the cider comes from Julian Temperley at Burrow Hill. Great value.

Gascoyne Place
Bath

"Functional yet ornate" is how Marty Grant and Wayne Taylor hoped Gascoyne Place would be – and so it is. And, bang opposite the Theatre Royal, it's steeped in history. The old city wall intrudes on the lower floor, there's a Georgian hoist near the main staircase and an Edwardian match-board ceiling. This sympathetic restoration includes vivid green hand-glazed tiles over the chimney breast, a Victorian mahogany bar from an East End pub and 1930s opaline lights. There are five seating areas in all: a snug, a small public bar, a mezzanine area and two fine-dining rooms. Food is simple, British and based around produce sourced from local farms. Pluck a pint of Butcombe bitter to accompany your Rainbow Wood Farm braised shin of beef stew with thyme dumplings, or one of 90 delicious wines. A thoroughly contemporary space.

Meals	12pm-3pm; 6pm-10pm; no food Sun eve. Main course £8.50-£15.
Closed	3pm-5pm. Open all day Sat & Sun.
Directions	5-minute walk from Bath railway & bus stations, opposite Bath Theatre Royal.

Meals	12pm-3pm (4pm Sun); 5.30pm-10pm; bar menu available all day. Main courses £5.95-£17.95; bar meals up to £9.95.
Closed	Open all day.
Directions	5-minute walk from Bath railway & bus stations, next to Bath Theatre Royal.

Charlie & Amanda Digney
Garricks Head,
8 St John's Place, Bath BA1 1ET
Tel   01225 428096
Web   www.garricksheadpub.com

Marty Grant & Wayne Taylor
Gascoyne Place,
1 Sawclose, Bath BA1 1EY
Tel   01225 445854
Web   www.gascoyneplace.co.uk

Entry 1 Map 3

Entry 2 Map 3

The Old Green Tree
Bath

Right in the centre, the cosy pub, whose staff are fanatical about ale (at least six guest beers chalked up on the board outside), hums with life even before midday. Deep in conversation, old regulars clutch pint jars to their chests as you squeeze through the narrow planked bar into a cabin-like room. Undecorated since the panelling was installed in 1928, the pub is part of our heritage and has no intention of changing – Tim and Nick refuse any form of modernisation. In three little, low-ceilinged rooms, a mosaic of foreign coins are stuck up with yellowing sellotape behind the bar – along with artists' work. The menu includes huge sarnies and adventurous twists on old English dishes. They have a devoted following and drink is not limited to beer: there are malts, wines, Pimms and hot toddies.

The Salamander
Bath

The main bar, like a Victorian apothecary, is stacked with bottles on a Welsh dresser, hand pumps gleam under the glass fluted lights and looking up is hoppy heaven. The narrow room stretches from the Parisian café-style front window to the moody orange recesses of the back. Bath Ales dominate, though the bottled beer list is eclectic (Leffe, Erdinger), and there are the usual oddities such as an old beer tap collection; the Salamander has become one of the most popular boozers in Bath. Up a set of creaky stairs hides the 'dining room', which has recently had a refit. From an open kitchen flow dishes both traditional and with a global slant, from cheddar and jalapeno soup to Spa Ale battered haddock with chips. A fine pub without the spittle, and live folk sessions take place every other night.

Meals	12pm-3pm.
	Main courses £5.50-£10.
Closed	Open all day.
Directions	Green Street, off Milsom Street. Bath city centre.

Meals	12pm-2.30pm (3pm Sun); 6.30pm-9.30pm (12pm-3pm Sun); no food Sun eve.
	Main courses £8.95-£11.95; bar meals £3.95-£7.50.
Closed	Open all day.
Directions	Behind Jollys in Bath city centre, off Milsom Street.

T Bethune & F N Luke
The Old Green Tree,
12 Green Street,
Bath BA1 2JZ
Tel   01225 448259

Tim Wilkins
The Salamander,
3 John Street, Bath BA1 2JL
Tel   01225 428889
Web   www.bathales.com

Entry 3 Map 3

Entry 4 Map 3

Bath & N.E. Somerset

King William
Bath

Named after the king who was on the throne when the Duke of Wellington passed his Beer Act (in a bid to wean people off nasty foreign spirits, anyone with two guineas could open a beerhouse), the little corner pub known as the King Billy has a chilled café/bar feel and a terrific range of wines and beers. They get into gastropub gear at lunch; the food's so popular Charlie and Amanda have created extra space in the intimate dining room upstairs (booking advised). Ingredients are locally sourced and largely organic, dishes are simple and modern – terrine of pigeon and rabbit, wild bass with roast fennel, local unpasteurised cheeses. Bare boards, village hall furniture, gold flock velvet curtains and background reggae and soul pull in an art-funky, Walcot Street crowd. And the staff couldn't be nicer.

Meals	12pm-3pm; 6.30pm-10pm; no food Sun eve. Main courses £24-£29; bar meals £6-£15.
Closed	3pm-5pm. Open all day Sat & Sun.
Directions	Short walk from Walcot Street, off London Road.

Charlie & Amanda Digney
King William,
36 Thomas Street, Bath BA1 5NN
Tel   01225 428096
Web   www.kingwilliampub.com

Entry 5 Map 3

Bath & N.E. Somerset

The Star Inn
Bath

Listed on the National Inventory of Historic Pubs, a serious boozer and museum piece wrapped into one. A pub since 1760, it is partitioned off into three numbered rooms, each with rough planks, panelled walls, ancient settles and opaque toplights. A real coal fire pumps out the heat and you can still get a free pinch of snuff from the tins on the ledge above the wall... you can almost imagine the Victorian regulars pressing their lips to their pewter tankards. To this day Bass is served in four-pint jugs which you can take away for a small deposit. There are no meals, just the odd bap from a basket on the bar. What counts is the beer, so much so that Alan has started brewing his own Abbey Ales and has since scaled the heady heights of the real ale world to win several awards for his Bellringer tipple. A jewel.

Meals	Fresh rolls served all day. Rolls from £1.90.
Closed	2.30pm-5.30pm. Open all day Sat & Sun.
Directions	On A4 (London Road) in Bath.

Alan Morgan
The Star Inn, 23 Vineyards,
The Paragon, Bath BA1 5NA
Tel   01225 425072
Web   www.star-inn-bath.co.uk

Entry 6 Map 3

The Wheatsheaf Inn
Combe Hay

A hidden valley, a pretty village, a gorgeous inn, three fabulous rooms. Views from the lush terraced garden – replete with veg plot and hens – stretch across to a fine ridge of trees, the manor house and church jutting out of the woods below. In summer there are barbecues, lazy lunches, horses clopping by. This is a 15th-century farmhouse with later additions – it's all but impossible to notice the join – whose exterior comes clad in Farrow & Ball creams. Outside there are Indian benches with seagrass cushions; inside, big sofas in front of the fire. Gastropub interiors have neutral colours to soak up the light, sandblasted beams, halogen spotlights and Lloyd Loom wicker dining chairs. Steps outside lead down to three deeply comfy bedrooms in a stone building. All come in contemporary rustic style with light wood furniture, flat-screen TVs, Egyptian cotton and deluge showers; there are White Company oils and bath robes too. Climb back up for seriously good food, perhaps risotto of Dorset crab, fillet of Buccleuch Scotch beef, hot raspberry soufflé. Bath is a hike across the fields.

Rooms	3 doubles. £95–£110.
Meals	12pm–2pm; 6pm–9.30pm (10pm Fri & Sat). Main courses £16.50–£20; bar meals £5–£9.
Closed	3pm–6pm & Mon all day.
Directions	South from Bath on A367, then left in Combe Down onto B3110. Straight ahead for 1.5 miles, then right for Combe Hay.

Ian & Adele Barton
The Wheatsheaf Inn,
Combe Hay, Bath BA2 7EG

Tel	01225 833504
Web	www.wheatsheafcombehay.com

Entry 7 Map 3

Wheelwrights Arms
Monkton Combe

A pub for all seasons. In winter, grab the table in front of the ancient fire where the wheelwright worked his magic; in summer, skip outside for a pint on the terrace. You're in the country, two miles from Bath, so drop down to the nearby Kennet & Avon canal and cycle or walk through glorious country into the city. The Wheelwrights dates to 1750. Inside, beautiful contemporary colours mix with soft stone walls and exposed timber frames. Logs are piled high in the alcoves, there's a wonderful snug, the daily papers are left on the bar and the food is delicious. Try roasted smoked salmon with braised fennel and crayfish sauce, steak and kidney pie, a trio of crème brûlées; on summer nights, dine in the garden illuminated by lights in the trees. Airy bedrooms in what was the wheelwright's annexe come in fresh, original style. Expect dark wood floors, shuttered windows, old-style radiators, flat-screen TVs; wooden beds are covered in immaculate linen, bathrooms come with L'Occitane lotions. They hold two season tickets for Bath Rugby Club at cost price, and more tickets for Bath's Thermae Spa: book early!

Rooms	7: 5 doubles, 1 twin, 1 single. £120–£145. Singles from £95.
Meals	8am–10am; 12pm–3pm; 6pm–10pm. Main courses £9.50–£14.90; lunch, 2 courses, £10 (Mon–Fri); Sunday roast £10.
Closed	Open all day.
Directions	A36 south from Bath for 4 miles, then right, signed Monkton Combe. Over x-roads, into village, on left.

David Phillips–White
Wheelwrights Arms,
Church Lane, Monkton Combe,
Bath BA2 7HB
Tel   01225 722287
Web   www.wheelwrightsarms.co.uk

White Hart
Bath

A short walk from Bath Spa Station, in sought-after Widcombe, this large detached pub has a pleasant courtyard garden and a backpackers' hostel above. Despite its reputation as one of the best places to eat in town, it still feels pubby, with a jolly bar, a pleasingly plain dining room and a mixed bag of tables. On rugby day it heaves, as pints of Butcombe Bitter and Wye Valley Butty Bach are downed. Chef Rupert Pitt has worked in some of Bath's best restaurants and his menu is short and to the point, with five starters and six mains. The food, well-priced and following the seasons, is delicious. Try the marinated feta with Mediterranean bulgur wheat salad, the baked sea bass with lemon and saffron butter, and the tender slow-braised pork belly with mashed potato and cider gravy.

Oakhill Inn
Oakhill

The Digneys, owners of the inimitable King William and the Garrick's Head in Bath, have given the old village inn a sympathetic brush up and a fresh look, by taking the pool and the skittles out and encouraging a new crowd (families, dogs, food-lovers) in. Wood-burning stoves, original parquet floors and various fine features are the backdrop to a rotating selection of local ales from the likes of Newman's and Stonehenge breweries, complemented by a well-priced menu of robust British dishes. So you may expect 'old-fashioned but modern' salt beef sandwiches with chips; steak and kidney pudding with greens; and the most comforting of comfort puddings – jam roly poly with custard, treacle tart with cream, and rhubarb crumble... served seasonally, of course. All this and Matt the barman, who's a star.

Meals	12pm-2pm; 6pm-10pm; no food Sun eve. Main courses £10-£13.	Meals	12pm-3pm; 6pm-9pm. Main courses £12-£15.
Closed	Open all day. Closed Sun eve in winter.	Closed	3.30pm-6pm. Open all day Sat & Sun.
Directions	Where the A3604 becomes Claverton Street, the pub is on the right, at junction of Widcombe Road & Prior Park Road.	Directions	Just off A367 Bath to Shepton Mallet road, 3 miles north of Shepton Mallet.

	Jo Lucas White Hart, Widcombe Hill, Bath BA2 6AA
Tel	01225 338053
Web	www.whitehartbath.co.uk

	Charlie & Amanda Digney Oakhill Inn, Fosse Road, Oakhill, Bath BA3 5HU
Tel	01749 840442
Web	www.oakhillinn.co.uk

Entry 9 Map 3

Entry 10 Map 3

Bedfordshire

The Plough at Bolnhurst
Bolnhurst

A tavern has stood here since the 1400s, but 16 years ago the last one burnt down; tradition lives on in this happy reincarnation. The Plough subtly holds on to its heritage, employing reclaimed blackened beams and cast-iron chimney. Overlaying this is a modern touch – stripped boards, hewn-wood bar and crisp white walls. Food is equally sophisticated; chef-patron Martin Lee's grounding was with Raymond Blanc. Braised pork belly with black pudding mash, roast pumpkin tart, Neal's Yard cheeses... 'gutsy flavours but restrained formulation' are the order of the day, and, going by the heaving crowd of happy foodies, they've got it right. Come to dine rather than pop in for a pint – the wines are impressive, though the well-kept Village Bike bitter also slips down a treat. A bright light in the desert that is Bedfordshire.

Bedfordshire

Hare & Hounds
Old Warden

The food may be fabulous but the Hare & Hounds is first and foremost a pub. There's always a welcome and a buzz, you can drop by for a glass of wine (or a jar of chutney) and the aromas from the kitchen mingle irresistibly with the woodsmoke from the fire. The beer's good too (Eagle Bitter, Bombardier). On a Sunday in summer, when they fly a Shuttleworth Spitfire from the grass airstrip next door, you could find the ice rattling in your G&T; otherwise the garden is blissfully quiet. No barbecues, just a few drinkers' tables and a smokers' gazebo. Inside are low timbered ceilings and four distinct areas: a funky snug with sofas, two rooms for eating, and a family room beyond. Game and poultry come from the village estate, veg and herbs from the allotment, cheeses are proudly British and the puddings are a treat.

Meals	12pm-2pm (2.30pm Sun); 6pm-9.30pm (6pm-10pm Fri & Sat). Main courses £11.50-£18.50; bar meals £4.50-£12.50.
Closed	3pm-6.30pm, Sun eves & Mon all day.
Directions	On B660 north of Bedford; pub in village centre.

Meals	12pm-2pm (3pm Sun); 6.30pm-9pm; no food Sun eve. Main courses £10-£18.
Closed	3pm-6pm & Mon (except Bank Hols).
Directions	Off B658 & A6001 3 miles west of Biggleswade; pub next to village hall.

Martin & Jayne Lee & Michael Moscrop
The Plough at Bolnhurst,
Kimbolton Road, Bolnhurst,
St Neots MK44 2EX
Tel   01234 376274
Web   www.bolnhurst.com

Jane Hasler
Hare & Hounds,
Old Warden, Bedford SG18 9HQ
Tel   01767 627225
Web   www.hareandhoundsoldwarden.co.uk

Entry 11 Map 9

Entry 12 Map 9

Bedfordshire

The Black Horse
Ireland

In Ireland – in Bedfordshire – is a welcoming pub. Stone dogs guard the front door, bollards linked by ships' rope divide terrace from car park and the door opens to a sweep of open-plan, split-level space. There's floor to ceiling glass at one end – looking out to palms, sculptures and ferns – and more formal dining areas at the other. The bar top is solid slate, smart banquettes edge tables both sides of a wood-burning stove but, in spite of the modernity, traditional features remain: fireplaces in excellent order and refurbished beams from which downlighters shine. This is a place for diners not drinkers, unless you've found a perch outside: food ranges from chicken on the griddle to pollack with a tiger prawn brochette, the puddings are more-ish, and Michael Winner, we are told, enjoyed his Sunday roast.

Meals	12-2pm; 6.30pm-9.30pm (12pm-5pm Sun). Main courses £8.95-£15.95.
Closed	3pm-6pm & Sun eve.
Directions	Pub signed from the A600 Shefford to Bedford road.

Darren Campbell
The Black Horse,
Ireland, Shefford SG17 5QL
Tel 01462 811398
Web www.blackhorseireland.com

Entry 13 Map 9

Berkshire

The Dundas Arms
Kintbury

The Dalzell-Pipers have run this delightfully old-fashioned inn for 40 years. At the junction of river and canal, dabbling ducks entertain diners while narrowboats glide by and summer crowds fill the waterside patio. People come mainly for the food. The carpeted small bar has a traditional feel; the restaurant to the side is crisp with white napery; both are a stage for some wholesome country cooking. Using fresh ingredients, notably estate game and prime meats from local dealers, David's lunchtime blackboard menus support old favourites like Cumberland sausages with mash, onion gravy and peas, steak-and-ale pie, and bread-and-butter pudding with cream. There's a decent wine list, too, and Morlands, Butts and West Berkshire's beers. The little station stands right opposite: in an hour you could be back in London.

Meals	12pm-2pm; 7pm-9pm; no food Mon eve or Sun all day. Main courses £12-£14; bar meals £4.95-£13.50.
Closed	2.30pm-6pm & Sun eve.
Directions	1 mile off A4 between Newbury & Hungerford.

David Dalzell-Piper
The Dundas Arms, 53 Station Road,
Kintbury RG17 9UT
Tel 01488 658263
Web www.dundasarms.co.uk

Entry 14 Map 3

Crown and Garter
Inkpen

An unreformed country local. On the night we stayed Gill was serving at the bar, her father was keeping an eye on the fire and her son was running through questions for the pub quiz. Gamekeepers and village footballers come for a pint of Good Old Boy, Mr Chubbs or Timothy Taylor's Landlord. Cockerels crow in the fields and in summer life spills onto a stone terrace and into the pretty garden. Inside you get wooden floors, thick red curtains and a huge settle by the fire. There's a small restaurant serving scrummy homemade pies, Thai curries, lamb shank, fillet steak; you can tuck in here, or in the bar, or, on sunny days, on the new outside patio. James II is said to have visited which might account for the wooden throne by the front door. Bedrooms, in a single-storey building around a garden, are spacious and airy and have painted floorboards, blended voiles, and brass or wooden beds. Two rooms interconnect for families, piping hot water flows in super little bathrooms. You can walk from the front door, try your luck at Newbury Races or watch the early morning gallops at Lambourne.

Rooms	8: 6 doubles, 2 twins. £90. Singles £59.50.
Meals	12pm–2pm (2.30pm Sun); 6.30pm–9.30pm; no food Sun eve. Main courses £7.95–£16.95; bar meals from £6.95; Sunday roast £10.95.
Closed	3pm–5.30pm (5pm–7pm Sun), Mon & Tues lunch.
Directions	A4 for Hungerford. After 2 miles, left for Kintbury & Inkpen. In Kintbury, left at corner shop onto Inkpen Road; inn on left after 2 miles.

Gill Hern
Crown and Garter,
Great Common, Inkpen,
Hungerford RG17 9QR
Tel 01488 668325
Web www.crownandgarter.com

Entry 15 Map 3

Berkshire

Pheasant Inn
Shefford Woodlands

It may look like it's seen better days but don't be put off: this is a cracking place with a reputation among the horse-racing set. This may explain the certain shabby gentility (rustic tiling, blood red walls, big mirrors, pine tables, heavy drapes) and certainly explains the TV tuned into the racing – often drowned out by the hubbub of jockeys and trainers. Butt's Jester, Loddon Hoppit and Wadworth 6X help charge the atmosphere, backed up by several wines by the glass. As for food, good ingredients are used in comfortingly familiar ways. A short menu delivers simple but careful home cooking: carrot and coriander soup, excellent meaty burgers; for dinner, grilled fillet of turbot with rosemary roast potatoes and asparagus, ginger and shellfish sauce. It's the best M4 pit-stop for miles.

Meals	12-2.30pm (12.30-2.30pm Sun); 7pm-9.30pm (9pm Mon & Sun; 7.30pm-10pm Sat). Main courses £9.95-£20.50.
Closed	Open all day.
Directions	M4 exit 14; A338 towards Wantage; 1st left onto B4000 for Lambourn; pub on right.

	John Ferrand
	Pheasant Inn, Ermin Street,
	Shefford Woodlands,
	Hungerford RG17 7AA
Tel	01488 648284
Web	www.thepheasantinnlambourn.co.uk

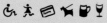

Entry 16 Map 3

Berkshire

The Red House
Marsh Benham

This well-groomed dining pub has an upmarket style. Just a stone's throw from the Kennet and Avon Canal, perched on the edge of a hamlet pretty near the A4, it's quite a find. Vibrant red walls, wide blond floorboards and fashionable leather dining chairs create an upbeat, unbuttoned atmosphere in the L-shaped bistro-bar – muddy boots no problem! – while the airier dining room strikes a more formal note with its red carpeting and round-back chairs. The food is the main thrust here, the modern brasserie-style repertoire living up to the surroundings. So dishes may include foie gras parfait with onion marmalade and brioche, and bream served with a bisque of hand-dived scallops. But there's plenty of informality too, what with lunch and dinner fixed price menus, handpumped ales and a front terrace for summer,

Meals	12pm-3pm; 6pm-10pm. Main courses £12.50-£19.95; bar snacks £4.75-£6.95; set menu £13.95 & £17.95.
Closed	3pm-6pm; Sun & Mon eves.
Directions	M4 junc 13; A4 between Newbury & Hungerford (10 mins from M4).

	Xavier Le-Bellego & Alan Morrison
	The Red House,
	Marsh Benham,
	Newbury RG20 8LY
Tel	01635 582017
Web	www.redhousemarshbenham.co.uk

Entry 17 Map 3

Carnarvon Arms
Burghclere

Fears that the beloved old pub would become another nondescript restaurant have proved to be unfounded. There are still ales on tap, wines by the glass, a bar menu listing bangers and mash (locally sourced, naturally) and a friendly welcome. The thoroughly modern renovation of this once rambling coaching inn near the gates of Highclere Castle is a spruce, stylish and upbeat affair. Expect fresh vibrant colours, bare boards and deep sofas in lounges, and a swishly traditional bar. In the light, high-vaulted dining room are painted beams, rug-strewn boards, a feature fireplace and Egyptian motifs inspired by collections at the Castle. Group executive chef Rob Clayton oversees the menu, the carte covering dishes such as braised shoulder of venison with a beetroot and goats' cheese gratin, and grilled fillet of sea bream with sun-blushed tomato and a basil cream sauce. Bedrooms are equally smart, dressed in fashionably neutral fabrics and tones, accompanied by plasma screens, WiFi connections and posh tiled bathrooms.

Rooms	23 twins/doubles. £79.95-£89.95. Singles £69.95-£79.95.
Meals	12pm-2.30; 6pm-9.30. Main courses £9.95-£19.95; bar meals £4.50-£12.95; set lunch £9.95 & £14.95.
Closed	Open all day.
Directions	Leave A34 at Tothill Services south of Newbury; signs to Highclere Castle; pub on right.

Harwood Warrington
Carnarvon Arms,
Winchester Road, Whitway, Burghclere,
Newbury RG20 9LE

Tel	01635 278222
Web	www.carnarvonarms.com

Berkshire

The Pot Kiln
Frilsham

TV chef Mike Robinson drank his very first pint in this remote and determinedly old-fashioned ale house – and jumped at the chance to buy it. A sprucing up of the dining room has not altered the faded character one jot, and you still find thirsty agricultural workers crowding the tiny, basic bar (bare tables, dartboard, filled rolls) with foaming pints of Brick Kiln Bitter. Perfectly lovely in summer – the garden looks onto fields – it's also wonderful in winter, when log fires and a menu strong on game come into their own. In the restaurant expect "European country cooking". That means rich pumpkin soup with fontina cheese fondue, warm salad of wood pigeon, daube of slow-cooked oxtail, sticky toffee pudding. The wine list is serious and affordable and the service is everything it should be. Expect a wait at weekends.

Meals	12pm–2pm; 7pm–9pm. Main courses £13–£18; set lunch £12.50 & £14.95 (weekdays only).
Closed	3pm–6pm. Open all day Sat & Sun.
Directions	In Yattendon, turn opposite church for Frilsham. Cross motorway; on for Bucklebury; on right after 0.5 miles.

Mike & Katie Robinson
The Pot Kiln,
Frilsham, Yattendon RG18 0XX
Tel 01635 201366
Web www.potkiln.co.uk

Entry 19 Map 4

Berkshire

The Bell Inn
Aldworth

The Bell has the style of village pubs long gone and has been in the Macaulay family for 200 years. Plain benches, venerable dark-wood panelling, settles and an outside gents: it's an unspoilt place to which folk flock. There's an old wood-burning stove in one room, a more impressive hearth in the public bar, and early evening drinkers cluster around a glass hatch. Fifty years ago the regulars were agricultural workers; today piped music and mobile phones are fervently opposed. The food fits the image and they keep it simple: choose from warm rolls filled with thick slices of home-baked ham, salt beef or crab, good puds and winter soups of the day. Drink prices are another draw; the ales come from the local Arkell's and West Berkshire breweries and the house wines are well-priced. There's also a great big garden.

Meals	11am–2.30pm (12pm–3pm Sun); 6pm–9.30pm (7pm–9.30pm Sun). Bar meals £2.50–£3.25.
Closed	3pm–6pm (7pm Sun) & Mon (except bank hols).
Directions	Off B4009, 3 miles W of Streatley.

H E Macaulay
The Bell Inn,
Aldworth,
Reading RG8 9SE
Tel 01635 578272

Entry 20 Map 4

Berkshire

Hind's Head
Bray

When the Tudor tavern across the road from Heston's Fat Duck (in posh Bray) came on the market, the world-famous chef snapped it up. Once again the old Hind's Head is the most genuine of village pubs (polished panelling, open fires) with one striking difference: terrific food. Expect a short slate of British classics... pea and ham soup, potted shrimps with watercress salad, mushroom and ale pie, the trademark triple-cooked chips, and revivals of historic puds (Quaking Pudding, Eton Mess). **Barry Dawson** heads the kitchen and never loses the focus: to maximise the taste of the finest materials. Side dishes are extra so it's not cheap – and service can be slow. Bar food includes Scotch quail eggs, coffee comes with chocs. Book if you want a table in the restaurant, or a private room, perfect for parties.

Berkshire

The Royal Oak
Paley Street

Modest at first glance, it has star quality inside. Nick Parkinson (son of Michael) may have given this small inn a contemporary and stylish lift, but he has cleverly managed to keep much of the traditional character. There are scrubbed wooden floors and stripped beams, timbers and panelling, and a collection of cricketing mementos, along with photographs of star personalities and Dad's interviewees: Mohamed Ali, Victoria Beckham, Sting. The bar is cosy and inviting, with solid wooden furniture, an open fire and a couple of armchairs. A snack menu is available at lunchtime, while the dining room's food, beautifully cooked by Dominic Chapman, is modern and classy, with a good choice of wines. And you can get a lovely pint of London Pride. The Royal Oak is friendly and well-run, opening its door to drinkers and diners with equal enthusiasm.

Meals	12pm-2.30pm (4pm Sun); 6pm-9.30pm; no food Sun eve. Main courses £12.95-£18.50; bar meals £1.50-£7.50
Closed	Open all day.
Directions	On B3028 in Bray.

Meals	12pm-2.30pm (3.30pm Sun); 6.30pm-10pm. Main courses £9.50-£20.
Closed	3pm-6pm & Sun eve.
Directions	On B3024 west of Paley Street, between A330 south of Maidenhead & Twyford.

Heston Blumenthal
Hind's Head, High Street,
Bray, Maidenhead SL6 2AB
Tel   01628 626151
Web   www.hindsheadhotel.co.uk

Nick Parkinson
The Royal Oak,
Paley Street, Maidenhead SL6 3JN
Tel   01628 620541
Web   www.theroyaloakpaleystreet.com

Entry 21 Map 4

Entry 22 Map 4

Berkshire

Greene Oak
Oakley Green

With a background in London gastropubbery, Henry and Katherine Cripps could not fail at their first solo venture, a swishly renovated dining pub close to Windsor, Ascot and foodie Bray. Enter an interior of wood and slate floors and soft green hues, antique French light fittings and big country mirrors. Most people come to eat and the style is traditional with a contemporary twist, a mix of British classic dishes and fashionable modern. Lunch may include pheasant and pistachio terrine with chilli jam and Caesar salad, or homemade beefburger with tomato and chilli relish. In the evening, potted crab and brown shrimp perhaps, roast belly pork with wok-fried Asian greens, fillet steak with béarnaise – polished off by a Valrhona chocolate pot with mascarpone. Service, wines and beers are as elegant as the rest.

Meals	12pm-3pm (3.30pm Sun); 6.30pm-9.30pm; no food Sun eve. Main courses £7.90-£16.90.
Closed	Open all day.
Directions	On B3383 south of A308, 2 miles west of Windsor.

Henry & Katherine Cripps
Greene Oak,
Oakley Green, Windsor SL4 5UW
Tel   01753 864294
Web www.thegreeneoak.co.uk

♿ 🏃 📖 🍷

Entry 23 Map 4

Berkshire

Two Brewers
Windsor

In the royal town, next to the Home Park gates and the famous Long Walk, small rooms meander around a tiny panelled bar and come quaintly decked with dark beams and wooden floors. One room with big shared tables reveals deep red walls and matching ceilings; the other two have more intimate seating areas. There are magazines to dip into and walls crammed with posters, press-cuttings, pictures and mirrors. On a blackboard above the fire, anecdotes commemorating each day are chalked up in preference to menu specials. Reserve a table and you won't go hungry: the compact menu follows a steady pub line, with daily specials, roasts on Sundays, and informal tapas on Friday and Saturday evenings. Beer, champagne, fine wines... and a sprinkling of pavement tables to tempt you after the rigours of The Big Tour. *No under-18s.*

Meals	12pm-2.30pm (4pm Sat & Sun); 6.30pm-10pm (tapas menu only Fri & Sat eve). Main courses £8-£13.50; Sunday roast £10.
Closed	Open all day.
Directions	Off High Street, next to Mews.

Robert Gillespie
Two Brewers,
34 Park Street,
Windsor SL4 1LB
Tel   01753 855426

♿ 📖 🐕 🍺 🍷

Entry 24 Map 4

Bristol

Bag o'Nails
Bristol

A five-minute walk from the harbourside and centre, this is a one-room drinkers' pub with a big reputation. Gas lamps, a tiled Victorian bar, a bare-boarded floor with three 'portholes' surveying the cellar, the odd game of draughts… it's that rare thing, a traditional boozer. And the sight of nine shiny hand pumps offering real ales from across the UK makes it a honeypot for CAMRA types (take a pint home). There's also a fabulous selection of bottled beers and ciders from independent breweries at good prices and a formidable range of ports. Dispensers for draught lager are camouflaged on the wall, the food menu stops at filled rolls, and there's no jukebox, simply the landlord's radio in the background. A serious temple for all things malt and hops, but with just five tables, get there early or expect to stand at the bar.

Meals	Rolls available all day.
Closed	Open from 5.30pm–11.30pm Mon-Weds. Open all day Thurs–Sun.
Directions	Right on Hotwells roundabout, opp. SS Great Britain.

Paul Dean & Amanda Ross
Bag o'Nails,
141 St Georges Road, Hotwells,
Bristol BS1 5UW
Tel   0117 940 6776

Entry 25 Map 3

Bristol

Cornubia
Bristol

This characterful inn, one of central Bristol's best-kept secrets, used to be two Georgian houses; now, after several recent changes of ownership, it has been rescued by Wiltshire's Hidden Brewery and given a new lease of life. Out goes the brown paintwork and the notoriously threadbare and sticky carpet, in comes a fresh a lick of paint and a function room upstairs. Surrounded by modern office blocks, this is a drinkers' pub at heart with up to eight ales available at any one time; stout's on draught and there are always a couple of west country ciders on tap. Food is basic – pies, baguettes, sandwiches – but with so many local beers to chose from, the Cornubia is driven more by conversation than gastronomy. A boozer with soul – and popular with office workers and *Evening Post* scribes.

Meals	12pm–8pm Mon–Fri. Hot pies 5pm–11pm. Main courses £4–£7.
Closed	Sat & Sun lunch. Open all day Mon–Fri.
Directions	5-min walk from Temple Meads station. From Victoria St, right into The Countershop, right again into Temple St.

Ross Nicol & Karen Beesley
Cornubia,
142 Temple Street,
Bristol BS1 6EN
Tel   0117 925 4415

Entry 26 Map 3

Bristol

The Hare on the Hill
Bristol

Not much to encourage you from the outside, but step through the doors and you're in a pub that knows its business. Bath Ales took on the corner boozer ten years ago for a total overhaul and served it up in unpretentious Bath Ales style – it feels as if it's been like this for a hundred years. Wooden floors, simple furniture and a fuss-free décor create a low-key charm while the cosmopolitan/student crowd are clearly happy with what the landlord prides himself on: good beer and conversation. It was CAMRA Pub of the Year the moment Bath Ales moved in. The place is full of nooks and crannies so you can easily find a quiet spot for a chat and a cider on tap, a pint of Bath Gem – or, if you're lucky, Rare Hare. Homemade soups, Spanish chicken and roasts on Sundays are prepared and cooked on the spot.

Bristol

Star and Dove
Bristol

In a funky, hilly suburb of Bristol, this once unloved boozer has been youthfully revived. And its owner carries a history: Eamon Fullalove used to chef at Jamie Oliver's Fifteen. His first solo venture since leaving the Jamie stable is this – a red-brick, early 20th-century neighbourhood pub with parquet floors and fireplaces intact. There are battered leather armchairs, rickety village hall chairs and a 'cor blimey' piano in the left-hand bar – a laid-back shabby chic. The bar menu concentrates on traditional pub dishes – lamb burger with hand-cut chips, fisherman's pie – with antipasti and charcuterie as an added treat; upstairs, the peaceful restaurant presents an Italian-inspired menu with classics such as peppered rib-eye steak, spedini of scallops and generous platefuls of homemade pasta.

Meals	12pm-2pm (5pm Sun); 6pm-9pm; no food Sun eve. Main courses from £5.45; bar snacks from £3.45.
Closed	2.30pm-5pm. Open all day Fri-Sun.
Directions	At top of Nine Tree Hill overlooking Stokes Croft.

Meals	12pm-3pm (4pm Sat & Sun); 6pm-10pm. Main courses £3-£15.
Closed	Open all day.
Directions	10-min walk from Bristol Temple Meads station. From York Road, left into St Luke's Road, past Victoria Park.

Paul & Dee Tanner
The Hare on the Hill, Dove St,
Kingsdown, Bristol BS2 8LX
Tel   0117 908 1982
Web   www.bathales.com

Eamon Fullalove & Christiane Jones
Star and Dove,
75 St Luke's Road, Totterdown,
Bristol BS3 4RY
Tel   0117 300 3712

Entry 27 Map 3

Entry 28 Map 3

Bristol

Robin Hood's Retreat
Bristol

An ordinary red-brick pub on bustling Gloucester Road; inside is special. Owner and chef Nathan Muir started his career working under Simon Hopkinson at Bibendum and his beautifully executed food is delivered from a broom cupboard-sized kitchen at the back. The refurb is classy, the cuisine modern European with occasional Asian influences, the menus driven by the seasons and the best produce available. Muir majors on bold flavours, often conjured from the humblest of ingredients, be they lambs' tongues with salsa verde or slow-braised mutton. Desserts include a much-loved treacle tart with English custard. Accompany these with a pint of real ale from a constantly changing selection of up to a dozen, mainly from West Country breweries, or an excellent wine. Sunday lunches are fabulous.

Meals	12pm-3pm; 6pm-9.30pm. Main course from £10; set lunch, 2 courses, £10; Sunday lunch £15 & £18.50.
Closed	Open all day.
Directions	North of the city centre on the main Gloucester Road.

Nathan Muir
Robin Hood's Retreat,
Gloucester Road, Bishopston,
Bristol BS7 8BG

Tel   0117 924 8639
Web   www.robinhoodsretreat.co.uk

Entry 29 Map 3

Bristol

The Albion
Bristol

Like Bath but without the tourists: Clifton village is Georgian to the core. Restaurants and delis abound but no-one had, until 2005, quite mastered the gastropub idea. Step forward Owain George who has given the student boozer down the pretty cobbled alley the classiest of makeovers. Outside, vast parasols; inside, a long stylish bar serving Butcombe and monthly guest ales, a winter log fire and a discreet wooden staircase leading to a restaurant that feels like a private room. A chef with a pedigree has been installed and the place attracts Clifton's loudest and proudest, but the Albion is still a pub, its menu available at every table. There are light bites at lunch and posh nosh at dinner (Jerusalem artichoke soup, roast tranche of turbot, Yorkshire grouse, pig's trotter). Book ahead at weekends.

Meals	12pm-3pm; 7pm-10pm; no food Sun eve. Main courses £12-£18.50; bar meals £6-£10.
Closed	Open all day. From 5pm on Mon.
Directions	In centre of Clifton village. (Tricky) on-street parking.

Owain George
The Albion,
Boyces Avenue, Clifton,
Bristol BS8 4AA

Tel   0117 973 3522
Web   www.thealbionclifton.co.uk

Entry 30 Map 3

Bristol

White Hart
Littleton upon Severn

Park at the back but go in at the front: it's worth it for the door alone. Step into a panelled vestibule with a 16th-century turned staircase; there are some great old fireplaces too in these rambling, ex-farmhouse rooms. Hops hang from main bar beams, tables, chairs and cushioned settles are scattered across flagged floors, and it's packed on Sundays. Outside are a sheltered terrace and a splendid front garden for summer revels and peaceful views. No music, just vintage billiards in the back bar, shelves of books and a much better than average family room. Meals continue to be generous and bursting with flavour, from ploughman's and baguettes to Sunday roasts and nursery puds. The ingredients are carefully sourced, the beers are good and the staff are friendly; new manager Jamie is doing a grand job.

Alastair Sawday's guides are about individuality, and our quest is to seek out the quirky, the unusual and the little-known.

Meals	12pm-2pm (2.30pm Sat); 6.30pm-9.30pm (12pm-2.30pm; 6pm-9pm Sun). Main courses £8.95-£15.95; Sunday roast £8.95.
Closed	Open all day.
Directions	From old Severn Bridge for Avonmouth, then Thornbury. 1st left at Elberton.

Jamie Reed
White Hart,
Littleton-on-Severn,
Thornbury BS35 1NR
Tel   01454 412275

Entry 31 Map 3

Bristol

32 The King's Head 60 Victoria Street, Bristol BS1 6DE
0117 927 7860
In Bristol's heart, untouched Victorian inside, 1660 out. A rare period narrow bar and an entirely panelled rear snug, a splendid mirrored back bar, photos of old Bristol and gallons of Smiles.

33 Wellington Inn Gloucester Rd, Horfield, Bristol BS7 8UR
0117 951 3022
Imposing red-brick pub a drop-kick from the Memorial Stadium. Something of a flagship for Bath Ales, plus solid pub food, a buzzing atmosphere and occasional live blues and folk.

34 Hope & Anchor 38 Jacobs Wells Road, Hotwells, Bristol BS8 1DR
0117 929 2987
Unpretentious and with a dedicated following, from arty youth to well-shod Cliftonites, who come for tasty pub grub and ales that change according to the landlord's whim.

35 The Merchants Arms 5 Merchants Road, Cliftonwood, Bristol BS8 4PZ
0117 904 0037
Bare-boarded and real, done-up without a whiff of modern pretension. Simple, friendly, civilised and Bath Ales-owned, with excellent beers and good snacks.

36 Old Duke 45 King Street, Bristol BS1 4ER
0117 927 7137
There's a New Orleans speakeasy, British-pub feel to this shrine to jazz and blues not far from Bristol Old Vic. Music is served up nightly along with the occasional curry or stew.

Photo: Jo Boissevain

Buckinghamshire

Swan Inn
Milton Keynes

A 13th-century gem in the heart of a sprawling New Town; across roundabouts and through housing estates you arrive at the clearly signed 'Milton Keynes Village'. Recently spruced up in gastropub style, keeping its beams, fireplaces and layout, the Swan has cool colours, scatter cushions and pews, chic chairs in its Snug and a glowing wood-burner in its bar. In the cosy dining room – wooden floors, chunky tables, open-to-view kitchen – Italian cured meats with chutney and homemade bread are on the menu alongside English pot-roasted chicken and cottage pie. Some produce comes from local allotments (in return for a pint or two), while imaginative evening meals include the likes of venison carpaccio with sweet onion jam. In summer you may eat outside, on the covered sun terrace or in the orchard garden.

Buckinghamshire

The Crooked Billet
Newton Longville

The twin talents of a former Sommelier of the Year, John Gilchrist, and head chef Emma have put the 16th-century pub on the county's culinary map. With innovative menus and a 400-bin wine list (all, astonishingly, available by the glass), you may imagine it's more restaurant than pub but it's an exemplary local with a great bar, weekly-changing ales, a log-fired inglenook and a great pubby atmosphere. Munch sandwiches, salads or steak and chips in the beamed bar at lunch; or crayfish Caesar salad, crispy pork belly with mustard mash, cabbage and bacon, and treacle and ginger parkin in the restaurant – inviting with its deep red walls, candles and country prints. Delicious cheeses come with fig and walnut cake and Emma's seasonal menus make full use of produce from first-class suppliers, villagers included.

Meals	12pm-10pm. Main course £7-£16.
Closed	Open all day.
Directions	Follow signs to Milton Keynes Village off V11 between junctions H6 & H7, 5 mins from town centre.

Meals	7pm-10pm (12.30pm-3pm Sun); bar meals 12pm-2pm Tues-Sat; no food Sun eve. Main courses £12.50-£22.50; bar meals £5.75-£10; tasting menu £55.
Closed	2.30pm-5.30pm; Mon lunch.
Directions	From Milton Keynes A421 for Buckingham, left for N. Longville.

	Steve Wilkins
	Swan Inn,
	Broughton Road, Milton Keynes Village, Milton Keynes MK10 9AH
Tel	01908 665240
Web	theswan-mkvillage.co.uk

Entry 37 Map 9

	John & Emma Gilchrist
	The Crooked Billet,
	2 Westbrook End, Newton Longville, Milton Keynes MK17 0DF
Tel	01908 373936
Web	www.thebillet.co.uk

Entry 38 Map 9

Buckinghamshire

Five Arrows Hotel
Waddesdon

Spires, turrets, ornamental ironwork outside; woven carpets, antique furnishings and paintings from Lord Rothschild's collection within. It is part of the model village built in 1887 by the Baron – along with Waddesdon Manor. The recent Pugin-style refurbishment creates an indulgent mood in keeping with the lofty ceilings and open fires. No bar to prop up but, from a wing-back armchair or a leather chesterfield, pints of Fuller's London Pride or a glass of champagne may be savoured. In the dining room, carefully sourced produce is subtly transformed into escalope of pork with cream and wild mushroom sauce, roasted sea bass with fennel and parmesan crisps, and honeycomb ice cream, while the magnificent wine list focuses on Rothschild interests around the world. Retire to a bed in a stout oak frame, smartly dressed in chintz or William Morris brocade: the late Victorian theme mirrors that of the manor. In the shadow of the vast mock-Elizabethan barley-twist chimney stacks is the exceptional garden, all manicured lawns and gravelled pathways. And the service is impeccable.

Rooms	11: 8 twins/doubles, 2 suites, 1 single. £85-£150. Singles £65.
Meals	12pm-2.15pm; 7pm-9.15pm (12pm-7pm Sun). Main courses from £13.50; bar meals from £6.50.
Closed	Open all day.
Directions	In village centre on A41, 6 miles west of Aylesbury.

Simon Offen
Five Arrows Hotel,
Waddesdon, Aylesbury HP18 0JE

Tel	01296 651727
Web	www.waddesdon.org.uk

Buckinghamshire

The Green Dragon
Haddenham

In what was once a manorial courthouse by Haddenham's pretty green, fabulous modern food is created. In the open-plan bar, with its laid-back medley of furniture and open fire, relax over a pint of village-brewed Notley Ale or one of several good wines by the glass. Graze on a decent lunchtime sandwich or a platter of organic cheeses, or settle down to something more substantial; the imaginative menu never stays still and set lunch (Tuesday to Thursday) is a snip at £12.95. Look forward to canon of lamb with spring greens, white beans and basil dressing, or halibut with creamed bacon (they have 18 different ways with fish). Sweet tooths will be happy with a pretty plateful of peach tarte tatin or a cappuccino crème brûlée. Families come for Sunday lunch and there's a sheltered courtyard for al fresco meals.

Meals	12pm-2pm; 7pm-9.30pm. Main courses £9.95-£18.00; set menu £12.95 (Tues-Thur); Sunday lunch £17.95.
Closed	3pm-6.30pm & Sun from 4pm.
Directions	2 miles from Thame; follow signs for Haddenham & Thame Parkway station.

Peter Moffat
The Green Dragon,
8 Churchway,
Haddenham HP17 8AA
Tel 01844 291403
Web www.eatatthedragon.co.uk

Entry 40 Map 9

Buckinghamshire

The Polecat Inn
Prestwood

A quirky place packed with character. Chintzy curtains, low lighting and beams, button-backed chairs, cosy corners, rugs and a fireplace stacked with logs make the 17th-century Polecat Inn feel more home than pub. The unusual flint bar serves several real ales, including Morland Old Speckled Hen and Marstons Pedigree, and there is an impressive selection of malts, and 16 wines by the glass. Among ticking clocks and happy banter, walkers and families tuck into tempting dishes such as steak and kidney pie, seafood hotpot, or roast duck with orange and cognac sauce. The chocolate and hazelnut tart with fudge sauce might just finish you off, so take one of the walking maps thoughtfully provided by John and work off any over-indulgence in the Chiltern Hills. It's a beautifully run place, and has a gorgeous garden.

Meals	12pm-2pm; 6.30pm-9pm. Main courses £9.20-£14; bar meals £3.90-£5.90.
Closed	2.30pm-6pm & Sun from 3pm.
Directions	On A4128 between Great Missenden & High Wycombe.

John Gamble
The Polecat Inn,
170 Wycombe Road,
Prestwood HP16 0HJ
Tel 01494 862253

Entry 41 Map 9

Buckinghamshire

Three Horseshoes Inn
Radnage

London may only be an hour's drive, but this is lost down a leafy lane. Red kites circle a deep bowl of countryside, smoke curls from cottages below, and the inn surveys the idyllic scene from on high. Inside are flagstones and an open fire in the tiny bar, and exposed timbers and pine settles in the restaurant. Simon, chef turned patron, has cooked at Le Gavroche and all the best places; dinner is delectable and the homemade piccalilli worth the trip alone. Come for lunch and baked camembert with garlic and rosemary, stay for dinner and tiger prawns, roasted sea bass, bread and butter pudding with marmalade ice cream. If you're here for the night, private stairs lead to super attic rooms (and more in the annexe) with silky quilts, goose down pillows, deluge showers, funky furniture and Farrow & Ball walls. Breakfast indulgently, drink in the views, hike in the hills, walk by the Thames. There's jazz and tapas once a month and in summer you can eat on the terrace at the back while ducks circle a sunken phone box in the pond. Great value set lunches, and sandwiches for passing walkers.

Rooms	6: 2 doubles, 1 suite, 1 single, 2 garden rooms. From £85.
Meals	12pm-2.30pm; 7pm-9.30pm. Main courses £10.50-£18.50; bar meals (lunch) £3.75-£13.50.
Closed	3pm-6pm & Mon. Open all day Sun till 8pm.
Directions	M40 junc. 5, A40 south thro' Stokenchurch, left for Radnage. After 2 miles, left to Bennett End. Sharp right, up hill, on left.

Simon Crawshaw & Tracey Button
Three Horseshoes Inn,
Bennett End, Radnage,
High Wycombe HP14 4EB
Tel   01494 483273
Web   www.thethreehorseshoes.net

Buckinghamshire

The Old Ship
Cadmore End

Down the steps to this wonderful, laid-back place just a few feet from the main road. Inside is a tiny space with furniture from the 80s, a red and brown patterned carpet, red draylon covered stools, wood panelling and dado rails. But none of this matters! It's the menu on the board that inspires (pea and Berkshire ham soup, Cadmore End rabbit pie) along with the jugs of beer brought up from the cellar and Rob and Sarah's infectious enthusiasm. Ninety per cent of the food is sourced within five miles of the pub and local allotment owners grow the vegetables. Just a small choice of house wine but if you want anything different you can choose from a selection of bin ends all labelled and priced. There's a large basset hound padding about and a roaring wood-burner; impromptu musical evenings are not uncommon.

Meals	12.15pm-2pm; 6.30pm-9pm; no food Sun eve. Main courses £8.50-£13.50.
Closed	3pm-6pm (7pm Sun) & all day Mon.
Directions	On B482 between Marlow & Stokenchurch & M40 junc 5.

Rob Jennings
The Old Ship,
Marlow Road, Cadmore End,
High Wycombe HP14 3PN
Tel   01494 883496

Entry 43 Map 4

Buckinghamshire

Old Queens Head
Penn

David and Becky Salisbury's mini-empire now contains this pub by the green. Dating from 1666 it has character and charm while inside, old beams and timbers in the rambling bar and dining areas blend perfectly with a stylish and contemporary décor – rug-strewn flags, polished boards, classic fabrics, lovely old oak. Food follows the successful formula of the Alford Arms, Frithsden, The Swan at Denham and the Royal Oak at Marlow, innovative seasonal menus and chalkboard specials mixing classic pub recipes with modern British flair. Choices range from 'small plates' – pan fried squid and chorizo on cannellini bean and parsley salad – to big dishes of slow-roast pork belly on black pudding fritter or wild mushroom, beetroot and Barkham Blue strudel. Great puddings too, and a glorious summer garden.

Meals	12pm-2.30pm (3pm Sat; 4pm Sun); 7pm-10pm. Main courses £10.75-£15.25.
Closed	Open all day.
Directions	From High Wycombe (M40 junc. 4), A40 towards Beaconsfield, then left for 1.5 miles into Hammersley Lane; pub on right, opposite church.

David & Becky Salisbury
Old Queens Head, Hammersley Lane,
Penn, High Wycombe HP10 8EY
Tel   01494 813371
Web   www.oldqueensheadpenn.co.uk

Entry 44 Map 4

Buckinghamshire

The Swan Inn
Denham

Swap the bland and everyday for the picture-book perfection of Denham village and the stylish Swan. Georgian, double-fronted, swathed in wisteria, the building has had a makeover by David and Becky Salisbury (of the Alford Arms, the Old Queens Head and the Royal Oak). It has been transformed by rug-strewn boards, chunky tables, cushioned settles, a log fire and a fabulous terrace for outdoor meals. Food is modern British. If pressed for time, choose from the 'small plates' list – sautéed pigeon breast with creamed shallots or salt and pepper squid with citrus mayonnaise. If you've nothing to rush for, linger over braised Henley venison with thyme mash accompanied by a pint of Courage Best or one of 19 wines by the glass. The owners have thought of everything, and the gardens are large enough for the kids to go wild in.

Meals	12pm-2.30pm (3pm Sat; 4pm Sun); 7pm-10pm. Main courses £11.25-£15.25.
Closed	Open all day.
Directions	From A412 (M25 junc. 17 or M40 junc. 1) follow signs for Denham.

David & Becky Salisbury
The Swan Inn,
Village Road, Denham UB9 5BH
Tel   01895 832085
Web   www.swaninndenham.co.uk

Entry 45 Map 4

Buckinghamshire

The Ostrich
Colnbrook

The Ostrich is an ancient, rambling place, within a mile of the motorways. Cross Oak Inns must have balked at the prospect of refurbishment, and the wonky timbered façade remains, but step through the huge glass doors and you enter a world in which old blends vibrantly with new. There's a glittering scarlet and steel bar that picks up the colour in the original stained glass, while the floors are slate-tiled and the furniture chunky. Expect sandblasted beams, original standing timbers and, in the atmospheric dining room, bowed, putty-coloured walls. Food is modern British and the menu wide-ranging, so pitch up for salads and sandwiches, ham hock terrine, herb-crusted lamb rump with red wine jus, and chocolate chilli parfait with mango compote. Take a peek upstairs at the lofty, tightly raftered function room – amazing.

Meals	12pm-2.15pm; 6pm-9.15pm (6.30pm-8.45pm Sun). Main courses £8.75-£18.50; sandwiches from £4.95 (Mon-Fri).
Closed	3pm-5.30pm (3pm-6pm Sat).
Directions	Colnbrook is signed off M4 (junc. 5) & A4 east of Slough.

Natalie Sydenham
The Ostrich,
High St, Colnbrook, Slough SL3 0JZ
Tel   01753 682628
Web   www.theostrichcolnbrook.co.uk

Entry 46 Map 4

Buckinghamshire

The Hand and Flowers
Marlow

It's almost Shakespearean. Ludlow's claim to the culinary crown of England is under challenge from prosperous Marlow; instead of arrows falling from the sky, Michelin stars are tumbling down. Chief instigator is Tom, whose incredible cooking has attracted interest in only two years; locals now fill the place day and night. Step into these airy 18th-century cottages and find flagged floors under low beams – it's remarkably easy-going. There's no froth on the menu, no dress code in the restaurant, just ambrosial food that elates. Try perfectly cooked salmon with frozen horseradish, sausages from pigs that munch windfalls in the orchards of a Suffolk estate, vanilla crème brûlée washed down by a honey-sweet beer chaser. Four stylish rooms stand 30 paces along the road in two refurbished cottages (expect a little noise). Beth, a sculptor, oversaw their creation; you get exposed beams, cow hide rugs, Egyptian cotton and flat-screen TVs. One room has a hot tub on a private terrace, another has a telescope and a window for stargazing. The Thames is close for revitalising walks. Special.

Rooms	4 doubles. £140-£190.
Meals	12pm-2.30pm; 7pm-9.30pm.
	Main courses £12.50-£21;
	bar lunch from £7.50.
Closed	25 & 26 December.
Directions	M4 junc. 9; A404 north; into Marlow; A4155 dir. Henley; on edge of town on right.

Tom & Beth Kerridge
The Hand and Flowers,
126 West Street, Marlow SL7 2BP
Tel 01628 482277
Web www.thehandandflowers.co.uk

Buckinghamshire

Royal Oak
Marlow

The old whitewashed cottage stands in a hamlet on the edge of the common. It's one of a thriving quartet of dining pubs owned by David and Becky Salisbury (the Alford Arms, Hertfordshire; the Swan Inn and the Old Queens Head, Buckinghamshire) and the relaxed but professional staff make it special. Beyond the terrace is a stylish, open-plan bar, cheerful with terracotta walls, rug-strewn boards, cushioned pews and crackling log fires. Order a pint of local Rebellion ale or one of the 17 wines available by the glass and check out the daily chalkboard or printed menu. Innovative pub grub comes in the form of 'small plates' (crispy duck leg on bean sprout and coriander salad) and main meals (seared Henley venison loin on parsnip dauphinoise): fresh and delicious. The sprawling gardens are perfect for summer.

Our inspectors appreciate a genuine welcome from hands-on publicans, a respect for local, seasonal or organic food, an enthusiastic staff, character and charm.

Meals	12pm-2.30pm (3pm Sat; 4pm Sun); 7pm-10pm. Main courses £10.75-£15.25.
Closed	Open all day.
Directions	From Marlow A4155; right signed Bovingdon Green.

Trasna Rice-Giff
Royal Oak,
Frieth Road, Bovingdon Green,
Marlow SL7 2JF

Tel	01628 488611
Web	www.royaloakmarlow.co.uk

Entry 48 Map 4

Buckinghamshire

49 Stag & Huntsmen Hambleden, Henley-on-Thames RG9 6RP
01491 571227
The setting's the thing and the picture-book village is popular with film crews. Bars are small and traditional, carpeted and lively; the dining room modern. Hearty food, excellent ale and invigorating walks into the Chilterns.

50 The White Horse Village Lane, Hedgerley, Slough SL2 3UY
01753 643225
Super local in easy reach of the M40 (junc. 2). Swap the service station for flagstones, inglenook, beamed bar and a perfect ploughman's lunch. Seven real ales are tapped from the barrel.

51 King of Prussia Blackpond Lane, Farnham Royal, Slough SL2 3EG
01753 643006
A great little place on a quiet country road close to Cliveden and Burnham Beeches. Relax with the papers and a pint in the revamped bar, or tuck into modern pub dishes in the informal dining rooms.

52 The Mole and Chicken Easington, Long Crendon HP18 9EY
01844 208387
Stunning views and quirky blackboard menus are two of the seductive charms that await those who beat a path to this door. A really cosy winter pub, so come on a damp Sunday and settle in for the day.

53 The Swan 2 Wavendon Road, Salford, Milton Keynes MK17 8BD
01908 281008
Innovative Peach Pubs have revamped this ordinary village boozer with style and panache; escape the M1 for great antipasti nibbles and enjoyable modern pub food, served all day.

54 The Crown Crown Lane, Little Missenden, Amersham HP7 0RD
01494 862571
An unspoilt brick-cottage pub in a pretty village, run by the same family for over 90 years. Excellent beers, good wines and sandwiches, a big garden and walking all around.

55 Lions of Bledlow Church End, Bledlow, Princes Risborough HP27 9PE
01844 343345
An ideal base for tackling one of the local walks into the Chiltern Hills, this time-worn 16th-century village pub delivers a good range of real ales, a pleasant garden, and hearty pub food.

Red Lion
Hinxton

In pretty Hinxton, close to Cambridge, the rambling, pink-washed Red Lion is a popular stopover in an area deprived of good food pubs. And its big garden overlooks the church: a lovely spot for peaceful summer sipping. Another draw is the buzzy atmosphere Alex Clarke has instilled in the beamed bar with its deep green chesterfields, worn wooden boards, cosy log fire and ticking wall clock. Ales from City of Cambridge, Adnams and Woodforde's add to the appeal, as do eclectic menus that list a range of classic pub dishes and more inventive specials, all at good prices. Pop in for a beef and horseradish sandwich or linger over pot-roasted rabbit. Puddings are to die for: sticky toffee pudding with caramel sauce, English trifle and passion fruit pavlova... Irresistible.

Meals	12pm-2pm (2.30pm Fri & Sat); 6.45pm-9pm (9.30pm Fri & Sat; 7pm-9pm Sun). Main courses £8.95-£17.50; bar meals £4.95-£9.95; Sunday roast £8.95-£10.50.
Closed	3pm (3.30pm Fri & Sat)-6pm; 4.30pm-7pm Sun.
Directions	Hinxton is signed off A11, 2 miles from M11 junc. 9, 8 miles south of Cambridge. Follow A1301 north, then turn left into village.

	Alex Clarke
	Red Lion,
	High Street, Hinxton,
	Cambridge CB10 1QY
Tel	01799 530601
Web	www.redlionhinxton.co.uk

Entry 56 Map 9

The Queen's Head
Newton

David and Juliet Short have run the Queen's Head for a quarter of a century and are now joined by son Robert who shares their commitment. There's a timeless appeal in the almost spartan main bar where clattering floorboards, plain wooden tables and aged paintings are watched over by a vintage clock that keeps the beat. A tiny carpeted lounge with dark beams and well-worn furniture is a cosier alternative when its fire is blazing. The whole interior is unusual and utterly unspoilt, a genuine backdrop for shove ha'penny, cribbage and beef dripping on toast. Yes, the food is simple, but deliciously so: rare roast beef sliced wafer-thin, ham on the bone, a mug of rich brown soup, locally baked bread – dispensed with slow deliberation and accompanied by Adnams ales tapped from the cask. A real pub with a loyal following.

Meals	12pm-2.15pm; 7pm-9.30pm. Bar meals £3.30-£5.80.
Closed	2.30pm-6pm (3pm-7pm Sun).
Directions	M11 junc. 11; A10 for Royston; left on B1368.

	David & Juliet Short
	The Queen's Head,
	Newton,
	Cambridge CB2 5PG
Tel	01223 870436

Entry 57 Map 9

Cambridgeshire

Hole in the Wall
Little Wilbraham

Hiding down a hundred lanes, it was just another pretty pub. In the hands of veteran chef Stephen Bull it has been transformed, with Jenny Chapman perfect front of house. It's clearly well-loved; regulars drop by for a swift half in the big timbered bar, and gather for lunch in the country-style restaurant at the back. In the bar are horse brasses and country prints, junk-shop find tables and several winter log fires. In contrast to this old-fashioned rusticity the food is decidedly modern: ingredients are as local and as organic as can be and the blackboard specials change regularly. Chris Leeton's cooking embraces many ideas, from classic chargrilled rump steaks with hand-cut chips and brandy sauce to butternut squash and tomato strudel. On summery days, the front garden is glorious.

Meals	12pm-2.30pm (2pm Sun); 7pm-9.30pm
	Main courses £10.50-£17.50; bar meals £3.75-£8.
Closed	3pm-6.30pm, Sun eve & Mon.
Directions	Take the Stow cum Quy turn off A14, then A1303 Newmarket road & follow signs to Little Wilbraham.

Stephen Bull
Hole in the Wall,
2 High Street, Little Wilbraham,
Cambridge CB1 5JY
Tel   01223 812282
Web   www.the-holeinthewall.com

Entry 58 Map 9

Cambridgeshire

Three Horseshoes
Madingley

From the outside, the thatched pub looks old-worldy; push the door and you embrace the new century. Here is a simple, stylish, open feel in pale wooden floors and furniture and soft sage and cream paintwork; there is space and light yet the familiar features of the old pub remain. The bar has local ales such as Cambridge Boathouse Bitter, a modern open log fire and a blackboard menu packed with Italian country dishes and imaginative combinations. Chef-patron Richard Stokes has run this classy gastropub for over 14 years and he serves some of the best food in the region. Excellent service matches the laid-back atmosphere of the busy bar while formality and white linen come together in the conservatory dining room, popular with business lunchers. In either room the choice of wines is superb — pity the designated driver.

Meals	12pm-2pm (2.30pm Sat & Sun); 6.30-9.30pm (6pm-8.30pm Sun).
	Main courses £10.95-£24.95; bar meals £7.95-£10.95; set menu £10.95 & £15.95.
Closed	3pm-6pm. Open all day Sat & Sun in summer.
Directions	Off A1303, 2 miles west of Cambridge.

Richard Stokes
Three Horseshoes,
High Street, Madingley,
Cambridge CB3 8AB
Tel   01954 210221
Web   www.threehorseshoesmadingley.co.uk

Entry 59 Map 9

Cambridgeshire

The Cock
Hemingford Grey

The young licensees have stripped the lovely 17th-century village pub back to its original simplicity. Step directly into an attractive bare-boarded bar, cosy with low beams and log-burner, and sup award-winning East Anglian ales: Highwayman, Golden Jackal and a monthly local guest. For food, move into the airy restaurant where buttermilk walls and modern prints sit beautifully with wooden floors and tables. The menu is strong on pub classics and the chef makes his own sausages, served with a choice of mash with horseradish or black pudding and delicious sauces (wild mushroom, wholegrain mustard). Duck parcel with sweet and sour cucumber is a favourite starter, while fish and game dishes reveal a refreshing, modern view. The British and continental cheeses should not be missed, and Sunday lunch is much praised.

Cambridgeshire

The Crown
Broughton

There's been a pub cum saddler's shop in this peaceful hamlet since medieval times; villagers saved the Crown from residential conversion in 2001 and now you find one of Cambridgeshire's best gastropubs. Inside: huge terracotta floor slabs; a long lightwood bar aimed at drinkers; white wines under ice in a vast brass trough bucket. Round the side of the chimney breast is a dining room with fresh blooms, tall wood-burner and orange check curtains – impressively 21st-century. If the twice-cooked beef with curly kale and red wine sauce and the treacle tart with cinnamon ice cream is anything to go by, Simon Cadge's food, refined and unshowy, is worth travelling the distance for. Children have capacious lawns to play on in summer, and conkers from majestic chestnuts to plunder.

Meals	12pm-2.30pm; 6.30pm-9pm (9.30pm Fri & Sat, 8.30pm Sun). Main courses £9.95-£15.95; light lunch £6.95-£12.95.
Closed	3pm-6pm (4pm-6.30pm Sun).
Directions	From A14 south for Hemingford Grey; 2 miles S of Huntingdon.

Meals	12pm-2pm; 6.30pm-9pm (9.30pm Fri & Sat) 12pm-3pm; 7pm-9pm Sun. Main courses £9.50-£17; bar meals £9.50-£16.
Closed	3pm-6pm; Mon & Tues. Open all day Sun.
Directions	Broughton is signed off A141 north east of Huntingdon.

Oliver Thain & Richard Bradley
The Cock,
47 High Street, Hemingford Grey,
Huntingdon PE28 9BJ

| Tel | 01480 463609 |
| Web | www.cambscuisine.com |

Entry 60 Map 9

Simon Cadge
The Crown,
Bridge Road, Broughton,
Huntingdon PE28 3AY

| Tel | 01487 824428 |
| Web | www.thecrownbroughton.co.uk |

Entry 61 Map 9

Cambridgeshire

The George Inn
Spaldwick

The rambling, buttermilk building dates from the 1500s and overlooks the village green. Inside, walls are hung with contemporary art, leather sofas and chunky wood tables speak 'modern brasserie', old timbers are exposed and floors are bare boards. The uncluttered styling blends beautifully with the history of the place. Modern variations on traditional dishes fit the bill – black pudding and seared scallops with chive and tomato butter sauce, calves' liver with red wine jus, and warm Valrhona chocolate mousse with pistachio ice cream. This is simple, robust food based on first-rate ingredients. The relaxed feel extends to the several eating areas in the rambling bar and the magnificent high raftered restaurant, and to drink there's Adnams Broadside or Greene King IPA. Or one of a slate of 24 wines by the glass.

Meals	12pm-2.30pm; 6pm-9.30pm. Main courses £5.95-£15.95.
Closed	Open all day.
Directions	Beside A141, off A14, 7 miles west of Huntingdon.

Nick Thoday & Louise Smith
The George Inn,
High Street, Spaldwick,
Huntingdon PE28 0TD
Tel   01480 890293

Entry 62 Map 9

Cambridgeshire

The Pheasant
Keyston

After running The Pheasant for the Huntsbridge group for two years, Jay and Taffeta bought the leasehold in 2007. Here you have a menu that is modern British, with the emphasis on local, seasonal produce. Add an enterprising list of wines and expertly kept ales and you have the Pheasant to a T. This textbook country pub does beams, open fires and comfy sofas better than anyone, and the cooking is as restorative as the surroundings; confit garlic, thyme and almond risotto, roast mallard with braised puy lentils, and treacle sponge and custard. The light lunch and early supper menu is tremendous value, and if you don't want a full-blown meal, there's bar food and beautiful unpasteurised British cheeses. The Pheasant never forgets it's a pub; Adnams ales, together with two or three guest ales, are always on hand pump.

Meals	12pm-2.30pm; 6.30pm-9.30pm (9pm Sun). Main courses £12.95-£19.95; bar meals £8.95-£10.95; Sunday lunch £18.50 & £22.50.
Closed	3pm-6pm.
Directions	Keyston off A14, halfway between Huntingdon & Kettering.

Taffeta & Jay Scrimshaw
The Pheasant,
Village Loop Road, Keyston,
Huntingdon PE28 0RE
Tel   01832 710241
Web   www.thepheasant-keyston.co.uk

Entry 63 Map 9

Cambridgeshire

The Anchor Inn
Sutton Gault

A real find, a 1650 ale house on Chatteris Fen, run by good people. Wedged between the bridge and the raised dyke, the little inn was built to bed and board the men conscripted to tame the vast watery tracts of swamp and scrub. These days cosy luxury infuses every corner. There are low beamed ceilings, timber-framed walls, raw dark panelling and terracotta-tiled floors. A wood-burner warms the bar, so stop for a pint of cask ale, then pick from a menu that is light, imaginative and surprising: hand-dressed crabs from Cromer in spring, asparagus and Bottisham hams in summer, wild duck from the marshes in winter. Breakfast is equally indulgent. Four spotless rooms up the narrow stair fit the mood exactly: not posh, supremely comfy, with trim carpets, wicker chairs, crisp white duvets, Indian throws, candles by the bath. The suites have a sofabed each and three rooms have fen and river views. Footpaths flank the water; stroll down and you might see mallards or Hooper swans, even a seal – the river is tidal to the Wash. Don't miss Ely (the bishop comes to eat).

Rooms	4: 1 double, 1 twin, 2 suites. £59.50-£155. Singles from £59.50.
Meals	12pm-2pm (2.30pm Sun); 7pm-9pm (6.30-9.30pm Sat; 6.30-8.30pm Sun). Main courses £9.50-£19.95; lunch, 2 courses, £11.95 (Mon-Fri).
Closed	3pm-7pm (6.30pm Sat & Sun).
Directions	West from Ely on A142. Left in Sutton onto B1381 for Earith. On south fringes of Sutton, right signed Sutton Gault. 1 mile north on left at bridge.

Adam Pickup & Carlene Bunten
The Anchor Inn,
Bury Lane,
Sutton Gault, Ely CB6 2DB
Tel   01353 778537
Web   www.anchorsuttongault.co.uk

Crown Inn
Elton

Conkers, hundreds of them, harden to a deep russet brown in the late summer sun by the front door and under the towering chestnut tree. Beneath which huddles The Crown; the setting is idyllic. The ancient sandstone inn looks across the green of this Wolds village that harbours the equally beautiful Elton Hall. The bar, beamed, and painted in pastel hues, with a huge oak mantle and grate, is the epitome of Old England. Here you may enjoy a pint of Golden Crown and a light meal. In the 'snug', seated by the big log fire on a wintery night, what nicer than to settle into chicken liver and brandy parfait with homemade chutney or fillets of seabass and red mullet with prawn and courgette risotto. Lunch is more traditional: ale battered haddock and chips, beef, ale and mushroom pie. Weekend dining is in the octagonal conservatory, which opens to a large decked area, great for summer. As for the bedrooms, they're brand new and gorgeous (plantation-style shutters for privacy, king-size beds, great lighting) with snazzy en suites. Two overlook the front, two are tucked away at the back.

Rooms	4 twins/doubles. £90. Singles £60
Meals	12pm-2.30pm (3pm Sun); 6.30pm-9pm; no food Sun eve or Mon all day. Main courses £8.95-£19; bar meals from £4.50; Sunday lunch £12.50 & £19.95.
Closed	Mon (bar open in eve). Open all day.
Directions	Village signed off A605, 6 miles SW of Peterborough. Pub on village green on Nassington Rd.

Marcus & Rosalind Lamb
Crown Inn,
8 Duck Street, Elton, Peterborough PE8 6RQ
Tel   01832 280232
Web   www.thecrowninn.org

Cambridgeshire

66   The Old Bridge Hotel 1 High Street, Huntingdon PE18 6QT
01480 424300
A smart hotel with battalions of devoted locals who come for the informal pubby bar (good local ales), the food (delicious), the wines (exceptional) and the hugely comfortable interiors.

67   Dyke's End 8 Fair Green, Reach, Cambridge CB5 0JD
01638 743816
Real community hamlet whose "splendid pub" (to quote the Prince of Wales) is owned by the village. A lovely old place, formerly a farmhouse, now with candlelit bars and interesting bar food.

68   White Pheasant Market Street, Fordham, Ely CB7 5LQ
01638 720414
Very welcoming dining pub with bare boards, wooden tables, crackling logs, fresh fish and farmhouse cheeses. Handpumped local Milton ales and a dozen wines by the glass. Reports welcome.

69   Cambridge Blue 85 Gwydir Street, Cambridge CB1 2LG
01223 361382
Away from the centre, this simple local has a warm atmosphere, stacks of rowing paraphernalia and a large garden. A wide choice of ales, among them Adnams and Elgoods, and straightforward bar food.

Cheshire

Hanging Gate
Sutton

High above Macclesfield, the heather moors of the Dark Peak fracture into steep, finger-like ridges; this very old pub hangs from the western slope. A staircase of tiny rooms drops sharply from a sublime little tap room via brass, copper and watercolour-dressed snugs to the 'View Room', where picture windows unveil an inspiring panorama that stretches to the West Pennine Moors. Several open fires add to the timelessness created by the wizened beams, flagged or carpeted floors and cosy corners where beers from Hydes of Manchester complement the splendid home-cooked food. Game from local estates, meat and fowl from nearby farms are crafted into unfussy, fulfilling meals with a strong local following. It's popular, too, with ramblers from the nearby Gritstone Trail and Macclesfield Forest. A brilliant place.

Cheshire

The Ship Inn
Wincle

The red sandstone building houses a small and well-loved local. Its two little taprooms are utterly simple, one with half barrels as ends for its counter, the other with stone flags and a cast-iron range. Food is taken seriously in the new dining room extension; ingredients are local and booking essential at weekends. There are sandwiches at lunchtime, and beer-battered haddock; fancier dishes include canon of lamb with date and herb crust and rosemary jus, and turbot and sea bass on crab linguine with roasted tomato sauce. The Ship is loved too for its beers: four on hand pump and a traditional cider or perry. The little country garden has tables and chairs shaded by mature trees; you're on the edge of the Peaks so the walks stretch in every direction. Giles is full of enthusiasm and knows what makes a pub tick.

Meals	12pm-2.30pm; 7pm-9.30pm; Sun 12pm-5pm, 6pm-9.30pm. Main courses £7.50-£17.50.		Meals	12pm-2.30pm (4pm Sat & Sun); 6pm-10pm. Main courses £10.95-£16.95; sandwiches from £4.95.
Closed	3pm-5pm. Open all day Sat & Sun.		Closed	3pm-6.30pm Tues-Thurs & Mon all day (except bank hols). Open all day Sat & Sun.
Directions	From A54 follow signs to Langley at Fairway Motel.		Directions	From Congleton A54 for Buxton for 7 miles; right at Clulow Cross for Wincle, 1.5 miles.

	Ian Rottenbury Hanging Gate, Meg Lane, Higher Sutton, Macclesfield SK11 0NG			Giles Meadows The Ship Inn, Wincle, Macclesfield SK11 0QE
Tel	01260 252238		Tel	01260 227217

Entry 70 Map 8

Entry 71 Map 8

Cheshire

The Plough
Eaton

The food at the Plough is fields ahead of much of the competition – but that's not all. This attractive red-brick building on a busy stretch of road has been serving ales since the 17th century; it started out as a coaching inn. Eat or drink in rooms arranged around a central bar; all are smart and comfortable, with antiques, prints and a convivial air. Then there's the Old Barn Restaurant – all rustic beams and centuries-old atmosphere – which was brought, plank by plank, all the way from Wales, then reconstructed here. Outside is a lawned raised garden. Specials might include asparagus brûlée topped with goat's cheese and caramelised onions, grilled sardines in a garlic tomato sauce, and roast pheasant with cognac, mushroom and bacon sauce. Puddings are a homemade treat – to be squeezed in after generous portions.

Meals	12pm-2.30pm; 6pm-9.30pm (12pm-8pm Sun). Main courses £7.95-£17.95.
Closed	Open all day.
Directions	Beside A536, 2.5 miles north west of Congleton.

Mujdat Karatas
The Plough,
Macclesfield Road, Eaton,
Congleton CW12 2NH
Tel   01260 280207

Entry 72 Map 8

Cheshire

Harrington Arms
Gawsworth

The creeper-covered, red-brick building started life as a farmhouse in 1663 and could still be part of a working farm. The outside may have grown but the inside has barely changed – and it wasn't long ago that they were serving beer here just from the cask. Off the passageway are a bar and a quarry-tiled snug – big enough to fit a settle, a table and an open fire. Then two more public rooms: the traditionally furnished Top Parlour, and the Tap Room where Friday's folk club sessions take place. The Wightmans took over in 2006 and have changed little. That includes the quality of the ale: it's said you won't get a finer pint of Robinsons than at the Harrington. Home-cooked meals and snacks are of the traditional pork pie, ploughman's and slab-sandwich variety – simple and good.

Meals	12pm-2.30pm; 5pm-7.30pm. Bar meals £2.99-£9.75.
Closed	3pm-5pm.
Directions	On A536, 2.5 miles from Macclesfield.

Andy & Caroline Wightman
Harrington Arms,
Church Lane, Gawsworth,
Macclesfield SK11 9RR
Tel   01260 223325

Entry 73 Map 8

Cheshire

The White Lion
Barthomley

An inn since 1614 and a siege site in the Civil War, the character-oozing White Lion – wonky black and white timbers, thick thatched roof – stands beside a cobbled track close to a fine sandstone church. Step in to three gloriously unspoilt rooms, all woodsmoke and charm, wizened oak beams, ancient benches and twisted walls, tiny latticed windows and quarry-tiled floors. No music or electronic wizardry, just the crackling of log fires and a happy hubbub. Lunchtime food is listed on chalkboards as walkers and locals settle down on ancient settles at scrubbed wooden tables for hot beef and onion baguettes with chips, hearty ploughman's and Sunday roasts, washed down with well-kept pints of Cheshire-brewed Burtonwood Top Hat. Summer seating is at picnic benches on the cobbles, with pretty views onto the village. Gorgeous!

Meals	12pm-2pm (2.30pm Sun); no food in the eve. Main courses £3.75-£6.95.
Closed	Open all day.
Directions	M6 junc. 16; 3rd exit for Alsager; left for Barthomley.

Laura Condliffe
The White Lion,
Barthomley,
Crewe CW2 5PG
Tel   01270 882242

Entry 74 Map 8

Cheshire

Bhurtpore Inn
Aston

The extended old Cheshire-brick village farmhouse trumpets 11 real ales, countless bottled continental beers, one hundred malts, and farmhouse ciders and perry. Whatever you choose, you can soak it up with something excellent from the ever-changing menu. The pub was named after an Indian city besieged by a local army commander, and multitudinous maps, paintings and ephemera spread through the warren of rooms vividly recall this deed. Low beams sag beneath myriad water jugs, and open fires crackle in the cosy lounge, where a mongrel-mix of furniture and seating, settles, a longcase clock and absorbing local bric-a-brac add tremendous character. The home-cooked food is really tasty, with local produce to the fore, the portions generous, the choice vast, and there are curries – galore! One great little place.

Meals	12pm-2pm (2.30pm Sat); 6.45pm-9.30pm (12pm-9pm Sun). Main courses £7.95-£13.
Closed	2.30pm-6.30pm. Open all day Sun.
Directions	Off A530, 5 miles SW of Nantwich. Follow signs for Wrenbury from turn in Aston near pottery.

Simon George
Bhurtpore Inn, Wrenbury Road,
Aston, Nantwich CW5 8DQ
Tel   01270 780917
Web   www.bhurtpore.co.uk

Entry 75 Map 7

The Dysart Arms
Bunbury

It is one of those rare places — all things to all people. With separate areas clustered round a central bar, it feels open and cosy at the same time. The 18th-century brick building protects a listed interior — rooms have scrubbed floorboards, good solid tables and chairs, pictures, prints and plants, and French windows opening to the terrace and garden. There's an inglenook packed with logs, a dining area in a library, and the beers and wines are superb. They're proud, too, of their food, and rightly so: game casserole with herb dumplings; salmon and smoked haddock fishcakes with tartare sauce; roast plum and almond tart; the cheeses are taken as seriously as the cask ales (try the local Weetwood Bitter) and the wines are thoughtfully chosen. Warm, intimate, friendly… the place runs on well-oiled wheels.

The Grosvenor Arms
Aldford

Pretty Aldford is all prim cottages and farms with barleysugar-twist chimneys and chequerboard brickwork. Not far from the old church and castle is the imposing brick and Victorian half-timber village local rejuvenated by Brunning & Price as their flagship pub. Something for everyone here in this most relaxing and classy pastiche: a traditional taproom and snug with log fire, tiled floor and a wonderful old photo of drunks in the stocks, an imposing part-panelled Library Room and a verdant conservatory. There are rustic kitchen tables on boards, tiles and rugs, a panoply of seating choices and a dark-wood bar groaning beneath hand pumps dispensing local beers. The ever-reliable B&P menu carries something for everyone and you can eat in summer on huge tree-shaded lawns next to the village cricket pitch.

Meals	12pm-9.30pm (9pm Sun). Main courses £8.50-£14.50.		Meals	12pm-10pm (9pm Sun). Main courses £7.95-£18.95.
Closed	Open all day.		Closed	Open all day.
Directions	Off A49, 3.5 miles from Tarporley.		Directions	6 miles south of Chester on B5130 to Farndon & Holt.

Darren & Elizabeth Snell
The Dysart Arms, Bowes Gate Road, Bunbury, Tarporley CW6 9PH
Tel   01829 260183
Web   www.dysartarms-bunbury.co.uk

Gary Kidd
The Grosvenor Arms, Chester Road, Aldford, Chester CH3 6HJ
Tel   01244 620228
Web   www.grosvenorarms-aldford.co.uk

Entry 76 Map 7

Entry 77 Map 7

Albion Inn
Chester

Chester's last unspoilt Victorian corner pub. Many a young man would have spent his shilling in the public bar, before he left to sign up for King and Country. The Albion is dedicated to the memory of those who fought. To a background of William Morris wallpaper, leather sofas and soft glowing lamps there is Great War memorabilia aplenty – and a 1928 Steck Player piano that occasionally entertains. There are four cask ales, a flurry of malts, decent wines and 'Trench Rations' in un-trench-like portions – boiled gammon and pease pudding, sausages from Penrith – often organic and locally sourced. Yummy Staffordshire oatcakes from Tunstall with all sorts of fillings are a house special; desserts include rice pudding with a dollop of jam. Do stay: the bedrooms at the top, reached via a separate entrance, are compact, cosy and en suite, with good antique furniture and super-comfortable beds. You are very welcome to bring the dogs (cold water and sausages available) but not the children. With the same landlord for 37 years, the Albion is that rare thing: a traditional city pub with an individual streak.

Rooms	2: 1 double, 1 twin. £75. Singles £65.
Meals	12pm-2pm; 5pm-8pm (6pm-8.30 Sat); no food Sun eve. Main courses £4.95-£8.90.
Closed	3pm-5pm (6pm Sat; 7pm Sun). Open all day Fri.
Directions	Opp. city walls between The Newgate & River Dee.

Michael Mercer
Albion Inn,
Park Street, Chester CH1 1RN
Tel   01244 340345
Web   www.albioninnchester.co.uk

Cheshire

The Pheasant Inn
Higher Burwardsley

After a hike along the Sandstone Trail, come and stand before the largest fireplace in Cheshire with a pint of Weetwood Old Dog. Or sit out on the terrace and gaze across the Cheshire Plain all the way to North Wales. Gloriously positioned up in the Peckforton Hills, the Pheasant has been stylishly re-vamped inside. The old laid-back feel has survived the smartening up of the big, beamed and wooden-floored bars, and food is informally served in both bar and restaurant. Seared scallops with lime and dill dressing, smoked haddock and salmon fishcakes, lambs' liver, smoked bacon and onion gravy, and sticky toffee pudding with toffee sauce should satisfy the most ravenous walker, while lunchtime's hot beef sandwiches are equally hearty. There are four ales and 12 wines by the glass but it's the views that you'll come back for.

Meals	12pm-9.30pm (10pm Fri & Sat; 8.30pm Sun); no food 3pm-6pm Mon. Main courses £8.50-£18.95; bar meals £3.95-£8.50.
Closed	Open all day.
Directions	Call for directions.

Andrew Nelson
The Pheasant Inn, Higher Burwardsley,
Tattenhall, Chester CH3 9PF
Tel 01829 770434
Web www.thepheasantinn.co.uk

Entry 79 Map 7

Cheshire

The Boot Inn
Willington

Prettily ivy-strewn, a row of country cottages turned pub. Set against wooded hills in the middle of fruit farming country, the village local looks west towards the Welsh Hills and south over the Cheshire plain. It's a gorgeous, sheltered spot with walks nearby. Inside, the pub has been opened up with the bar at the hub. Old quarry tiles, some panelling, characterful beams and a log-burning stove pull the walkers and talkers in. The stone-flagged dining room opens onto a garden you can spill into on warm days, there's a log fire in winter, and donkeys and cats to keep children entertained. Popular food ranges from sandwiches, baguettes and panini at the bar to local lamb with roast vegetables and sea bass deep-fried in sesame batter. Local Weetwood Ales are on draught, and there are a number of wines.

Meals	10am-2.30pm; 6pm-9.30pm Mon-Thurs; 10am-9.30pm Fri-Sun. Main courses £8.50-£12.95.
Closed	3pm-6pm. Open all day Fri-Sun.
Directions	Chester-Manchester A54; right for Willington; 2 miles, left at T-junc. for Boothsdale.

Mike Gollings
The Boot Inn,
Boothsdale, Willington,
Tarporley CW6 0NH
Tel 01829 751375

Entry 80 Map 7

Cheshire

The Fox & Barrel
Cotebrook

So called because a former landlord let a persued fox escape to the cellar, this busy, roadside pub throngs with drinkers and diners in equal measure. Inside, a comfortable mix of snug corners, interesting ornaments, pictures and prints on bay-windowed walls, a large open brick fire stacked with logs, and quarry tiles covered with traditional patterned rugs. There's also a large and pleasant dining room in cream; tables are candlelit and easy on the eye, and gentle background music plays. There are several cask ales, good wines and enjoyable food generously served: goat's cheese terrine with apple chutney, lamb rump with cranberry and redcurrant jus, steak and kidney pie, bouillabaisse – all homemade. Service is exemplary and the staff are attentive, whether you're in for a swift half or a slap-up meal.

Meals	12pm-2.30pm; 6pm-9.30pm (12pm-8pm Sun); no bar meals Fri & Sat eve & Sun.
	Main courses £8.95-£16.15; bar snacks from £4.95; Sunday lunch £9.50 & £14.50.
Closed	3pm-5.30pm. Open all day Sat & Sun.
Directions	On A49 near Oulton Park.

Chris Crossley
The Fox & Barrel, Forest Road,
Cotebrook, Tarporley CW6 9DZ

Tel	01829 760529
Web	www.thefoxandbarrel.com

Entry 81 Map 7

Cheshire

Chetwode Arms
Lower Whitley

The 400-year-old, Cheshire-brick roadside inn hides a warren of small rooms and passageways. There's the bar room itself, tiny, with an open coal fire, and four more; the snuggest may be used as a private dining room. Expect low ceilings, exposed brick and beams, fresh flowers and mirrors, oodles of atmosphere and tasty food. In the dining room – opening onto a terrace that overlooks the pub's own bowling green – contented locals tuck into local game pie, beef Wellington with wild mushroom sauce, salmon fishcakes with homemade chips and herb mayonnaise, and steaks cooked on hot rocks. There are lunchtime sandwiches, salads and ploughman's, four changing guest ales on tap and the wine list favours some top vineyards from Richard's home country – South Africa. Great for judicious drinkers of wine and beer, and a super dining pub.

Meals	12pm-2.30pm; 6pm-9.30pm (11.30am-9.30pm Sat & Sun). Main courses £10.75-£17.95.
Closed	3.30pm-5.30pm. Open all day Sat & Sun.
Directions	On A49 2 miles from M56 junc. 10.

Richard Starnok
Chetwode Arms, Street Lane,
Lower Whitley, Warrington WA4 4EN

Tel	01925 730203
Web	www.chetwodearms.com

Entry 82 Map 7

Cheshire

83   The Buffet Bar Stalybridge Station, Stalybridge SK15 1RF
0161 303 0007
Only a handful of these charming Victorian establishments survive
– this extraordinary, narrow little bar is an integral part of the busy
Stalybridge Station. Renowned for its choice of real ale, pies and
puddings.

84   Oddfellows Arms 73 Moor End Road, Mellor, Stockport SK6 5PT
0161 449 7826
Folk travel from miles around and ramblers tumble down footpaths
from the moors, for winter log fires and eclectic modern food.
Now the mellow gritstone pub has new owners; reports welcome.

85   The Old Harp Quayside, Little Neston, Wirral CH64 0TB
01513 366980
Small and unassuming in a stunning spot on the edge of the Dee
Marshes. Watch marsh harriers or little egrets as you down real ales
and gaze over the estuary to North Wales.

86   Old Harkers Arms Russell Street, Chester CH1 5AL
01244 344525
A buzzy atmosphere and a great range of microbrewery ales at this
beautifully converted warehouse down by the canal. Run by
Brunning & Price pubs, so expect good modern pub food.

87   The Cholmondeley Arms Cholmondeley, Malpas SY14 8BT
01829 720300
Gabled Victorian schoolhouse standing opposite Cholmondeley
Castle: expect an airy 'schoolroom' feel with raftered, vaulted
ceilings and educational relics. These days the chalk boards list
classy bar food.

88   Blue Bell Inn Bell o' th' Hill, Tushingham, Whitchurch SY13 4QS
01948 662172
Charismatic, mossy-tiled, wonkily beamed pub with a beautifully
lived-in feel. Super taproom, pints of Shropshire Gold, generous
pub food, and a peaceful garden with verdant views.

89   Dusty Miller Wrenbury, Nantwich CW5 8HG
01270 780537
Hugely popular pub in a beautifully converted watermill beside the
Shropshire Union Canal. Local food is ever-present on the
imaginative menus. Super al fresco areas.

90   Nags Head Long Lane, Haughton Moss, Tarporley CW6 9RN
01829 260265
Spic-and-span 17th-century pub with a real fire and all the
trimmings. Conservatory extension combines views with fresh
local food, and there's a big garden and bowling green.

The Gurnard's Head
Zennor

The coastline here is magical and the walk up to St Ives is hard to beat. Secret beaches appear at low tide, cliffs tumble down to the water and wild flowers streak the land pink in summer. As for the pub, you couldn't hope for a better base. It's earthy, warm, stylish and friendly, with airy interiors, colourwashed walls, stripped wooden floors and fires at both ends of the bar. Logs pile up in an alcove, maps and art hang on the walls, books fill every shelf; if you pick one up and don't finish it, take it home and post it back. Rooms are warm and cosy, simple and spotless, with superb mattresses, throws over armchairs, Roberts radios and, in the suite, a lovely big tub. Downstairs, super food, all homemade, can be eaten wherever you want: in the bar, in the restaurant or out in the garden in good weather. Snack on rustic delights – pork pies, crab claws, half a pint of Atlantic prawns – or tuck into more substantial treats: fresh asparagus with a hollandaise sauce, fish stew with new potatoes, rhubarb crème brûlée. Picnics are easily arranged and there's bluegrass folk music in the bar most weeks.

Rooms	7: 4 doubles, 3 twins/doubles. £80-£140. Singles from £60.
Meals	12.30pm-2.30pm; 6pm-9.30pm. Main courses £4.50-£10.95 (lunch), £4.50-£14 (dinner).
Closed	Open all day.
Directions	West from St Ives on B3306. On right at head of village.

Charles & Edmund Inkin
The Gurnard's Head,
Treen, Zennor, St Ives TR26 3DE
Tel   01736 796928
Web   www.gurnardshead.co.uk

Entry 91 Map 1

Cornwall

The Star Inn
St Just

Entrenched in the wild landscape close to Land's End is the 'last proper pub in Cornwall'. This 18th-century gem, owned by the ex-mayor of St Just and its oldest and most authentic inn, proudly shirks the trappings of tourism and remains a drinkers' den. Bands of locals sink pints of Tinners Ale in the low-beamed, spick-and-span bar, old pub games thrive and the place is the hub of the local folk scene, with live music at least ten nights a month, singalongs and joke-telling all part of the Monday evening entertainment. The dimly-lit bar is jam-packed with interest and walls are littered with seafaring and mining artefacts; coals glow in the grate on wild winter days. Come for St Austell ale and the 'craic'. A free juke box, mulled wine in winter and that pub rarity: a great family room.

Meals	No food served.
Closed	Open all day.
Directions	A3071 from Penzance. On right-hand side of square in centre.

Johnny McFadden
The Star Inn,
Fore Street, St Just,
Penzance TR19 7LL
Tel   01736 788767

Entry 92 Map 1

Cornwall

Tinner's Arms
Zennor

Under landlords Grahame and Richard, one of Cornwall's most historic pubs has been given a welcome shot in the arm. Close to the church in the coastal hamlet of Zennor, the 13th-century inn is pretty unspoilt with its flagstone floors, whitewashed walls and fabulously long, well-stocked bar. The food and drink have moved sharply up a gear, with lunch and evening menus changing daily – Newlyn crab, local cheeses, ales from St Austell, Sharp's and Skinners, Burrow Hill ciders from Somerset. The Tinners Arms remains a proper inn bursting with character and open log fires and will always be a popular stop for walkers heading for the nearby coastal paths. It's packed in summer – sit out in the large garden overlooking the sea. Off-season, you could be alone in the bar – just you and the dog.

Meals	12pm-2.30pm; 6pm-9pm. Main courses £6.50-£14.50.
Closed	Open all day.
Directions	Off B3306 St Ives-St Just road, 4 miles west of St Ives.

Grahame Edwards & Richard Motley
Tinner's Arms,
Zennor, St Ives TR26 3BY
Tel   01736 796927
Web   www.tinnersarms.com

Entry 93 Map 1

Cornwall

Angarrack Inn
Angarrack

Personality alone would earn the Angarrack a place in this guide. It starts with David, the landord, and ends with a bizarre assortment of paraphernalia -bagpipes, a clarinet, plates, photos, horns... to list all would risk incredulity. The pub is exquisitely cosy, with small spaces, sometimes squashed – a snug around a coal fire, a couple of small dining areas, dark walls and ceilings. The food is cheap, cheerful, generous – 'school dinner' of the best kind, with the addition of an excellent game paté for a touch of sophistication. Ingredients are locally grown, there is an emphasis on local beer, and the cider is delicious. Plonked beneath a massive Victorian railway viaduct the pub has an unusual site, while David and Jackie's enthusiasm for doing things honestly and without pretence is a tonic.

Meals	12pm-2pm; 6.30pm-9pm. Main courses £6.50-£14.95; sandwiches from £2.95; Sunday roast £7.50.
Closed	3pm-6pm (7pm Sun).
Directions	In village centre, 0.5 miles from A30 north of Hayle.

David & Jackie Peake
Angarrack Inn,
12 Steamers Hill, Angarrack,
Hayle TR27 5JB
Tel   01736 752380

Entry 94 Map 1

Cornwall

The Pandora Inn
Mylor Bridge

Yachtsmen moor at the end of the pontoon that reaches into the creek. The building, too, is special: thatched and 13th-century. Originally The Passage House, it was renamed in memory of the *Pandora*, a naval ship sent to Tahiti to capture the mutineers of Captain Bligh's *Bounty*. The pub keeps the traditional layout on several levels, along with some panelled walls, polished flagged floors, snug alcoves, three log fires, loads of maritime mementos – and amazingly low wooden ceilings. The bar food has something to please everyone, with fresh seafood dominating the 'specials' board. Arrive early in summer – by car or by boat; the place gets packed and parking is tricky. On winter weekdays it's blissfully peaceful, and the postprandial walking along wooded creekside paths easy.

Meals	12pm-3pm; 6.30pm-9pm (9.30pm Fri & Sat). Main courses £8.50-£14.95; bar meals £4.75-£14.95.
Closed	Open all day.
Directions	A39 from Truro; B3292 for Penryn & Mylor Bridge; descend steeply to Restronguet.

John Milan
The Pandora Inn, Restronguet Creek,
Mylor Bridge, Falmouth TR11 5ST
Tel   01326 372678
Web   www.pandorainn.com

Entry 95 Map 1

Cornwall

The Roseland Inn
Philleigh

Beside a peaceful parish church, two miles from the King Harry Ferry, a cob-built Cornish treasure. The front courtyard is bright with blossom in spring, climbing roses in summer. Indoors: old settles with scatter cushions, worn slate floors, low black beams and winter log fires. Local photographs, gig-racing memorabilia and a corner dedicated to rugby trophies scatter the walls. The place is spotlessly kept and run with panache by brother and sister team, William and Ella Richards, and attracts locals and visitors in search of good food such as local farm meats and fish landed at St Mawes. Dishes range from decent sandwiches to game terrine, salmon and prawn fishcakes, rib-eye steak and whole sea bass. Staff are full of smiles – even when the pub doubles as the Roseland Rugby Club clubhouse on winter Saturday nights.

Meals	12pm-2.30pm (3pm Sun); 6pm-9pm (7pm-9pm Sun). Main courses £8-£16; sandwiches from £5; Sunday roast £8.
Closed	3pm-6pm.
Directions	Off A3078 St Mawes road or via King Harry Ferry from Truro (Feock) to Philleigh.

William & Ella Richards
The Roseland Inn,
Philleigh, Truro TR2 5NB
Tel   01872 580254
Web   www.roselandinn.co.uk

Entry 96 Map 1

Cornwall

Kings Head
Ruan Lanihorne

A pub with a heart. Niki and Andrew are warm, friendly and love what they do. Find pine-backed stools, a comfy old sofa, a real fire. An impressive collection of tea cups hangs from the ceiling, a window sparkles with a display of coloured bottles and all is quirky and fun. Off the main bar are a second room with maps and wood-burner and a homely, carpeted dining room with gleaming tables and Windsor chairs. Ales are from Skinners in Truro, fish from St Mawes. Tuck into venison casserole with parsley mash and finish with lemon posset, and a fabulous sirloin of beef on Sundays, with Yorkshire pudding. The quiet little village on the old coach road from Penzance to London has a church with a Norman font and a creek that is a haven for waders and waterfowl... behind is the Roseland countryside.

Meals	12.30pm-2pm; 6.30pm-9pm. Main courses £8.95-£17.75.
Closed	Mon all day Nov-Mar.
Directions	Village signed off A3078 Tregony-St Mawes road.

Andrew & Niki Law
Kings Head,
Ruan Lanihorne, Truro TR2 5NX
Tel   01872 501263
Web   www.kingsheadruan.co.uk

Entry 97 Map 1

Cornwall

The Plume of Feathers
Mitchell

It was an inspired move to transform the old 16th-century coaching inn where John Wesley once preached into a warm and stylish pub-restaurant with rooms. The imaginative cooking draws an appreciative crowd and, in summer, food is available all day. Low stripped beams, half-panelled walls hung with modern art, fresh flowers, candle-studded pine tables and soothing lighting make this place a pleasure to walk into; it feels novel and fun. Delightful staff serve Scottish beef and local vegetables and fish at sensible prices – take roasted whole sea bass with crispy fennel and basil salad and grilled Dover sole with lemon butter, thick steak sandwiches at lunch and delicious puddings, perhaps chilled vanilla rice pudding with spiced pineapple. The central bar is lively with TV, piped music and Sharps Doom Bar on tap.

Meals	12pm-10pm.
	Main courses £8.95-£14.95.
Closed	Open all day.
Directions	Off junction of A30 & A3076.

Vicky Powell
The Plume of Feathers,
Mitchell, Truro TR8 5AX
Tel 01872 510387
Web www.theplume.info

太 🛏 🐈 🍺 🍷

Entry 98 Map 1

Cornwall

The Crown Inn
Lanlivery

You are on the bucolic Saint's Way, along which Irish drovers used to 'fat walk' their cattle from Padstow to Fowey before setting sail for France. Walkers still stop by for sustenance. Most of the 12th-century longhouse's flagged floors have been carpeted, but the deep granite-lined clome oven remains and a country mood prevails – the Crown is the hub of the village. Five areas ramble: the largest for dining, the conservatory for the sun, and three small bars. Tasty food comes courtesy of fine Cornish produce, and is cooked to order: crayfish cocktail, seared scallops with lemon and garlic butter, creamy steak and ale pie, Cornish rump steak with all the trimmings. There's a decent wine list, and handpumped ales include one brewed specially for the pub, Crown Inn Glory. The pretty garden has a view of the church tower.

Meals	12pm-2.30pm; 6pm-9.15pm.
	Main courses £6.95-£15.95;
	bar meals £3.95-£7.95.
Closed	Open all day.
Directions	Signed off A390 between
	Lostwithiel & St Blazey.
	Pub opp. church.

Andy Brotheridge
The Crown Inn,
Lanlivery, Bodmin PL30 5BT
Tel 01208 872707
Web www.wagtailinns.com

♿ 太 🛏 🐈 🍺 🍷

Entry 99 Map 1

Slipway Hotel
Port Isaac

If the tide is in, leave your car at the top and approach on foot. To arrive unflustered (the streets are narrow) is the best way to appreciate this charming Cornish fishing village. At the Slipway, a modest bar area plays second fiddle to the front terrace with its prime views of the working harbour, beach and sea. Sup Sharps ales as seagulls wheel overhead before tucking into the freshest of fresh crab sandwiches (we're talking 'food feet' here, not miles!). If walking the coast path or surfing has drummed up more of an appetite then move into the galleried restaurant – once a chandlery – for some serious fishiness. You could start with steamed Fowey mussels with red onion, chilli, parsley and white wine cream before diving into a whole grilled gilt head bream on artichoke hearts. If that wasn't enough, finish with crème brulée infused with fresh blackberries and cointreau, or a Cornish cheese board with red onion chutney. Bedrooms offer true shelter from a storm, havens of modernity with stylish bathrooms and wooden furniture. Ask for a balcony and a sea view.

Rooms	10: 8 twins/doubles, 2 family suites. £90–£170. Singles £67.50–£97.50.
Meals	12pm–2.30pm; 6.30pm–9pm. Main courses £6.25–£8.95 (lunch), £13.25–£17.45 (dinner).
Closed	Open all day.
Directions	Opposite harbour & beach in village centre.

Mark & Kep Forbes
Slipway Hotel,
Harbour Front, Port Isaac PL29 3RH

Tel	01208 880264
Web	www.portisaachotel.com

The Mill House Inn
Trebarwith

You coast down a steep winding lane to the 1760s mill house in its woodland setting: these seven lovely acres are its own. The woodland in turn leads to a spectacular beach – Trebarwith's. What a setting! Back at the inn, the bar combines the best of Cornish old and Cornish new: big flagged floor, whitewashed beams, wooden tables, chapel chairs, two leather sofas by a wood-burning stove. The dining room over the mill stream has light, elegance and a bistro feel: sea blues, white linen. Settle down to baked local mushrooms stuffed with spinach and sun-dried tomatoes and topped with Tesyn cheese, Cornish haddock with crayfish risotto, Michaelstow beef on a bed of roast vegetables; the locally sourced dishes are updated daily and the chef trained with Jamie Oliver. The pub's uncluttered bedrooms vary in size and have a contemporary feel, in sympathy with the peaceful setting. The beach, all surf and sand, is a ten-minute walk, while coastal trails lead to Tintagel, official home of the Arthurian legends… walking, biking, surfing, you couldn't possibly be bored.

Rooms	9: 7 doubles, 1 single, 1 family room. £70–£120. Singles £40–£60.
Meals	12pm–2.30pm (3pm Sun); 6.30pm–8.30pm (9pm Fri & Sat). Main courses £7.50–£10.95 (lunch), £12–£17(dinner).
Closed	Open all day.
Directions	From Tintagel, B3263 south, following signs to Trebarwith Strand. Inn at bottom of steep hill.

Mark & Kep Forbes
The Mill House Inn,
Trebarwith, Tintagel PL34 0HD

Tel	01840 770200
Web	www.themillhouseinn.co.uk

Cornwall

St Kew Inn
St Kew Churchtown

Lost down a maze of lanes in a secluded wooded valley, the St Kew is a grand old inn originally built for the masons working on the church; though its stone walls go back 600 years it has been welcoming visitors for a mere 200. Reputedly haunted by a Victorian village girl discovered buried beneath the main bar, it is an irresistibly friendly, chatty place with a huge range and a warming fire, a dark slate floor, winged settles and a terrific unspoilt atmosphere – no pub paraphernalia here. Meat hooks hang from a high ceiling, earthenware flagons embellish the mantelpiece, fresh flowers brighten the bar. Local St Austell ales are served in the traditional way, straight from the barrel, and the legendary steaks are delicious. In summer, the big streamside garden is the place to be.

Meals	12pm-2pm; 7pm-9.30pm. Main courses £7.25-£13.95.
Closed	2.30pm-6pm (3pm-6pm Sun). Open all day July-Aug.
Directions	From Wadebridge for Bude on A39 for 4 miles; left after golf club. 1 mile to St Kew Churchtown.

Philip & Lanie Calvert
St Kew Inn,
St Kew Churchtown,
Bodmin PL30 3HB
Tel   01208 841259

Entry 102 Map 1

Cornwall

The Bush Inn
Morwenstow

After a blowy walk along the cliffs this ancient pub makes the perfect resting place. Local farmer Rob Tape has sympatheticallyy updated the Bush, one of Cornwall's oldest smugglers' haunts. Once a monastic rest house, parts date back to AD950; note the Celtic piscina carved from serpentine in one wall. Slate-flagged floors, a huge stone fireplace and lovely old wooden furnishings in the bar preserve the timeless character of this immutable place. Food is served all day in two charming, contemporary dining rooms and includes beef and lamb from neighbouring farms, seafood from Widemouth Bay, and crispy duck confit with sautéed potatoes and red wine sauce. Weary walkers are revived by excellent beers and robust snacks. There's seating on the front lawn, wooden play equipment for kids and a view out to sea.

Meals	12pm-9pm (9.30pm summer). Main courses £5.50-£16.
Closed	Open all day.
Directions	Follow signs for Morwenstow off A39, 9 miles north of Bude.

Rob & Edwina Tape
The Bush Inn, Crosstown,
Morwenstow, Bude EX23 9SR
Tel   01288 331242
Web   www.bushinn-morwenstow.co.uk

Entry 103 Map 1

Cornwall

104 The Maltsters Arms Chaple Amble, Polzeath PL27 6EU
01208 812473
Away from the busy beaches around Rock is this inviting 16th-century pub, with fun and funky eating areas and a good all-round menu including excellent fresh-fish specials. Reports please.

105 The Rashleigh Polkerris, St Austell PL24 2TL
01726 813991
A pub *on* the beach, in a tiny cove! The old coastguard station is cosy in winter, unbeatable in summer, so down a pint of real ale and watch the sun set across St Austell Bay.

106 The Blue Peter Quay Road, Polperro PL13 2QZ
01503 272743
Unspoilt little fishing pub built into the cliffside by Polperro's harbour. Dark and cosy wood-floored bar with hidden corners, nautical artefacts, tip-top Cornish ales, and sea views.

107 The Falcon Inn St Mawgan, Newquay TR8 4EP
01637 860225
Wisteria-draped, utterly unspoilt and a summer haven for those escaping the bucket-and-spade beach. Decent pub food in the rug-strewn dining room or the splendid garden.

108 The Driftwood Spars Hotel Trevaunance Cove, St Agnes TR5 0RT
01872 552428/553323
New owners for this 17th-century pub, yards from sheltered sandy Trevaunance Cove. Big traditional bar with stone walls, roaring log fires and homebrewed ale; modern restaurant with fishy menu. Reports welcome.

109 The White Hart Churchtown, Ludgvan, Penzance TR20 8EY
01736 740574
Granite-stone 14th-century pub with ochre-coloured walls, low beams and real ale from the cask. Come for intimate boxed seating areas and log-burning fires.

110 The Ship Porthleven, Helston TR13 9JS
01326 564204
A hit with holidaymakers and locals, this harbourside pub revels in its fun, smuggler-meets-fishing boat interior, and offers surprisingly good food alongside Cornish ales.

Cornwall

111 Halzephron Gunwalloe, Helston TR12 7QB
01326 240406
Opera singer Angela Thomas put this remote smugglers' inn up for sale late in 2007. Famous for the cosy interior, the freshly cooked food and the big sea views – reports please.

112 Cadgwith Cove Inn Cadgwith, Ruan Minor, Helston TR12 7JX
01326 290513
Smack on the coastal path, in a thatched fishing hamlet, sits this old smugglers' inn. Decked with seafaring mementos, there's a fishy menu and five ales on tap. Views reach across the cove from the sun-trap terrace.

113 The New Inn Manaccan, Helston TR12 6HA
01326 231323
Unfussy thatched village local with that 'lost in the old country' feel. Walk over from Helford for heart-warming pub grub, pints of Doom Bar and a natter with the locals.

114 The Shipwright's Arms Helford, Helston village TR12 6JX
01326 231235
Park in the car park and walk down to the creek, to this pretty thatched pub in its gorgeous terraced garden of flowers and palms. Yachtsmen tie up outside and there's always a buzz, but changes are afoot.

115 Seven Stars The Moor, Falmouth TR11 3QA
01326 312111
Unchanging, unspoilt and rather quirky town-centre pub with splendid narrow tap room, racked Sharp's and Skinner's ales and snug back bar. Run by a priest for over 50 years.

Cumbria

The Wheatsheaf
Beetham

A sweet timelessness pervades the village of Beetham. The Wheatsheaf traces its origins to the 16th century: note the leaded windows, dark panelling, fine mouldings and wide open stairs. Comfortable furnishings, pictures and flowers add warmth. Beyond the cocooning bar is a classic tap room with a big open fire and old prints while the first-floor dining rooms have a country-house feel. Bar food ranges from generous sandwiches to potted shrimps, warm black pudding with smoked bacon salad and Cumberland sausages with creamy mash. Lamb noisettes with redcurrant jus and Lytham line-caught sea bass with pea and bacon risotto make an appearance in the evening. Cask ales from Bryson's and Jennings keep drinkers happy and Kendal is a 15-minute drive – unless you get stuck behind a tractor or sheep!

Meals	12pm-2pm; 6pm-9pm; 12pm-8.30pm Sun. Main courses £10-£17; Sunday lunch £11.95 & £13.95.
Closed	3pm-5.30pm. Open all day Sat & Sun.
Directions	Off A6, 1 mile south of Milnthorpe.

	Richard & Jean Skelton The Wheatsheaf, Beetham, Milnthorpe LA7 7AL
Tel	015395 62123
Web	www.wheatsheafbeetham.com

Entry 116 Map 11

Cumbria

Strickland Arms
Sizergh

Right beside the gates to Sizergh Castle, this old pub was desperate for attention. Now it is jointly run by Martin Ainscough and the National Trust. Behind the stark stone exterior are two civilised rooms decked out in best NT style: earthy Farrow & Ball colours, rugs on slate and wooden floors, an eclectic mix of antiques. Order a pint of Coniston Bluebird, pick a seat by a glowing coal fire, peruse the papers while you wait, then tuck into delicious food that bears no resemblance to normal pub fare. From local and organic ingredients come baked field mushrooms with concassed tomatoes, sea bass fishcakes with sweet chilli dressing, chump of lamb with port and shallot sauce. There's a lovely flagged front terrace for summer with pretty views (and just a slight hum from the dual carriageway).

Meals	12pm-2pm; 6pm-9pm (12pm-8.30pm Sun). Main courses £9.95-£15.50; bar lunch £5-£8.95.
Closed	3pm-5.30pm. Open all day Sat & Sun.
Directions	Just off A590 north of Kendal, by Sizergh Castle gates.

	Martin Ainscough Strickland Arms, Sizergh, Kendal LA8 8DZ
Tel	01539 561010

Entry 117 Map 11

Cumbria

Wheatsheaf
Brigsteer

Brigsteer is a jumble of old cottages and new houses – a spill-over from bustling Kendal – and this long, whitewashed pub has been sitting on the crossroads since 1762. Now it has bright hanging baskets and a little bit of garden over the road with some tables and chairs for sunnier days. It also has a vamped-up downstairs with subtle lighting, wooden floors and smooth plaster walls. Chef Gareth Webster cooks everything from scratch with flair – no fast food here. Don't fill up on crisps, wait for slow-cooked Cumbrian rabbit with braised leeks, shortcrust pastry and Cumberland mustard cream, or slowly braised saddleback pork belly with black pudding and smoked garlic roast potatoes. There's a sound wine list, two cask ales and port by the glass: cheese fans can unleash their excitement over Allerdale, Keldthwaite Gold and Blengdale Blue. Upstairs are three comfortable bedrooms, not swish but squeaky clean and with solid pine beds, shower rooms and views onto the village. You are near to Kendal for lots of shops and the Lakes for strolling, birdwatching or boating.

Rooms	3 doubles. £85.
Meals	12pm-2pm (2.30pm Sat & Sun); 5.45pm-9pm.
	Main courses £10.95-£16.95; bar lunches from £3.95.
Closed	3pm-5.45pm.
Directions	From M6 junc. 36, A591 towards Kendal; Brigsteer is signed left after 5 miles; pub in village centre.

Lee Rowbotham
Wheatsheaf,
Brigsteer, Kendal LA8 8AN

Tel	01539 568254
Web	www.brigsteer.gb.com

The Mason's Arms
Strawberry Bank

A perfect Lakeland inn tucked away two miles inland from Lake Windermere. You're on the side of a hill with huge views across lush fields to Scout Scar in the distance. In summer, all pub life decants onto a spectacular terrace – a sitting room in the sun – where window boxes and flowerbeds tumble with colour. The inn dates from the 16th century and is impossibly pretty. The bar is properly traditional with roaring fires, flagged floors, wavy beams, a cosy snug... and a menu of 70 bottled beers to quench your thirst. Rustic elegance upstairs comes courtesy of stripped floors, country rugs and red walls in the first-floor dining room – so grab a window seat for fabulous views and order delicious food, anything from a sandwich to Cumbrian duck. Self-catering cottages and apartments come with fancy kitchens (breakfast hampers can be arranged), cool colours, fabulous beds, gleaming bathrooms and Bang & Olufsen TVs. Best of all, you have your own private terrace; order a meal in the restaurant and they'll bring it to you here. Brilliant.

Rooms	3 + 2: 3 suites. £55-£105. 2 cottages (1 for 4, 1 for 6). Cottages £105-£175.
Meals	12pm-2pm; 6pm-9pm (12pm-9pm Sat & Sun). Main courses £10.25-£14.95; bar meals from £5.95.
Closed	Open all day.
Directions	M6 junc. 36; A590 west, then A592 north. 1st right after Fell Foot Park. Straight ahead for 2.5 miles. On left after sharp right-hand turn.

John & Diane Taylor
The Mason's Arms,
Strawberry Bank, Cartmel Fell LA11 6NW
Tel   01539 568486/ 01282 842450
Web   www.strawberrybank.com

Cumbria

The Punch Bowl Inn
Crosthwaite

You're away from Lake Windermere in a small village encircled by a tangle of lanes that defeat most tourists. A church stands next door; the odd bride ambles out in summer, bell ringers practise on Friday mornings. But while the Punch Bowl sits in a sleepy village lost to the world and doubles up as the local post office, it is actually a seriously fancy inn. It was rescued from neglect by Paul and Steph, who own the impeccable Drunken Duck, and after a top-to-toe renovation it now sparkles. Outside, honeysuckle climbs on old stone walls, inside four fires keep you warm in winter. A clipped elegance runs throughout: leather sofas in a beamed sitting room, candles in vases on dining room tables, an old farmhouse table in the restaurant crammed with brandies and malts. You can dine on succulent roast Cumbrian lamb with duck-fat potatoes, creamed leeks and a mint jus, then retire to a fabulous room with bold fabrics, flat-screen TV, Roberts radio and a bathroom with a heated floors. Four rooms have huge views down the Lyth valley; readers are full of praise.

Rooms	9: 1 twin/double, 5 doubles, 2 four-posters, 1 suite. £110-£195. Suite £225-280. Singles from £82.50.
Meals	12pm-3pm; 6pm-9pm. Main courses £10-£22.95.
Closed	Open all day.
Directions	M6 junc. 36, then A590 for Newby Bridge. Right onto A5074, then right for Crosthwaite after 3 miles. Pub on southern flank of village.

Jenny Sisson
The Punch Bowl Inn,
Crosthwaite, Kendal LA8 8HR
Tel   015395 68237
Web   www.the-punchbowl.co.uk

Entry 120 Map 11

Cumbria

The Watermill Inn
Ings

The converted bobbin mill is Tardis-like outside. Inside: beams, open stonework, open fires and lots of traditional pubby stuff to give the idea they've been serving beer for centuries. Everyone loves the Watermill: locals, tourists, walkers, dogs. They come for the 50 malt whiskies, the heady farm ciders and the mind-boggling range of 16 real ales served in award-winning condition, including cracking beers brewed in the pub's own microbrewery. There's a sunny front bar good for families, a dimly-lit drinkers' bar and several eating areas that overlook the rushing stream. Tuck into tasty pub food locally supplied: fish and chips, chicken with mustard and rosemary, ale pie, cheddar platter. The pub is on the edge of good walking country and handy for Windermere, and a late night bus back to Kendal is the icing on the cake.

Meals	12pm-4.30pm; 5pm-9pm. Main courses £7-£14.95.
Closed	Open all day.
Directions	Just off A591 in Ings, midway between Kendal & Windermere.

Brian Coulthwaite
The Watermill Inn,
Ings Village, Windermere LA8 9PY
Tel   01539 821309
Web   www.watermillinn.co.uk

Entry 121 Map 11

Cumbria

Hole in t'Wall
Bowness

Known in 1612 as the New Inn, the name was later changed, thanks to the landlord's habit of passing beer though the wall to the blacksmith's next door. It's a good, old-fashioned tavern, not plain but not plush, packed with tourists in season and prepared for walkers all year round. The slate flagstones and fireplace have been uncovered and restored, the black beams are heavy with hops, chamber pots and pretty plates, and the flagged front terrace makes a cheery suntrap in summer. You get two bars downstairs, one long and narrow with that characterful log fire, the other small and snug with an old range, and a third room up. Food is straightforward, from prawn platter to curry of the day; there are jacket potatoes, sandwiches, real ale and mulled wine. Lake Windermere is a three-minute walk.

Meals	12pm-2.30pm; 6pm-8.30pm. 12pm-7pm Fri & Sat; no food Sun eve. Main courses £6.25-£9.95.
Closed	Open all day.
Directions	From Windermere A592; fork off right onto Fallbarrow Rd for Lowside before A592 joins A5074.

Susan Burnet
Hole in t'Wall,
Lowside,
Bowness-on-Windermere LA23 3DH
Tel   015394 43488

Entry 122 Map 11

Cumbria

Tower Bank Arms
Sawrey

Just across from the ferry, next to Hilltop – Beatrix Potter's farm – is Jemima Puddleduck's inn. (She may not have caroused here, but she did waddle by.) Today the National Trust are its sympathetic custodians. Jumbles of whitewashed buildings make up the legendary village of Sawrey; a courteous staff handles the summer crowds. Enter a slate-flagged bar with a grand open range that throws out the heat on chilly days; further in it is carpeted and cosy. Flowers and shining bits and bobs make the place homely; the oak-floored dining room is set with white linen napkins and polished cutlery. Four local ales accompany dishes to please walkers: beef casseroled in ale, trout from Esthwaite, Cumbrian lamb in various guises. The puddings are scrumptious and the cheeses reflect Cumbria's producers. Special.

Key to the survival of Britain's rural ale houses is the provision of good food – and, increasingly, bedrooms.

Meals	12pm–2pm; 6pm–9pm (8pm Sun). Main courses £7–£11.
Closed	3pm–5pm. Open all day Sat & Sun and in summer.
Directions	On B5285 2 miles south east of Hawkshead; towards the Windermere Ferry.

Anthony Hutton
Tower Bank Arms,
Sawrey, Ambleside LA22 0LF
Tel 015394 36334
Web www.towerbankarms.co.uk

Entry 123 Map 11

Drunken Duck Inn
Barngates

Afternoon tea can be taken in the garden, where lawns run down to Black Tarn and Greek gods gaze upon jumping fish. You're up on the hill, away from the crowds, cradled by woods and highland fell. Huge views from the terrace shoot off for miles to towering Lakeland peaks. Roses ramble on the veranda, stone walls double as flower beds and burst with colour. As for the Duck, she may be old, but she sure is pretty, so step into a world of airy interiors: stripped floors in a beamed bar, timber-framed walls in the restaurant. Wander at will and find open fires, grandfather clocks, rugs on the floor, exquisite art. They brew their own beer, have nine bitters on tap and the food is utterly delicious: diver-caught scallops, roasted and served with slow confit of pork; fillet of monkfish with crab risotto and sauce gribiche. Bedrooms are dreamy, smartly dressed in crisp white linen, with colours courtesy of Farrow & Ball and peaty water straight off the fell. Rooms in the main house are snug in the eaves; those across the courtyard are crisply uncluttered and indulgent.

Rooms	17: 15 doubles, 2 twins. £120-£250. Singles from £90.
Meals	12pm-2.15pm; 6pm-9pm. Main courses £13.95-£23.95; bar meals £4.50-£8.95.
Closed	Open all day.
Directions	West from Ambleside on A593, then left for Hawkshead on B5285. After 1 mile, left, signed. Up hill to inn.

Stephanie Barton
Drunken Duck Inn,
Barngates, Ambleside LA22 0NG

Tel   015394 36347
Web   www.drunkenduckinn.co.uk

Entry 124 Map 11

Cumbria

White Hart Inn
Bouth

The main bar has a counter dripping with brass, hops and beer pumps; walls and shelves are strewn with clay pipes, old photos, taxidermy and tankards. It's a friendly, sleepy-village local, where regulars mingle with visitors over pints of Black Sheep and Hawkshead Bitter. There are loads of malts, too, and a no-nonsense menu that includes rare-breed meat from Aireys of Ayside, local lamb cooked in fresh thyme and red wine, and wild mallard and pheasant from the shooting parties that congregate in the pub car park on winter Saturdays. They source locally, and offer small portions to children. A sloping flagged floor reflects the light from the window; fires at both ends are log-fuelled in cold weather. The walking's marvellous and pub and village fit snugly into the ancient landscape of wooded valleys and tight little roads.

Meals	12pm-2pm; 6pm-8.45pm. Main courses £9.25-£14.95.
Closed	Mon & Tues lunch (except bank hols). Open all day Sat & Sun.
Directions	Off A590 Barrow road after Lakeside & Haverthwaite Steam Railway.

Nigel & Kath Barton
White Hart Inn,
Bouth, Ulverston LA12 8JB
Tel 01229 861229
Web www.bed-and-breakfast-cumbria.co.uk

Entry 125 Map 11

Cumbria

Manor Arms
Broughton-in-Furness

Unspoilt, grey-stoned Broughton-in-Furness — with village stocks — is a market town that feels like a village. In a corner of its Georgian square stands the 18th-century Manor Arms, a modest inn that has been in the family for 19 years. This is not a foodie's pub, though snacks are on tap all day — hot and cold rolls, homemade soup and the like. Its main fascination lies in its traditional bar and its eight handpumped ales; try Yates, Copper Dragon, Roosters… there are more in the cellar. In their quest for perfection, David Varty and son Scott go to some lengths to ensure the beers are in perfect condition. Cosy up on the bay window seat with children's books and games — little ones are welcome here. Logs burn in a rare 'basket' fireplace into whose oak mantel drinkers have scored their names down the centuries.

Meals	Bar snacks 12pm-10pm (9pm Sun).
Closed	Open all day.
Directions	On A593, 10 miles south west of Coniston.

David & Scott Varty
Manor Arms, The Square,
Broughton in Furness LA20 6HY
Tel 01229 716286
Web www.manorarmsthesquare.co.uk

Entry 126 Map 11

Cumbria

Blacksmiths Arms
Broughton Mills

An utterly unspoilt little local. In the land of rugged hills and wooded valleys, you approach down a winding lane between high hedges; once you are round the final bend, the low-slung farmhouse-inn comes into view. Inside are four small, slate-floored rooms with beams and low ceilings, long settles and several log fires. The bar is strictly for drinking – indeed, there's not much room for anything else; there are three cask ales (two local, one guest) and traditional cider in summer. Across the passage, a room serving proper fresh food, snacks or full meals, and two further dining rooms that sparkle with glass and cutlery. The blackboard advertises dishes with a contemporary slant plus beef and Herdwick lamb reared in the valley. The food is seriously good, so it gets busy; in summer you can spill onto the flowery terrace.

Meals	12pm-2pm; 6pm-9pm. Main courses £6.95-£14.95; bar meals from £2.95.
Closed	2.30pm-5pm Tues-Fri (winter only) & Mon lunch. Open all day Sat & Sun.
Directions	Off A593, Broughton to Coniston.

Michael & Sophie Lane
Blacksmiths Arms, Broughton Mills,
Broughton-in-Furness LA20 6AX
Tel   01229 716824
Web www.theblacksmithsarms.com

Entry 127 Map 11

Cumbria

The Langstrath Country Inn
Borrowdale

A magnet for walkers: just a track up the Langstrath to the Lakes' highest peaks. Mike and Sara Hodgson are settling in well. Vertical timbers create cosy stable-like corners, carpeting and a crackling fire add warmth, and there are fascinating old photos of local characters and scenes to peruse over your pint. The slate-topped bar with its polished brass rail sports four hand-pulls for Jennings, Black Sheep, Hesket Newmarket and Hawkshead; good wines are available by the glass; a couple of dozen malts enliven the varnished rack. The changing dinner menu indicates an enthusiasm for local produce – Rosthwaite Herdwick lamb, Lune Valley steak, Morecambe Bay shrimps (potted); lunch is a soup and sandwich affair. A popular refuelling stop on the Coast to Coast path and the Cumbrian Way.

Meals	12pm-2.30pm; 6.30pm-9pm. Main courses £9.50-£14.95; bar lunch from £4.50.
Closed	Open all day April-Oct. Check opening times in winter.
Directions	From Keswick B5289 to Borrowdale. Village on left between Rosthwaite & Seatoller. Tricky parking.

Mike & Sara Hodgson
The Langstrath Country Inn,
Stonethwaite, Borrowdale,
Keswick CA12 5XG
Tel   01768 777239
Web www.thelangstrath.com

Entry 128 Map 11

Cumbria

Kirkstile Inn
Loweswater

Hard to imagine a more glorious setting than that of the Kirkstile Inn, tucked in among the fells, next to an old church and a stream, a half mile from the lakes of Loweswater and Crummock. Roger Humphreys is well up to the job of hosting this legendary bar. The whole place is authentic, traditional, well looked after: whitewashed walls, low beams, solid polished tables, cushioned settles, a well-stoked fire, plants, flowers and the odd horse harness to remind you of the past. Come for afternoon tea, or settle down with an unforgettable pint of Coniston Bluebird Bitter or their own excellent Melbreak Bitter. Five chefs use local produce for unfussy traditional dishes such as steak and ale pie, chicken breast stuffed with Cumberland sausage with an onion sauce, and sticky toffee pudding.

Meals	12pm-2pm; 6pm-9pm. Main courses £7.50-£13; bar snacks £4-£7.
Closed	Open all day.
Directions	Lorton road from Cockermouth; follow signs to Loweswater.

Roger Humphreys
Kirkstile Inn, Loweswater,
Cockermouth CA13 0RV
Tel   01900 85219
Web   www.kirkstile.com

Entry 129 Map 11

Cumbria

Old Crown
Hesket Newmarket

In a dreamy village and with porter on tap! The old pub is owned by a cooperative of 147 souls and is run by Malcolm and Pat. Its tiny front room with bar, settles, glowing coals, thumbed books, pictures and folk music (the first Sunday of the month) squeezes in a dozen; a second room houses darts and pool; a third and fourth are dining rooms. Not only is this the only pub where you can sample all of Hesket Newmarket's beers brewed in the barn at the back – ask about tours – but it is the focal point of the community, even supporting the post office whose postmistress repays in puddings and pies. The Old Crown is also known for its fine curries and Sunday roasts. Its authenticity draws people from miles around, Prince Charles dropped by (twice) to launch the *Saving Your Village Pub* guide, walkers come for the Caldbeck Fells.

Meals	12pm-2.30pm Fri-Sun; 6pm-9pm. Main courses £6-£13; bar meals £2.50-£6.50.
Closed	2.30pm-5.30pm Fri-Sun. Open from 5.30pm Mon-Thurs.
Directions	M6 junc. 41 for Wigton on B5305. 6.5 miles turn for H. Newmarket.

Malcolm & Pat Hawksworth
Old Crown, Hesket Newmarket,
Carlisle CA7 8JG
Tel   01697 478288
Web   www.theoldcrownpub.co.uk

Entry 130 Map 11

Cumbria

Highland Drove
Great Salkeld

Yards from the Norman church with its keep-like tower (protection against marauding Scots), the timber porch leads to a flagged bar – cosy, warm, civilised. There's a bar-dining area with easy leather chairs and pine tables, and a popular games room with pool. With open log fires, tartan, brick and timber, this is a spruce, 21st-century inn that pleases drinkers, diners and walkers. Named after the waters ('kyloes') that the cattle drovers crossed on their way to Scottish market, the dining room has a Highland lodge feel, its great windows gazing to the lush Pennines. Tuck into rack of lamb, pan-fried Nile perch, chargrilled beef fillet with port and thyme jus, and toffee and banana crumble. Beers are from the cask, wines are well-chosen. Or keep things simple with a fresh baguette in the bar.

Meals	12pm-2pm; 6.15pm-7.45pm (5.45pm-7.15pm Sat); restaurant 6.30pm-9pm only. Main courses £6.25-£10.95 (bar); £9.95-£18.50 (dinner).
Closed	2.30-6pm. Mon lunch (except bank hol). Open all day Sat & Sun.
Directions	Just off B6412 in Great Salkeld.

Donald & Paul Newton
Highland Drove,
Great Salkeld, Penrith CA11 9NA
Tel   01768 898349
Web   www.highland-drove.co.uk

Entry 131 Map 11

Cumbria

The Gate
Yanwath

It was built as a toll gate in 1683 – hence the name. Known to locals as the Yat, the old pub has gained a reputation for its food, locally sourced and served in hearty portions. The place is immaculate, the young staff are attentive and the landlord remains loyal to the pub's roots, so you may eat anywhere, including the sunny sheltered patio at the back. Walk in to a characterful, dimly-lit bar, all cosy corners and crackling fire, background music and happy chatter. Beyond is a light, airy and raftered dining room. The menu depends on fresh deliveries every day including Cumbrian meat and plenty of fish, and there's homemade food for children, from pizza to beefburgers and fishcakes. Wines come from an excellent merchant's in Kendal, beers include the fruity and full-flavoured Doris's 90th Birthday Ale.

Meals	12pm-2.30pm; 6pm-9pm. Main courses £12-£25.
Closed	Open all day.
Directions	On B5320 south-west of A6 & Penrith; 2.5 miles from M6 junc. 40.

Matt Edwards
The Gate,
Yanwath, Penrith CA10 2LF
Tel   01768 862386
Web   www.yanwathgate.com

Entry 132 Map 11

Cumbria

Brackenrigg Inn
Ullswater

The terrace and bay windows of this 18th-century inn have breathtaking views across Ullswater to the fells. Attention to detail is noticeable here, and the service is swift and friendly. The part-panelled bar with polished old boards, darts and open fire has a homely feel, as does the carpeted lounge-dining room where families are welcome. There are several local beers on tap, and a good long wine list. Menus have a modern British slant. In the bar, try mussels cooked in white wine, garlic and cream sauce, or superb Cumberland sausages with mash and onion gravy; in the restaurant, spicy fish soup, sea bass with pea purée and basil oil, and guinea fowl stuffed with black pudding and thyme, served with bubble and squeak and a redcurrant sauce. Sunday lunch is brilliant value, and the treacle toffee pudding sensational.

In the Worth a Visit sections you will find top-flight pubs that have recently changed hands, pubs that we believe are on the up, and great little locals that didn't make a full entry but are still worth seeking out.

Meals	12pm-2.30pm; 5pm-9pm.
	Main courses £11.95-£17.95; bar meals £4.25-£13.95; Sunday lunch £9.95 & £12.95.
Closed	Open all day.
Directions	M6 junc. 40; A66 for Keswick; A592 for Ullswater; Watermillock 5 miles.

	Michael Evans
	Brackenrigg Inn,
	Ullswater, Penrith CA11 0LP
Tel	01768 486206
Web	www.brackenrigginn.co.uk

Entry 133 Map 11

Mardale Inn @ St Patrick's Well
Bampton

Though close to the M6 at Shap, this area east of the Lakes is much overlooked, with its high fells and romantic Haweswater. The hub of the village is its newly restored pub – all modern stone flags on the floor, exposed stone and brickwork, beams and open fireplaces, nifty lighting and good use of space. Big chunky wooden tables and chairs encourage a look at the menu: try potted Morecambe Bay shrimps, smoked haddock fishcakes with herb mayonnaise and wild mushroom and pea risotto. If you're a sweet sort of person finish with toffee pudding and caramel sauce, or a local cheese platter – nothing a dose of harsh fell walking wouldn't put right. Or you could just fall into one of the calming bedrooms upstairs; uncluttered with pale oatmeal carpets and spanking new bathrooms. Young friendly staff are buzzing about and the feeling is modern, but this is still 'the local' to folk nearby so you'll be rubbing shoulders with proper Cumbrians and there'll be live music some nights. You can walk to Haweswater from here; the last breeding golden eagles in this country soar high above its dark surface.

Rooms	4 twins/doubles. £70–£100. Singles £45.
Meals	12pm–9pm. Main courses £7.50–£14.50.
Closed	Open all day.
Directions	Bampton is signed from A6 at Shap or B5320 south of Penrith.

Seb Hinley
Mardale Inn,
Bampton, Penrith CA10 2RQ
Tel   01931 713244
Web   www.mardaleinn.co.uk

Entry 134 Map 11

The Sun Inn
Kirkby Lonsdale

Set in a narrow street and with the historic parish church behind, The Sun is a fine example of an old inn: step under the ancient portico and into the low-ceilinged bar full of warmth, soft colours and a jolly mix of tables and chairs. Upstairs are some stylish bedrooms with exposed stone work, old timber beams and splashes of contemporary fabric; bedside and dressing tables are hand-made, mattresses are wide, towels thick and bathrooms generous. Food is also lavish: push the boat out and sit in the smart brasserie-style dining room for cold roast fillet of beef served pink with homemade horseradish sauce, or oven roasted monkfish tail with chive potato cake and creamed spinach. And polish it all off with chocolate and pear pancakes layered with fresh cream if you have any room left. There are plenty of cask ales to keep serious beer drinkers happy, but the wine list is sublime and there are good organic choices, some by the glass. Pootle around Kirkby Lonsdale with its interesting mix of shops or strike out further for some grand walking; you're on the edge of the Yorkshire Dale National Park.

Rooms	11 twins/doubles. £80-£130. Singles £55-£110.
Meals	12pm-2.30pm; 7pm-9pm. Main courses £9.95-£16.95; bar meals from £5.35.
Closed	Open all day.
Directions	M6 junc. 36; A65 for 5 miles following signs for Kirkby Lonsdale; pub in town centre.

Mark & Lucy Fuller
The Sun Inn,
6 Market Street,
Kirkby Lonsdale LA6 2AU
Tel   015242 71965
Web   www.sun-inn.info

Cumbria

136 The Sun Inn Main Street, Dent, Sedbergh LA10 5QL
01539 625208
Dent is an unspoilt Dales village of cobbles and cottages. After an invigorating walk, pile into The Sun for log fires and pints of Dent beers, brewed up the valley.

137 Bay Horse Winton, Kirkby Stephen CA17 4HS
01768 371451
Traditional local overlooking the green, with cosy stone-flagged bar, open fires, Hawkshead ales on tap and hearty food. Rare-breed meats are supplied by renowned local farmer Peter Gott, the chef-owner's uncle.

138 Mill Inn Mungrisdale, Penrith CA11 0XR
01768 779632
By a tumbling burn at the foothills of Blencathra, a homely village inn with a solid northern feel, a warming fire and a bar dispensing Jennings ales and country food to locals and walkers.

139 The Pheasant Bassenthwaite Lake, Cockermouth CA13 9YE
01768 776234
The wonderful snug has a ceiling coloured by 300 years of tobacco and polish, there are open fires, good bar food and cracking Jennings beers on tap. A country-cottage garden, too.

140 Old Dungeon Ghyll Great Langdale, Ambleside LA22 9JY
015394 37272
To hikers ruddy from the day's exertions, the infamous, barn-like Walkers' Bar serves decent grub, mugs of tea, and God's own beer, Yates. The atmosphere is infectious.

141 Britannia Inn Elterwater, Ambleside LA22 9HP
01539 437210
With Great Langdale Beck tumbling into the tarn, a brilliant starting point for walkers. Return for pints of foaming Cumbrian ale, hearty food, views from the terrace. Being everyone's secret, the pub is always busy.

142 The Sun Hotel & Inn Coniston LA21 8HQ
015394 41248
A no-nonsense little pub at the back of an Edwardian hotel, with stone flags and walls, old settles, local ales from the cask and hearty pub food. Great views from the garden.

143 Queens Head Hotel Townhead, Troutbeck, Windermere LA23 1PW
015394 32174
Crouching at the foot of the Kirkstone pass, a famous pub that is a warren of fascinating rooms. Sweeping views, seriously good food and blazing logs on the fire. Robinson's brewery took over late 2007 – reports please.

Derbyshire

Three Horseshoes
Breedon-on-the-Hill

Opposite the villagers' old 'lock up', a listed village inn. Ian Davison and Jennie Ison have revitalised the old place and introduced a relaxed modern feel and a menu to match. Expect painted brickwork, seagrass matting, antique tables, Windsor chairs, an eclectic mix of pictures and masses of space. Smaller rooms include a simple quarry-tiled bar and an intimate red dining room with three tables, while pride of place goes to a handsome Victorian bar counter picked up years ago and stored in anticipation of the right setting. Dishes are chalked up on boards in the bar and the award-winning formula offers halibut with garlic and prawn sauce, lamb shank with mustard mash, and bread and butter pudding. Marston's Pedigree and Theakstons on hand pump should satisfy those in for a swift half. Outside: a sheltered patio at the back.

Meals	12pm-2pm; 5.30pm-9.15pm (12pm-3pm Sun). Main courses £13.50-£19.50; bar meals £4.95-£7.95.
Closed	2.30pm-5.30pm & Sun from 3pm.
Directions	Follow signs off A42 between Ashby de la Zouch & Castle Donington.

Ian Davison & Jennie Ison
Three Horseshoes,
Breedon-on-the-Hill,
Derby DE73 8AN
Tel   01332 695129
Web   www.thehorseshoes.com

Entry 144 Map 8

Derbyshire

The Red Lion Inn
Hognaston

Jason and Jenny took over this endearing and enduring village local and have changed little. The open-plan, L-shaped bar room quakes with quarry tiles and mature floorboards, on which stands a Pandora's box of classic tables, pews and settles overseen by umpteen artefacts, from an HMV-style gramophone to a ship's gimbal hanging from a low-slung beam. The original and imposing wood-panelled bar sweeps between levels warmed by capacious log fires, dispensing ales from Marston's or from one of a raft of craft breweries that have exploded in Derbyshire. Filling fodder, from light bites to hearty creations, includes crab cakes, beef stroganoff, orange and tarragon duck, and lamb dishes that are the signature of the place. A fine old pub for the traditionalist – in walking and shooting country.

Meals	12pm-3pm; 6.30pm-9.30pm. Main courses from £8.50; bar snacks from £6.95.
Closed	3pm-6pm. Open all day Sun.
Directions	Off the B5035 between Ashbourne & Wirksworth.

Jason & Jenny Waterall
The Red Lion Inn,
Hognaston,
Ashbourne DE6 1PR
Tel   01335 370396

Entry 145 Map 8

Derbyshire

The Bear Inn
Alderwasley

The best of olde England, in the back of beyond and not easy to find! Inside the dressed-stone pub is a bare-boarded, atmospheric warren – a long passageway, a comfy lobby (replete with budgies and cockatoos: fun for families), and a solid old door to a delightful snug with high-backed settles, old pews and stools, low beams, clutches of farmers and chinwagging locals. Yet more rooms, more alcoves, old brass scales, gilt-framed prints, a dresser packed with porcelain, horsey ephemera, ancient clocks, candles, stone fireplaces and aromatic log fires. The blackboard menu is long, with up to 30 main courses available all day and great Sunday roasts, there are six handpumps with a changing array of beers, and plenty of wines. Great staff make this an extremely popular place; book your table for evenings and weekends.

Meals	12pm-9.30pm (9pm Sun).
	Main courses £8.95-£17.95;
	bar meals £3.95-£5.95.
Closed	Open all day.
Directions	From B5025 east of Wirksworth, turn off at Wirksworth Moor at the Malt Shovel pub. Continue for 1 mile.

Nicola Fletcher-Musgrave
The Bear Inn,
Alderwasley,
Belper DE56 2RD
Tel   01629 822585

Entry 146 Map 8

Derbyshire

The Barley Mow
Kirk Ireton

Sunlight streams through the stone mullioned windows of this Jacobean pub. Outside, its resplendent sundial is dated 1681. So authentic is the Barley Mow that Sir Isaac Newton could be penning the last words of a thesis in the parlour. The tiled tap room floor is framed by simple wall benches and dotted with old stools; barrels of ale are racked neatly behind the bar; it is austere, dimly lit, addictive. To the side, up a few steps from the front parlours, are adjoining rooms that include the original kitchen with its huge 17th-century working bread oven. A selection of fresh cobs is available at lunchtime while suppers are for residents only. As you sip your Thatchers cider or Whim Hartington IPA, you will notice the slate-topped tables with a missing corner and wonder why? For drinkers, ramblers and historians, sheer delight.

Meals	Rolls available 12pm-2pm, £1.
Closed	2pm-7pm.
Directions	Signed off B5023 Wirksworth to Duffield road.

Mary Short
The Barley Mow,
Kirk Ireton,
Ashbourne DE6 3JP
Tel   01335 370306

Entry 147 Map 8

Derbyshire

Ye Olde Gate Inne
Brassington

One of the most exquisite pubs in Derbyshire, built from timber salvaged from the wrecks of the Armada. Furnishings are plain: ancient settles, rush-seated chairs, gleaming copper pans, a clamorous clock, a collection of pewter. In winter a fire blazes in the blackened range that dominates the quarry-tiled bar. In the dim yet wonderfully atmospheric snug are a glowing range and flickering candlelight. There's a short, changing blackboard menu and traditional tucker: ploughman's, baguettes (delicious roast beef with onions and mushrooms), venison casserole, homemade bread and butter pudding. Come too for superbly kept Marstons Pedigree on hand pump and a number of malts. Mullioned windows look onto a sheltered back garden – perfect for the popular evening barbecues that are held from Easter until October.

Meals	12pm-2pm (12.30pm-2.30pm Sun); 6.30pm-9pm; no food Sun eve. Main courses £7.95-£18.95; bar meals £3.85-£10.95.
Closed	2.30pm-6pm (7pm Sun); Mon (except bank hols) & Tues lunch.
Directions	Midway between Ashbourne & Wirksworth off B5035.

Peter Scragg
Ye Olde Gate Inne,
Well Street, Brassington,
Matlock DE4 4HJ
Tel   01629 540448

Entry 148 Map 8

Derbyshire

Druid Inn
Birchover

A strange, enticing countryside of tors, crags, wooded knolls and stone circle-strewn moors erupts high above Matlock. In the midst of this morphological mayhem stands the Druid Inn, its mellow stone exterior disguising an ultra-chic gastropub and a menu drawing on traditional British and the best of European; ham hock, black pudding and Stilton terrine, monkfish with tomato, chorizo and butter bean stew, rice pudding with gingerbread ice cream, crab mayonnaise sandwiches. Shadows of the old village local remain: a quarry-tiled snug with open fire, antique seats and beers brewed by the Leatherbritches brewery – but the general atmosphere is that of bistro-in-the-country, with a minimalist décor in the split-level restaurant rooms. Suntrap patios promise village views, and ramblers rub shoulders with epicures.

Meals	12pm-2.30pm (3pm Sun); 6pm-9pm. Main courses £9-£16; sandwiches from £6.
Closed	Mon in winter; Sun from 4pm. Open all day.
Directions	From A6; B5056; signs for Birchover.

Michael & Bryan Thompson
Druid Inn,
Main Street, Birchover DE4 2BL
Tel   01629 650302
Web   www.thedruidinn.co.uk

Entry 149 Map 8

Devonshire Arms
Beeley

Classic Peak District scenery surrounds Beeley's stone cottages and this public house. Converted from three cottages in 1747, it became a coaching inn that was visited by Edward VII and is popular now because of its proximity to great Chatsworth House. In 2006 it was taken over by the Duke and Duchess of Devonshire. Always a civilised lunch spot for well-heeled locals, it now verges on the opulent. Along with the beams, log fires and settles are candy-stripe tub chairs in vibrant hues and cushions tucked into cosy crannies. In a room where floor-to-ceiling windows overlook the beck are snazzy bar stools, a glass-fronted wine store and more enticing colours. Bar and brasserie serve traditional and modern food and meat from the estate – all delicious – while the wine list reaches the dizzy heights of Château Petrus. In a stone-flagged tap room, walkers are refreshed with expertly kept ales. (Walk through the woods to Chatsworth; if you're staying, entry is free.) Bedrooms, equally vibrant, stylish and understated, are full of comfort and joy. The staff are lovely and breakfasts are a treat.

Rooms	4: 3 doubles, 1 suite. £145–£185.
Meals	12pm-9.30pm. Main courses £9.95–£19.50; bar meals £5.95–£12.95.
Closed	Open all day.
Directions	Follow signs for Chatsworth off A6 at Rowsley Bridge.

Alan Hill
Devonshire Arms,
Beeley, Matlock DE4 2NR
Tel   01629 733259
Web   www.devonshirebeeley.co.uk

SPECIAL
AWARD
see pages 18-19

Pubs with rooms

Entry 150 Map 8

Derbyshire

Old Poets' Corner
Ashover

Old Poets' Corner has something for every one and it has been achieved with effortless style. Inside this mock-Tudor village-centre inn, ideally placed for forays into the Peaks and Dales, is a whirlwind of activity that pulls together live music, eight real ales, one perry, an ever-changing range of five ciders and an Arts and Crafts interior. And, living up to its name, there's a regular poets' night for local rhymesters. From good hefty farmhouse settles and pine tables, music-loving regulars sup ale brewed in the pub's own microbrewery and ciders such as Broadoak Moonshine (8.4% abv)… And with that in mind the menu is more than substantial, trumpeting chillis, pastas, pies, casseroles and a carvery on Sundays. Sit back, relax and be entertained by the energy and good vibes surrounding you.

Meals	12pm-2pm; 6.30pm-9pm; 12pm-3pm Sun. Main courses £4.25-£14; bar meals £3.25-£9.50; Sunday roast £6.95.
Closed	Open all day.
Directions	Ashover is just off B6036, between Kelstedge & Woolley Moor.

Kim & Jackie Beresford
Old Poets' Corner, Butts Road,
Ashover, Chesterfield S45 0EW
Tel   01246 590888
Web   www.oldpoets.co.uk

Entry 151 Map 8

Derbyshire

The Bull's Head
Ashford-in-the-Water

Lovely carved settles, cushions, clocks and country prints – this is pub heaven. There are newspapers and magazines to read, light jazz hums in the background, coals glow in the grate. The busy Bull's Head has been in Debbie Shaw's family for half a century and she and Carl have been at the helm for the past eight. Carl cooks, proudly serving "bistro food, not a laminated menu"; even the bread and the cheese biscuits are homemade. With a strong emphasis on local and seasonal produce, there could be steak and Old Stockport pie with braised red cabbage, pan-fried calves' liver with bubble-and-squeak and red wine gravy, sticky toffee pudding with black treacle sauce. Service is swift and friendly and, this being a Robinson's pub, Unicorn Best Bitter, Old Stockport and Wards are on hand pump – a brilliant place.

Meals	12pm-2pm; 6.30pm-9pm (7pm-9pm Sun); no food Thurs pm. Main courses £10-£17.50.
Closed	3pm-6pm (7pm Sun).
Directions	Off A6, 2 miles north of Bakewell. 5 miles from Chatsworth.

Debbie Shaw
The Bull's Head, Church Street,
Ashford-in-the-Water,
Bakewell DE45 1QB
Tel   01629 812931

Entry 152 Map 8

Derbyshire

Three Stags Heads
Wardlow Mires

As you weave your way across the moor you could easily miss this collection of cottages, modestly housing a pottery and a pub. The pub is a gem inside, and couldn't be plainer: two small rooms, one heated by a fire, the other by a coal-burning kitchen range, nice for drying out waterproofs. So settle into a pint of Abbeydale's Black Lurcher, the house bitter with an 8% ABV, named in memory of one of the dogs. The menu really is a case of what is available from the surrounding countryside and features a lot of game. (It has been known for squirrel to have gone into the pot.) Opening times are restricted depending on whether you're here for pottery or a pint, and a plate of something hot and wholesome from the chalked board. Soaked in history it's no museum – the hosts, the dogs and the impromtu music see to that!

Meals	1pm-3.30pm; 7pm-9pm. Main courses £8.50-£10.50.
Closed	Mon-Thur all day & Fri until 7pm. Open all day weekends & bank hols.
Directions	At junction of A623 & B6465 south east of Tideswell.

Geoff & Pat Fuller
Three Stags Heads,
Wardlow Mires,
Tideswell SK17 8RW
Tel   01298 872268

🐾 🍺

Entry 153 Map 8

Derbyshire

The Chequers Inn
Froggatt Edge

The setting is almost alpine in its loveliness – impossible to pass this pub by. Once four stone-built cottages going back to the 16th century, the Tindall's ancient whitewashed inn has been sympathetically modernised, recently refurbished and is full of homely touches. Wooden floorboards, pine and country prints, cottage furniture and interesting objets give character to rooms that radiate off a stone-walled, timber-ceilinged bar. While blackboards promise modern bistro-style dishes – crab and pea linguine, pan-fried calves' liver with celeriac purée and red pepper sauce – the standard menu lists doorstep sandwiches and traditional casseroles and pies. From the raised garden behind, a path leads straight up through woods to stunning Froggatt Edge; the walking is marvellous.

Meals	12pm-2pm; 6pm-9.30pm; 12pm-9.30pm Sat (9pm Sun). Main courses £8-£18.
Closed	2.30pm-6pm. Open all day Sat & Sun.
Directions	On A625 8 miles northwest of Chesterfield, 9 miles southwest of Sheffield.

Jonathan & Joanne Tindall
The Chequers Inn, Froggatt Edge,
Hope Valley, Calver S32 3ZJ
Tel   01433 630231
Web   www.chequers-froggatt.com

💳 🍺 🍷

Entry 154 Map 8

Derbyshire

The Plough
Hathersage

You'll find a big welcome from Bob, Cynthia and their team at their isolated 16th-century free house, once a corn mill, on the banks of the river. Acres of grounds and a riverside garden high in the National Park form a perfect backdrop to a popular inn. The atmosphere is convivial in the cosy, carpeted, split-level bar, where walkers and talkers unwind against a backdrop of log fires, exposed beams, stone walls, good solid furniture; beyond is a plush country restaurant. With over 40 dishes to choose from, this is very much a dining pub. Tasty food, from lamb sweetbreads with pancetta to lemon sole with papardelle, is the order of the day, there's a range of hand-pulled ales and fine wines for connoisseurs. You're on a main road but in nine private acres; the sloping gardens are lovely, and have valley views.

Devon

Rose & Crown
Yealmpton

Delicious smells tempt you the moment you enter this big, bustling, open-plan pub. People travel miles for the food: chef Daniel Gillard cut his teeth at the Carved Angel. Cheerful staff dispatch good-looking dishes to softly-lit tables in one of two dining areas. A step or two down are squashy cow-hide sofas around an open fire, cream-washed open-stone walls and wooden Venetian blinds – perfect simplicity. The best wines represent the best value, and the ales and the menu change monthly. Curried prawn wontons in a clear consommé are just one example of a beautifully executed Pacific Rim menu, but you can have pork and leek sausages too, and roasted skate wing with chestnut mushrooms, and west country cheeses, and poached apple with calvados ice cream. *Seafood restaurant in neightbouring barn.*

Meals	11.30am-2.30pm; 6.30pm-9.30pm (Sat 11.30am-9.30pm, Sun 12pm-9pm). Main courses £12.95-£19.95; bar meals £9.95-£12.95.
Closed	Open all day.
Directions	On B6001, 1 mile south from Hathersage towards Bakewell.

Meals	12pm-2pm (3pm Sun); 6.30pm-9pm. Main courses £9.95-£18; set lunch £9.95 & £12.95.
Closed	Closed 3pm-6pm. Open all day Sun.
Directions	On A379, 7 miles south-east of Plymouth.

Bob & Cynthia Emery
The Plough, Leadmill Bridge,
Hathersage S32 1BA
Tel 01433 650319
Web www.theploughinn-hathersage.co.uk

John Stevens
Rose & Crown, Market Street,
Yealmpton, Plymouth PL8 2EB
Tel 01752 880223
Web www.theroseandcrown.co.uk

Entry 155 Map 8

Entry 156 Map 2

Devon

The Ship Inn
Noss Mayo

At the head of a tidal inlet, a 16th-century pub remodelled with a nautical twist. While visiting boats can tie up alongside (with permission!), high-tide parking is trickier. When the tide is in, you enter via the back door on the first-floor level; when out, it's a quick stroll over the 'beach' and in at the front. Downstairs are plain boards, a wooden bar, solid wood furniture and walls richly caparisoned with maritime prints. Open fires, books and newspapers add to the easy feel. Upstairs the Galley, Bridge and Library areas have views and a happy, dining buzz. The menu strikes a modern chord: shank of Devon lamb with rosemary and garlic sauce and pan-fried duck breast alongside pumpkin and pea risotto and chocolate mousse. Take your drink to the sunny patio at octagonal tables and relish the watery views.

Meals	12pm-9pm (9.30pm Sat). Main courses £9.75-£17.95; bar meals £5.25-£11.95.
Closed	Open all day.
Directions	South of Yealmpton, on Yealm estuary.

Charles & Lisa Bullock
The Ship Inn,
Noss Mayo, Plymouth PL8 1EW
Tel   01752 872387
Web   www.nossmayo.com

Entry 157 Map 2

Devon

Dartmoor Union
Holbeton

Don't be deceived by the unassuming plaque next to the front door of this former cider press and village union room. Inside is stylish, welcoming and full of surprises. The leather sofas, chopped logs and glossy piles of *Country Living* in the flagstoned bar create a comfortable farmhouse feel, while the burgundy walls of the dining area add a bistro touch. The pub is part of the Wykeham Inns group who also own the Rose & Crown at Yealmpton – so broad and keenly priced daily menus appeal to all tastes, with some judicious sourcing of ingredients. Tuck into partridge with spicy lentils and parsnip purée or crab crostini. Another surprise: they have a microbrewery in the enclosed garden, producing two ales from a Kentish blend of Goldings, Brambling Cross and Fuggles hops. Beaches and walks beckon…

Meals	12pm-2pm (3pm Sun); 6.30pm-9pm (9pm Sun). Main courses £9.95-£18.95; bar meals £6.95-£11.95.
Closed	3pm-5.30pm. Open all day Sun.
Directions	Village signed off A379, 10 miles east of Plymouth.

Anthony Russell
Dartmoor Union, Fore Street,
Holbeton, Plymouth PL8 1NE
Tel   01752 830288
Web   www.dartmoorunion.co.uk

Entry 158 Map 2

Devon

Fortescue Arms
East Allington

Tom and Werner are the 'highlights' here. Canadian Tom is maitre d' and has looked after heads of state; Austrian Werner has cheffed in starred kitchens. Double doors fling open in summer and the wine corks pop in the bar. Your hosts welcome locals and visitors alike, and provide fabulous food. Portions are generous, quick to arrive, great value and, if the rabbit and pumpkin stew is anything to go by, delicious. Emphasis is on local produce so there's venison steak with red wine and berry gravy; pheasant stuffed with chestnuts; tuna with red wine and caper sauce; apfelstrüdel with crème patissière. The dark panelled and flagstoned bar is where Tom holds court, the restaurant is inviting with terracotta walls and glowing candles, and the outdoor decked area is smartly spotlit at night.

Meals	12pm-2pm; 7pm-9.30pm. Main courses £9.95-£17.65; bar meals £6.80-£12.95.
Closed	2.30pm-6pm & Mon lunch.
Directions	Village signed off A361 between Totnes & Kingsbridge.

Werner Rott & Tom Kendrick
Fortescue Arms,
East Allington, Totnes TQ9 7RA
Tel 01548 521215
Web www.fortescue-arms.co.uk

Entry 159 Map 2

Devon

Victoria Inn
Salcombe

Separated from the rock pools and the sea by a modest car park, this fully revamped inn has won awards under chef-proprietor Andrew Cannon. Local pictures and nautical *objets* acknowledge the location and history – as does the menu, whose range is broad. Pop in for a pint and a sandwich and chips or stay for a daily fish special served in generous portions. Young and cheery staff make all ages welcome and the large three-tiered garden, with super wooden play area, makes this an excellent family venue in summer. Salcombe's yachties and second-home owners mean that star-spotters may get lucky – though you might be better off having a nautical natter with the sea dogs at the bar. Flowers and white linen in the restaurant, log fires and malt whiskies in the bar, coastal walks to make the heart soar.

Meals	12pm-2.30pm; 6pm-9pm. Main courses £7.95-£15.95.
Closed	Open all day.
Directions	By the harbour in town centre.

Andrew Cannon
Victoria Inn,
Fore Street, Salcombe TQ8 8BU
Tel 01548 842604
Web www.victoriainnsalcombe.co.uk

Entry 160 Map 2

Devon

The Mill Brook Inn
South Pool

Arrive before the boats do. They drop anchor a step away and their first port of call is this popular local – a little pub with a big heart. Good food and hospitality are positively worshipped here, and in the best seasonal and local style. Feast on legendary crab sandwiches and hand-cut chips, a paean to the humble potato. In winter, a log fire warms the immediate bar area while padded settles and wheelback chairs cluster comfortably around tables in several snugs. The stream-side terrace is tiny but guarantees entertainment in summer once the Aylesbury ducks are at play, so sit back and relax with a pint of Bass or Palmers Ale. Owners Ian and Diana have ambition and integrity and are determined to deliver some of the best food and drink in the area. They do so with enthusiasm and charm.

Meals	12pm-2pm; 7pm-9pm. Main courses £6.50-£10 (lunch), £10-£15 (dinner).
Closed	Open all day.
Directions	From Frogmore on A379 east of Kingsbridge follow signs south to South Pool; pub in village centre.

Ian Dent & Diane Hunt
The Mill Brook Inn,
South Pool, Kingsbridge TQ7 2RW
Tel 01548 531581
Web www.millbrookinnsouthpool.co.uk

Entry 161 Map 2

Devon

Pig's Nose Inn
East Prawle

Winding lanes with high hedges weave from the main road to the edge of the world. There are an awful lot of porcine references round these parts (South Hams, Gammon Head, Piglet Stores) and the Pig's Nose is Devon's most southerly pub. Filled with character, a wood-burner and quirky ephemera, it has an atmosphere all of its own. A pie, pint and a paper at lunchtime can give way at night to the entire pub joining in a singalong; Peter's connections entice legendary acts – The Yardbirds, Wishbone Ash – to play in the adjacent hall. If your teenagers fail to join in, a ready supply of 50p coins will keep them entertained in the pool room. Your hosts have a terrific sense of fun and faithful visitors return again and again, while the sea-view village has barely changed since the Thirties.

Meals	12pm-2pm; 6.30pm-9pm (7pm-9pm in winter). Main courses £5.50-£11.
Closed	2.30pm-6pm (7pm in winter), Sun eve & Mon all day in winter.
Directions	A379 Kingsbridge-Dartmouth; at Frogmore, right over bridge opp. bakery; signs to East Prawle. Pub by green.

Peter & Lesley Webber
Pig's Nose Inn,
East Prawle, Kingsbridge TQ7 2BY
Tel 01548 511209
Web www.pigsnoseinn.co.uk

Entry 162 Map 2

Devon

Tradesmans Arms
Stokenham

This 14th-century, part-thatched pub, formerly a brewhouse with three cottages, stands in a sleepy village inland from Slapton Sands and takes its name from the tradesmen who used to call in for a jug of ale while trekking the coastal bridlepath. You may still find a tradesman or two here today, downing a pint in the main bar. Beamed and attractively rustic, it has an open fire and antique dining tables, while gilt framed pictures fill the Georgian dining room; both have views that reach across the valley. The menu and daily chalkboard specials list some innovative pub food. As well as the usual lunchtime sandwiches, the daily-changing and seasonal selection includes fresh Brixham fish, scallops from the bay and game. You'll find six real ales on hand pump, including Brakspear Bitter – Nick's favourite tipple.

Devon

The Tower Inn
Slapton

Despite the drawbacks of hidden access and tricky parking, this 14th-century inn attracts not just locals but visitors from Slapton Sands. Standing beside the sinister ivy-clad ruins of a chantry tower, the pub is a flower-bedecked classic, and hugely atmospheric inside. Dark and gloomy by day, the low-beamed and stone-walled interior – all rustic dark-wood tables, old pews and fine stone fireplaces – is hugely atmospheric by night, thanks to the flickering light from candles and fires. Golden, bitter-sweet St Austell Brewery Tribute from the handpumps could be accompanied by a plateful of black bream with a warm fennel and orange salad, or local beef, seasonal game, venison and lamb. A lovely, sleepy village setting – and a super landscaped garden at the back with views of the parish church and the eerie tower.

Meals	12pm-2.30pm; 6.45pm-9.30pm. Main courses £7.95-£15.95; bar meals £3.95-£7.95.
Closed	3pm-5.30pm. Open all day Sun.
Directions	1 mile from Slapton Sands & Torcross, off A379.

Meals	12pm-2pm; 7pm-9pm. Main courses £10-£19
Closed	2.30pm-6pm & Mon lunchtime.
Directions	Off A379 between Torcross & Dartmouth. Signed.

	Nicholas Abington Abbott
	Tradesmans Arms,
	Stokenham, Kingsbridge TQ7 2SZ
Tel	01548 580313
Web	www.thetradesmansarms.com

	Thea Butler & Dan Cheshire
	The Tower Inn,
	Slapton, Kingsbridge TQ7 2PN
Tel	01548 580216
Web	www.thetowerinn.com

Entry 163 Map 2

Entry 164 Map 2

Devon

Kings Arms
Strete

Tempting to visit on a dark and rainy night – but a shame to miss the glorious views of Start Bay. Rob Dawson has revitalised the Edwardian hotel-turned-pub, bringing a natural warmth and a fine menu. A modest bar and a few tables greet you, then up the pine stair to a mezzanine dining room. Delicious smells waft from the kitchen – of seared scallops with pea mousses and Serrano ham, brill with red wine glaze and garlic confit, poached pears with Devon Blue ice cream and port jelly. Oysters are gathered from the river Dart, lobsters and crabs come from the bay, the cheeses are local and the wines are wide-ranging with an excellent number by the glass. The Kings Arms and its garden fill up at summer weekends as holiday-cottagers get wind of the place, and return – for the food, the friendliness and the views.

Meals	12pm-2pm (3pm Sun); 6.30pm-9pm. Main courses £9.50-£19.95.
Closed	2.30pm-6pm (3pm-7pm Sun). Sun eves & Mon all day in winter.
Directions	Between Dartmouth & Torcross on the A379.

Rob Dawson
Kings Arms, Dartmouth Road,
Strete, Dartmouth TQ6 0RW

| Tel | 01803 770377 |
| Web | www.kingsarms-dartmouth.co.uk |

Entry 165 Map 2

Devon

The Normandy Arms
Dartmouth

The Commercial of the 1850s became The Normandy 90 years later – named after the landings; some of the sailors who died were buried on a farm in this parish. With its charming slate bar and floor, open wood beams, lovely red corner seating and bright, friendly staff, The Normandy is, in spite of its brilliance with food, still a pub. Peter, who cut a dash at the Dorchester and the Blue Ball at Triscombe, is chef; Sharon does front of house. Both are splendidly hands-on. People come from Kingsbridge, Totnes, Dartmouth for the food. Our meal of pigeon breasts with dauphinoise potatoes and red cabbage, followed by warm plum tarte tatin, was a winning blend of restraint and indulgence. West country cheeses come with homemade chutney, fish comes from Brixham and the wine list is long. Spoiling all round.

Meals	12pm-2pm; 7pm-9pm; no bar food Fri & Sat eve. Main courses £9.95-£16.95; bar meals £7.50-£13.95.
Closed	3pm-7pm, Tues lunch, Sun eve & Mon all day Dec-Feb.
Directions	Village signed off A3122 5 miles west of Dartmouth.

Peter Alcroft & Sharon Murdoch
The Normandy Arms,
Chapel Street, Blackawton,
Totnes TQ9 7BN

| Tel | 01803 712884 |

Entry 166 Map 2

Devon

The Ferry Boat Inn
Dittisham

The only inn right on the river, it used to serve the steamers plying between Dartmouth and Totnes – you can still arrive by boat. Big windows show off the view to the wooded banks of the Greenway Estate (once Agatha Christie's home, now owned by the NT: shake the bell and catch the ferry). Arrive early for the best seats in the rustic, unspoilt little bar with its bare boards, crackling log fire, nautical bric-a-brac and all-important 'high tides' board; if you've missed the village car park, negotiated the steep lane and parked on the 'beach', then check the board before ordering your pint. Similarly, the tide dictates whether or not you can dine outside in summer. Expect a rousing welcome, live music sessions and decent home-cooked pub food. Gents can 'spray and pray' next door in the converted chapel.

Devon

Turtley Corn Mill
Avonwick

The mill's six acres slope down to a lake, so there's space for a multitude of picnic tables (order your hampers in advance). And, more unusually, boules, croquet, jenga and a ginormous chess set. Inside has been revamped to create a series of spacious inter-connected areas: the bar with its dark slate floors and doors to the garden; the wooden-floored 'library' lined with books; the mill room with the turning wheel right outside – plus wood-burner, prints on pristine white walls and oriental rugs. The food is traditional and homemade, be it crab sandwiches on granary bread or fillet of sea bass served on chorizo mash. Side orders are extra, a paper menu is printed off every day, and wines start at £11.95, plus several by the glass. A cosy pub for a rainy day, and with outdoor space to roam in summer.

Meals	12pm-2pm; 7pm-9pm. Main courses £6.95-£12.
Closed	Open all day.
Directions	Off A3122, 2 miles west of Dartmouth.

Meals	12pm-9.30pm (9pm Sun). Main courses £7.50-£16.
Closed	Open all day.
Directions	A38 eastbound, turn for South Brent/Avonwick; 1st right to Avonwick, on B3372. Bear left following signs for Totnes; pub 100m on left.

	Ray Benson The Ferry Boat Inn, Manor Street, Dittisham, Dartmouth TQ6 0EX
Tel	01803 722368

	Bruce & Lesley Brunning Turtley Corn Mill, Avonwick, South Brent TQ10 9ES
Tel	01364 646100
Web	www.avonwick.net

The Maltsters Arms
Tuckenhay

The setting is spectacular – down on the quay of the wooded and beautiful Bow Creek – so pick a table outside. The 1550s pub was once owned by 'gastronaut' Keith Floyd and is a friendly and cheerfully informal place; get cosy in winter, and convivial in summer. Interconnecting rooms have deep red walls, scrubbed tables, boarded floors, log fires and big windows looking up the creek. The quayside bar, with barbecue, is ever-open and a boon on warm days. Daily menus use local ingredients; you may find West Country ploughman's, game pie, skate with lemon and caper butter, and banoffee bread and butter pudding, all of it tasty. Behind the bar, local ales and farm ciders vie for attention among wines, spirits and organic juices. The rooms, though now some years old, still have Floyd's pizzazz and a touch of exotic luxury; one has a nautical theme, the 'Duke's Room' has a masculine air, and 'Khun Akorn' reveals a Thai décor and a huge draped bed. Children and dogs get a proper welcome – it's that sort of place.

Rooms	4 doubles. £85-£110.
Meals	12pm-3pm (4pm Sundays); 7pm-9.30pm. Main courses £8.95-£19.95.
Closed	Open all day.
Directions	Off A381, 2.5 miles south of Totnes.

Denise & Quentin Thwaites
The Maltsters Arms,
Bow Creek, Tuckenhay, Totnes TQ9 7EQ
Tel   01803 732350
Web   www.tuckenhay.com

Entry 169 Map 2

The White Hart Bar
Dartington

Down a long, long drive past farmland and deer, Dartington Hall finally peeps into view: the college, conference centre, arts centre, dairy farm and 14th-century hall built for a half-brother of Richard II. Tucked into the corner of the courtyard – dotted with picnic tables in summer – is the White Hart. The bar and restaurant is informally 21st century, with chunky beams, York stone floor, smouldering log fires, round light-oak tables and Windsor chairs. Organic and local produce are the mainstay of the menus, from soups to stews with dumplings. In the trestled dining hall: Start Bay crab cake; river Exe mussels; chocolate and coffee tart. Beers are from Otter Brewery, there are excellent wines and organic juices and ciders. Walk off a very fine lunch with a stroll through the parkland that borders the Dart.

Meals	12pm-2pm; 6pm-9pm; snacks 2pm-5pm. Main courses £7-£14.95.
Closed	Open all day.
Directions	Off A385, 2 miles north west of Totnes.

John Hazzard
The White Hart Bar, Dartington Hall,
Dartington, Totnes TQ9 6EL
Tel   01803 847111
Web   www.dartingtonhall.com

Entry 170 Map 2

The Church House Inn
Marldon

The old village pub is a civilised place, popular with retired locals and ladies that lunch. With a welcoming bar, several dining areas and lovely sloping garden, it's a proper all-rounder. The feel is one of a well-crafted, rustic elegance – stonework and beams, original bell-shaped windows, crisp table settings and smiling service. The central bar has been partitioned into three areas, plus one four-tabled candlelit snug, perfect for a party. The chef has been here years and the diners keep coming, and the food is modern British and locally sourced (including naturally reared Exmoor steak). Others come just for a pint of well-kept Dartmoor Best and a chat by the fire. The pub originally housed the artisans who worked on Marldon Church, and its ancient tower overlooks the hedged garden.

Meals	12pm-2pm (2.30pm Sun); 6.30pm-9.30pm (9pm Sun). Main courses £8.50-£17.95.
Closed	2.30pm-5pm (3pm-5.30pm Sun).
Directions	Marldon off Torquay-Brixham ring road. Pub at bottom of village, signed.

Julian Cook
The Church House Inn,
Marldon,
Paignton TQ3 1SL
Tel   01803 558279

Entry 171 Map 2

Bickley Mill
Kingskerswell

The microclimate of the English Riviera is never more apparent than in the garden of this 13th-century flour mill. David and Tricia have orchestrated a total refurbishment and their stylishly cosy interiors are just the ticket. Come for wood floors, stone walls, hessian rugs, cushioned sofas. Three fires burn in winter, there are Swedish benches, colourful art and a panelled breakfast room in creamy yellow. Everywhere you look something lovely catches the eye, be it a huge sofa covered with mountainous cushions, old black and white photos hanging on the walls or a decked terrace at the side for a pint or two in the summer sun. Bedrooms have a simple beauty in warm colours, pretty pine, trim carpets, crisp white linen – and with reasonable prices they're an absolute steal. Downstairs you'll find helpful staff, local ales and loads to eat (light bites to a three-course feast) perhaps devilled kidneys, salmon fishcakes, banana and toffee pancakes; there's a menu for children and baby chairs, too. A small inn full of good things.

Rooms	8: 5 doubles, 2 twins, 1 family room. £70–£80. Singles £55.
Meals	12pm-2pm (2.30pm Sat); 6.30pm-9pm (9.30pm Fri & Sat); 12pm-8pm Sun. Main courses £9.55–£15.95.
Closed	3pm-6pm. Open all day Sun.
Directions	South from Newton Abbot on A381. Left at garage in Ipplepen. Left at T-junc. after 1 mile. Down hill, left again, pub on left.

David & Tricia Smith
Bickley Mill,
Stoneycombe, Kingskerswell TQ12 5LN

Tel	01803 873201
Web	www.bickleymill.co.uk

Entry 172 Map 2

Devon

The Rock Inn
Haytor Vale

Originally an ale house for quarrymen and miners, the 300-year-old Rock Inn stands in a tiny village high on Dartmoor's windswept slopes. Run by the same family for over 20 years, this civilised haven oozes character; there are polished antique tables and sturdy settles on several levels, a grandfather clock, pretty plates and fresh flowers, cosy corners and at least two fires. Settle down with a pint of Dartmoor Best in the beamed and carpeted bar and peruse the supper menu that highlights local, often organic, produce. All that fresh Dartmoor air will have made you hungry, so tuck into rib-eye steak with black peppercorn and brandy sauce, then chocolate, orange and cointreau tart. Lunchtime meals range from soup and sandwiches to local sausages in onion gravy. There's a pretty beer garden, too.

Meals	12pm-2pm; 7pm-9pm. Main courses £7.50-£13.95 (lunch); £15.95-£18 (dinner); sandwiches £4.95.
Closed	Open all day.
Directions	At Drumbridges roundabout A382 for Bovey Tracey; B3387 to Haytor. Left at phone box.

Christopher & Susan Graves
The Rock Inn, Haytor Vale,
Widecombe-in-the-Moor TQ13 9XP
Tel 01364 661305
Web www.rock-inn.co.uk

Entry 173 Map 2

Devon

Rugglestone Inn
Widecombe-in-the-Moor

Beside open moorland, within walking distance of the village, is a 200-year-old stone pub whose two tiny rooms lead off a stone-floored passageway. Few of the daytrippers who descend on this idyllic village in the middle of Dartmoor make it to the Rugglestone. Low beams fill the old-fashioned parlour with its simple furnishings and deep-country feel. Both rooms are free of modern intrusions, the locals preferring cribbage, euchre and dominoes. The tiny bar serves local farm cider; Butcombe Bitter and St Austell Dartmoor Best are tapped from the cask. From the kitchen comes proper home cooking, from ploughman's lunches and soups to lamb shanks and fresh fish — and not a deep-fat fryer in sight. Across the babbling brook at the front is a lawn with benches and peaceful moorland views. A little piece of heaven.

Meals	12pm-2pm; 7pm-9pm. Main courses from £6.95-£10.95.
Closed	3pm-6pm. Open all day Sat & Sun.
Directions	600 yards from centre of Widecombe; signed.

Richard Palmer & Vicki Moore
Rugglestone Inn,
Widecombe-in-the-Moor,
Bovey Tracey TQ13 7TF
Tel 01364 621327

Entry 174 Map 2

The Elephant's Nest
Horndon

Overseas visitors will give a rapturous smile as they enter the main bar, all polished oak beams, flagstone floors and crackling fires... you almost imagine a distant Baskerville hound baying. This is an atmospheric inn that serves properly home-cooked food – very local, very seasonal and British with a twist: perhaps antipasto of pastrami, rosette saucisson and Black Forest ham, or South Devon sirloin with mushrooms, vine tomatoes and French fries; sweet tooths can drool over Mrs Cook's fabulous lemon posset with blueberry compote. When suitably sated, slip off to the new annexe and a nest of your own in one of three rather fun, wonderfully quiet and extremely comfortable rooms. Wake to a pretty garden with views to Brentor church and Dartmoor, even, perhaps, a cricket match to watch: the pub has its own ground and club. So settle back to the thwack of willow on leather with a pint of Palmer's IPA – or Copper Ale, Jail Ale from Princetown, and guest ales from O'Hanlon's, Otter, Cotleigh, Teignworthy and Butcombe.

Rooms	3 twins/doubles. £75.
Meals	12pm-2.15pm; 6.30pm-9pm.
	Main courses £8.95-£16.95.
Closed	3pm-6.30pm.
Directions	Pub signed off A386 between Okehampton/Plymouth at the Mary Tavy Inn in Mary Tavy; follow signs for Horndon.

	Hugh & Denise Cook
	The Elephant's Nest,
	Horndon, Mary Tavy, Tavistock PL19 9LQ
Tel	01822 810273
Web	www.elephantsnest.co.uk

Devon

The Halfway House
Grenofen

'Twixt Plymouth and Launceston – the journey once took two days! – this old travellers' resting place, a row of six cottages, has embraced the millennium. In the bar are smooth pale wooden floors, spot-lit stone walls and modern leather sofas before a friendly log fire. Sharp's Doom Bar, London Pride and Tribute go down well with walkers; the river Walkham is nearby and the walking is magnificent in autumn. Fancy a meal? You're in good hands. In an elegant slate-floored dining room, to tables set with white linen and candles, delicious food is ferried. Try smoked mackerel with celeriac rémoulade, or pan-seared fillet of bass on saffron risotto with flamed red pepper sabayon. Everything is prepared and cooked to order and that includes the old-fashioned pub classics and the tapas on the bar menu.

Meals	12pm-2pm; 5.30pm-9pm. Main courses £10.95-£18.95; set lunch & early evening menu £10.50 & £13.95.
Closed	Open all day.
Directions	Beside A386 in Grenofen, midway between Plymouth & Launceston.

Peter Storey
The Halfway House,
Grenofen, Tavistock PL19 0JE
Tel   01822 612960
Web   www.thehalfwayhouseinn.com

Entry 176 Map 2

Devon

The Harris Arms
Lewdown

You are welcomed on the way in and thanked on the way out. The passion Andy and Rowena have for food and wine is infectious and the awards they are gathering is proof of their commitment. Expect a long bar, a fire at one end, a patterned carpet, maroon walls and a big strawberry blond cat named Reg. A large new decked area at the back has rich rolling views. The Whitemans are members of the Slow Food movement so real food is their thing: cheeses are the west country's finest, fish, meat, vegetable and dairy produce come from exemplary local suppliers, and wines are chosen from small growers. Flavoursome food is what the chefs deliver and whether it be roast belly pork with cider jus, fish and chips or rump of Devon lamb with redcurrant and mint jus, it is consistently good. Great value, too.

Meals	12pm-2pm; 6.30pm-9pm (7pm-9pm Sun). Main courses £8.50-£9.50 (lunch), £11.50-£17.50 (dinner).
Closed	3pm-6pm; Mon (except bank holidays) & Sun eve in winter.
Directions	On old A30 between Lewdown & Lifton; leave A30 at Broadwoodwidger exit & head south.

Andy & Rowena Whiteman
The Harris Arms,
Portgate, Lewdown EX20 4PZ
Tel   01566 783331
Web   www.theharrisarms.co.uk

Entry 177 Map 2

The Dartmoor Inn
Lydford

There aren't many inns where you can sink into Zoffany-clad winged armchairs in the dining room, snooze on a hand-painted bed under a French chandelier, or shop for Swedish tableware while you wait for the wild sea bass to crisp in the pan. You can here: the inn is the template of deep-country chic, a fairytale inn dressed up as a country local. True, walkers and dogs stride in from the moors and squeeze into the bar for Dartmoor Best Bitter, organic bottled cider, fish and chips or a hearty steak sandwich, but then again the walls are coated in textured wallpaper, the settles are smartly sandblasted, gilded mirrors sit above smouldering fireplaces and upstairs a soft velvet throw is spread out across a pretty sleigh bed. Add to this wonderful staff and Philip's ambrosial food (saffron scrambled eggs for breakfast, ham hock terrine for lunch, free-range duck for dinner) and you have a very spoiling place. Triple-glazed bedroom windows defeat road noise and the moors are on your doorstep – nearby is the thrilling Lydford Gorge – so walk in the wind, then eat, drink and sleep.

Rooms	3 doubles. £115-£125.
Meals	12pm-2pm; 6.45pm-9pm.
	Main courses £9.50-£22.50;
	bar menu £4.95-£12.95.
Closed	2.30pm-6.30pm, Sun eve &
	Mon lunch.
Directions	North from Tavistock on A386.
	Pub on right at Lydford turnoff.

Karen & Philip Burgess
The Dartmoor Inn,
Lydford, Okehampton EX20 4AY
Tel 01822 820221
Web www.dartmoorinn.com

Devon

Sandy Park Inn
Chagford

A small thatched pub in a tiny village on Dartmoor. The Teign runs through the valley, so follow its path for views that lift the soul. Those of a more sedentary disposition can sit in the beer garden and take in the view while sampling local delicacies. This is a cracking country boozer, loved by locals, and with food that punches above its weight; Barry the butcher brings in slow-grown pork off the moor, the cod comes battered in beer, the cheeses are local. Come for benched snugs and oriental rugs, worn flagstones and crackling logs, delicious smells and a happy hum. Standing room only at the bar at weekends; local musicians occasionally drop in to play on Sunday nights. Bedrooms sparkle with unexpected treats – flat screen TVs, CD players, padded headboards, colourful throws – but the bar is lively, and a night here will only suit those who want to have some fun. Most rooms have pretty views over the village and some are en suite, others not – come to practise the dying art of smiling at strangers on the landing. Also: kippers at breakfast, maps for walkers and dog biscuits behind the bar.

Rooms	5: 1 twin, 1 double, each en suite; 3 doubles each with separate bath/shower. £92. Singles £59.
Meals	12pm-2.30pm; 6.30pm-9.30pm. Main courses £7.50-£14.
Closed	Open all day.
Directions	A30 west from Exeter to Whiddon Cross. South 2 miles to Sandy Park. Pub on right at x-roads.

Nick Rout
Sandy Park Inn,
Sandy Park, Chagford TQ13 8JW

Tel   01647 433267
Web   www.sandyparkinn.co.uk

Entry 179 Map 2

Devon

Duke of York
Iddesleigh

Built to house the 14th-century stonemasons working on the church next door, the thatched Duke of York is the most genuine of locals, big-hearted and generous. It serves comforting food, real ale and Sams Cider from Winkleigh – along with a great welcome from a farmer-pub landlord and his wife. Scrubbed oak tables carry fresh flowers and candles, there are village photographs on the walls, bank notes on the beams, rocking chairs by the log fire – it's rustic and enchanting. Thanks to fish fresh from Clovelly and Brixham and locally sourced beef, lamb and pork, you tuck into the heartiest home cooking: tureens of homemade soup, steak and kidney pudding, lamb chops with rosemary and garlic gravy, whole baked sea bass with lemon butter, scrumptious puddings. And the all-day breakfasts are not for the faint-hearted.

Meals	12pm-10pm (9.30pm Sun) . Set menu, 3 courses, £24; bar meals £4.50-£14.
Closed	Open all day.
Directions	On B3217 between Exbourne & Dolton, 3 miles NE of Hatherleigh.

Jamie Stuart & Pippa Hutchinson
Duke of York,
Iddesleigh,
Winkleigh EX19 8BG
Tel   01837 810253

Entry 180 Map 2

Devon   Award winner 2008

The Lamb Inn
Sandford

Animal paintings brighten the bar, the ladies' loo is a gorgeous pink, the Portuguese chef is passionate about provenance and Bob and Tiny (the dogs) are a delight. The old posting inn is the hub of the village. There are three open fires in winter and carpeting for cosiness, stubby white candles on plain tables, tankards filled with roses and, upstairs, a long window seat that looks onto the village below. (Skittles and darts too, a big screen for films and sporting events, and a brilliant open mic night once a month.) The unplush décor is matched by a blackboard menu free of affectation, the scrumptious-sounding dishes ranging from a platter of west country cheeses to a Mediterranean cassoulet. All is locally sourced and made from scratch, and that includes the pastas and the breads. Bedrooms follow in 2008.

Meals	12pm-2pm; 6.30pm-9.30pm. Main courses £6.50-£12.
Closed	Open all day.
Directions	From A3072 follow signs for Sandford; pub in village centre.

SPECIAL
AWARD
see pages 18-19

Community pub

Mark Hildyard
The Lamb Inn, Village Square,
Sandford, Crediton EX17 4LW
Tel   01363 773676
Web   www.lambinnsandford.co.uk

Entry 181 Map 2

Devon

The Grove Inn
Kings Nympton

The pub is in the heart of old Nympton: a 'natural sacred grove'. A place of celebration for our pagan ancestors, and you should raise a glass to your good fortune in being here. There are paintings of the superb countryside by local artists, a picture gallery of faces past and present, beams hung with bookmarks, stone walls, a slate floor, and a wood-burner. Old and new combine with understated ease. New landlord Robert has already grasped the fundamentals of hospitality by the horns and Deborah his wife uses the freshest local produce to create her menus. Try individual Devon beef wellington served with dauphinoise potatoes or Lundy plaice with herb butter. Ales are from Cotleigh, Exmoor, Tarka, ciders are Sam's Dry Real, wines are from the Sharpham Estate. As they say round these parts – proper job!

Meals	12pm-2pm; 7pm-9pm; no food Mon, or Sun eve. Main courses £8-£17; Sunday lunch £8 & £14.75.
Closed	3pm-6pm & Mon lunch.
Directions	Off B3226 south of South Molton; pub in village centre.

Robert Smallbone
The Grove Inn, Kings Nympton,
South Molton EX37 9ST
Tel 01769 580406
Web www.thegroveinn.co.uk

Entry 182 Map 2

Devon

The Masons Arms Inn
Knowstone

Leaving windswept Exmoor behind, arrive through fern or twisting lane. Wood is stacked against the 13th-century walls, you are drawn to enter. The beamed, flagged bar fills with dogs and walkers in wellies, in for a natter and a pint of Cotleigh Tawny ale. But who would imagine, down worn stone steps, a cosy lounge with deep sofas and a restaurant extension complete with mural? Served at candlelit tables is food fit for kings. Mark Dodson spent 18 years working at Bray's celebrated Waterside Inn, 13 of those as head chef. Short menus accompanied by French and New World wines major in classic French and British dishes and are concocted from the finest regional produce; try pan-fried scallops with pear and vanilla or Devon beef fillet with rich oxtail and parsnip purée. The rear terrace has wonderful views to Exmoor.

Meals	12pm-2pm; 7pm-9pm. Main courses £14.00-£18.50; Sunday lunch £29.50.
Closed	3pm-6pm, Sun eve & Mon all day.
Directions	M5 junc. 27; A361 for Barnstaple; Knowstone signed after 16 miles. Into village, right at bottom of hill & pub on left.

Mark Dodson
The Masons Arms Inn, Knowstone,
South Molton EX36 4RY
Tel 01398 341231
Web www.masonsarmsdevon.co.uk

Entry 183 Map 2

Culm Valley Inn
Culmstock

Don't be put off by the unprepossessing exterior of Richard Hartley's pub by the lovely river Culm. The old station hotel may not be posh but it's warm, easy and charming: deep pink-washed walls, glowing coals, flickering oil lamps and candles. From bar stools the locals sample microbrewery beers while the gentry drop by for unusually good food. Easy-going chef-patron Richard and his merry band make this place zing. Look to the chalkboard for south coast seafood, weekend fish specials, Ruby Red Devon beef from nearby farms, and tapas. From the English elm bar you can order from a fantastic array of rare and curious spirits, French wines from specialist growers and up to ten local beers tapped from the cask. Richard plans an extra huge bedroom with a swish bathroom, aimed at families; the other three are simple and cheerful, with white bed linen and vibrant walls, and share two spotless bathrooms. In the words of one reader: "Fantastic host, great wine, superb homemade everything, lovely room, and an offer of taking the dogs for a walk the next day."

Rooms	4: 1 double, 1 twin, 2 family rooms. £60-£100. Singles £30.
Meals	12pm-2pm; 7pm-9.30; no food Sun eve. Main courses £7-£20; bar meals £6-£10.
Closed	3pm-7pm winter (except Sat & Sun).
Directions	On B3391, 2 miles off A38 west of Wellington.

Richard Hartley
Culm Valley Inn,
Culmstock, Cullompton EX15 3JJ
Tel   01884 840354

Entry 184 Map 2

Devon

The Quarryman's Rest
Bampton

There's something for everyone here. Real ale for beer buffs, a dining room for foodies, a fruit machine for gamblers, pool for the football team, and a shelter with scatter cushions in the garden, for smokers. The garden is lovely, too, and overlooks fields. Back in the pub, it's spacious inside, with dark panelling and sofas in one area, lightness and sunshine in another, and a separate carpeted dining room for quiet meals. All the produce is local, from the beer, cider and perry to the beef – you can see the cows from the window. It's not unknown either for regulars to swap a pheasant or a box of tomatoes for a pint. Along with the art on the walls (all for sale) you get proper shepherd's pie, steak and kidney pudding, pumpkin and wild mushroom risotto, ginger parkin – fantastic food, and really well priced.

Devon

The Cadeleigh Arms
Cadeleigh

It's a steep climb to get here but the car will drive itself back down the hill – and the sloping garden has wonderful views. From the glittery seats in the ladies' loo to the white wines from Bickleigh a mile down the road, this pub combines fabulous produce with a big dose of fun. Jeremy is head chef and the food is done brilliantly, be it moules marinière, risotto of roasted squash, liver and lambs' kidneys or an English pud. The menu varies day to day, according to what is in season. Jane and Elsbeth are a great team and a woman's touch is clearly at work here: antique pine tables and modern art, magazines and background jazz, games in the cupboard, logs by the grate. In the skittle alley they hold plays and serve suppers in the interval – and the coffee comes with milk in white china-cow jugs. Special.

Meals	12pm-2pm; 6pm-9.30pm (12pm-4pm Sun). Main courses £8.95-£12.95.
Closed	Open all day.
Directions	From A396 follow signs to Bampton; pub just as you enter the village.

Meals	12pm-2pm (2.30pm Sun); 7pm-9pm. Main courses from £8.95.
Closed	Sun eves & Mon.
Directions	From A396 just after Bickleigh Mill, turn right; signed.

Paul & Donna Berry
The Quarryman's Rest, Briton St, Bampton, Tiverton EX16 9LN

Tel	01398 331480
Web	www.thequarrymansrest.co.uk

Elspeth Burrage
The Cadeleigh Arms, Cadeleigh, Bickleigh EX16 8HP

Tel	01884 855238
Web	www.thecadeleigharms.co.uk

Entry 185 Map 2

Entry 186 Map 2

Devon

The Drewe Arms
Broadhembury

The Burge family run a relaxed ship – the secret of their long success. The 15th-century pub is the cornerstone of a thatched Devon village. By the fire are the day's papers; on the bar, local Otter ales tapped straight from the cask and wines beyond reproach. Beams are oak-carved, walls plank-panelled, there are country tables, wood carvings and a log-fired inglenook that crackles in winter. Food is way above average for a country pub, with fish from Branscombe, Exmouth and Newlyn. Go for spicy crab soup, whole Dover sole or Lyme Bay lobster. Plenty of classy modern touches, too, in sea bream with orange and chilli, hand-dived scallops seared to perfection, and, for carnivores, roast partridge or beef fillet with Café de Paris butter. All this, and a garden that's as dreamy as a country garden can be.

Meals	12pm-2pm; 7pm-9pm. Main courses £10-£20.
Closed	3pm-6pm (from 5pm Sun).
Directions	M5 junc. 28; A373 Honiton to Cullompton.

Kerstin & Nigel Burge & Andrew Burge
The Drewe Arms,
Broadhembury, Honiton EX14 3NF
Tel   01404 841267

Entry 187 Map 2

Devon

The Jack in the Green
Rockbeare

Bustle and buzz in the dark wood bar, and good local brews on tap – Otter Ale, Cotleigh Tawny, Branscombe Vale Bitter. But this is more restaurant than pub: "For those who live to eat," reads the sign. In a series of smart, brightly lit, blue-motif carpeted rooms, Devon Chef of the Year (2007) Matthew Mason's bar menu goes in for modern and mouthwatering variations of tried and trusted favourites: braised faggot with creamed potato, steamed venison pudding with port and juniper jus… even the ploughman's is impressive. More ambition on display in the restaurant, where seared fillet of salmon with sorrel and hollandaise sauce and roasted Creedy Carver duck breast with griottine cherries make for succulent seasonal choices. Paul Parnell has been at the helm for years and he and his staff do a grand job.

Meals	11.30am-2pm (2.30pm Fri & Sat); 6pm-10pm (9.30pm Mon); 12pm-9.30pm Sun. Main courses £12.50-£22.50; bar meals from £7.50.
Closed	2.30pm-5.30pm (3pm-5.30pm Fri, 3pm-6pm Sat). Open all day Sun.
Directions	5 miles east of M5 (exit 29) on old A30 just past Exeter Airport.

Paul Parnell
The Jack in the Green,
Rockbeare, Exeter EX5 2EE
Tel   01404 822240
Web   www.jackinthegreen.uk.com

Entry 188 Map 2

Devon

Devon

The Bridge Inn
Topsham

Unchanged for most of the century – and in the family for as long – the 16th-century Bridge is a must for ale connoisseurs. And for all who love a pub furnished in the old-style: just high-back settles, ancient floors, a simple hatch. (The Queen chose the Bridge for her first official 'visit to a pub'.) Years ago it was a brewery and malthouse; Caroline's great-grandfather was the last publican to brew his own here. This is beer-drinker heaven, with up to ten real ales served by gravity from the cask. There's cider and gooseberry wine, too. Cradle your pint to the background din of local chatter in the Inner Sanctum, or out in the garden by the steep river bank. With bread baked at the local farm, home-cooked hams, homemade chutneys and Devon cheeses, the sandwiches and ploughman's are first-class.

Digger's Rest
Woodbury Salterton

A 500-year-old, fat-walled former cider house built of stone and cob – surely the quintessential thatched Devon inn. A good-looking makeover has revived the timbered interior: fresh lemon walls and an eclectic mix of old dining tables, subtle wall lighting, tasteful prints. Arrive early to bag the sofa by the log fire. In addition to the local Otter and guest ales, the good list of wines and the relaxing atmosphere, there are organic soft drinks, Italian Gaggia coffee, soothing piped jazz, baby-changing facilities, newspapers and a one-hour lunch promise. The brilliant pub menu employs the best local produce, so treat yourself to Diggers fish pie, Devon Ruby Red beef (21-day hung rib-eye with red wine butter) and local Kenniford Farm pork, roasted for Sunday lunches. A beautifully landscaped patio garden, too.

Meals	12pm-1.45pm.
	Bar meals £3-£6.90.
Closed	2pm-6pm (7pm Sun).
Directions	M5 exit 30; A376 to Exmouth; 2 miles, right to Topsham; Elmgrove Road into Bridge Hill.

Meals	12pm-2.30pm; 6.30pm-9.30pm (Sat 12pm-9.30pm; Sun 12pm-9pm).
	Main courses £7.25-£14.95; bar meals £2.95-£14.95.
Closed	3pm-6pm. Open all day Sat & Sun.
Directions	Off A3052, 3 miles east of Exeter & 3 miles from M5 junc. 30.

Caroline Cheffers-Heard
The Bridge Inn,
Topsham, Exeter EX3 0QQ
Tel 01392 873862
Web www.cheffers.co.uk

Stuart Hawthorne & James Birch
Digger's Rest, Woodbury Salterton,
Exeter EX5 1PQ
Tel 01395 232375
Web www.diggersrest.co.uk

Entry 189 Map 2

Entry 190 Map 2

Masons Arms
Branscombe

Approach straggling Branscombe down narrow lanes to this creeper-clad inn. The 14th-century bar has a traditional feel with dark ship's timbers, stone walls, slate floor and a fireplace that cooks spit-roasts to perfection. Quaff pints of Otter Bitter or Branscombe Vale Brannoc by the fire; on warm days, head for the sun-trap terrace. Nothing is too much trouble for the staff, whose prime aim is for you to unwind. Local produce, including crab and lobster landed on Branscombe's beach, is the focus of the modern British menu. There's Ruby Red beef casserole with horseradish mash and whole line-caught sea bass, local crab ploughman's and roast leg of organically reared lamb with pancetta and tomato jus. No need to drive home; bed down instead in a room upstairs, or climb the steps to one of the cottages behind. Bedrooms are comfortably traditional while suites are vast and characterful: four-posters, deep sofas, thick carpets, antiques. The pebbly beach is a 12-minute stroll across National Trust land and coastal path walks reward the adventurous.

Rooms	21 twins/doubles. £80–£165.
Meals	12pm–2pm (2.15pm Sat & Sun); 7pm–9pm. Main courses £9.95–£13.95; bar meals £3.95–£7.50; set menu £27.50.
Closed	3pm–6pm in winter. Open all day Sat & Sun, every day in summer.
Directions	Off A3052 between Sidmouth & Seaton.

Colin & Carol Slaney
Masons Arms,
Main Street, Branscombe, Seaton EX12 3DJ
Tel   01297 680300
Web   www.masonsarms.co.uk

Entry 191 Map 2

Devon

192 Fountain Head Street, Branscombe, Seaton EX12 3BG
01297 680359

Be charmed by big flagstones, wood-clad walls, dim-lit corners, good pub grub and village-brewed beers. No fruit machines, just local babble and possibly a snoozing dog – walking country by the sea.

193 The Blue Ball Sandygate, Exeter EX2 7JL
01392 873401

Handy for the motorway, the colourwashed, thatched, roadside inn offers a welcoming respite. Brasserie-style food in a contemporary interior, and beams, flagstones and log fires in the rustic bar.

194 The Turf Hotel Exminster, Exeter EX6 8EE
01392 833128

Reached only on foot (20-min walk), by bike or by boat, a unique, rambling old pub overlooking the estuary mudflats. Bareboard bar with big bay windows for winter wader-watching and top-notch Otter Ales. Closed Dec-Feb.

195 Nobody Inn Doddiscombsleigh, Exeter EX6 7PS
01566 783331

Andy & Rowena Whiteman from the Harris Arms took over this famous old inn in '08. Expect few changes to the black beams and horse-brasses interior, local-food menus and fine wines. Reports please.

196 The Drewe Arms The Square, Drewsteignton EX6 6QN
01647 281224

Long, low and thatched, an unpretentious and well-loved village local in a pretty square by the church. Local ales still served from hatchways, and home cooking for walkers. Castle Drogo is nearby.

197 The London Inn Molland, South Molton EX36 3NG
01769 550269

Honest and unpretentious village local in the Exmoor foothills full of locals, dogs, hunters and shooters. Few frills in rambling flagstoned rooms, hearty food and great beer.

198 The Rydon Inn Holsworthy EX22 7HU
01409 259444

Much extended and refurbished old Devon longhouse with an impressive vaulted dining room, modern menus that champion local suppliers, and super views across rolling farmland.

199 The Warren House Inn Postbridge, Moretonhampstead PL20 6TA
01822 880208

Old tin miners' pub, high and alone, in a remote part of Dartmoor. No frills, just plain and simple, with Otter on tap and log fires warming the panelled bar. Visit on a clear day – the view sails for 20 miles.

200   The Peter Tavy Inn Peter Tavy, Tavistock PL19 9NN
01822 810348
Atmospheric 15th-century inn on the flanks of desolate
Dartmoor. Masses of charm in black beams, polished slate, long
pine tables and wood-burners in huge hearths. Cracking beer and
walks from the door.

201   Pilchard Inn Burgh Island, Bigbury-on-Sea TQ7 4BG
01548 810514
Walk across the sand or take the sea tractor to this atmospheric
smugglers' pub on the tidal island made famous by Agatha
Christie. Beams, flagstones, roaring log fires, barbecues, views,
cliff walks. Unique!

202   Cricket Inn Beesands, Kingsbridge TQ7 2EN
01548 580215
Unassuming outside, open-plan within, but a real local feel. Yards
from the beach, and lots of local fish. Expect jazz with Sunday
lunch (that's two fabulous roasts with all the trimmings).

203   The Start Bay Inn Torcross, Kingsbridge TQ7 2TQ
01548 580553
Packed the minute it opens (arrive late at your peril), this modest
14th-century beachside inn serves the best fresh fish and chips in
Devon. Dressed crab too. Arrive hungry.

204   The Cherub 13 Higher Street, Dartmouth TQ6 9RB
01803 832571
Dartmouth's oldest pub (1380) creaks with age: a magnificent
timbered house with an overhanging beamed façade. Good ales in
tiny bar with inglenook; pub food in restaurant.

205   Kingsbridge Inn 9 Leechwell Street, Totnes TQ9 5SY
01803 863324
Top-of-the-town treasure dating from the 13th-century, tucked down
a narrow street. Cosy beamed bar with fires and flagstones,
imaginative changing menus and jazz Sunday lunches. Reports please.

206   The Chasers Stokeinteignhead, Torquay TQ12 4QS
01626 873670
The reward for finding this thatched Devon longhouse is Darren
Bunn's inspired modern cooking. Seasonal menus brim with local
goodies – and lovely service from wife Hayley.

207   The Anchor Inn Cockwood, Dawlish EX6 8RA
01626 890203
Fine views of Cockwood's harbour from this 460-year-old former
fisherman's cottage. Rather fitting then to find an awesome 30
mussel dishes on a long, fishy menu. Good ale but tricky parking.

The Shave Cross Inn
Marshwood Vale

Fancy a pint of Branoc and a spicy salad of jerk chicken? Once a busy stop-off point for pilgrims and monastic visitors (who had their tonsures trimmed while staying), the cob-and-flint pub now sits dreamily off the beaten track at the end of several very narrow lanes. It was rescued from closure by the Warburtons, back from the Caribbean. Life has stepped up a gear and the old tavern thrives – thanks largely to the exotic and delicious cuisine, and the swish bedrooms in a new stone building next door. Where else in deep Dorset can you tuck into Louisiana blackened chicken with cream and pepper sauce? There's simple pub grub for less adventurous palates, while surroundings remain strictly traditional: flagged floors, low beams, country furniture and vast inglenook. Named after the surrounding hills, those seven smart bedrooms flourish big sleigh beds and grand four-posters, stone floors and oak beams and a host of pleasing extras – fresh coffee, plasma screens, bathrobes, posh smellies. The meandering garden, with goldfish pool, wishing well and play area, is gorgeous.

Rooms	7 doubles. £160–£190. Singles £95.
Meals	12pm-2.30pm (3pm Sun); 6pm-9pm (9.30pm summer); no food Sun eve in winter. Main courses £9.95–£16.50; set menus £22.50 & £26.
Closed	3pm-6pm & Mon (except bank holidays). Open all day Jun-Aug.
Directions	B3162 for Broadwindsor; left in 2 miles for Broadoak. Follow unclassified road for 3 miles.

Roy & Mel Warburton
The Shave Cross Inn,
Shave Cross, Marshwood Vale,
Bridport DT6 6HW
Tel   01308 868358
Web   www.theshavecrossinn.co.uk

Entry 208 Map 3

The Bull Hotel
Bridport

Urban-chic meets rural simplicity at Richard and Nikki's Regency-style coaching inn. Funky and fun sums up this vibrant place and you feel good the moment you step through the door. Escape Bridport's bustle, kick off your shoes and plonk yourself down on a squashy sofa with a pint of Otter ale. The bar is open all day, for hearty English breakfasts and cappuccino and cake, for lunchtime sandwiches and kids' high tea. For seriously good food, there's a candlelit restaurant; for summer lunches, a Victorian courtyard. Daily menus are contemporary and work with the seasons while organic ingredients are locally sourced: Lyme Bay scallops with black pudding and garlic sauce, Mapperton lamb cutlets with red wine. Enjoy vanilla rice pudding and handmade cheeses. And the bedrooms! Classic period features mix serenely with modern pieces and antiques, there are Designer Guild fabrics and Milo sofas, plasma screens and big comfy beds, Tivoli radios and white waffle robes, roll-top baths and Neal's Yard smellies. A boon for arty Bridport – and the fantastic Jurassic coast is a mile away.

Rooms	14: 10 doubles, 1 twin, 1 single. £70–£180. 2 family rooms. £145–£250. Singles from £60.
Meals	8.30am-10pm; 12pm-3pm; 6.30pm-9.30pm Sun. Main courses £8.50-£11.95 (lunch), £11.95-£15.95 (dinner).
Closed	Open all day.
Directions	In town centre.

Nikki & Richard Cooper
The Bull Hotel,
34 East Street,
Bridport DT6 3LF

Tel	01308 422878
Web	www.thebullhotel.co.uk

European Inn
Piddletrenthide

Mark Hammick has returned, with his wife Emily, to his Dorset roots – in the glorious Piddle Valley. The inn is a gem, with its beamed bar and dining room, old pine tables, charming watercolours, wood-burning stove and pints of Goldfinch brewed in Dorchester. As for the menus, they are short, seasonal, gutsy and champion local producers. The family farm at Wraxall and Genesis Farmers in Buckland Newton supply the meat; try loin of lamb served with garlic and rosemary juices and slow-braised Halstock Dexter beef with horseradish mash and red wine. Vegetables come from local allotments and gardens, there are Portland scallops, Mappowder gooseberries (in crumble) and a board laden with handmade organic cheeses. 'Red' and 'Green' bedrooms are warm, cosy and ooze style and comfort – big beds, crisp linen, colourful cushions and throws, antique furnishings and tempting extras: fresh coffee and homemade shortbread, a decanter of sherry, a flat-screen TV, just-picked flowers. Handmade toiletries and roll-top baths await in plush bathrooms... gorgeous to come home to after a day exploring the Dorset coast.

Rooms	2 doubles. £80. Singles £55.
Meals	12pm-2pm; 7pm-9pm; no food Sun eve. Main courses £8-£14.
Closed	3pm-6pm; Sun eves & Mon.
Directions	On B3143 between Dorchester & Sherborne, 5 miles north of Dorchester.

Mark & Emily Hammick
European Inn,
Piddletrenthide, Dorchester DT2 7QT
Tel   01308 348308
Web www.european-inn.co.uk

Dorset

The Brace of Pheasants
Plush

In a sleepy hamlet surrounded by rolling downland, this thatched brick and flint building is Dorset's prettiest pub (or a close contender). Originally two 16th-century cottages linked to the smithy, it became an inn in the mid-1930s and displays an unusual sign – a brace of pheasants in a glass case. Beyond the latch door, the traditional low-beamed main bar has real charm and character, with an inglenook big enough to plonk yourself down in, a further impressive fireplace with a winter log fire, and an assortment of tables and chairs. Foaming pints of Ringwood and Otter are tapped straight from the cask to accompany plates of warming seasonal food – maybe crab, gruyère and saffron cream tart, or wood pigeon stroganoff. There's a peaceful back garden for summer sipping, and great walks straight from the door.

Meals	12pm-2.30pm; 7pm-9.30pm. Main courses £9-£16.
Closed	3pm-7pm, Sun eve & Mon.
Directions	Plush is signed off B3143 Dorchester-Sherborne road, just north of Piddletrenthide.

	Phil & Carol Bennett
	The Brace of Pheasants,
	Plush, Dorchester DT2 7RQ
Tel	01300 348357
Web	www.braceofpheasants.co.uk

Entry 211 Map 3

Dorset

The Square & Compass
Worth Matravers

The name honours all those who cut stone from the nearby quarries. This splendid old pub has been in the family for 100 years and remains gloriously unchanged. A narrow (and rare) drinking corridor leads to two hatches from where Ringwood and guest ales are drawn from the cask. With a pint of farmhouse cider and a homemade pastie, you can chat in the flagged corridor or settle in the parlour with its painted wooden panels, wall seats, local prints and cartoons. The wood-burner will warm you on a wild night. The stone-walled main room has live music; there's cribbage and shove ha'penny; the family's fossil museum is next door. Gazing out across fields to the sea, the pub and its sunny front terrace – dotted occasionally with free-ranging hens – is a popular stop for coastal path hikers. A treasure.

Meals	Pasties and pies only, £2.50.
Closed	3pm-6pm. Open all day Sat & Sun & every day July-Sep.
Directions	B3069 east of Corfe Castle; through Kingston; right for Worth Matravers.

	Charlie Newman & Kevin Hunt
	The Square & Compass,
	Worth Matravers,
	Swanage BH19 3LF
Tel	01929 439229

Entry 212 Map 3

Dorset

Coventry Arms
Corfe Mullen

Hard to beat if you're looking for a great little pit-stop en route to the coast; it's right by the A31. The Coventry Arms may not resemble the 15th-century watermill it once was but the rustic and rambling rooms, the sagging oak beams the worn flagstones and the cosy nooks and crannies lend a clue as to its age. And there's a lovely, comforting, laid-back feel: terracotta walls are lined with tasteful pictures and fishing paraphernalia, logs crackle in the grate, chunky candles glow on old dining tables. The modern British menu focuses on local produce, every small supplier is named and praised on the list of specials, and seafood is a speciality. There are trout and whiting fishcakes with horseradish cream, Angus beef for Sunday lunch, four ales pulled from the cask, and a streamside garden for summer.

Meals	12pm-2.30pm; 6pm-9.30pm; all day on Sun.
	Main courses £10-£20; bar meals £5-£10.
Closed	3pm-5.30pm. Open all day Sat & Sun.
Directions	A31 between Dorchester & Wimborne; 2 miles west of Wimborne.

John Hugo
Coventry Arms, Mill Street,
Corfe Mullen, Wimborne BH21 3RH
Tel 01258 857284
Web www.coventryarms.co.uk

Entry 213 Map 3

Dorset

The Museum Inn
Farnham

In a village with roses round every door is one of the finest inns in the south of England. Pub entrepreneur David Sax plans to keep the atmosphere warm and happy, following a gentle upgrade. The big 17th-century bar has a period feel – all flagstones, inglenook, fresh flowers and a fashionable mismatch of tables and chairs. Popular with the barbour bunch and their dogs, it is quietest out of season. Expect cosy alcoves to hide in, a book-filled drawing room to browse and a smart, white-raftered dining room. Chef Matthew Davey is Michelin-trained and his sophisticated dishes range from smoked haddock fishcake with creamed leek and split-pea velouté to roasted local estate venison with butternut squash mash and sour cherry jus. Prune and armagnac pudding comes with clotted cream, lemon tart with berry compote. Fabulous.

Meals	12pm-2pm (2.30pm Sat & Sun); 7pm-9.30pm (9pm Sun).
	Main courses £14-£18.50; bar snacks (lunch) £6.50-£7.50.
Closed	3pm-6pm (7pm Sun).
Directions	From Blandford, A354 for Salisbury for 6.5 miles, then left, signed Farnham. Inn on left in village.

David Sax
The Museum Inn, Farnham,
Blandford Forum DT11 8DE
Tel 01725 516261
Web www.museuminn.co.uk

Entry 214 Map 3

The Talbot
Iwerne Minster

The early 20th-century exterior opens to an exceedingly good pub-with-rooms. Key to the Talbot's success is that it keeps its locals happy: drinkers come for the pints of Badger, the pool table and the screen, foodies for the lounge and dining room, comfortably decorated with rugs and candlelit tables. Monthly menus and daily dishes reflect the seasons and make brilliant use of local supplies – game from surrounding estates, fish from Dorset day boats, meats and sausages from the village butcher. At lunch you can tuck into roast beef and horseradish sandwiches or homemade pork pie, then push the boat out in the evening with carpaccio of peppered Ranston estate beef fillet, venison braised in red wine, orange and thyme, and steamed pear pudding topped with Dorset ice cream. As for the bedrooms, recently spruced up and named after local hills, they're as fine as the rest, with crisp cotton sheets and colourful throws, armchairs and painted wooden beds, feature fireplaces and spacious bathrooms. Follow a proper English breakfast with a hike to the top of Hambledon Hill – and be wowed by the views.

Rooms	5: 4 twins/doubles, 1 family room. £90–£120. Singles £70.
Meals	12pm-2pm; 6.30pm-9.30pm. Main courses £8.50–£17.50.
Closed	2.30pm-6pm.
Directions	On A350 Blandford/Shaftesbury road, 4 miles north of Blandford.

Lester & Jane Wareham
The Talbot,
Iwerne Minster, Blandford Forum DT11 8QN
Tel   01747 811269
Web   www.the-talbot.com

Entry 215 Map 3

Dorset

Stapleton Arms
Buckhorn Weston

An inn with a big heart. There are no pretensions here, just kind, knowledgeable staff committed to running the place with informal panache. A facelift has brought a streak of glamour back to this old coaching inn, and a delightful garden at the back. Downstairs are sofas in front of the fire, a piano for live music in the bar and a restaurant in Georgian blue with shuttered windows and candles in the fireplace. You can eat wherever you want. Pork pies (to eat in or take out), Serrano ham and Tête de Moine cheese all wait at the bar, but if you want a three-course feast you must book – it gets packed out. There are salmon and crab fishcakes, home-baked Dorset ham, banana tarte tatin, even a beer menu; ale matters here. On Sundays groups can order their own joint of meat, and there's always a menu for kids. Rooms above are soundproofed to ensure a good night's sleep. They're comfy-chic with Egyptian linen, fresh flowers, happy colours, perhaps a claw-foot bath. Also: maps and picnics, wellies if you want to walk, games for children, DVDs for all ages. Wincanton is close for the races.

Rooms	4: 3 doubles, 1 twin/double. £80–£120. Singles £72–£96.
Meals	12pm-3pm; 6pm-10pm (9.30pm Sun). Main courses £8.90–£14; bar meals from £5; Sunday roast £11.50.
Closed	3pm-6pm. Open all day Sat & Sun.
Directions	A303 to Wincanton. Into town, right after fire station, signed Buckhorn Weston. Left at T-junc. after 3 miles. In village, left at T-junc. Pub on right.

Kaveh Javvi
Stapleton Arms,
Church Hill, Buckhorn Weston,
Gillingham SP8 5HS

Tel	01963 370396
Web	www.thestapletonarms.com

Entry 216 Map 3

Dorset

217 Ship Inn West Stour, Gillingham SP8 5RP
01747 838640
Spruced up roadside inn with stripped oak boards, scrubbed farmhouse tables, big bow windows and a buzz. Cracking ales on tap and a chalkboard menu listing fish specials and seasonal game.

218 Rose & Crown Trent, Sherborne DT9 4SL
01935 850776
A rural Dorset gem – thatched and unpretentious with rug-strewn stone floors, log fires, four ales on tap and views across open fields to rolling hills. Peacefully at the end of the lane by the church.

219 Crown Inn Ibberton, Blandford Forum DT11 0EW
01258 817448
True old Dorset local in a sleepy village under Bulbarrow Hill. Kick off your hiking boots in the lovely garden, savour local ciders and real ales, refuel on fabulous, well-priced food.

220 The Royal Oak 23 Long Street, Cerne Abbas DT2 7JG
01300 341797
Crackling log fires throughout the three flagstoned rooms add to the charm of this creeper-clad, thatched and historic pub. Four Badger beers, wines by the glass and seasonal menus.

221 The Greyhound Sydling St Nicholas, Dorchester DT2 9PD
01300 341303
Having made a success of The West Bay down by the sea, John Ford and Karen Trimby (plus chef) moved inland to this rambling village local in a valley north of Dorchester. The fish should be good – reports welcome.

222 The Fox Inn Corscombe, Dorchester DT2 0NS
01935 891330
Everything about this idyllic thatched inn is lovely: the food, the people, the setting. Expect stuffed owls in glass cases, gingham tablecloths, flowers, flagstones, fires and six fish dishes a day.

223 Marquis of Lorne Nettlecombe, Powerstock DT6 3SY
01308 485236
Isolated inn with gardens (suitable for kids) at the base of Eggardon Hill. Worth the trip down tortuous lanes for log fires, Palmers ales, lovely food and valley views.

224 The Three Horseshoes Powerstock, Bridport DT6 3TF
01308 485328
Victorian stone inn in a drowsy village down twisting lanes below Eggardon Hill. Fresh food and tip-top Palmers ale, best savoured on a balmy evening on the terrace watching the sun slide over the valley.

Dorset

225   The Anchor Inn Seatown, Chideock DT6 6JU
      01297 489215
      A terrific coastal path watering-hole below Golden Cap. The big
      sun terrace and clifftop gardens overlook a pebbly beach. Open
      fires, pints of Palmers, crab sandwiches.

226   Vine Inn Vine Hill, Pamphill, Wimborne BH21 4EE
      01292 882259
      Former bakehouse run by the Sweatland family for generations,
      now owned by the National Trust. Two timeless bars, London
      Pride on tap and sandwiches for sustenance. Close to Kingston
      Lacy House.

227   The Anchor West Street, Shapwick, Blandford Forum DT11 9LB
      01258 857288
      Little lanes through the Stour Valley lead to Shapwick and the new-
      look Anchor. Expect scrubbed tables on quarry tiles, Ringwood ales
      and imaginative food. Handy for Kingston Lacy (NT). Reports please.

228   Ship in Distress Stanpit, Mudeford, Christchurch BH23 3NA
      01202 483997
      Quirky and crammed with nautical clutter, this entertaining local
      is a fish fancier's dream. Arrive early for Mudeford crab or grilled
      scallops, great fish and chips or a tureen of Breton-style fish soup.

The Victoria Inn
Durham

In the centre of lovely old-fashioned Durham – all cobbled streets, riverside walks, Cathedral – is a Victorian public house with small rooms, high ceilings, marble fireplaces, three coal fires, etched and cut glass and a collection of Victoriana. Once upon a time, shawled women popped in for a porter or an errant husband, now it's frequented by builders, students, families and academics. Virtually unaltered since it was built in 1899, the Vic has been in the Webster family for years and has a strong local following. The three traditional rooms are spick and span; above the bar servery is an unusual gallery with shining figurines and ornaments of Queen Victoria and the Prince Consort. Simple snacks are available but it is the Darwins Ghost Ale and other local and Scottish beers, the whiskies and the camaraderie that makes this place enticing. Upstairs bedrooms are warm, cosy, comfortable, traditionally furnished and good value, breakfasts are relaxed and generous and there's off-street parking and garaging. Original, timeless and welcoming.

Rooms	5: 3 doubles, 1 twin, 1 family room. £60–£65. Singles £48–£65.
Meals	12pm–3pm. Toasted sandwiches only.
Closed	Open all day.
Directions	5-minute walk over Kingsgate Bridge from cathedral, castle & market place.

Michael Webster
The Victoria Inn,
86 Hallgarth Street, Durham DH1 3AS
Tel   0191 386 5269
Web   www.victoriainn-durhamcity.co.uk

Entry 229 Map 12

Durham

Black Bull Inn
Frosterley

An enticing village pub run as its owners like it. It is atmospherically lit, with solid tables and high-back settles (cushioned for comfort), stone flags, ticking clocks, glowing ranges, warmth and good cheer. No lagers, but coffee and scones from 10.30am, cider from the cask and beers from a few villages away. The hop is treated with reverence here – dark malty porter from Wylam Brewery, bitter from Allendale – and the good value food is a joy. Rather than devising a menu then searching for suppliers, Diane and Duncan source the produce first: local as much as possible, and in tune with the seasons. A shin of Broomhill Farm beef braised in ale on root vegetables with dumplings is the sort of thing they love here. Every Tuesday local musicians play classical, folk or jazz…hey, this place even has its own peal of bells.

Meals	12pm-2.30pm; 7pm-9pm; no food Sun or Mon eve. Main courses up to £13.95; Sunday roast £7.95.
Closed	Open all day. Closed Sun & Mon eve.
Directions	Beside A689 in Weardale between Wolsingham & Stanhope.

Duncan & Diane Davis
Black Bull Inn,
Bridge End,
Frosterley DL13 2SL
Tel   01388 527784

Entry 230 Map 12

Durham

The County
Aycliffe

Having won a Raymond Blanc scholarship in 1995, and worked with Gary Rhodes in London, Andrew Brown brought his skills north and restored the fortunes of a once run-down pub overlooking Aycliffe's pretty green. Bare boards and fresh walls help create a pleasing minimalist feel. The award-winning food draws an eager crowd, while the open-plan bar is still the focal point of the community. Eat here, or in the stylish bistro. There are open sandwiches at lunchtime, and sausages with black pudding mash; in the bistro, crab and prawn risotto with lobster sauce, confit shoulder of lamb with Mediterranean vegetables, grilled tuna with fennel and a tomato ragout. The touch is light, bringing out textures and flavours superbly. Several real ales are on hand pump, wines are mostly New World, and service is swift, young and friendly.

Meals	12pm-2pm (2.30pm Sun); 6pm-9.15pm (6.45pm-9.15pm Sat). Main courses £12.50-£19.95; bar meals £5-£10.50.
Closed	2pm-5.30pm (6.30pm Sat). Open 12pm-2.30pm Sun.
Directions	North of junc. 59 A1 (M), by A167.

Andrew Brown
The County, 13 The Green,
Aycliffe, Darlington DL5 6LX
Tel   01325 312273
Web   www.the-county.co.uk

Entry 231 Map 12

Rose and Crown
Romaldkirk

An idyllic village of mellow stone where little has changed in 200 years. The Rose and Crown dates from 1733 and stands on the green, next to the village's Saxon church. Roses ramble above the door in summer, so pick up a pint and search out the sun on the gravelled forecourt. Inside is just as good. You can sit at settles in the tiny locals' bar and roast away in front of the fire while reading the *Teesdale Mercury*, or seek out sofas in the peaceful sitting room and tuck into afternoon tea. Bedrooms are lovely. Those in the converted barn have padded headboards and tumble with colour; those in the main house come with antique pine, padded window seats and warm country colours. All have crisp white linen, Bose sound systems and quietly fancy bathrooms. Fabulous food can be eaten informally in the brasserie (smoked salmon soufflé, confit of duck, sticky toffee pudding) or grandly in the panelled dining room (farmhouse ham with fresh figs, grilled sea bass, honey and whisky ice cream). High Force waterfall and Hadrian's Wall are close and there's a drying room for walkers.

Rooms	12: 6 doubles, 4 twins, 2 suites. £135–£190. Singles from £85.
Meals	12pm-1.30pm; 6.30pm-9.30pm (9pm Sun). Main courses £10–£15.25.
Closed	Open all day.
Directions	From Barnard Castle, B6277 north for 6 miles. Right in village towards green. Inn on left.

Christopher & Alison Davy
Rose and Crown,
Romaldkirk, Barnard Castle DL12 9EB
Tel   01833 650213
Web   www.rose-and-crown.co.uk

Entry 232 Map 12

Durham

Durham

Bridgewater Arms
Winston

A Victorian schoolhouse with views rising across fields to distant woods is the slightly quirky setting for this fun and welcoming modern bar and restaurant. The memory of the old school is carefully retained in the bar, with its high ceiling, decorative leaded windows, shelves of books and photos of past pupils. The names of the children that took part in 1957's *Jack and the Beanstalk* are inscribed in big letters above the bar, adding charm and a touch of history. Adjoining half-panelled dining rooms are warmly decorated and furnished in contemporary style. Blackboards and daily printed menus place firm emphasis on the local, seasonal, fresh and organic, the choice of dishes ranging from traditional Yorkshire with a modern twist to Asian-inspired. Outside is a garden for whiling away a couple of hours in the sun.

The Morritt Arms Hotel
Greta Bridge

Peace and quiet are the keynotes of the Dickens Bar of this well-loved coaching inn; the novelist stayed here while researching *Nicholas Nickleby*. The imposing building, invitingly floodlit after dark, has been welcoming travellers on the long road from Scotch Corner to Carlisle and Scotland since the 17th century. It's a warm and stylish stopover: the interior is effortlessly homely, polished block floors are graced with colourful rugs and deep chintz armchairs front open log fires — a cosy spot for afternoon tea and homemade cakes. The Dickens Bar has three local cask ales, views across the lawn to the river, and a wonderful mural painted in 1946 by John Gilroy, who selected well-known local figures and created a Dickensian theme around them. Bar snacks in the bar, elaborate modern dishes in the restaurant and bistro.

Meals	12pm-2pm; 5.30pm-9pm; no food Sun eve. Main courses £9.50-£17.
Closed	2.30pm-5.30pm & Mon. Open all day Sun.
Directions	Just off A67 between Darlington & Barnard Castle; at entrance to village.

Meals	12pm-9.30pm. Main courses £10-£19.
Closed	Open all day.
Directions	Off A66, 10 miles west of Scotch Corner.

Claire & Barry Dowson
Bridgewater Arms,
Winston, Darlington DL2 3FY

| Tel | 01325 730302 |
| Web | www.bridgewaterarms.com |

Barbara-Anne Johnson
The Morritt Arms Hotel, Greta Bridge,
Barnard Castle DL12 9SE

| Tel | 01833 627232 |
| Web | www.themorritt.co.uk |

Durham

Number Twenty 2
Darlington

It is young, yet it is Darlington's most classic pub. Just off the town centre, the Victorian-styled 'Traditional Alehouse & Canteen' looks no different from the neighbouring shop fronts. Inside, a high ceiling and raised areas in the front bays give a vault-like impression; Number Twenty 2 is licensed for the sale of ales, wines and a limited range of spirits. There are five changing guest ales alongside eight regular beers, nine continental beers on tap, and a good choice of wines chosen for easy quaffing; it's a civilised place favoured by local business folk, and the staff know their stuff. At the back of the long bar is a seating area known as the 'canteen' at lunchtimes, and the food is good and uncomplicated. It may be closed on Sundays, but for the rest of the week Darlington has a very fine local.

Meals	12pm-2pm.
	Main courses £4.95-£9.95.
Closed	Open all day. Closed Sun.
Directions	Just west of Darlington town centre. Coniscliffe Road leads into A67 to Barnard Castle.

Ralph Wilkinson
Number Twenty 2, Coniscliffe Rd, Darlington DL3 7RG
Tel   01325 354590
Web   www.villagebrewer.co.uk

Entry 235 Map 12

Essex

The Viper
Mill Green

Isolated, but not lonely, this little pub sits in magnificent woodland on an empty road. The snug, neat, open-plan front bar is warm and jolly and the locals will tell you, with pride, that these plain simple rooms have barely changed for 60-odd years. One blackboard lists a regularly changing selection of East Anglian real ales, such as Mighty Oak's intriguingly named Jake the Snake and Nethergate's Viper Ale; another lists a decent choice of wines. The classic, good-value bar snacks are served at lunchtime only – sandwiches, pies, soup, chilli, ploughman's – and there's a choice of roasts on Sunday. The setting is so peaceful you can ignore the nearby road, tables on the lawn overlook a cottage garden, resplendent in summer with flowers and shrubs, and excellent walks start from the door.

Meals	12pm-2pm (3pm Sat & Sun).
	Main courses £3-£5.95; Sunday roast £7.95.
Closed	3pm-6pm. Open all day Sat & Sun.
Directions	From A12 for Margaretting; left up Ivy Barn Lane; pub at top.

Donna Torris
The Viper,
The Common, Mill Green,
Ingatestone CM4 0PT
Tel   01277 352010

Entry 236 Map 9

The Bell Inn & Hill House
Horndon-on-the-Hill

A 600-year-old timber-framed coaching inn, as bustling today with happy locals as it was when pilgrims stopped on their way to Canterbury. Everything here is a delight: hanging lanterns in the courtyard, stripped boards in the bar, smartly dressed staff in the restaurant, copious window boxes bursting with colour. This is a proper inn, warmly welcoming, with thick beams, country rugs, panelled walls and open fires. Stop for a pint of cask ale in the lively bar, then potter into the restaurant for sensational food, perhaps Stilton ravioli, grilled Dover sole, orange and passion fruit tart. Christine grew up here, John joined her 35 years ago; both are much respected in the trade, as is Joanne, Master Sommelier and loyal manager of many years. An infectious warmth runs throughout this ever-popular inn. As for the bedrooms, go for the suites above the shop: cosy, traditional, individual, rather wonderful. In the morning stroll up the tiny high street to breakfast with the papers at elegant Hill House, then head north into Constable country, or east to the pier at Southend.

Rooms	15: 7 doubles, 3 twins, 5 suites. £40–£100.
Meals	12pm–1.45pm (2.30 Sun); 6.30pm–9.45pm (from 7pm Sun); no food bank holiday Mon. Main courses £9.50–£14.95; bar meals £7.95–£10.50.
Closed	2.30pm–5.30pm (3pm Sat; 4pm–7pm Sun).
Directions	M25 junc. 30/31. A13 for Southend for 3 miles, then B1007 to Horndon-on-the-Hill. On left in village.

Christine & John Vereker
The Bell Inn & Hill House,
High Road,
Horndon-on-the-Hill SS17 8LD

| Tel | 01375 642463 |
| Web | www.bell-inn.co.uk |

Entry 237 Map 5

Essex

The Cricketers
Clavering

It achieved fame as the family home and training ground of Jamie Oliver and, as such, draws a few passers-by... but this big 16th-century inn on the edge of Clavering handles its glory with good humour. Trevor and Sally Oliver's pub has low beams, original timbers and a contented, well-cared for air; light floods in, reflected in the highly polished tables and gleaming brass and glass. A serious commitment to seasonal food is obvious the moment you see the printed menu: steamed mussels with white wine and shallots, wild char-grilled venison with quince and redcurrant sauce, organic salmon with a red peppercorn crust on green beans with fresh salsa verdi, shank of lamb with root vegetables. Blackboards list daily specials and good value wines of the month, many served by the glass.

Meals	12pm-2pm; 6.30pm-9.30pm. Main courses £10-£18; set menu £22 & £27.50.
Closed	Open all day.
Directions	On B1038 between Newport & Buntingford.

Trevor & Sally Oliver
The Cricketers, Clavering,
Saffron Walden CB11 4QT
Tel 01799 550442
Web www.thecricketers.co.uk

Entry 238 Map 9

Essex

Axe & Compasses
Arkesden

At the heart of a highly desirable village of thatched cottages with a stream running down its middle, the 400-year-old building resembles the perfect Essex pub. The rambling interior is a classic too: beamed ceilings, timbered walls, panelling, open fires, comfy sofas – and that's just the lounge bar. Thanks to attentive service and a well-loved, lived-in feel, this is a popular place. It's all down to the Christou family, with father Themis at the head, whose respect for the traditions of English inn-keeping puts many English landlords to shame. Local Greene King ales are excellent; food is either good English – steak and kidney pie, chicken supreme, wing of skate – or recognises the family's Greek Cypriot roots, with moussakas and Greek salads. It may not be cheap but it's freshly cooked and generously served.

Meals	12pm-2pm; 6.45pm-9.30pm. Main courses £11.95-£17.50; bar meals £4.95-£14.95; Sunday lunch £19.
Closed	2.30pm-6pm (3pm-7pm Sun).
Directions	On B1038 between Newport & Clavering.

Themis & Diane Christou
Axe & Compasses,
Arkesden,
Saffron Walden CB11 4EX
Tel 01799 550272

Entry 239 Map 9

The Sun Inn
Dedham

An idyllic village made rich by mills in the 16th century. These days you can hire boats on the river, so order a picnic at the inn, float down the Stour, then tie up on the bank for lunch al fresco. You're in the epicentre of Constable country; the artist attended school in the village and often returned to paint St Mary's church with its soaring tower; it stands directly opposite. As for the Sun, you couldn't hope to wash up in a better place. Step in to find log fires in grand grates, board games on old tables, stripped floors and an easy elegance. A panelled lounge comes with sofas and armchairs, the bar is made from a slab of local elm and the dining room is beamed and airy, so settle in for grilled rib-eye steak with artichokes, fish from British waters, local cheeses and children's portions of whatever they fancy. Bedrooms are gorgeous: creaking floorboards, a panelled four-poster, timber-framed walls, decanters of sherry. There's afternoon tea on arrival, a garden for summer barbecues and the inn owns Victoria's Plums, a tiny shop selling locally grown fruit and veg next door.

Rooms	5: 4 doubles, 1 four-poster. £85–£130. Singles £60–£130.
Meals	12pm–2.30pm (3pm Sat & Sun); 6.30pm–9.30pm (10pm Sat). Main courses £8.50–£16.50; bar meals £4.50–£8.50.
Closed	Open all day.
Directions	A12 north past Colchester. 2nd exit, marked Dedham.

Piers Baker
The Sun Inn,
High Street, Dedham,
Colchester CO7 6DF
Tel   01206 323351
Web   www.thesuninndedham.com

The Mistley Thorn
Mistley

In Constable country: an unexpectedly chi-chi village where Georgian cottages gather around a river estuary with wide, light views of water, bobbing boats and green hills beyond. David and Sherri (who have a cookery school next door) run the place beautifully: staff are young and very good, there are plenty of locals tossed into the mix downstairs and some impeccably behaved children too. The mood is laid-back city wine bar rather than country pub. Colours are soft and easy, the tables are of various shapes, candles flicker, modern art rubs along well with the odd antique and food is taken seriously but with no grim reverence. There's lots of good local fish and seafood – smoked haddock chowder, crab linguine with chilli, chunky fishcakes, brilliant chips – and a pudding list that includes cheesecake from Sherri's mum. Bedrooms are calm with cream carpets, big beds, pale green paintwork and some have views over the water. Bathrooms have a Turkish feel with tiny beige and cream tiles, spotless white baths and overhead showers. It's all entirely charming.

Rooms	5: 3 doubles, 2 twins/doubles. £70-£95. Singles £60-£80.
Meals	12pm-2.30pm; 6.30pm-9.30pm; 12pm-4pm; 6pm-9.30pm Sat & Sun. Main courses £8.95-£15.95; bar meals £4.25-£8.95.
Closed	3pm-6.30pm. Open all day Sat & Sun.
Directions	From A12 Hadleigh/East Bergholt exit north of Colchester. Thro' East Bergholt to A137; follow signs to Manningtree, drive thro' to Mistley High Street.

David McKay & Sherri Singleton
The Mistley Thorn,
High Street, Mistley,
Colchester CO11 1HE

Tel	01206 392821
Web	www.mistleythorn.co.uk

Entry 241 Map 10

Compasses at Pattiswick
Pattiswick

Jono and Jane Clark's transformation of this old pub is a huge success. Slick and sophisticated bars mix flagstones with floorboards, modern furniture and soft lights with creams and sages. At heart it remains a local, with plenty of space for drinkers in for a pint of Woodforde's Wherry or Abbot Ale. Yet the food is the major draw, served in the bar or the elegantly beamed and spacious restaurant. Old favourites such as Gloucester Old Spot bangers with mash and onion gravy are founded on well-sourced raw materials, for the kitchen cultivates a network of small local producers. More modern dishes might include chicken breast with creamy goat's cheese, and leek and bacon pasta; for pudding, who could resist spotted dick with Bird's custard? Outside: a terrace and an adventure play area so children may romp.

The Swan
Little Totham

In a village of 300 souls with no shop, post office or bus service, the highpoint has to be the pub with the award-winning ales. Little Totham is lucky: Gavin takes his role as publican seriously. He's taken over the running of the Swan from his parents, so you could say it's in the blood, and the pretty, listed, 400-year-old cottage inn is as merry as can be. There are quiz nights, live music events of folk, Irish and contemporary music and a choice of old pub games. Lunchtime food ranges from toad-in-the-hole to scampi and chips to roast on Sundays. No glamour, no frills, just a lovely, lively local with low beams, open fires, soft lighting and bar room chat. Once you're here it's a job to tear yourself away. There's a splendid dining room too, ideal for family gatherings, and the front beer garden is a lively spot in summer.

Meals	12pm-3pm (4pm Sun); 6pm-10pm. Main courses £6.75-£14.75 (lunch), £9.95-£16.95 (dinner).
Closed	Open all day.
Directions	B1024 towards Coggeshall from A12, then left on A120 towards Braintree & take 2nd right for Pattiswick.

Meals	12pm-2.30pm (3pm Sun); no food Mon. Main courses £4.95-£8.95.
Closed	Open all day.
Directions	Leave A12 at Rivenhall for Great Braxted, right onto B1022, then immed. left into Loamy Hill Road; 2 miles, on right, in village centre.

	Jono & Jane Clark
	Compasses at Pattiswick,
	Pattiswick, Braintree CM77 8BG
Tel	01376 561322
Web	thecompassesatpattiswick.co.uk

	Gavin Pascoe & Rebecca Davis
	The Swan,
	School Road,
	Little Totham CM9 8LB
Tel	01621 892689
Web	www.theswanpublichouse.co.uk

Entry 242 Map 10

Entry 243 Map 10

Gloucestershire

Ostrich Inn
Newland

In the village of Newland the Ostrich is where the beer drinkers go. Across from All Saints Church, that 'Cathedral of the Forest', you'll mix with all sorts before a log fire. Huntsmen and trail bikers pile in for the massive portions of delicious food, from the Newland bread and cheese platter to rib-eye steak with lashings of fresh béarnaise. The nicotine-brown ceiling that looks in danger of imminent collapse is supported by a massive oak pillar in front of the bar where the locals chatter and 1940s jazz CDs keep the place swinging. The weekly menu, served throughout the pub, takes a step up in class, and is excellent value. Energetic Kathryn and her chef Sue keep the place buzzing. To the back is a walled garden – and the loos, 'just by there', beyond the coal sacks and guarded by the pub pooch Alfie.

Gloucestershire

The Old Spot
Dursley

Nudged by a car park and Dursley's bus station is the old and lovely Old Spot. Built in 1776 as a farm cottage, the pub has since gained national recognition among ale buffs, who make pilgrimages to sample the brews. Indeed, the Old Spot has become something of a showcase for the beers of Uley Brewery, including Pig's Ear and Old Ric, the latter named after a former landlord. Real ciders include Weston's and Ashton Press. For a pub named after a rare-breed pig, it comes as no surprise that there are porcine figurines and pictures dotted around the place, as well as a few old prints and posters. Food is simple and pubby – BLT sandwiches, bangers and mash, home-baked pies with shortcrust pastry lids. Friendly, no-nonsense, traditional, and on the Cotswolds Way. For ale-lovers, sheer joy.

Meals	12pm-2.30pm; 6.30pm-9.30pm (6pm-9.30pm Sat). Main courses £12.50-£18.50; bar meals £5.50-£9.50.	
Closed	3pm-6.30pm (6pm Sat).	
Directions	Signed on lane linking A466 at Redbrook & at Clearwell between B4228 Coleford & Chepstow road.	

Meals	12pm-8pm Mon-Thurs; 12pm-3pm Fri-Sun. Bar meals £2.95-£7; Sunday roast £6.95.
Closed	Open all day.
Directions	100 yards from Dursley town centre.

	Kathryn Horton Ostrich Inn, Newland, Coleford GL16 8NP
Tel	01594 833260
Web	www.theostrichinn.com

	Steve Herbert The Old Spot, Hill Road, Dursley GL11 4JQ
Tel	01453 542870
Web	www.oldspotinn.co.uk

Entry 244 Map 7

Entry 245 Map 8

Gloucestershire

The Lodge
Minchinhampton

Lording it on a high and ancient piece of common ground is this former hunting lodge to Henry VIII. The cattle roam free; you too can wander and gaze on the views of five valleys. Outside is traditional; inside is striking. Expect bold art, classical columns, acres of smooth oak and honey-coloured stone walls; sofas sprawl around low coffee tables, fireplaces crackle, the conversation is lively. Still with a pub feel, albeit an up-to-the-minute one, the bar serves Budding from Stroud Brewery alongside Abbotts, IPA and Otter. In the restaurant, large and open plan with floor-to-ceiling windows for the view, an ancient carved stone lion presides over various freshly sourced delights, such as seared scallops with apple and celeriac truffle dressing, and braised Cotswold pork belly with sauté potatoes.

Meals	12pm-3pm; 6pm-10pm. Main courses £8.95-£15.95.
Closed	Open all day.
Directions	In the middle of Minchinhampton Common - 300 yds off common road; signed.

Nick Beardsley
The Lodge,
Minchinhampton, Stroud GL6 9AQ
Tel   01453 832047
Web   www.thelodgeminchinhampton.com

Entry 246 Map 8

Gloucestershire

The Butcher's Arms
Sheepscombe

Tracking down this delightful local involves an "are you sure this is the right road?" adventure down narrow winding lanes – to tiny Sheepscombe, one of Laurie Lee's favourite places. If the weather's fine, and you haven't had one too many pints of Hooky, find the most level spot you can in the garden and relish the views. Inside: flowery curtains at mullioned windows, beams, brasses and bentwood chairs. So grab a perch by the wood-burning stove or a table in the tiny dining room; while you tuck into flavoursome food packed with local ingredients – a roast of Longridge lamb, a vegetarian 'pie of the day' – you'll find yourself rubbing shoulders with walkers, cyclists and locals. Inside or out, this is a place to savour. No plans for trendification, just a friendly down-to-earth place doing the thing it does best.

Meals	12pm-2.30pm; 6.30pm-9.30pm (12-9.30pm Sat; 12pm-9pm Sun). Main courses £7.95-£15.95
Closed	3pm-6pm. Open all day Sat & Sun.
Directions	Off A46 north of Painswick.

Mark & Sharon Tallents
The Butcher's Arms,
Sheepscombe, Painswick GL6 7RH
Tel   01452 812113
Web   www.butchers-arms.co.uk

Entry 247 Map 8

Gloucestershire

White Horse Inn
Frampton Mansell

A quirky-chic bar and restaurant, with good ales and first-class food. Emma and Shaun have filled it with candlelit tables on seagrass floors, modern art on vibrant walls, Indian curios inspired by their travels. Expect an informal atmosphere and a big smile from Emma as she pulls pints of Uley Bitter and oversees the restaurant. Fresh food is the mainstay of Shaun's imaginative modern menus: tuck into pigeon breast with bacon, black pudding and chestnuts, followed by red mullet fillets with roasted cherry tomatoes and crayfish tails. All this and lobsters, oysters, crabs and clams fresh from the tank (seasonal) and puddings to entice you (sticky toffee pudding with butterscotch sauce). It may not be very lovely and it may be next to a petrol station in the middle of nowhere – but what a pity to pass it by.

Gloucestershire

The Bell at Sapperton
Sapperton

This elegant pub attracts wine-lovers, foodies, ramblers and riders. Inside is a spacious but intimate décor that spreads itself across several levels – stripped beams and wood-burners, modern art on stone walls, old settles and church chairs, fresh flowers and newspapers. Sup on local Cotswold lager or Butcombe ale, dine on fresh local produce and rare breed meats. Specials are chalked up above the fireplace and the food is generous in its range: local pigeon and Cotswold crayfish, lamb from Lighthorne, poached plums with crème brulée, a delicious local goat's cheese called Rachel. Not a typical family pub but Sunday roast lunches are hugely popular and the wine list is expertly conservative to match the clientele. Summer eating can be outside on the well-tended terrace and spills over into the sun-trapping courtyard.

Meals	12pm-2.30pm (3pm Sun); 7pm-9.45pm. Main courses £10.95-£16.25; bar meals £3.95-£9.95; set menu £14.25 & £15.95.
Closed	3pm-6pm & Sun from 4pm.
Directions	On A419, 6 miles W of Cirencester.

Meals	12pm-2pm; 7pm-9.30pm (9pm Sun). Main courses £11.95-£16.95; ploughman's £7.25; Sunday lunch £13.50 & £17.50.
Closed	2.30pm-6.30pm (3pm-7pm Sun).
Directions	Off A419, 6 miles west of Cirencester.

	Shaun & Emma Davis
	White Horse Inn,
	Cirencester Road,
	Frampton Mansell, Stroud GL6 8HZ
Tel	01285 760960

	Paul Davidson & Pat Le Jeune
	The Bell at Sapperton,
	Sapperton, Cirencester GL7 6LE
Tel	01285 760298
Web	www.foodatthebell.co.uk

♿ 🚶 💳 🐾 🍻

Entry 248 Map 8

♿ 🚶 💳 🐾 🐕 🍻

Entry 249 Map 8

Gloucestershire

The Tunnel House Inn & Barn
Coates

Emerge via the portico tunnel of the Stroudwater canal to find a gracious Bath stone house in the clearing; it was built in the 1780s to house the canal workers. Its latest conversion has been well considered. Not only are there wheelchair-accessible toilets but a delightfully quirky, bareboarded décor: scrubbed tables and huge faded sofas in front of a fire, a cacophony of bric-a-brac in the bar (most on the ceiling!), an Ogygian juke box with decent tunes. In the dining room choose from a seasonal menu: beef and horseradish sandwiches, spiced potted pheasant, rabbit pie, haddock and chips, sticky toffee pudding. Uley Bitter and Hook Norton will keep ale fans happy, and there are several wines. Outside, a big garden with open-field views – great for kids – and a rather smart terrace.

Meals	12pm-2.15pm; 6.45pm-9.30pm. Main courses £8-£13.
Closed	3pm-6pm. Open all day Fri-Sun.
Directions	Off A433 Cirencester to Tetbury road; follow brown signs to pub.

Rupert Longsdon
The Tunnel House Inn, Tarlton Rd,
Coates, Cirencester GL7 6PW

Tel	01285 770280
Web	www.tunnelhouse.com

Entry 250 Map 8

Gloucestershire Award winner 2008

Five Mile House
Duntisbourne Abbots

In 300 years the interior has changed not a jot. Here are planked floors, open fires, two curving settles, a sunny lounge bar, newspapers and cribbage. There's a flagstoned 'poop deck' of a snug for locals and a galley a few steps below; a more genteel wardroom – once the owner's private parlour – stands across the hall. Here you may review the pick of the day's produce: perhaps splendidly thick sandwiches of roast beef with horseradish, or roast lamb with rosemary jelly. All is cooked to order by Johann and his team. Deserving more consideration than the proverbial swift half, the beer, which includes guests and Taylor's Landlord, is seriously good. There are serene views to the valley below and above, a busy main road, mercifully concealed by a bank and burgeoning hedgerows. You can hardly go wrong here.

Meals	12pm-2.30pm, 6pm-9.30pm; 7pm-9pm Sun. Main courses £8.50-£16.95.
Closed	3pm-6pm (4pm-7pm Sun).
Directions	On A417, turn at D. Abbots Services; down road past petrol station.

SPECIAL AWARD
see pages 18-19

Authentic Pub

Jo & Jon Carrier
Five Mile House, Old Gloucester Rd,
Duntisbourne Abbots,
Cirencester GL7 7JR

Tel	01285 821432
Web	www.fivemilehouse.co.uk

Entry 251 Map 8

Bathurst Arms
North Cerney

Young James Walker has worked hard to breathe new life into this handsome inn on the Bathurst Estate. Once unloved, the 17th-century building now exudes warmth and energy as locals, walkers and travellers drop in for pints of Wickwar Cotswold Way and unpretentious and delicious pub food. The stone-flagged bar is the hub of the place, warmed by a crackling log fire. Eat here or head next door to James's pride and joy, the revamped restaurant, with open kitchen and a sitting area that displays an organic wine list – pluck a bottle from the shelf. Allotment vegetables, Cerney goat's cheese, game from Withington and local farm beef are championed – so try mixed breads with Italian olive oil, beef and real ale pie with suet crust, Bathurst burgers with barbecue sauce, baked apple crumble with homemade custard – the best of British. Spruced-up bedrooms provide a homely base for city folk escaping to the Cotswolds: clean, comfortable, freshly painted, well-equipped (WiFi available) and TV-free. Readers are full of praise.

Rooms	6 twins/doubles. £75. Singles £55.
Meals	12pm-2pm (2.30pm weekends); 6-9pm (9.30pm Sat; from 7pm Sun). Main courses £9.95-£16.95; bar meals £3.95-£8.95.
Closed	3pm-6pm (7pm Sun). Open all day Sat & Sun in summer.
Directions	Beside A435 Cirencester-Cheltenham road, 4 miles north of Cirencester.

James Walker
Bathurst Arms,
North Cerney, Cirencester GL7 7BZ
Tel   01285 831281
Web   www.bathurstarms.com

Green Dragon
Cockleford

Hidden down a sleepy lane somewhere off the A435, this mellow Cotswold stone building, festooned with honeysuckle and hanging baskets, was a cider house three centuries ago. It's still beautifully traditional inside. So settle down with a pint of Hooky in the stone-flagged bar, all warm mustard walls and glowing candles, logs crackling in the inglenook, hops hanging from blackboards and beams. Furnishings are hand-crafted by 'Mouseman' Thompson (look for the mouse trademark signature) and the food is comforting and freshly cooked. Tuck into a bowl of chilli or a tuna niçoise salad, or, in winter, something more substantial, a hearty mutton stew or a steak and kidney pudding with minted mushy peas. The pick of the courtyard bedrooms, kitted out in modern pine and named after Gold Cup winners, is the St George's Suite, a vast room with deep leather sofas and a king-size bed, a flat-screen TV, books, magazines and a huge tiled bathroom with free-standing bath and walk-in shower. Wonderful walks start from the front door.

Rooms	9: 8 twins/doubles, 1 suite. £85–£140. Singles £65.
Meals	12pm–2.30pm (3pm Sat; 3.30pm Sun); 6pm–10pm (9.30pm Sun). Main courses £7.50–£15.95.
Closed	Open all day.
Directions	Cockleford is signed off A435 at Elkstone south of Cheltenham.

Simon & Nicky Haly
Green Dragon,
Cockleford, Cowley,
Cheltenham GL53 9NW

Tel	01242 870271
Web	www.green-dragon-inn.co.uk

Inn at Fossebridge
Fossebridge

A vast two-acre lake, hog roasts in summer, a glorious old bar – such details set the Inn at Fossebridge apart. Inside all is super-rustic and cosy – flagstone floors, stone walls, open fires, beamed ceilings – and there's a terrific hubbub at lunchtime. Throw in real ales, roast lunches and a welcome for all and you have somewhere worth going out of your way for. The Jenkins family run this gorgeous old coaching inn and draw in lovers of good food with blackboard specials of potted prawns with anchovies and garlic chilli; sausages with bacon mash; sticky toffee pudding. The two bars – one with darts board and stag's head – are divided by stone archways; the dining room has a gentler Georgian feel. And there's a cosy sitting room in country-house style. Outside is just as fine: a great decked and fenced terrace to the side, a five-acre garden, with lake, bordering the river Coln, and a tyre swing for kids. Bedrooms, country-smart, range from smallish to spacious, with coordinated fabrics, striped walls, Gilchrist & Soames goodies, flat-screen TVs. Fabulous.

Rooms	8: 7 twins/doubles, I family suite. £80–£115. Singles £70–£100. Breakfast £10.
Meals	12pm–3pm; 6.30pm–10pm (9.30pm Sun). Main courses £8.95–£18.50; bar meals £5.95–£8.50; Sunday roast £11.75.
Closed	Open all day.
Directions	Beside A429 between Cirencester & Northleach.

Robert & Liz Jenkins
Inn at Fossebridge,
Fossebridge,
Cirencester GL54 3JS
Tel   01285 720721
Web   www.fossebridgeinn.co.uk

Gloucestershire

Puesdown Inn
Northleach

Leave the A40 behind and step into this stylish roadside Cotswold inn. Who would not be cheered by the log fires, the fresh flowers, the plump sofas, the scattered magazines and the wandering puss? The owners are charming, the interior is upbeat and the airy shuttered brasserie is a favourite. Chef-patron John creates daily menus of modern British dishes based on high quality ingredients: mutton from the Highgrove estate, game from local shoots, beef from Gloucestershire, fish delivered daily from Brixham and cheeses from the region. Tuck into super-fresh tian of crab and avocado followed by fillet of wild sea bass with julienne of vegetables with saffron mash, finish with a light bread and butter pudding or a trio of chocolate desserts. There are traditional pub favourites too; the quality of the ingredients shines through and the wine list is short but well chosen. Do stay. Next door are three compact but beautiful rooms – a chic leather armchair, a pretty brass bed, white Italian bathrooms and showers that drench. A great little place.

Rooms	3 doubles. £85-£95. Singles £50-£60.
Meals	12pm-3pm; 6pm-10.30pm (6pm-9.30pm Sun). Main courses £10-£18; bar meals £4.25-£12.50.
Closed	3pm-6pm, Sun & Mon eve in winter. Open all day Sat & Sun.
Directions	Beside A40 15 miles east of Cheltenham.

John & Maggie Arnmstrong
Puesdown Inn,
Compton Abdale,
Northleach GL54 4DN
Tel   01451 860262
Web   www.puesdown.cotswoldinns.com

Gloucestershire

Seven Tuns Inn
Chedworth

In 1610, and for a few centuries after that, the Seven Tuns was a simple snug; then they diverted the river and built the rest. Part-creepered on the outside, it rambles attractively inside, past open fires, aged furniture, antique prints and a skittle alley with darts. After a gentle walk to Chedworth's Roman Villa, buried in the wooded valley nearby, there's no finer place to return to for a pint of Young's Bitter. Mingle with cyclists, walkers and locals in the little lounge or rustic bar. If you're here to eat you can do so overlooking the garden through two gorgeous mullioned windows; a little further, across the road, is a raised terrace by a waterwheel and babbling brook. Pub grub is listed on daily menus, from slow roast pork belly to confit of duck. This is still the village hub, just as it should be.

Gloucestershire

The Victoria Inn
Eastleach Turville

The golden-stoned Victoria pulls in the locals — whatever their age, whatever the weather — propping up the bar, welly-clad with dogs or indulging in home-cooked grub by the log fire. A simple village hostelry on the outside, it's deceptively spacious inside. The Richardsons, in spite of opening up the interior, have kept much of the character and cosiness intact. The low-ceilinged and flagstoned bar offers darts, conversation and pints of Arkells 3B, while the L-shaped dining room is the setting for delicious platefuls of freshly prepared food: salmon fishcakes; pork and leek sausages; slow-roasted lamb shank with garlic potatoes and red wine sauce. There are picnic tables out at the front, from where you can look down onto the pretty stone cottages of two villages. A lovely spot for a country stroll.

Meals	12pm-2.30pm (3pm Sat & Sun); 6.30pm-9.30pm (9pm Sun). Main courses £7.95-£14.95.
Closed	3pm-6pm. Open all day Sat & Sun in winter, every day in July & Aug.
Directions	Off A429, north of Cirencester.

Meals	12pm-2pm; 7pm-9.30pm (9pm Sun). Main courses £7.95-£14.75.
Closed	3pm-7pm.
Directions	Off A361 between Burford & Lechlade.

Alex Davenport-Jones
Seven Tuns Inn,
Queen Street, Chedworth,
Cirencester GL54 4AE

Tel   01285 720242

Entry 256 Map 8

Stephen & Susan Richardson
The Victoria Inn,
Eastleach Turville,
Fairford GL7 3NQ

Tel   01367 850277

Entry 257 Map 8

Gloucestershire

The White Hart Inn
Winchcombe

After a period of Swedish ownership the White Hart has returned to its English coaching inn roots. Gone is the Gustavian furniture and the sisal matting, in have come quarry tiles, scrubbed pine and framed cricket memorabilia – including England wicket keeper Jack Russell's 1990 Ashes sweater. Peter Austen used to run the successful Clifton Sausage in Bristol and the good old British banger rules the roost here. Although it's been gastrofied, this is still a pub, and whether you're eating in the restaurant or the front bar, you order at the counter. Choose one of three real ales to accompany a succulent Old Spot pork pie with grape chutney – or order from the main menu, awash with local produce and a list of suppliers. The small wine shop means almost 200 good wines at cost price, plus corkage – a nice touch.

Meals	12pm-9.30pm.
	Main courses £8.50-£16;
	bar meals £1.50-£6.50.
Closed	Open all day.
Directions	From Cheltenham, B4632 to Winchcombe. Inn on right.

Peter Austen
The White Hart Inn,
High Street, Winchcombe GL54 5LJ
Tel 01242 602359
Web www.the-white-hart-inn.com

Entry 258 Map 8

Gloucestershire

The Beehive
Cheltenham

There are few pubs of character in Cheltenham but this one shines like a beacon in the bohemian backstreets of Montpellier. Owned by the team in charge of The White Hart in Winchcombe, this is the place to come for lively conversation, well-kept beer and hearty food. It's also very popular with the racing crowd during the Gold Cup. Hidden among antique shops and cafés, the lovely Beehive has a pubby bar and two dining areas, the usual scrubbed floors, mismatched wooden tables and the summery bonus of a courtyard at the back. There are three regular real ales on tap – including the locally brewed Goff's Jouster – and generous portions of gastropub favourites like as Old Spot sausages with mustard mash and gravy – and the more exotic-sounding grilled cod with a merguez, chorizo and chickpea stew.

Meals	12pm-2.30pm; 6pm-8.30pm
	(7pm-10pm Thur-Sat);
	no food Sun eve.
	Main courses £8.95-£16;
	Sunday lunch £13.50 & £15.50.
Closed	Open all day.
Directions	Montpellier Villas is off Suffolk Road.

Matt Walker
The Beehive,
1-3 Montpellier Villas,
Cheltenham GL50 2XE
Tel 01242 702270

Entry 259 Map 8

Ebrington Arms
Ebrington

The glorious gardens at Hidcote Manor and Kiftsgate Court are a ramble across fields from the Ebrington Arms. This is a relaxed and rustic Cotswold stone pub that has been restored and revived by Claire and Jim. Little has changed in the 18th-century bar, the hub of the community, cosy with low beams and winter fires. Bag a seat and share pints of Purity with the regulars, or seek out the cosy dining room next door. Worn stone floors, a mishmash of tables and chairs, cushioned window seats and fresh flowers set the scene for some terrific pub food cooked from fresh local produce. Dishes are simple yet full of flavour, so dive in to spiced lentil and roasted pepper soup, rump of Cotswold lamb with rosemary jus, and walnut tart with vanilla ice cream. No need to negotiate the route home when you can bed down here; bedrooms (up steepish stairs) are quirky and full of charm, with chunky wooden beds, colourful throws and plump pillows, deep window seats with village or country views, and the odd antique. A properly unpretentious country pub, run by the nicest people.

Rooms	3: 1 twin, 1 double, 1 four-poster. £90-£100.
Meals	12pm-2.30pm; 6.30pm-9pm (9.30pm Fri & Sat). Main courses £9.50-£14.50.
Closed	3pm-6pm & Mon. Open all day Sun.
Directions	West from Shipton-on-Stour on B4035. Across A429. After a mile, bear right at sharp left-hand bend; village signed.

Claire & Jim Alexander
Ebrington Arms,
Ebrington, Chipping Campden GL55 6NH
Tel   01386 593223
Web   www.theebringtonarms.co.uk

Entry 267 Map 8

Gloucestershire

Westcote Inn
Nether Westcote

Westcote is a recently renovated 300-year-old stone malthouse, with stunning views across the Evenlode valley, and Regency Cheltenham up the road. Rub shoulders with trainers and jockeys in the Tack Room bar, with its Gold Cup mementos and TV for big racing days; dine in the contemporary, vaulted restaurant, sprinkled with paintings and sculptures by local artists, illuminated by windows that make the most of the wide-ranging view. It may be smart and Cotswold chic but the character remains and the atmosphere is nicely low-key, what with Hooky on tap, a terrace for spit-roasts and a garden large enough to play croquet and football. Menus are traditional British: tuck into braised lamb shank or grilled lemon sole in the bar. The restaurant carte steps up a gear with terrine of suckling pig, foie gras and lentils, John Dory with lobster and artichoke vinaigrette, and superb Cotswold cheeses (Little Wallop, Crudges Cheddar). Gorgeous bedrooms have big beds with colourful throws, flat-screen TVs, DVD players, coffee machines, alarm clocks with iPod connectors, fluffy robes and bubbles for deep soaks.

Rooms	4: 3 doubles, 1 family. £85–£110.
Meals	12pm-2.30pm; 7pm-9.30pm. Main courses £9.95–£18.50; sandwiches (lunch) from £5.95.
Closed	Open all day.
Directions	From A40 at Burford, A361 then A424 dir. Stow-on-the-Wold. After 6 miles, right for Nether Westcote; signs to inn.

Julia Reed
Westcote Inn,
Nether Westcote,
Chipping Norton OX7 6SD

Tel	01993 830888
Web	www.westcoteinn.co.uk

Entry 268 Map 8

Gloucestershire

The Horse and Groom
Upper Oddington

Cotswold stone, hanging baskets, hefty beams and flagstone floors, chunky logs around the double fireplace... is this the pub from central casting? It's 500 years old and Simon and Sally Jackson have rejuvenated without losing the traditional charm. There's a good selection of guest ales, some from nearby microbreweries, including Wye Valley Best, Butty Bach and Hereford Pale Ale, Barley Mole and Banks's Best. The menu takes a Cook's tour of Europe, with a good serving of trad-English: pan-fried sea bream fillets with fresh egg tagliatelle, Moroccan spiced chicken, lamb and pancetta casserole, roast duck breast with apple and potato boulangère, game from the Adlestrop Estate. Produce is organic and local whenever possible, breads and puddings are all homemade. No fewer than 25 wines are available by the glass.

Meals	12pm-2pm; 6.30pm-9pm (7pm-9pm Sun). Main courses £12-£19.75.
Closed	3pm-5.30pm.
Directions	Village signed off A436 east of Stow-on-the-Wold.

Simon & Sally Jackson
The Horse and Groom,
Upper Oddington,
Moreton-in-Marsh GL56 0XH
Tel   01451 830584
Web   www.horseandgroom.uk.com

Entry 269 Map 8

Gloucestershire

The Boat Inn
Ashleworth

This extraordinary, tiny pub has been in the family since Charles II granted them a licence for liquor and ferry – about 400 years! It's a gem – a peaceful, unspoilt red-brick cottage on the banks of the Severn and an ale-lover's paradise. Settle back with a pint of Beowulf, Church End or Archer's in the gleaming front parlour – colourful with fresh garden flowers, huge built-in settle and big scrubbed deal table fronting an old kitchen range – or in the spotless bar. On sunny summer days you can laze by the languid river. Adjectives are inadequate: this place is cherished. Real ale straight from the cask, Weston's farm cider, a bar of chocolate, a packet of crisps... but don't feed Sam the dog, he's on a diet. There's no 'jus' here; lunchtime meals are fresh filled rolls with homemade chutney. Perfect.

Meals	12pm-2pm. Filled rolls (lunchtime only).
Closed	2.30pm-7pm (3pm-7pm Sat & Sun), Wed lunch & Mon.
Directions	On A417 1.5 miles from Hartpury, between Gloucester & Ledbury.

Ron & Elisabeth Nicholls
& Louise Beer
The Boat Inn, Ashleworth Quay,
Ashleworth, Gloucester GL19 4HZ
Tel   01452 700272
Web   www.boat-inn.co.uk

Entry 270 Map 8

Gloucestershire

The Kilcot Inn
Kilcot

The smart blue and sand-yellow exterior bodes well... then step in to a happy tumble of exposed stone walls, flagged floors, Tudor beams and three quirky 'tree-stump' chairs before a central fire. There's an open feel to this cosy inn, with the large bar dominating the drinking side. Beers include Cats Whiskers, Hobgoblin and Bass on hand pump; there are a couple of ciders, including Weston's Old Rose, and decent wines. The restaurant area has pine furniture, an eclectic mix of chairs, a new tapestry on the wall. Seasonal menus make good use of local organic and free-range produce, as seen in tiger prawns with pak choi, chilli, ginger and garlic, grilled goat's cheese with pears poached in honey and mustard, local ice creams and cheeses and homemade puds. Work it all off with a good walk – and bring the dogs and children.

Meals	12pm-2.30pm; 6pm-9.15pm (12pm-3pm; 7pm-9pm Sun). Main courses £11.75-£17.95; bar meals £5.50-£12.50; Sunday roast from £7.95.
Closed	3pm-6pm. Open all day Sun & in summer.
Directions	Kilcot signed off B4421 between Newent & Gorsley.

Sue Harper
The Kilcot Inn,
Ross Road, Kilcot,
Newent GL18 1NG
Tel   01989 720663

Entry 271 Map 8

Gloucestershire

The Glasshouse Inn
Longhope

If you are a fan of Fuller's London Pride and Butcombe, Weston's ciders and all good, nature-blessed produce, come here. Ramshackle tables and open log fires are considered modern at this converted 15th-century brick cottage where glass was once blown in wood-fired ovens and cider pressed in the shed. Guinness adverts, cartoons and horse racing prints decorate the place as do autographed England rugby shirts – and the chiming clock never serves as an invitation to leave. Say landlords Steve and Jill: "We buy the best available produce locally, so chefs can provide our customers with generous portions of tasty, interesting, homemade food." Expect authentic Thai curries or pork fillet stuffed with apricots with a cider sauce, a lovely calm atmosphere, a terrific little garden for summer sipping and super local walks.

Meals	12pm-2pm; 7pm-9pm; no food Sun eve. Main courses £7.50-£15.
Closed	3pm-6.30pm & Sun eve.
Directions	North off A40 between Gloucester & Newent at Longhope, signed Clifford Mesne: through Glasshouse, pub at bottom of hill on right.

Steve & Gill Pugh
The Glasshouse Inn,
May Hill,
Longhope GL17 0NN
Tel   01452 830529

Entry 272 Map 8

The King's Arms Inn
Didmarton

The spruced-up roadside village inn sports slate floors, stone lintels, mellow walls, and oak settles in the bar, and a cheekily bright front room adorned with lithographs of the area. In the dining room are terracotta walls, carved panels, chunky wooden tables and high-backed chairs. There's a big old fireplace for winter, darts and dominoes for fun, a walled garden for summer and a boules pitch that people travel some way for. For a light lunch consider a wholemeal sandwich of Wiltshire ham and coleslaw, or rare roast beef and horseradish. 'Classics' on the menu might include haddock in beer batter or roast venison with red wine and juniper berry sauce, while daily dishes could highlight sea bass with tomato and prawn risotto – all delicious. 'If they don't serve beer in heaven, then I'm not going', reads the sign behind the bar, so Uley Bitter stands alongside guest ales. Rooms upstairs are cosy, stylish and inviting, with colourful throws on comfortable beds, plasma screens and spotless shower rooms; the self-catering cottages are in the coaching stable. A perfect place in the Cotswolds.

Rooms	4 + 3: 3 doubles, 1 single. 3 cottages. £95. Single £65.
Meals	12pm-2.30pm; 6pm-9.30pm (12pm-8pm Sun). Main courses £8.95-£16.95; bar meals £4.95-£9.95.
Closed	Open all day.
Directions	On A433 between Tetbury & the M4, junc. 18.

Alastair & Sarah Sadler
The King's Arms Inn,
The Street, Didmarton, Badminton GL9 1DT
Tel 01454 238245
Web www.kingsarmsdidmarton.co.uk

Entry 273 Map 3

Gloucestershire

Fine 16th-century stone pub set back from a deep-cut Cotswold lane. Enticing with its tiny windows, low beams, open fires and inventive menu. Sunny south-facing terrace.

Quietly civilised bar/brasserie attached to the Calcot Manor Hotel. Cosy up by the log fire in the elegant bar; take your pick of local ales, good wines and imaginative food. Westonbirt Arboretum is up the road.

Everything is done with simplicity and integrity and that includes the interior of bare boards, cream walls and open fires. New chef Martin Caws has a brilliant pedigree. Reports please.

Impressive, creeper-clad 15th-century stone inn close to Cotswold Water Park. Rambling rustic interior with roaring log fires, red walls, four real ales and decent food.

Quirky backstreet pub with glowing fires, scrubbed pine tables and rugs on old tiled floors. Character landlord, decent fresh fodder and five cracking real ales. A must for beer drinkers.

Well-preserved time-warp beside A417 east of Cirencester. Hatch bar, handpumped Hook Norton, two simple flagstoned rooms with log fires, and long-serving landlord. Closed weekday lunchtimes.

A Cotswold stone pub in a pretty village and a gastropub of note, with fireside tables, Hooky on tap and an open theatre kitchen serving modern pub food. New owner – reports welcome.

A roaring log fire, a sober décor, a relaxed mood and a skittle alley for locals – on the village green that everyone dreams of. Long a jewel in the Cotswolds culinary crown but a new chef and management early 2008 – reports please.

The Peat Spade

Longstock

Hampshire is as lovely as any county in England, deeply rural with lanes that snake through verdant countryside. As if to prove the point, the Peat Spade serves up a menu of boundless simplicity and elegance. First there's this dreamy thatched village in the Test valley, then there's the inn itself, packed to the gunnels with lip-licking locals for Sunday lunch in early February (and there's a 4pm sitting to satisfy demand). Behind the lozenge-paned windows a Roberts radio on the bar brings news of English cricket, gilt mirrors sparkle above smouldering fires, fishing rods hang from the ceiling, and a fishing tackle shop is on site. There's a horseshoe bar, a sitting room for those who stay, a roof terrace for summer breakfasts and two bedrooms above the bar. The rest are in Peat House next door, and are as lovely as you'd expect. Fired Earth colours, sisal matting, big wooden beds, Roberts radios, crisp white linen – the works. There's no space left to describe how fabulously wonderful the food is, but be assured it is.

Rooms	6 doubles. From £110.
Meals	12pm–2pm (4pm Sun); 7pm–9.30pm; no food Sun eve Dec-April. Main courses £11.50–£17.
Closed	Open all day.
Directions	A3057 north from Stockbridge, then left after a mile for Longstock. In village.

Lucy Townsend & Andy Clarke
The Peat Spade,
Longstock, Stockbridge SO20 6DR

Tel	01264 810612
Web	www.peatspadeinn.co.uk

SPECIAL
AWARD
see pages 18-19

Pubs with rooms

Hampshire

The Greyhound
Stockbridge

Civilised, one-street Stockbridge is England's fly-fishing capital, and the colour-washed Greyhound reels in fishing folk and foodies. The 15th-century coaching inn is a dapper, food-and-wine-centred affair and one of fine pedigree: John Howe produces modern dishes based on skill and impeccable produce. Charming staff serve the likes of line-caught sea bass with salsify and brown shrimp risotto and artichoke velouté, while desserts might see a plum and star anise tarte tatin alongside liquorice ice cream. In the lounge are low dark beams, modern armchairs and sofas and a big inglenook; in the open-plan dining area, wooden floors, solid trestle-style tables, contemporary leather chairs, more beams. Bedrooms above also manage to blend character with comfort, so you will find spotlights alongside auction antiques, classy bathrooms and flat-screen TVs. Five minutes down the road Longstock Park Water Garden is open on the first and third Sunday of the month in summer; back at the inn, a small garden at the back overlooks the Test. Rest here awhile with a glass of chablis – or cast a line.

Rooms	8: 4 twins, 3 doubles, 1 single. £90–£120. Singles £70.
Meals	12pm-2pm (2.30pm Fri-Sun); 7pm-9pm (9.30pm Fri & Sat). Main courses £17.95–£20.25; set lunch £18.25 & £23.50.
Closed	3pm-6pm.
Directions	A303, A34 south, then A30 into Stockbridge. Pub on right on west end of high street.

John Howe
The Greyhound,
31 High Street,
Stockbridge SO20 6EY

Tel	01264 810833
Web	www.thegreyhound.info

White Star Tavern & Dining Rooms
Southampton

Placing the city firmly on the gastropub-with-rooms map, the old seafarers' hotel has been stylishly revived. Large etched windows carry the White Star logo, while a cluster of lounges at the front come decked out with gleaming leather chesterfields. The place is stocked, as is the fashion, with a heady mix of real ales, continental lagers, premium spirits and cocktails. Around the big darkwood bar, to a backdrop of original wood panelling, is booth-like seating for casual dining; shipping photographs and original chandeliers add to the metropolitan mood. The more formal dining area comes with a softer approach: expect stylish wallpaper and sophisticated lighting. The cooking hits all the right notes, with a dedicated bar menu as well as à la carte; dishes include such delights as sautéed calves' liver with red cabbage, chestnuts and cream potatoes. The bedrooms above – named after White Star Line ships or America's Cup yachts – are individually styled and continue the upbeat modern theme, while bathrooms are decked out with roll tops and big showers. And there's a guests' sundeck, too. Young and fun.

Rooms	13 twins/doubles. £79-£99.
Meals	12pm-2.30pm (3pm Fri & Sat); 6.30pm-9.30pm (10pm Fri & Sat); 12pm-9pm Sun. Main courses £9.50-£19; bar meals £4.50-11.
Closed	Open all day.
Directions	A33 to Southampton city centre & head for Ocean Village & Marina.

Mark Dodd & Matt Boyle
White Star Tavern & Dining Rooms,
28 Oxford Street,
Southampton SO14 3DJ
Tel   023 8082 1990
Web   www.whitestartavern.co.uk

Entry 284 Map 3

The Rose & Thistle
Rockbourne

Rockbourne is the kind of village where you might find Miss Marple trimming a rose bush. The pub is dreamy too, and, like many, started life as two cottages; the two huge fireplaces are no surprise. It is a great mix of oak beams and timbers, carved benches, flagstones and tiles. Add country-style fabrics and tables strewn with magazines and you have an enchanting place to return to after visiting Rockbourne's Roman villa. Tim Norfolk has a reputation for his steaks and sauces and his ever-changing specials make use of fresh local produce: estate game in season, south-coast fish. In summer you can dine in the garden, on smoked salmon and scrambled eggs, prawns by the pint and classic steak and kidney pudding. The more elaborate evening menu favours fish, such as monkfish wrapped in pancetta. Delightful.

The Royal Oak
Fritham

Small, ancient, thatched and secluded – an ale-lover's retreat. No fruit machines here: just quiet, old-fashioned bonhomie. Locals sup pints and exchange stories around the bar; ramblers and dogs are welcome. Huge fires crackle through the winter, enticing you to linger. Neil and Pauline McCulloch believe in local produce and deliver honest, unpretentious pub lunches: ploughman's with homemade pâté, French dressed local crab, sausages from their pigs, no chips. Though rustically simple, the three small rooms are well turned out, with light floorboards, solid tables and spindleback chairs, homely touches, darts, dominoes and cribbage. Five local beers are drawn straight from the cask, including Hop Back Summer Lightning and Ringwood Best. Also: a large garden for summer barbecues and a September beer festival.

Meals	12pm-2.30pm; 7pm-9.30pm. Main courses £8.75-£19.50; bar meals from £5.
Closed	3pm-6pm (Sun from 8pm Nov-Mar).
Directions	3 miles NW of Fordingbridge, off B3078.

Meals	12pm-2.30pm (3pm Sat & Sun). Main courses £4.50-£8.50.
Closed	3pm-6pm. Open all day Sat & Sun.
Directions	M27 junc. 1; B3078 to Fordingbridge; turn for Fritham after 2.5 miles. Follow signs.

	Tim Norfolk The Rose & Thistle, Rockbourne, Fordingbridge SP6 3NL
Tel	01725 518236
Web	www.roseandthistle.co.uk

	Neil & Pauline McCulloch The Royal Oak, Fritham, Lyndhurst SO43 7HJ
Tel	023 8081 2606

Entry 285 Map 3

Entry 286 Map 3

The East End Arms
East End

The name may conjure up images of a Londoner's local, but this is about as far from the average city boozer as you can get. Hidden down narrow New Forest lanes, it's winningly unpretentious; owned by John Illsley of the band Dire Straits, its walls are lined with photographs of the famous. Walkers, wax jackets and the odd gamekeeper congregate in the earthy Foresters Bar – or in the lounge/dining room, carpeted-comfortable with sturdy tables, sofa and log fire. Locally sourced fish and seafood dishes flow from the kitchen, such as 'catch of the day' with mixed salad and French fries, or a whole grilled seabass with creamed potatoes. In the small garden are picnic benches and a big green brolly. At first glance this plain little pub might not warrant a second; in fact, it's all a pub should be.

The Bugle
Hamble

Hamble's famous pub, celebrated by yachtsmen the world over, was saved in 2005 by the people behind Southampton's White Star. Using traditional materials and methods they have remodelled the Bugle's 16th-century heart – so you find new-oak beams and standing timbers, stripped-back brick fireplaces and open fires, natural flagstone floors and polished boards. The atmosphere is relaxed, the bar throngs with drinkers and diners on sailing days, there's a simply adorned dining area for escaping the bustle and an intimate private room upstairs. Space and a wide-ranging clientele informs the style of the food. Sit at the bar with a pint of Deuchars and a pork pie, or go the whole hog and order ham, egg and chips or calves' liver with pancetta mash. Or slip off to the super front terrace for views of bobbing boats on the Hamble.

Meals	12pm-2.30pm; 7pm-9.30pm. No food Sun & Mon eve. Main courses £8-£17.50.
Closed	3pm-6pm. Open all day Sun.
Directions	Off B3054, 3 miles east of Lymington; follow signs for Isle of Wight ferry & keep going.

Meals	12pm-2.30pm (3pm Fri); 6.30pm-9.30pm (6pm-10pm Fri); 12pm-10pm Sat (9pm Sun). Main courses £10-£15; bar meals from £3.95-£6.50.
Closed	Open all day.
Directions	M27 junc. 8; signs to Hamble, right at mini-r'bout & follow cobbled street down to riverside car park.

	Joanna Dydak & Jeremy Willcock
	The East End Arms,
	East End, Lymington SO41 5SY
Tel	01590 626223
Web	www.eastendarms.co.uk

	Matthew Boyle & Mark Dodd
	The Bugle,
	High Street, Hamble SO31 4HA
Tel	023 8045 3000
Web	www.buglehamble.co.uk

Entry 287 Map 3

Entry 288 Map 4

Hampshire

The Black Boy
Winchester

Quirky pubs with personality, real ale and fine food are worth tracking down. Winchester's example is best reached on foot – following the riverside path from the NT's Winchester Mill. The landlord has created an unassuming tavern that is pleasingly off the wall. Fascinating paraphernalia ranges from fire buckets and old signs to a 'library' crammed with books, oddities greet the eye at every turn. It's the easiest place in the world to while away an hour or three. Choose a pint of Flower Pots Bitter (one of five handpumped ales) and a cosy corner with a deep sofa and a log fire to relish it in. Lunchtime peckish? Tuck into beer-battered cod, shepherd's pie or sandwiches. In the evening, pop across the road to The Black Rat restaurant (also owned by David) and splash out on something a touch more inventive.

Meals	12pm-2pm; 7pm-9pm; no food Mon all day, Sun eve & Tues lunch. Main courses £5.50-£8.50.
Closed	3pm-5pm (7pm Sun).
Directions	Head south out of city along Chesil Street; Wharf Hill 1st road on right; parking off Chesil Street.

David Nicholson
The Black Boy,
1 Wharf Hill, Winchester SO23 9NQ
Tel   01962 861754
Web   www.theblackboypub.com

Entry 289 Map 4

Hampshire

Running Horse
Littleton

Littleton saw its old pub close in 2003. The following year saw the horse 'up and running', with a sleek new look and an emphasis on the food. Now, in the experienced hands of Richard and Kathryn Crawford (they run the hugely successful Plough in Sparsholt) this revitalised local is set to thrive. Pop in for a pint of Palmers or Ringwood in the bar with polished boards, leather chairs and subtle uplighting; settle down to a lunchtime sandwich or a ploughman's on the fabulous terrace. Or head off to the slate-floored restaurant extension for some serious dining (there are outside tables at the back). The board is chalked up daily – perhaps Thai fishcakes with Asian dressing, shoulder of lamb with red wine jus, or sea bass with anchovy, caper and lemon butter. Staff are welcoming and happy to chat.

Meals	12pm-2pm; 6pm-9pm (9.30pm Fri & Sat); 6pm-8.30pm Sun. Main courses £11.75-£17.50; sandwiches from £4.95.
Closed	3pm-5.30pm. Open all day Sat & Sun.
Directions	Village signed off A272 just west of Winchester.

Richard & Kathryn Crawford
Running Horse,
88 Main Road, Littleton,
Winchester SO22 6QS
Tel   01962 880218

Entry 290 Map 4

Hampshire

The Flower Pots Inn
Cheriton

Ramblers and beer enthusiasts beat a path to Pat and Jo Bartlett's door, where award-winning pints of Flower Pots Bitter and Goodens Gold are brewed in the brewhouse across the car park. Open fires burn in two traditional bars: one a wall-papered parlour, the other a quarry-tiled public bar with scrubbed pine and an illuminated, glass-topped well. Ales are tapped from casks behind the counter hung with hops, and drunk to the accompaniment of happy chat; music and electronic games would be out of place here. In keeping with the simplicity of the place, the menu is short and straightforward: baps with home-cooked ham, sandwiches toasted or plain, home-cooked hotpots, spicy chilli with garlic bread, hearty winter soups. Curry-lovers come on Wednesday evenings for authentic Punjabi dishes; Morris dancers drop by in summer.

Meals	12pm-2pm; 7pm-9pm (6.30pm-10pm Weds); no food Sun eve & bank hol eve. Main courses £3.50-£7.50.
Closed	2.30pm-6pm (3pm-7pm Sun).
Directions	Village signed off A272 east of Winchester; pub off B3046 in village centre.

Joanna & Patricia Bartlett
The Flower Pots Inn,
Cheriton,
Alresford SO24 0QQ
Tel   01962 771318

Entry 295 Map 4

Hampshire

The Yew Tree
Lower Wield

Tim Gray's experience at the Masons Arms, Branscombe has proved invaluable. He has totally revitalised this hard-to-find but worth-tracking-down inn. The re-worked, stone-flagged and beamed bar is immediately welcoming: a winter fire, a chiming clock, walls festooned with character prints, a happy mishmash of furniture. There's a slightly more formal note to the dining area off to one side. As for Tim, he is "fuelled by passion and fun." On summer weekends it's especially buzzy as beer flows and the local cricket team play on the pitch opposite; if cricket's not your thing, bag a seat in the peaceful front garden, in the shade of the eponymous yew. Good fresh dishes are chalked up daily, so be cheered by steak, ale and mushroom pudding with rich onion gravy, and sea bass served with parsley and sun-dried tomato butter.

Meals	12pm-2pm; 6.30pm-9pm (8.30pm Sun). Main courses £8.95-£17.95.
Closed	Mon.
Directions	4.5 miles north of Alresford, off B3046.

Tim Gray
The Yew Tree, Lower Wield,
Alresford SO24 9RX
Tel   01256 389224
Web   www.the-yewtree.org.uk

Entry 296 Map 4

The Sun Inn
Bentworth

Stonehenge Pigswill, Badger Tanglefoot, Ringwood Best, Fuller's London Pride... a parade of hand pumps pulls the boys in. There's charm, too: this friendly, flower-decked local was once a pair of 17th-century cottages. Surprisingly little has changed. On ancient bricks and bare boards is a rustic mix of scrubbed pine tables and oak benches and settles; beams are hung with brasses, walls adorned with prints and plates; there are fresh and dried flowers, candelight and smart magazines. Three cosy log-fired inglenooks warm the interlinking bars. Food is mostly perfect English: onion and cider soup, pheasant braised in black beer and raisin wine, Sunday roasts, wicked puddings. Hidden down a tiny lane on the edge of a village in deepest Hampshire the Sun could scarcely be more rural. Footpaths radiate from the door.

The Wellington Arms
Baughurst

Lost down a web of lanes, the 'Welly' draws foodies from miles. Cosy, compact and decorated in style — wall benches, rustic pictures, terracotta floor — the single bar-dining room has just seven tables (do book!). Jason's modern British cooking is first-class and inventive, the boards are chalked up daily and the produce, mainly organic, is sourced within five miles. Kick off with crispy fried pumpkin flowers stuffed with ricotta and feta, follow with a rack of lamb chops with potato rosti and mint sauce, finish with a sensational sticky toffee pudding. (Or a rhubarb, strawberry and elderflower jelly with 'fairy floss'!). The mood is easy and there's Wadworth 6X on tap. Migrate to the huge garden for summer meals and views of seven bee hives and 35 rare-breed chickens; the eggs can be bought at the bar. Wonderful.

Meals	12pm-2pm; 7pm-9.30pm. Main courses £7.95-£14.95; Sunday roast £8.95-£10.95.
Closed	3pm-6pm. Open all day Sun.
Directions	Off A339, 2 miles from Alton.

Meals	12pm-2.30pm; 6.30pm-9.30pm. Main courses £10.50-£19.50; set lunch £15 & £18 (Wed-Fri).
Closed	3pm-6.30pm, Tues lunch, Sun eve & Mon all day.
Directions	Baughurst is signed off A340 at Tadley, or A339 east of Kingsclere.

	Mary Holmes The Sun Inn, Sun Hill, Bentworth, Alton GU34 5JT
Tel	01420 562338

	Jason King & Simon Page The Wellington Arms, Baughurst Rd, Baughurst RG26 5LP
Tel	0118 982 0110
Web	www.thewellingtonarms.com

Entry 297 Map 4

Entry 298 Map 4

Hampshire

The Hawkley Inn
Hawkley

A chatty mix of locals, farmers and walkers fill this no-frills inn. In a sleepy village at the end of plunging lanes, the Hawkley's front bars remain delightfully scruffy (a 'listed' carpet, nicotine-stained walls, a mad moose head above the log fire) while the rear extension adds a touch of modernity. So bag one of the rustic scrubbed tables and quaff amazing local beers – Ballards Wassail, Dark Star Espresso, and at least eight others from the local Bowman brewery. Or tuck into country food from a spanking new kitchen and arrive early at weekends, it's a popular place. Food ranges from soups and ploughman's to spinach and ricotta tart and Sussex beef stew – and you can book ahead for Sunday roast beef served 'pink'. Well worth the detour, once you've found it. Chawton, famous for Jane Austen's house, is nearby.

Hampshire

Harrow Inn
Steep

The 16th-century Harrow is a gem. Unspoilt, brick-and-tiled, it hides down a country lane that dwindles into a footpath by a little stream (not easy to find!). It has been in Claire and Nisa McCutcheon's family since 1929 and they keep it very much as it must always have been. Where nicer to sup a pint than within these two small rooms with their timbered walls, scrubbed elm tables and brick inglenook fireplace aglow in winter. Behind a hatch-like serving counter, barrels of local ale rest on racks, bundles of drying hops hang above. There's a small, wild orchard garden – only the distant hum of the hidden A3 disturbs the bucolic calm. Food is limited to generously filled sandwiches, fresh soups, homemade quiches, a ploughman's platter, treacle tart – served with a smile. Loos are a quick dash across the lane.

Meals	12pm-2pm (3pm Sat & Sun); 7pm-9.30pm (9pm Sun). Main courses £7.50-£13.50; bar snacks £5; Sunday roast £9.95.
Closed	3pm-5.30. Open all day Sat & Sun.
Directions	After A3/B3006, thro' Burgates, right into Hawkley Road & back over A3; 2 miles to hairpin bend; next left is Pococks Lane.

Meals	12pm-2pm; 7pm-9pm; no food Sun eve. Bar meals £4.30-£11.
Closed	2.30pm-6pm (3pm-6pm Sat, 3pm-7pm Sun); Sun eve Oct-Apr.
Directions	Off A272 at Steep west of Petersfield, left opp. garage; left at church; cross A3 to reach pub.

Jeannie Jamieson
The Hawkley Inn, Pococks Lane, Hawkley, Liss GU33 6NE
Tel   01730 827205
Web   www.hawkleyinn.co.uk

Entry 299 Map 4

Claire & Nisa McCutcheon
Harrow Inn,
Steep,
Petersfield GU32 2DA
Tel   01730 262685

Entry 300 Map 4

The White Horse Inn
Priors Dean

Known as 'The Pub with No Name' – the cradle on the nearby road being sign-less – this isolated pub is fiendish to find. But worth the effort for its candlelit Jacobean charm. Untouched by modernity, its two splendid bars have open log fires, a medley of old tables, clocks and agrarian implements and a patina on the walls achievable only by age. The ticking of a grandfather clock and the gentle motion of the rocking chairs before the fire transport one to another era. It is blissfully cosy in winter; in summer you can sprawl in the garden. Hampshire's highest pub stands 750 feet up on the top of the Downs, with views rolling out on every side. Up to eight real ales are accompanied by homemade pies, pan-fried pheasant and beer battered with hand-cut chips, and there's a decent range of wines.

The Trooper Inn
Petersfield

Any reservations about the slightly awkward exterior of this 17th-century roadside inn melt away on entering the large open bar with its optics and beer handles – and Hassan, your impeccable host. Choose a table by the crackling log fire in winter or in the sunny, old-fashioned conservatory overlooking fields. Walls are dense with photographs, posters and pubby paraphernalia; engaging staff mix efficiency with chat as they serve pints of Sharps or Ringwood and deliver delicious food to the table. Starters might include fig, feta and Parma ham or homemade confit duck with red onion and cumin; local wild boar might follow, or poached mussels cooked in coconut, chilli and lemongrass to tickle a jaded palette; traditional puds – spotted dick, treacle sponge – keep everyone happy. A dining pub everyone will enjoy.

Meals	12pm-2.30pm; 6.30pm-9.30pm (from 7pm in winter). Main courses £8.95-£14.95; sandwiches from £4.95.
Closed	2pm-6pm. Open all day Sat & Sun.
Directions	Between Petersfield & Alton. 6 miles from Petersfield, beyond Steep.

Meals	12pm-2pm (2.30pm Sun); 7pm-9pm (9.30pm Fri & Sat). Main courses £10-£18.
Closed	3pm-5pm & Sun eve.
Directions	From A3 take exit for Winchester (A272); left at r'bout for Petersfield, then 1st exit left at next r'bout for Steep; up hill for 3 miles; pub on right.

Paul & Georgie Stuart
The White Horse Inn,
Priors Dean, Petersfield GU32 1DA
Tel   01420 588387
Web   www.stuartinns.com

Hassan Matini
The Trooper Inn, Alton Road,
Froxfield, Petersfield GU32 1BD
Tel   01730 827293
Web   www.trooperinn.com

Entry 301 Map 4

Entry 302 Map 4

Hampshire

The Thomas Lord
West Meon

Named after the founder of Lord's, it seems right that this unpretentious rural gem be filled with cricketing paraphernalia. The dark, beamed and half-panelled bar walls are decorated with old cricket bats, caps, pads and associated prints, while well-used sofas and the odd leather armchair draw up to a fire in winter. There's an endearing miscellany of weathered, wooden furniture, big fat candles and a herringbone floor, drinkers, dogs and a small back room weighed down by books. This friendly pub is loved by a (mostly) well-heeled local crowd, while the kitchen's robust country cooking draws on excellent local suppliers listed alongside the dishes... the pork and black pepper sausages with onion gravy were delicious. True to form, an array of Hampshire ales follows the local theme. A great country inn.

Meals	12pm-2pm; 7pm-9pm (9.30pm Fri & Sat); no food Sun eve. Main courses £9.95-£15; sandwiches £5.
Closed	3pm-6pm. Open all day Sat & Sun.
Directions	Just off A32 between Alton & Wickham. Signed.

David Thomas & Richard Taylor
The Thomas Lord, High Street,
West Meon, Petersfield GU32 1LN
Tel 01730 829244
Web www.thethomaslord.co.uk

Entry 303 Map 4

Hampshire

The Royal Oak
Langstone

Twitchers regularly beat a path to the door of this waterside pub. The views across Chichester Harbour are stunning... of rare birds and moored boats, magical on a fine summer's evening. From your bench at the water's edge you can watch the tide ebb and flow and study the waders in the mudflats; at spring tide the water laps the front door. The pub, licenced since 1725, was once a row of 16th-century cottages lived in by workers at Langstone Mill next door; they used to have a 'tidal licence' allowing travellers a drink while waiting for the tide to ebb. When inclement weather forces you inside and away from the view you'll find rambling rooms with flagstone and pine floors, beams, an open fire. There are real ales, traditional pub grub, roasts on Sundays and sandwiches all day.

Meals	12pm-9pm. Main courses £6.95-£14; bar snacks from £2.95; Sunday roast £7.95.
Closed	Open all day.
Directions	Beside Chichester harbour, off A3023 before bridge to Hayling Island. Parking can be tricky.

Chris Ford
The Royal Oak,
19 Langstone High Street,
Langstone, Havant PO9 1RY
Tel 023 9248 3125

Entry 304 Map 4

Hampshire

305 The Jolly Sailor Lands End Rd, Old Bursledon, Southampton SO31 8DN
023 8040 5557
Reached via 45 steps or by boat, this former shipbuilder's house overlooks the river Hamble. Watch all things nautical from the terrace and from big windows in the newly furbished bars.

306 Brushmakers Arms Shoe Lane, Upham, Bishops Waltham SO32 1JJ
01489 860231
Park by the duck pond and stroll up the lane – to a buzzy beamed bar filled with chatty locals, Ringwood and Hampshire ales on tap and hearty portions of proper pub food.

307 Hampshire Bowman Dundridge Lane, Dundridge, Bishops Waltham
SO23 1GD 01489 892940
Rustic country local set beside a winding lane. Draws an eclectic crowd for farm cider and Hampshire ales tapped from the barrel in the time-worn bar, hearty home cooking, and super orchard garden.

308 The Tichborne Arms Tichborne, Alresford SO24 0NA
01962 733760
Real ales from the cask, homely pub food and a glorious summer garden draw folk to this thatched pub in a serene hamlet. The Wayfarer's Walk and the Itchen Way almost pass the door.

309 The Anchor Inn Lower Froyle, Alton GU34 4NA
01420 23261
Like its older sibling, the successful Peat Spade in Longstock, the smartly revamped Anchor offers classic English food, local ales and great wines in an informal setting.

310 The Fleur de Lys Pilley Street, Pilley, Lymington SO41 5QB
01590 672158
History is as much of a pull as a good pint at this thatched pub serving classy modern food in beamed bars. Roaring fires, lovely garden, forest walks from door. Reports on the new regime, please.

311 The Oak Inn Pinkney Lane, Bank, Lyndhurst SO43 7FE
023 8028 2350
New Forest walks radiate from this friendly, low-beamed, 18th-century pub. Walkers, cyclists and locals pour in, for ale tapped from the cask, the mix of hearty pub dishes and great local fish – reports please.

312 The Mayfly Testcombe, Wherwell, Andover SO20 6AX
01264 860283
Unrivalled river scenes draw summer crowds to this beamed old farmhouse on the banks of the fast-flowing Test. Comfortable bar, pubby food, splendid riverside terrace. Arrive on foot (or bike) via the Test Way.

The Boot

Orleton

Part and parcel of the village, The Boot earned its name from its previous life as a cobblers, when it also housed a cider house and a butchers. A rich history is to be expected in a 16th-century building and this charming black and white village inn has it in spades. In the lovely large garden is the smallest house in the county – now in disrepair (its last inhabitants were, suitably, jockeys) but there are plans afoot to revive it as a curiosity. Inside the pub: masses of space for its many fans. Locals cluster around the large open fire in the quarry-tiled bar to share crosswords and banter, along with well-kept ales. It's all very welcoming and homely. Food in the carpeted bars is homemade and filling – hot baguettes, steak and ale pie, lasagne – with things getting a little fancier in the evening.

The Riverside Inn

Aymestrey

Edward IV had a celebratory noggin here after a decisive incident in the Wars of the Roses. He was declared King soon afterwards. It is much altered: to an easy mix of antiques, fresh flowers, hops and pine. Menus change with the seasons and the seductive dishes include rack of lamb with fondant potato and red wine jus, and Ludlow venison with spiced red cabbage and walnuts. Wander from the bar into linked rooms with log fires; order a pint of Wye Valley Ale from Stoke Lacy or a house wine from Italy, Chile, Spain. And look for the map of the kitchen gardens from which so much of the fruit and vegetables come. The setting is bucolic, tucked back from a stone bridge over the river Lugg, alive with river trout, waterside seats and a lovely terraced garden. And the Mortimer Trail passes the front door.

Meals	12pm-2pm; 7pm-9pm.
	Main courses £10.95-£13.25.
Closed	3pm-6pm.
Directions	Village signed off B4361 between Ludlow & Leominster

Meals	12pm-2pm; 7pm-9pm (6.30pm-8.30pm Sun).
	Main courses £9.95-£19.95; bar meals from £4.
Closed	3pm-6pm.
Directions	On A4110 18 miles north of Hereford.

	Philip & Jane Dawson The Boot, Orleton, Ludlow SY8 4HN
Tel	01568 780228

	Richard & Liz Gresko The Riverside Inn, Aymestrey, Leominster HR6 9ST
Tel	01568 708440
Web	www.theriversideinn.org

Entry 313 Map 7

Entry 314 Map 7

Herefordshire

Bell Inn
Yarpole

The pub car park fills up fast these days. And a peep through the window reveals chefs in pristine whites calling "service" as great-looking dishes are ferried off to tables. The kitchen is in the hands of Mark Jones, whose daily chalked-up menu announces fish and chips with mushy peas and ploughman's with robust fillings. Crispy crab cakes rub shoulders with coq au vin, and there's butternut squash and chestnut lasagne for vegetarians. But it's still a village pub where locals meet over a pint of Wye Valley, dogs doze and children play in the large leafy garden. Large and reassuringly traditional, there are plush red benches, beams, horse brasses and a roaring log fire. You can eat where you like, in the bar or the gloriously converted barn. Children have mini-portions of real food, and the staff are charming.

Meals	12pm-2.30pm (3pm Sun). Main courses £13.50-£14.95.
Closed	3pm-6.30pm & Mon.
Directions	Yarpole signed off B4361 between Ludlow & Leominster.

Claude & Claire Bossi
Bell Inn,
Yarpole,
Leominster HR6 0BD
Tel   01568 780359

Entry 315 Map 7

Herefordshire

The Stagg Inn
Titley

It took some courage for Steve Reynolds to take on a tiny village pub in the back of beyond and, defying all odds, become a Herefordshire food hero. What strikes you is the attention to detail on the daily boards: the only thing you're not told is the name of the bird from which your pigeon breast (perfectly served with fig and port sauce) came. And most of the produce is organic. They fully deserve their Michelin star, won in 2001: the first for a British inn. Come for seared scallops on parsnip purée with black pepper oil, traditional roast grouse with game chips and bread sauce, and an ancient Caerphilly that arrives in the mail because the lane leading to the farm where it's made is impassable. The intimate, flag-stoned bar is perfect and dog-friendly, there's beer from Hobsons, cider from Dunkerton's and some very classy wines.

Meals	12pm-2pm; 6.30pm-9pm (9.30pm Fri & Sat). Main courses £13.50-£17.50; bar meals £8.50-£10.90.
Closed	3pm-6.30pm, Sun eve & Mon all day.
Directions	On B4355 between Kington & Presteigne.

Steve & Nicola Reynolds
The Stagg Inn,
Titley, Kington HR5 3RL
Tel   01544 230221
Web   www.thestagg.co.uk

Entry 316 Map 7

Herefordshire

The New Inn
Pembridge

Perfect for English heritage lovers with big appetites. The food is generously portioned, the building is as old as can be (1311), and Pembridge is a remarkable survivor; its market hall (where you can sup pints in the summer) could be in deepest France. It is a simple but great pleasure to amble in to this ancient inn, order a drink and squeeze into the curved back settle in the flagstoned bar; when the fireplace logs are lit, it's heaven. This is the most timeless of old locals, with photos of village shenanigans up on the wall and a darts board put to good use. Upstairs has floral carpets, books and sofa; it's a reassuring spot in which to tuck into reassuringly familiar smoked chicken and avocado salad, steak and ale pie and seafood stew. Jane Melvin is happy doing what she does best.

Herefordshire

Old Black Lion
Hay-on-Wye

Heaven for historians, book lovers and foodies in equal measure. Oliver Cromwell lodged here while laying siege to Hay Castle – the main building heaves with oak beams, ancient artefacts and conspiratorial nooks and crannies. Dolan Leighton has changed little at this popular dining pub, where cheerful staff pull pints of the eponymous Black Lion bitter. Seasonal bar favourites keep the kitchen working through every session as diners feast on trout grilled with prawns and Morrocan lamb casserole with fig compote. In the evening, pick a table in the cosy 20-seat restaurant to sample beef wellington or steak and kidney pie with cabbage and smoked bacon. There's a well-priced wine list and a good list of halves. Don't miss the 13th-century Mappa Mundi in Hereford Cathedral – or the town's 30 bookshops.

Meals	12pm-2pm; 6.30pm-9pm (7pm-8.30pm Sun). Main courses £6.95-£12; bar meals £4.95-£8.50.
Closed	3pm-6pm.
Directions	Just off A44 in Pembridge. In centre next to Market Square.

Meals	12pm-2.30pm; 6.30pm-9.30pm. Main courses £10-£18; bar meals from £5; Sunday roast £10.95.
Closed	Open all day.
Directions	2-minute walk from centre of Hay.

	Jane Melvin The New Inn, Market Square, Pembridge HR6 9DZ
Tel	01544 388427

	Dolan Leighton Old Black Lion, 26 Lion Street, Hay-on-Wye HR3 5AD
Tel	01497 820841
Web	www.oldblacklion.co.uk

Entry 317 Map 7

 Entry 318 Map 7

Herefordshire

The Pandy Inn
Dorstone

Going back to 1165, a half-timbered Herefordshire gem, a contender for 'oldest pub in the land'. Inside are heavy beams, a worn flagstoned floor, much smoke-stained stone, a vast oak lintel over an old log grate and an intimate dining room beyond the red velvet curtain. This is the county of Dorothy Goodbody and Butty Bach ales, Old Rosie and 'cloudy' scrumpy. On the menu are mussels, big Hereford beef steaks and seasonal British specials, while for hungry walkers there are filled baguettes, hearty vegetable soup and homemade chicken-liver pâté with first-class bread. Families feel welcome here and children may spill into the garden with its picnic tables and play area in summer. You are in the 'Golden Valley', so set off for Abbey Dore, Arthur's Stone or bookish Hay-on-Wye, a short drive away.

Meals	12pm-3pm; 6pm-9pm. Main courses £5.95-£12.50; Sunday roast £8.95.
Closed	3pm-6pm (6.30pm Sun) & Mon all day in winter. Open all day Sat.
Directions	Signed from B4348 Hereford to Hay-on-Wye, 5 miles from Hay.

Bill Gannon
The Pandy Inn,
Dorstone, Hay-on-Wye HR3 6AN
Tel 01981 550273
Web www.pandyinn.co.uk

Entry 319 Map 7

Herefordshire

The Wellington
Wellington

The austere frontage hides a welcoming bar and memorable food. At banquettes around the fire, Wye Valley HPA, Landlords and Hobsons ales can be sampled; beyond is a dining room of exposed brickwork, old beams and Herefordshire hops. A list of suppliers is on show, the chef is a stickler for seasonality and visiting celebrities like Franco Taruschio (ex Walnut Tree, now Barnsley House) have left their mark. So pitch up for *vincisgrassi Maceratese* (Parma ham and porcini lasagne finished with truffle oil), monkfish tail and chorizo braised in red wine, and wild mushroom risotto with parmesan shavings... there's a notable Italian accent. Puddings might include cinnamon roasted fig and madeira trifle, the cheeses are local and the Sunday roasts magnificent. Be sure to book: Wellington is a hungry village.

Meals	12pm-2pm (12.30pm-2pm Sun); 7pm-9pm. Main courses £10.50-£16.75; bar meals £4.95-£7.95; Sunday lunch £12.50 & £17.50.
Closed	3pm-6pm (7pm Sun) & Mon lunch.
Directions	Village signed off A49, 4 miles north of Hereford.

Ross & Philippa Williams
The Wellington,
Wellington, Hereford HR4 8AT
Tel 01432 830367
Web www.wellingtonpub.co.uk

Entry 320 Map 7

Herefordshire

The Railway
Hereford

What a discovery: the old railway tavern on the slopes of Dinmore Hill has become a gastropub. Work up an appetite as you mount the Ziggurat steps from the car park to the top terrace (there are easier routes on the other side!) where sweeping views of the countryside compete with two Victorian railway bridges. Inside: a contemporary mix of old and new, with smooth plaster walls painted in muted tones alongside original stones. Pull yourself up from the leather sofa to enter a bistro-like dining room serving some tasty food: locally made breads with salty Welsh butter, pretty parcels of Lay & Robson smoked salmon with cream cheese, succulent Gloucester Old Spot chops, carved and fanned across the plate and served with a whole poached pear. Service can be diffident but is always charming.

Meals	11.30am-2.30pm (12pm-3pm Sun); 7pm-9pm.
	Main courses £9.50-£19.50; bar meals £2.25-£10.50.
Closed	2.30pm-6.30pm; Sun from 3.30pm; Tues lunch & Mon all day.
Directions	On A49 between Leominster & Hereford, 4 miles south of Leominster.

Gill Morris
The Railway,
Dinmore,
Hereford HR1 3JP
Tel   01568 797053

Entry 321 Map 7

Herefordshire

The Crown & Anchor
Lugwardine

Locals, families, couples, walkers – all sorts gather here, drawn by the happy buzz. Three miles from the centre of Hereford, the old pub is countrified and atmospheric. Intimate rooms are cosy with red quarry tiles scattered with rugs, solid pine tables, corner settles and comfy sofas in corners. Pastoral prints dot the walls, bookshelves spill with books, bottles and jars. There's a big log fire and a hop-decorated bar from which Butcombe, Worthy Pedigree and Timothy Taylor beers flow; Nick offers malts from Oban and Talisker and a good few wines, and Julie oversees an excellent kitchen. Whether you choose a cheddar sandwich or a fillet of pollock with parsley sauce and mash, it will be fresh and good. There's plenty for vegetarians, too, and bread and butter pudding with custard. The garden is pretty in summer.

Meals	12pm-2pm; 7pm-10pm (9.30pm Sun).
	Main courses £8.50-£14.
Closed	Open all day.
Directions	From Hereford A438 to Ledbury. In Lugwardine, 1st left into Cotts Lane.

Nick & Julie Squire
The Crown & Anchor,
Cotts Lane, Lugwardine,
Hereford HR1 4AB
Tel   01432 851303

Entry 322 Map 7

Herefordshire

The Butchers Arms
Woolhope

Martin produces good food from a spanking new kitchen, there are log fires and smiling Cheryl to settle you in. Surrounded by walking country, opposite Marcle Ridge and close to the Forestry Commission's Haugh Woods, this half-timbered 'magpie' house (once owned by equestrian streaker Lady Godiva) goes back to the 14th century – and the ceiling beams just about reach the level of your nose. Taken over by returning locals it has undergone a restoration that it deserved long ago. From the central bar, cosy with Windsor armchairs, hung with Weston's cider lithos and sepia prints, French windows slide open to a charming terrace and a garden. In the evening, dine by candlelight in the restaurant from a menu that offers big salads in summer and, in winter, local game and warming rabbit pie with sage and bacon.

Meals	12pm-2pm; 6.30pm-9pm. Main courses £8.95-£19.95; bar snacks (lunch) from £3.95; Sunday roast £9.25.
Closed	3pm-6.30pm & Mon lunch in winter.
Directions	Off B4224 between Hereford & Ross-on-Wye.

Martin & Cheryl Baker
The Butchers Arms,
Woolhope,
Hereford HR1 4RF
Tel   01432 860281

Entry 323 Map 7

Herefordshire

The Lough Pool Inn
Sellack

The pool and stream by which the pub once stood, deep in the bosky folds of Herefordshire, have long run dry. Expect a hearty greeting from David and Janice Birch, a cosy fire, a glowing bar, hop-strewn and head-ducking beams and a refreshingly unshowy dining room – solid tables, comfortable chairs – in which to enjoy daily-changing dishes. Seasonal menus successfully balance comfort food and modern treatments of superb local ingredients, be it split pea and ham hock soup served with homemade bread, beef and oxtail suet pudding with root vegetable mash, or grilled mixed fish with saffron mayonnaise. Stock-in-trade are good real ales from Wye Valley Brewery, strong draught ciders, wines by the glass of surprising quality; try the French fizz. A relaxed and civilised place to be.

Meals	12pm-2pm; 7pm-9pm. Main courses £4.85-£12.95 (lunch & specials), £10.95-£18.95 (dinner).
Closed	3pm-6.30pm; Sun eve & Mon Oct-Feb.
Directions	Off A49, 3 miles north-west of Ross-on-Wye on Ross-Hoarwithy road; Sellack & pub signed.

David & Janice Birch
The Lough Pool Inn,
Sellack, Ross-on-Wye HR9 6LX
Tel   01989 730236
Web   www.loughpoolinn.co.uk

Entry 324 Map 7

The Saracens Head
Symonds Yat East

This is an adventure before you've booked in. The bar staff still, obligingly, run the old, hand-cranked ferry across the lovely limpid river. The old inn dates from the 16th century and became a pub in the 18th but has a entirely 21st-century buzz now, thanks to its excellent young staff and its modern brasserie. Dishes are chalked up on the blackboard by the bar – exotic sandwiches and bruschettas, pheasant terrine, wild boar with chive mash, Welsh goat's cheese panna cotta, crème brulée – all so delicious that people travel down from Birmingham for the experience. The terraces by the water attract a crowd in summer and lend a seaside-holiday feel; sit back with your Theakston's Old Peculiar and watch the canoeists float by. In winter, the public bar is a warm haven; pool tables attract young punters and trippers come for Symonds Yat. A shame not to stay: upstairs and in The Boathouse are a flurry of new oak-floored bedrooms, stylishly finished and furnished, beautifully cared for; ask for a room with a view up *and* down the river. Breakfast is one of the best.

Rooms	10: 7 doubles, 2 twins, 1 family room. £74–£130. Singles from £50.
Meals	12pm-2.30pm; 6.30pm-9pm. Main courses £11.95-£18.95 (lunch); £10-£18 (dinner); bar meals £4.25-£13.95.
Closed	Open all day.
Directions	A40 Ross-on-Wye to Monmouth; exit at Little Chef; signs for Symonds Yat East.

	Chris & Peter Rollinson
	The Saracens Head,
	Symonds Yat East, Ross-on-Wye HR9 6JL
Tel	01600 890435
Web	www.saracensheadinn.co.uk

Entry 325 Map 7

New Inn
St Owens Cross

The New Inn has been refuelling travellers on the old Ross to Abergavenny road since the 16th century. Its well-worn entrance, just off the crossroads, leads to a magnificent bar – part antique dresser, part architectural salvage – with an original pewter bar top and inlaid brass hand pulls. The inglenook warms the quarry-tiled floor, a padded settle sits beneath antlers and fox trophies. Beyond: dark tables and chairs on the best kind of pub carpet and the cosiest little snug for many a mile; get in there with a pint of Wadworths or Jennings ale. The impeccable kitchen is run by Emma, one of the youngest head chefs in the region, a self-confessed pudding fanatic whose rhubarb and custard cheesecake is renowned. She keeps the 'Old Favourites' board local and lively and her Madgett's Farm duck breast comes with a honey and whisky sauce and beetroot compote. After a turn in the garden with views to the Black Mountains, step up the creaky stairs to a pair of wonderfully beamed bedrooms complete with four-posters and antiques, one large enough to dine (or breakfast) in.

Rooms	2 doubles. £70–£80. Singles £40–£45.
Meals	12pm–9pm.
	Main courses £8.25–£14.25.
Closed	Open all day.
Directions	At junction where A4137 crosses B4521, 4 miles NW of Ross-on-Wye.

Nigel & Tee Maud
New Inn,
St Owens Cross HR2 8LQ

Tel 01989 730274
Web www.newinn.biz

The Mill Race
Walford

A surprise to push open the 'ecclesiastical' door and find yourself in a bold stylish space. The central log fire is the focus of the room, a blackboard lists the local suppliers and a stainless steel kitchen glistens beyond the granite-topped bar. Relax in a black bucket chair as you browse the papers or gaze on the hills from the terrace. An eclectic choice of music may play in acknowledgement of a mostly young clientele, but foodies of all ages come here for the chef, Aaron Simms, who trained at Le Manoir aux Quatres Saisons. It's the best of modern British pub food. For lunch there are steak burgers with onion marmalade and quiche of the day, for dinner, 'real' prawn cocktail, wild mushroom risotto and Herefordshire steak and kidney pie. It looks great on the plate and it's jolly good value.

The New Harp Inn
Hoarwithy

The Old Harp was lost to temperance and thus began the New Harp to keep the ale flowing. And flow it does. Cask ales change with the seasons, Belgian beers are on tap, there are 80 bottled beers from around the world and a Broome Farm Cider fermented in rum casks. Inside all is crisp and contemporary: a new slate floor and a mix of furniture, art and light pouring in through the bay windows from where you can see the Italianate church overlooking the village. Walk up an appetite beside the river Wye across the field before surveying a menu where a terrine of local rabbit with pancetta, dates, pistachios and chilli tomato jam leads on to How Caple partridge braised with spiced pears and served with cabbage parcels of chestnut purée and bacon. In short, a buzzy country pub where you are massively indulged.

Meals	12pm-2pm; 6.30pm-9.30pm. Main courses £4.50-£16.50.
Closed	3pm-5pm. Open all day Fri-Sun.
Directions	Walford is on B4234 3 miles south of Ross-on-Wye.

Meals	12pm-2.30pm; 6pm-9.30pm (9pm Sun). Main courses £9.50-£17.55.
Closed	3pm-6pm. Open all day in summer.
Directions	A49 from Ross, second right turn to Hoarwithy; village 4 miles through lanes.

Rebecca Bennett
The Mill Race,
Walford, Ross-on-Wye HR9 5QS
Tel   01989 562891
Web   www.millrace.info

Entry 327 Map 7

Andrew & Fleur Cooper
The New Harp Inn,
Hoarwithy, Hereford HR2 6QH
Tel   01432 840900
Web   www.newharpinn.co.uk

Entry 328 Map 7

Herefordshire

Carpenter's Arms
Walterstone

A little chapel-side pub in the middle of nowhere, hard to find but worth it, superb in every way. Vera has been dispensing Wadworth 6X and Breconshire Golden Valley from behind the corner hatch for years and everyone gets a welcome: locals, walkers, families, babies. Through an ancient oak doorway is a tiny bar with a log-fired range and a dining area to the side. Floors are Welsh slate, settles polished oak, tables cast iron, walls open stone; it's as cared for as can be. On the menu are fishcakes and salad, chicken breast stuffed with stilton and wrapped in bacon, syrup and stem ginger pudding – proper homemade food, some organic. Beer is served from the drum, cider and perry from the flagon. In summer, spill into the grassy garden and gaze up at the Skirrid, then pull on the hiking boots and climb it.

> A pub is a pub when you find three or more (often local) real ales, a welcome for those popping in just for a pint, a menu that includes ploughman's or other old-fashioned pub classics, and an easy-going, convivial atmosphere.

Meals	12pm-3pm; 7pm-10pm. Main courses £10.95-£14.95; bar meals from £5.
Closed	Open all day.
Directions	Village signed from Pandy; Pandy signed from A465 from Abergavenny.

Vera Watkins
Carpenter's Arms,
Walterstone, Hereford HR2 0DX
Tel   01873 890353

Entry 329 Map 7

Herefordshire

330 The Cottage of Content Carey, Hereford HR2 6NG
01432 840242

Décor is pared-down traditional: flagstones in the bar, polished wood beyond, Windsor chairs, pine tables and pews. A walkers' food pub in the heart of Herefordshire. New owners – reports please.

331 Three Crowns Inn Bleak Acre, Ullingswick HR1 3JQ
01432 820279

Lost down lanes, it's worth any number of missed turns. Beams and settles, open fires, candles on tables, wonderful chalked up menus that brim with local and organic produce. Don't miss the monthly farmers' market.

332 Salutation Inn Market Pitch, Weobley HR4 8SJ
01544 318443

Lording it at the top end of the village green, the old cider house creaks with age. Drop by for a pint of Butty Bach by the fire in the timbered bar. New owner – reports please.

333 The Tram Eardisley, Hereford HR3 6PG
01544 327251

Ancient timbered local delivering interesting food from locally sourced produce, and changing real ales. Settle into the cosy beamed bar and the warmly decorated dining areas.

Worth a visit

Photo: dreamstime.com

Hertfordshire

The Alford Arms
Frithsden

It isn't easy to find, so be armed with a detailed map or precise directions before you set out – David and Becky Salisbury's gastropub is worth any number of missed turns. It's in a hamlet enfolded by acres of National Trust common land. Inside, two interlinked rooms, bright, airy, with soft colours, scrubbed pine tables on wooden or tiled floors. Food is taken seriously and ingredients are as organic, free-range and delicious as can be. On a menu that divides dishes into small plates and main meals, there is home-smoked duck breast on celery choucroute, Cornish fish stew with saffron potaoes, treacle tart with lemongrass créme fraîche. Wine drinkers have the choice of 17 by the glass, while service is informed and friendly. Arrive early on a warm day to take your pick of the teak tables on the sun-trapping front terrace.

Meals	12pm-2.30pm (3pm Sat; 4pm Sun); 7pm-10pm. Main courses £11-£15.25.
Closed	Open all day.
Directions	A4146 Hemel Hempstead to Water End; 2nd left after Red Lion to Frithsden; left after 1 mile at T-junc., then right; on right.

David & Becky Salisbury
The Alford Arms,
Frithsden,
Hemel Hempstead HP1 3DD
Tel 01442 864480
Web www.alfordarmsfrithsden.co.uk

Entry 334 Map 9

Hertfordshire

The Valiant Trooper
Aldbury

Named in honour of the Duke of Wellington who, it is said, held a meeting here during the Napoleonic Wars, the dear little brick and tiled cottage has been serving ale since 1752. Now it caters for booted ramblers, diners escaping town and families – there's a play house in the garden. You'll find dark beams on rough-plaster walls, bare brick, blazing log fires, tiled floors, an old-fashioned feel and a big welcome from landlord Tim O'Gorman, who's been pleasing customers for over 20 years. Walkers can slake a thirst with a decent pint of ale from a chalked-up choice of five and refuel on ciabatta sandwiches. The light and airy stable restaurant bustles with lunchers on Sundays. Come for roasts and proper English dishes: peppered mackerel with horseradish relish, and bread and butter pudding.

Meals	12pm-2.15pm; 6.30pm-9.15pm; no food Sun & Mon eve. Main courses £8-£12; bar meals £5; Sunday roast £9-£11.
Closed	Open all day.
Directions	North of Berkhamsted off B4506 towards Aldbury Common.

Tim O'Gorman
The Valiant Trooper,
Trooper Road, Aldbury,
Tring HP23 5RW
Tel 01442 851203

Entry 335 Map 9

Hertfordshire

339 Bull at Cottered Cottered, Buntingford SG9 9QP
01763 281243
Refurbished and extended food pub in a pretty village setting. Call in for decent wines, Greene King ales, warming fires and interesting food served in low-beamed rooms furnished with antiques. Reports welcome.

340 The Old Mill London Road, Berkhamsted HP4 2NB
01442 879590
Hot off the press from vibrant Peach Pubs – a beautifully restored old mill, with natural oak furnishings and deep sofas in classy rooms, and menus to match. Great canal-side terrace.

341 The Holly Bush Potters Crouch, St Albans AL2 3NN
01727 851792
An immaculate 18th-century country pub elegantly furnished with antiques and big oak tables candlelit at night. Fabulous Fuller's ales, straightforward food, nice garden.

342 The Bricklayers Arms Hogpits Bottom, Flaunden HP3 0PH
01442 833322
A pretty, 18th-century building with low beams, blazing winter fire and timbered walls tucked away in the exotically named Hogpits Bottom. Excellent beers, 50 wines and menus listing home-smoked fish and steak and kidney pie. Reports please.

Worth a visit

Seaview Hotel
Seaview

Everything here is a dream. You're 50 yards from the water in a small seaside village that sweeps you back to a nostalgic past. Locals pop in for a pint, famished yachtsmen step ashore for a meal, those in the know drop by for a luxurious night in indulging rooms. When the weather is warm, have a pre-dinner drink in the front garden and watch the sun go down over the Solent – perfect. In the bar, order island-brewed Goddard's Special and the famous hot crab ramekin; if you're here on a Sunday, don't miss the roast. Afterwards, retire to a sitting room for binoculars and views of the sea. The pitch pine bar has a roaring fire and every conceivable nautical curio nailed to its walls, the terrace buzzes with island life in summer, the restaurants hum with the contented sighs of happy diners. Some bedrooms come in super-smart country-house style (upholstered four-posters, padded headboards), others are more contemporary (Farrow & Ball colours, fancy bathrooms). Ask for details about wine-tasting, cycling and adventure breaks.

Rooms	Main house: 14 twins/doubles, 3 four-posters. Seaview Modern: 4 doubles, 3 twins/doubles. £120-£199.
Meals	12pm-2.30pm; 7pm-9.30pm. Main courses £7-£14; Sunday lunch £13.95 & 16.95.
Closed	Open all day.
Directions	From Ryde, B3330 south for 1.5 miles. Hotel signed left.

Andrew Morgan
Seaview Hotel,
High Street, Seaview PO34 5EX
Tel   01983 612711
Web   www.seaviewhotel.co.uk

Isle of Wight

The New Inn
Shalfleet

Built in 1746, this old fishermen's haunt is worth more than a passing nod – especially if you are on the 65-mile coastal path trail. Or have got here by boat and moored at Shalfleet Quay. The place now draws a cheery mix of tourists, walkers and sailors to a spick-and-span bar with 900-year-old flagstones, beams and old fireplaces, and a series of pine-tabled dining rooms decked with nautical bits and bobs. Refreshment includes pints of island-brewed ales and fabulously fresh seafood marked up on the daily-changing chalkboard. The huge platter is a treat; other (cheaper) fish choices might include sea bass cooked with lemon or simply grilled plaice. The crab sandwiches are memorable, as is the lobster salad. And carnivores are not forgotten, with prime steak, game in season and traditional pub grub.

Meals	12pm-2.30pm; 6pm-9.30pm. Main courses £6-£20.
Closed	Open all day.
Directions	On A3054 between Yarmouth & Newport.

Martin Bullock
The New Inn, Main Road,
Shalfleet, Yarmouth PO30 4NS
Tel 01983 531314
Web www.thenew-inn.co.uk

Entry 344 Map 3

Kent

Shipwright's Arms
Faversham

It's been called the loneliest pub in the world. Surrounded by salt marshes, the below-sea-level-building and boatyard are protected by a dyke from inundation by the tidal creek above. Its isolation calls for self-sufficiency: water is still drawn from a well and propane gas used for cooking. Plain and simple just about sums up the three tiny bar rooms separated by standing timbers and wooden partitions, all warmed by open fires or stoves, with booths formed by black-panelled settles and there's no shortage of boating paraphernalia. Beers are from Kent brewers Goachers and Hopdaemon and are expertly kept, food sustains sailing folk and walkers on the Saxon Shore Way, and Derek and Ruth are lovely people. Join the summer crowd in the garden and sup a pint on the sea wall. Worth the trek.

Meals	12pm-2.30pm; 7pm-9pm; no food Sun eve. Main courses £6.95-£12.95.
Closed	3pm-6pm & Mon all day in winter.
Directions	From A2 for Sittingbourne. Through Ospringe, right at r'bout on to western link road; right at end (T-junc.). Left opp. school in 0.25 miles. Cross marsh to pub.

Derek & Ruth Cole
Shipwright's Arms,
Hollowshore,
Faversham ME13 7TU
Tel 01795 590088

Entry 345 Map 5

Kent

The Pepper Box
Ulcombe

Off a country lane, surrounded by fields of corn, the 15th-century Pepper Box has far-reaching views across the Kentish Weald from a glorious decked terrace. Once the haunt of smugglers, it takes its name (apparently unique) from their favourite weapon, the Pepper Box pistol. A series of traditional dining areas rambles round the central bar, carpeted, cosy, low-beamed, with a sofa-fronted inglenook and glowing log fire. Drinks include foaming pints of Shepherd Neame Porter and Master Brew, local apple juice and decent wines by the glass. Menus are wide ranging and portions not for the shy! Tuck into a big bowl of chilli or a plateful of monkfish in garlic butter; pot-roasted pheasant or calves' liver in sage butter. And what could be nicer than to sup a summer pint on the terrace as the sun sinks into the Weald? *A Shepherd Neame pub.*

Meals	12pm-2.15pm (3pm Sun); 7pm-9.45pm. Main courses £7.50-£17; sandwiches from £4.
Closed	3.30pm-6.30pm. Closed from 5pm Sun.
Directions	From M20 junc 8, take A20 towards Ashford; right for Fairbourne Heath in Harrietsham. Keep ahead at crossroads; pub in 200 yds.

Geoff & Sarah Pemble
The Pepper Box, Fairbourne Heath,
Ulcombe, Maidstone ME17 1LP

Tel	01622 842558
Web	www.shepherdneame.co.uk

Entry 346 Map 5

Kent

Dining Room at the Railway Hotel
Faversham

This extraordinary hostelry opposite the station combines the elements of a town boozer (bar billiard table, Shepherd Neame beers) with classy food from a skilled duo. Talent, imagination and the freshest ingredients they can get their hands on result in some unexpectedly unpubby pub grub. The menu changes every six weeks or so to reflect the seasons and the raw materials come mostly from local farms and shoots with a preference for the organic and the odd foraged find. So a gorgeous salad of apple and foraged leaves may accompany your confit duck. Anthony's passion-fruit jelly with blackberry sorbet is a sensation, and the superb English cheeses come from Canterbury's Goods Shed. It's an enticing room, too, with its mix of wooden tables, fresh flowers and chic chandeliers. Worth missing the train for. *A Shepherd Neame pub.*

Meals	12pm-2.30pm (3.30pm Sun); 6.30pm-9pm; no food Sun eve, Mon & Tue. Main courses £11.80-£15; set lunch £12.50 & £15.50.
Closed	Open all day.
Directions	Opposite Faversham railway station.

Anthony North & Jonny Butterfield
Dining Room at the Railway Hotel,
Preston Street, Faversham ME13 8PE

Tel	01795 533173
Web	www.railwayhotelfaversham.co.uk

Entry 347 Map 5

The Sportsman
Seasalter

Slip off to Seasalter for a meal you won't forget. Brothers Phil and Steven Harris's pub is a gastronomic haven amid marshlands, beach huts and caravan sites with the North Sea somewhere behind. In defiance of the pub's bleak surroundings, happy eaters fill three light-filled rooms that spread across stripped pine floors topped with chunky reclaimed-wood tables built and a log fire. The blackboard menu, short and sweet, promises everything seasonal and a passion for fish. (Try the tasting menu, Tuesday to Friday.) There's Thornback ray with balsamic vinaigrette, new-season lamb with pommes Anna, apple parfait with blackberry sorbet and hazelnuts... they make their own salt, churn their own butter and, in 2008, netted a Michelin star. Expect good wines by the glass and Shepherd Neame on hand pump. Exceptional. *A Shepherd Neame pub.*

Meals	1pm-2pm; 7pm-9pm; no food Sun & Mon. Main courses £13.95-£19.95.
Closed	3pm-6pm.
Directions	On coast road between Faversham & Whitstable.

Phil Harris
The Sportsman, Faversham Road,
Seasalter, Whitstable CT5 4BP
Tel 01227 273370
Web www.thesportsmanseasalter.co.uk

Entry 348 Map 5

The Red Lion
Stodmarsh

In an enchanting village, reached down rutted lanes that wind through bluebell woods, is a 15th-century pub with tiny rooms. Walk into an interior of bare boards, log fires, draped hops, prints, menus, old wine bottles, milk churns, trugs, baskets, candles on every table and a very bossy cat. Then there's the landlord, Robert Whigham, a legend in his own time. A basket of freshly laid eggs (chickens roam the garden, of course), chutney and a sign for the sale of locally smoked ham add to the rustic, rural feel. Greene King IPA and Old Speckled Hen are tapped from barrels behind the bar and everyone here is a regular, or looks like one. The blackboard menu changes according to what arrives from the farms and shoots, food arrives on huge painted plates and the quality is high. It doesn't get much better than this!

Meals	12pm-2.30pm (3pm Sun); 6.30pm-9.30pm; no food Sun eve. Main courses £9.95-£15.95.
Closed	Open all day.
Directions	Off A257 Canterbury to Sandwich road.

Robert Whigham
The Red Lion,
High Street, Stodmarsh,
Canterbury CT3 4BA
Tel 01227 721339

Entry 349 Map 5

Kent

Fitzwalter Arms
Goodnestone

The 16th-century village pub stands on a sleepy road that dwindles to a footpath bordering Goodnestone Park where Jane Austen was a visitor. There's no standing on ceremony in these two tiny, unspoilt bars. Claire greets you warmly as you rub shoulders with all manner of folk, from local drinkers to walkers and foodies. There are logs fires and delicious bar food – omelettes, mushrooms on toast – all of which wash down nicely with a pint of Shepherd Neame. Then there's an intimate dining room with its own log fire and views through leaded windows to the churchyard. The menu chalks up such delights as wild mallard leg with red cabbage and soured cream, and pork belly with crackling and apple sauce. Chef Dave ensures vegetables are organic, meat free-range and fish delivered daily from Hythe. A gem. *A Shepherd Neame pub.*

Meals	12pm-2pm; 7pm-9pm.
	Main courses £9.50-£17.50;
	Sunday roast £13.50.
Closed	3pm-6pm & Sun eve.
	Open all day Thurs-Sat.
Directions	From Canterbury, A257 to
	Wingham, then B2046 signed
	Aylesham; follow signs to
	Goodnestone.

	Dave Hart
	Fitzwalter Arms, The Street,
	Goodnestone, Canterbury CT3 1PJ
Tel	01304 840303
Web	www.shepherd-neame.co.uk

Entry 350 Map 5

Kent

The Griffin's Head
Chillenden

Jerry and Karen's hugely attractive Shepherd Neame pub – a Wealden hall house from the 14th century – will charm you. Dominated by a log fire in the tiny, flagstoned, central bar and back-to-back with its doppelganger hearth in the snug, attractive restaurant, this is a superb winter pub. Pale beams and standing timbers are everywhere, ceilings are low and the beams above the bar are a mass of glass beer mugs. Lovers of fizz know they've come to the right place the moment they step in and spot the blackboard listing champagne. Wine is taken seriously too, with a fair choice by the glass – six reds, six whites. Good country cooking is of the creamy garlic mushrooms, steak and kidney pie, roast partridge in cranberry sauce variety.. In spring the gorgeous garden is surrounded by wild roses. *A Shepherd Neame pub.*

Meals	12pm-2pm; 7pm-9.30pm;
	no food Sun eve.
	Main courses £7.95-£18.50.
Closed	Open all day. Closed Sun eves.
Directions	A2 from Canterbury; left on
	B2068 for Wingham;
	Chillenden signed.

	Jeremy Copestake
	The Griffin's Head,
	Chillenden,
	Canterbury CT3 1PS
Tel	01304 840325

Entry 351 Map 5

New Flying Horse Inn
Wye

Nothing is too much trouble for these affable hosts: the day's papers, ales from Shepherd Neame, wines by the glass, a friendly chat. A crackling log fire in the main bar adds to the charm, along with oak beams, timbers and a sprinkling of horse brass and pub paraphernalia. It is a genuine village local, with a difference: in summer you can marvel at Julian Dowle's award-winning Chelsea Flower Show garden, a nostalgic version of wartime Blighty that includes vegetable plots and flower boarders, imported oak trees and a thatched cottage, and a magnificent patio with a flagpole and play area. Food is correspondingly traditional: ham, double egg and chips, perhaps, or beef lasagne, supplemented by a specials board of more exotic offerings such as tempura hake with stir-fry vegetables and noodles with hoisin sauce. The pub was built in the 17th century – as a posting house – so the bedrooms and bathrooms vary in size. Fresh decorated, they come in neutral colours with the occasional low beam or desk area tucked behind a chimney breast. The quieter, smaller rooms are in the stable block. *A Shepherd Neame pub.*

Rooms	9: 8 twins/doubles, 1 single. £90. Single from £55.
Meals	12pm–2pm; 6pm–9pm (6.30pm Sun). Main courses £4.95–£8.95 (lunch), £9.25–£14.50 (dinner).
Closed	3pm–5.30pm Mon–Fri in winter. Open all day Sat, Sun and in summer.
Directions	A mile off A28 north of Ashford; follow one-way system into Wye; Upper Bridge St is 2nd turning on right after High Street.

Cliff Whitbourne
New Flying Horse Inn,
Upper Bridge Street,
Wye, Ashford TN25 5AW

Tel	01233 812297
Web	www.newflyinghorsewye.co.uk

Entry 352 Map 5

Kent

Royal Hotel
Deal

Whether out on the decked terrace listening to the waves raking the beach, or in the lounge bar cosy with leather chairs, chesterfields and fire, you can follow in the footsteps of Lord Nelson and Emma. They stayed here in the winter of 1801. It was an inspired move by Shepherd Neame – the oldest brewery in the country – to rescue and transform this run-down seaside hotel. The new look is understated and stylish, especially in the bedrooms where a gentle nautical theme plays. Colours are softly modern and the attention to detail (flat-screen TVs, slick modern bathrooms) runs throughout. The best rooms have a sea view balcony and a claw-foot bath placed in the room. With food available all day, the Royal has proved a hit with families drawn by the beach and the please-all menu of pub classics – yours to peruse wherever you sit. As for the deckside colonial-style bar, it makes a popular 19th hole inside and out; golfers come to play the celebrated Open Championship course Royal St George's, as well as qualifying courses Prince's and Royal Cinque Port. *A Shepherd Neame pub.*

Rooms	19: 12 twins/doubles, 1 single. £90–£160. 5 family rooms £110–£145.
Meals	12pm-9pm. Main courses £6.75–£11.95.
Closed	Open all day.
Directions	On seafront close to town centre.

Sara Smith
Royal Hotel,
Beach Street, Deal CT14 6JD
Tel   01304 375555
Web   www.theroyalhotel.com

Kent

The Granville
Lower Hardres

From the same stable as the Sportsman in Seasalter, the Granville mirrors its older sibling, straddling the divide between restaurant and pub. Rugs are strewn, leather sofas fill one corner and there's a big beer garden outside. It's a pleasure to sit back in this laid-back place, downing rock oysters with shallot vinegar and a pint of stout (or a well-chosen wine). Overseeing it all is Gabrielle Harris, aided by chef Jim Shave heading an open-to-view kitchen that deals in modern uncontrived dishes. Chalked up on blackboards are tried-and-trusted favourites like whole roast wild sea bass with garlic and rosemary. There's homemade bread to dip, and a flourless chocolate cake that will charm those even without allergies. Ingredients are impeccably sourced. Great for walkers, foodies, families – and the Channel tunnel. *A Shepherd Neame pub.*

Kent

Froggies at the Timber Batts
Bodsham

Winding lanes lead, finally, to Bodsham, with glorious views of the North Downs. Wander into the splendidly rural Timber Batts – built in 1485 – and you are in for a surprise. Along with the bar menu is a slateboard of British and Gallic specialities, chalked up in French, and the Loire house wine comes from the vineyard of the owner-chef's cousin. So sit yourself down at an old pine table and be cheered by platefuls of local game, Rye Bay fish, free-range egg and crispy thin French fries, confit de canard, roast rack of lamb with herbs, and café Liègoise. In winter, nurse a whisky by one of three fires, in summer enjoy the garden with its lush Kentish views. And make the most of delicious local and French produce at the last-Sunday-of-the-month market in the car park.

Meals	12pm-2pm (2.30pm Sun); 7-9pm; no food Sun or Mon eve. Main courses £11.95-£16.95; bar meals £4.95-£11.95.
Closed	3pm-5.30pm. Open all day Sun.
Directions	On B2068 just outside Canterbury.

Meals	12pm-2.30pm (12.30pm Sun); 7pm-9.30pm; no food Sun eve. Main courses £14-19; Sunday lunch £16 & £20.
Closed	3pm-6.30pm & Mon (Tues if bank hol Mon). Open all day Sat & Sun.
Directions	B2068 for Canterbury; left for Wye & Bodsham; 1st left fork; 1.5 miles; right for Wye; right for Bodsham; 300 yds up on top of hill.

	Phil & Gabrielle Harris
	The Granville,
	Street End, Lower Hardres,
	Canterbury CT4 7AL
Tel	01227 700402

	Joel Gross
	Froggies at the Timber Batts,
	School Lane, Bodsham,
	Wye TN25 5JQ
Tel	01233 750237
Web	www.thetimberbatts.co.uk

Entry 354 Map 5

Entry 355 Map 5

The Dering Arms
Pluckley

Pluckley is possibly the most haunted village in England (16 ghosts at the last count) and the gothicky Dering Arms contributes its share. The former hunting lodge is hidden down country lanes almost two miles from the village. Owner/chef James Buss has given this civilised place a fantastic reputation for food and drink. There are stone floors, blazing logs, old wooden tables and chairs and two bars garlanded with hops, farming implements, guns and prints, so feast amid it all on fine produce and fish that will have you hooked (whole Dover sole, crab salad, tuna pan fried with garlic and lemon butter). Or dine in the pretty restaurant, candlelit at night. The blackboard also lists seasonal game, pie of the day, confit of duck. Dering Ale on hand pump is brewed for the pub by Goachers of Maidstone, and there are wines and whiskies galore. James has smartened up the three simple bedrooms, adding good shower rooms to two (the third has a private bathroom) and individual pieces of furniture: a grand sleigh bed in one, an antique brass bed in another.

Rooms	3 doubles. £50–£75. Singles £40–£60.
Meals	12pm-2pm; 7pm-9.30pm.
	Main courses £10–£21.95.
Closed	3pm-6pm;
	Sun eves from 5pm & all day Mon.
Directions	8 miles west of Ashford (M20 south junc. 8). Signed from Pluckley, by railway station.

James Buss
The Dering Arms,
Station Road, Pluckley TN27 0RR
Tel   01233 840371
Web   www.deringarms.com

The Black Pig
Tunbridge Wells

Rustic menus brimming with organic and biodynamic foods put Julian Leefe-Griffiths's George & Dragon on Kent's culinary map. Keen to replicate the success, he took on the Orson Welles in 2007, spruced it up in his own eclectic style and re-named it after a tasty rare-breed pig. Now there's a relaxed informality and a funky feel. In the bar are leather chairs, contemporary wall coverings and a chandelier; in the dining areas, earthy colours and planked floors. From the open-to-view kitchen flow pork sausages with mash and onion gravy, slow-roasted belly pork with roasted vegetables and Three Little Pigs, a board laden with English, Italian and Spanish hams. Non-porcine dishes include crab and scallop fettucine and rump of Sussex Red beef, and there are 13 wines by the glass. Pig heaven in Tunbridge Wells.

The Hare
Langton Green

As you negotiate the green and the surrounding roads in the quest for somewhere to park, you'd be forgiven for thinking The Hare is hardly Kent's best-kept secret. Don't be put off. The feel inside is stylish and relaxed and the food among the best in the area. Large, light rooms create marvellous eating areas, with gleaming, well-spaced tables on polished floorboards, and character from old prints, paintings and books. The blackboard menu has pub classics such as steak and ale pie with braised cabbage and good sandwiches, plus more ambitious dishes like shoulder of lamb with red wine sauce, and slow-roast belly pork with dauphinoise potato. Cheerful staff dispense Greene King Abbot Ale and guest beers such as Ruddles County and Archers. Wine is taken seriously too; the well-balanced wine list has 17 by the glass.

Meals	12pm-2.30pm (4pm Sun); 7pm-9.30pm; no food Sun eve. Main courses £6-£12.50 (lunch), £11.50-£14.50 (dinner).
Closed	Open all day.
Directions	Town centre; Grove Hill Road is almost opposite the railway station entrance, to the right of Hoopers Store.

Meals	12pm-9.30pm (9pm Sun). Main courses £7.50-£16.50.
Closed	Open all day.
Directions	On A264 3 miles west of Tunbridge Wells.

Julian Leefe-Griffiths
The Black Pig, 18 Grove Hill Rd,
Tunbridge Wells TN1 1RZ

Tel 01892 523030
Web www.theblackpig.net

Chris Little
The Hare, Langton Green,
Tunbridge Wells TN3 0JA

Tel 01892 862419
Web www.brunningandprice.co.uk

Entry 361 Map 5

Entry 362 Map 5

George & Dragon
Speldhurst

"We buy from people not companies,'" says Julian Leefe-Griffiths – before launching into an exuberant description of the produce he finds in the local woods and the beers that come from Westerham. Meat, game and vegetables are local and often organic; cheeses come mostly from Sussex. Rescuing one of the oldest inns in southern England from years of mediocrity is no easy task, but they've made a fine start. It's a characterful old pub, loved for its massive flagstones, doors, inglenook and beams. Gutsy food is the biggest treat: crisp, salty sea purslane cooked with creamy soft scallops, wood sorrel with seared local wood pigeon breast, smoked eel on toast with poached duck egg and confit garlic, Valrhona chocolate tart. The atmosphere is easy, the staff friendly, and there's a lovely rear garden.

Meals	12pm-3pm (4pm Sun). Main courses £9.50-£15.50; bar meals £5.50-£9.50.
Closed	Open all day.
Directions	In centre of village opposite church.

Julian Leefe-Griffiths
George & Dragon, Speldhurst Hill,
Speldhurst, Tonbridge TN3 0NN
Tel   01892 863125
Web   www.speldhurst.com

Entry 363 Map 5

Spotted Dog
Smarts Hill

Everyone loves this 16th-century English pub... walkers, grannies, dogs. It is rambling, low-beamed, nooked and crannied to the hilt. But there's nothing traditional about the short daily-changing menu, a well-priced blending of country dishes with current trends. And it's good – whether a plate of Weald Smokery Parma ham, olive roasted skate with a beurre noisette, game stew with parsley dumplings, or a simple BLT sandwich. Sit back with an expertly kept pint of Larkins or Harveys Best by an inglenook fire – there are several – and admire the tiny doors and the mullioned windows, the rough hewn beams and the ancient panelling; this is a textbook English pub. In summer, stroll into one of the tiered beer gardens at the front and back, then pop into the pub's wonderful farm shop next door. Fun, friendly and charismatic.

Meals	12pm-2.30pm; 6pm-9.30pm (12pm-4pm; 6pm-9pm Sun). Main courses £8.95-£14.95.
Closed	4pm-6pm. Open all day Sat.
Directions	Off B2188, 1.5 miles from Penshurst.

Colette O'Reilly
Spotted Dog,
Smarts Hill,
Penshurst TN11 8EE
Tel   01892 870253

Entry 364 Map 5

The Beacon
Tunbridge Wells

Everything ticks over beautifully at the Beacon. The spacious late-Victorian interior is a work of art, brimful of magnificent oak panelling, stained glass and ornate plaster ceilings. Good beers, an impressive range of wines by the glass and open fires lure drinkers to the clubby bar; in summer, take to the terrace with its famed panorama of the Weald of Kent – stunning. In every season, the food, served in the bar or the formal dining room, draws people from far and wide. Whether you are here for the Sunday roast, the haddock fillet battered in Harveys Ale or a three-course feast (game and apricot terrine wrapped in pancetta, honey and mustard glazed lamb rack with truffle polenta and chargrilled vegetables, sticky toffee pudding with butterscotch sauce) you should go home happy. And there are beds for the night, in three serene rooms at the top of the grand wooden staircase. In the Georgian Room, elegant colours and a roll-top slipper bath, in the Colonial Room, exquisite African fabrics. Wake to views of spectacular grounds – woods, lakes, wildlife and a genuine Tunbridge Wells chalybeate spring.

Rooms	3: 2 doubles, 1 single. £97. Single £68.50.
Meals	12pm-2.30pm; 6.30pm-9.30pm (12pm-9pm Sun). Main courses £9.25-£15.
Closed	Open all day.
Directions	Tea Garden Lane signed off A264 1 mile west of Tunbridge Wells.

John Cullen
The Beacon,
Tea Garden Lane, Rusthall,
Tunbridge Wells TN13 9JH
Tel   01892 524252
Web   www.the-beacon.co.uk

The Bullfinch
Sevenoaks

The old roadside boozer has been transformed by Geronimo Inns. The framework is still there – rambling rooms, beams – but the designers have swept in with a fresh modern broom. Now it is enticing, thanks to sweeping floors of stone and wood, a huge central chimney-piece, comfy sofas, big chunky tables and food based on the best local produce. Good-quality beers and wines, too. The dining area is huge, light and airy with decking to handle the overflow and lawns for lazy days. Menus parade lunchtime steak sandwiches with caramelised onion, horseradish mayo and fat chips along with chunky bacon and cheese burgers; dinner lists garlic and parsley snails and roasted rack of lamb with dauphinoise. The Bullfinch has become one of the most popular places for dining out in Kent – and one of the chic-est.

Meals	12pm-3pm; 6pm-9.30pm (10pm Fri); 12pm-10pm Sat (8pm Sun). Main courses £8.50-£15.25.
Closed	Open all day.
Directions	On A224 1 mile north of Sevenoaks.

Karen & Steve Jordan
The Bullfinch,
Riverhead, Sevenoaks TN13 2DR
Tel   01732 455107
Web   geronimo-inns.co.uk

Entry 366 Map 5

The Harrow
Ightham Common

The continuing, hands-on approach of John Elton and Claire Butler is reaping rewards. Their Kent ragstone country pub looks the part, with cottage garden flowers outside, candlelight and a roaring winter fire within. The cooking is based on sound supplies, from local game to wild mushrooms, and the food adds enough spice to provoke interest without being overpowering: mustard and chive sauce with home-baked ham, fillet of chicken with Cajun spices. Some of the starters might make a meal in themselves: spicy vegetable and lentil soup comes with a whole loaf, and tomato and anchovy salad is a heaped pile. A separate restaurant, that spreads into a small conservatory, has a more formal feel to match the starched white cloths on the bookable tables. It's first-come, first-served for tables in the bar – and this is a popular place!

Meals	12pm-2pm (3pm Sun); 6pm-9pm. Main courses £9.50-£17; bar meals £6.50-£17.
Closed	3pm-6pm, Sun eve & Mon all day.
Directions	Ightham Common signed off A25.

John Elton & Claire Butler
The Harrow,
Ightham Common,
Sevenoaks TN15 9EB
Tel   01732 885912

Entry 367 Map 5

Kent

The Swan on the Green
West Peckham

West Peckham may be the back of beyond – a well-heeled beyond – but there's nothing backward about Gordon Milligan's pub. People are drawn by its reputation for good food and its beer from the microbrewery at the back. The décor is fresh, contemporary and open-plan: blond wood, rush-seated chairs, modern black and white photographs. Under the Swan Ales label, half a dozen brews are funnelled from the central bar: Ginger Swan, Swan Mild, Trumpeter Best, Fuggles, Bewick, Cygnet. Menus are a compendium of updated pub classics and the likes of tomato and root vegetable chowder, red mullet with mussel broth, and crispy duck confit with red wine jus. Gordon and his team have created a balanced mix of drinking bar and dining areas in a 16th-century pub. You may even borrow a rug and eat on the village green.

> Regionality is gaining momentum... lamb is not just lamb, it's Lancastrian and heather-reared. Asparagus is English and served in season. Pork is Tamworth and free-range, and individual farms are sometimes named on the menu.

Meals	12pm-2pm; 7pm-9pm; no food Sun & Mon eve. Main courses £9.95-£15.95; bar meals £5.65-£12.95.
Closed	3pm-6pm; check Sun eves in winter.
Directions	From A26 north east of Tonbridge, north on B2106; 1st left for West Peckham; pub by green & church.

	Gordon Milligan The Swan on the Green, West Peckham, Maidstone ME18 5JW
Tel	01622 812271
Web	www.swan-on-the-green.co.uk

Entry 368 Map 5

Kent

369   The Great House Gills Green, Hawkhurst TN18 5EJ
01580 753119
Former Elizabethan cottages with an alluring mix of beams, furnishings and open fires in the rambling bar or cool Orangery dining room. Fresh brasserie food best enjoyed on the Mediterranean terrace.

370   King William IV The Street, Benenden, Cranbrook TN17 4DJ
01580 240636
16th-century tile-hung inn, upmarket in style, reflecting its location. Scrubbed wooden tables, crackling logs in the old inglenook, Shepherd Neame ales, good country cooking, a relaxed lived-in air.

371   George Inn 44 The Street, Newnham, Faversham ME9 0LL
01795 890237
At this tile-hung 16th-century pub, fine rugs on stripped wooden floors, big lamps and candles on scrubbed tables and log fires in inglenooks create a civilised setting for pub grub and pints of Master Brew.

372   The Gate Inn Boyden Gate, Marshside, Canterbury CT3 4EB
01227 860498
A charming rural local, run for years by a landlord who resists change. Two small, well-worn bars, log fires, Shepherd Neame tapped from the cask, and simple hearty food.

373   The Tiger Stowting, Ashford TN25 6BA
01303 862130
Hard-to-find, civilised country boozer with friendly locals, rugs on bare boards, candles on scrubbed tables, roaring winter fire, real ales (festival in summer) and splendid live jazz evenings. Reports please.

374   The Woolpack Brookland, New Romney TN29 9TJ
01797 344321
An isolated medieval pub on the edge of windswept Romney Marsh. Seek refuge and warmth by the log fire in the low-ceilinged bar, quaff Shepherd Neame in tip-top condition, tuck into hearty pub food.

375   Rock Inn Hoath Corner, Chiddingstone Hoath, Tonbridge TN8 7BS
01892 870296
Timeless, tile-hung brick cottage in a glorious position. Scuffed and charmingly laid-back, the perfect walker's stop for a pint of Larkins and a satisfyingly thick sandwich.

Lancashire

The Rams Head Inn
Denshaw

High on the moors between Oldham and Ripponden – you're on the border here – with glorious views, the inn is two miles from the motorway but you'd never know. Unspoilt inside and out, there's a authentic, old-farmhouse feel. The small rooms, cosy with winter log fires, are carpeted, half-panelled and beamed and filled with interesting memorabilia. Until recently beer was served straight from the cask; there's still an old sideboard behind the bar to remind you of former days. Blackboards announce a heart-warming selection of tasty and well-priced food cooked to order: game and venison in season, seafood specialities and great steaks. A wonderfully isolated Lancashire outpost, staffed by people who care, and with a farm shop, deli and tea rooms. Well-behaved children are very welcome most evenings – but watch the open fires!

Meals	12pm-2.30pm; 6pm-10pm (12pm-8.30pm Sun). Main courses £8.95-£17.95; set menu £10.95; sandwiches £3.95-£7.95.
Closed	2.30pm-6pm Tue-Sat; Sun from 8.30pm & Mon all day (except bank holidays).
Directions	M62 junc. 22 for Oldham & Saddleworth; 2 miles on right.

G R Haigh
The Rams Head Inn,
Denshaw, Saddleworth OL3 5UN
Tel   01457 874802
Web   www.ramsheaddenshaw.co.uk

Entry 376 Map 12

Lancashire   Award winner 2008

The Highwayman
Burrow

Hot on the heels of the Three Fishes at Mitton, the Highwayman is poised to repeat the Fishes' success. In this stylishly revamped old stone inn in the beautiful Lune valley, Nigel Haworth raids the rich borderlands of Cumbria and Yorkshire in his continuing pursuit of good produce; his regional heroes are showcased on the menus and the walls. So look forward to Farmer Sharp's Herdwick mutton pudding, Cumbrian fell-bred rib-eye steak, warm Flookburgh shrimps, and Lancashire curd tart with organic lemon cream. There are a raft of classy wines by the glass and Thwaites Lancaster Bomber on tap. Knowledgeable staff add attentive service to a gloriously informal country interior of stone and wooden floors, eclectic old tables and cosy corners with crackling log fires. For summer: a fantastic terrace and garden.

Meals	12pm-2.30pm; 6pm-9pm (from 5.30pm Sat); 12pm-8.30pm Sun. Main courses £9.50-£16.95.
Closed	Open all day.
Directions	On A683 2 miles south of Kirkby Lonsdale towards Lancaster.

SPECIAL AWARD
see pages 18-19

Local, seasonal & organic produce

Nigel Haworth & Craig Bancroft
The Highwayman,
Burrow, Kirkby Lonsdale LA6 2RJ
Tel   01524 274249
Web   www.highwaymaninn.co.uk

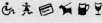

Entry 377 Map 12

Bay Horse Inn
Forton

The Wilkinsons have been in the saddle for a number of years during which their son Craig has become an accomplished chef. Lancashire produces some marvellous ingredients and Craig takes full advantage of them in his modern British cooking – so tuck into fish pie with cheese mash, Bowland lamb hotpot with pickled red cabbage, and roast Lune Valley venison with honey sauce. Although the Bay Horse takes its food seriously and is dedicated to quality (right down to its home-grown herbs and veg) it has not lost sight of its pubbiness; the atmosphere is easy and Moorhouses, Pendle Witches Brew and Black Sheep are on tap. Interconnecting areas are comfortably furnished with a mix of old chairs and cushioned seating in bay windows, the dining room sparkles and the bar is warm and inviting. Gentle background jazz, quirky ephemera and a winter fire add to the mood and the service is friendly and professional. And, in the lovely old Corn Store over the way, are three fabulous bedrooms with bathrooms to match: chic patterned wallpaper, Roberts radios, Arran Aromatics. It couldn't be nicer.

Rooms	3: 2 double, 1 suite. £89-£110.
Meals	12pm-2pm (3pm Sun); 7pm-9.15pm; no food Sun eve.
	Main courses £11.95-£19.95; Sunday lunch £15.95 & £19.95.
Closed	3pm-6.30pm & Mon all day.
Directions	From M6 junc. 33; A6 for Preston, 2nd left; pub on right.

Craig Wilkinson
Bay Horse Inn,
Forton, Lancaster LA2 0HR
Tel   01524 791204
Web   www.bayhorseinn.com

Millstone Hotel
Mellor

Modern meets traditional – this time, in a handsome 18th-century coaching inn in a pretty village on the edge of the Ribble valley. There's a welcoming glow in the bar, with its oak beams and panelling, richly patina'd furniture, grandfather clocks and smart carpeting. Get cosy by the roaring fire with a pint of local Thwaites Bitter and a crispy duck spring roll. Or eat in the welcoming dining room, resplendent with chandeliers, red carpeting and white linen. Local ingredients are carefully sourced – poultry from Goosnargh, lamb from Pendle, shrimps from Morecambe Bay. The food is wholesome and unpretentious, including the chutney that bursts with fruit from Balderstone, served with Eccles cake and crumbly cheese. Then there's Ribblesdale goat's cheese and avocado salad, spiced salmon fishcakes with chilli jam and grilled lime, and Farnsworth of Whalley sausages with black pudding, mash and onion gravy. Bedrooms ooze comfort: sumptuous fabrics and luxurious linen, Roberts radios and plasma TVs, top-spec bathrooms, padded coat hangers, umbrellas for wet days. A marvellously popular inn.

Rooms	23 twins/doubles. £125-£155. Singles £109-£124.
Meals	12pm-9.30pm (9pm Sun). Main courses £8.95-£14.95; set menus £23.95 & £29.95.
Closed	Open all day.
Directions	M6 junc. 31; A59 dir. Clitheroe past British Aerospace; right at r'bout signed Blackburn/Mellor; signs to Mellor.

	Anson Bolton
	Millstone Hotel,
	Church Lane, Mellor BB2 7JR
Tel	01254 813333
Web	www.millstonehotel.co.uk

Entry 379 Map 12

Lancashire

The White Bull
Ribchester

The Ribble babbles through the Bowland Fells, and you can just about make out the remains of the Roman baths in this cobbled corner of Ribchester. A further short stroll brings you to the ancient, stately pub. The moment you enter the grandly pillared door you know you're in for a treat: a warm glow emanates from the gleaming oak bar, the dark beams, the polished brass rail, the fire in the grate. In the cosy snug, two huge old oak tables create an ideal space for a group; and there's a smart pool room with a firmament of stars overhead. The Bells are protégées of celebrity chef (and neighbour) Paul Heathcote, so while Kath pulls pints of Bowland Brewery Hen Harrier and does friendly front of house, Chris concocts simple marvels in the kitchen. Poultry comes from Reg Johnson in Goosnargh, pork and lamb from Pinfold Farm up the road, vegetables from allotments in the village; traceability is key. After all this, a shame not to stay: three very lovely and contemporary bedrooms have crisp linen, top TVs, the odd beam, and sweet views over the village and beyond. Great value.

Rooms	3 doubles. £70. Singles £50.
Meals	12pm-2.30pm; 6pm-9.30pm (12pm-8pm Sun). Main courses £8.50-16.50; Sunday lunch £16.50.
Closed	Mon (open in eve). Open all day.
Directions	A59 from Clitheroe dir. Preston; B6245 signed Longridge until Ribchester.

Chris & Kath Bell
The White Bull,
Church Street, Ribchester,
Blackburn PR3 3XP
Tel   01254 878303
Web   www.whitebullrib.co.uk

Lancashire

The Lunesdale Arms
Tunstall

A soft, wide, undulating valley, the Pennines its backdrop – this is the setting of The Lunesdale Arms. A traditional pub with a fresh, modern feel: Pimms in the summer, mulled wine in the winter, good ales and good cheer. Comfort is deep: big sofas and wood-burning stoves, cushioned settles, newspapers to browse and oil paintings to consider – even to buy. A big central bar separates drinkers (three local cask ales, whiskies and wines) from diners. Sit down to locally reared produce, home-baked bread and seasonal, often organic, vegetables at tables away from the bar. Chef Richard Price delivers wholesome food full of flavour – spinach, pea and mint soup with home-baked bread, roast Cumbrian smoked ham hock with mash and parsley sauce, chocolate brownie – and encourages children to have small portions.

Meals	12pm-2pm (2.30pm Sat & Sun); 6pm-9pm. Main courses £8.50-£14.50; bar meals £4-£14.50.
Closed	3pm-6pm & Mon all day. Open all day Sat.
Directions	M6 junc. 34; A683 for Kirkby Lonsdale.

Emma Gillibrand
The Lunesdale Arms,
Tunstall, Kirkby Lonsdale LA6 2QN
Tel   01524 274203
Web   www.thelunesdale.co.uk

Entry 381 Map 12

Lancashire

The Three Fishes
Mitton

The producers, suppliers and growers are the heroes of this venture, named and proclaimed on the back of every menu; Lancashire is a hotbed of food artisans. The 17th-century village pub in the lovely Ribble Valley is taking gastropubbery to a mouthwatering new level. The long whitewashed public house has been restyled in rustic-smart 21st-century fashion and is vast: up to 130 people inside, a further 60 out. Walls are pale brick, floors stone, furniture sober, lighting subtle and winter logs glow. Wines are gorgeous, local pints and real ciders are served and the beer-friendly food includes ignored but once-popular British delicacies. Delicious are the slow-baked succulent pigs' trotters, the hotpot from heather-reared lamb, the orange and bitter chocolate pudding. Sunday lunch is an institution.

Meals	12pm-2pm; 6pm-9pm (5.30pm-9pm Sat); 12pm-8.30pm Sun. Main courses £8.50-£16.95.
Closed	Open all day.
Directions	From M6 junc. 31 onto A677, then follow A59 into Whalley; B6246 for Great Mitton.

Nigel Haworth & Craig Bancroft
The Three Fishes, Mitton Road,
Mitton, Whalley BB7 8PQ
Tel   01254 826888
Web   www.thethreefishes.com

Entry 382 Map 12

Red Pump Inn
Bashall Eaves

Down meandering lanes in the stunning Ribble valley is this handsome roadside pub, its south-facing terrace tumbled with flowers. In the bar: stone floors, an open fire, richly worn oak settles and tables, books scattered here and there, shuttered windows with green views – the new owners have transformed the old place into a great country inn. Beers include Grindleton Ribble Rouser brewed down the road in Clitheroe; pints are downed by the local shoot during the season. For lunch there are two rooms to choose from: one cosy with dark red walls, the other with stripped pine and a wooden floor. In the evening, sit in the large, beamed, candlelit restaurant. The menu is big in season on local game (with a rare sighting of jugged hare!). There's slow-roasted duck leg with homemade orange marmalade, roasted belly pork in seriously big portions, and their own sausages made with herbs from the garden, served with delicious champ and minted gravy. White-painted bedrooms have chocolate silk bedspreads, luxurious linens, spic and span bathrooms with thick snowy towels. And those glorious views.

Rooms	3 twins/doubles. £70–£85. Singles £50–£70.
Meals	12pm-2pm; 6pm-9pm (12pm-7pm Sun). Main courses £9.50-£17.95; bar meals from £4.50.
Closed	2.30pm-6pm & Mon (except Bank Hols). Open all day Sun.
Directions	From Clitheroe, B6243 following signs to Edisford Bridge. Cross bridge & turn right, signed Bashall Eaves.

	Jonathan & Martina Myerscough
	Red Pump Inn, Clitheroe Road,
	Bashall Eaves, Clitheroe BB7 3DA
Tel	01254 826227
Web	www.theredpumpinn.co.uk

Lancashire

The Freemasons Arms
Wiswell

Nothing fazes Ian Martin. He cooks brilliantly, serves great ales, vintage cognacs and malt whisky, and must have one of the finest wine lists in the country. All this in a tiny pub in a village in Lancashire. Formerly three small cottages, one of which was a freemasons' lodge, its small beamed bars are simply and freshly decorated in green, pink and white with not a flounce in sight – just fresh flowers and modern art. The cooking is equally contemporary, allowing the flavours and textures to speak for themselves. Smoked bacon and lentil soup followed by salmon fishcakes with homemade tartare sauce make for a fantastic value two-course lunch. Potted Goosnargh duck and Bowland ham comes with apple and ale chutney, there are fine cheeses and the vintage clarets – 120 of them – go back 30 years. Extraordinary.

Meals	12pm-2pm; 6pm-9.30pm (12pm-8pm Sun). Main courses £8.95-£16.95.
Closed	3pm-6pm, Mon & Tues all day. Open all day Sun.
Directions	From A59, 2 miles south of Clitheroe, take A671 to Blackburn. After 0.5 miles, 1st left to Wiswell.

Ian Martin
The Freemasons Arms,
8 Vicarage Fold, Wiswell,
Whalley BB7 9DF

Tel   01254 822218

Entry 384 Map 12

Lancashire

Craven Heifer
Chaigley

Walk in on a chilly day after a romp through damp Lancashire fields; the welcome is a warm as the wood-burning stove in the bar. Leave your wellies in the porch and flop into a battered leather sofa with a pint of Golden Trough brewed up the road. The glowing parquet plundered from a church in Liverpool, the undressed stone walls, the specials chalked up on boards and the jugs of fresh flowers – all create a sense of ease. Nick Warfe trained with Pauls Heathcote and Rankin, and locally sourced ingredients are thoughtfully prepared. Ham and Lancashire cheese risotto with rocket pesto arrives steaming and fragrant, with a good glass of wine from the impressive list. Polish it all off with pan-fried spotted dog with vanilla ice cream, then venture out into the rolling hills outside the door.

Meals	12pm-2.30pm; 6pm-9pm (Breakfast 11am-12pm; 12pm-8pm Sun). Main courses £8.50-£16.50; Sunday lunch £18.
Closed	Mon & Tues. Open all day Sun.
Directions	M6 exit 31A Longridge; signs for Chipping (Trough of Bowland); before Chipping, right for Chaigley. Right at end, right again; 500 yds.

Nick & Ali Wharf
Craven Heifer, Chipping Road,
Chaigley, Clitheroe BB7 3LX

Tel   01254 826215
Web   www.cravenheiferchaigley.co.uk

Entry 385 Map 12

Lancashire

Assheton Arms
Downham

Assheton is the family name of the Lords of Clitheroe and Downham is their village. In the best traditions of country life, the pub stands opposite the church – the community's hub. The rambling, low-beamed bar bustles more often than not with village regulars and hikers ruddy from exertion; it's just below Pendle Hill. Diners drop by for the fresh oysters, the moules and frites, the pan-fried monkfish and the hearty puddings. Plenty of regional dishes on offer too with Lancashire hotpot, Morecambe Bay shrimps and a Lancashire cheese platter. The atmosphere of an old inn has been preserved, right down to the majestic stone fireplace and the horse brasses on the walls. Sit at solid oak tables on wing-back settles and bask in the absence of electronic games. In summer the front terrace entices you with pastoral views.

Meals	12pm-2pm (2.30pm Sun in winter); 7pm-9.30pm; 12pm-9pm Sun in summer. Main courses £8.50-£15.50.
Closed	3pm-7pm. Open all day Sat & Sun.
Directions	Off A59, 3 miles NE of Clitheroe.

David Busby
Assheton Arms,
Downham, Clitheroe BB7 4BJ

Tel	01200 441227
Web	www.assheton-arms.co.uk

Entry 386 Map 12

Lancashire

The Inn at Whitewell
Whitewell

The old deerkeeper's lodge sits just above the river Hodder with views across parkland to rising fells in the distance. Merchants used to stop by and fill up with wine, food and song before heading north through notorious bandit country. Now barbours and muddy dogs mix with posh frocks and suits. You can eat in the bar but the long restaurant and the outside terrace drink in the view – which will only increase your enjoyment of Bowland lamb with cassoulet of beans and root vegetables, homemade ice cream and fine wines (including their own well-priced Vintner's). In the bar, antiques, bric-a-brac, peat fires, old copies of *The Beano*, fish and chips, warm crab cakes and local bangers. At weekends it get packed; if you want a table, the more formal restaurant takes bookings. A perfect place.

Meals	12pm-2pm; 7.30pm-9.30pm. Main courses £8-£13.75 (bar) £14-£23 (restaurant); bar meals from £3.65-£8.50.
Closed	Open all day.
Directions	M6 junc. 31a, B6243 east through Longridge, then follow signs to Whitewell for 9 miles.

Charles Bowman
The Inn at Whitewell,
Whitewell, Clitheroe BB7 3AT

Tel	01200 448222
Web	www.innatwhitewell.com

Entry 387 Map 12

Lancashire

Mulberry Tree
Wrightington

A big jewel in Lancashire's crown, with a Wrightington-born chef who headed the kitchen at Le Gavroche, the Mulberry Tree is a vast, rambling place with a fresh, modern look to match the cooking. There's a smart lounge with a long bar, a private dining room and an open-plan eating area – subtly lit, softly hued, warmly carpeted. Whether you order something simple like rump steak with pepper sauce from the bar, or book for a serious meal, you'll be impressed by the presentation and the finesse. Start with Tuscan white bean soup with pesto, move onto breast of wood pigeon with wild mushrooms and rich merlot sauce. Lush puddings include bread and butter pudding with apricot coulis, and rhum baba with chantilly cream. Chef-patron Mark Prescott's verve in the kitchen makes this one of the best gastropubs in the north-west.

Meals	12pm-3pm; 5pm-9.30pm (12pm-10pm Sat & Sun). Main courses £14.95-£19.95; bar meals £5.50-£14.95; Sunday roast £14.50 & £18.
Closed	3pm-6pm. Open all day Sat & Sun.
Directions	M6 junc. 27; B5250 for Eccleston; 2 miles, on right.

Mark Prescott
Mulberry Tree,
9 Wrightington Bar, Wrightington,
Wigan WN6 9SE

Tel   01257 451400

Entry 388 Map 11

Lancashire

The Eagle & Child
Bispham Green

There's an old-fashioned pubbiness here *and* a sense of style – an informality touched with zing. The candlelit main bar welcomes you in with its rug-strewn flagged floors, hop-decked beams and open fire; another room has hessian carpeting and burgundy walls; another, as engaging, and cosy, a cast-iron fireplace. Hand pumps line the bar (with beers from lesser-known brewers like Beartown Brewery) while the shelves parade an army of malts and the wine cellar has some fine offerings. The staff seem to enjoy themselves as much as the customers and the food has won awards; there's Lancashire hotpot, roast suckling pig with apple and cider gravy, partridge with porcini and madeira sauce. The pub's reputation lies, too, with its cask ales, and the beer festival in May packs the place out. Marvellous.

Meals	12pm-2pm; 5.30pm-8.30pm (9pm Fri & Sat); 12pm-8.30pm Sun. Main courses £10-£16.50; bar meals £3.75-£7.
Closed	3pm-5.30pm. Open all day Sun.
Directions	From M6 junc. 27, A5209 for Parbold; right along B5246; left for Bispham Green. Pub in 0.5 miles.

Martin Ainscough
The Eagle & Child, Malt Kiln Lane,
Bispham Green, Ormskirk L40 3SG

Tel   01539 561010
Web   www.ainscoughs.co.uk

Entry 389 Map 11

Leicestershire

The Queen's Head
Belton

Take a village pub by the scruff of its neck and renovate it from top to toe. The result: a cool, relaxed drinkers' bar, all leather sofas, blond wood and low-slung tables, a bistro with a welcoming fire and a dining room of wood, suede and leather, with a canopied al fresco extension. Add spacious, spotless and warmly carpeted bedrooms with a similarly stylish feel and you have a well-nigh perfect coaching inn. (The bedrooms are reached via a discreet door at the side.) The Weldons deserve applause for not losing sight of tradition: the Queen's Head serves its own beer from the local Wicked Hathern brewery, plus outstanding wines. Printed menus and blackboard dishes point to diverse ideas that are beautifully executed, from burgers and relish in the bar to roasted scallops with langoustine risotto, beef fillet with morel mushroom sauce, divine puddings and a good value set menu in the restaurant. Watch out for the summer Real Ale and Gourmet Barbecue weekend, and the Champagne and Lobster night. Lovely staff, too.

Rooms	6: 4 doubles; 2 twins sharing bath. £70–£100. Singles £65.
Meals	12pm–2.30pm (4pm Sun); 7pm–9.30pm (10pm Fri & Sat). Main courses £13.50–£19.50; bar meals £4–£9.50; set menu £12–£16; Sunday lunch £13 & £16.
Closed	3pm–7pm; Sun from 5pm.
Directions	In Belton, just off B5234, 6 miles west of Loughborough.

Henry & Ali Weldon
The Queen's Head,
2 Long Street, Belton,
Loughborough LE12 9TP

Tel	01530 222359
Web	www.thequeenshead.org

Entry 390 Map 8

Leicestershire

The Cow & Plough
Oadby

A pub-restaurant housed in the former milking sheds of a working farm. The Lounts founded it in 1989 and filled it with good beer and a hoard of brewery memorabilia: the two back bars are stuffed with period signs, mirrors and bottles. It later became an outlet for their range of Steamin' Billy ales (named after Elizabeth's Jack Russell who 'steamed' after energetic country pursuits). When the foot and mouth epidemic closed the farm's visitor centre, they established a restaurant there instead. Most of their dishes are made with local produce such as rib-eye steak with red wine, chestnut and thyme sauce and honey-glazed Tamworth ham. The pub has built up a great reputation, winning awards and becoming a place for shooting lunches. And there's a conservatory with piano and plants and beams decked with dried hops.

Meals	12pm-3pm (5pm Sun); 6pm-9pm; no food Sun & Mon eve. Main courses £7.75-£16.95; Sunday lunch £14.95 & £16.95; bar meals £4.95-£10.95.
Closed	3pm-5pm. Open all day Sat & Sun.
Directions	On B667 north of town centre & A6.

	Barry Lount
	The Cow & Plough,
	Stoughton Farm Park, Oadby,
	Leicester LE2 2FB
Tel	0116 272 0852
Web	www.steamin-billy.co.uk

Entry 391 Map 8

Leicestershire

Red Lion Inn
Stathern

Quirky stylishness and cheerful service. The rambling Red Lion feels like a home, with its books and papers, deep sofas and open fires; gamekeepers frequent the flagstoned bar. A trusted network of growers and suppliers fills the kitchen with game from the Belvoir estate, cheeses from the local dairy, fruits and vegetables from nearby farms. Menus are on blackboards, with a choice that leaps between fashion and tradition: potted prawns and melba toast; village-made sausages with mustard mash; pan-fried halibut with squid ink linguine, olives, pine nuts and saffron dressing; chocolate and pecan pie with apple and cinnamon ice cream. The set Sunday lunch is great value. The wine list is imaginative; beers include village-brewed Brewsters Bonnie and children have homemade lemonade. The outdoor play area will please them, too.

Meals	12pm-2pm (3pm Sun); 7pm-9.30pm. Main courses £10.50-£17.50; Sunday lunch £16.50.
Closed	3pm-6pm; all day Mon & Sun from 6.30pm. Open all day Fri & Sat.
Directions	Off A607 north east of Melton Mowbray; through Stathern; past Plough; pub signed on left.

	Ben Jones & Sean Hope
	Red Lion Inn,
	Red Lion Street, Stathern LE14 4HS
Tel	01949 860868
Web	www.theredlioninn.co.uk

Entry 392 Map 9

Leicestershire

The Manners Arms
Knipton

The Duke and Duchess of Rutland are the landlords of this village inn, a pint's throw from the family seat at Belvoir Castle. It's their local too. The pub was originally built as a hunting lodge and so is no stranger to playing host to an array of guests. The Beaters Bar is rustic rural with Windsor chairs, log fire and polished boards; the Red Coats Restaurant is more intimate with swagged floral fabrics and deep red walls; and the pristine bedrooms, each with its own décor, are smartly feminine, the furnishings having been chosen by the Duchess herself. Each is named after family members past and present. Menus are seasonal, the produce sourced locally, much of it from the estate, and children get half portions at half price: brilliant. Although the style is traditional the young team here have been innovative in their thinking, with inventive dishes on the menu and jolly jazz barbecues in the summer months. Breakfast is served in a rather lovely conservatory opening to a sun terrace – a delightful spot for afternoon tea.

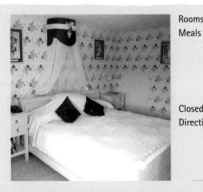

Rooms	10: 8 doubles, 2 singles. £55–£120.
Meals	12pm-3pm; 6pm-9pm (12pm-9pm Sat; 8pm Sun). Main courses £15.95-£21.95; bar meals £4.95-£14.50; lunch, 2 courses, £12.95; Sunday lunch £15.95.
Closed	Open all day.
Directions	From A607 Grantham to Leicester road, follow Knipton signs from Croxton Kerrial.

Alex Grainger
The Manners Arms,
Croxton Road, Knipton,
Grantham NG32 1RH

Tel	01476 879222
Web	www.mannersarms.com

Entry 393 Map 9

Leicestershire

Tollemache Arms
Buckminster

Awards have been won for the food at this imposing Victorian inn in an estate village on the Lincolnshire border. But make no mistake, the Tollemache is still an inn. As the chef-patron says in his book of recipes, "If we have a dozen ladies lunching, it's a restaurant; if the locals are filling the bar on a Friday night it's a pub. Often it's both." Real ales are from Grainstore in Oakham and much of what lands on your plate comes via local shoots, like seared hare loin with figs steeped in mulled wine. Or their take on fast food: pigeon breast on toast with onion marmalade and a sauce of port and red wine. This is served in a restaurant/brasserie setting, smartly set about with high-back chairs and hide sofas, polished floorboards, modern works of art and tables set well apart.

Leicestershire

The Old Barn
Glooston

This is in prime hunting country and delightfully tranquil – old stone cottages opposite; church and rectory next door. The lane itself, a dead-end, is variously named Andrew Lane, Cow Lane, Main Street, Gartree Road and Adelphi Row. And the Old Barn comes into sight. No hint of what lies inside. Gnarled oak timbers, a blackened range, walls in contemporary pastels and creams: enter a front bar where light lunches, old world wines and a pint of Greene King Abbot are served. A step down is the cellar restaurant, crisp with white linen, fresh flowers and real fire. Choose from traditional dishes such as local game casserole, beef wellington or Lincolnshire pork cutlet with stilton, fig and cider jus. It's a concise menu prepared to order, and served by a friendly staff.

Meals	12pm-2pm; 6.30pm-9pm
	Main courses £9.50-£14;
	set menu £10 & £14.
Closed	3pm-6pm; Sun eve & Mon all day.
Directions	4 miles west of A1 on
	B676 towards Melton Mowbray.

Meals	12pm-2pm (4pm Sun);
	6pm-9.30pm; no food Mon.
	Main courses £9.95-18.95;
	bar meals £4.95-£9.95.
Closed	3pm-6pm.
Directions	From B6047 at Tur Langton follow
	signs to Cranoe, then fork left
	after 1.5 miles to Glooston.

	Mark Gough
	Tollemache Arms,
	48 Main Street, Buckminster,
	Melton Mowbray NG33 5SA
Tel	01476 860007
Web	www.thetollemachearms.com

♿ 🕴 📧 🐾 🍷

Entry 394 Map 9

	Guy Oliver
	The Old Barn,
	Main Street, Glooston,
	Market Harborough LE16 7ST
Tel	01858 545215

🕴 📧 🐾 🍷

Entry 395 Map 9

Leicestershire

The Baker's Arms
Thorpe Langton

A sleepy-village treasure with oodles of atmosphere beneath 16th-century thatch. A series of intimate little areas have been kitted out with cottagey scrubbed pine tables, antique pews and settles, paintings and prints on warm terracotta walls. The Baker's is more foodie than boozy though the pubbiness remains and if you're looking for a pint of Baker's Dozen you won't be disappointed. But most come for Kate Hubbard's first-rate cooking (do book) and use of impeccable produce. Chalked up daily on the boards are pan-fried scallops with a honey, mustard and lemon dressing, confit of duck leg and breast with parsnip and apple compote, baked sea bass with spinach, mushrooms and prawn jus, white chocolate and raspberry trifle. Wines, too, are good, and may come mulled in winter. Great staff make the Baker's Arms close to perfect.

Meals	12pm-2.30pm Sat & Sun; 6.30pm-9.30pm (6pm-9.30pm Sat). Main courses £11.50-£18.50.
Closed	All day Mon; Tues-Fri lunch; Sat 2.30pm-6pm & Sun eve.
Directions	On A6, 10 miles south of Leicester.

Kate Hubbard
The Baker's Arms, Thorpe Langton,
Market Harborough LE16 7TS
Tel   01858 545201
Web   www.thebakersarms.co.uk

Entry 396 Map 9

Lincolnshire

The Chequers Inn
Woolsthorpe-by-Belvoir

A coaching inn for 200 years, the Chequers has built a reputation as a top dining pub in recent years. There's contemporary luxury and deep comfort, a flurry of open fireplaces, three dining areas and two bars, rug-strewn floors, heavy oak tables, leather sofas, linen drapes and Farrow & Ball colours. You have two ales on hand pump, 30 wines by the glass, 50 whiskies, several fruit pressés and a humidor on the bar. Robust dishes – clam, squid and salmon risotto, calves' liver with mash, bacon and onion marmalade, chocolate tart with bitter orange sorbet – taste as good as they look, the weekday evening menu is a steal (three courses, £15). In summer the pub hosts the village cricket team on what must be one of the slopiest pitches in England. The Vale of Belvoir and its grand castle are as beautiful as they sound.

Meals	12pm-2.30pm (4pm Sun); 6pm-9.30pm (8.30pm Sun). Main courses £9.50-£19; bar meals £4.95-£8.95; Sunday lunch £10.95; set lunch £11.50 & £15.
Closed	3pm-5.30pm. Open all day Sat & Sun.
Directions	Off A52, west of Grantham.

Justin & Joanne Chad
The Chequers Inn, Main Street,
Woolsthorpe-by-Belvoir,
Grantham NG32 1LU
Tel   01476 870701
Web   www.chequers-inn.net

Entry 397 Map 9

Houblon Inn
Oasby

The word 'civilised' springs to mind, as befits the pedigree of the place. The pub is named after one of the landowners in the area, John Houblon, first governor of the Bank of England – you'll find him honoured on the back of the £50 note. Hollyhocks round the door and pretty sash windows greet you; low beams, stone walls and a crackling fire wait inside. 'Houblon' is also Flemish for 'hop' and ale-lovers will not be disappointed. Craft-brews Belly Dance, Oldershaw Old Boy and Surrender will take your fancy as you perch at the bar and scan the simple yet stylish menu – moules marinières; lamb rump with roast shallots; apple and pear crumble. Owner Hazel makes this pub special; quietly passionate about the place, she left 'the smoke' years ago and thrives on the business. Outside is a gravel garden dotted with good wooden furniture and parasols; across the courtyard, in a converted barn, are four cosy, peaceful and well-equipped bedrooms. Bang in the middle of a conservation village, the Houblon Inn is honest, unaffected and intelligently run.

Rooms	4: 3 doubles, 1 twin. £60-£70. Singles £40-£45.
Meals	12pm-2pm; 6.30pm-9.30pm; no food Sun eve. Main courses £6.95-£16.95; bar meals £4.50-£9.95.
Closed	2pm-6.30pm (3pm-7pm Sun) & Mon (open bank hol lunch).
Directions	From A1, B6703 to Ancaster; right to Welby, follow road to Oasby.

Hazel Purvis
Houblon Inn,
Oasby, Grantham NG32 3NB
Tel　01529 455215
Web　www.houblon-inn.co.uk

Lincolnshire

Brownlow Arms
Hough-on-the-Hill

Standing proudly in the centre of a hilltop village, this magnificent building is said to have been the servants' quarters to the Manor. Now it has the feel of an intimate country house. Winged Queen Anne chairs in autumnal hues invite you to settle in by the open fire amid deep rich oak beams and polished panelling; regulars sup Marstons Burton ale as chatter flows around the central bar. In the intimate restaurant, the food, revealing a French classical influence, is accomplished as befits such a setting – soufflés, foie gras, duck confit, panache of pink bream. Desserts range from refreshing rhubarb parfait to comforting jam roly-poly. It's blowy up here with idyllic open countryside all around but there is a sheltered, landscaped terrace for a quiet pint and an early supper. The mood of baronial elegance continues upstairs with four superb bedrooms that reveal sumptuous fabrics and drench showers. Note that this is very much a grown-ups place, not suitable for under 14s – and make sure when using the car park you don't park in the neighbours' drive!

Rooms	4 doubles. £96. Singles £65.
Meals	6.30pm-9.30pm Tues-Sat; Sun lunch 12pm-2pm. Main courses £13.95-£22.50.
Closed	Tues-Sat lunch, Sun eve & Mon all day.
Directions	On A607 6 miles north of Grantham.

Paul & Lorraine Willoughby
Brownlow Arms,
High Road, Hough-on-the-Hill,
Grantham NG32 2AZ

Tel	01400 250234
Web	www.thebrownlowarms.com

Lincolnshire

Wig & Mitre
Lincoln

Three decades on, Michael, Valerie and the pub are still here, sandwiched between the cathedral and the courts. (They could have called it the Mitre & Wig: though lawyers dine here, the first pint was drawn by the Bishop.) Downstairs has a French café feel: old oak boards, exposed stone, sofas to the side – a civilised place for late breakfast and the papers. Upstairs, a cosy series of dining rooms and an open fire. In the Seventies it was hard to find decent food in a pub, let alone one in Lincoln. Valerie's kitchen became one of the most exciting in the area, serving a mix of dishes – was this the first gastropub? Today there are dishes like braised blade of beef with mustard mash, and pan-fried pork fillet with black pudding and celeriac purée. More restaurant than pub, there are also some excellent wines.

Meals	8am-11pm.
	Main courses £9.95-£21.95.
Closed	Open all day.
Directions	On Steep Hill just down from the Cathedral.

Michael & Valerie Hope
Wig & Mitre,
32 Steep Hill, Lincoln LN2 1LU
Tel   01522 535190
Web   www.wigandmitre.com

Entry 400 Map 9

Lincolnshire

The Bluebell
Belchford

High in the Wolds, amid the vast openness of the Lincolnshire farms, is the Bluebell in Belchford – warmth and cosiness hit you as you enter. To a traditional backdrop of deep polished oak is a bar sporting chintz curtains with neat ties, floral sofas and wing-back chairs; in one of two dining areas are gilt-framed oil paintings on deep red walls, in the other, an airy modernity. They're proud of their food here, and so they should be: almost all the produce is locally sourced (Lincolnshire Red beef, fish from Grimsby). At lunch there are filled ciabattas and beef and guinness pie, while things step up a gear at dinner with dishes such as charred calves' liver with roast garlic mash. It's as friendly as can be and as cosy as a steamed sponge pudding with custard – and you might tuck into one of those, too.

Meals	11.30am-2.30pm; 6.30pm-9.30pm
	(12pm-4pm Sun).
	Main courses £9.95-£17.
Closed	3pm-6pm; Sun eve & Mon.
Directions	Village signed off A153 between Horncastle & Louth.

Darren & Shona Jackson
The Bluebell,
Main Road, Belchford,
Horncastle LN9 6LQ
Tel   01507 533602

Entry 401 Map 9

London

Swag & Tails
Knightsbridge

Down a pretty mews in one of the smartest spots in town, the little pub with black shutters and well-clipped topiary is an easy walk – even in your Manolos – from the Harvey Nichols-Harrods drag. Escape the crowds and rest weary feet in the warm, yellow-and-blue interior where wooden floors and swagged curtains make a fresh and glamorous alternative to the heavy trimmings of your usual Knightsbridge boozer. The tiled conservatory at the back is a delightful spot in which to tuck into seared king scallops with lemon dill sauce or roast venison with crushed sweet potatoes; the food is stylish, modern and very good. Staff are full of smiles and, if it takes an explorer to find this little place, the wonderful photograph of Nare's Arctic expedition of 1875 is a fitting first reward for your perseverance.

Meals	12pm-3pm; 6pm-10pm. Main courses £10.95-£15.95; bar meals £5.25-£9.95.
Closed	Open all day. Closed Sat & Sun.
Directions	Nearest tube: Knightsbridge.

Annemaria Boomer-Davies
Swag & Tails, 10-11 Fairholt Street,
Knightsbridge SW7 1EG

Tel	020 7584 6926
Web	www.swagandtails.com

Entry 402 Map 4

London

The Thomas Cubitt
Belgravia

As well-upholstered as Belgravia itself. The handsome ground-floor bar has high ceilings, oak-block floors, tall windows that open to tables in the street, and a bit of panelling thrown in for good measure. A cords and cashmere crowd is drawn by the classic country-house feel, the real ales, the superb wines, and the kitchen, which puts more thought into what it produces than many a full-blown restaurant. In the bar is a reassuring selection of pub favourites – organic beef burgers, grilled sausages with roasted red onion gravy and buttery mash – and the organic Sunday roasts are fabulous. In the über-elegant dining room upstairs the food is fiercely modern (take sea bass with fennel, and a caviar and chive velouté). It's popular, and the friendliness of the staff, even under pressure, is a pleasure.

Meals	Bar: 12pm-11pm. Restaurant: 12pm-3pm (Mon-Fri); 6pm-11pm. Main courses £9.50-£14.50; bar meal from £6.
Closed	Bar open all day. Restaurant closed Sun.
Directions	Nearest tubes: Victoria; Sloane Square.

Ryan Moses
The Thomas Cubitt, 44 Elizabeth St,
Belgravia SW1W 9PA

Tel	020 7730 6060
Web	www.thethomascubitt.co.uk

Entry 403 Map 4

London

Duke of Wellington
Marylebone

An unexpected London find – in a charming backstreet in Marylebone. Until recently it was looking tired, even exhausted; now The Duke is a funky little gastropub. The light, spacious single bar has hung on to its boarded floor, ornate ceiling (painted a deep blood red) and dark wood bar, while a wall of gilt framed mirrors and modern artworks create a bohemian feel (check out the glitter-encrusted bust of the Iron Duke on your way to the loo). While Fuller's London Pride is one of two real ales on tap, the Duke's reputation now rests on its food. The style is robust modern British and the ingredients are the freshest: carrot and coriander soup with cumin, chargrilled 45-day aged rump of beef with mustard and tarragon butter. Upstairs is a wonderfully intimate dining room with a slightly extended menu.

London

The Builders Arms
Chelsea

Who would expect such a tasty little pub in the back streets off the King's Road? The country living room feel is so seductive you could happily move in. So settle back with a glass of proscecco or a pint of London Pride among worn leather sofas and mixmatched chairs, board games and books, soft green walls and a ruby-red snug behind the bar. 'Never trust a builder without a tattoo' reads the sign on the wall, but you won't find many builders in The Builders: it's stylish at heart (even if labelling the loos 'Builders' and 'Ballerinas' is a touch twee). The food is delicious modern British and well presented: pea and ham soup, roast salmon and basil risotto, and peppered sirloin steak with wilted spinach and mash. The area is a shoppers' dream but don't expect a table on Friday lunchtimes: it's packed!

Meals	12pm-3pm (4pm Sat & Sun); 6.30pm-10pm (7pm-9pm Sun). Main courses £12.50-£16 (bar), £13-£19.75 (restaurant).
Closed	Open all day.
Directions	Nearest tube: Marylebone.

Meals	12pm-2.30pm (4pm weekends); 7pm-10pm Mon-Weds; 7pm-11pm Thurs-Sat; 7pm-9pm Sun. Main courses £8-£15.
Closed	Open all day.
Directions	Nearest tubes: Sloane Square; South Kensington. Behind King's Road, between Sydney Street & Chelsea Green.

Jamie Prudom
Duke of Wellington,
94a Crawford Street,
Marylebone W1H 2HQ
Tel   020 7723 2790

Entry 404 Map 4

Rupert Clevely
The Builders Arms,
13 Britten Street, Chelsea SW3 3TY
Tel   020 7349 9040
Web   www.geronimo-inns.co.uk

Entry 405 Map 4

London

Chelsea Ram
Chelsea

A quiet residential street off the Lots Road seems an unlikely place to find a corner pub bursting with bonhomie. It used to be a junk shop; now the fine arched shop windows with etched glass are complemented by soft greens and terracottas, a dark green wooden bar and local art. A carpeted area to the back has small alcoves, soft lighting and thumbed books – an intimate spot for some enticing food. Salmon fishcakes with crab and citrus bisque, perhaps, or confit duck leg on roasted garlic mash and braised red cabbage, all great value. Scrubbed tables see lively card games (bring your own) over coffee, chirpy staff run a fast-paced bar. Close to the large storage depot of Bonhams the auctioneers, this much-loved pub is worth the few minutes' walk from the end of the King's Road.

London

The Atlas
Fulham

Up high, golden letters on wooden panelling proclaim London Stout, Burton Bitter and mild ales. The Atlas is a great little place in which to delve into more modern brews: Fuller's London Pride, Caledonian Deuchars IPA, Adnams Broadside. A glazed wooden partition divides the bar in two, and other Thirties' features remain: floorboards, attractive black and white tiling around the foot of the bar and three brick fireplaces, two of which add a glow in winter. The third has been converted into a serving hatch for superb dishes that change twice a day – grilled sardines and Tuscan sausages, pot-roast poussin – and the wine list trumpets 24 wines by the glass. Doors lead to a walled beer garden where folk flock under the rain cover. Great atmosphere, great food, great staff – a genuine cracker.

Meals	12pm-3pm (4pm Sun); 6.30pm-10pm (9pm Sun). Main courses £9-£14.50.
Closed	Open all day.
Directions	Nearest tubes: Fulham Broadway; Sloane Square.

Meals	12.30pm-3pm (4pm Sun); 7pm-10.30pm (10pm Sun). Main courses £9.50-£14; bar meals £4.50-£8.
Closed	Open all day.
Directions	Nearest tube: West Brompton.

James Symington
Chelsea Ram,
32 Burnaby Street,
Chelsea SW10 0PL

Tel   020 7351 4008

Entry 406 Map 4

**George & Richard Manners
& Toby Ellis**
The Atlas, 16 Seagrave Road,
Fulham SW6 1RX

Tel   020 7385 9129
Web   www.theatlaspub.co.uk

Entry 407 Map 4

London

The Carpenter's Arms
Hammersmith

An unexpected find: an extraordinary distillation of gastropub and local in a charming backwater between King Street and the Great West Road (aka the A4). The glorious single bar has fashionably bare boards, plain tables, a fire that glows on chilly days and doors giving onto a sheltered little garden. And it's done well for itself, being a popular spot for a discerning mix while managing (just) to hold on to its pubby feel, in spite of the emphasis on dining. An ever-changing seasonal menu sees inventive dishes popping up every day. So you get seared scallops with butterbeans, pine nuts and saffron; rib-eye steak with fries and café de Paris butter; apple tart 'fine' with nutmeg ice cream. Service is exuberant and warm, the atmosphere is laid back. It's a satisfying place to dine.

London

Cat's Back
Putney

Down a backstreet, away from waterside development, a gem. There's an appealing eccentricity here, among the cosy-red walls, mix 'n' match tables, African masks, disco glitter ball, portrait of Audrey Hepburn and all manner of flotsam and jetsam – presents from regulars and treasures picked up on the family's travels. It's mellow and fun and everyone and his dog pops by – locals, builders, business folk. At night, moody candlelight, chilled music and good food. The wines are better than the beers but you may expect excellent organic meats and vegetables – try shrimp tempura with oyster sauce and roast shoulder of pork, finish with tiramisu. Coloured lights in the stairwell lead to a lovely sash-windowed restaurant and a small but lavish private dining room beyond. Friendly and much-loved.

Meals	12pm-3pm (4pm Sun); 7pm-10pm (7.30pm-9.30pm Sun). Main courses £8.75-£15.
Closed	Open all day.
Directions	Between King Street & the A4; nearest tube Stanford Brook.

Meals	11am-10.30pm. Main courses £8.50-£11.50; bar meals from £4.50.
Closed	Open all day.
Directions	Nearest tube: Putney.

Simon Cherry & Matt Jacomb
The Carpenter's Arms,
91 Black Lion Lane,
Hammersmith W6 9BG
Tel   0871 703 2881

Entry 408 Map 4

Roger Martin
Cat's Back, 86 Point Pleasant,
Putney SW18 1NN
Tel   020 8877 0818
Web   www.thecatsback.com

Entry 409 Map 4

London

Spencer Arms
Putney

They fly the Slow Food flag here – with passion. And it's all so delicious: the roast rainbow trout, the rib-eye steak, the ham hock risotto, the 'British tapas' (venison carpaccio, potted shrimps). The lamb is from Cornwall because it tastes nicer and they love their chutneys; take some home. The stage for all this good humour is a pretty Victorian tavern with a big open room of sturdy tables and painted boards, a blackboard of wines and a sofa by the fire. Add bookshelves and games chest, chilled music for quieter moments, tailor-made orders for unfaddy children and cider punch with calvados and you have one amazing place. The staff are brilliant and chef Adrian Jones (ex Shibden Mill) cycles 20 miles along the river to work each day, such is his enthusiasm. Finish it off with a walk on Barnes Common.

London

The Ship
Wandsworth

Drinking a pint of Young's Special next to a concrete works doesn't sound too enticing, but the riverside terrace by Wandsworth Bridge is a dreamy spot. Chilly evenings still draw the crowds to this super old pub, cosy inside with its warm-red and sage-green walls, and its conservatory with central chopping-board table and wood-burning stove. No music, just happy chat, newspapers, tall blackboards and fresh flowers. Chef Peter Murray sources fresh ingredients to create his seasonal menus which may include crispy pork belly braised oriental style with pak choi, potato spaghetti rösti and star anise jus, or tian of Portobello mushrooms, red onions, mixed peppers and herb cream sauce. The Ship opens its arms to all, there are live music and quiz nights, and families merrily gather in summer.

Meals	12pm-2.30pm (3pm Sat; 4pm Sun); 6.30pm-10pm (9pm Sun). Main courses £7.50-£17.50; bar meals & tapas from £3.50.
Closed	Open all day.
Directions	Nearest rail: Putney; Barnes.

Meals	12pm-10pm. Main courses £9.95-£19.95.
Closed	Open all day.
Directions	Nearest rail: Wandsworth.

Jamie Sherriff
Spencer Arms,
237 Lower Richmond Rd,
Putney SW15 1HJ
Tel 020 8788 0640
Web www.thespencerarms.co.uk

Entry 410 Map 4

Oisin Rogers
The Ship, Jews Row,
Wandsworth SW18 1TB
Tel 020 8870 9667
Web www.theship.co.uk

Entry 411 Map 4

London

The Fentiman Arms
Kennington

Toffee-coloured walls, a relaxed mood, well-thumbed books and games: a decent place to nurse a hangover on a Saturday morning, along with the Fentiman brunch menu. This busy pub, designed by proprietor Rupert Clevely's wife Jo, echoes the cosmopolitan themes and earthy colours of their beloved South Africa. Smart regulars gather over pints of Bombardier and a menu that stretches beyond the confines of brunch. Chicken liver parfait with red onion marmalade, braised pork belly with apricot and thyme potato rösti, and date and walnut slice with rum ice cream are devoured in cosy corners amongst fat velvet cushions and suede bolsters. The upstairs function room, with high ceilings and large windows, is a popular place for big gatherings; so too is the trendy outdoor terrace. Arrive early on Sundays.

Meals	12pm-3pm (4pm Sat); 6.30pm-10pm (10.30pm Fri & Sat; 12.30pm-9pm Sun). Main courses £7.95-£13.95.
Closed	Open all day.
Directions	Nearest tubes: Oval; Vauxhall.

Rupert Clevely
The Fentiman Arms,
64 Fentiman Road,
Kennington SW8 1LA
Tel   020 7793 9796
Web   www.geronimo-inns.co.uk

Entry 412 Map 4

London

The Garrison Public House
Bermondsey

Do dinner and a movie – there's a cinema downstairs for private hire, and a great little restaurant up. Gastropub veterans Clive Watson and Adam White have taken on an old boozer, kept the engraved glass windows and remodelled the rest into a light, airy, bare-boarded space. The furniture is silver-sprayed, lamps and objects fill every cranny. Fresh food, from apricots to Orkney mussels, arrives from the market down the road. A glass of rioja or a bottle of St Peter's goes down beautifully with rib-eye steak with watercress and roquefort butter, or seabass with crab and baked potatoes. And the pub is open daily for breakfast. The kitchen is open, staff are laid-back, decibels are high, tables are crammed. Forget hushed conversation: the place bounces with bonhomie. More eaterie than pub.

Meals	8am-11.30am, 12pm-3.30pm, 6.30pm-10pm Mon-Fri; 9am-11.30am, 12.30pm-4pm, 6.30pm-10pm Sat (6pm-9.30pm Sun). Main courses £9.80-£16.
Closed	Open all day.
Directions	Nearest tube: London Bridge.

Clive Watson & Adam White
The Garrison Public House,
99 Bermondsey St,
Bermondsey SE1 3XB
Tel   020 7089 9355
Web   www.thegarrison.co.uk

Entry 413 Map 4

London

Anchor & Hope
Southwark

One of the first bistropubs to champion below-stairs food. Come for some of the plainest yet gutsiest cooking in London; chef Jonathan Jones attracts droves. The food is described as 'English bistro', and give or take the odd foreign exception (a chorizo broth, a melting pommes dauphinoise), it is just that. The menu is adventurous yet striking in its simplicity: warm snail and bacon salad, smoked herring with fennel and orange, slip soles with anchovy butter, rabbit with pearl barley and sherry, homemade liqueurs, blackberry merangue. The beer comes from Charles Wells, the wine list has 18 by the glass. Staff are youthful – and may be rushed. Décor is 1930s sober and the restaurant area glows by candlelight. No bookings (bar Sunday lunch) and massively popular, but arrive early or late and you may get a table.

Meals	12pm-2.30pm; 6pm-10.30pm; Sun 2pm (bookings only). Main courses £10-£20; Sunday lunch £30.
Closed	Mon lunch & Sun eve. Open all day Tues-Sat.
Directions	Nearest tubes: Southwark; Waterloo.

Robert Shaw
Anchor & Hope,
36 The Cut,
Southwark SE1 8LP
Tel   020 7928 9898

Entry 414 Map 4

London

Greenwich Union
Greenwich

Master brewer Alastair Hook has turned this Greenwich boozer into a shrine to his lagers and beers. The golds and browns of the interior reflect the hues of the ales he painstakingly creates at the nearby Meantime Brewery; the Red, White, Golden, Amber and Chocolate beers slip down so easily that Sainsbury's has made them part of their range. (If you're not sure which pairs with which food, helpful staff behind the bar will give you a taster.) And this quirky little pub is a great place to eat, the chef willing to concoct tapas at short notice. He is also a dab hand at roasted chicken breast with sweet shallots, and chestnut gnocchi with porcini mushrooms. Sandwiches include homemade 'piadina' (flat bread from Romagna) served with brie and rocket salad. All are welcome, from families to dogs.

Meals	12pm-4pm (4.30pm weekends); 5.30pm-10pm (9pm Sat). Main courses £6.90-£12.90; bar meals £3.95-£12.90.
Closed	Open all day.
Directions	Exit Greenwich station, left & 2nd right (Royal Hill), pub on right.

Alastair Hook
Greenwich Union,
56 Royal Hill, Greenwich SE10 8RT
Tel   020 8692 6258
Web   www.meantimebrewing.com

Entry 415 Map 4

London

The Gun
Docklands

It's fiendishly difficult to find, but persevere. The front room, dominated by a dark panelled bar, is hugely atmospheric – a planked floor, settles, battered leather sofas, the smell of truffles in the air. The restaurant area is pristine, and a loose nautical theme runs through the prints and paintings. Bag a table by the fire; settle in till the sun sets over the river, on a gorgeously candlelit terrace. There's a reassuring selection of pub favourites – fish pie, beef shin burger with fat chips – in the bar while the restaurant menu is fiercely modern: pan fried haddock with scallops and a champagne velouté; fillet of veal with dumplings, spinach purée and baby morels. Weekend brunch from 11.30am to 1pm is hugely popular – do book; Portuguese barbecues trumpet Billingsgate fish. Amazing.

Meals	12pm-3pm (11.30am-4pm Sat & Sun); 6pm-10.30pm (9.30pm Sun). Main courses £11.95-£18; bar meals £4.50-£12.50.
Closed	Open all day.
Directions	Just off A1206 (Prestons Road); turn into Managers Street; right turn at the end.

Tom & Ed Martin
The Gun, 27 Coldharbour,
Docklands E14 9NS
Tel 020 7515 5222
Web www.thegundocklands.com

Entry 416 Map 4

London

The Princess
Clerkenwell

Bare boards, bare tables and a mix of suits and bohemians – another Clerkenwell boozer turned gastropub. This one is cool, charismatic and romantically candlelit at night. In the downstairs bar, British classics nudge Mediterranean dishes – choose fish 'n' chips or risotto, or book a big table for a long, lazy, entirely British Sunday lunch. For more formality and adventurous cooking, trip up the spiral staircase in the corner to the restaurant above, where some daring and accomplished dishes – pan-fried queen scallops with piri piri butter and rocket; duck breast with roast pumpkin pilau and mint yogurt – are served by a likeable staff. Well-kept Timothy Taylor and Fuller's London Pride are on hand pump if you're popping in for a drink, and they make the best Bloody Marys in town. A good solid pub.

Meals	12.30pm-3pm (1pm-4pm Sun); 6.30pm-10.30pm; no food Sun eve. Main courses £11.95-£14.95; bar meals £5-£10.50.
Closed	Open all day.
Directions	Nearest tube: Farringdon.

Zim Sutton
The Princess,
76 Paul Street,
Clerkenwell EC2A 4NE
Tel 020 7729 9270

Entry 417 Map 4

London

The Easton
Clerkenwell

Home from home for the Amnesty International crowd, whose headquarters are down the street, this corner pub may look like the classic London tavern but inside it is airy and modern. Bare boards, plain windows, a long bar topped with fresh flowers, funky wallpaper at the far end… drinkers and diners mingle over pints of Timothy Taylor and global house-white and wonder what to pick from the ever-changing chalk board. The kitchen goes in for rustic portions of chargrilled lemon and thyme pork chops; roast tomato and chorizo stew; Springbok sausages with spring onion champ, braised red cabbage and pancetta gravy. It's a godsend for the area, with pub tables spilling onto the pavement and a genuinely local feel. Staff are charming – even on Fridays when the drinkers descend, and hearty dishes are replaced with tapas.

London

Coach & Horses
Clerkenwell

Gone are the days when the Edwardian pub was a corner boozer; now it fills with a media crowd. Savour a pint of London Pride in the small panelled bar as you check out a blackboard that lists some of the best gastropub food in London. British dishes are devised with enthusiasm and ingredients burst with flavour: venison and partridge terrine with chutney; sea bream with lentils, fennel and salsa verde; quince and almond tart with clotted cream. Rare-breed meats are reared at Long Ghyll farms in Lancashire, fish is delivered daily. The bar specialises in malt whiskies and attentive staff lay on nibbles of toasted pumpkin seeds in keeping with the pub's logo, a pumpkin pulled by four mice. Note: most tables have a reserved sign on them on busy nights, so drinkers may be confined to the bar.

Meals	12.30pm-3pm (1pm-4pm Sun); 6.30pm-10pm (9.30pm Sun). Main courses £7.95-£12.95.
Closed	Open all day.
Directions	Nearest tube: Farringdon.

Meals	12pm-3pm; 6pm-10pm. Main courses £10.75-£14; bar meals £3-£6.
Closed	Open all day. Closed Sat lunch & Sun eve.
Directions	Nearest tube: Farringdon.

Jeremy Sutton & Andrew Veevers
The Easton,
22 Easton Street,
Clerkenwell WC1X 0DS
Tel   020 7278 7608

Giles Webster
Coach & Horses, 26-28 Ray Street,
Clerkenwell EC1R 3DJ
Tel   020 7278 8990
Web   www.thecoachandhorses.com

Entry 418 Map 4

Entry 419 Map 4

Jerusalem Tavern
Clerkenwell

There's so much atmosphere here you could bottle it up and take it home – along with one of the beers. Old Clerkenwell has reinvented itself; the quaint little 1720 tavern epitomises all that is best about the place. Its name is new, acquired nine years ago when the St Peter's Brewery of Suffolk took it over and stocked it with their ales and fruit beers. Step in to a reincarnation of a nooked and crannied interior, candlelit at night with a winter fire; come before six if you'd prefer a table. Lunchtime food is simple and English – bangers and mash, a roast, a fine platter of cheese – with ingredients from Smithfield Market down the road. Staff are friendly and know their beer, and the full range of St Peter's ales is all there, from the cask or the specially designed bottle. Heaven.

The White Swan
Holborn

It had spent the previous ten years as the Mucky Duck; then, in 2003, brothers Tom and Ed transformed the old journalists' den. The bar evokes a classic, cramped, city pub feel; at plain tables on fashionably unpolished boards, City traders enjoy real ales and fine wines. Upstairs is a smart restaurant with some unusually good modern European cooking ranging from the robust (roast leg of rabbit with tomato compote, herb dumplings and mustard cream sauce) to the subtle (roast halibut with Savoy cabbage, clams and white wine sauce). Cheese and wine lists are encyclopaedic and regulars get lockers to store their unfinished spirits. The daily bar menu takes in pub classics, perhaps Denham Estate pork sausages with mash and onion gravy, open steak sandwich, brilliant fish and chips .

Meals	12pm-3pm; 5pm-9.30pm (Tue-Thurs). Main courses £4.50-£8.50.
Closed	Open all day. Closed Sat & Sun.
Directions	Nearest tube/rail: Farringdon.

Meals	12pm-3pm; 6pm-9.45pm. Main courses £15-£18; bar meals from £8-£15.
Closed	Open all day Mon-Fri. Private parties only Sat & Sun.
Directions	Nearest tube: Chancery Lane.

Colin Cordy
Jerusalem Tavern, 55 Britton Street,
Clerkenwell EC1M 5UQ
Tel   020 7490 4281
Web   www.stpetersbrewery.co.uk

Tom & Ed Martin
The White Swan,
108 Fetter Lane, Holborn EC4A 1ES
Tel   020 7242 9696
Web   www.thewhiteswanlondon.com

Entry 420 Map 4

Entry 421 Map 4

London

The Eagle
Clerkenwell

Still mighty, after all these years. No tablecloths, no reservations, just delicious food ordered from the bar. With its real ales and decent choice of wines, the appeal is as much for drinkers as for diners and at peak times it heaves. The atmosphere is media-bohemian and the offices of the *Guardian* lie next door. In spite of the rustic appeal of scuffed floors, worn leather chairs, mix-and-match crockery, background Latin music and art gallery upstairs, the Eagle's reputation rests on its edible, seasonal bounty. The long bar counter is dominated by a stainless steel area at which Mediterranean vegetables, cuttlefish and pancetta are prepared. Pasta, risotto, peasant soups, spicy steak sandwiches... and vibrant Spanish hustle and bustle. Worth the trek to get here.

Meals	12.30pm-3pm (3.30pm Sat & Sun); 6.30pm-10.30pm. Main courses £7.50-£14.50.
Closed	Open all day. Closed Sun eve.
Directions	Nearest tube: Farringdon.

Michael Belben
The Eagle,
159 Farringdon Road,
Farringdon EC1R 3AL
Tel   020 7837 1353

Entry 422 Map 4

London

Charles Lamb Public House
Islington

Everyone's welcome at Camille and Hobby's small pub, hidden down a tangle of Georgian streets behind Camden Passage. It's a dear little place that keeps its pubby feel, with two unshowy bar rooms and well-kept ales on hand pump. So the blackboard menu — fresh, short, ever-changing — is the biggest surprise. Eat informally at plainly set tables in either bar, on Serrano ham with celeriac remoulade, or Lancashire hot pot. (Camille is French so there may be a crispy duck confit too.) Best of all is Sunday's all-day roast beef and Yorkshire pudding with all the trimmings. It's brilliant home-cooked food, but you need to get here early: tables cannot be booked. Walk it all off with a stroll along the bosky banks of the Regent's Canal, and seek out the house where essayist and poet Charles Lamb lived, two streets away.

Meals	12pm-3pm Wed-Fri (4pm Sat); 6pm-9.30pm (12pm-6pm Sun). Main courses £8-£12; Sunday roast £10.50-£12.
Closed	Open all day (open from 4pm Mon & Tues).
Directions	Nearest tube: Angel.

Hobby & Camille Limon
Charles Lamb Public House,
16 Elia Street, Islington N1 8DE
Tel   020 7837 5040
Web   www.thecharleslambpub.com

Entry 423 Map 4

London

The Duke of Cambridge
Islington

Thanks to pioneering Geetie Singh, 'organic' and 'sustainable' are the watchwords at London's first all-organic pub, and British rustic the style. Wines, beers, spirits are certified organic and they buy as locally as they can to cut down on food miles. Most of the beers are brewed in nearby Shoreditch, meat comes from two farms, fish is purchased from sustainable sources. Impeccable produce and menus that change twice a day. It's a sprawling, airy space with a comfortable, easy, shoestring minimalism, so sit back and take your fill of lentil and pancetta soup, mussels with chorizo, fennel and chives, game pie with braised red cabbage, venison steak with redcurrant jus, crusty bread, fruity olive oil, quince crumble and cream – in here, or in the large restaurant. Justifiably rammed.

Meals	12.30pm-3pm (3.30pm Sat & Sun); 6.30pm-10.30pm (10pm Sun). Main courses £9-£18.
Closed	Open all day.
Directions	Nearest tube: Angel.

Geetie Singh
The Duke of Cambridge,
30 St Peter's St, Islington N1 8JT
Tel   020 7359 3066
Web   www.dukeorganic.co.uk

Entry 424 Map 4

London

The Lansdowne
Primrose Hill

Worth crossing postcodes for. It's buzzing, laid-back, open-plan and atmospherically lit, with big wooden tables and dark blue décor – and manages, downstairs, to keep its pubby feel. Upstairs is an elegant and charming 60-seat restaurant where a cool crowd is treated to some adventurous food – homemade pasta dishes, sea bass en papillotte, belly of pork with mash and shallots, juicy rib-eye steak with fat chips and béarnaise. Though the serious dining goes on up here, you can also eat down where the decibels are high, the atmosphere shambolic and everyone loves the pizzas (kids included). There are two draught ales and one real cider, but really this is a wine, lager and olives place. Outside in summer is a little oasis to which you can retreat and leave the city behind.

Meals	12pm-3pm (9.30am-3.30pm Sat & Sun); 6pm-10pm (9.30pm Sun); pizzas all day. Main courses £9-£17; bar meals £5-£16.50.
Closed	Open all day.
Directions	Nearest tube: Chalk Farm.

Amanda Pritchett
The Lansdowne, 90 Gloucester Ave,
Primrose Hill NW1 8HX
Tel   020 7483 0409
Web   www.thelansdownepub.co.uk

Entry 425 Map 4

London

The Engineer
Primrose Hill

Isambard Kingdom Brunel once had an office here, today the place is run by a painter and an actress. Behind the half-stuccoed 1850 edifice lies a cheerful, friendly gastropub with a smart bohemian feel and a reputation for food. It is particularly strong on fish cooked with a touch of the Mediterranean – sea bass with minted couscous and aubergine relish, say – but there are organic steaks with béarnaise, fat homemade chips and creamy and chocolatey desserts to love too. Wines look to the New World and beer is excellent. Eat up or down: the front bar is relaxed, bright and buzzing, the restaurant upstairs has white plates on white cloths, mirrors in gilt frames and art for sale. In summer, the large lush garden catches the sun. The service is often praised, the parking is easy.

London

Dartmouth Arms
Highgate

Sitting unobtrusively in a Highgate side street, the Dartmouth Arms may look smartly unexceptional but inside is another story. There's personality in the front bar, wooden tables are junk-shop simple and the flat-screen TV attracts fans for the footie. The back room, where champagne bottles hang from a chandelier, is a more peaceful space. Come for three perfectly kept cask ales, loads of small-producer ciders, several wines by the glass and a modern British menu displayed on boards – landlord Nick is passionate about food and beer. Expect something for everyone here: wild mushroom soup, sausages with tomato sauce and mash, steaks, Sunday roasts, croque monsieur, generous salads. The background music is noisy at times, there are quizzes on Tuesdays and an ever-lively crowd.

Meals	9am-3pm; 7pm-10.30pm.
	Main courses £12.50-£16.50.
Closed	Open all day.
Directions	Nearest tube: Camden Town.

Meals	11am-3pm; 6pm-10pm
	(10am-10pm Sat & Sun).
	Main courses from £7.50.
Closed	Open all day.
Directions	Nearest tube: Tufnell Park.

	Karen Northcote
	The Engineer, 65 Gloucester Ave,
	Primrose Hill NW1 8JH
Tel	020 7722 0950
Web	www.the-engineer.com

	Nick May
	Dartmouth Arms, 35 York Rise,
	Darmouth Park NW5 1SP
Tel	020 7485 3267
Web	www.dartmoutharms.co.uk

Entry 426 Map 4

Entry 427 Map 4

London

Holly Bush
Hampstead

Down a Hampstead cul-de-sac, stables once owned by painter George Romney have become a hugely loved pub. A labyrinth of corridors leads to cosy corners, painted settles and big tables set with board games and pints of Harvey's Sussex. Ale rules at the Holly Bush, where the chef cooks not with wine but with beer. Through the open kitchen, the aromas of beef and Harvey's pie prove a temptation for drinkers to become diners. Adnams rarebit or a pint of prawns – followed by hot chocolate, marmalade and malt whisky fondant – is intended to educate the beer lover's palate. Dishes are seasonal and fresh, with game and organic meats from Winchelsea and a superb selection of English cheeses. Upstairs in the dining room, all pistachio walls and wooden floors, the celebration of all things British continues.

> Cooking standards in pubs have risen in recent years and a growing number of pubs are sourcing the best ingredients from the best producers, but this is no excuse for pubs to charge restaurant prices.

Meals	12pm-10pm (9pm Sun). Main courses £8-£15; bar meals £3.50-£6.
Closed	Open all day.
Directions	Nearest tube: Hampstead.

Jesus Anorve
Holly Bush, 22 Holly Mount,
Hampstead NW3 6SG

Tel	020 7435 2892
Web	www.hollybushpub.com

Entry 428 Map 4

London

429 The Seven Stars 53 Carey Street, Holborn WC2A 2JB 020 7242 8521
Right by the Law Courts, the narrow bar has hung on to its boarded floors, low beams and old mirrors; framed vintage legal film posters bedeck red walls. The menu is short, bistro-like and English with inspired flourishes.

430 Portobello Gold 95-97 Portobello Rd, Notting Hill W11 2QB
020 7460 4910
A gastro-hotel in Notting Hill: bar, restaurant, internet café and groovy place to stay. In the bar are tiled floors, an open fire, exhibitions of photography and music on Sunday evenings; at the back, a restaurant with a retractable glass roof and jungle planting.

431 The Fat Badger 310 Portobello Rd, Kensington W10 5TA 020 8969 4500
At the scruffy end of Notting Hill, a good-natured bohemian pub with beaten-up leather chesterfields and funky chandeliers. Works well as a boozer and a place for a plate of something tasty – pork pie and pickle, roast partridge and red cabbage.

432 Havelock Tavern 57 Masbro Rd, Shepherds Bush W14 0LS
020 7603 5374
No music, no fuss, just plain floorboards and tables squeezed around the main bar, luscious smells from the hatch (the menu changes twice daily!) and a happy, noisy, friendly crowd. As cheap as chips (rather good ones) for Brook Green. Brilliant.

433 The Pig's Ear Old Church Street, Chelsea SW3 5BS 020 7352 2908
Off the King's Road, a nice little corner spot that still looks like a pub, serving Uley Pig's Ear on tap and a perfect Bloody Mary. Rousing rustic cooking: roast belly pork, braised ox tongue, roast cod with puy lentils and chorizo salsa.

434 The Anglesea Arms 15 Selwood Terrace, South Kensington SW7 3QG
020 7373 7960
Traditional floral wallpaper, heavy velvet curtains, pints of Adnams, the Sunday papers and, in the little restaurant downstairs, deeply, comfortingly English food in the posh heart of South Ken.

435 The White Horse 1-3 Parson's Green, Fulham SW6 4UL
020 7736 2115
'The Sloany Pony' may be a hotbed of Fulhamites but it's also reputed to have the best-kept beers in Europe. Comfy sofas, log fires, slatted blinds, a big terrace, and a menu that suggests the best accompanying liquor.

436 The Idle Hour 62 Railway Side, Barnes SW13 0PQ 020 8878 5555
A small haven tucked away down a little alley in Barnes, with a fresh, contemporary décor and a predominantly organic menu. Sundays are legendary, with a winter fire and roasts brought to the table.

London

437   The Fox & Hounds 66 Latchmere Rd, Battersea SW11 2JU
020 7924 5483

A bright little corner pub in Battersea, a foodie destination and a shrine to the golden brew. Mediterranean-style dishes flow from the open-to-view kitchen; a great atmosphere, and a garden for summer.

438   The Gunmakers 13 Eyre Street Hill, Clerkenwell EC1R 5ET
020 7278 1022

In cool Clerkenwell, low ceilings, bare boards and good cheer fill this tiny, unspoilt pub commemorating Hiram Maxin (who produced the first automatic machine gun nearby). Blackboard menus and Wells Bombardier please a mixed bunch.

439   The Peasant 240 St John Street, Islington EC1V 4PH 020 7336 7726

A Victorian gin palace with a reputation for splendid food, wines, beers and cocktails. Tapas, mezze and the daily papers downstairs; pretty restaurant up. Brilliantly positioned for antique shops, the Design Centre and Sadler's Wells.

440   The Narrow 44 Narrow Street, Limehouse E14 8DP 020 7592 7950

Gordon Ramsay's first pub, in an Edwardian dockmaster's house on a gorgeous bend of the Thames. Good range of real ales and ciders and the best of gutsy British food. Sensibly short menu and reasonable prices.

441   Drapers Arms 44 Barnsbury Street, Islington N1 1ER 020 7619 0348

It's won a hatful of awards for its food and is friendly, airy and scrupulously clean. A nice place in which to settle down on a comfy leather sofa with a jug of Bloody Mary. Outside, a lovely little garden.

442   The Junction Tavern 101 Fortess Rd, Kentish Town NW5 1AG
020 7485 9400

From the open-to-view kitchen flows food that is modern European and wide-ranging. While half the pub is restaurant, the rest is old-fashioned bar, serving over ten real ales a week and an August beer festival. A joy in laid-back Kentish Town.

443   The Flask 77 Highgate West Hill, Highgate N6 6BU 020 8348 7346

This Hogarthian warren (he stayed here) may be 350 years old but its candlelit crannies have a stylish feel, the pies are handmade and the beer pulls are marked with handwritten labels. Much loved, mobbed in summer and right by Hampstead Heath.

444   The Bull 13 North Hill, Highgate N6 4AB 0845 456 5033

The plain listed Georgian façade gives way to an inspired interior for rustic-simple dishes with huge depth of flavour. A chic retreat in Highgate – and a vintage American pool table for a bit of fun.

Worth a visit

The White Hart
Lydgate

Decay was setting in at this 18th-century ale house overlooking Saddleworth Moor when Charles Brierley took it over, over a decade ago. It has since been transformed into a charming restaurant-pub. Relax in the bar with a glass of Timothy Taylors Landlord, toast your toes by the wood-burning stove and admire the sleek décor. It's a comfortable backdrop for British cheeses, platters of oysters, 'Saddleworth' sausages (five, with five different kinds of mash). Move upstairs to the restaurant, where delicacy combines with robustness in some unusually fine cooking: chilli squid with saffron and garlic mayonnaise, braised lamb with pickled red cabbage, pan-fried cod with tomato compôte. This is a beautiful village and, on a fine day, you can stretch your eyes all the way to the distant Cheshire Plain.

The Swan
Dobcross

Immerse yourself in the epitome of a traditional Yorkshire village pub, in a lush, comely landscape. Slabbed stone floors and colourwashed ceilings pitch like a dinghy in a storm, and rooms warmed by huge log fires hive off in all directions from the lobby bar – sparingly dressed with toby jugs, local paintings and some fascinating old documents concerning the building, once the village court and gaol. Outside, the tiny patio overlooks an absurdly picturesque village square from which lanes plummet down into the Tame Gorge, backed by forbidding moors. On the door lintel are the initials of the Wrigley chewing-gum family who once lived here. Today's visitor can chew on good homemade pea and ham soup, cheese and onion pie and chilli with rice, helped down by the full range of Jennings' beers and guests.

Meals	12pm-2.30pm; 6pm-9.30pm (1pm-7.30pm Sun). Main courses £5.50-£21.
Closed	Open all day.
Directions	From Oldham E on A669 for 2.5 miles. Before hill right onto A6050; 50 yds on left.

Meals	12pm-2pm (2.30pm Sunday); 5.30pm-8pm; no food Sunday evenings. Main courses £7.95-£8.95.
Closed	3pm-5.30pm (3.30pm Thurs-Sun).
Directions	Off A670, 4 miles north-east of Oldham near Uppermill; signs for Saddleworth, then Dobcross.

Charles Brierley
The White Hart, 51 Stockport Road, Lydgate, Oldham OL4 4JJ
Tel 01457 872566
Web www.thewhitehart.co.uk

Howard Mellor & Simon Thrower
The Swan,
The Square, Dobcross,
Oldham OL3 5AA
Tel 01457 873451

Entry 445 Map 12

Entry 446 Map 12

Merseyside

The Philharmonic
Liverpool

The Phil was built by Liverpool brewers Robert Cain & Co in the style of a gentlemen's club: a place for bodily refreshment after the aesthetic excitements of the Philharmonic Hall opposite. There's ornate Victorian extravagance at every turn, high ceilings, elaborate embellishment, etched glass; the gents is decked in marble and mosaic, its porcelain fittings of historical importance. Sweep through the columned entrance into the imposing central bar, gawp at the scale. Beyond, a succession of small rooms and snugs separated by mahogany partitions, then a Grand Lounge with a stately frieze and table service for lunch: settle down to baked potatoes or fish and chips. Very popular with students, the Philharmonic is a great pub serving excellent beers, wines and whiskies and a huge dose of cheer.

Norfolk

Gin Trap Inn
Ringstead

An actor and a lawyer run this old English Inn. Steve and Cindy left London for the quiet life and haven't stopped since, adding a conservatory dining room at the back and giving the garden a haircut. The Gin Trap dates to 1667, while the horse chestnut tree that shades the front took root in the 19th century; a conker championship is in the offing. A smart whitewashed exterior gives way to a beamed locals' bar with a crackling fire and the original dining room in Farrow & Ball hues. There are fortnightly quiz nights on Sundays but most come for the food: Norfolk mussels, organic burgers, beer-battered haddock and chips, poached winter fruits; walkers will find great comfort here. Ringstead — a pretty village lost in the country — is two miles inland from the coastal road, Sandringham is close and fabulous beaches beckon.

Meals	12pm-10pm.
	Main courses £5-£15.
Closed	Open all day.
Directions	City centre; between cathedrals at corner of Hardman Street.

Meals	12pm-2pm (2.30pm Sat & Sun); 6pm-9pm (9.30pm Fri & Sat).
	Main courses £8-£15.95; sandwiches (lunch) from £5.
Closed	2.30pm-6pm. Open all day in summer.
Directions	North from King's Lynn on A149. Ringstead signed right in Heacham. Pub on right in village.

Marie-Louise Wong
The Philharmonic,
36 Hope Street,
Liverpool L1 9BX
Tel   0151 7072837

Entry 447 Map 11

Steve Knowles & Cindy Cook
Gin Trap Inn, High Street,
Ringstead, Hunstanton PE36 5JU
Tel   01485 525264
Web   www.gintrapinn.co.uk

Entry 448 Map 9

Norfolk

The Rose and Crown
Snettisham

Roses round the door and twisting passages within, it is gloriously English. Homemade burgers with red onion relish and fish and chips with minted mushy peas should please the traditionalists, but the menu soon spirals into the dizzy realms of pressed wild salmon with caviar cream, and seared calves' liver with fried polenta, baby gem lettuce and fig vinaigrette. It's great value. In spite of 30 wines on the list, half available by the glass, the Rose and Crown is still proud to be a pub; fine beers on hand pump and a hands-on feel. The walled garden was once the village bowling green and children will enjoy the wooden play fort and the weeping willows. Inside are a warren of rooms with low ceilings and uneven floors, old beams and log fires, a family-friendly garden room and a flurry of rather stylish bedrooms, the quietest in the extension off the courtyard. Golfers have Brancaster and Hunstanton, shoppers Burnham Market, birdwatchers Snettisham. For walkers and families the beaches of Wells on the Sea and Holkham are stupendous.

Rooms	16 twins/doubles. £90–£110. Singles £70–£90.
Meals	12pm-2pm (2.30pm Sat & Sun); 6.30pm-9pm (9.30pm Fri & Sat). Main courses £8.50-£14.50.
Closed	Open all day.
Directions	Village signed off A149 10 miles north of King's Lynn. Turn right at r'bout into village & then 1st left, pub 100yds on left.

Anthony & Jeannette Goodrich
The Rose and Crown,
Old Church Road,
Snettisham PE31 7LX

Tel	01485 541382
Web	www.roseandcrownsnettisham.co.uk

Entry 449 Map 9

The Dabbling Duck
Great Massingham

After a tireless campaign by the villagers to buy their local, the Rose & Crown has become the Dabbling Duck and has been revived with panache. The duck-egg blue inn stands prettily by the green and the big duck pond. Business has been brisk, the draw being the wonderful food chalked up on the boards, the beers from the barrel (well-kept Adnams and Woodforde's) and the easy country feel. The bar has been cut from a single slice of ancient Norfolk oak, there are high-backed settles by a blazing log fire, rug-strewn wooden floors, chunky candles on scrubbed kitchen tables, shelves lined with books and board games, and village green views. The food is locally sourced: bowls of Brancaster mussels, Cley prawns with basil mayonnaise, thick sirloin steaks from the Holkham Estate, ham, egg and chips. The care and attention to detail extends to gorgeous bedrooms with big brass beds, colourful cushions and throws, plasma screens, Roberts radios and wood-floored bathrooms – and homemade cookies and fresh coffee on tap. All this, 20 minutes from the beach and the bird-rich saltmarshes. Superb.

Rooms	3 doubles. £90. Singles £60.
Meals	12pm-2.30pm (3pm Sun); 6.30pm-9pm; no food Sun eve. Main courses £4.75-£15.50.
Closed	Open all day.
Directions	Village signed south off A148 at Harpley between King's Lynn & Fakenham.

Sunee McKelvey
The Dabbling Duck,
11 Abbey Road, Great Massingham,
King's Lynn PE32 2HN
Tel   01485 520827
Web   www.thedabblingduck.co.uk

Entry 450 Map 10

The Kings Head Hotel
Great Bircham

A Victorian inn – once part of the Sandringham estate – with a red roof and trimmed lawns. The sort that you might imagine would be filled with chintz. Instead, find a huge hall with a cream ceramic floor, low spotlights, suede sofas and, at the end, a dramatic wall with squares of bevelled mirror above a black table with black and gold lamps. The restaurant is pure Notting Hill with square white plates and stainless steel; the food is excellent – locally sourced as much as possible – be it seared Szechuan tuna with a sushi roll or Cromer crab. Grab a comfortable chair in the wooden-floored drawing room with cream rugs and a roaring fire – or retire to your room. It will be swish and spotless with a huge bed, a flat-screen TV, a port decanter, fresh milk and homemade biscuits. Bathrooms are filled with goodies from the Natural Soap Company in Wells. An acre of lawned garden has a play area for kids and plenty of places for sitting, so eat out here if the weather is fine. Staff are efficient and naturally smiley. You'll be well looked after.

Rooms	12 doubles. £125-£225. Singles from £69.50.
Meals	12pm-2pm (3pm Sun); 7pm-9pm. Main courses £7.75-£22.50; bar meals £4.95-£14.95.
Closed	Open all day.
Directions	From King's Lynn, A148 to Fakenham. Turn left on B1153 after Hillington village. Drive through Flitcham. As you come into Bircham, the hotel is on left hand side.

Mark Orton
The Kings Head Hotel,
Great Bircham PE31 6RJ

Tel	01485 578265
Web	www.the-kings-head-bircham.co.uk

The White Horse
Brancaster Staithe

The setting is magical. Fabulous views reach across the marshes and the water with its moored boats, and dinghies sailing on the evening high tide. The coastal path starts right outside this neat inn with its benches, parasols and troughs of plants and flowers: the perfect spot for a pint after a stroll. Inside, the fishy theme continues but in a modern, crisp way: seascape colours, natural materials, pictures of boats, bowls of pebbles and shells, big windows to the views. Bedrooms are beautiful. Those upstairs capture the ever-changing light; those on the ground floor have flower-filled terraces and a New England feel and lead straight onto the marshes. From here you can spot fishing boats and ringed plovers, several species of tern and, in winter, geese; don't forget your binoculars. Dine by candlelight on mussels and oysters from yards away, homemade bread and ice creams, all of it as local and seasonal as possible. Huge sunsets, fine food, big breakfasts, and a real welcome for children and dogs.

Rooms	16: 12 doubles, 4 twins. £85-£180.
Meals	12pm-2pm; 6.30pm-9pm; bar food 9am-9pm. Main courses £9.50-£18; bar meals £6.50-£9.50.
Closed	Open all day.
Directions	Midway between Hunstanton & Wells-next-the-Sea on the A149 coast road.

Cliff Nye
The White Horse,
Brancaster Staithe PE31 8BY
Tel   01485 210262
Web   www.whitehorsebrancaster.co.uk

Norfolk

The Hoste Arms
Burnham Market

Nelson was once a local. Now it's farmers, fishermen and film stars who jostle at the bar and roast away on winter evenings in front of a roaring fire. In its 300-year history the Hoste has been a court house, a livestock market, a gallery and a brothel. These days it's more a pleasure dome than an inn and even on a grey February morning it buzzes with life, the locals in for coffee, the residents polishing off leisurely breakfasts, diligent staff attending a wine tasting. The place has a genius of its own with warm bold colours, armchairs to sink into, panelled walls, its own art gallery. Fancy food can be eaten anywhere and anytime, so dig into local oysters with orange and rice wine vinegar, oriental beef broth or honey-glazed ham hock. In summer, life spills out onto tables at the front or you can dine on the terrace in the garden at the back. Rooms are all different, the quietest away from the bar: a tartan four-poster, a swagged half-tester, leather sleigh beds in the Zulu wing. Burnham Market is gorgeous and the magnificent north Norfolk coast on your doorstep. Bring the shrimping nets.

Rooms	36: 12 twins/doubles, 4 four-posters, 5 singles, 7 suites. Zulu Wing: 5 doubles, 3 suites. £122–£216. Singles from £90. Suites £158–£273. Half-board from £73 p.p.
Meals	12pm-2pm; 7pm-9pm. Main courses £9.75–£23.50; sandwiches (lunch only) from £3.95; Sunday roast £10.50.
Closed	Open all day.
Directions	On B1155 for Burnham Market. By green & church in village centre.

Emma Tagg
The Hoste Arms,
The Green,
Burnham Market PE31 8HD
Tel   01328 738777
Web   www.hostearms.co.uk

Entry 453 Map 10

The Crown
Wells-next-the-Sea

The interior of this handsome 16th-century coaching inn has been neatly rationalised yet is still atmospheric with its open fires, bare boards and easy chairs. And it's run by Chris Coubrough, an enterprising landlord who knows how to cook. Order pub food at the bar and eat it in the lounges or the lovely modern conservatory: a hearty serving of Brancaster mussels, paella with monkfish, crab claws, squid, clams and chorizo. Or, simple, the Crown beefburger with pepper relish and a pint of local brew Adnams Bitter. Bold colours, modern art and attractively laid tables give life to the restaurant too, where local ingredients are translated into global ideas: steamed cod with ginger lemongrass and lime; Thai marinated duck breast with seared scallops and chilli jam. Uncluttered bedrooms have a cool, minimalist feel and a fresh white theme – plump pillows and crisp linen on good wooden beds, flat-screen TVs; larger rooms have squashy sofas and DVD players. Beaches and bracing salt marsh walks are mere minutes away.

Rooms	12: 10 twins/doubles, 2 family suites. £90-£155.
Meals	12pm-2.30pm; 6.30pm-9.30pm. Main courses £9.95-£14.95; set menus £29.95 & £34.95.
Closed	Open all day.
Directions	Wells-next-the-Sea is on B1105, 10 miles north of Fakenham; pub by the south of town centre.

Chris Coubrough
The Crown,
The Buttlands,
Wells-next-the-Sea NR23 1EX

Tel   01328 710209
Web   www.thecrownhotelwells.co.uk

Entry 454 Map 10

The Globe Inn
Wells-next-the-Sea

Set back a few hundred yards from the bustling harbour at Wells, the Globe sits on leafy Buttlands Green. The 19th-century coaching inn has been given a thorough makeover by Tom and Polly Coke, who transformed the Victoria on their family estate at Holkham — expect the best. It's a big hit with visitors and locals alike, a warm mishmash of old furniture, wooden boards, big wood-burner and antique lighting. The restaurant, in New England style, has a good reputation for food that's unstuffy, fresh, modern. Lots comes from the estate and only the season's finest will do: spring lamb with fresh asparagus, roasted sea bass, wild partridge (a rare treat). On sunny days you can take your plates and your pints (Adnams and Woodforde's) out into the red-brick courtyard, bordered on one side by a vast, as yet, unused, ballroom. Bedrooms are a treat — as fresh and untraditional as can be, with oak floors, blinds, velvet cushions, big baths and monsoon showers. The ones at the front get the views. Children and dogs like it too, what with child-size pies, crabbing on the quay and walks on the hugest beach ever.

Rooms	7: 5 doubles, 2 twins. £65–£130.
Meals	12pm-2.30pm; 7pm-9pm.
	Main courses £8.50–£14.
Closed	Open all day.
Directions	North from Fakenham on B1105.
	Hotel on green in centre of town.

Tom Coke
The Globe Inn,
The Buttlands,
Wells-next-the-Sea NR23 1EU

Tel	01328 710206
Web	www.globeatwells.co.uk

Norfolk

The Orange Tree
Thornham

This place knows what a contemporary food pub should be. From funky wicker fencing fronting the garden to sage-splashed walls, the approach from the village green says it all. Step inside – to chunky seagrass floors, light wood, bright walls and log-stuffed fireplaces. Snuggle up at a cheeky *table à deux* at the bar, or retire to one of two relaxed dining rooms. There's a faint waft of Norfolk 'money' on the air, but something for everyone on the Ivy-esque menu – from game broth and dumplings to sautéed halibut with a warm salad of pumpkin, mussels and kale. This is a fabulous area for food, and the pub sources locally and well. Adnams and Greene King are on hand pump, and the wine list does a decent job. Come for urban chic, a particularly happy feel and great food.

Meals	12pm-2pm; 6.30pm-9pm (9.30pm Fri & Sat); 12pm-6pm Sun. Main courses £9-£15.50.
Closed	Open all day.
Directions	On A149 in village centre; from Hunstanton, pub on left-hand side.

Richard Golding
The Orange Tree, High Street,
Thornham, Hunstanton PE36 6LY
Tel   01485 512213
Web   www.theorangetreethornham.co.uk

Entry 456 Map 9

Norfolk

Carpenter's Arms
Wighton

Regulars and newcomers love this pub for all the right reasons: good beer, good food and hands-on owners. It looks modest enough from the outside, three knocked-together cottages in traditional knicker-pink render. But a courageous hand with the paint pot has transformed the interior: tables and chairs in terracotta, navy and duck-egg blue, a jolly blue in the hallway, and walls in a dining room that would make Barbie blink. Kelims, leather-style sofas and a bold paintings create a happy mishmash of textures, a big double-sided wood-burner heats the bar and dining room and there's a grassy sun-trap around the back. A pint of well-kept Nelson's Revenge slips down a treat with hot crab linguine with mint and chilli, or skate wing with buttered samphire, or calves' liver and bacon with red wine jus.

Meals	12pm-2.30pm (6pm Sun); 6pm-9.30pm; no food Sun eve or Mon in winter. Main courses £7.95-£12.95.
Closed	2.30pm-5.30pm. Open all day Sat & Sun.
Directions	Village signed off A149 at Wells-next-the-Sea.

Gareth & Rebecca Williams
Carpenter's Arms,
High Street, Wighton,
Wells-next-the-Sea NR23 1PF
Tel   01328 820752

Entry 457 Map 10

Norfolk

Red Lion
Stiffkey

Tucked into the side of a hill, overlooking the meadows where beef cattle graze, is a cosy inn that is a pleasure to step into. Enter a warren of three small rooms with bare floorboards and 17th-century quarry tiles, 'clotted cream' walls, open log fires and an unpretentious mix of stripped wooden settles, old pews and scrubbed tables. The pub attracts a loyal crowd for its fresh seafood – crab from Wells boats, mussels from Johnny Dowsing in the village and fresh beer battered cod – and its first-rate ales from local brewers: Woodforde's Wherry, Yetmans Orange. Locals rub shoulders with booted walkers and birdwatchers recovering from the rigours of the Peddars Way path and Stiffkey's famous marshes. After a day on the beach the large and airy conservatory is popular with families; dogs, too, are welcomed.

Meals	12pm-2.30pm; 6.30pm-9pm. 12pm-9pm Sun. Main courses £8.95-£13.
Closed	Open all day.
Directions	From Wells, 2 miles along coast road towards Cromer.

Andrew Waddison
Red Lion, 44 Wells Road, Stiffkey,
Wells-next-the-Sea NR23 1AJ

Tel   01328 830552
Web   www.stiffkey.com

♿ 🚶 ✉ 🐾 🍺 🍷

Entry 458 Map 10

Norfolk

The Anchor
Morston

Taste the salty sea – Morston mussels, Thornham oysters, Blakeney crab – and wash it all down with Norwich's Winter Brewery Golden ale... or a nice cup of Royal tea. All a village pub should be, this flintwork and whitewashed building re-opened last year following a serious fire. It's a warren of intimate, loved and lived-in rooms, each with its own story to tell: a random collection of tables and chairs, old fishing pics and faded newspaper clippings. There's even a cosy old 'front room' resplendent with stuffed birds and armchairs. Around every corner are enthusiastic birders, chattering locals and relaxed tourists lapping it up. Honest pub cooking with fine local ingredients matches the decent beers and inexpensive wines. On a sunny day stretch out in the secluded beer garden. Book a seal trip while you sup.

Meals	12pm-2.30pm; 6pm-9.30pm; 12pm-8pm Sun. Main courses £8.95-£18.95.
Closed	Open all day.
Directions	In the centre of Morston on the A149, 2 miles west of Blakeney.

Nick Handley
The Anchor,
The Street, Morston,
Holt NR25 7AA

Tel   01263 741392

♿ 🚶 ✉ 🐾 🍺 🍷

Entry 459 Map 10

Norfolk

Norfolk

White Horse Hotel
Blakeney

The smart hub of this small coastal village attracts its share of switched-on custom; Blakeney is the jewel in north Norfolk's crown. The lamp-lit windows of the bar beckon; Adnams Bitter and Woodforde's Wherry are served to those in search of a pint. But stay for more: dressed local crab, filled ciabattas, sea bass with crayfish butter and rocket salad are all served in the polished bar, while local Cley Smokehouse smoked salmon, Morston mussels and seasonal ingredients are given a decidedly contemporary treatment in the sunny-coloured restaurant. With its airy conservatory and sheltered courtyard, Dan Goff's friendly inn is a pleasant place to rest weary limbs following a bracing coast path walk. At the bottom of the steep, narrow high street are marshes of sea lavender, natural mussel beds and seals a ferry ride away.

The Pigs
Edgefield

If passion and pedigree go hand in hand then The Pigs' patrons are onto a winner. Running the old pub (once known as the Bacon Arms) is a partnership of restaurateurs fighting the corner for real food locally sourced – some of which comes directly from the patrons' gardens. The enterprising menu, a retro version of British classics, encourages indecision; be tempted by beef dripping on toast with cock-a-leekie soup, marmalade-glazed ham hock with mustard mash, and Horlicks rice pudding with Earl Grey-stewed prunes. Homemade pork scratchings, colonial spiced almonds and mixed pickle pots are further enticements, along with old-fashioned pub games, decent cask ales and a fabulous children's menu. No hushed gastronomic museum this, more of a "traditional bar with continental leanings."

Meals	12pm-2.15pm (bar meals only); 6pm-9pm. Main courses £10.95-£18.95.
Closed	Open all day.
Directions	Just up from quay, in village; off A149 10 miles west of Sheringham.

Meals	12pm-2.30pm (3pm Sun); 6pm-9pm. Main courses £9.95-£14.95.
Closed	3pm-6pm; Sun eve & all day Mon.
Directions	Edgefield on B1149, 3 miles south of Holt; pub south side of village.

Dan Goff
White Horse Hotel,
4 High Street, Blakeney NR25 7AL
Tel   01263 740574
Web   www.blakeneywhitehorse.co.uk

Gary Long
The Pigs, Norwich Road,
Edgefield, Holt NR24 2RL
Tel   01263 587634
Web   www.thepigs.org.uk

Entry 460 Map 10

Entry 461 Map 10

Norfolk

The Wiveton Bell
Wiveton

This is a new enterprise for a couple of Nottingham-based restaurateurs. The pull of the great outdoors led them to this Norfolk pub, with a backdrop of village green and church. The setting may be bucolic but Wiveton is no backwater; on highdays and holidays these coastal outposts of North Norfolk get livelier than Chelsea, such is the influx of city escapees. And they will find much to please them here, for a stunning, simple-rustic makeover has transformed the interior of the charming whitewashed inn – beams, chunky tables, polished plank floors – that suits the bistro-pub ethos down to the ground. And the menu is seductive, ranging from slow roast pork belly, bangers and mustard mash to Thai fish cakes and chilli dipping sauce. It's all so lovely you'll want to stay the night. Four lovely new bedrooms have antique beds with crisp linen and goose down pillows, flat-screen TV/DVDs, mini CD players, iPod docks, broadband and books; cosy bathrooms have bathrobes and top toiletries; fresh croissants are delivered to the door. Marvellous.

Rooms	4 doubles. £85–£110.
Meals	12pm-2.15pm; 6pm-9.15pm.
	Main courses £8.95-£15.95.
Closed	3pm-5.30pm.
Directions	Wiveton signed off A149 at Blakeney; pub opposite church.

Berni Morritt & Sandy Butcher
The Wiveton Bell,
Blakeney Road, Wiveton,
Holt NR25 7TL

Tel	01263 740101
Web	wivetonbell.co.uk

Saracens Head
Wolterton

A true country inn with nourishing food, real ale, good wines, a big courtyard garden, enchanting and enclosed, and Norfolk's bleakly lovely coast – this is why people come. But it's the food that's the deepest seduction. Robert and his team cook up "some of Norfolk's most delicious wild and tame treats". Tuck into Morston mussels with cider and cream, pigeon, Cromer crab, venison. Vegetarians are pampered too, a rare thing. Then Robert works his magic on old favourites such as bread and butter pudding... The bar with wood-burners is as convivial as a bar could be, a welcome antidote to garish pub bars with their fruit machines – Robert will have none of them. There's a parlour room that is decidedly civilised: terracotta walls with friezes, candles in bottles, a black leather banquette, open log fires. Retire to a countrified bedroom with bold colours, sisal floors, linen curtains, pretty touches; wake to a fabulous, generous breakfast. The whole mood is of quirky, committed individuality – slightly arty, slightly unpredictable and in the middle of nowhere.

Rooms	6: 5 doubles, 1 twin. £90. Singles £50.
Meals	12.15pm–2pm; 7.15pm–9.30pm. Main courses £11.95-£15.95; bar meals £5.50-£8.80.
Closed	3pm-6pm (7pm Sun).
Directions	From Norwich, A140 past Aylsham, then left, for Erpingham. Don't bear right for Aldborough, go straight through Calthorpe. Over x-roads. On right after about 0.5 miles.

Robert & Rachel Dawson-Smith
Saracens Head,
Wolterton,
Erpingham NR11 7LZ

Tel	01263 768909
Web	www.saracenshead-norfolk.co.uk

Entry 463 Map 10

The Walpole Arms
Itteringham

The Walpole is one of a select band of renowned food pubs in north Norfolk. Ex-*Masterchef* producer Richard Bryan may have gone but Andy Parle, once head chef to Alastair Little, continues to oversee the menus, and the daily chalkboard reflects the seasons and brims with local produce – Cromer crab, Morston mussels, venison from the Gunton estate, farm-fresh fruits and vegetables. Enjoy the likes of Jerusalem artichoke soup with wilted rocket and truffle oil, black bream with herb-crushed potatoes and velouté, and poached quince and frangipane tart. You can eat in the bar, all rough brick walls, beamed ceilings, standing timbers and big open fire, or in the stylish dining room. There are fine East Anglian ales from Adnams and Woodforde's, a first-class list of wines, and a glorious vine-covered terrace for summer.

The Wildebeest Arms
Stoke Holy Cross

In the 1990s Henry Watt introduced good food to this country inn – a rarity then. Today the Wildebeest is one of the most popular dining pubs in Norfolk. The 19th-century building may be no great shakes on the outside but the atmosphere is special. Modernised to create one long room split by a central bar, there are rich yellow walls, dark oak beams, a winter fire and an African theme to match the pub's name. Ales include Adnams, there's a good choice of wines by the glass and the food is up-to-the-minute and freshly made. Tuck into the rich delights of pan-seared haunch of venison with fondant potato, crispy parma ham and dark chocolate sauce. Chef Daniel Smith may enjoy a bit of leonine bravura but he is wonderfully at home with old English favourites like sausage and mash and sticky toffee pudding.

Meals	12pm-2pm (2.30pm Sun); 7pm-9pm; no food Sun eve. Main courses £9.95-£15.95.
Closed	3pm-6pm (4pm-7pm Sun).
Directions	From Aylsham towards Blickling, then 1st right to Itteringham.

Meals	12pm-2pm; 7pm-10pm. Main courses £7.50-£16.50; set menu, 2 courses, £15.
Closed	3pm-6pm.
Directions	Off A140, 3 miles south of Norwich.

Christian Hodgekinson
The Walpole Arms, The Common, Itteringham, Norwich NR11 7AR
Tel 01263 587258
Web www.thewalpolearms.co.uk

Henry Watt
The Wildebeest Arms, 82-86 Norwich Rd, Stoke Holy Cross, Norwich NR14 8QJ
Tel 01508 492497

Entry 464 Map 10

Entry 465 Map 10

The Mulberry Tree
Attleborough

Urbane, contemporary and soothing, this is just perfect for ladies (or shy gentlemen) who lunch, and it wouldn't matter if you arrived alone. There are lots of seating areas in the bar, along with bay windows, high ceilings, huge church candles in glass lanterns and dark leather sofas to guarantee comfort. There's good food, too. Choose from the bar menu (Suffolk ham with free-range eggs and hand-cut chips) or go the whole hog in the restaurant (potted Cromer crab, pan-fried sea bass). Gooey chocolate squares with butterscotch sauce and vanilla ice cream could finish you off, but retire to one of the lovely bedrooms upstairs and you can recover in comfort. The feel is New England/French colonial, with huge arty rococo mirrors, willow twigs in vases, slatted blinds and rich autumnal fabrics. This sophisticated pub is right in the middle of a sleepy market town and the local bowls club have their grounds behind; in summer, simple seating with parasols are set up behind the bar area with its big windows. Forests, beaches, market towns and nature reserves are near to explore.

Rooms	5: 4 doubles, 1 twin/double. £80. Singles £69.
Meals	12pm-2pm; 6.30pm-9pm. Main courses £10.95-£16.95; bar meals £5.45-£9.50.
Closed	Open all day.
Directions	On one-way system around town centre at junction with Station Road.

Philip & Victoria Milligan
The Mulberry Tree,
Station Road, Attleborough NR17 2AS

Tel	01953 452124
Web	www.the-mulberry-tree.co.uk

Norfolk

467 **King's Head** Harts Lane, Bawburgh, Norwich NR9 3LS
01603 744977

Unprepossessing yet with a terracotta façade, Anton Wimmer's old pub is full of low-beamed charm. Delight in East Anglian ales, wines by the glass and piped jazz. New chef – reports please.

468 **Fat Cat** 49 West End Street, Norwich NR2 4NA
01603 624364

Victorian corner pub and beer drinkers' heaven: 30 real ales with some on hand pump, others tapped from cask. The owners proudly keep this a traditional and simple drinking pub.

469 **Mad Moose Arms** 2 Warwick Road, Norwich NR2 3LD
01508 492497

The more relaxed, less polished sister pub to the Wildebeest Arms. Tall windows, red walls, darkwood panelling, funky wide-screen TV, good modern pub food and ale from Wolf Brewery.

470 **Buckinghamshire Arms** Blickling, Aylsham NR11 6NF
01263 732133

Handsome, NT-owned Jacobean inn close to the gates of the grand hall. Glowing wood-burners in old-pine furnished bars; tourists fill the lawns in summer. New landlords – reports please.

471 **The George** Cley-next-the-Sea, Holt NR25 7RN
01263 740652

The Norfolk Naturalists Trust was formed at this rambling Edwardian inn overlooking the saltmarshes. Refurbishment is on-going under Dan Goff (of the White Horse in Blakeney) and menus champion local produce.

472 **The Three Horseshoes** Warham All Saints, Warham NR23 1NL
01328 710547

Plain rooms that have barely changed since the 1930s – gas lights, rough deal tables, Victorian fireplaces. East Anglian ales tapped from the cask, good home cooking favouring old Norfolk recipes.

473 **The Lord Nelson** Walsingham Rd, Burnham Thorpe, Kings Lynn
PE31 8HN 01328 738241

Ancient benches and settles, worn brick, tile floors, and a serving hatch instead of a bar distinguish this marvellous place. Be tempted by a tot of Nelson's Blood or a pint of Woodforde's. Imaginative food and a family-friendly garden.

474 **The Lifeboat Inn** Ship Lane, Thornham PE36 6LT
01485 512236

The glowing lamps and open fires of this bags-of-character inn beckon. It's been an ale house since the 16th century – and they still serve a decent pint. The sea is a brisk, bracing walk across fields.

Northamptonshire

George & Dragon
Chacombe

It's an old pub – the building dates from 1640 and has been added to over the centuries – but a relative newcomer given that Chacombe appears in the Domesday Book. One wonders what they did for a drink until 1640. There's a great atmosphere at the George & Dragon, with its flagstones, low beams, simple furnishings, crackling log fire and mellow front festooned with flowers in summer. Like so many successful country pubs, it's reputation has been built on its food. Roast beef sandwiches, game terrine, steak and kidney pie, Norfolk crab salad, lamb Wellington, bread and butter pudding – this is good, comforting, English food. Almost all the ingredients are local, and there are real ales from Everards and several wines by the glass. Chacombe is a delightful conservation village and a world away from the M40 just over the hill.

Meals	12pm-2.30pm (3pm Sun); 6pm-9.30pm; no food Sun eve. Main Courses £7.50-£15.
Closed	Open all day.
Directions	M40 junc. 11; A361 for Daventry; Chacombe signed in 1 mile.

Richard Phillips
George & Dragon,
Silver Street, Chacombe,
Banbury OX17 2JR
Tel   01295 711500

Entry 475 Map 8

Northamptonshire

Royal Oak
Eydon

Everyone's welcome at the small and unpretentious Royal Oak. Walkers drop by to refuel, children are welcome in the games room, dogs amble freely. No music, just the hum of happy eaters. The menu – fresh, short, regularly changing – is the big attraction and you'll find not only the best of British – Gloucester Old Spot belly pork stuffed with black pudding, Cornish hake supreme – but also a touch of the exotic (eg. spicy vegetable tagine). The pretty, 17th-century honey-stone pub has old flagstones, exposed stone walls, a wood-burner in the inglenook and a Sunday-papers-and-a pint feel. The long bar is propped up by ale-quaffing regulars, the rest is made over to the games room and three small eating areas. There are picnic seats out in front and Eydon, though only seven miles from the motorway, feels as remote as can be.

Meals	12pm-2pm; 7pm-9pm; no food Mon. 1 course £14.50; 2 courses £19.95; 3 courses £23.95.
Closed	2.30pm-6pm (3pm-7pm Sun).
Directions	Off A361 midway between Banbury & Daventry.

Justin Lefevre
Royal Oak,
6 Lime Avenue, Eydon,
Banbury NN11 3PG
Tel   01327 263167

Entry 476 Map 8

Northamptonshire

Fox and Hounds
Great Brington

Near Althorp House – home of the Spencers – the pub is also known as the Althorp Coaching Inn. Decked with flowers inside and out, resting in the heart of an multi-thatched estate village, it is a popular place. There's an enclosed courtyard within earshot of the cricket green, a nice spot for a pint of Langton Bowler (alongside many other wonderful ales) and, when the nights draw in, the fires burn brightly in the restaurant and bar, glowingly traditional with its floorboards, flagstones and plentiful bric-a-brac. The regulars appreciate the good value meals and the baguettes from the bar, while the restaurant serves beef and game from the farm estate, cooked in an unfussy manner. Major sporting events – Silverstone is up the road – are shown (discreetly) in the bar, and Tuesday evenings see live music.

Meals	12pm-2.30pm; 6.30pm-9.30pm. Main courses £9.25-£16.75.
Closed	Open all day.
Directions	From Northampton, A428; then 1st left after Althorp; pub near Althorp Hall.

Jacqui Ellard
Fox and Hounds,
Main Street, Great Brington,
Northampton NN7 4JA
Tel   01604 770651

Entry 477 Map 8

Northamptonshire

The Wollaston Inn
Wollaston

It was once the Nag's Head: U2 played here and John Peel DJ'd. But then the local Doc Martens factory closed, and when the boots walked, so did the pub's rockin' clientele. When Chris Spencer took it on a few years ago it was a real dive. His aim was to clean up its act, and the result is as far from spit-and-sawdust as you can get – creamy walls, high ceilings, comfy sofas. The beer garden is now a courtyard patio with bay trees in terracotta pots. Chris is serious about his food, especially seafood, which changes daily. That doesn't mean pretentious: he won't have any truck with "drizzling", or "beds" of this or that. Instead, he does a Mediterranean saffron fish stew and hake steak – as well partridge, venison, ploughman's and steamed syrup pudding. The wine list is one to wade around in.

Meals	11am-9.30pm (10.30pm Sat & Sun). Main courses £8.50-£25; bar meals from £6.50.
Closed	Open all day.
Directions	Village signed off A509 south of Wellingborough.

Chris Spencer
The Wollaston Inn, 7 London Road,
Wollaston, Northampton NN29 7QS
Tel   01933 663161
Web   www.wollaston-inn.co.uk

Entry 478 Map 9

Northamptonshire

Snooty Fox
Lowick

If it weren't for the sign, this could be a manor house. (It was, four centuries ago.) Nowadays it's patronised as both pub and restaurant. The bar, with polished dining tables, caramel leather sofas and open fire, is separate from the dining room proper; both are beamed, flagged and open-stone-walled. And it's notably family friendly, with a toy box for children and a slide in the garden. There are Greene King IPA and Fuller's London Pride on tap but what sets this place apart is its chef-patron. Delicious pub favourites like homemade pork pie with chutney and bangers and mash are served in the bar, while in the restaurant there's a more upmarket rotisserie-grill menu – dry-aged steaks cut to order alongside such treats as braised belly pork with parmesan polenta and fresh crab tagliatelle. Very well worth seeking out.

Meals	12pm-2pm; 6pm-9.30pm. Main courses £10.50-£13.95.
Closed	Open all day.
Directions	A14 junc.12; follow A6116 for 2 miles.

Clive Dixon
Snooty Fox,
Main Street, Lowick NN14 3BH
Tel   01832 733434
Web   www.snootyinns.com/snootyfox/

Entry 479 Map 9

Northamptonshire

The Queen's Head
Bulwick

A mellow old stone pub in a lovely village – you'll wish this was your local. The simple beamed and flagstoned bar rambles into several country-styled dining rooms. This may be the owners' first pub venture, but their natural friendliness and instinct to keep things simple has worked in their favour. Bar food features the very good Grassmere Farm ham with local free range eggs, or try a steak and stilton toasted sandwich washed down with Rockingham Ales from the village microbrewery. The short à la carte menu is full of more extravagant enticements: whole roasted teal wrapped in prosciutto ham with spiced red cabbage and apple, honey-glazed turnips and celeriac crisps; roast monkfish with mussel, cockle and potato chowder; roast haunch of local wild venison rubbed in rosemary, garlic, lemon and juniper.

Meals	12pm-2.30pm; 6pm-9.30pm; no food Sun eve. Main courses £8.50-£19.95; bar snacks from £4.95.
Closed	3pm-6pm (7pm Sun) & Mon all day.
Directions	Just off A43, between Stamford & Corby.

Geoff Smith & Angela Partridge
The Queen's Head,
Main Street, Bulwick,
Corby NN17 3DY
Tel   01780 450272

Entry 480 Map 9

Northamptonshire

The Falcon
Oundle

The Falcon is a smashing place serving wonderful food. Discreetly, stylishly modernised, it keeps its pubby feel – darts in the tap bar, an open fire in the main bar and well-kept Adnams on hand pump. The extras are undoubtedly spoiling: high-back tapestry-covered chairs, candlelight and fresh flowers. Richard III was born in Fotheringhay Castle and Mary Queen of Scots was executed here; now the castle is a mound but the church is worth a visit and the Falcon picks up on the history in the prints in the bar. For a change of mood, head for the elegant, double conservatory. Cooking is stylishly simple, whether it's fillet of seabass with fennel, whole roast partridge with fondant potaotes, or linguine with salmon, chilli and crème fraîche. Wines are as good, with a surprising 18 by the glass.

Meals	12pm-2pm (3pm Sun); 6.15pm-9.15pm (8.30pm Sun). Main courses £13.95-£19.95; bar meals £4.95-£10.95.
Closed	Open all day.
Directions	Off A605 4 miles NE of Oundle.

Harry & Sally Facer
The Falcon, Fotheringhay, Oundle,
Peterborough PE8 5HZ
Tel   01832 226254
Web   www.thefalcon-inn.co.uk

Entry 481 Map 9

Northumberland

The Manor House Inn
Carterway Heads

No wonder it's a popular place. Cheerful young staff, tasty food, a good bar with four cask ales and a cask cider, eight wines by the glass, a raft of malts. The large, light lounge bar, with wood-burning stove and blackboard menu, is a great spot for meals, though there's a dining room if you prefer. Chicken liver pâté comes with onion marmalade, scallops with chilli jam, pigeon breast with mushroom and juniper sauce. In the smallish public bar, modestly furnished with oak settles and old pine tables, is a big open fire; owners Chris and Moira Brown add a further warm touch. Take your pint of Theakstons Best into the garden in summer where the eye sweeps over the Derwent valley to the Durham moors. There's a shop/delicatessen selling a wide range of goodies – puddings, chutneys, ice cream – much of it home-produced.

Meals	12pm-9.30pm. Main courses £6.75-£15; sandwiches from £3.95.
Closed	Open all day.
Directions	Beside A68 at junction with B6278; 3 miles west of Consett.

Moira & Chris Brown
The Manor House Inn,
Carterway Heads,
Shotley Bridge DH8 9LX
Tel   01207 255268

Entry 482 Map 12

Northumberland

The Feathers Inn
Hedley on the Hill

Since taking over in 2007, Helen and Rhian have built on the Feathers' reputation as a destination for good food, yet this pub keeps its old-fashioned pubby feel. It is a rare treat west of Newcastle to find such an authentic little place. In the two bars are old beams, exposed stone, Turkey rugs, simple furnishings, open fires and a cottagey feel; you'd feel as much at home browsing the papers here as enjoying a fireside chat. Beer is excellent, with four cask beers from local or microbreweries; wines are taken as seriously. The delicious food – wild Holy Island mussels cooked in cider with thyme and parsley; venison and game pie with braised red cabbage; roast Muggleswick grouse with bread sauce and game gravy – is cooked with skill and passion by Rhian from locally sourced produce. A star in the making.

Meals	12pm-3pm; 6pm-9pm; no food Mon. Main courses £9-£15; bar meals £3.
Closed	Open all day. Closed Mon lunch.
Directions	From Consett, B6309 north to New Ridley; follow signs to Hedley on the Hill.

Helen Greer & Rhian Cradock
The Feathers Inn, Hedley on the Hill,
Stocksfield NE43 7SW
Tel 01661 843607
Web www.thefeathers.net

🚶 🍽 🍺 🍷

Entry 483 Map 12

Northumberland

Dipton Mill
Hexham

Less than a ten-minute drive out of town along a rollercoaster road, Geoff Brooker's old inn squats in a deep hollow next to a stone bridge and a babbling brook. Formerly a mill house built around 1750, it's been updated but within the tiny interior there's still a single warm and intimate bar with panelled walls, low ceilings, small leaded windows and blazing winter log fires. Food is home-cooked: warming soups and steak and kidney pie, or ploughman's with a rare choice of British and local cheeses. Real-ale fans will know that the Dipton Mill is the brewery tap for Hexhamshire Brewery ales, Geoff being both landlord and head brewer. For summer: a big walled garden with a wooden bridge over the mill stream. For winter, a word of warning: if there's ice, you may get down the hill you may not get up again! A fantastic pub.

Meals	12pm-2pm; 6.30pm-8.30pm. Main courses £5.50-£8.00.
Closed	2.30pm-6pm & Sun eve.
Directions	From Hexham B6306 for Blanchland; 2nd right onto Dipton Mill Road to Whitley Chapel & Racecourse; pub 2 miles on.

Geoff Brooker
Dipton Mill,
Dipton Mill Road,
Hexham NE46 1YA
Tel 01434 606577

♿ 🚶 🐕 🍺 🍷

Entry 484 Map 12

Northumberland

The Angel
Corbridge

Even older than Hadrian's Wall, quaint Corbridge is a pretty place with the 17th-century Angel, full of history and character, at its heart. Step straight into the splendid panelled lounge, cosy with its leather armchairs, heavy drapes, big open fire and newspapers to browse. Off to the left, a plush dining room – deep carpeting, polished tables, sparkling glassware; to the right, the bar. This is a big room, simply decorated in brasserie style with a bright and contemporary feel. Cask beers are available and the menu, chalked on a blackboard over the fire, announces sunblush tomato soufflé as well as more traditional dishes, and the Angel's legendary Yorkshire pudding. There's a beer garden at the back, more places to sit at the front. A comfortable stopover on the long journey from north to south.

Meals	12pm-9pm (9.30pm Fri & Sat; 12pm-4pm Sun); no food Sun eve. Main courses £7.95-£12.50 (lunch), £8.95-£19.95 (dinner); sandwiches from £4.25.
Closed	Open all day.
Directions	In Corbridge, 2 miles off A69.

John Gibson
The Angel,
Main Street, Corbridge,
Hexham NE45 5LA
Tel 01434 632119

Entry 485 Map 12

Northumberland

Queens Head Inn
Great Whittington

A warm refuge in a wild country of moors, sheep and vast skies. The mellow bar is charming, its 1930s hunting mural satisfactorily yellowed by open fires. Gleaming beer engines disburse High House Farm Brewery ale from down the road; hunting prints hint at local interests; a background tape plays. Toast your toes from the carved oak settle before the fire, then up steps to a traditional lounge and another log-filled grate for those bitter Northumbrian days. Gill Jackman greets all who enter from the cold, staff are still gently charming and people come for the food; chef Steven Murran uses the best available produce, including local beef and lamb. Daily menus may include seared red mullet with coriander and lime dressing, crisp pork belly with apple and cider jus, and dark chocolate steamed pudding.

Meals	12pm-2pm; 5.30pm-9pm (6pm-9.30pm Fri & Sat); 12pm-8pm Sun. Main courses £7.95-£19.95; bar meals from £4.50.
Closed	Open all day.
Directions	Off B6318, 4 miles north of Corbridge.

Ron & Gill Jackman
Queens Head Inn,
Great Whittington,
Corbridge NE19 2HP
Tel 01434 672267

Entry 486 Map 12

Battlesteads Hotel
Wark

In the land of castles, stone circles and fortified towers is Battlesteads, an old inn given a fresh lease of life by energetic new owners. Enter a large, cosy, low-beamed and panelled bar with a fire in the brick hearth and local cask ales on hand pump. A step further and you find a second bar, more spacious; further still, a big formal dining area: leather chairs at dark wood tables, blue drapes at tall windows, a sweep of new floor. And now there's a spanking new conservatory dining room that reaches into the sunny walled garden. The menus show a commitment to sourcing locally, and that includes lamb, beef and fish landed at North Shields. The food is flavoursome, one example being home-cured Angus beef with juniper berries, peppercorns and herbs, meltingly tender; another is 'two-day duck' with a rich bacon and pea jus. The housekeeping is exemplary so bedrooms are spotless as well as spacious, carpeted and comfortable, and the newest, with wheelchair access, are on the ground floor. Hadrian's Wall is marvellously close.

Rooms	17 twins/doubles. £90–£110. Singles £50–£60.
Meals	12pm-3pm; 6.30pm-9pm (9.30pm Fri, Sat & Sun). Main courses £8.95-£18.50; bar meals £4.95-£9.50.
Closed	Open all day.
Directions	From A69 at Hexham, A6079 to Chollerford, then A6320 for Bellingham; Wark is halfway.

Richard & Dee Slade
Battlesteads Hotel,
Wark, Hexham NE48 3LS

Tel	01434 230209
Web	www.battlesteads.com

The Pheasant Inn
Stannersburn

A super little inn run with an instinctive understanding of its traditions. The stone walls hold old photos of the community; from colliery to smithy, a vital record of its past. The bars are wonderful: brass beer taps glow, anything wooden has been polished to perfection and the clock above the fire keeps perfect time. The house ales are expertly kept – Timothy Taylor's, Theakston's Black Sheep – and Robin cooks with relish, nothing too fancy, but more than enough to keep a smile on your face: Thai potato soup, fish simply grilled, no chips. As for Sunday lunch, *The Observer* readers voted it one of the best in the North. Bedrooms in the purpose-built annexe and the old hay barn are simple and tidy, not grand but cosy, and you'll get a piping hot breakfast the next morning – accompanied maybe by a view of the sheepdogs bringing the herd in for shearing. This is the glorious Northumberland National Park – no traffic jams, no rush – and don't miss the sculpture at Kielder. Then hire bikes and cycle round the lake, or saddle up on a pony and take to the hills.

Rooms	8: 4 doubles, 3 twins, 1 family room. £80–£85. Singles £45–£50.
Meals	12pm-2pm (2.30pm Sun); 7pm-9pm. Main courses £9.50–£14.50; bar meals £7.50–£8.50.
Closed	3pm-6.30pm (7pm Sun); Mon & Tues Nov-Mar.
Directions	From Bellingham follow signs west to Kielder Water & Falstone for 7 miles. Hotel on left, 1 mile short of Kielder Water.

Walter, Irene & Robin Kershaw
The Pheasant Inn,
Stannersburn,
Kielder Water NE48 1DD

Tel	01434 240382
Web	www.thepheasantinn.com

Entry 488 Map 14

The Ship Inn
Low Newton-by-the-Sea

An authentic coastal inn with tongue and groove boarding and flooring, old settles, scrubbed tables and a solid-fuel stove. Step in and step back a hundred years. Landlady Christine Forsyth fell in love with the simplicity of the place and gives you provender to match. The home-brewed beer and fair trade coffee and chocolate blend beautifully with a menu built around the best local produce – simple, fresh, satisfying. Local hand-picked-crab rolls, lobster from over the way, Craster kippers from two miles down the coast, ploughman's with local unpasteurised cheddar and Turnbulls free-range ham. In the evenings there's often a choice (venison, grilled red mullet) but do book first. Park on a compulsory plot back from the beach and take the short walk to the sand, green and pub. Worth every step.

The Olde Ship
Seahouses

The Glen dynasty has been at the helm of this nautical gem for close on a century. The inn sparkles with maritime memorabilia to remind you of Seahouses' fine heritage and the days when Grace Darling rowed through huge seas to rescue stricken souls. Settle into the atmospheric main bar by the glowing fire with a decent pint – there are eight ales to choose from – and gaze across the harbour to the Farne Islands and the Longstone Light (later, take the ferry). In the smaller 'cabin' bar you can get stuck into some hearty food – lentil and tomato soup, wild boar terrine with Cumberland sauce, beef stroganoff, fish chowder, lamb curry, bread and butter pudding. Dinner in the restaurant is a set four-course affair. The place positively creaks with history – retreat here after a bracing coastal walk to Bamburgh Castle.

Meals	12pm-2.30pm; phone for evening opening & food times. Main courses £7-£22; bar meals £2-£6.95.
Closed	4pm-6pm Mon-Thurs. Open all day weekends & school hols.
Directions	From Alnwick B1340 for Seahouses for 8 miles to crossroads; straight over, follow signs.

Meals	12pm-2.30pm; 7pm-8.30pm Main courses £7.50-£13.25; bar meals £4.25-£13.25
Closed	Open all day.
Directions	B1340 off A1 8 miles north of Alnwick; inn above harbour.

Christine Forsyth
The Ship Inn, The Square,
Low Newton-by-the-Sea,
Alnwick NE66 3EL
Tel   01665 576262

A & J Glen, D Swan & J Glen
The Olde Ship,
Main Street, Seahouses NE68 7RD
Tel   01665 720200
Web   www.seahouses.co.uk

Entry 489 Map 14

Entry 490 Map 14

Nottinghamshire

Ye Olde Trip to Jerusalem
Nottingham

As much a museum piece as a pub. Parts of the building date from 1037 and certainly there has been brewing on the site since the 1170s (to supply the needs of the castle above), while the crusaders probably met here en route to Jerusalem. An amazing place carved into solid rock on which the castle sits. There are rickety staircases, ancient chimneys that were cut up through the rock to assist medieval brewing, and a cursed galleon, hairy with dust because the last three people who cleaned it died. The Rock Lounge, with its sandstone ceiling and chimney, is aptly named, the cellars stretch more than 100 feet beneath the castle, and there's a small courtyard for those who choose daylight. The Trip (meaning 'resting place') serves a mixed crowd – locals, tourists, students – and the food is standard pub grub.

Nottinghamshire

Cock & Hoop
Nottingham

Opposite the law courts – now an award-winning museum – the old ale house once gave sanctuary to judges preparing for the hangings that took place outside. The pub is a happier place today, shoppers, city workers and trendies making a bee-line for the most civilised spot in town. There are two rooms, one at ground level, one below. Below is larger and softly lit; ground-level has an open fire and a tiny bar. Both have wooden panelling and bare-brick walls, plush furnishings, armchairs, benches, club chairs. Friendly staff know their stuff, beers are well-kept (Black Sheep, London Pride) and there's an unexpectedly good selection of whiskies and wines. Food takes in club sandwiches, homemade soups, roast salmon, sticky toffee pudding, all courtesy of the stylishly informal hotel next door.

Meals	12pm-8pm.
	Main courses £5.55-£8.95.
Closed	Open all day.
Directions	From inner ring road follow A6005 'The North' to Castle Boulevard; right into Castle Road.

Meals	12pm-10pm.
	Main courses £8.95-£11.95.
Closed	Open all day.
Directions	From city centre, follow brown signs for Lace Market; next to Lace Market Hotel.

Allen Watson
Ye Olde Trip to Jerusalem,
1 Brewhouse Yard,
Nottingham NG1 6AD

Tel   0115 947 3171
Web   www.triptojerusalem.com

Entry 491 Map 8

Andrew Hunt
Cock & Hoop, 25 High Pavement,
Nottingham NG1 1HE

Tel   01158 523231
Web   www.cockandhoop.co.uk

Entry 492 Map 8

Nottinghamshire

The Victoria
Beeston

A large picture of Queen Victoria rules the main bar of this unpretentious and bustling city-suburb pub. It's an ex-Victorian railway hotel with bags of character, and its awesome raft of ales, wines by the glass and malt whiskies pulls in a crowd. The civilised main bar, with fire, newspapers on racks and etched windows, sets the tone for the other rooms, all plainly painted in magnolia with woodblock flooring and scrubbed dark-wood or brass-topped tables. Blackboards give the food and booze headlines. You get Sicilian pork, cottage pie and veggie dishes to delight even non-vegetarians (pasta with goat's cheese and rocket pesto). At the back, there's a heated marquee area for cooler summer nights; dine as the trains go by. Service is efficient and friendly. Try to catch the summer festival of ale, food and music.

Meals	12pm-8.45pm (7.45pm Sun). Main courses £6.95-£11.95.
Closed	Open all day.
Directions	Off A6005 at the bottom of Dovecote Lane. Follow signs to Beeston station.

Neil Kelso & Graham Smith
The Victoria,
Dovecote Lane, Beeston NG9 1JG
Tel   0115 925 4049
Web   www.victoriabeeston.co.uk

Entry 493 Map 8

Nottinghamshire

Martin's Arms
Colston Bassett

An Elizabethan farmhouse that became an ale house around 1700, and an inn 100 years later. Today it is a deeply civilised pub. The front room exudes so much country-house charm – scatter cushions on sofas and settles, crackling logs in Jacobean fireplaces, 18th-century prints – that the bar seems almost an intrusion. Fresh, seasonal menus change daily. Bar snacks include special sandwiches, warm salads and splendid ploughman's lunches with Colston Bassett stilton from the dairy up the road (do visit). In the restaurant, the highlight of the winter menu is Park Farm Estate game shot by Salvatore the chef. Polish it all off with raspberry and mascarpone shortbread with stem ginger. Behind the bar is an impressive range of well-kept real ales, cognacs, wines and malts from Adnams. Superb.

Meals	12pm-2pm; 6pm-10pm; no food Sun eve. Main courses £12.50-£21.95; bar meals £9.95-£21.95.
Closed	3pm-6pm (7pm Sun).
Directions	Off A46, east of Nottingham. Take Owthorpe turning.

Lynne Strafford Bryan
& Salvatore Inguanta
Martin's Arms, School Lane,
Colston Bassett NG12 3FD
Tel   01949 81361

Entry 494 Map 9

Nottinghamshire

Waggon & Horses
Halam

Enthused by its fantastic reputation for food, chef Roy Wood jumped at the chance to buy the Whites' share of the business in 2007. Enticing menus change with the seasons and almost everything is sourced locally, while the fish arrives daily from Cornwall. So try braised monkfish wrapped in Parma ham with seared scallops and saffron linguine, and venison loin with grilled polenta and marinated pears; even lunchtime's rolls are worth travelling for. This spotlessly maintained pub is small, oak beamed and softly lit with low ceilings and bold walls. In the cosy but open-plan bar, rush-seated chairs pull up to sturdy tables; there's the odd settle and masses of cricket memorabilia. It's a Thwaites' tied house, friendly and expertly run; they also do catering for parties. Sit outside and watch the Halam world go by.

Meals	12pm-2.30pm (3pm Sun); 6pm-9.30pm; no food Sun eve. Main courses £9-£16; set menu (lunch & early eve) £12 & £15.
Closed	3pm-5.30pm Mon-Sat. Sun eves.
Directions	Halam is signed off A612 or B6386 in Southwell.

Roy & Laura Wood
Waggon & Horses, Mansfield Road, Halam, Newark NG22 8AE
Tel   01636 813109
Web   www.thewaggonathalam.co.uk

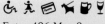

Entry 495 Map 9

Nottinghamshire

Caunton Beck
Caunton

Having hatched the successful Wig & Mitre in Lincoln, the Hopes looked for a rural equivalent and found one in Caunton. The pub was lovingly reconstructed from the skeleton of the 16th-century Hole Arms and then renamed. A decade on and it is a hugely popular pub-restaurant, opening at 8am for breakfast – orange juice, espresso, scrambled eggs. Later, there are sandwiches, mussels with pickled ginger and coriander laksa and pot-roasted guinea fowl; the puddings are fabulous. It's all very relaxed and civilised, the sort of place where newspapers and magazines take precedence over piped music and electronic wizardry. Come for country chairs at scrubbed pine tables, rag-rolled walls and a fire in winter, parasols on the terrace in summer. Well-managed ales are on hand pump, and the village is pretty.

Meals	8am-11pm. Main courses £9.50-£19.95.
Closed	Open all day.
Directions	6 miles NW of Newark past sugar factory on A616.

Michael & Valerie Hope
Caunton Beck, Main Street, Caunton, Newark NG23 6AB
Tel   01636 636793
Web   www.wigandmitre.com

Entry 496 Map 9

Nottinghamshire

497 Bottle & Glass High Street, Harby, Newark NG23 7EB
01522 703438

Quirky village pub now owned by the Hopes from Lincoln's famous Wig & Mitre. Victorian features blend with soft furnishings and chalkboard menus list soup to Sevruga caviar, all-day breakfast and 38 wines by the glass.

498 Robin Hood High Street, Elkesley, Worksop DN22 8AJ
01777 838259

A far better pit-stop than the roadside 'restaurants' on offer: take the Elkesley turning off the A1 for a decent ploughman's or a lamb confit with mint pesto, garlic and thyme sauce.

499 Black Horse Caythorpe, Nottingham NG14 7ED
0115 966 3520

A tiny, carpeted bar where Sharron Andrews sells beer brewed on the premises and the fish menu is so popular that booking is essential. Dick Turpin once hid in the gents, apparently.

500 Larwood and Voce Fox Road, Trent Bridge, Nottingham NG2 6AJ
0115 981 9960

Thriving town-centre 'pub and kitchen' next to Trent Bridge cricket ground. Come for the smart modern bar, cricket on the plasma screen, live jazz and decent gastropub food. The bar throngs on match days.

Worth a visit

Photo: istockphoto.com

Oxfordshire

The Lamb
Satwell

'Real ale, real food and real people,' reads the sign. Close to watery Henley-on-Thames, the 16th-century beamed cottage is owned by TV chef Anthony Worrall Thompson – and the words on the sign ring true. Enter a gorgeously low-beamed bar: scrubbed pine tables on tiled floors, logs crackling in the grate, local ales on hand pump. Arrive early to bag a seat by the fire (no bookings) or settle into the cosy dining room next door; be treated to steaming plates of home-cooked pies, casseroles and stews very fairly priced. There's classic fish pie, Irish stew, steak and kidney pie and Wozza'a own Middlewhite pork sausages with mash and onion gravy. So start with half a pint of prawns, finish with rhubarb crumble; it's all scrumptiously English and don't miss the Sunday roasts. There's a secluded garden, too.

Meals	12pm-2.30pm (4pm Sat); 6pm-9.30pm (10.30pm Fri & Sat); 12pm-9pm Sun. Main courses £7.95-£9.95; Sunday roast £9.95.
Closed	3pm-6pm. Open all day Sat & Sun.
Directions	A4130 north from Henley; 5 miles; 1st exit at r'bout near Nettlebed onto B481 to Highmoor; thro' village; 1 mile to Satwell.

	William McCord
	The Lamb, Satwell,
	Shepherd's Green,
	Henley-on-Thames RG9 4QZ
Tel	01491 628482
Web	www.awtonline.co.uk

Entry 501 Map 4

Oxfordshire

Rising Sun
Witheridge Hill

Much-loved landlady Judith Bishop is back with Brakspear and loving every minute of it. In this creamy cottage-pub, tucked up a gravel track on the edge of the Chilterns, her magic touch is clearly to be seen... in the rambling dining area and in the cosy bar, with its bare boards, terracotta walls, scrubbed pine tables, deep sofa by the crackling fire and no end of lovely touches – books, magazines and huge vases of flowers. Eager to do something different on the food front, Judith has introduced tapas dishes and 'grazing' plates (Indian or mezze) to share – as well as stilton and guinness paté, pigeon breast wrapped in Parma ham with sherry gravy, and a classic beef and beer pie. Great ales, a secluded garden and a deli corner selling homemade and local goodies add to the pleasure.

Meals	12pm-2.30pm (3pm Sun); 7pm-9.30pm; no food Sun eve in winter. Main courses £8.95-£15.50; £5 lunch dish (Mon-Thurs).
Closed	3pm-6pm. Open all day Sat & Sun.
Directions	Witheridge Hill is signed off B481 east of Stoke Row.

	Judith Bishop
	Rising Sun,
	Witheridge Hill,
	Henley-on-Thames RG9 1AH
Tel	01491 640856

Entry 502 Map 4

Oxfordshire

The Five Horseshoes
Maidensgrove

This pub-cottage sits up high in a remote spot in the Chilterns, on a tiny lane that winds its way past Russell's Water near Stonor House. Arrive early in summer for the best seat in the garden and the finest view in Oxfordshire. As you gaze on rolling hills, pint of Brakspears to hand, red kites wheel overhead and steaks sizzle on the weekend barbecue. Windows in the conservatory dining room also get the view, so you can relish it all year round – or head into the rambling, low-ceilinged bar where a wood-burning stove warms the cockles. Cosy and carpeted, with cushioned settles and scrubbed tables, it's a perfect place for tucking into the comforting pub food. The focus is on fresh, local produce. Try the game terrine or wild Oxfordshire venison, and there's roast beef and pork on Sundays. Then head off into the hills.

Oxfordshire

The Crooked Billet
Stoke Row

Dick Turpin apparently courted the landlord's daughter and Kate Winslet had her wedding breakfast here. Pints are drawn direct from the cask (there is no bar!) and the rusticity of the pub charms all who manage to find it: beams and inglenooks, old pine, walls lined with bottles and baskets of spent corks. In the larger room, red walls display old photographs and mirrors; shelves are stacked with books... by candlelight it's irresistible. You come here to eat and the menu is Italian/French provincial, and long: beef fillet with seared foie gras and red wine jus, venison with roast figs and port and juniper, chocolate tart with mint ice cream. It's founded on supremely well-sourced raw materials and bolstered by a satisfying wine list. Occasional jazz, and a big garden bordering the beech woods where children can roam.

Meals	12pm-2.30pm (3pm Sat, 4pm Sun); 6.30pm-9.30pm.
	Main courses £8.50-£16; bar meals £5-£9.75; Sunday roast £13.75.
Closed	3.30pm-6pm & Sun from 6pm. Open all day Sat.
Directions	Maidensgrove signed off B481 north of Nettlebed, & B480 4 miles north of Henley.

Meals	12pm-2.30pm; 7pm-10.30pm (12pm-10.30pm Sat & Sun).
	Main courses £12.50-£20.
Closed	2.30pm-7pm. Open all day Sat & Sun.
Directions	5 miles W of Henley, off B481 Reading to Nettlebed road.

Nataliina Langlands-Pearse
The Five Horseshoes, Maidensgrove,
Henley-on-Thames RG9 6EX
Tel   01491 641282
Web   www.thefivehorseshoes.co.uk

Entry 503 Map 4

Paul Clerehugh
The Crooked Billet,
Newlands Lane, Stoke Row,
Henley-on-Thames RG9 5PU
Tel   01491 681048
Web   www.thecrookedbillet.co.uk

Entry 504 Map 8

The Cherry Tree Inn
Stoke Row

A cherry orchard flourished here 400 years ago and farm workers lived in these brick and flint cottages. Five trees survive on the sprawling lawn at the front, so come in spring for the blossom. Beds of lavender lead up to the front door, inside you find ancient stone flagging and low beamed ceilings, plus board games in a cupboard, fairylights in the fireplace and a different colour on the walls in each room. Beers are from Brakspear and there's a very decent selection of wines by the glass but it's the food that's the draw. Huge bowls of mussels flow from the kitchen, plates of rare roast beef and updates of classic puddings; our tarte tatin came with a calvados sauce. Rooms in the next-door barn are good value for money, stylish and private, with walls of colour, creamy carpets, silky red throws and leather headboards. Two have high beamed ceilings, bathrooms with slate floors are just the ticket, and each room has its own thermostat. A breakfast club for locals runs on the first Saturday of each month, so you may have company. Expect kippers, scrambled eggs, the full works.

Rooms	4 doubles. £95.
Meals	12pm-3pm (4pm Sat & Sun); 7pm-10.30pm. Main courses £7.50-£13.50 (lunch), £10.50-£15.50 (dinner).
Closed	Open all day. Closed Sun from 4pm.
Directions	A4070 north from Reading. After four miles, right, through Checkendon, to the village of Stoke Row.

Richard Coates & Paul Gilchrist
The Cherry Tree Inn,
Stoke Row,
Henley-on-Thames RG9 5QA

Tel	01491 680430
Web	www.thecherrytreeinn.com

Oxfordshire

Sweet Olive @ The Chequers Inn
Aston Tirrold

Expect more than a hint of Gallic charm at this homely village local close to the Ridgeway Path: the owners and all the staff are French, which gives it a great deal of style. In the locals' bar, a central pillar and beam are lined with old wooden wine boxes, there's Hooky on hand pump and first-class French country cooking (with a hint of North Africa) in the rustic bistro dining room with its quarry tiled floor, roaring fire and old oak furniture. The blackboard menu changes daily with much emphasis placed on seasonal and organic food: oxtail in puff pastry with red burgundy sauce, escalope of venison with creamed cabbage and port wine. Children's meals are prepared from the same menu, simple snacks and fresh baguettes are served at lunch time, the wine list is mainly French, and the coffee is perfect.

Meals	12pm-2pm; 7pm-9pm.
	Main courses £11.95-£15.50.
Closed	3pm-6pm; Sun eve & all day Weds.
Directions	Aston Tirrold is signed off
	A417 between Streatley &
	Wantage.

Stephane Brun & Olivier Bouet
Sweet Olive @ The Chequers Inn,
Aston Tirrold, Didcot OX11 9DD
Tel   01235 851272
Web   www.sweet-olive.com

Entry 506 Map 4

Oxfordshire

The Bull & Butcher
Turville

Landlady Lydia Botha ensures this little pub quenches the thirsts of all who come to visit – and many do – one of the most bucolic film locations in Britain. The Vicar of Dibley has strutted Turville's streets, suspects from *Midsomer Murders* have propped up the bar. There's bags of atmosphere here, and style, in cream walls, latched doors, fresh flowers. It's a jolly place in which to down a pint of Brakspear's finest and indulge is some good modern British food: lamb casserole, sea bass with red pepper risotto, a superb steak and kidney pudding. There's no piped music, no games, no pubby paraphernalia, just fine 17th-century beams, working log fires, a unique function room, and friendly people. Londoners descend at weekends, there's a garden to spill into and great walks through the Chiltern beech woods.

Meals	12pm-2.30pm (4pm Sun);
	6.30pm-9.30pm (7pm-9pm Sun);
	12pm-9.30pm Sat.
	Main courses £10-£14;
	bar meals £6-£10.
Closed	Open all day.
Directions	M40 junc. 5; through Ibstone;
	for Turville at T-junction.

Lydia Botha
The Bull & Butcher, Turville,
Henley-on-Thames RG9 6QU
Tel   01491 638283
Web   www.thebullandbutcher.com

Entry 507 Map 4

Oxfordshire

Fox and Hounds
Christmas Common

In a hamlet in the hills – a few grand houses and this 15th-century brick and flint cottage: the civilised Fox and Hounds. Once it was a rustic rural ale house, but Brakspears have transformed it into a thriving food pub under the guidance of chef-landlord Kieron Daniels. Enter a beamy bar full of simple benches, cosy corners, logs glowing in a vast inglenook (always lit), cribbage and cards and pints of Brakspear tapped direct from the cask. The foodie action takes place in the restaurant, with its open-to-view kitchen and French windows to the garden. Farm-reared meats and local fruit and vegetables result in such dishes as mussel and brown shrimp risotto, roast partridge with cranberry gravy, panna cotta and candy ginger. Make time for walks through the beech woods, look out for soaring red kites.

Meals	12pm-2.30pm (3pm Sat & Sun); 7pm-9.30pm. Main courses £10-£18.
Closed	3pm-5pm in winter & Sun eves. Open all day Sat.
Directions	From M40 junc. 5 follow old A40.

Kieron Daniels
Fox and Hounds,
Christmas Common,
Watlington OX49 5HL
Tel   01491 612599

♿ 🚶 ▦ 🐾 🍷
Entry 508 Map 4

Oxfordshire

The Lord Nelson
Brightwell Baldwin

The back-lane setting of Brightwell Baldwin lives up to expectations; cottages tumbling down the hill, a church perched on a bank, a rambling old inn festooned with flowers, flags on Trafalgar Day. The creamy façade and front veranda entice you into a civilised interior, all wooden floors, wonky beams, logs fires, cosy corners and charm. Antiques, fine old prints and Nelson memorabilia keep the eye entertained. Most come to dine and dine well you can, on chicken liver parfait with homemade chutney, monkfish with mustard beurre blanc, lemon tart with raspberry coulis. Retire to the snug (deep sofas, table lamps, a country-house feel) for coffee and a little doze. And there's more – Brakspear on tap, 20 wines by the glass, friendly, smiley service and a wonderful rear terrace for summer sipping.

Meals	12pm-2.30pm; 6.30pm-10pm (7pm-9.30pm Sun). Main courses £12.95-£18.95; set lunch £10.95.
Closed	3pm-6pm.
Directions	Village signed off B4009 between Benson & Watlington.

Roger & Carole Shippey
The Lord Nelson, Brightwell Baldwin,
Watlington OX49 5NP
Tel   01491 612497
Web   www.lordnelson-inn.co.uk

♿ 🚶 ▦ 🐾 🍷
Entry 509 Map 4

Oxfordshire

The Mole Inn
Toot Baldon

The Mole continues to wow discerning Oxford foodies – it is packed most days. Expect an impeccable stone exterior, a landscaped garden and a ravishing bar. Be delighted by stripped beams and chunky walls, black leather sofas, logs in the grate and a dresser that groans with breads and olive jars. Chic rusticity proceeds into three dining areas: fat candles on blond wooden tables, thick terracotta floors and the sun angling in on a fresh plateful of beef casserole with garlic and bacon dauphinoise. Daily specials point to a menu that trawls the globe for inspiration, and whether you go for light salad and pasta bowl lunches or monkfish and king prawn stir fry with egg noodles and sweet chilli, you'll eat well. Scrumptious ice creams, British cheeses, good wines, local Hook Norton ale and polite staff complete the picture.

Meals	12pm-2.30pm (4pm Sun); 7pm-9.30pm (6pm-9pm Sun). Main courses £9.50-£15.95; bar meals £5.95-£9.95.
Closed	Open all day.
Directions	From A4074, 5 miles south of Oxford; turn at Nuneham Courtenay for Marsh Baldon & Toot Baldon.

Gary Witchalls
The Mole Inn,
Toot Baldon, Oxford OX44 9NG
Tel 01865 340001
Web www.themoleinn.com

Entry 510 Map 8

Oxfordshire

The Half Moon
Cuxham

A new venture for Andrew and Eilidh in this thatched house on the main street of the village. Cleverly they have retained the feel of a pub – quarry tiles, floorboards, farm implements, warming fires and a mishmash of settles and rush-seated chairs – whilst serving the most contemporary of British food (duck hearts or lambs kidneys on toast, local pheasant stew, curly kale and bacon). There are over 30 bins to choose from, or try a pint of Brakspears. Step outside to a small area with seating for barbecues on sunny days, then a herb garden and a polytunnel where as many vegetables as possible are grown; they also prepare and deliver food to homes in the village to take the hard work out of entertaining. A lovely, informal place – no wonder Henry the springer spaniel makes an appearance most evenings.

Meals	12pm-2pm (3pm Sun); 6pm-9pm. Breakfast 9am-11am Sat; Sunday brunch 10am-2pm; no food Sun eve. Main courses £9.50-£18.50.
Closed	2.30pm-5.30pm. Open all day Sun.
Directions	M40 junc 6; follow B4009 south to Watlington, then right along B480 to Cuxham.

Andrew Hill & Eilidh Ferguson
The Half Moon,
Cuxham, Watlington OX49 5NF
Tel 01491 614151
Web www.thehalf-moon.com

Entry 511 Map 4

Oxfordshire

The Fishes
Oxford

Location, location, location – The Fishes has it all. Three acres of gardens, minutes from the A34, and walking distance from the dreaming spires. It's run by Peach Pubs, the most innovative small pub group in the land; where else can you borrow a rug for the garden, order a Pimms and a picnic basket for two and spread out by a river? Just arrive early on fine days. Order (by midweek) a family roast beef platter for the weekend, on Sunday sit down to it on the veranda. The successful Peach food formula is reproduced here: the deli board selection, the starters of pumpkin and sage risotto and Caesar salad, the main dishes of fish stew, salmon Wellington and braised blade of beef with baby onion jus. Greene King ales, decent wines by the glass and a passion for locally sourced produce complete this very rosy picture.

Meals	12pm-10pm (9.30pm Sun). Main courses £8.75-£15.50; Sunday roast £10.50.
Closed	Open all day.
Directions	North on A34; left junction after Botley Interchange, signed to Rugby Club. From south, exit A34 at Botley & return to A34 south; then as above.

	Ben Matthews The Fishes, North Hinksey, Oxford OX2 0NA
Tel	01865 249796
Web	www.fishesoxford.co.uk

Entry 512 Map 8

Oxfordshire

The White Hart
Fyfield

Incredible to think that when Henry VIII came to the throne this building was already 70 years old. Stone mullioned windows, huge oak timbers and a magnificent arch-braced roof are the backdrop for oak settles, wrought-iron candle holders, white linen napkins, fresh flowers and delicious food cooked by Mark. The menu is extensive and modern: antipasti, mezze and fish boards for one or to share, then roast fillet of venison with beetroot gratin, savoy cabbage and bacon. Specials may include a plate of three-year-aged Iberico ham from wild acorn-fed black pigs, and suppliers are mentioned on the menu so you can see where everything comes from. Enjoy four real ales and Cheddar valley cider, and staff who are capable and knowledgeable (they were all taken to Hook Norton recently to see how the beer was brewed).

Meals	12pm-2.30pm (3pm Sat & Sun); 7pm-9.30pm (6.30pm-9pm Sun). Main courses £11.95-£19.50; lunch £13.95 & £16.95.
Closed	3pm-5.30pm; Mon all day. Open all day Sat & Sun.
Directions	Fyfield is just off A420 Oxford to Swindon road, 7 miles south west of Oxford; pub in village centre.

	Mark & Kay Chandler The White Hart, Main Road, Fyfield, Abingdon OX13 5LW
Tel	01865 390585
Web	www.whitehart-fyfield.com

Entry 513 Map 8

The Trout at Tadpole Bridge
Buckland Marsh

A 17th-century Cotswold inn on the banks of the Thames, so pick up a pint, drift into the garden and watch life float by. The Trout is a drinking fisherman's paradise, walls are busy with bendy rods, children are liked and dogs can doze in the flagstoned bars. The downstairs is open plan and timber-framed, there are gilt mirrors and logs piled high in alcoves. Gareth and Helen have cast their fairy dust into every corner: super bedrooms, oodles of style, fabulous modern food. Bedrooms at the back are away from the crowd; three open onto a small courtyard where wild roses ramble on creamy stone – but you may prefer to stay put in your room and indulge in funky fabrics, trim carpets, monsoon showers (one room has a claw-foot bath), DVD players, a library of films. Sleigh beds, brass beds, beautifully upholstered armchairs… one room even has a roof terrace. You can watch boats pass from the breakfast table, feast on local sausages, tuck into homemade marmalade courtesy of Helen's mum. Food is as local as possible, and there are maps for walkers to keep you thin. Bliss!

Rooms	6: 4 doubles, 1 twin, 1 suite. £110-£140. Min. 2 nights weekends.
Meals	12pm-2pm; 7pm-9pm. Main courses £11.25-£17.50; bar snacks from £5.95; Sunday lunch £10.95.
Closed	3.30pm-6pm & Sun eve in winter.
Directions	A420 southwest from Oxford for Swindon. After 13 miles, right for Tadpole Bridge. Pub on right by bridge.

Gareth & Helen Pugh
The Trout at Tadpole Bridge,
Buckland Marsh, Faringdon SN7 8RF
Tel 01367 870382
Web www.trout-inn.co.uk

Pubs with rooms

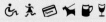

The Fleece
Witney

If you need to be in Oxford, staying at the Fleece is an attractive alternative; a cheaper one, too. Lee Cash and Victoria Moon dug deep into their pockets to buy the lease on the Georgian Fleece – and thus launched the hugely successful Peach Pub Company. Expect a sparkling gastropub interior: wooden floors, plum walls, squashy sofas, low tables – and continental opening hours that start with coffee and bacon sarnies at 8.30am. Moving the bar to the front has worked wonders, drawing in casual drinkers for pints of Greene King. They don't believe a pub is the place for leather-bound tomes either so what you get is a regularly changing wine list at sensible prices. Thumbs-up too for the all-day sandwiches, salads and deli-board menu: starters of cheese, charcuterie, fish, olive tapenade, marinated chillies, stone-baked pizzas too, and modern brasserie-style dishes such as braised shoulder of lamb with roasted winter roots. Delightful bedrooms are big enough to hold an armchair or two and beds are extremely comfortable; we'd recommend one at the front overlooking charming Witney's green.

Rooms	10: 1 twin/double, 8 doubles, 1 single. £80-£90.
Meals	12pm-2.30pm; 6.30pm-10pm; snacks served 2.30pm-6.30pm. Main courses £9-£16; bar meals £4-£12.
Closed	Open all day.
Directions	Witney is off A40 between Oxford and Burford; pub on green, near church.

Aimee Moore
The Fleece,
11 Church Green,
Witney OX28 4AZ
Tel   01993 892270
Web   www.fleecewitney.co.uk

🏃 💳 🐕 🍷

Entry 515 Map 8

The Boar's Head
Ardington

A dapper estate village with a church, a pub and a post office, the pub being the home of the village cricket club. It's a civilised place with a battalion of locals and barbour-clad walkers who come for open fires, the daily papers, local ales, gorgeous food. Sunday lunch rolls on to six and the bar is lively most evenings, making it the hub of a small community. Gilt mirrors and old oils hang on the walls. There are big oak tables in the restaurant and doors onto a terrace for al fresco summer suppers. Rooms upstairs are unmistakably smart. The small double has a beamed ceiling, the big double comes with a claw-foot bath, the suite has a sofa for kids and views over the village. All have good beds, crisp linen and piles of cushions. Passion bursts from the kitchen, the food is popular as a result. Everything is homemade: bread, pasta, pastries, ice cream, so try hot onion and gruyère tart, Cornish mussels with a spinach gratin, stuffed pheasant and mustard mash, bread and butter pudding with Bailey's ice cream.

Rooms	3: 2 doubles, 1 suite. £85-£130. Singles £75-£95.
Meals	12pm-2pm; 7pm-9.30pm. Main courses £17-£20; bar meals £7.95-£14.95.
Closed	3pm-6.30pm Sat (7pm Sun).
Directions	A417 west from Didcot for Wantage. Through West Hendred & Ardington signed left. In village, left by bus stop; on left.

Bruce & Kay Buchan
The Boar's Head,
Church Street, Ardington,
Wantage OX12 8QA

Tel	01235 833254
Web	www.boarsheadardington.co.uk

Entry 516 Map 3

Oxfordshire

The Rose & Crown
Shilton

Small, cosy, friendly and run with panache. In a mellow Cotswold stone village, the pub's setting could not be more idyllic. The 16th-century Rose & Crown holds just two rooms: the bar room itself, simple and unadorned, and a fractionally larger extension built in 1701, where you eat. There's an open fire in the inglenook and a medley of kitchen tables and chairs, making the once rundown local a most atmospheric and civilised public house. Be charmed by low beams, exposed stone walls, a terracotta floor, fresh flowers and good food. You'll find a happy crowd sitting down to pigeon terrine with beetroot chutney, pork and duck cassoulet with red cabbage, and good old ham, egg and chips. This is a gorgeous, sheltered spot and there's a garden you can drift into on warm days.

Meals	12pm-2pm (2.45pm Sat & Sun); 7pm-9pm; no food Sun eve in winter. Main courses £6-£9.50 (lunch), £9-£14.50 (dinner).
Closed	3pm-6pm. Open all day Sat & Sun.
Directions	Shilton is signed off B4020, 2 miles SE of A40 at Burford.

Martin Coldicott
The Rose & Crown,
Shilton,
Burford OX18 4AB
Tel   01993 842280

Entry 517 Map 8

Oxfordshire

The Swan
Swinbrook

No pool tables, no juke boxes, no fruit machines, no soggy dogs – though "dry and on a lead" will do. This old water mill going back to the 15th century, in a lovely village on the Devonshire Estate, has been charmingly restored by the Duchess and Archie and Nicola Orr-Ewing – owners of the King's Head at Bledington. In the three interconnecting rooms of this listed building you may expect well-nurtured pints of Hook Norton and modern pub food. Local ingredients dominate an enticing menu – pheasant with celeriac and parsnip mash, lamb hotpot, lunchtime salt beef sandwiches – while open fires will warm the cockles of anyone's heart. In summer, the new, oak-beamed, high-raftered conservatory comes into its own. Flagstones, settles, cheerful chatter and the idly-flowing river Windrush across the road – a nigh-on perfect place.

Meals	12pm-2pm (2.30pm Sun); 7pm-9pm (9.30pm Fri & Sat). Main courses £10.95-£17.50; sandwiches (lunch) from £5.25; Sunday roast £11.95.
Closed	3pm-6pm. Open all day Sat & Sun.
Directions	From Oxford A40, through Witney. Village signed right, off A40.

Archie & Nicola Orr-Ewing
The Swan,
Swinbrook, Burford OX18 4DY
Tel   01993 823339
Web   www.theswanswinbrook.co.uk

Entry 518 Map 8

Oxfordshire

The Carpenters Arms
Fulbrook

Near popular Burford, this roadside inn hides a warren of rooms. But the building has been transformed by Paul and Mandy Griffith, who attract a cosmopolitan crowd in search of good beer, real food and a great buzz. Drinking and eating co-exist happily in beamed, atmospheric rooms, stylish with cushioned window seats, wood-burners, exposed stone walls and heritage colours. Greene King ales are on tap and the rolling menu changes with the day's supplies; the ingredients are sourced with care. So look to the chalkboard for delicious homemade faggots and fishcakes, and rib-eye steak with gorgonzola butter and skinny fries. Lunchtime brings a good-value set lunch: tasty Old Spot bacon chops, smocked haddock and crayfish mornay. And there's a conservatory at the back where summer doors open to a pretty rear garden.

Meals	12pm-2.30pm (3.30pm Sun); 6.30pm-9.30pm. Main courses £8-£16; set lunch, 2 courses, £12.50.
Closed	3pm-6.30pm; Sun from 4pm & Mon.
Directions	On A361 2 miles north of Burford.

Paul & Mandy Griffith
The Carpenters Arms, Fulbrook Hill, Fulbrook, Burford OX18 4BH
Tel   01993 823275
Web   thecarpentersarmsfulbrook.co.uk

Entry 519 Map 8

Oxfordshire

Royal Oak
Ramsden

Blazing winter fires, piles of magazines and well-thumbed books by the inglenook make this the perfect place for a pint of real ale, so tuck into a corner filled with plump scatter cushions. Some brilliant food can be had in the pubby bar – open-stone walls, cream and soft-green windows – as well as in the extension beyond, where glass doors open to a pretty terrace with wrought-iron chairs and outdoor heaters for chilly evenings. Dishes such as roast half shoulder of Westwell lamb with rosemary and garlic sauce, roast cod with tapenade crust and sweet pepper sauce and chocolate and brandy ice cream should put a smile on your face; in winter, there's lots of game. Well-behaved children and dogs are welcome, the staff are delightful and the village is a stunner. You won't hear a bad word said about this place.

Meals	12pm-2pm; 7pm-10pm. Main courses £7.50-£18; Sunday lunch £16.95.
Closed	3pm-6.30pm.
Directions	On B4022, 3 miles north of Witney.

Jon Oldham
Royal Oak,
Ramsden,
Chipping Norton OX7 3AU
Tel   01993 868213

Entry 520 Map 8

Oxfordshire

Kings Arms
Woodstock

Standing proud in historic Woodstock, the Kings Arms is a refuge from town bustle. David and Sara Sykes's passion for this Georgian building has seen it restored to former glory – a lovely combination of old and new. Tradition can be found downstairs in the classic bar – all boarded floors, leather banquettes, carved wooden settle, stained-glass panels – then it's through to the vaulted dining room for high-backed leather chairs, fat candles on chunky tables, rustic mirrors, bold art and wooden artefacts. Equally up-to-date are the menus, a typical meal reeling in cod and cured ham fishcakes, braised shin of beef with a shallot and red wine sauce, and apricot and walnut tart. More modernity in the bedrooms, which ramble over three floors and have a minimalist feel. Be spoiled by low-slung solid-wood beds with firm mattresses and richly coloured throws, leather bucket chairs, super bathrooms, thick fluffy towels and Molten Brown toiletries. Boutiques abound around town and Blenheim Palace is on the doorstep. *No children under 12 overnight.*

Rooms	15: 14 doubles, 1 twin. From £140. Singles from £75.
Meals	12pm-2.30pm; 6.30pm-9.30pm (12pm-9.30pm Sun). Main courses £11.50-£17.75.
Closed	Open all day.
Directions	On A44 at corner of Market Street in town centre.

David & Sara Sykes
Kings Arms, 19 Market Street,
Woodstock OX20 1SU

Tel	01993 813636
Web	www.kings-hotel-woodstock.co.uk

The White Horse
Stonesfield

Unremarkable on the outside, inside is a civilised tavern. Low ceilings, painted beams, wooden floors, stone and terracotta walls: contemporary mixes with old. A coal fire, a large sofa and a retro espresso machine dominate the bar while a Grecian head fills the fireplace in the dining room, adding to the quirky chic. Owner Richard Starnowski has put in a lot of work to achieve this look and atmosphere; hard to believe the White Horse was boarded up for four years. Now it's a charming place loved by all ages, with friendly staff, Hook Norton beers and delicious food. The kitchen is known for its seasonal focus and generous portions, from shepherd's pie to confit of duck, and there are occasional jazz evenings in the function room and skittle alley. A very happy mix of restaurant and pub.

Meals	12pm-2pm (4pm Sun); 6.30pm-10pm. Main courses £9.95-£16.75; bar meals £4.95-£9.95; set lunch £10 & £12.95.
Closed	3pm-6pm; Sun eve & Mon. Open all day Sat.
Directions	Take B4437 off A44 north of Burford then follow signs for Stonesfield; tricky to find.

Richard Starnowski
The White Horse,
The Ridings, Stonesfield,
Chipping Norton OX29 8EA
Tel   01993 891063
Web   www.thewhitehorse.uk.com

Entry 522 Map 8

Nut Tree Inn
Murcott

The menu reads like a posh London restaurant, but you can get supper and a pint for a tenner on Sunday nights and there are pigs out the back. Imogen and Mike are friendly and fun and operate their own version of 'The Good Life' down here in their idyllic whitewashed, thatched pub, and grow a lot of their own food. The bar is soothing with an open fire, white linen, natural stripped oak beams, stone walls and leather chesterfields. Choose from well-priced bar food (smoked salmon with scrambled eggs, artisan cheeses) or take a look at the specials board: tea-smoked wild goose with mango purée, cucumber and pickled ginger salad; chopped venison steak and wild mushroom risotto. There's real ale, draught cider, a long wine list and a pretty rear terrace for summer days with views over the smallholding.

Meals	12pm-2pm; 7pm-9pm (6pm-8pm Sun). Main courses £14-£22; bar meals £4.50-£9.
Closed	Sun eve in winter. Open all day.
Directions	Murcott is 5 miles south of Bicester, signed off A41 towards Aylesbury.

Michael & Imogen North
Nut Tree Inn,
Main Street,
Murcott OX5 2RE
Tel   01865 331253

Entry 523 Map 8

Oxfordshire

White Hart
Wytham

Who says the traditional and the contemporary don't mix? At the White Hart, bold colours and modern art mingle with flagged floors and stone fireplaces. And the different areas have distinctive characters: the 'Parlour' room has a French feel with painted floors and furniture and a central bread block laid with fresh loaves; the cosy bar has exotic coloured walls and velvet cushions. The upstairs bar is all open brickwork, plain floorboards, log fire and walls bearing framed tomatoes. The rustic terrace has Greek terracotta wood-burners and a 15th-century dovecote. There are real ales and a raft of wines by the glass in the bar and modern cooking from the kitchen. Monthly specials might include local wild venison with black cherry jus, and roast halibut on saffron and herb risotto with tomato confit and green chilli salsa.

Meals	12pm-3pm (3.30pm Sat); 6.30pm-10pm (12pm-9pm Sun). Main courses £10.50-£19.95; set dinner, 2 courses, £12.50.
Closed	3.30pm-5.30pm. Open all day Sat & Sun.
Directions	A34 to Oxford, off at Botley interchange.

David Peevers
White Hart,
Wytham, Oxford OX2 8QA
Tel 01865 244372
Web www.thewhitehartoxford.co.uk

Entry 524 Map 8

Oxfordshire

The Oxford Arms
Kirtlington

A robust 19th-century dining pub tucked away down a lane in a village eight miles from Oxford – the coat of arms above the door shows an Ox walking through a ford. Pretty windows are painted pale green grey and window boxes are coloured with geraniums. The main bar faces south, the floors are flagged and boarded, wood smoke tinges the air; the perfect place to decide what to eat while you sip a half of Hook Bitter or something from the excellent wine list. To one side is a candlelit dining area with large tables and comfy sofas, the other is more pubby and informal with bar stools and farmhouse chairs. Wherever you decide to eat there will be the convivial rumble of chat in the background and the food is a treat: splash out on potted shrimps with toast, then salmon and prawn fish cakes with sweet chilli sauce.

Meals	12pm-2.30pm; 6.30pm-9.30pm. Main courses £9.50-£16.
Closed	3pm-6pm & Sun eve.
Directions	On A4095 between A44 south of Woodstock & Bicester.

Bryn Jones
The Oxford Arms, Troy Lane,
Kirtlington, Oxford OX5 3HA
Tel 01869 350208
Web www.oxford-arms.co.uk

Entry 525 Map 8

Falkland Arms
Great Tew

Five hundred years on and the fire still roars in the stone-flagged bar under a low-slung timbered ceiling that drips with tankards and jugs. Tradition runs deep: the hop is treated with reverence, ales are changed weekly, old pump clips hang from the bar and they stock endless tins of snuff with great names like Irish High Toast and Crumbs of Comfort. In summer Morris Men jingle in the lane outside and life spills out onto the terrace at the front and into the lovely big garden behind. This lively pub is utterly down-to-earth and in very good hands. Dig into pork pies and plates of cheese in front of the fire or hop next door to the tiny beamed dining room for Paul's home-cooked delights. Bedrooms are cosy, some verging on snug; the attic room is wonderfully private. Brass beds and four-posters, maybe a bit of old oak and an uneven floor; you'll sleep well. It's all blissfully short on modern trappings, nowhere more so than in the bar, where mobile phones meet with swift and decisive action. Perfect pub, perfect village: though archetypal Cotswolds, Chipping Norton is truly unspoilt.

Rooms	5 doubles. £80–£120.
Meals	12pm–2pm (bar meals only); 7pm–8pm; no food Sun eve. Main courses £11.95–£16.95; bar meals £8.95–£11.95.
Closed	2.30pm–6pm (from 3pm Sat; 3pm–7pm Sun). Open all day weekends in summer.
Directions	North from Chipping Norton on A361, then right onto B4022, signed Great Tew. Inn by village green.

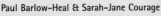

Paul Barlow-Heal & Sarah-Jane Courage
Falkland Arms,
Great Tew, Chipping Norton OX7 4DB

Tel	01608 683653
Web	www.falklandarms.org.uk

Entry 526 Map 8

Oxfordshire

The Kings Head Inn
Bledington

About as Doctor Dolittle-esque as it gets. Achingly pretty Cotswold stone cottages around a village green with quacking ducks, a pond and a perfect pub with a cobbled courtyard. Archie is young, affable and charming with locals and guests, but Nic is his greatest asset – a milliner, she has done up the bedrooms on a shoestring and they look fabulous. All are different, most have a stunning view, some family furniture mixed in with 'bits' she's picked up, painted wood, great colours and lush fabrics. The bar is lively – not with music but with talk – so choose rooms over the courtyard if you prefer a quiet evening. The pretty flagstoned dining room (exposed stone walls, Farrow & Ball paints, pale wood tables) is inviting; and you can lunch by the fire in the bar – on devilled kidneys, sausage and mash, ale and root-vegetable pie pie; there are homemade puds and serious cheeses, too. And there are lovely unpompous touches like jugs of cow parsley in the loo. Loads to do round these parts: antiques in Stow, walking and riding in gorgeous countryside, even a music festival in June.

Rooms	12: 10 doubles, 2 twins. £70–£125. Singles £60.
Meals	12pm-2pm; 7pm-9pm (9.30pm Fri & Sat). Main courses £9.95–£18; bar meals from £4.50.
Closed	3pm-6pm. Open all day Sat & Sun.
Directions	East out of Stow-on-the-Wold on A436, then right onto B4450 for Bledington. Pub in village on green.

Archie & Nicola Orr-Ewing
The Kings Head Inn,
The Green, Bledington OX7 6XQ

Tel	01608 658365
Web	www.kingsheadinn.net

Entry 527 Map 8

Oxfordshire

The Crown Inn
Church Enstone

Tony was head chef at the Three Choirs Vineyard; now he has his own place. With his wife Caroline, he decided to head for the Cotswolds and found this striking inn. It's a mellow-stone, 17th-century dream, off the beaten track in a sleepy village close to the river Glyme. Step in to a cosy, cottagey bar with old pine tables on a seagrass floor, rough stone walls, and a log fire crackling in the inglenook. At lunchtime, walkers and weekenders drop in for pints of Hook Norton and generous plates of home-cooked pub food; warming soups, steak and Hooky pie, fish and chips are listed on the blackboard. Cooking moves up a gear in the evening and fish is Tony's speciality; sea bass may be on the menu, with scallops, chilli and garlic dressing. Food is locally sourced and Sunday lunch is terrific; be sure to book.

Meals	12pm-2pm; 7pm-9pm; no food Mon. Main courses £7.95-£16.95; bar meals £4.75-£12.95; Sunday lunch £14.95 & £17.95.
Closed	3pm-6pm; Mon lunch & Sun from 4pm.
Directions	3.5 miles south east of Chipping Norton.

Tony & Caroline Warburton
The Crown Inn, Mill Lane,
Church Enstone,
Chipping Norton OX7 4NN
Tel 01608 677262
Web www.crowninnenstone.co.uk

Entry 528 Map 8

Oxfordshire

The Chequers
Churchill

Eye-catching with an immaculate stone frontage, the 18th-century Chequers stands smartly on the village lane. The Goldings took it on in 2003 and months of refurbishment followed before the reincarnation was unveiled. Prepare for a dramatic, airy and open-plan interior of bare boards and pine tables, cleverly partitioned dining areas, stone walls, roaring wood-burner and stacked logs, and chunky tables topped with candles and flowers. Soaring rafters and a vast dresser racked with wine bottles create an impression in the dining extension. No music, just a buzz when busy, and excellent food — red snapper and shrimp bouillabaisse, rib-eye steak with red wine sauce, lemon and raspberry posset. Book for the crispy duck night (Thursday) and roast Sunday lunches. Upstairs are a lounge and a private dining area.

Meals	12pm-2pm (3pm Sun); 7pm-9.30pm (9pm Sun). Main courses £4-£16.50.
Closed	Open all day.
Directions	Churchill on B4450 between Chipping Norton & Stow-on-the-Wold.

Peter & Asumpta Golding
The Chequers,
Church Road, Churchill,
Chipping Norton OX7 6NJ
Tel 01608 659393

Entry 529 Map 8

The Kingham Plough
Kingham

Overlooking a pretty green, this sturdy Cotswold inn resembles the perfect English pub. The food is exemplary modern British and much of what you eat comes from within ten miles. Scan the chalkboards in the bar if you're after a snack: a homemade pork pie with chutney, perhaps, simple and delicious with a pint of Hook Norton or a glass of Weston's pear cider. Up a few steps and you're into the beamed and vaulted dining area, for rustic platefuls of warm pork belly and watercress salad, slow-cooked haunch of venison with port and chestnut sauce, spicy pears poached in mulled wine. Chef-patron Emily Watkins, once sous-chef at the Fat Duck, is another young cook who has swapped the glamour of Michelin stars for her own kitchen in the country. Everything here is done with simplicity and integrity and that includes the interior of slate, brick and wood floors, exposed stone walls, beams, open fires and wooden tables. Bedrooms are as fresh and comfortable as can be – in one is a magnificent claw-foot bath – while white linen, digital screens and homemade flapjacks add to the treats.

Rooms	7 twins/doubles. £75–£95. Singles £65–£75.
Meals	12pm–2.30pm; 7pm–9pm. Main courses £10–£16.
Closed	Open all day.
Directions	Signed off B4450 between Chipping Norton & Stow-on-the-Wold.

SPECIAL
AWARD
see pages 18-19

Local, seasonal & organic produce

Emily Watkins & Adam Dorrien-Smith
The Kingham Plough,
Kingham,
Chipping Norton OX7 6YD
Tel   01608 658327
Web   www.thekinghamplough.co.uk

Oxfordshire

Mason's Arms
Swerford

The village of Swerford was once owned by a unfortunately-named henchman of William the Conqueror, one Robert D'Oily. It may be low on roadside appeal but the Mason's interior reveals a cottagey chic décor: duck-egg blue beams, clotted-cream walls, olive checked curtains, and rugs and seagrass hugging the floors. A wardrobe is stacked with wine bottles, background music plays, candles glow in the restaurant and drinkers nurse their Hooky Best. As for the food, it's locally sourced best-of-British. Chef-patron Bill, who's worked for Ramsay and lives to tell the tale, delivers soft herring roes on toast, braised shin of beef, user-friendly steaks and roast shoulder of Oxford Down lamb. Children are not indulged with nuggets 'n' chips but offered mini-portions of real food – and a garden to romp in.

Meals	12pm-2.15pm (2.30pm Sun); 7pm-9.15pm (9pm Sun). Main courses £10.95-£13.95; bar meals £6.50-£9.95; set menus £12.95 & £17.95.
Closed	3pm-6pm (7pm Sun). Open all day in summer.
Directions	On A361 north-east of Chipping Norton.

Bill & Charmaine Leadbeater
Mason's Arms, Banbury Road,
Swerford, Chipping Norton OX7 4AP

Tel	01608 683212
Web	www.masons-arms.com

Entry 531 Map 8

Oxfordshire

Black Boy Inn
Milton

In 2007 Merchant Inns snaffled up this 16th-century gem, next to the parish church in sleepy Milton. The results are impressive. The single long room oozes original features and charm: oak beams and exposed stone walls by the bar, a red and black tiled floor, cosy terracotta colours, seagrass matting, scrubbed pine tables – and a log-burning stove in the inglenook at the posh dining end. Beyond, a swish conservatory dining area overlooks a courtyard of upmarket brollies and teak tables. Really good food embraces pub classics like sausages and mash as well as more modern dishes like crab, lime and chilli cakes with ginger and lemongrass sauce. Heart-warming puds include dark chocolate fondant and sticky toffee pudding; daily papers, Greene King ales and landscaped gardens are further treats.

Meals	12pm-3pm; 6.30pm-9pm (9.30pm Fri & Sat); no food Sun eve. Main courses £9.95-£16.95; bar meals £7.95-£11.50; Sunday lunch £15 & £20.
Closed	Open all day.
Directions	From Banbury take A4260 towards Oxford; turn right after Adderbury for Bloxham & Milton; pub on right-hand side.

Brendan Eschle
Black Boy Inn,
Milton, Banbury OX15 4HH

Tel	01295 722111
Web	www.blackboyinn.com

Entry 532 Map 8

Oxfordshire

Wykham Arms
Sibford Gower

Gordon Ramsay got his first job here. Later, under the name The Moody Cow, it lost some of its popularity; now the listed free house is a thoroughly modern inn. Having seen the Cotswold village, you'd be forgiven for expecting cushions and chintz; instead you get creams and deep reds, flagged floors and farmhouse furnishings. The menu, served through a warren of connected rooms, spills over with local and seasonal produce; flavours are strong, clean and uncomplicated. So tuck into Cornish scallops with celeriac remoulade, salmon with beetroot and marinated artichoke salad, and wild boar and apple sausages with beer mustard mash. Lots of wines by the glass, from a list that is excellent and affordable, and families and dog owners are made very welcome. For summer there's a big patio and a wooded garden.

A well-loved pub with a big welcome, a crackling fire and the landlord's personality etched into the very fabric of the building lifts the spirits. Add heart-warming food and fine beer and you are in heaven.

Meals	12pm-3pm; 7pm-9.30pm; no food Sun eve. Main courses £15-£18; bar meals £7.50-£10.
Closed	3pm-6pm & Mon all day.
Directions	Between Brailes & Swalcliffe; on B4035, follow signs to Sibford Gower.

Damian & Deborah Bradley
Wykham Arms, Colony Lane,
Sibford Gower, Banbury OX15 5RX
Tel   01295 788808
Web   www.thewykhamarms.co.uk

Entry 533 Map 8

Oxfordshire

534 Olde Reindeer Inn 47 Parsons Street, Banbury OX16 5NA
01295 264031
Banbury's oldest pub has a reputation for good value, home-cooked lunches and cracking Hook Norton ale, in a cosy bar with polished boards and a magnificent carved fireplace. Don't miss the panelled Globe Room.

535 The Bull Inn Sheep Street, Charlbury OX7 3RR
01608 810689
Handsome 16th-century inn overlooking the main street of this charming Cotswold town. Flagstones, fires and Hook Norton in the rustic bar; fresh daily menus in the warmly decorated dining room.

536 Lamb Inn High Street, Shipton-under-Wychwood OX7 6DQ
01993 830465
A gorgeously done-up dining pub with antique furnishings, stripped stone walls, huge flowers and log fires. Good wines, Greene King ales, quirky bedrooms, special food. New owners – reports please.

537 The Boot Inn Barnard Gate, Eynsham OX29 6XE
01865 881231
Enjoy a pint of Hook Norton and fresh, flavourful food to a backdrop of standing timbers, bare board floors, good country tables, candlelight at night, a huge log fire… and walls covered with a rare collection of celebrity footwear.

538 The Angel 14 Witney Street, Burford OX18 4SN 01993 822714
Hook Norton has bought this 16th-century coaching inn, a short stroll from Burford's historic high street, added real ale and turned it back into a classy old inn. Lovely atmosphere and good food.

539 Masons Arms South Leigh, Witney OX29 6XN
01993 702485
Gerry Stonhill's pub is more gentleman's club than quintessential thatched inn – three Dickensian rooms filled with hessian-clad walls, crackling log fires and spent wine bottles. No beer but proper English food, at a price.

540 Turf Tavern Bath Place, Oxford OX1 3SU 01865 243235
Classic 18th-century tavern where ale reigns supreme – a dozen on tap and 200 guest beers served annually. A warren of small bars, three flagged courtyards, winter braziers and chestnuts, simple bar food. Generally heaves.

541 Rose & Crown 14 North Parade Avenue, Oxford OX2 6LX
01865 510551
No music or mobile phones at this characterful, three-room Victorian pub in North Oxford – just great ales, traditional lunchtime food, a heated back yard and an interesting clientele.

Worth a visit

542 The Bear 6 Alfred Street, Oxford OX1 4EH
01865 728164
Oxford's oldest boozer, popular with town and gown, has a miniscule and shambolic interior, many years' worth of framed, frayed ties (it's a long story), tasty hamburgers and cracking ale.

543 The Goose Britwell Salome, Watlington OX49 5LG
01491 612304
Thriving pub-restaurant at the base of the Chilterns, with a Michelin star. Remodelled, informal and relaxing, more restaurant than pub and with a pump-free bar – although Hook Norton is straight from the cellar.

544 King William IV Hailey, Wallingford OX10 6AD
01491 681845
Take an OS map to locate this rural treat tucked down single-track lanes in the Chilterns. Spick-and-span traditional interior, the full range of Brakspear ales, grassy front garden with peaceful views – super after a hike in the hills.

545 Black Horse Burncote Lane, Checkendon RG8 0TE
01491 680418
Persevere up the rutted lane to this old-fashioned country local and enter another age. The pub has been run by the same family for 100 years; come for local ales from the cask, filled rolls, pickled eggs and a peaceful garden.

546 Perch and Pike The Street, South Stoke, Reading RG8 0JS
01491 872415
Thames-side walkers and those in the know beat a path to this serenely restyled village inn for foaming pints of Brakspears, winter log fires and hearty food in the low-beamed bar.

547 The White Lion Crays Pond, Goring Heath RG8 7SH 01491 680471
A smart Henley and Goring crowd is drawn by the imaginative and daily-changing menus that mix old favourites with new ideas. Call in for breakfast, or relax over the papers with a pint of Greene King.

548 The Greyhound Gallowstree Road, Rotherfield Peppard RG9 5HT
0118 972 2227
Hugely attractive, ancient and cosy pub north of Reading. Impressive country venue for TV celebrity chef Anthony Worrall Thompson and his grill-restaurant formula – 35-day aged beef steaks and his own suckling pigs.

549 The Baskerville 7 Station Road, Lower Shiplake, Henley-on-Thames RG9 3NY 0118 940 3332
Rambling, brick-built 1930s pub close to the Thames Path in an upmarket village. Very good food served throughout classy and comfortable panelled rooms, plus local ales and summer barbecues.

The Olive Branch
Clipsham

This is not your usual chi-chi ex-boozer in a sleepy village; a relaxed pub personality is pinned here to a Michelin star. The casual mood is created by old beams, exposed stone walls, loosely arranged tables and a warm medley of books, furniture and roaring log fire – a rustic-chic informality rules and makes a visit here a joy. Chalk boards on tables in the restaurant reveal the names of the evening's diners, while the English food – cauliflower soup, roast rib of beef, caramelised lemon tart – is the greatest treat. So are the hampers of terrine, cheese and homemade pies that you can whisk away for picnics in the country. Bedrooms in Beech House across the lane are impeccable. Three have terraces, one has a free-standing bath, all come with crisp linen, pretty beds, Roberts radios, real coffee. Super breakfasts – smoothies, boiled eggs and soldiers, the full cooked works – are served in a smartly renovated barn, with flames leaping in the wood-burner. The front garden fills in summer, the sloe gin comes from local berries, and bridle paths lead out across peaceful fields. Superb.

Rooms	6: 5 doubles, 1 family. £80–£160. Singles from £65.
Meals	12pm-2pm (3pm Sun); 7pm-9.30pm (9pm Sun). Main courses £10.50-£22.50; set lunch £19.50; Sunday roast £14.50.
Closed	3pm-6pm. Open all day Sat & Sun.
Directions	2 miles off A1 at Stretton (B668 junction).

Ben Jones & Sean Hope
The Olive Branch,
Main Street, Clipsham LE15 7SH

Tel	01780 410355
Web	www.theolivebranchpub.com

Entry 550 Map 9

Rutland

Finch's Arms
Upper Hambleton

Alone on its peninsula surrounded by Rutland Water, the Finch's has the greatest of rural views. Colin Crawford could have sat back and twiddled his thumbs and people would still have poured in. But he has not been idle, and has created a terrific team in the kitchen led by David Bailey. Décor in the Garden Room is ultra-elegant, with food to match; choose from lamb confit with crispy pancetta and mash, turbot with salmon mousse, fresh Cornish mussels, and rib-eye steak with horseradish. Or sausages with mash and onion... the bar and restaurant menus change frequently, and local produce is used where possible. There's a small, bustling bar with log fires, a fine selection of ales, a great wine list, and a garden and a hillside terrace for summer with wonderful watery views. Staff are friendly and efficient.

Meals	12pm-2.30pm; 6pm-9.30pm (12pm-8pm Sun). Main courses £8.50-£25.
Closed	Open all day.
Directions	Off A606, east of Oakham.

Colin & Celia Crawford
Finch's Arms, Oakham Road,
Upper Hambleton, Oakham LE15 8TL

Tel	01572 756575
Web	www.finchsarms.co.uk

♿ ☺ ☐

Entry 551 Map 9

Shropshire

New Inn
Baschurch

Outside, jolly hanging baskets and a plain, whitewashed frontage. Inside, a sensitive stripping back to old brick and beams, a bright and open space. There are comfortable sofas at one end, light-oak dining chairs and tables at the other and a big traditional bar in between. In spite of the 48 covers, a well-placed wall and brick fireplace give the dining areas a certain intimacy; outside, sun shades and decking invite summer drinkers and diners. Four ales on the pump and good house wines are served by Jenny Bean and her charming staff. In the kitchen, Marcus prepares such delights as tempura tiger prawns with sweet chilli sauce; beef and Shropshire ale pie; pan fried guinea fowl breast stuffed with goat's cheese and figs; caramelised lemon tart with clotted cream. All villages should have a pub like this.

Meals	12pm-2pm (3pm Sun); 6.30pm-9.30pm (7pm-9pm Sun). Main courses £9.25-£18.95; bar meals £5.95-£9.25.
Closed	3pm-6pm (4pm-7pm Sun).
Directions	Pub just off B5067 in Baschurch, 5 miles north west of Shrewsbury.

Marcus & Jenny Bean
New Inn, Church Road, Baschurch,
Shrewsbury SY4 2EF

Tel	01939 260335
Web	www.thenewinnbaschurch.co.uk

♿ ☺ ☐

Entry 552 Map 7

The Inn at Grinshill
Grinshill

A ridge of pine soars high above the village; bring the boots and take to Shropshire's wild hills. Down at the inn, nothing but good things; this is a wonderfully welcoming bolthole, a top-to-toe renovation which now shines. Wander at will and you find an 18th-century panelled family room with rugs and games, a 19th-century bar with quarry-tiled floors and a crackling fire, and a 21st-century dining room, serene in cream, flooded with light courtesy of glazed coach-house arches. Bedrooms upstairs are just as good, with piles of pillows, crisp white linen and wispy mohair blankets or shiny quilted eiderdowns, and technology hidden behind mirrors. Back downstairs, ambrosial delights pour from the kitchen – the breast of duck served with an orange and lemon marmalade was faultless. A grand piano gets played on Friday nights and life spills out into the garden in summer. Church bells peal, roses ramble, there's cricket in the village at the weekend and the Shropshire Way passes by outside. Don't miss the magical follies at Hawkstone Park.

Rooms	6: 3 doubles, 2 twins, 1 single. £60-£120.
Meals	12pm-2.30pm; 6pm-9.30pm. Main courses £9.95-£20; bar meals £4.95-£18; Sunday roast £9.95.
Closed	3pm-6pm; Sun from 4pm & Mon Jan-Easter.
Directions	A49 north from Shrewsbury. Grinshill signed left after 5 miles.

Kevin & Victoria Brazier
The Inn at Grinshill,
High Street, Grinshill, Shrewsbury SY4 3BL
Tel   01939 220410
Web   www.theinnatgrinshill.co.uk

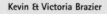

Entry 553 Map 7

The Fox
Chetwynd Aston

As you wander from room to room you realise just how vast this 1920s pub is. Yet there are plenty of nooks to be private in. Fires crackle in magnificent fireplaces, heavy cast-iron radiators add warmth, Turkey rugs are scattered on stained-wood floors and summer promises a great big garden with rolling views. Pews, solid oak tables and chairs – there's a happy mix of furniture and a bistro feel. It's a grown-ups' pub and attracts a civilised crowd, appreciative of the good selection of wines by the glass and the six regularly changing guest ales. Choose a table, then browse the daily-changing menu: there are ploughman's with local cheeses, salted duck breast with an orange, watercress and fennel salad, venison steak with roasted vegetables, warm chocolate brownies and very good coffee.

All Nations
Madeley

The old Victorian pub, spruce and white, could be an extension of the Industrial Open Air Museum on the other side of the bridge. Step across the threshold and you're into timeworn-tavern territory – cast-iron tables, leatherette benches, coal fire at one end, log fire at the other. Old photographs of Ironbridge strew the walls, secondhand paperbacks ask to be taken home (donations to charity accepted), dogs doze and spotless loos await outside. It's a chatty, friendly ex-miners' ale house and some of the locals could have been here forever. Drink is own-brew, well-kept, low-cost Dabley from the hatch plus three others and a cider, while the menu encompasses several sorts of roll – black pudding perhaps, or cheese and onion, with tomato on request. Catch it before it's gone.

Meals	12pm-10pm (9.30pm Sun). Main courses £7.95-£15.95.
Closed	Open all day.
Directions	Just off A41 south of Newport,

Meals	Rolls available all day, £1.70-£3.
Closed	Open all day.
Directions	Off Legges Way, near entrance to Blists Hill Museum.

	Samantha Malloy
	The Fox, Pave Lane,
	Chetwynd Aston, Newport TF10 9LQ
Tel	01952 815940
Web	www.brunningandprice.co.uk

	Jim Birtwistle
	All Nations,
	20 Coalport Road, Madeley,
	Telford TF7 5DP
Tel	01952 585747

Entry 554 Map 8

Entry 555 Map 8

Shropshire

The Hundred House Hotel
Norton

Henry is an innkeeper of the old school, with a sense of humour – he once kept chickens, but they didn't keep him. Having begun its life in the 14th century, the place rambles charmingly inside as well as out. Enter a world of blazing log fires, soft brick walls, oak panelling and quarry-tiled floors. Dried flowers hang from beams, herbs sit in vases, blackboard menus trumpet prime Shropshire sirloin, venison casserole with herb dumplings and salmon fishcakes with lobster bisque. In the restaurant, Sylvia's wild and wonderful collage art hangs on wild and wonderful walls, and there's live music in the barn. Wander out with a pint of Heritage Mild and share a quiet moment with a few stone lions in the beautiful garden, full of herbaceous plants and a working herb garden with over 50 varieties – a real summer treat.

Meals	12pm-2.30pm; 6pm-9.30pm (7pm-9pm Sun). Main courses £7.95-£20.95.
Closed	3pm-5.30pm.
Directions	In village of Norton midway between Bridgnorth & Telford on A442.

The Phillips Family
The Hundred House Hotel,
Norton, Shifnal TF11 9EE
Tel 01952 730353
Web www.hundredhouse.co.uk

Entry 556 Map 8

Shropshire

Pheasant Inn
Linley Brook

The only traffic you're likely to encounter on the way here are a couple of horses clopping along – or, if things hot up a bit, a tractor. The Pheasant has been here for centuries and is wondrously unspoilt. Expect a wood-burning stove, an open fire, wooden benches... and fox masks, fox brushes and polished horse brasses on low beams. In a second room, past the hatch, are bar billiards. Simon and Liz Reed run the Pheasant single-handedly; they cook, clean, serve, stoke the fire *and* find time to chat to customers. Walkers and locals pop in for a quiet pint and simple, very good pub food: toasted sandwiches, local gammon and steaks, sticky toffee pudding. Even the beers have names that belong to another age: Wye Valley Butty Bach, Salopian Heaven Sent, Cannon Muzzle Loader and Shropshire Gold.

Meals	12pm-2pm; 6.30pm-9pm. Bar meals £5.25-£8.50.
Closed	2.30pm-6.30pm (from 3pm Sat & Sun); from 10pm Mon, Tues & Sun.
Directions	Just off B4373 Bridgnorth-Broseley road, 4 miles north of Bridgnorth.

Simon & Liz Reed
Pheasant Inn,
Linley Brook, Bridgnorth WV16 4TA
Tel 01746 762260
Web www.the-pheasant-inn.co.uk

Entry 557 Map 8

Shropshire

Riverside Inn
Cressage

There's a great buzz in this large comfortable huntin', shootin' and fishin' inn – standing on a magnificent bend of the Severn, looking gloriously out to the Wrekin and beyond. It's worth seeking out for its crackling wood-burner in winter and its dining conservatory with views all year round. In summer there's a pretty garden smartly furnished, and you can fish from the bank for salmon and trout. The seasonal monthly menu might start with steamed leek and cheddar pudding – a tasty modern take on an old country dish – and move on to whole roast trout with almonds or steak and kidney pie. There's port to accompany your cheese, and lovely Salopian beers and homemade puddings, sorbets and ice creams. It's all good value and comfortingly traditional. And there's no need to hurry home: upstairs are a number of well-proportioned Georgian bedrooms. Doubles and twins are cosy, spacious 'executive' rooms have river views from sash windows and all are in excellent order. The service, as in every good pub, is both relaxed and efficient.

Rooms	7: 6 doubles, 1 twin. £60-£70. Singles £45.
Meals	12pm-2.30pm; 6.30pm-9.30pm. Main courses £7-£12.
Closed	3pm-6pm. Open all day Sat & Sun May-Sept.
Directions	South from Shrewsbury on A458, through Cross Houses to Cressage; pub on left.

Peter Stanford Davis
Riverside Inn,
Cressage, Shrewsbury SY5 6AF
Tel   01952 510900
Web   www.theriversideinn.net

Entry 558 Map 7

Shropshire

Feathers Inn
Brockton

Once two Elizabethan cottages built from ship-salvaged timber, the Feathers stands in prime walking country. And the rambling, characterful interior comes as a surprise. Walk in to tiled and wooden floors, whitewashed stone walls, painted beams, a vast inglenook, stone busts, grand swagged curtains, chunky church candles and colourful art for sale. Order a pint of Hobson's or an excellent wine to accompany some great pub food: chef-patron Paul Kayiatou comes from London's top kitchens, so sit back and enjoy pan-fried Scottish scallops with crispy bacon and caesar salad, roast belly pork with black pudding and apple and cinnamon chutney, and warm chocolate fondant. There's a good value early evening supper menu and local roast beef on Sundays. Mellow, warm and satisfying after a long hike along Wenlock Edge.

Meals	12pm-2.30pm; 6.30pm-9.30pm. Main courses £8.95-£15.95; set menu £12.95 & £14.95 (Tues-Fri before 8pm); Sunday lunch £10.95 & £13.95.
Closed	3pm-6.30pm & Mon all day.
Directions	On B4378 Much Wenlock to Craven Arms road, 5 miles south-west of Much Wenlock.

Paul & Anna Kayiatou
Feathers Inn,
Brockton, Much Wenlock TF13 6JR
Tel   01746 785202
Web   www.feathersatbrockton.co.uk

Entry 559 Map 7

Shropshire

White Horse Inn
Pulverbatch

The drive to get here is the biggest treat. And the White Horse, in a village mentioned in the Domesday Book, is an ancient place – parts date back to the 14th century, when it was a farmhouse. There's a more recent restaurant add-on at the back but the old main bar is the most seductive, all wonky flagstoned floors, roaring fire in a big old grate and deep-hued walls. It's the perfect setting for Steve Bruce's excellent, robust cooking. Walkers and cyclists, on their way to the glorious Long Mynd, could do a lot worse than recuperate with a trio of local-farm sausages on whole grain mustard mash or a casserole of Shropshire lamb, all washed down with a well-kept ale or a decent wine. There's no garden at the inn – a shame in an area as stunning as this – but there are picnic benches at the front.

Meals	12pm-2pm; 6.30pm-9.30pm (12pm-9.30pm Fri & Sat; 9pm Sun) Main courses £7.25-£14.95.
Closed	2pm-6.30pm & Mon. Open all day Sat, Sun & Bank Hols
Directions	Pulverbatch signed off A49 south of Shrewsbury & A488 Knighton road SW of Shrewsbury.

Steve & Debbie Bruce
White Horse Inn,
Pulverbatch, Shrewsbury SY5 8DS
Tel   01743 718247
Web   www.whitehorsepulverbatch.co.uk

Entry 560 Map 7

Crown Country Inn
Munslow

Richard and Jane Arnold bought this listed Tudor inn (variously a courtroom, doctor's surgery and jail in previous lives) in a parlous state. Now it's a happier place, where locals gather for a chat and a pint of Cleric's Cure at dark polished tables in a winter-cosy, log-stoved bar. The upstairs function room and outside terrace are also well-used. The secret of the inn's success is revealed on the rustic walls of the bar, adorned with food awards and a map of suppliers: proprietor and chef Richard is passionate about local produce and the menu is stuffed with it. Try crostini ('little toasts') of local black pudding with Wenlock Edge Farm bacon, or griddled local sirloin steak with organic smoked butter. And the cheeseboard is a treat of lesser-known British cheeses – including Hereford Hop, rolled in hops.

Three Tuns
Bishops Castle

Beer deliveries are a cinch for the Three Tuns. There's been a licensed brewery next door (in a listed Victorian tower) since 1642. Pub and brewery are now under separate ownership but the pub still exclusively sells four of their beers and very good they are too. The place has an unassuming air, like the rest of this time-warp town. The separate snug, public bar and lounge have been simply redecorated with pale green paintwork, scrubbed tables and no airs and graces. (In contrast to some impressive marble loos...) A more recent addition is the oak-framed, conservatory dining room where tasty dishes may feature some unusual touches, such as chargrilled tuna in red Thai curry sauce with fried pasta. A great mix of regulars, from suits to bohemians, a real fire in the stone fireplace, and live music at weekends.

Meals	12pm-1.45pm; 6.45pm-8.45pm.. Main courses £11.50-£16.50; bar meals £4-£15.95.
Closed	Sun eves & Mon all day.
Directions	On B4368 to Bridgnorth, at extreme western end of Munslow.

Meals	12pm-3pm; 7pm-9pm; no food Sun eve Main courses £5.95-£9.25.
Closed	Open all day.
Directions	Town on B4385 off A488 12 miles north of Knighton; pub in town centre

	Richard & Jane Arnold Crown Country Inn, Munslow, Craven Arms SY7 9ET
Tel	01584 841205
Web	www.crowncountryinn.co.uk

	Tim & Catherine Curtis-Evans Three Tuns, Salop Street, Bishops Castle SY9 5BW
Tel	01588 638797

Entry 561 Map 7

Entry 562 Map 7

Shropshire

The Unicorn Inn
Ludlow

Ludlow, full of timber-framed houses and artisan shops, looks and tastes delicious. As for the Unicorn, it hides at the bottom end of town on the east bank of the river as you approach the Shrewsbury road and, unlike its more distinguished restaurant neighbours, does not have to be booked weeks in advance. Along with well-priced bar snacks there's proper food and plenty of it (own-recipe sausages with bubble and squeak, chicken roulade with sweet and sour sauce, syrup sponge and custard). You eat at scrubbed tables in the dining rooms or in the beer garden by the stream, or, best of all, before a log fire in the panelled, beamed bar where floor and ceiling slope drastically. Ceremony here is about as out-of-place as Formula One tyres on a family Ford and the beer is expertly kept: no wonder it remains popular.

Shropshire   Award winner 2008

Fighting Cocks
Stottesdon

As you tail tractors and horses on the lane to get here, you pass the farm that supplies the kitchen with its excellent meat. Sandra Jeffries wears multiple hats: jolly landlady, enthusiastic chef, manager of the great little shop next door. So step into the bar and choose a velour-topped seat or a settle or a sofa by the fire. The décor is haphazard, the carpet patterned, the piano strewn with newspapers and guides (Shropshire's ancient hills beckon) and the copper-topped bar hung with tankards. Up steps is a room for darts, dominoes and TV, and a function room. The dining room is as unpretentious as can be and a match for the cooking; you'll love the gamey (and spicy) casseroles, the organic salmon, scrumptious pies and tempting nursery puddings. A true community pub, with a welcome that embraces outsiders.

Meals	12pm-2.15pm; 6pm-9.15pm. Main courses £9.25-£19.59; Sunday roast from £8.95; sandwiches from £4.50.
Closed	Open all day.
Directions	From A49, B4361 to Ludlow. After lights & bridge, bear right; bear left up hill. Next right after lights at bottom of hill. 50 yds on left.

Meals	7-9pm (12-2.30pm; 7-9pm Sat); no food Mon & Sun. Main courses £8-£15.
Closed	Mon-Fri lunch. Open all day Sat & Sun.
Directions	Village signed off A4117 & B4363 east of Ludlow at Cleobury Mortimer.

SPECIAL AWARD
see pages 18-19

Community pub

Graham Moore
The Unicorn Inn,
Lower Corve Street, Ludlow SY8 1DU
Tel   01584 873555
Web   www.unicorninnludlow.co.uk

Sandra Jeffries
Fighting Cocks,
1 High Street, Stottesdon,
Bridgnorth DY14 8TZ
Tel   01746 718270

Entry 563 Map 7

Entry 564 Map 7

Shropshire

The Clive
Bromfield

It doesn't really matter whether you're in the mood for old or new; this pub does both. Inside the old redbrick farmhouse on the Ludlow-Shrewsbury road you discover a chic restaurant on one side and a bar on the other. The bar starts life all chrome tables and blonde wood floors, then turns a corner and changes mood, becoming an elegant collection of antique chairs, rugs and pictures dotted around a huge old stone fireplace. The food remains resolutely modern. Prime ingredients, from Corvedale lamb to Nash venison, are the star players in a menu glittering with talent and clever combinations. It's not just fancy footwork though – the food is terrific, be it wild mushroom, borlotti and pinto bean tagliatelle with roast garlic, basil and gorgonzola, or seared fillet of Shropshire beef with buckwheat noodles, wasabi and oyster sauce. And then there are the bedrooms in converted outbuildings, all of them stylish and impeccable visions of unfussy modern comfort within a framework of gnarled oak beams. Bathrooms are white and pristine, the furniture contemporary, the outlook blissfully rural.

Rooms	14: 13 twins/doubles. £85-£110. 1 family suite. £110-£200.
Meals	12pm-3pm; 6.30pm-9.30pm (12pm-9.30pm weekends). Main courses £9.95-£17.95.
Closed	Open all day.
Directions	2 miles north of Ludlow on A49.

Paul Brooks
The Clive,
Bromfield, Ludlow SY8 2JR
Tel   01584 856565
Web   www.theclive.co.uk

Entry 565 Map 7

Shropshire

566 Sun Inn Rosemary Lane, Leintwardine SY7 0LP

No airs or graces at this terraced house beside the river: just two rooms with scrubbed tables, stone floors, barrels of beer and cider still aged in the kitchen. Unchanged since the Ark, and landlady Floss in her 90s. No phone.

567 Llanfair Waterdine Knighton LD7 1TU
01547 528214

The old Welsh longhouse in a hamlet by the river is a fine spot for Ken Adams's innovative modern British cooking. With impeccable local produce and Woods ale on tap, this is more restaurant-with-rooms than pub.

568 The Miners Arms Priest Weston, Shrewsbury SY7 8EW
01938 561352

On the wild Welsh borders, an unspoilt pub, the hub of hamlet life – they sell dog food, groceries and gas, hold folk nights, marrow competitions and harvest thanksgiving. Wonderful bar with big inglenook and beer brewed in Bishops Castle; food on request.

569 The Royal Oak Cardington, Church Stretton SY6 7JZ
01694 771266

At the foot of Caer Caradoc, a 500-year-old pub loved by muddy-booted ramblers who come for its dependable range of real ales, cider and inexpensive daily specials from local suppliers.

570 Bottle & Glass Picklescott, Church Stretton SY6 6NR
01694 751345

Warm and inviting with log fires, fresh flowers, chunky candles and a bookcase full of novels. Foaming pints and hearty helpings for walkers, happily ensconced in the wild hills of Shropshire. Up for sale in 2007 – reports please.

571 White Hart The Wharfage, Ironbridge TF8 7AW
01952 432901

Just down from the 'Ironbridge', overlooking the Severn, a pub with a modern rustic feel: colourful pictures, stripped floorboards, stylish shades of off-white and grey. A crowd-pleasing menu keeps things simple.

Worth a visit

Somerset

Woods Bar & Dining Room
Dulverton

It hasn't been a pub for ever – indeed, it used to specialise in tea and cakes – but it is in the centre of a lively village, and wine buffs and foodies have much to be grateful for. Landlords Sally and Paddy are friendly and welcome families and dogs. A stable-like partition divides the space up into two intimate seating areas, beyond which is a smart, soft-lit, deeply cosy bar: two wood-burners, lots of pine, a few barrel tables and exposed stone walls. Outside, a small paved area and a couple of cast-iron tables. Ales include Exmoor Gold, Otter and St Austell – but the wines are the thing here, with many by the glass. Expect fine modern British dishes, with the emphasis on food in season. Hard to resist breast of pheasant with chestnut purée and port sauce – or a slab of Montgomery's cheddar with homemade chutney.

Meals	12pm-2pm; 7pm-9.30pm (9pm Sun). Main courses £6.95-£14.95.
Closed	3pm-6pm (7pm Sun).
Directions	From Tiverton, A396 N; left on B3222 for Dulverton; near church & bank.

Sally & Paddy Groves
Woods Bar & Dining Room,
4 Bank Square,
Dulverton TA22 9BU
Tel   01398 324007

Entry 572 Map 2

Somerset

Tarr Farm Inn
Dulverton

Come for rare peace – no traffic lights, no mobile signals, not for miles. Tucked into the Barle valley, a short hop from the ancient clapper bridge at Tarr Steps, this well-established 16th-century inn is surrounded by beautiful woodland above the hauntingly high spaces of Exmoor National Park. The blue-carpeted, low-beamed main bar has plenty of comfy window seats and gleaming black leather sofas; Exmoor Ale and Mayner's cider flow as easily as the conversation. To fill the gap after a bracing walk the menu draws heavily on local game – hunting and shooting are big sports here – so you get venison and rabbit casserole, pan-roasted partridge and a hundred French and New World wines. The garden views are sublime; where better to try the best West Country cheeses followed by perfect coffee?

Meals	12pm-3pm; 6.30pm-9.30pm (cream teas 3pm-5pm). Main courses £12.95-£17.50; bar meals £6.95-£12.50.
Closed	Open all day.
Directions	From Dulverton, take B3223 north, left to Tarr Steps & Inn is signed.

Judy Carless & Richard Benn
Tarr Farm Inn , Tarr Steps,
Dulverton, TA22 9PY
Tel   01643 851507
Web   www.tarrfarm.co.uk

Entry 573 Map 2

Royal Oak Inn
Luxborough

Five miles south of Minehead, as the pheasant flies, is Luxborough, tucked under the lip of the Exmoor's Brendon hills. This is hunting country and from September to February the bar hums with the sound of gamekeepers, beaters, drivers and picker-uppers from the nearby Chargot shoot. Often they stay to dine, very well: on potted ham hock; fish from St Mawes; vegetables from local growers; and beef, lamb and venison that's almost walked off the hills. Two low-beamed, log-fired, dog-dozed bars (with locals' own table) lead to a warren of dining rooms kitted out with polished dining tables and hunting prints on deep green walls. (In spate, the river Washford has been known to take a detour!). A shelf heaves with walking books and maps; James and Siân lend them freely, all are returned. The village is small but people have been coming here all their lives, for a pint and a chat over cribbage, backgammon, scrabble. For those lucky enough to stay, bedrooms ramble around the first floor (one below has a private terrace) and are individual, peaceful, homely and great value.

Rooms	11: 8 doubles, 2 twins, 1 single. £65–£95.
Meals	12pm–2pm; 7pm–9pm. Main courses £11.95–£15.95; bar meals £4.95–£10.95.
Closed	2.30pm–6pm.
Directions	Luxborough is signed off A396 from Dunster.

James & Siân Waller
Royal Oak Inn,
Luxborough, Dunster TA23 0SH
Tel   01984 640319
Web   www.theroyaloakinnluxborough.co.uk

Entry 574 Map 2

Somerset

Lord Poulett Arms
Hinton St George

In a ravishing village, a ravishing inn, French at heart and quietly groovy. Part pub, part country house, with walls painted in reds and greens and old rugs covering flagged floors, it fuses classical design with earthy rusticity. A fire burns on both sides of the chimney in the dining room; on one side you can sink into leather armchairs, on the other you can eat under beams at antique oak tables while candles flicker. Take refuge with the daily papers on the sofa in the locals' bar or head past a pile of logs at the back door and discover an informal French garden of box and bay trees, with a piste for boules, a creeper-shaded terrace, a hammock. Bedrooms upstairs come in funky country-house style, with fancy flock wallpaper, perhaps crushed velvet curtains, a small chandelier or a carved-wood bed. Two rooms have slipper baths behind screens in the room; two have claw-foot baths in bathrooms one step across the landing; Roberts radios add to the fun. Brilliant food includes summer barbecues, Sunday roasts and the full works at breakfast. Great value and friendly to all – dogs included.

Rooms	4: 2 doubles, each en suite; 2 doubles, each with separate bath. £88. Singles £59.
Meals	12pm-2pm; 7pm-9pm. Main courses £9-£16.
Closed	3pm-6.30pm.
Directions	A303, then A356 south for Crewkerne. Right for West Chinnock. Through village, 1st left for Hinton St George. Pub on right in village.

Steve & Michelle Hill
Lord Poulett Arms,
High Street, Hinton St George,
Crewkerne TA17 8SE

Tel	01460 73149
Web	www.lordpoulettarms.com

Entry 581 Map 3

Royal Oak Inn
Luxborough

Five miles south of Minehead, as the pheasant flies, is Luxborough, tucked under the lip of the Exmoor's Brendon hills. This is hunting country and from September to February the bar hums with the sound of gamekeepers, beaters, drivers and picker-uppers from the nearby Chargot shoot. Often they stay to dine, very well: on potted ham hock; fish from St Mawes; vegetables from local growers; and beef, lamb and venison that's almost walked off the hills. Two low-beamed, log-fired, dog-dozed bars (with locals' own table) lead to a warren of dining rooms kitted out with polished dining tables and hunting prints on deep green walls. (In spate, the river Washford has been known to take a detour!). A shelf heaves with walking books and maps; James and Siân lend them freely, all are returned. The village is small but people have been coming here all their lives, for a pint and a chat over cribbage, backgammon, scrabble. For those lucky enough to stay, bedrooms ramble around the first floor (one below has a private terrace) and are individual, peaceful, homely and great value.

Rooms	11: 8 doubles, 2 twins, 1 single. £65–£95.
Meals	12pm–2pm; 7pm–9pm. Main courses £11.95–£15.95; bar meals £4.95–£10.95.
Closed	2.30pm–6pm.
Directions	Luxborough is signed off A396 from Dunster.

James & Siân Waller
Royal Oak Inn,
Luxborough, Dunster TA23 0SH
Tel   01984 640319
Web   www.theroyaloakinnluxborough.co.uk

Somerset

The Rock Inn
Waterrow

Perambulating along the Somerset and Devon borderlands in search of country cooking and a comfortable bed, you could do no better than to chance upon this coaching inn. Lost along the back road between Taunton and South Molton, built into the rock face by the river in a green valley, it is run by a mother and son team. Joanna (chef) and Matt (ex Hotel du Vin) have restored the fortunes of the old timbered inn. Good home-cooked food, served at pine tables in the rustic bar or the bistro-style dining room, draws the farmers from the hills and taps into a network of quality local suppliers: free-range pork, craft cheeses, beef from Joanna's farm down the valley. So tuck into double-baked Jubilee Gold soufflé; beef, red wine and onion pie; Exmoor venison steak with port and berry sauce; and Ladram Bay lobster with salad. Local extends to the ales: very well-kept Cotleigh Tawny and Exmoor Gold. Simple, homely bedrooms are warm and comfortable, with crisp cotton sheets on old pine or brass beds, and flat-screen TVs; the largest has a leather sofa and a wood-burning stove, quite a treat on a winter's night.

Rooms	8 twins/doubles. £70. Singles £40.
Meals	12pm-2.30pm; 6.30pm-9.30pm (7pm-9pm Sun). Main courses £7.50-£15.95.
Closed	3pm-6pm.
Directions	On B3227 between Bampton & Wiveliscombe.

Matt Harvey & Joanna Oldman
The Rock Inn,
Waterrow, Wiveliscombe,
Taunton TA4 2AX
Tel   01984 623293
Web   www.rockinn.co.uk

Entry 575 Map 2

Somerset

Three Horseshoes
Langley Marsh

A proper, traditional local and proud of it. Come for good beer and good food, kept and cooked by Mark and Julia. Otter Bitter, Cotleigh Tawny and Palmers IPA are tapped from the cask and there's Thatcher's Gold cider on tap. Lunches and dinners have been described as "home-cooked food from heaven" and Julia uses fish and game from Exmoor and locally reared beef. The pies, soup and sandwiches and the daily specials – lamb's liver and bacon, venison steak with red wine gravy, plaice with prawns in a white wine sauce – are freshly made, there are no chips on the menu and the vegetables are fresh from the garden. In the bustling front room a timeless atmosphere prevails, with polished tables, dominoes and cards and an organ; in the dining room are old settles; in the garden, tables and neat lawns.

Meals	12pm-1.45pm; 7pm-9pm. Main courses £5.50-£11.95.
Closed	2.30pm-7pm; Sun eve & Mon.
Directions	Off B3227 Wiveliscombe; turn in front of White Hart towards Huish Champflower; 1 mile on right.

Mark & Julia Fewless
Three Horseshoes,
Langley Marsh,
Wiveliscombe TA4 2UL
Tel   01984 623763

Entry 576 Map 2

Somerset

Carew Arms
Crowcombe

Freddie Connor-Muir is the new torchbearer at this thoroughly authentic pub in a pretty village south of the Quantock Hills. The front room with its hatch bar, original flagstones, large inglenook and assorted hunting memorabilia – beware of low-flying antlers – is as unspoilt as a bar can be. Otter and Exmoor ales get the conversation going, as does the robust wine list. The old skittle alley is now a bar-dining room with French windows leading to a gloriously sunny back terrace with woodland views; the new skittle alley, complete with old horse stalls, makes a good family area. Menus use fresh ingredients and everything is made in-house, so there's Exmoor lamb steak with minted mashed potatoes and madeira wine gravy, and smoked haddock in dill cream sauce with potatoes, carrots and asparagus. Dogs get a good welcome.

Meals	12pm-2pm; 7pm-9pm. Main courses £8.75-£14.95.
Closed	3.30pm-5pm. Open all day Sat & Sun.
Directions	Off A358 between Taunton & Minehead. In centre of village.

Freddie Connor-Muir & Helen Holden
Carew Arms, Crowcombe,
Taunton TA4 4AD
Tel   01984 618631
Web   www.thecarewarms.co.uk

Entry 577 Map 2

Somerset

Blue Ball Inn
Triscombe

Not so long ago the Blue Ball was 'rolled' down the hill; now the old thatched buildings join the ancient stables below. Thanks to craftsmen's skills and plenty of vision, it has metamorphosed into a rather smart pub. Climb the fabulous beech stairs to a swishly carpeted central bar that leads to two dining areas, both with country furnishings and fabrics and high-raftered ceilings. Menus are imaginative, produce local. Treat yourself to ham hock and apricot terrine with watercress salad or slow cooked belly pork with kale, black pudding and crackling. At the bar, lunchtime crusty rolls and excellent cheese ploughman's make this a popular walkers' pit-stop. There are four ales, wines by the glass and local farm ciders, best enjoyed in summer in the multi-tiered garden with glorious views across Taunton's vale.

Meals	12pm-1.45pm; 7pm-8.45pm. Main courses £7.95-£16.95.
Closed	4pm-6pm.
Directions	From Taunton A358 for Minehead; past Bishops Lydeard, right to Triscombe.

Gerald & Sue Rogers
Blue Ball Inn, Triscombe,
Bishops Lydeard, Taunton TA4 3HE
Tel   01984 618242
Web   www.blueballinn.co.uk

Entry 578 Map 2

Somerset

The Rising Sun Inn
West Bagborough

In 2002 the Sun rose from the ashes of a fire and shines more brightly than ever. It sits in sleepy West Bagborough on the flanks of the Quantock Hills. Constructed around the original 16th-century cob walls and magnificent door, its reincarnation is bold and craftsman-led, with 80 tons of solid oak timbers and windows and a slate-floored bar. Add Art Nouveau features, spotlighting and swagged drapery and you find one very smart pub. There's Exmoor Fox and Cotleigh Tawny to sample, modern art to buy, and, high in the rafters, a dining room with views that unfurl to Exmoor and the Blackdown Hills. It's an impressive setting for impressive food: game and foie gras terrine with quince jelly; saddle of Exmoor lamb with pancetta; ham, duck egg and chips; sticky ginger ale cake. Worth walking down the hill for.

Meals	12pm-2pm (3pm Sun); 6.30pm-9.30pm (7pm-9pm Sun). Main courses £4.95-£17.
Closed	3pm-6pm.
Directions	Off A358 Taunton-Minehead road, 8 miles north-west of Taunton.

Jon & Christine Brinkman
The Rising Sun Inn,
West Bagborough, Taunton TA4 3EF
Tel   01823 432575
Web   www.theriser.co.uk

Entry 579 Map 2

Farmer's Inn
West Hatch

You don't often trek into deepest Somerset and wash up at a deeply groovy inn, but that's what you get at the Farmer's, so brave the narrow country lanes and head to the top of the hill. All the country treats are on hand. Outside, cows in the fields, cockerels crowing and long clean views; inside, friendly people, open fires and a timber-framed bar. It's all the result of a total renovation, and one airy room now rolls into another giving a sense of colour and comfort, space and light. Imagine terracotta-tiled floors and beamed ceilings, yellow tongue-and-groove panelling, old pine dining tables dressed with pots of rosemary and logs piled high in the alcoves. Stay the night in off-beat but elegant and big rooms with distinctive beds (all antique) and expansive, gleaming wooden floors. There are power showers and claw-foot baths, one room has a daybed, others have sofas, another a courtyard. Super food flies from the kitchen – grilled sardines, rib-eye steak, chocolate and mint mousse – and you can eat on the terrace in summer. The pub is also on a new circular bridle path funded by English Heritage.

Rooms	5: 4 doubles, 1 twin. £90-£120. Singles £70-£100.
Meals	12pm-2pm (2.30pm Sat & Sun); 7pm-9pm (9.30pm Fri & Sat). Main courses £10.75-£16; bar meals £5.50-£10.75.
Closed	2.30pm-6pm (3pm-7pm Sat & Sun).
Directions	M5 junc. 25, then south on A358. Right at Nag's Head pub, up hill for two miles, following signs towards RSPCA. On left.

Debbie Lush
Farmer's Inn,
Slough Green, Higher West Hatch,
Taunton TA3 5RS

Tel	01823 480480
Web	www.farmersinnwesthatch.co.uk

Lord Poulett Arms
Hinton St George

In a ravishing village, a ravishing inn, French at heart and quietly groovy. Part pub, part country house, with walls painted in reds and greens and old rugs covering flagged floors, it fuses classical design with earthy rusticity. A fire burns on both sides of the chimney in the dining room; on one side you can sink into leather armchairs, on the other you can eat under beams at antique oak tables while candles flicker. Take refuge with the daily papers on the sofa in the locals' bar or head past a pile of logs at the back door and discover an informal French garden of box and bay trees, with a piste for boules, a creeper-shaded terrace, a hammock. Bedrooms upstairs come in funky country-house style, with fancy flock wallpaper, perhaps crushed velvet curtains, a small chandelier or a carved-wood bed. Two rooms have slipper baths behind screens in the room; two have claw-foot baths in bathrooms one step across the landing; Roberts radios add to the fun. Brilliant food includes summer barbecues, Sunday roasts and the full works at breakfast. Great value and friendly to all – dogs included.

Rooms	4: 2 doubles, each en suite; 2 doubles, each with separate bath. £88. Singles £59.
Meals	12pm-2pm; 7pm-9pm. Main courses £9-£16.
Closed	3pm-6.30pm.
Directions	A303, then A356 south for Crewkerne. Right for West Chinnock. Through village, 1st left for Hinton St George. Pub on right in village.

Steve & Michelle Hill
Lord Poulett Arms,
High Street, Hinton St George,
Crewkerne TA17 8SE

Tel	01460 73149
Web	www.lordpoulettarms.com

Rose & Crown Inn (Eli's)
Huish Episcopi

Quirky, unspoilt and in the family for 140 years. The layout has evolved, gradually taking over the family home. There's no bar as such – you choose from the casks – but who cares when the locals are so lovely, the cider so rough and the beer so tasty. Walk in and you step back to the Fifties. There are worn flagstones, aged panelling and coal fires in five low parlours radiating off a central tap room. The 'gentleman's kitchen' is the oldest and cosiest, the pool, darts and juke box room the largest and newest. They do crib nights and occasional quiz nights and Morris dancers drop by in summer. The food is brilliant value: creamy winter vegetable soup, a tasty pork, apple and cider cobbler, chicken breast with tarragon, chocolate and rum torte. Everyone's happy and children like the little play area outside.

Halfway House
Pitney Hill

Somerset's mecca for beer and cider aficionados. No music or electronic wizardry to distract you from the serious business of sampling up to eight ales tapped straight from the drum, heady Hecks' ciders and bottled beers from around the globe. Local clubs gather for chess, music, hockey. In the two simple and homely rooms is a friendly, hoorah-Henry buzz: there are old benches and pews, scrubbed tables, stone-slabbed floors, three crackling log fires and the daily papers to nod off over. A quick lunchtime pint can swiftly turn into two hours of beer-fuelled bliss – so blot up the alcohol with a ploughman's or a salmon steak straight from the pub's smokery. In the evenings the Halfway's revered homemade curries are gorgeous and go down very nicely with pints of Butcombe, Branscombe and Hop Back ales.

Meals	12pm-2pm; 5.30pm-7.30pm; no food Sun eve. Main courses £3-£6.95.
Closed	2.30pm-5.30pm Mon-Thurs. Open all day Fri-Sun.
Directions	300 yards from St Mary's Church. On left-hand side towards Wincanton on leaving Huish.

Meals	12pm-2.30pm; 6.30pm-9.30pm; no food Sun. Main courses £3.95-£9.95.
Closed	3pm-5.30pm (7pm Sun).
Directions	Beside B3153, midway between Langport & Somerton.

Eileen Pittard
Rose & Crown Inn (Eli's),
Huish Episcopi,
Langport TA10 9QT
Tel   01458 250494

Julian Litchfield
Halfway House,
Pitney Hill, Langport TA10 9AB
Tel   01458 252513
Web   www.thehalfwayhouse.co.uk

Entry 582 Map 3

Entry 583 Map 3

Somerset

Devonshire Arms Hotel
Long Sutton

A lively English village with a well-kept green; the old school house stands to the south, the church to the east and the post office to the west. The inn (due north) is 400 years old and was once a hunting lodge for the Dukes of Devonshire; a rather smart pillared porch survives at the front. These days open-plan interiors are warmly contemporary with high ceilings, shiny blond floorboards and fresh flowers everywhere. Hop onto brown leather stools at the bar and order a pint of Crop Circle, or sink into sofas in front of the fire and crack open a bottle of wine. In summer, life spills onto the terrace at the front, the courtyard at the back and the lawned garden beyond. Upstairs, a flurry of large, light and absolutely fabulous bedrooms, with low-slung wooden beds, seagrass matting, crisp white linen and freeview TV. The hosts are engaging and the food's a joy; choose from ploughman's with homemade chutney or grilled sardines with truffle mayonnaise, linger over wild mallard with parsnip chips and Italian speck. Then take to the nearby Somerset levels and walk off your indulgence in style.

Rooms	9: 8 doubles, 1 family room. £75-£130. Singles from £65.
Meals	12pm-2.30pm; 7pm-9.30pm (9pm Sun). Main courses £12.95-£18.50; bar meals £4.20-£12.50.
Closed	3pm-6pm.
Directions	A303, then north on B3165, through Martock, to Long Sutton. Pub by village green.

Philip & Sheila Mepham
Devonshire Arms Hotel,
Long Sutton, Langport TA10 9LP
Tel   01458 241271
Web   www.thedevonshirearms.com

Entry 584 Map 3

The Queen's Arms
Corton Denham

Stride across rolling fields, feast on Corton Denham lamb, retire to a perfect room. Buried down several Dorset and Somerset-border lanes, this 18th-century stone pub has an elegant exterior – more country gentleman's house than pub. Delightful Londoners Rupert and Victoria Reeves have not let it lose its countrified feel. The bar, with its rug-strewn flagstones and bare boards, pew benches, deep sofas and crackling fire, has not lost its country feel. In the dining room – big mirrors on terracotta walls, new china on old tables – robust British dishes are distinguished by fresh ingredients from local suppliers. Try smoked haddock and spinach tart with a glass or two of Jim Barry's Aussie shiraz, follow with pan-fried Old Spot pork with balsamic strawberries... and find room for a comforting crumble. The bedrooms and bathrooms are beautifully designed in gorgeous colours; a duck-egg blue wall here, red and cream checked curtains there. All have lovely views and the bathrooms are immaculate. A friendly labrador, Butcombe on tap, comfort and authenticity.

Rooms	5: 4 doubles, 1 twin. £75–£120.
Meals	12pm-3pm (3.30pm Sun); 6pm-10pm (9.30pm Sun). Main courses £8.60-£14.95; bar meals from £5.25.
Closed	3pm-6pm. Open all day Sat & Sun.
Directions	From A303 take Chapel Crosse turning, through South Cadbury village. Next left & follow signs to Corton Denham. Pub at end of village, on right.

Rupert & Victoria Reeves
The Queen's Arms,
Corton Denham DT9 4LR

Tel	01963 220317
Web	www.thequeensarms.com

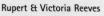

Entry 585 Map 3

Somerset

The Montague Inn
Shepton Montague

The O'Callaghans' 17th-century public house has been a stables, livery, grocery; now it is an inn in the true sense of the word. Small remains beautiful, with regional guest ales from Butcombe, Bath Ales and Blindman's Brewery, a wood-burner in the bar, candles on stripped pine tables and organic produce from neighbouring farms. Master Chef John McKeever's food is simple yet imaginative. There are lunchtime ploughman's of local cheeses while daily specials could mean a hot pot on Tuesday and fresh fish in beer batter and chips on Friday. And then there's grilled local goat's cheese in a celery, apple and walnut salad, and chargrilled fillet of local beef with garlic cream mash, bacon and lentil jus — all of it brilliant. The restaurant and rear terrace have bosky views to Redlynch and Alfred's Tower.

Meals	12pm-2.30pm; 7pm-9pm. Main courses £13.50-£19.50; bar meals £5.95-£8.50.
Closed	3pm-6pm (3.30pm Sun); Mon all day & Sun eve.
Directions	Off A359 2 miles east of Castle Cary, towards Bruton.

Sean & Suzy O'Callaghan
The Montague Inn,
Shepton Montague,
Wincanton BA9 8JW
Tel 01749 813213

Entry 586 Map 3

Somerset

Red Lion
Babcary

The Red Lion is a Somerset revival that combines the best of pub tradition with excellent food. There is a single central bar with a locals' snug behind dispensing Glastonbury Hedge Monkey ale, local cider and house wines from France and Oz. To one side, hair-cord carpets, sofas and the cast-iron stove give a welcome to the bright bar/lounge, while to the far right a dozen well-spaced country dining tables plainly set out on original flagstone flooring are part of an immaculate reconstruction. Daily menus offer as little or as much as you'd like, from wild boar terrine with red cabbage chutney or wild mushroom soup to pork and herb sausages with mash and mustard jus, chicken with Tuscan bean stew and chorizo, and braised lamb shank. Best to book at weekends, though.

Meals	12pm-2.30pm; 7pm-9pm (9.30pm Fri & Sat). Main courses £9.50-£16.
Closed	2.30pm-6pm & Sun eve.
Directions	Off A37 & A303 7 miles north of Yeovil.

Clare & Charles Garrard
Red Lion,
Babcary,
Somerton TA11 7ED
Tel 01458 223230

Entry 587 Map 3

The Pilgrim's at Lovington
Lovington

"The pub that thinks it's a restaurant with rooms" delivers a unique style. It's thoroughly civilised yet distinctly informal, serving Cottage Champflower on hand pump and good modern dishes that draw on the best local produce. Choose a table in the original part of the building, all low beams, flagstones, rustic walls lined with watercolours and a log fire. Jools is passionate about using the best Somerset has to offer and his menus highlight suppliers and growers. So there's Michael Brown's smoked eel served with Denhay bacon on Charles Dowding's organic leaves, and Dorset-caught sea bass with creamed potatoes and pernod sauce. Local farms supply the meat, ice creams are made in Lovington, veg is home-grown, bread is homemade using locally milled flour. And then there are the rooms in the converted Cider Store, stunning with their French sleigh or brass bedsteads, plasma screens and touch-activated lamps, fresh coffee and big bathrobes. Ample bathrooms come with roll top baths and 'wet-room' style showers – or both. Wake to delicious breakfasts under posh brollies in summer.

Rooms	5 twins/doubles. £80–£110.
Meals	12pm-2pm; 7pm-9pm. Main courses £7–£18.
Closed	3pm-7pm; Sun eves & Mon all day.
Directions	On B3153 between Castle Cary & Somerton.

Julian & Sally Mitchison
The Pilgrim's at Lovington,
Lovington, Castle Cary BA7 7PT

Tel	01963 240597
Web	www.thepilgrimsatlovington.co.uk

The Manor House Inn
Ditcheat

The hub of Dicheat has a just-renovated feel – in 2007 two new landlords swept in with a youthful broom – but authenticity will follow. In the bar – big, unscuffed and open plan – there's a good fire blazing. Settle back with something tasty from local breweries and tune into chatter of weather, sump oil and stock. The skittle alley has had a makeover too – skittles clatter merrily in the background – and now doubles up as a sports bar and function room. In the meantime, enticing aromas encourage you to check out the chalked boards and the game and fish specials. On the regular carte are chargrilled steaks, prawns in garlic butter, stilton and wild mushroom tart, roasted belly pork on a sage and apple risotto with a red wine sauce. Staying the night? Behind the inn, in the Old Mews, smart and generous bedrooms lie. Named after racehorses trained in the village, all three have a traditional look that's cosy and cottagey; beds are comfortable and modern, bath and shower rooms a treat. In the morning, after a full English breakfast, you'll discover a picture-perfect village amid gently rolling hills.

Rooms	3: 2 doubles, 1 twin. £90. Singles £50.
Meals	12pm-2pm; 7pm-9.30pm; no food Sun eve. Main courses £7.95-£16.95; bar meals £5.25-£11.95.
Closed	3pm-5.30pm. Open all day Fri-Sun.
Directions	Between A37 & A371, in Ditcheat next to church.

Mark Phillips & Neil Chant
The Manor House Inn,
Ditcheat, Shepton Mallet BA4 6RB

Tel	01749 860276
Web	www.manorhouseinn.co.uk

Somerset

The Three Horseshoes
Batcombe

Down a web of country lanes, the Woods' honey-stoned coaching inn sits in a lovely village. Step into a long, low bar, its beams cream, its pine scrubbed, its pink-sponged walls hung with local views. There are cushioned window seats, an inglenook with a wood-burning stove, pretty courtyards and grassed areas, even a play area. It's truly relaxing, a treat for locals, walkers and families. The modern British menu uses local organic produce, much from the vegetable garden, and is full of promise: start with homemade pâté de campagne, move on to shoulder \of local lamb with red wine jus or sea bass fillet with tomato and herb salsa, finish with a trio of English puds. Plus regular wine tastings, and Bats in the Belfry made specially for the pub by Blindmans Brewery. *Children welcome at lunchtime.*

Meals	12pm-2pm; 7pm-9pm; no food Sun eve. Main courses £10.50-£18.50; lunch from £8.75; bar meals from £6.75.
Closed	3pm-6.30pm (7pm Sun) & Mon (except bank hols).
Directions	Off A359 between Frome & Bruton, 7 miles south west of Frome.

Bob & Shirley Wood
The Three Horseshoes,
Batcombe, Shepton Mallet BA4 6HE
Tel   01749 850359
Web   www.3horseshoesbatcombe.co.uk

Entry 590 Map 3

Somerset

The Talbot Inn at Mells
Mells

Even in fog the village is lovely. Huge oak doors open to a cobbled courtyard and rough-boarded tithe barn bar on one side, and dining rooms and bedrooms on the other. Inside, a warren of passageways, low doorways, nooks, crannies and beams – all you'd hope for from a 15th-century inn. Butcombe Bitter flows from the cask and there are wines galore including five by the glass; it's a great drinking pub and, with a garden with views, a big draw for tourists in summer. Soak up any excess with Brixham crab soup, confit duck leg with braised red cabbage and peppercorn sauce, or local ham, eggs and chips, then head down to the brook and converse with the ducks. Dinner under the hop-strewn rafters highlights fresh Brixham fish such as brill fillets in nut-brown butter. The effortless hospitality is a further plus.

Meals	12pm-2pm; 7pm-9pm. Main courses £11.95-£17.95.
Closed	2.30pm-6.30pm (3pm-7pm Sun).
Directions	From Frome A362 for Radstock; left signed Mells.

Rob Rowlands
The Talbot Inn at Mells, Selwood St,
Mells, Frome BA11 3PN
Tel   01373 812254
Web   www.talbotinn.com

Entry 591 Map 3

Somerset

Tucker's Grave Inn
Faulkland

If only the essence of Tucker's could be bottled and preserved; 'to be used as emergency tonic for the despairing' the label would read. In an unassuming, almost-unsigned 17th-century stone building, Tucker's is defiantly informal. A narrow, extremely wiggly corridor leads in from the garden door; it's like walking into someone's living room as you stoop to enter the warmth. No bar, just four beer casks and containers of local cider sitting in their jackets in the bay (no draught) and a stack of crisp boxes against the wall. A small open fire lends cosiness to the no-frills room next to the tiny wooden serving room. The interiors are basic but the atmosphere is roaring at weekends. In the words of one regular: "you can't come here without chatting to someone". And now there's a skittles room in the big back garden.

Meals	Sandwiches available. Sandwiches from £2.
Closed	3pm-6pm (7pm Sun).
Directions	A366 Radstock-Frome; left onto A362; through Faulkland, pub near next junction.

Glenda & Ivan Swift
Tucker's Grave Inn,
Faulkland,
Radstock BA3 5XF

Tel   01373 834230

Entry 592 Map 3

Somerset

The Black Horse
Clapton-in-Gordano

The Snug Bar once doubled as the village lock-up and, if it weren't for the electric lights and the cars outside, you'd be hard pushed to remember you were in the 21st century. All flagstones and dark moody wood, the main room bears the scuffs of centuries of drinking. Settles and old tables sit around the walls; cottage windows with wobbly shutters let a little of the outside in. The fire roars in its vast hearth beneath a fine set of antique guns — so pull off your muddy boots and settle in. Sepia prints of parish cricket teams and steam tractors clutter the walls and cask ales pour from the stone ledge behind the hatch bar. The food is unfancy bar fodder, with daily specials. Ale takes pride of place; beneath a chalkboard six jacketed casks squat above drip pans. There are fine wines too, and plenty of garden.

Meals	12pm-2pm; no food Sun. Main courses £3.50-£6.95.
Closed	Open all day.
Directions	M5 junc. 19 for Portbury & Clapton. Left into Clevedon Lane.

Nicholas Evans
The Black Horse, Clevedon Lane,
Clapton-in-Gordano,
Portishead BS20 7RH

Tel   01275 842105

Entry 593 Map 3

Bear & Swan
Chew Magna

It is a four-square Victorian pub in the middle of Chew Magna – a desirable village in fine walking country. Inside: a roomy and airy bar and a damned good restaurant. Reclaimed floorboards in the bar, nestling tables, wooden pews and big log fires create a simple, sophisticated feel; in the restaurant are oriental rugs and ladderback chairs, candlelight and flowers and bottles racked on the wall – gorgeous. Beers (Butcombe and Bath Ales), 15 wines by the glass and an irresistible menu draw people from near and far. Pop in for a goat's cheese and chorizo baguette (not on Sundays: hot meals only) or stay a while to savour the delights of black pudding with caramelised apples and beetroot sauce, tuna with fondant sweet potato and star anise dressing, summer puddings and pecan tarts. The chalkboard changes daily, much is organic and the staff are delightful. Upstairs are two spacious bedrooms, cosy and comfortable with floral curtains, carpeted floors, charming period furniture, stylish bathrooms and an open-plan living area (with kitchen and breakfast bar) to share. This would be perfect for families.

Rooms	2 doubles. £80. Singles £50.
Meals	12pm–2pm (3pm Sun); 7pm–9.45pm; no food Sun eve. Main courses £9.50–£18.50; bar meals £4.50–£12.
Closed	Open all day.
Directions	On B3130 between A37 & A38.

Nigel & Caroline Pushman
Bear & Swan,
13 South Parade, Chew Magna BS40 8SL
Tel 01275 331100
Web www.bearandswan.co.uk

Somerset

The Crown
Churchill

Once a coaching stop between Bristol and Exeter, then the village grocer's, now an unspoilt pub. Modern makeovers have passed it by and beer reigns supreme, with up to ten ales tapped from the barrel. For years landlord Tim Rogers has resisted piped music and electronic games; who needs them in these beamed and flagstoned bars? The rustic surroundings and the jolly atmosphere draw both locals and walkers treading the Mendips hills. Find a seat by the log fire, cradle a pint of Butcombe or RCH PG Steam Bitter, be lulled by the hum of regulars at the bar. If you're here at lunchtime you'll find a short, traditional, blackboard menu: warming bowls of soup, thick-cut rare roast beef sandwiches, winter casseroles, treacle pud. Evenings are reserved for the serious art of ale drinking, and it's packed at weekends.

Somerset

Wookey Hole Inn
Wookey Hole

On the edge of the Mendip hills: a traditional façade, a funky décor, excellent food and no end of choice behind the kitsch-with-style bar. The whole place throngs, particularly in summer when the big garden comes into its own. It's also relaxed and properly child-friendly with toys and wax crayons for doodling on (paper) tablecloths. Terracotta tiles, open fires, stripped wood and wooden panelling, splashes of strong colour, arty lamps, photos and interesting *objets*. The atmosphere is laid-back, the cool levels boosted by live jazz at Sunday lunch times, and the food, which has good local credentials, is seriously tasty and imaginative: onion jam and goat's cheese bruscetta, fillet of beef with Exmoor blue cheese, spiced lamb burgers with smoked cheddar. The puddings are seductive, too.

Meals	12pm-2.30pm.
	Main courses £3.40-£7.50.
Closed	Open all day.
Directions	From Bristol A38 to Churchill, right for Weston S.M. Immed left in front of Nelson Pub, up Skinners Lane, pub on bend.

Meals	12pm-2.30pm; 7pm-9.30pm; no food Sun eve.
	Main courses from £8.50 (lunch), £12.75-£19.50 (dinner).
Closed	Sun eve.
Directions	Follow brown tourist signs for Wookey Hole off A371 or A39 in Wells.

Tim Rogers
The Crown,
The Batch, Churchill,
Congresbury BS25 5PP
Tel   01934 852995

Michael & Richard Davey
Wookey Hole Inn,
Wookey Hole, Wells BA5 1BP
Tel   01749 676677
Web   www.wookeyholeinn.com

Entry 595 Map 3

Entry 596 Map 3

Somerset

597 Blue Flame West End, Nailsea BS48 4DE
01275 856910
Spartan, well-worn rural local favoured by farmers and real ale and cider fans. Two basic rooms, a coal fire, barrels on stillage, filled rolls, pub games and big garden; open all day in summer. A one-off!

598 Ring O'Bells Hinton Blewett
01761 452239
Snug and cosy village local tucked away by the old church and brimming with cheer and hospitality. Come for cracking Bath ales, honest home-cooked food and a fun time.

599 Carpenter's Arms Stanton Wick, Pensford
01761 490202
Beams and stone walls are jazzed up by a tartan carpet, and the gleaming country style bar bristles with beverages at this classy inn set high above the Chew Valley. Good food and fine wines, too.

600 Kings Arms Litton, Radstock BA3 4PW
01761 241301
Big changes at the rambling old village pub, revamped in style: a sumptuous décor complements worn flagstones and roaring fires. Great British food takes in braised mutton suet pudding and Sunday roasts.

601 The Hunters' Lodge Priddy, Wells BA5 3AR
01749 672275
On the windswept crossroads, a stark little treasure. Mr Dors is its proudest fixture, administering ale and just-made bowls of chilli to cavers, pot-holers, hikers and the odd local. An unpretentious treat.

602 Kingsdon Inn Kingsdon, Somerton TA11 7LG
01935 840543
Picture-postcard thatched inn only minutes from the A303 (Podimore roundabout). Charming single bar with bending beams and a blazing fire – the perfect refuge for homecooked meals and pints of Butcombe.

603 Cat Head Inn Chiselborough, Stoke-sub-Hamdon TA14 6TT
01935 881231
Striking hamstone pub in countryside close to Montacute. Spotless flagstoned rooms, fresh imaginative food, Otter bitter on tap and attractive gardens with views over the village.

604 The Helyar Arms East Coker, Yeovil BA22 9JR
01935 862332
Fine gastropub worth a detour – for the handsome feudal village it lives in, and the food that goes from strength to strength. Real ales, local cider, global wines – all well priced.

Worth a visit

Staffordshire

The George
Alstonefield

Green sward ripples endlessly in this remote limestone village with its old church perched on a plateau between the remarkable gorges of the rivers Dove and Manifold. Set amidst this verdant Eden, the George is an ultra-reliable local, in the family for four decades, and lovingly managed. Small, timeless rooms of beams, quarry tile and log fire carry benches and Britannia tables, fascinating old photos and polished plate. It's an unhurried place, where everyone knows everyone else (or soon will), ramblers cram the benches and tables out front and time passes slowly. In the newly redecorated dining room a young chef gets creative with seasonal produce, so there are scallops with pea purée, haunch of venison and homemade puds. Outside at the back is a peaceful courtyard shaded by an immense ash.

Staffordshire

Yew Tree
Cauldon

The Old Curiosity Shop meets *The Antiques Road Show*. For over 40 years, landlord Alan East has squirreled away enough artefacts to make Michael Aspel weep. Behind the tiny leaded windows of this unassuming, 300-year-old pub every space is filled: longcase clocks and flintlocks, penny-farthings and valve radios, synphonions and polyphons (insert 2p and retire), old pews and marvellously carved benches. Pianolas lie half-buried in their paper-scroll programs (there's one playing most of the time). Josiah Wedgwood would find ceramics he may have handled (and his four-poster bed), and Queen Victoria her hosiery. Look for the Serpent (a medieval church instrument); wince at the ACME dog carrier. A floor-to-ceiling treasure trove – plus local pork pies, hot baps and sandwiches, Bass, Burton Bridge Bitter and Grays Mild.

Meals	12pm-2.30pm; 7pm-9pm. Main courses £8-£15.50; bar meals £3.50-£9.
Closed	3pm-6pm. Open all day Sat & Sun.
Directions	Village signed off A515, 7 miles north of Ashbourne.

Meals	Bar snacks 70p-£3.50.
Closed	2.30pm-6pm (3pm-6pm Sat, 3pm-7pm Sun).
Directions	Off A523 Leek to Ashbourne road at Waterhouses.

	Ben & Emily Hammond The George, Alstonefield, Ashbourne DE6 2FX
Tel	01335 310205
Web	www.thegeorgeatalstonefield.com

	Alan East Yew Tree, Cauldon, Waterhouses, Stoke-on-Trent ST10 3EJ
Tel	01538 308348

Entry 605 Map 8

Entry 606 Map 8

Staffordshire

The Holly Bush Inn
Stafford

Geoffrey Holland came to the Holly Bush some years ago and has turned it into a thriving local. Indeed, all the emphasis is local, especially where food is concerned. Cheeses, vegetables, meat and game are local and almost exclusively organic; herbs are fresh from the garden. Even a few of the recipes, such as the 'oatcakes' (that's pancakes not biscuits), are strictly Staffs. Only the fish and some of the beers are from further afield. But people travel miles for the home-smoked salmon with hollandaise sauce and the steak and ale pie. The 'second oldest licensed pub in the country' is a characterful little place, quirky even, with open fires and the odd carved beam and settle. Out on the big back lawn, a wood-oven bakes pizzas in summer, and the village, listed in the Domesday Book, should charm you.

Meals	12pm-9.30pm (9pm Sun). Main courses £7.25-£13.95; bar snacks £2.25-£3.25.
Closed	Open all day.
Directions	Off A51 south of Stone & A518 north east of Stafford.

	Geoffrey Holland The Holly Bush Inn, Salt, Stafford ST18 0BX
Tel	01889 508234
Web	www.hollybushinn.co.uk

Entry 607 Map 8

Suffolk

Duke's Head
Somerleyton

Hugh Crossley's shabby-chic gastropub overlooks the Somerleyton Estate; visit the grand hall, explore the glorious grounds. This 17th-century village inn has been restored in a simple, understated style with a laid-back feel: bare boards and beams, roaring log fire, warmly cosy bar. Next door, in the rambling, simply adorned dining area, good, gutsy, seasonal food is served. Daily menus use produce grown and shot on the estate, ranging from stilton and plum chutney sandwiches to pigeon breast with beetroot relish and Duke burgers with hand-cut chips. Delicious desserts include marmalade bread and butter pudding; at Sunday lunch, the family roast is brought to the table ready to carve. The Duke's Head is great in summer, too, so plonk yourself down on a rustic al fresco bench and relish the views.

Meals	12pm-3pm; 6pm-10pm. Main courses £8.50-£12.50; sandwiches from £3.
Closed	Open all day.
Directions	Village & pub signed off B1074, 5 miles NW of Lowestoft.

	Hugh Crossley Duke's Head, Slugs Lane, Somerleyton, Lowestoft NR32 5QR
Tel	01502 730281
Web	www.somerleyton.co.uk

Entry 608 Map 10

Suffolk

The Crown
Southwold

The Crown has an eye for metropolitan sophistication. Ceilings are elegantly beamed, the walls of the big, laid-back bar are colourwashed and uncluttered – fitting for a town known as Kensington-on-Sea. The food comes as bar snacks in full modern-brasserie mode: tempura Brancaster oysters, tapas, confit duck leg, salt pollock hash with poached egg. Fresh flowers sit on kitchen-style tables, there are newspapers to read, Adnams ales on hand pump and fine wines to try. There's no pretentiousness and a fascinating mix of customers – suits, locals, trendies, grannies, families. There's a smart, sunny restaurant, and a smaller, pubbier panelled back bar keeps hard-core traditionalists happy. All in all, The Crown has succeeded in being simultaneously a simple pub and brasserie-wine bar with serious aspirations.

Suffolk

The Anchor
Walberswick

Seeking sea air, beer guru Mark Dorber and wife Sophie are doing wonders at this Adnams boozer. To the sound of the sea crashing on the beach beyond, the vast lawn hosts summer barbecues – and the homemade burgers draw an appreciative crowd. Inside, sand, stone and aqua tones are redolent of the sea and open skies and add a contemporary touch, while Sophie's menus overflow with produce sourced from a rich vein of organic farms and top local butchers. They have put fresh food firmly back on the menu, and doubled the allotment at the back. Menus match beer with food: try Adnams Broadside with a melting Irish stew. A summer treat would be fruits de mer with a draught wheat beer, out on the new sun terrace overlooking allotments, beach huts and distant sea.

Meals	12pm-2pm; 6.30pm-9pm.	
	Main courses £10-£15.	
Closed	Open all day.	
Directions	From A12, A1095 to Southwold.	
	Inn on High Street.	

Meals	12pm-3pm; 6pm-9pm	
	(all day Sat in July & Aug).	
	Main courses £10.25-£17.75.	
Closed	4pm-6pm.	
	Open all day Sat in July & Aug.	
Directions	From A12 south of Southwold;	
	B3187 to Walberswick.	

	Francis Guildea
	The Crown,
	High Street, Southwold IP18 6DP
Tel	01502 722275
Web	www.adnamshotels.co.uk

	Mark & Sophie Dorber
	The Anchor, Main Street,
	Walberswick, Southwold IP18 6UA
Tel	01502 722112
Web	www.anchoratwalberswick.com

Entry 609 Map 10

Entry 610 Map 10

The Westleton Crown
Westleton

This is one of England's oldest coaching inns, with 800 years of continuous service under its belt. It stands in a village two miles inland from the sea at Dunwich, with Westleton Heath running east towards Minsmere Bird Sanctuary. Inside, you find the best of old and new. A recent refurbishment has introduced Farrow & Ball colours, leather sofas and a tongue-and-groove bar, while the panelled walls, stripped floors, ancient beams and spindle-back chairs remain. Weave around and find nooks and crannies in which to hide, flames flickering in an open fire, a huge map on the wall for walkers. You can eat wherever you want, and a breakfast room in the conservatory opens onto a terraced garden for summer barbecues. Fish comes straight off the boats at Lowestoft, local butchers provide local meat. Lovely bedrooms are scattered about and come in cool lime white with comfy beds, Egyptian cotton, flat-screen TVs. Super bathrooms are fitted out in Fired Earth; the most stylish have claw-foot baths. Aldeburgh and Southwold are close by.

Rooms	25: 20 doubles, 2 twins, 2 family rooms, 1 single. £110-£170. Singles £85-£95.
Meals	12pm-2.30pm; 7pm-9.30pm. Main courses £9.50-£19.50; bar meals £4.25-£9.95.
Closed	Open all day.
Directions	A12 north from Ipswich. Right at Yoxford onto B1122, left for Westleton on B1125. On right in village.

Matt Goodwin
The Westleton Crown,
The Street, Westleton,
Southwold IP17 3AD

Tel	01728 648777
Web	www.westletoncrown.co.uk

Entry 611 Map 10

Suffolk

The Queens Head
Bramfield

Another chef-landlord with an interest in provenance – and Mark Corcoran's menus make reassuring reading. Recent dishes include peppered swordfish with garlic, mint and lemon dressing, and Denham Estate venison steak with red wine and wild mushroom sauce; rest assured that half the ingredients will be organic and locally sourced. Lighter bites may include grilled dates wrapped in bacon on a mustard sauce, and tasty soups. All this plenty is served in a high-raftered bar with dark timbered walls, scrubbed pine tables and a fireplace ablaze with logs in winter. A rustically cosy room lies next door. There are small portions for children and the drinks are exemplary: Adnams ales, ciders, wines and local elderflower pressé. Enjoy the lovely terraced courtyard and the garden with bantams and bower – and the pretty church next door.

Meals	12pm-2pm; 6.30pm-9.15pm; 7pm-9pm Sun. Main courses £8.95-£15.95.
Closed	2.30pm-6.30pm (3pm-7pm Sun).
Directions	2 miles north of A12 on A144 Halesworth road.

Mark & Amanda Corcoran
The Queens Head, The Street,
Bramfield, Halesworth IP19 9HT

Tel	01986 784214
Web	www.queensheadbramfield.co.uk

Entry 612 Map 10

Suffolk

The King's Head
Laxfield

Known locally as the Low House because it lies in a dip below the churchyard, the 600-year-old pub is one of Suffolk's treasures. Little has changed in the last 100 years and the four rooms creak with character – all narrow passageways, low ceilings, wood panelling and tiny fires for cold nights. The simple parlour is dominated by a three-sided, high-backed settle and there's no bar – far too new-fangled a concept for this place. Instead, Adnams ales are served from barrels in the tap room. In keeping with the authenticity, the food is rustic, hearty and homemade, the short blackboard menu listing soup, sandwiches, hot dishes and puddings. It's the sort of place where folk music starts up spontaneously, while summer brings Morris men. The lovely garden overlooking the brook at the back was once a bowling green. Heaven.

Meals	12pm-2pm; 7pm-9pm. Main courses £6.50-£9; bar meals £3.95-£6.
Closed	3pm-6pm. Open all day in summer.
Directions	From Laxfield church, left down hill for 50 yards. Left; pub on right.

SPECIAL AWARD
see pages 18-19

Authentic pub

Robert Wilson
The King's Head, Gorams Mill Lane,
Laxfield IP13 8DW

Tel	01986 798395
Web	www.laxfield-kingshead.co.uk

Entry 613 Map 10

Sibton White Horse
Sibton

Drinkers rejoice! This is a traditional, brasses-and-blackened-beams sort of place and the bar is the most interesting room in the house: find an old oak servery, gleaming brass beer engines, old pews and settles and an inglenook fireplace roaring away. The landlord is passionate about real ale so there's plenty on tap but also weekly changing guest ales, over 30 wines and a good range of malts and liqueurs. Food is fresh and fairly seasonal with local game, homemade bread and meat from the next village: try roast Sibton pheasant breast with baked sweet potato rings or a Dingley Dell pork cutlet from Wickham Market. The listed building sits in rolling countryside just under a mile from the pretty village of Peasenhall; on sunny days folk spill outside onto big lawns. In a converted annexe are simple bedrooms with antique pine furniture, dried flowers, good beds and spotless modern shower or bathrooms; views are to open countryside. You are a 20-minute drive from both Aldeburgh and Southwold so this is perfect for days out at the seaside.

Rooms	6: 5 twins/doubles, 1 single. £80–£125. Singles £55.
Meals	12pm–2pm; 7pm–9pm. Main courses £6.95–£9.95 (lunch), £9.95–£17.95 (dinner); Sunday roast £8.95.
Closed	3pm–6pm & Mon lunch.
Directions	A1120 off A12 at Yoxford; at Peasenhall, turn right opposite Creasey's butchers; pub signed.

	Neil & Gill Mason Sibton White Horse, Halesworth Road, Sibton, Saxmundham IP17 2JS
Tel	01728 660337
Web	www.sibtonwhitehorseinn.co.uk

Station Hotel
Framlingham

The railway disappeared long ago, the old buildings are now business units, but the 'hotel' continues to thrive. Cask ales (a classic Victorian Bitter, a sweet, wintry porter) are perfect accompaniments for gutsy cooking. Who would imagine, chalked up on the board on the edge of a market town somewhere in Suffolk, creamy baked vacherin cheese or pig's trotters stuffed with apple and black pudding? Or warm almond and orange polenta cake light as a cloud? Lunch is quiet but it bustles at night, helped along by the master of the kitchen, Mike Jones, and his friendly, laid-back team. The building is pretty in a shabby-boho way, the interior is charming. Expect blackened stripped boards, cream papered walls, a stuffed head, and bone-handled knives partnering paper serviettes – a characterful mix.

The Crown Inn
Snape

It's a Suffolk gem, this well-preserved 15th-century inn with beams and brick floors, a stroll from the Maltings and a short drive from Minsmere's birds. It claims to have the finest example anywhere of a double Suffolk settle, known as the 'old codgers'; for this it is worth the trip alone. But the real old codgers have long gone: this popular food pub now attracts a rather cosmopolitan crowd. Key to its success has always been fresh, local produce, particularly fish, game and seasonal ingredients; now Gary Cook (ex chef at Aldeburgh's renowned 152) has taken over. In his trusty hands the food side should flourish alongside, we suspect, the deliciously pubby atmosphere of old brick floors and roaring log fires. The real ales and the wines are supplied by Adnams, who own the place.

Meals	12pm-2pm; 7pm-9pm (9.30pm Fri & Sat). Main courses £4-£14.75; bar meals £3.25-£11.
Closed	2.30pm-5pm (7pm Sun).
Directions	From Wickham Market, 10 min off the A12.

Meals	12pm-2.30pm; 6pm-9.30pm (12pm-10pm Sat); no food Sun eve, or Mon in winter. Main courses £6.95-£12.
Closed	2.30pm-6pm (open all day Sat/Sun in summer).
Directions	From A12, A1094 for Aldeburgh; right at Snape Church onto B1069; follow 'Snape Maltings' sign. Pub on left at bottom of hill.

Mike Jones
Station Hotel, Station Road,
Framlingham, Woodbridge IP13 9EE
Tel   01728 723455
Web   www.thestationhotel.net

Gary Cook & Teresa Golder
The Crown Inn,
Bridge Road, Snape,
Saxmundham IP17 1SL
Tel   01728 688324

Entry 615 Map 10

Entry 616 Map 10

Suffolk

Kings Head
Orford

Standing in the shadow of the village church and windswept graveyard, the 16th-century King's Head is steeped in smuggling history: Orford's ancient quay is a stroll away. David and Ruth Watson, owners of the swish Crown & Castle across the square, have breathed new life into the place since taking over. This is no gastropub, however, but a proper, no-nonsense village local. A winter fire warms the beamed and carpeted traditional bar, and there's a homely dining room next door. In keeping, the food is classic pub grub – sourced entirely from locally sourced ingredients. Folk love the 'doorstop' Suffolk cured-bacon sandwiches, the steak and ale pies and the Orford smoked mackerel with mustard sauce. Or drop by for a cracking pint of Adnams Broadside – itself a meal in a glass.

Meals	12pm-2.30pm; 6.30pm-8.30pm. Main courses £6.95-£10.95; bar snacks from £3.95.
Closed	3pm-6pm (4pm-7pm Sun).
Directions	Leave A12 at Woodbridge; A1152 & B1084 to Orford; pub on main square.

David & Ruth Watson
Kings Head, Front Street, Orford, Woodbridge IP12 2LW
Tel   01394 450205
Web   www.kingshead-orford-suffolk.co.uk

Entry 617 Map 10

Suffolk

White Hart
Otley

Deep in Suffolk, the quintessence of community spirit. Lynda, Sarah and chef Sam have made the White Hart their own: free-spirited, utterly individual, a place to expect the unexpected. Scout leaders pop in for the warmth and the beer, the piano may be commandeered for a singsong at any time. At weekends children sprawl on the sofa or play battleships under the tables and anything goes; a dining room is tucked around the end of the very long bar but you can eat wherever you like. So kick off your shoes, pull up a chair and order a meal. There are sausages with mash and Aspall cider gravy, Sri Lankan fishcakes and red Thai fish curry, half a pint of prawns and sirloin steak with chips. They are even founder members of the Slow Food movement so the food bursts with flavour and the sourcing is impeccable. One of the best.

Meals	12pm-2.30pm; 6pm-9pm. Main courses £7.45-£12; Sunday roasts £3.95 (child-size), £6.95 & £8.95.
Closed	3pm-5pm, Mon lunch & Sun from 5pm.
Directions	B1079 from Otley, 0.5 miles north towards Helmingham, on left.

Lynda Saint
White Hart, Helmingham Road, Otley, Ipswich IP6 9NS
Tel   01473 890312
Web   www.thewhitehartotley.co.uk

Entry 618 Map 10

The Ship
Levington

The Levington Ship is a 14th-century thatched beauty overlooking the River Orwell. This alone makes it a popular watering hole, the low-ceilinged bar and flower-festooned rear terrace filling quickly with yachting types, locals and townies escaping to the country for lunch. Naturally, the bar emphasises a nautical theme, with pictures of barges, lifebuoys and a ship's wheel on the walls. Over the past few years chef-patron Mark Johnson's imaginative cooking has made its successful mark, his chalkboard menus listing fresh fish and locally reared meats – notably venison from the Suffolk Estate – as well as seasonal salads and local vegetables. Exemplary French cheeses come from the Rungis Market in Paris and superior real ales from East Anglian brewers Adnams and Greene King. Wonderful riverside walks also await.

The Crown
Stoke-by-Nayland

Several low-ceilinged but rambling rooms, one with a view of the kitchen, are decked in muted colours; the mood is warm, appealing and refreshingly music-free. There's space to prop up the bar and down a pint from Suffolk brewers Adnams, while the seasonal menu is a sympathetic combination of traditional and contemporary. Chefs dispatch exuberant renditions of salt and pepper squid with garlic and lemon mayonnaise, crispy pork belly with creamed leek mash, pan-fried calves' liver with bubble-and-squeak potato cake, crispy bacon and red wine sauce. Polish it all off with prune and armagnac tart with clotted cream or a platter of five British cheeses. The food is fairly priced and there's an outstanding wine list, with wines matched to the food and bottles to take home from the shop. And a glorious terrace with stunning views.

Meals	12pm-2pm (3pm Sun); 6.30pm-9.30pm (9pm Sun). Main courses from £7.75-£14.95.
Closed	2.30pm-6pm. Open all day Sat & Sun.
Directions	A12/A14 junction to Woodbridge; follow signs for Levington.

Meals	12pm-2.30pm; 6pm-9.30pm (10pm Fri & Sat); 12pm-9pm Sun. Main courses £8.95-£15.95.
Closed	Open all day.
Directions	Just off B1087 in Stoke-by-Nayland.

Stella & Mark Johnson
The Ship,
Levington,
Ipswich IP10 0LQ
Tel   01473 659573

Richard Sunderland
The Crown, Stoke-by-Nayland,
Colchester CO6 4SE
Tel   01206 262001
Web   www.eoinns.co.uk

Entry 619 Map 10

Entry 620 Map 10

Suffolk

Star Inn
Lidgate

The garden is glorious on a summer's day. For winter there are two blazing fires – and two snugs, each the centrepiece of an ancient-beamed bar. Indeed, the pretty Star, built in 1588, is one of the oldest buildings in the village. It is also as English as can be, yet landlady Maria Teresa Axon comes from Catalonia in Spain. The rich aromas that greet you may just as well come from boeuf en daube or venison in port as from Spanish-style roast lamb, fabada asturiana (Asturian pork and bean stew) or parillada of fish. Bring a good appetite as portions will be generous, and do book; proximity to Newmarket brings racing types in droves. There are darts and dominoes to get stuck into, Greene King beers on hand pump – ask about the unusual handles – and Spain is deliciously represented in brandies and wines.

We make no claims to pure objectivity in choosing these places. They are here simply because we like them. Our opinions and tastes are ours alone and we hope you will share them.

Meals	12pm-2.30pm; 7pm-10pm; no food Sun eve. Main courses £10.50-£18.95; bar meals £2.50-£6.90.
Closed	3pm-6pm.
Directions	On B1063, 7 miles south east of Newmarket.

Maria Teresa Axon
Star Inn,
The Street, Lidgate,
Bury St Edmunds CB8 9PP

Tel	01638 500275

Entry 625 Map 9

Suffolk

626   Old Cannon Brewery 86 Cannon Street, Bury St Edmunds IP33 1JR
01284 768769
Revitalised Victorian brewhouse-pub where boards clatter, the tables are plain and a huge mirror vies with two stainless steel brewing vessels. Great beer, modern pub food – worth the five-minute walk from town.

627   Angel Hotel Whitworth, Lavenham CO10 9QZ
01787 247388
Refurbished diners' pub and old inn overlooking Lavenham's market place and famous timbered guildhall. East Anglian ales and a daily-changing menu. New owner with big plans – reports please.

628   The Henny Swan Henny Street, Great Henny, Sudbury CO10 7LS
01787 269238
A stylish revamp at this middle-of-nowhere riverside pub. Appealing lunch and supper menus and Suffolk ales, and picnic tables on grass running down to the pretty river.

629   Anchor Inn 26 Court Street, Nayland CO6 4JL
01206 262313
The old country inn by the river has been thoroughly renovated – with some detriment to the atmosphere. But regulars and tourists are drawn by the fresh gastropub food.

630   Butt & Oyster Pin Mill, Chelmondiston, Ipswich IP9 1JW
01787 280245
In a charmingly untouristy sailing village, an old estuary pub with settles, tiled floors, summer terrace with barbecue and Adnams tapped from the cask. Arrive early if you want a window seat.

631   The Queens Head Erwarton, Ipswich IP9 1LN   01473 787550
Unassuming village local in the rural wilds of the Shotley peninsula, with views across fields and bobbing boats. Come for Suffolk ales and rustic pub food: fishcakes, steaks and homemade nursery puds.

632   The Ramsholt Arms Dock Road, Ramsholt, Woodbridge IP12 3AB
01394 411229
Idyllic – on the shore of the river Deben. Down a pint of Nethergate on the terrace, listen to the calls of the curlew. Cosy fires, game in season and great fish and chips.

633   The Dog Inn The Green, Grundisburgh, Woodbridge IP13 6TA
01473 735267
A nicely refurbished village dining pub run by enthusiastic brothers. Expect classic English dishes using top-notch seasonal produce from local suppliers: roast partridge with game chips; Ketley lamb pie and mash.

Suffolk

634 **Victoria** The Street, Earl Soham, Stowmarket IP13 7RL
 01728 685758

Inauspicious whitewashed village local by the green, famous for its home-brewed beers (Earl Soham Brewery). Few frills in the main bar but hearty pub food and a proper pint of Victoria Ale.

635 **Crown Inn** Great Glemham IP17 2DA
01728 663693

In their charming village pub, David and Georgie serve up the cream of the crop – not just the local Jersey dairy produce from Marybelle's Rendham farm but also well-bred Alde Valley lamb and superb Suffolk brews.

636 **Plough & Sail** Snape Maltings, Snape IP17 1SR 01728 688413

Set at the front of the Maltings, next to the road, this busy bustling Adnams pub-restaurant delivers a globally inspired menu to a vast array of tables. A tourist magnet on weekends and holidays.

637 **Eels Foot Inn** Eastbridge, Leiston IP16 4SN
01728 830154

A plain, backwater village pub delivering good honest food, Adnams ales, and a real craic on music nights. Close to Minsmere Bird Reserve; mobbed in summer.

638 **The Bell Inn** Ferry Road, Walberswick IP18 6TN
01502 723109

A 600-year-old inn set in a tiny summer-soft, winter-bleak fishing village. Come for good local ales and homely bar food to a backdrop of ancient beams, flagstones, wooden settles and open fires.

639 **The Randolph Hotel** Wangford Road, Reydon, Southwold IP18 6PZ
01502 723603

As good for a quick bite and a pint of Adnams as for a three-course meal that takes in local fish and game. This late Victorian pub-hotel has sleek modern good looks – and gardens for summer.

640 **The Swan** Low Street, Hoxne IP21 5AS
01379 668273

Still a feel of times past at this village local that goes back to the late 15th century. Expect acres of oak floorboards, carved timbers, colourwashed walls, Adnams on tap, and large helpings of homecooked food.

641 **St Peter's Hall** St Peter South Elmham, Bungay NR35 1NQ
01986 782288

The 13th-century moated manor thrives, brewing and bottling an exemplary range of bitters, fruit ales and porters. Take the weekend brewery tour or venture into the medieval hall to eat and drink like kings.

The Albert Arms
Esher

Jonathan Dunne's growing empire of eateries along Esher's bustling high street revolves around this dazzling white corner pub. The place buzzes from dawn to midnight, drawing in passers-by for breakfast, sports' fans for the screen, business people for the meeting rooms, and diners for classic English food. Not forgetting the live weekend jazz nights, the regular wine courses, and Jonathan's wine store a few doors down. In an oak-floored dining room with an elegant décor and an open-to-view kitchen you may choose from eight real ales and 36 wines by the glass the perfect match for your rack of lamb. Or your Dover sole, fish stew, calves' liver and bacon or 28-day matured Angus steak (a house speciality). Set lunch menus and delicious Sunday roasts add to the appeal. The stylishness extends to six classically simple bedrooms lying in the mews house to the side, so make the most of crisp sheets on good quality beds, mini hi-fi's and WiFi and shining wet rooms with drench showers. In the morning, set off to discover the history of Hampton Court Palace.

Rooms	6 doubles. £110.
Meals	12pm-2.45pm; 7pm-9.45pm (12pm-4pm Sun); no food Sun eve. Main courses £10.50-£22; Sunday lunch £12.50-£13.50.
Closed	Open all day.
Directions	In town centre.

Jonathan Dunne
The Albert Arms,
82 High Street,
Esher KT10 9QS
Tel   01372 465290
Web   www.albertarms.com

Surrey

The Inn @ West End
West End

Wine importer Gerry Price draws them in from all over Surrey. Stylishly revamped dining areas are light and modern with wooden floors and fine fabrics. The feeling is relaxed and friendly – quiz nights, film club, boules, barbecues; the homely bar has a wood-burning stove, handpumped ale comes from Fuller's and Young's and the list of wines is long, with a nod to Portuguese shores. Monthly menus have modern British choices ranging from salmon and dill fishcakes with tartare sauce to pot-roasted pork with cabbage and dauphinoise potatoes – and partridge, pheasant, woodcock and teal in winter. A pastry chef masterminds a select choice of desserts; cheeses are farmhouse best. Add good value set lunches, lunchtime wine-tasting sessions, an al fresco dining patio and popular wine dinners and you have a superbly run place.

Meals	12pm-2.30pm (3pm Sun); 6pm-9.30pm (9pm Sun). Set menus from £11.95; sandwiches from £5.25; Sunday lunch £22.95.
Closed	3pm-5pm Mon-Fri.
Directions	On A322 towards Guildford, 2 miles from M3 junc. 3.

Gerry & Ann Price
The Inn @ West End,
42 Guildford Road,
West End GU24 9PW
Tel   01276 858652
Web   www.the-inn.co.uk

Entry 643 Map 4

Surrey

Black Swan
Ockham

Geronimo Inns' boss Rupert Clevely must have jumped for joy when he completed the deal on the Black Swan, his first pub outside London. Minutes from the A3 yet deep in leafy Surrey, a grand makeover has seen the old bikers' boozer transformed into swish gastropub, the brick façade dwarfed by an amazing pavilion extension. Clever design pulls informal and open-plan drinking and dining areas together around a curving bar, with a classic bar for pints and an airy, high-ceilinged eating area that buzzes with diners. Décor may be ultra-modern but, with up to six ales on tap and a flurry of non-bookable tables, it is still a pub. Good food ranges from potted salmon with pickled cucumber or cider-battered cod and chips, to shepherd's pie and herb-crusted rack of lamb. The Black Swan is thriving.

Meals	12pm-10pm. Main courses £8-£17.50; bar snacks £5-£9.50.
Closed	Open all day.
Directions	Ockham is signed off A3 just south of M25 junc. 10. Pub just north of village at crossroads.

Kevin Ward
Black Swan, Old Lane, Ockham,
Guildford KT11 1NG
Tel   01932 862364
Web   www.geronimo-inns.co.uk

Entry 644 Map 4

Surrey

The Parrot
Forest Green

Having left their mini-empire of London pubs for a livestock farm in the Surrey hills, the Gottos also run this rambling, 17th-century pub overlooking the village green and cricket pitch. They are passionate about food, its provenance and quality, and the Parrot pub showcases meats reared on their farm — Shorthorn cattle, Middlewhite pigs and mutton — both on the short, imaginative menu and in the unique farm shop inside. Surely one of few pubs where you can tuck into game pie, lamb rump with minted pea purée and roast belly pork with mash and braised cabbage, and then buy the produce to take home (farm meats, free-range eggs, sausages, pickles, cheeses, pies). Elsewhere, beams, flagstones and lovely bits and bobs, old settles and blazing fires, Young's on tap and 16 wines by the glass. The value is outstanding.

Surrey

The King William IV
Mickleham

Open fires, fresh flowers and amazing views are a few of the reasons people make the steep stepped climb. The old alehouse was built for Lord Beaverbrook's estate staff – a hilltop eyrie that has long been a popular little pub in summer, when all and sundry spill into the terraced gardens. In winter it's super-snug and squeezes in two carpeted bars. The real badgers have gone (see the photos on the walls) but their namesake ale remains on tap as well as Sharps Doom Bar and those from The Hogs Back Brewery. Equal attention is paid to food. Chips are banned but nobody cares when delicious homemade pies, lamb shank with red wine sauce and Thai-style sea bass are brought to the table. There are steam puddings too: just what you need after a morning hiking over the hills. Arrive before midday to be sure of a seat.

Meals	12pm-3pm (6pm Sun); 6pm-10pm; no food Sun eve. Main courses £9.25-£13.50; Sunday roast £11.75.
Closed	Open all day.
Directions	Opposite the village green, off B2127 just west of junction with B2126, 5 miles south-west of Dorking.

Meals	12pm-2pm; 7pm-9.30pm (12pm-5pm Sun). Main courses £7.25-£16.75; sandwiches £5-£5.75; Sunday roast £11.95.
Closed	3pm-6pm. Open all day Sun.
Directions	A24 for Dorking. Just before Mickleham, pub on hill above Frascati restaurant. Ask about parking.

	Charles & Linda Gotto The Parrot, Forest Green, Dorking RH5 5RZ
Tel	01306 621339
Web	www.theparrot.co.uk

	Ian & Liz Duke The King William IV, Byttom Hill, Mickleham, Dorking RH5 6EL
Tel	01372 372590
Web	www.king-williamiv.com

Entry 645 Map 4

Entry 646 Map 4

Surrey

The Hare & Hounds
Lingfield

With proprietor-chef Fergus's collection of quirky collectables filling every corner, this place has an idiosyncratic air. Bar bustle can be surveyed from old cinema seats or one of a pair of throne-like chairs, while the cushion-laden banquettes make an ideal spot for viewing a menu studded with the names of the farms that supply much of the produce. Blackboard specialities may include pan-fried wild pheasant breast with braised leg and roast vegetables. On the printed menu: chargrilled swordfish with aubergine bhuna with tomato and garlic tzatziki, and gorgonzola and red wine risotto. Diners are as happy among the hop garlands and the greenery of the main bar as beneath the bold paintings of Fergus's artist wife in the lovely dining room. Nurse a summer pint of Abbot Ale in the partly decked garden.

Those who are familiar with our Special Places series know that we look for originality and authenticity, and disregard the anonymous and the banal.

Meals	12pm-2.30pm (12pm-3pm Sun); 7pm-9.30pm.
	Main courses £7.95-£18.95.
Closed	Open all day (closed Sun from 8pm).
Directions	From A22 towards Lingfield Racecourse into Common Road.

Fergus Greer
The Hare & Hounds,
Common Road,
Lingfield RH7 6BZ

| Tel | 01342 832351 |
| Web | www.hareandhoundslingfield.co.uk |

Entry 647 Map 4

The Swan Inn and Restaurant
Chiddingfold

Here are a sparkling dining room and a cool bar – wooden floors, chunky tables: this is more chic restaurant than timeworn boozer. Still, its pubby origins have not been forgotten: there's Hogs Back TEA and Fuller's London Pride for those in for a pint, and ham, egg and chips (the best, naturally) for those in for a bite. And then there are snails, carpaccio of beef, goat's cheese soufflé and fishcakes with smoked salmon sauce – dishes that promise a successful juggling of popular and modern. In the dining room a well-presented menu lists a tempting choice, from seared salmon with flageolet beans and a green peppercorn sauce to confit duck leg with dauphinoise potatoes and red wine sauce. If you're staying, contemporary bedrooms have a minimalist feel, with muted earthy colours, flat-screen TVs and trendy bathrooms with power showers and posh toiletries. The spacious suite has its bedroom upstairs and its sitting room down, and overlooks the prettily landscaped beer garden. All in all, a happy, relaxed revival of an old inn, popular with walkers and foodies alike.

Rooms	11: 9 doubles, 2 suites. £70–£140.
Meals	12pm-2.30pm; 6.30pm-10pm.
	Main courses £9.45–£19.95;
	bar meals £4.25–£7.95;
	Sunday roast £11.95.
Closed	Open all day.
Directions	South of village green beside A283 between Guildford & Petworth.

Daniel Hall & Darren Tidd
The Swan Inn and Restaurant,
Petworth Road, Chiddingfold,
Guildford GU8 4TY

Tel	01428 682073
Web	www.theswaninn.biz

Entry 648 Map 4

Surrey

649 Dog and Pheasant Haslemere Road, Brook, Haslemere GU8 5UJ
01428 682763
Rambling, low-beamed pub opposite the cricket green. Come for the atmosphere, the view and the food – moules and frites, fillet steak and pepper sauce, great tapas – cooked by Kiwi Buzz. Reports please.

650 The Stag Lower Eashing, Godalming GU7 2QG
01483 421568
With a lease dating back to 1771, this is an attractive, atmospheric place to stop off for very good home cooking – and the teak-furnished terrace by the water makes a languorous drinking spot.

651 Old School House Stane Street, Ockley, Dorking RH5 5TH
01306 627430
Fabulous fish and seafood: expect fresh Selsey crab and Loch Fyne oysters alongside Fuller's beers. Cosy and friendly (though once a boys' boarding school), but more restaurant than pub.

652 The Plough Coldharbour, Dorking RH5 6HD
01306 711793
The smell of woodsmoke wafting from The Plough's chimneys is hard to resist, as are the home-brewed Crooked Furrow and Tallywacker, the delicious pub food, and the leafy walks to the top of Leith Hill.

653 Stephan Langton Friday Street, Abinger Common, Dorking RH5 6JR
01306 730775
Secluded country pub at the bottom of leafy Leith Hill, with a handful of cottages and a hammer pond for company. Great refuelling spot after exploring Surrey's finest walks.

654 Punch Bowl Inn Oakwood Hill, Dorking RH5 5PU
01306 627249
15th-Century charm: a roaring inglenook, scrubbed tables and wonky flagged floors. The tile-hung pub is in superb walking country. Summer barbecues and Badger beers.

655 The White Cross Water Lane, Richmond TW9 1TJ
020 8940 6844
Real fires in cosy bars and huge windows overlooking the Thames – what views! Enjoy a pint or three on the river terrace, packed on a summer day. Bar food is swiftly served.

Sussex

The Stag
Balls Cross

The quintessential Sussex pub – some might say (and often do) it's the best pub in the world. Under 16th-century beams by a crackling log fire, or in the big garden in summer, riders, walkers and locals enjoy a natter over well-kept Badger and Sussex Bitter. Wholesome home-cooked food is another draw, the traditional recipe pies, pastries and casseroles being the greatest temptation. A sweet shop in a former life, this little inn still welcomes children: in a set-aside room youngsters may play undisturbed. There is also plenty for adults: the Stag has its own darts team, jazz nights outdoors in summer, carol singing and visits from the travelling Mummers at Christmas. There's a 17th-century stone-floored bar and a dining room that's carpeted and cosy. And a useful tethering post for those who come by horse.

Meals	12pm-2pm; 7pm-9pm; no food Sun eve. Main courses £7.50-£18; bar meals £4-£18.
Closed	3pm-6pm (7pm Sun).
Directions	2 miles from Petworth on Kirdford road.

Hamish Hiddleston
The Stag,
Balls Cross,
Petworth GU28 9JP
Tel   01403 820241

Entry 656 Map 4

Sussex

Hollist Arms
Lodsworth

Villager and proprietor George Bristow rescued this lovely pub a few years ago, injected fresh enthusiasm and stuffed the menu with great ingredients. Prawn and crayfish 'knickerbockers', duck breast in soy sauce with ginger, and a melt-in-the-mouth cottage pie – all are first-class. Villagers prop up the very long bar for a fine pint of King's Horsham Best, while civilised sofas by a huge inglenook encourage others to linger. The smaller, more intimate rooms of this former smithy have been kept: one, a cosy private dining room, another a sweet snug with armchairs, blazing fire and tables piled high with magazines and games. And there's a garden for summer. From the hand-cut, local-farm potato chips to the colourwashed walls, pretty feather-patterned curtains and soothing classical sounds, this Hollist oozes magic.

Meals	12pm-2pm (2.30pm Sat, 3pm Sun); 7pm-9pm (9.30pm Fri & Sat, 6.30-8pm Sun). Main courses £10-£16; bar meals £5-£10.
Closed	3pm-6pm (4pm-6pm Sun).
Directions	Halfway between Midhurst & Petworth; signed off A272.

George Bristow
Hollist Arms,
The Street, Lodsworth,
Petworth GU28 9BZ
Tel   01798 861310

Entry 657 Map 4

Sussex

Welldiggers Arms
Petworth

Once occupied by well-diggers, this rustic 300-year-old roadside cottage has little immediate appeal. But enter and you are greeted by Ted Whitcomb, landlord and larger-than-life persona, pulling pints of Young's and cracking jokes behind the bar for 50-odd years. Surprisingly, this is a dining-orientated pub, its low-ceilinged bar and snug packed with happy eaters at long settles and huge oak tables. Come for classic British food: king prawns in garlic, fresh mussels, whole Dover sole, and properly hung T-bone steaks. Alternatives may include braised oxtail and dumplings, calves' liver, black pudding and mash, seasonal game – and magnificent Sunday roasts. Popular with enthusiasts of racing (Goodwood), shooting and polo (Cowdray Park), so be sure to book. At the back is a patio with views over the South Downs.

Meals	12pm-2pm; 6pm-9pm; no food Sun eve. Main courses £7.50-£19.50; bar meals from £4.25.
Closed	3.30pm-6pm; Sun, Tues & Wed eve & Mon all day.
Directions	Beside A283 Pulborough road, 1 mile east of Petworth.

Ted Whitcomb
Welldiggers Arms,
Pulborough Road,
Petworth GU28 0HG
Tel   01798 342287

Entry 658 Map 4

Sussex

The Keepers Arms
Trotton

Nick Troth and the fledgling Weybourne Inns have now taken on the Keepers Arms at Trotton. High above the road, with a front terrace and views, it is equally pleasing inside. The warm, friendly bar has beams, polished floorboards, characterful tables, leather sofas and a winter fire – and a good range of changing ales from local breweries. Chef Matt Appleton has a fine pedigree so you may expect such delicacies as foie gras and ham hock terrine with a pea purée and a salad of pea shoots, and honey-roasted Gressingham duck with creamed savoy cabbage, shiitake mushrooms and puy lentils. You eat at candlelit tables in the dining room next to the bar, its warm colours, light tartan fabrics and modern high-backed chairs giving it an upbeat hunting lodge air. At lunch, blackboards announce much-loved pub classics, too.

Meals	12pm-2pm (2.30pm Sun); 7pm-9.30pm (9pm Sun). Main courses £11.95-£16.75.
Closed	3pm-6.30pm; Sun eves; Mon.
Directions	On A272 between Midhurst & Petersfield.

Nick Troth
The Keepers Arms,
Trotton, Petersfield GU31 5ER
Tel   01730 813724
Web   www.keepersarms.co.uk

Entry 659 Map 4

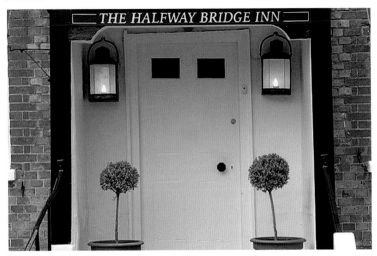

Halfway Bridge Inn
Halfway Bridge

Paul and Sue Carter bought this mellow old coaching inn in 2006 and have introduced a stylish feel. Keeping the classic three-room layout and the warren of cosy corners and split levels, they have added scrubbed tables, cushioned benches, big lilies and fat candles. Thirsts are quenched by Sussex beers and wines by the glass, and the food is good, a satisfying mix of traditional and modern with menus that change seasonally. Find a seat by the open fire and scan a menu that announces first-rate fish from Billingsgate alongside game suet pudding and canon of lamb. For summer there's a sheltered patio with posh tables and brollies. This would be a lovely place for a short break, so why not stay? Away from the busy road, over the lane from the inn, the old Cowdray barns have been converted into super rooms where deep beds, leather chairs, plasma screens and PlayStations "for the boys" sit alongside old beams and rustic brickwork. The attention to detail extends to big mirrors, fat fluffy towels, French lotions and potions – and torches attached to key fobs so you don't get lost in the dark!

Rooms	6: 2 doubles , 4 suites. £120–£130. Singles from £85. Suites £140–£160.
Meals	12pm–2.30pm; 6.30pm–9.15pm (8.30pm Sun). Main courses £10.95–£18.95; bar meals £5.95–£11.95.
Closed	Open all day.
Directions	On A272 halfway between Midhurst & Petworth.

Paul & Sue Carter
Halfway Bridge Inn,
Halfway Bridge, Midhurst GU28 9BP

Tel	01798 861281
Web	www.thesussexpub.co.uk

Entry 660 Map 4

Sussex

The Three Horseshoes
Elsted

Low beams, latched doors, high settles, deep-cream bowed walls, big log fires and home-cooked food: all that you'd hope for, and more. Built in 1540 as a drovers' ale house, it has no cellar, so staff pull ales from the barrel instead; the line of metal casks is visible in the lower open-timbered bar, formerly a butcher's shop and still with the ceiling hooks. Local seafood, meat and game appear on a tempting country menu – summer lobster and crab, pheasant in cider with shallots and prunes, steak and kidney in Guinness pie – and are served in snug rooms. In the main dining room with its wood-burning stove you can't miss the flock of chickens in china, pottery and wood. Landlady Sue has a passion for poultry and in summer her feathered friends cluck cheerily outside among the drinkers with their golden pints.

Meals	12pm-2pm; 6.30pm-9pm (7pm-8.30pm Sun). Main courses £8.95-£17.95; bar meals £6.95-£9.95.
Closed	2.30pm-6pm (3pm-7pm Sun).
Directions	From Midhurst A272 for Petersfield; Elsted signed left in 2 miles.

Sue Beavis & Michael Newton
The Three Horseshoes,
Elsted,
Midhurst GU29 0JY
Tel 01730 825746

Entry 661 Map 4

Sussex

The Star & Garter
East Dean

If fresh fish and seafood appeal then follow the winding Sussex lanes to this 18th-century brick-and-flint pub. Hidden in the folds of the South Downs, with miles of breezy walks from the front door, the old ale house now draws the well-shod from Goodwood and Midhurst. Seafood platters spill over with whole Selsey lobster and crabs, scallops, wild salmon, crevettes and prawns. There are big bowls of mussels, whole baked bass, venison pie and, in season, a mouthwatering game grill, with partridge from West Dean, pigeon from East Dean and local wild boar sausages. Drink fine Sussex ales straight from the cellar in the open-plan, wooden floored room, where hops adorn stripped beams, old village photographs line bare-brick walls and daily papers fill the rack by the door. In summer, head for the sun-trap patio or lawned gardens.

Meals	12pm-2.30pm; 6.30pm-10pm (12pm-10pm Sat; 9.30pm Sun). Main courses £10.50-£16.50; bar meals £5.50-£8.50.
Closed	Open all day Sat & Sun.
Directions	Village signed off A286 between Midhurst & Chichester at Singleton.

Oliver Ligertwood
The Star & Garter, East Dean,
Goodwood, Chichester PO18 0JG
Tel 01243 811318
Web www.thestarandgarter.co.uk

Entry 662 Map 4

The Foresters
Graffham

Friendly, savvy, youthful new owners have taken on Graffham's little pub. Their intelligently compact and straightforward menus reflect the seasons, change daily and are driven by good quality produce from within 50 miles. A list of suppliers accompanies the menu, while local microbrewery ales find a place at the hand pump. A thoughtfully chosen wine list has plenty by the glass as well as country wines from Lurgashall Winery. As for the pub, it dates from the 17th century, has beamed ceilings, a big crackling log fire, exposed bricks, darkwood floors and cottagey furniture and pews. Cosy bedrooms in a building next door are small and simple but nicely decorated with good linen, trim carpets, chunky beds and bathrooms with showers. Breakfast is 'English' continental, and you can choose to have it delivered to the room in a specially prepared hamper. Or have a table laid in the pub. As for Graffham, it's a cul-de-sac village an hour from London, and as English as the Foresters itself.

Rooms	2 doubles. £90.
Meals	12pm-2.30pm (3pm Sun); 6pm-9.30pm. Main courses £8.75-£22, lunch £3.95-£16.50; Sunday roast £10-£17.
Closed	3pm-6pm; Sun eve & Mon all day.
Directions	From Midhurst, 2 miles south on A286, then left for Heyshott/Graffham. Straight ahead, left at T-junc. in village; pub on right.

Robert & Clare Pearce
The Foresters,
The Street, Graffham,
Midhurst GU28 0QA

Tel	01798 867202
Web	www.forestersgraffham.co.uk

The Chilgrove White Horse
Chichester

A pub-restaurant with rooms hiding in the shell of an 18th-century inn that sits at the foot of the South Downs – lose yourself in gorgeous hills. Back at the pub you'll find ducks on the pond and a garden in which to watch the sun drop behind the hills so sit back with a pint of Ballards and a baguette (drinks are served with food). In the sparkling, timber-framed restaurant, tables are smartly dressed with crisp linen and gleaming glass, logs smoulder on the fire. Alcoves bust with hundreds of bottles and the bar is clad in old wine boxes – the White Horse's cellar is the biggest draw. There are more than 600 wines on the list, and 14 by the glass. They are also Green Tourism gold award winners, so the food is as local and organic as can be. As for the bedrooms, they open onto a private garden and have light colours, pretty rugs, fresh flowers, bins to recycle your rubbish; the bigger rooms have sofas and fridges and breakfast hampers are brought to you – enjoy your coffee and croissants in the garden when the sun shines. Chichester is close, as is the Witterings for sand dunes and sea.

Rooms	9 twins/doubles. £95–£160. Singles £75–£150.
Meals	12pm-2pm; 7pm-10pm. Main courses £14.95–£22.50; bar meals £7.95–£10.50.
Closed	3pm-6pm; Sun eve & Mon all day.
Directions	South from Midhurst on A286. Through West Dean, then right onto B2141. On right after 2 miles.

Charles & Carin Burton
The Chilgrove White Horse,
Chilgrove, Chichester PO18 9HX

Tel	01243 535219
Web	www.whitehorsechilgrove.co.uk

Entry 664 Map 4

Sussex

The Fox Goes Free
Charlton

King William III may have stopped off here to refresh his royal hunting parties but this 400-year-old flint pub, secreted away in the South Downs, is now home to some fine ales from small local breweries. Settle down by a big blazing fire under beamed ceilings for a pint of Ballards Best and the pub's own Fox Goes Free; in summer there's a garden with sweeping farmland views. The traditional bar food suits the surroundings, so sit at scrubbed tables and choir chairs for fresh butcher's sausages with mash, onion gravy and veg, followed by a comforting treacle sponge with custard. In the dining room — once a stable for race horses — are less familiar creations, perhaps pan-fried duck breast with stir-fry vegetables and hoi sin sauce. Goodwood racecourse is just up the hill and there are downland walks from the door.

Meals	12pm-2.30pm; 6.30pm-10pm; 12pm-10pm Sat (9.30pm Sun). Main courses £9.95-£16.95; bar meals £8.50-£9.95.
Closed	Open all day.
Directions	From Chichester follow A286 towards Midhurst. At Singleton right to Charlton.

David Coxon
The Fox Goes Free,
Charlton, Goodwood PO18 0HU
Tel   01243 811461
Web   www.thefoxgoesfree.com

Entry 665 Map 4

Sussex

Anglesey Arms at Halnaker
Halnaker

Laid back, relaxed, free of airs and graces, a Georgian brick pub in an affluent part of West Sussex. It's not a pie-and-a-pint pub or a chips-with-everything roadside diner — just a cracking good local run by Roger and Jools Jackson, genuinely committed to keeping it charming and old-fashioned. Expect varnished and stripped pine, flagstones, beams and panelling, crackling log fires, locals downing pints at the bar. Food is fresh and home-cooked using great local produce — crab and lobster from Selsey, traceable meats (organic South Downs lamb and pork, organic well-hung beef from the Goodwood Estate), venison and game from local shoots. Even the ciders, wines and spirits are organic. A great little local, with inter-pub cricket, golf and quizzes and regular 'moules and boules' events in the two-acre garden.

Meals	12pm-2.30pm; 6.30pm-9.30pm; no food Sun eve. Main courses £10.95-£17.95; bar meals £4.95-£12.95.
Closed	3pm-5.30pm. Open all day Sun.
Directions	On A285, 4 miles north east of Chichester.

Roger & Jools Jackson
Anglesey Arms at Halnaker,
Halnaker, Chichester PO18 0NQ
Tel   01243 773474
Web   www.angleseyarms.co.uk

Entry 666 Map 4

The Crab & Lobster
Sidlesham

The down-at-heel boozer has become a fabulous pub-with-rooms. This one is managed by Sam Bakose. The new-look 'Crab' – backing onto Pagham Harbour and bird-rich marshes – opened its doors in 2007 and the results are stunning. The ancient flagstones and inglenook fireplace blend effortlessly with the upholstered banquettes, the ornate mirrors and the vintage photos on the walls. There's a fishy focus to the menu, as you'd expect – crab and lobster ravioli; oganic sea trout with niçoise salad; Cornish sardines with black olive butter – while carnivores can tuck into the likes of Sussex lamb cutlets with roasted garlic and thyme jus. Wash it all down with a pint of local Harvey's and choose a seat on the back terrace for those views of sheep-grazed meadows and marshes. Bedrooms are for birdwatchers, particularly Room 4 with its perfectly placed telescope... there are handmade beds, planked floors and walk-in storm showers. Be delighted by heritage colours, fresh coffee and beautiful bathrooms sporting L'Occitane toiletries. A chic Sussex bolthole.

Rooms	4 + 1: 4 doubles, 1 cottage for two. £120-£140. Singles from £75.
Meals	12pm-2.15pm; 6pm-9.30pm. Main courses £11.50-£19.50.
Closed	Open all day.
Directions	Mill Lane is off B2145 Chichester to Selsey road, just south of Sidlesham; pub is close to Pagham Harbour.

Sam Bakose
The Crab & Lobster,
Mill Lane, Sidlesham, Chichester PO20 7NB
Tel   01243 641233
Web   www.thesussexpub.co.uk

Entry 667 Map 4

The Royal Oak Inn
Chichester

There's a cheery wine-bar feel to the Royal Oak; locals and young professionals come with their children and it's as countrified as can be. Inside, a modern-rustic look with traditional touches prevails: stripped floors, exposed brickwork, dark leather sofas, open fires, racing pictures on the walls; the inn was once part of the Goodwood estate. The dining area is big, light and airy, with a conservatory from which you can spill out onto a terrace that's warmed by outdoor lamps on summer nights. At scrubbed pine tables you can tuck into delicious salmon and chorizo fishcakes, Scottish rump beefburgers, wild mushroom risotto. Bedrooms are divided between three cottages, a nearby barn and upstairs at the back (ask for one with a view). All have CD players, plasma screens, a DVD library and top toiletries – the best of modern – along with excellent lighting, brown leather chairs and big comfy beds. Staff are attentive, breakfasts are good and fresh, a secret garden looks over cornfields, and you're well-placed for Chichester Theatre and the boats at pretty Bosham.

Rooms	8: 4 doubles, 1 twin, 3 cottages. £90–£130. Singles £65–£75.
Meals	12pm–2.30pm; 6.30pm–9pm. Main courses £11.50–£18; bar meals £5.25–£10.50.
Closed	Open all day.
Directions	From Chichester A286 for Midhurst. First right at first mini roundabout into E. Lavant. Down hill, pass village green, over bridge, pub 200 yds on left. Car park opposite.

Charles Ullman
The Royal Oak Inn,
Pook Lane, East Lavant,
Chichester PO18 0AX

Tel	01243 527434
Web	www.thesussexpub.co.uk

Sussex

The Chimney House
Brighton

The Victorian red-brick corner boozer has become a gastropub of note – the first pub venture of Lia Vittone. Taking its stylish lead from the bistro pubs of London it has not lost its community feel, so settle in to leather armchairs, scrubbed tables and an open kitchen from which classic British dishes flow. As you might expect, the produce is well-sourced and often organic; it's the sort of place where even the ketchup is homemade. Tuck into smoked haddock rarebit and roasted tomatoes with a blackfaced-lamb burger and mint yoghurt, or a pork chop with garlic new potatoes, rainbow chard and apple compote. Or just pop in for a bowl of hand-cut chips to soak up the excellent Harveys ales. Tables are filled on a first come, first-served basis – except on New Year's Eve and Valentine's Night!

Meals	12pm-2.30pm Fri & Sat (3.30pm Sun); 6pm-9.30pm. Main course £8.95-£14.95.
Closed	3pm-5pm (Mon-Thurs).
Directions	In the Seven Dials area, on the corner of Upper Hamilton Rd & Exeter St.

	Lia Vittone The Chimney House, Upper Hamilton Rd, Brighton BN1 5DF
Tel	01273 556708
Web	www.chimneyhouse.co.uk

Entry 669 Map 4

Sussex

The Fountain Inn
Ashurst

The 16th-century Inglenook Bar is a snug place to be on a cold and rainy night, as Paul McCartney and Wings thought when they made their Christmas video here. When the fireplace decides 'to blow' you're transported back centuries. In the flagstoned, candlelit bar, aromatic with woodsmoke from that wafting fire, be treated to wholesome food (steak, mushroom and ale pie, game sausages, nursery puds), along with a great selection of wines and three real ales. No need to bother with the wine list – just wander into the corridor where, on an ancient wonky wall, the bottles themselves are on display. In summer sup a pint of local Harvey's Sussex ale on the raised decking overlooking the pond. Although the annual classic car and motorbike meeting attracts those from afar, the Fountain firmly remains a local.

Meals	11.30am-2.30pm; 6pm-9.30pm (Sun 12pm-3pm). Main courses £7.50-£18.95; bar meals from £4.50.
Closed	Open all day.
Directions	On B2135, 4 miles north of Steyning.

	Craig Gillet The Fountain Inn, Ashurst, Steyning BN44 3AP
Tel	01403 710219

Entry 670 Map 4

Sussex

Royal Oak
Wineham

A rural survivor, the part-tiled, black-and-white-timbered cottage almost lost down a country road is six centuries old and has been refreshing locals for the last two. It is unspoilt in every way. In the charming bar and tiny rear room are brick and bare-boarded floors, a huge inglenook with winter log fires and sturdy, rustic furniture. Antique corkscrews, pottery jugs and aged artefacts hang from low-slung beams and walls. New landlord Michael Bailey plans to change little and continues to draw Harveys Best straight from the cask (no pumps) and, in keeping with ale house tradition, offers a menu of good, freshly made pub food using locally sourced produce; think sandwiches, generous ploughman's, and hearty soups and pies on chilly days. No music or electronic hubbub, just traditional pub games.

Meals	11am-2.30pm (12pm-4pm Sun); 5.30pm-11pm (6pm-11pm Sat, 7pm-10.30pm Sun). Main courses £8-£12; sandwiches £2.50-£3.50.
Closed	2.30pm-5.30pm (6pm Sat, 3pm-7pm Sun).
Directions	Off A272 between Cowfold & Bolney.

Michael Bailey
& Sharon Nettleton
Royal Oak,
Wineham, Henfield BN5 9AY
Tel   01444 881252

Entry 671 Map 4

Sussex

The Cat
West Hoathly

Father and son Nick and Mark White used to have the Fountain at Ashurst; now they have The Cat. And they're slowly upgrading the 16th-century building without losing the character – a medieval hall house with a Victorian extension. They've uncovered a well in one of the bars, and created a garden room leading out to a semi-walled garden at the back, furnished with teak and umbrellas. Inside, wooden panelling, beamed ceilings, planked floors and splendid inglenooks. Traditional pub food attracts a solid, old-fashioned crowd: retired locals and walkers on the High Weald Way. Our rare roast beef and horseradish salad came with hunks of bread fresh from the oven, and the pancakes with proper maple syrup. The owners are delightful, the setting is idyllic: in a pretty village opposite a 12th-century church.

Meals	12pm-2pm (2.30pm Sun); 6pm-9.30 (7pm-9pm Sun); 12pm-9.30 Sat. Main courses £8.95-£16.95; bar meals £5.50-£8.95.
Closed	2.30-6pm (3.30-7pm Sun) & all day Mon. Open all day Sat.
Directions	Village signed off B2028 6 miles north of Haywards Heath.

Mark & Nick White
The Cat, Queens Square,
West Hoathly, E. Grinstead RH19 4PP
Tel   01342 810369
Web   www.catinn.co.uk

Entry 672 Map 4

Sussex

The Coach & Horses
Danehill

With ale on tap from Harveys in Lewes, fresh fish from Seaford and lamb from the fields opposite, this is a very fine pub. The central bar is its throbbing hub, original wooden panelling and open fires accompanying the gentle pleasure of mulled wine in winter-cosy rooms. During the rest of the year the big raised garden comes into its own; spread yourselves on the new terrace under the boughs of a spreading maple. Whatever the weather, the food attracts folk from far and wide. In the stable block restaurant a changing seasonal menu from chef Lee Cobb places the emphasis on quality rather than quantity – honey roasted confit duck leg on chorizo, red pepper and chickpea ragout, seared queen scallops and tiger prawns with sweet chilli pak choi, broad bean risotto with parmesan and basil oil. A rural pub that is a true local.

Sussex

The Jolly Sportsman
East Chiltington

Deep in Sussex, a little place with a passion for beers, food and wine. Brewery mats pinned above the bar demonstrate Bruce Wass's support of small breweries, while the food has been described as "robust, savoury, skilled and unpretentious." In the stylish restaurant, where oak tables are decorated with flowers and candles, plates are filled with mussel, prawn and herb risotto, marinated Ditchling lamb rump, peppered red deer fillet. In the bar, dogs doze, the fire glows and there are winter snifters from Bruce's impressive whisky collection to try, including rarities bought at auction. Outside, ancient trees give shade to rustic tables and the idyllic garden has a play area for children. A team of talented enthusiasts run this pub; the Moroccan-tiled patio tables were even made by the pub's own 'washer-upper'.

Meals	12pm-2pm (2.30 Sat & Sun); 7pm-9pm (9.30pm Sat); no food Sun eve. Main courses £9.95-£15.50; bar meals £4.50-£5.50.
Closed	3pm-6pm. Open all day Sat & Sun.
Directions	From Danehill (A275) take School Lane towards Chelwood Common.

Meals	12.30pm-2.15pm (3pm Sun); 7pm-9.15pm (10pm Fri & Sat). Main courses £11.75-£19.50; set lunch £12.50 & £15.95; bar meals £4.90-£10.45.
Closed	3pm-6pm, Sun from 4pm & Mon all day. Open all day Sat.
Directions	From Lewes A275; B2166 for East Chiltington.

Ian Philpots
The Coach & Horses,
Coach & Horses Lane,
Danehill RH17 7JF

Tel 01825 740369
Web www.coachandhorses.danehill.biz

Entry 673 Map 4

Bruce Wass
The Jolly Sportsman,
Chapel Lane, East Chiltington,
Lewes BN7 3BA

Tel 01273 890400
Web www.thejollysportsman.com

Entry 674 Map 4

The Bull
Ditchling

In a picturesque village, a pretty inn, dark and cosy and warmed by cheery fires and candlelight. The rambling and atmospheric bar hasn't changed for years; the other areas have been stylishly transformed: pine, parquet and modern prints on mellow walls. And there's some rather upmarket food to match, like bouillabaisse or pork loin with apricot crumble, sage mash and mustard sauce. Even the ciabattas are filled with oaked smoked salmon and horseradish cream. Game comes from the Balcombe estate, lamb from Ditchling farms and for dessert, cherry panna cotta with raspberry coulis or Sussex pond pudding. Similar treats can be found on the separate children's menu. You can eat or drink wherever you like, including the snug at the back. Bring bikes and try out the high-level trails on the South Downs, then return to gorgeous bedrooms where new and old blend as successfully as below. Expect ancient beams painted white, bold silks, crisp linen, walk-in rain showers, fresh lilies. There's even a hot rail in the loos to dry out wet walkers' clothing.

Rooms	4: 3 doubles, 1 twin/double. £80-£120.
Meals	12pm-2.30pm (3pm Sat; 6pm Sun); 7pm-9.30pm; no food Sun eve. Main courses £9.50-£16; sandwiches £6.50.
Closed	Open all day.
Directions	In centre of village, by mini-r'bout at central crossroads.

Dominic Worrall
The Bull,
2 High Street, Ditchling BN6 8TA
Tel   01273 843147
Web   www.thebullditchling.com

The Griffin Inn
Fletching

A proper inn, one of the best, a community local that draws a well-heeled and devoted crowd. The occasional touch of scruffiness makes it almost perfect; fancy designers need not apply. The Pullan family run it with huge passion. You get cosy open fires, 400-year-old beams, oak panelling, settles, red carpets, prints on the walls... this inn has aged beautifully. There's a lively bar, a small club room for racing on Saturdays and two cricket teams play in summer. Bedrooms are tremendous value for money and full of uncluttered country-inn elegance: uneven floors, lovely old furniture, soft coloured walls, free-standing Victorian baths, huge shower heads, crisp linen, fluffy bathrobes, handmade soaps. Rooms in the coach house are quieter, those in next-door Griffin House quieter still. Smart seasonal menus include fresh fish from Rye and Fletching lamb; the food and the beers are as local as can be. There's a wood oven on the terrace and, on summer Sundays, a spit-roast barbecue — accompanied by ten-mile views stretching across Sheffield Park to the South Downs.

Rooms	13: 6 doubles, 7 four-posters. £85-£145. Singles £60-£80 (not weekends).
Meals	12pm-2.30pm (3pm Sat & Sun); 7pm-9.30pm (9pm Sun). Main courses £10-£18.50; bar meals £6.50-£14.50.
Closed	3pm-6pm. Open all day Sat & Sun.
Directions	From East Grinstead, A22 south, right at Nutley for Fletching. On for 2 miles into village.

Bridget, Nigel & James Pullan
The Griffin Inn,
Fletching, Uckfield TN22 3SS
Tel   01825 722890
Web   www.thegriffininn.co.uk

Entry 676 Map 4

Sussex

Ram Inn
Firle

The road runs out once it reaches Firle village... hard to believe now, but this quiet backwater was once a staging post. Built of brick and flint, the inn reveals a fascinating history – the Georgian part was once a courthouse and the kitchen goes back 500 years. Rescued from closure in 2006, the Ram Inn is once again thriving. Shaun Filsell has redecorated its three rooms in rustic-chic style – bare boards and parquet, coal fires in old brick fireplaces, chunky candles on darkwood tables. Walkers stomp in from the Downs for pints of Harvey's Sussex and hot steak sandwiches; foodies flock after dark for great fresh food, perhaps honey-glazed belly pork with roasted sweet potato and honey and thyme sauce, and dark chocolate truffle torte. And there's a splendid flint-walled garden for peaceful summer supping.

Meals	12pm-3pm; 6.30pm-9.30pm (12pm-9.30pm Sat; 12pm-6pm Sun). Main courses £7.95-£9.95 (lunch), £9.25-£14.95 (dinner).
Closed	Open all day.
Directions	Pub & village signed off A27 east of Lewes.

	Shaun Filsell
	Ram Inn,
	Firle, Lewes BN8 6NS
Tel	01273 858222
Web	www.theram-inn.com

Entry 677 Map 4

Sussex

George Inn
Alfriston

You can't miss the ancient façade of The George as you stroll down Alfriston's pretty little High Street. Step inside the creaky old inn, first licensed in 1397, and things become even more historic, thanks to worn planked floors, head-cracking beams, thick standing timbers, a huge inglenook with a crackling winter fire, and hop bines strewn above the bar. It is the cosiest possible setting for some tasty pub food and a foaming pint of Greene King. Share a rustic board for two laden with charcuterie and breads, roasted garlic and warm olive oil, or tuck into a brie and bacon sandwich. Then there are hearty steaks, mushroom and Guinness suet pudding, and, in the evening, dishes such as monkfish cassoulet. Lunch in the flint-walled garden, explore the village, hike the South Downs Way.

Meals	12pm-2.30pm; 7pm-10pm. Main courses £10.50-£16.95.
Closed	Open all day.
Directions	Alfriston is signed off A27 between Polgate & Lewes, 4 miles west of Polegate.

	Roland & Cate Couch
	George Inn, High Street,
	Alfriston, Lewes BN26 5SY
Tel	01323 870319
Web	www.thegeorge-alfriston.com

Entry 678 Map 5

Sussex

The Lamb Inn
Wartling

Landlord Rob and chef Alison have transformed The Lamb into a little place known for great ales, excellent food and good cheer. There's a bar with a wood-burner, a beamy snug with chunky candles and fresh flowers, a dining room with enough space for a couple of comfy sofas and a log fire, and no music, just chatter. Specialising in fresh fish and local produce from Chilley Farm, the menu announces fillet of local Limousin beef with red wine and mushroom sauce, braised shank of Sussex lamb with garlic mash and mint and redcurrant gravy, and fish pie. A good selection of cheeses will follow, along with temptations such as iced chocolate and Baileys parfait. Make a mental note of this secluded pub if you are planning a visit to nearby Herstmonceux Castle: the drive across the Pevensey Levels is worth it.

Meals	11.45am-2.15pm (12pm-2.30pm Sun); 6.45pm-9pm. Main courses £8.95-£17.95; bar meals £5.75-£12.95; set menu, 2 courses, £12.
Closed	3pm-6pm & Sun eve.
Directions	A259 to Polegate & Pevensey; 1st exit for Wartling; on right after 3 miles.

Robert & Alison Farncombe
The Lamb Inn,
Wartling, Hailsham BN27 1RY
Tel   01323 832116
Web   www.lambinnwartling.co.uk

Entry 683 Map 5

Sussex

The Gun
Gun Hill

Winding lanes lead to this 16th-century tiled and timbered farmhouse with glorious views across rolling countryside. Its name originates from the cannon foundries that were located at Gun Hill. Expect a neat open-plan interior with comfortably furnished alcoves, several log fires and an old kitchen Aga in the cosy main bar. Plank floors, thick candles on scrubbed tables, fresh flowers and bold artwork create a civilised feel, traditional menus champion local produce and every dish is freshly prepared. Kick off with a Sussex smokie, follow with a shortcrust pastry pie or a Sussex rib-eye steak with pepper sauce. And finish off with a visit to the farm shop/continental deli in the old coach house. The Gun is worth hunting down in all seasons, and has a terrace and lawn for lazy summer days.

Meals	12pm-3pm; 6pm-9.30pm; (12pm-9pm Sun). Main courses £8.95-£17.20; set menu £8.95 & £11.95.
Closed	Open all day.
Directions	From A267 south of Horam, take road right in 0.25 mile for Gun Hill; pub in 0.5 miles.

Martial Chaussy
The Gun,
Gun Hill, Horam TN21 0JU
Tel   01825 872361
Web   www.thegunhouse.co.uk

Entry 684 Map 5

The Star Inn
Old Heathfield

Built as an inn for pilgrims in the 14th century, with a rough, honey-stone façade, the Star has gained a few creepers over the centuries and its atmospheric interior has mellowed nicely. Low-beamed ceilings, wall settles and panelling, huge log-fuelled inglenook – it's cosy, candlelit and winter inviting. The appeal in summer is the peaceful, award-winning garden, bright with flowers and characterful with hand-crafted furniture; the gorgeous view towards the South Downs was once painted by Turner. The chalkboard lists grilled king prawn brochettes and game terrine with onion and date chutney, roast fillet of salmon with caviar and shrimp sauce and wild mushroom linguine. To drink, try Harveys Sussex Bitter from Lewes. And make time to visit the impressive church with its fine early-English tower.

The Horse & Groom
Rushlake Green

An idyllic setting for a small, traditional, personally run pub. Fiona Airey sets out to attract people looking for more than a pint and a packet of crisps, and the menu is long and tempting, listing seafood chowder, steak and mushroom pudding, stuffed pork fillet wrapped in pancetta with stilton sauce, and dressed Hastings crab. Generosity is a strong point, and Fiona insists that all dishes include a healthy selection of fresh vegetables. Shepherd Neame Masterbrew and seasonal guests are on hand pump and they have half a dozen wines and champagne by the glass. Two small bars glow with horse brasses; the Gun Room restaurant is nicely traditional with its Windsor chairs, log fire and hunting trophies; the garden – with handmade furniture and Weald views – is one of the nicest places for dining out in Sussex. *Shepherd Neame.*

Meals	12pm-2.15pm; 6pm-9.15pm; no food Sun eve. Main courses £9.50-£14.
Closed	3pm-5.30pm. Open all day Sat & Sun.
Directions	From A265 east of Heathfield, left onto B2096, then 2nd right.

Meals	12pm-2.15pm (2.30pm Sat & Sun); 7pm-9.30pm (9pm Sun). Main courses £7.50-£18.95.
Closed	3pm-5.30pm (7pm Sunday).
Directions	From Heathfield A265 for Burwash; B2096 for Battle. Right at Chapel Cross.

	Richard Sawyer The Star Inn, Church Street, Old Heathfield TN21 9AH
Tel	01435 863570
Web	www.thebestpubsinsussex.co.uk

	Fiona Airey The Horse & Groom, Rushlake Green, Heathfield TN21 9QE
Tel	01435 830320
Web	www.thehorseandgroom.eu

Entry 685 Map 5

Entry 686 Map 5

The George in Rye
Rye

Ancient Rye has a big history. It's a reclaimed island, a wealthy cinque port which once held its own army yet regularly fell into French hands. Henry James lived here, and the oldest working church clock in England chimes in a gracious square at the top of the hill. As for the George, it stands serenely on the cobbled high street. It was built in 1575 from reclaimed ships' timbers and its exposed beams and joists remain on display to this day. A contemporary revamp in classical style trumpets airy interiors, stripped floors, panelled walls and open fires – Jane Austen in the 21st century. There's a huge leather sofa in the bar by the fire, screen prints of the Beatles on the walls in reception, voile curtains and parquet floors in the restaurant. Divine bedrooms come in all shapes and sizes, but fabulous fabrics, Frette linen, flat-screen TVs and Vi-spring mattresses are standard, as are Aveda soaps by the bath and cashmere covers on hot water bottles. Superb food in the restaurant – seared scallops, Romney Marsh lamb, Seville orange ice cream – can be washed down by local English wines. Exceptional.

Rooms	24: 6 doubles, 13 twins/doubles, 5 suites. £125-£175. Suites from £225. Singles from £95.
Meals	12pm-3pm; 7pm-9.30pm. Main courses £12-£16; bar meals £5-£6.
Closed	Open all day.
Directions	Follow signs up hill into town centre. Through arch; pub on left. Parking at foot of hill.

Alex & Katie Clarke
The George in Rye,
98 High Street, Rye TN31 7JT
Tel   01797 222114
Web   www.thegeorgeinrye.com

Entry 687 Map 5

Sussex

688 White Horse Silverhill, Hurst Green TN19 7PU
01580 860235

Renovated roadside boozer with gastropub appeal – wooden floors, leather sofas, scrubbed tables and a posh outside terrace with serene views. Come for Harvey's Best on tap and a pedigree kitchen team. Reports please.

689 The Curlew Junction Road, Bodiam, Robertsbridge TN32 5UY
01580 861394

In the smart homely bar the wood-burner glows, Badger Bitter is on hand pump and the wine list flies the flag for Britain. Food ranges from posh baguettes to fillet steak with red onion rösti. Bodium Castle is next door. Up for sale late 2007 – reports welcome.

690 Merrie Harriers Cowbeech, Hailsham BN27 4JQ
01323 833108

The simple, part-panelled bar has a huge brick inglenook with logs at the ready, the red-carpeted restaurant extension has countryside views, and there's a nice garden at the back. New ownership – reports please.

691 Six Bells Chiddingly, Hailsham BN8 6HE
01825 872227

Gary Glitter, Led Zeppelin and Leo Sayer have all played in this quirky little boozer renowned for its music and atmosphere. Log fires, Harveys on hand pump, boules in the garden, great value food.

692 Blackboys Inn Lewes Road, Blackboys, Uckfield TN22 5LG
01825 890283

Splendid 14th-century black-weatherboarded pub overlooking an iris-covered pond. Rambling interior has bare boards, log fire, rustic benches and eclectic décor in the timeless bar. Extensive menus.

693 Rose Cottage Inn Alciston, Lewes BN26 6UW
01323 870377

Close to the South Downs Way, this wisteria-clad cottage is on a quiet lane to nowhere. Run by the Lewis family since 1960, it's a bolthole for ramblers in search of cosy bars, cushioned pews, a decent pint and fresh fish and game.

694 The Peacock Shortbridge, Piltdown, Uckfield TN22 3XA
01825 762463

The often-lit inglenook, its uneven lintel hung with horse brasses and horse tack, is worth the trip alone, the garden with slide is safe for children and the food is all homemade.

695 The Juggs The Street, Kingston, Lewes BN7 3NT 01273 472523
Made from two tiny 15th-century cottages, it oozes character –
low ceilings, rough black timbers, rustic benches. The Shepherd
Neame ales and Sunday roast lunches are worth leaving the South
Downs Way for.

696 The Royal Oak Inn The Street, Poynings, Brighton BN45 7AQ
01273 857389
A pretty village location below the South Downs for Paul Day's
revamped pub. Come for the lovely summer garden (great
barbecues), the local Harvey's bitter and the ambitious menus
brimming with local foods.

697 The Ginger Pig 3 Hove Street, Hove BN3 2TR 01273 736123
The third dining venue of the Gingerman group, housed in a fine
building close to the sea front. A swish informal bar and a buzzy
dining area decked with art. Great food, no bookings: arrive early.

698 Crown Inn Worthing Rd, Dial Post, Horsham RH13 8NH 01403 710902
New keen chef-landlord with big plans for this homely village inn
off the A24. Imaginative fresh food includes a good tapas menu –
washed down with local Kings Horsham Best. Reports please.

699 Black Jug 31 North Street, Horsham RH12 1RJ 01403 253526
Victorian town centre pub owned and revamped by Brunning &
Price. Expect classic wooden panelling, wooden floors, trademark
bookcases and modern pub food served all day.

700 Three Moles Selham, Midhurst GU28 0PN 01798 861303
Built to serve Selham Station in 1872, now an unspoilt and old-
fashioned rural local with simple furnishings. Great beer, farm
cider, monthly singalongs, long-serving landlady, no food.

701 Duke of Cumberland Arms Henley, Midhurst GU27 3HQ
01428 652280
Latch doors lead to two tiny bars that creak with character –
ancient scrubbed tables and log fires in the grate. Ales are drawn
from the cask, roasts are brought as a joint to the table, the garden
has great Weald views.

702 Noah's Ark The Green, Lurgashall, Petworth GU28 9ET 01428 707346
Refurbished 16th-century tile-hung pub with newish tenants in a
glorious position overlooking the cricket green and churchyard –
pick up a pint on a balmy summer's eve. Reports please.

703 The King's Arms Midhurst Road, Fernhurst, Midhurst GU27 3HA
01428 652005
New owners at this distinctive 17th-century stone pub have
introduced a light contemporary dining room and bedrooms. The
rest has a traditional feel: beams, local ales and a blackboard of
classic bar food. Lovely garden, too.

Warwickshire

The Inn at Farnborough
Farnborough

Turning a neglected inn into a pub-restaurant was an exciting prospect for chef Anthony and his wife Joanna. Their vision and dedication led to a change of name, a stylish revival and menus created daily from the best local suppliers. It's not just the food that is irresistible but the warm yellow walls, subtle lighting, open fires and rustic floors. The food is gorgeous: local Dexter beef with red wine and shallots, lamb confit with pea and mint purée, salmon fishcakes with hollandaise... Or there's a good value lunchtime and early evening menu. Add fine wines by the glass, posh bar nibbles and a fabulous landscaped garden... not everyone will be enamoured of the background music but it would be hard to find a more civilised pub. There's even a private dining room, with jaunty red walls, zebra-print chairs and a juke box.

Meals	12pm-3pm; 6pm-10pm.
	Main courses £8.95-£19.95;
	bar meals £5-£12.
Closed	3pm-6pm. Open all day Fri-Sun.
Directions	From junc. 11 on M40 follow signs
	for Banbury. At 3rd r'bout right
	onto A423 for Southam.

Anthony Robinson
The Inn at Farnborough,
Farnborough, Banbury OX17 1DZ

| Tel | 01295 690615 |
| Web | www.innatfarnborough.co.uk |

Entry 704 Map 8

Warwickshire

The Castle Inn
Edgehill

A splendid site! Charles I raised his battle standard here, before the battle of Edge Hill, and the pub sits inside the octagonal tower, built to commemorate the 100th anniversary of the battle. Unique and unusual, it opened as a pub in 1822, and later was bought by the Hook Norton Brewery. From the viewing balcony or the great big garden, spectacular views sweep over the steep scarp to the plain below and away to the Malvern Hills, some 40 miles away. In the public bar are darts, pool and a fruit machine; the octagonal walls of the lounge bar are decorated with all the Civil War maps and memorabilia you could wish for. Food is traditional English — sandwiches, steaks, home made beef and ale pie — washed down with perfect pints of Old Hooky, real cider and country wines. Malts are taken seriously, too.

Meals	12pm-2pm; 6.30pm-9pm;
	no food Mon eve in winter.
	Main courses £5-£14;
	bar meals £3-£8.
Closed	2.30pm-6pm (3pm-6pm Sat & Sun).
	Open all day in summer.
Directions	Off A422, 6 miles NW of Banbury.

Tony, Sue & Rory Sheen
The Castle Inn,
Edgehill, Banbury OX15 6DJ

| Tel | 01295 670255 |
| Web | www.thecastle-edgehill.com |

Entry 705 Map 8

The Red Lion
Long Compton

Dogs are welcome in this ancient warren of a pub; dog sketches adorn the walls. The pub's own, Cocoa ('The Landlady') is often around. But that doesn't mean the whiff of wet canine. Instead you will get the mouthwatering aroma of excellent, imaginative cooking from Sarah Keightley, co-manager and chef, who has come from the Howard Arms at Ilmington. Crispy-battered cod and chips are served here with caper berries and mushy peas served on *The Red Lion Times* (!), while herb-baked whole sea bass may be complimented by star anise and caramelised lemons. And you can stay, in five bedrooms that reflect the unfussy approach. With natural colours and crisp ginghams, their comfort and quality makes up for their size. In a place that goes back 250 years, bedrooms are not likely to be huge. Downstairs there's space for everyone, from the pool room to the restaurant to the beautiful flagged bar area warmed by a real fire and a wood-burning stove. The smart but sensitive refurb has not cost this village pub its character, nor its sense of community.

Rooms	5: 2 double, 1 twin, 1 single, 1 family room. £80-£110. Single £55.
Meals	12pm-2.30pm; 6-9pm (12pm-9.30pm Fri-Sun). Main courses £10.50-£17.95
Closed	2.30pm-6pm Mon-Thurs. Open all day Fri-Sun & bank holiday Mons.
Directions	Beside A3400 between Chipping Norton & Shipston-on-Stour.

Lisa Phipps & Sarah Keightly
The Red Lion,
Main Street, Long Compton CV36 5JS
Tel 01608 684221
Web www.redlion-longcompton.co.uk

Entry 706 Map 8

The Howard Arms
Ilmington

The Howard buzzes with good-humoured babble as well-kept beer flows from the flagstoned bar. Logs crackle contentedly in a vast open fire; a blackboard menu scales the wall above; a dining room at the far end has unexpected elegance, with great swathes of bold colour and some noble paintings. Gorgeous bedrooms are set discreetly apart from the joyful throng, mixing period style and modern luxury beautifully: one with a painted antique headboard and bleached beams, another more folksy (patchwork quilts, sunshine-yellow walls) and there's a large, lavish half-tester full of antiques. All are individual, all huge by pub standards. The village is a surprise, too, literally tucked under a lone hill, with an unusual church surrounded by orchards and an extended village green. Round off an idyllic walk amid buzzing bees and fragrant wild flowers with a meal at the inn, perhaps seared scallops with a sweet chilli sauce and crème fraîche, then beef, ale and mustard pie, finally spiced pear and apple flapjack crumble. From a blackboard menu the food is inventive, upmarket and very good.

Rooms	3: 2 doubles, 1 twin. £120–£138. Singles from £87.50.
Meals	12pm–3pm; 6.30pm–9.30pm (6.30pm–10pm Fri & Sat). Main courses £10.50–£16.
Closed	Open all day.
Directions	From Stratford, south on A3400 for 4 miles, right to Wimpstone & Ilmington. Pub in village centre.

Steve Wilkins
The Howard Arms,
Lower Green, Ilmington,
Stratford-upon-Avon CV36 4LT
Tel 01608 682226
Web www.howardarms.com

Entry 707 Map 8

Warwickshire

The Fox & Hounds Inn
Great Wolford

The gorgeous, honey-coloured pub has been trading since 1540 and dozes contentedly in a tiny community on the edge of the Cotswold hills. On entering the bar through a low oak door the pub opens out, captivatingly, before you. Bunches of dried hops are tucked into ancient beams, there are candlelit tables on flagstoned floors, polished oak settles and a huge stone fireplace that crackles with logs in winter. Flames flicker in the copper bar counter as you order a pint of Hook Norton and study the blackboard menu announcing such treats as Gressingham duck with parsnip mousse and caramelised apple, and halibut with herb crust on chive and leek risotto. The menu is kept short and fresh and changes each day. It couldn't be cosier, or more welcoming – a perfect country pub. And there's also a good terrace for summer.

Meals	12pm-2pm (2.30pm Sat & Sun); 6.30pm-9pm; no food Sun eve. Main courses £12-£16.
Closed	2.30pm-6pm & Mon.
Directions	Off A3400 between Shipston-on-Stour & Long Compton.

Gill & Jamie Tarbox
& Sioned Rowland
The Fox & Hounds Inn, Great Wolford,
Moreton-in-Marsh CV36 5NQ
Tel   01608 674220
Web   www.thefoxandhoundsinn.com

Entry 708 Map 8

Warwickshire

The One Elm
Stratford-upon-Avon

Stratford has a reputation for great pubs and drama – and was the birthplace of the first Slug and Lettuce. In the narrow building that The Slug once occupied stands The One Elm. Owned by Peach Pubs (of Warwick's Rose & Crown), it, too, is a cracker. The bar is light, airy and wooden-floored and the décor modern and stylish, with leather sofas and bar stools reminiscent of Giacometti sculptures. In the bar are good beers and great wines; outside, an attractive, sheltered terrace; at the back, the restaurant, with a private, secluded mezzanine and a short but mouthwatering menu. There's a chargrill section, a 'risotto of the week' and a deli board that's available all day. Being slightly off the tourist trail, this attracts a local crowd, and the friendly staff are on tap from breakfast until closing time.

Meals	12pm-10pm (9.30pm Sun). Main courses £8.50-£15.
Closed	Open all day.
Directions	In town centre on corner of Guild Street & Shakespeare Street.

Michael Montredmond
The One Elm, 1 Guild Street,
Stratford-upon-Avon CV37 6QZ
Tel   01789 404919
Web   www.peachpubs.com

Entry 709 Map 8

Warwickshire

Bell Inn
Stratford upon Avon

If things Elizabethan and Shakespearian entrance and inspire you, then the Bell will not disappoint, running alongside the village high street, set amongst the black and white timbered houses. There is a richness about the natural oak beams and settles, the stone floors partially covered with Persian rugs and the dog-grates cradling glowing embers. This is very much a historic village inn serving top-quality, locally sourced food, whether it be a simple pub favourite such as Lashford's pork and leek sausages on cheddar mash or, more adventurously, Cajun swordfish steak with pineapple and spring onion salsa. If you're into food provenance, every supplier is listed on the back of the menu and they are almost all small independents – bakers, butchers, brewers. Just like this thriving free house.

Meals	11.45am-2.30pm (3pm Sat); 6.30pm-9.30pm (6pm-10pm Sat); 12pm-9.30pm Sun. Main courses £9.95-£15.95; bar meals from £5; Sunday roast £10.95-£11.95.
Closed	3pm-6pm. Open all day Sat & Sun.
Directions	Leave A3400 south west of Stratford on B439; continue to Welford in 4 miles; Bell on right through village.

Colin & Teresa Ombler
Bell Inn, Binton Road,
Welford-on-Avon CV37 8EB
Tel   01789 750353
Web   www.thebellwelford.co.uk

Entry 710 Map 8

Warwickshire

The King's Head
Aston Cantlow

It is said that Shakespeare's parents had their wedding reception at the King's Head. One can imagine the scene at this long, low, rambling country inn with its small leaded windows, flagged floors and inglenook crackling with logs; perhaps they even tucked into the famous Duck Supper, a house speciality. More up-to-date delicacies join the menu today, and all is tasty, from the rare roast beef sandwiches with celeriac and horseradish to salmon, lemongrass and chive fishcakes, roast venison with calvados sauce, and the lemon cheesecake. Elderly ladies chat over pots of tea and diners come from miles around, notably well-heeled Brummies. In the bar, stylish with lime-washed beams, scrubbed pine and painted brick walls, are real ale and good wines. There's a small garden for summer and the walks start from the door.

Meals	12pm-2.30pm (12.30pm-3pm Sun); 6.30pm-9.30pm; no food Sun eve. Main courses £10-£15; bar meals £5-£8.
Closed	3pm-5.30pm. Sun eves after 7.30pm. Open all day Sat.
Directions	Off A46 for Aston Cantlow.

Peter & Louise Sadler
The King's Head, 21 Bearley Road,
Aston Cantlow,
Stratford-upon-Avon B95 6HY
Tel   01789 488242
Web   www.thekh.co.uk

Entry 711 Map 8

Warwickshire

The Bell
Tanworth-in-Arden

First it was a row of cottages, then a hotel. In the 1930s it was taken on by Jack Hood the boxer – now the pub on the green is post office, delicatessen, restaurant and B&B rolled into one. The main bar is contemporary and sleek: furniture from Italy, textured cushions, soft lighting, modish taupes and creams. The dining room has a boudoir glow, all silvery papered walls, vast chandelier and chocolate fountain (!)... the deli is at the end of the bar, the conference room doubles up as a Sunday school. It may be swish but it's flamboyant too, and fun – just like its owner, Ashley Bent. The menu trumpets smoked fish platter and seared monkfish with pea and mint risotto alongside game casserole, rump of lamb with herb mash and red pepper and olive jus, and apple pie and custard. And they do a great Sunday roast.

Meals	12pm-2pm (3pm Sun); 6.30pm-9pm. Main courses £6.95-£8.95 (lunch), £9.95-£15.95 (dinner); Sunday lunch, 2 courses, £13.95.
Closed	3pm-6pm & Sun eve. Open all day Sat in summer.
Directions	M42, junc. 3, then A435 south for Reddich. Tanworth signed left. In village on green.

Ashley Bent
The Bell,
The Green, Tanworth-in-Arden,
Henley-in-Arden B94 5AL
Tel 01564 742212
Web thebellattanworthinarden.co.uk

Entry 712 Map 8

Warwickshire

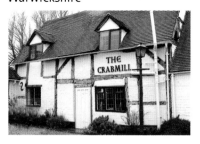

The Crabmill
Preston Bagot

The lovely, rambling building, with tiny leaded windows and wonderfully wonky beams, once contained a cider press. Later a pub, now it's a busy gastro haven with a dining room for every mood – one, pistachio-green and scented with lilies, another deep red, its walls hung with plump nudes, and another a candlelit mushroom-cream. There's a steely bar with sandblasted glass panels, great flagstones and a winter fire. At the back, a split-level lounge with wooden floors, deep leather sofas and a garden that heads off into open countryside. For summer there's stylish decking outside. The food is popular and the dishes imaginative and colourful, from simple croque monsieur and Cornish pasty to roast halibut with parsley and shallot rösti, steamed greens and lobster sauce. Fresh herbs are imported from France.

Meals	12pm-2.30pm (3.30pm Sun; sandwiches only 2pm-2.30 Sat); 6.30pm-9.30pm. Main courses £9.95-14.95.
Closed	Open all day. Closed Sun eve.
Directions	From Henley-in-Arden on A4189 towards Claverdon.

Sally Coll
The Crabmill,
Preston Bagot, Claverdon B95 5DR
Tel 01926 843342
Web www.thecrabmill.biz

Entry 713 Map 8

The Rose and Crown
Warwick

Peach Pubs' flagship Rose and Crown opens with bacon sarnies for breakfast (rather good ones) and stays open all day. Enter a cheery, airy, wooden-floored front bar with red and white walls, big leather sofas, low tables and a crackling winter fire. To the back is the big and bustling eating area and a private room that can be booked for parties. Almost all of the staff trained at Raymond Blanc's Petit Blanc restaurants; the food is good. Served all day, the tapas-style portions of cheeses, hams, marinated anchovies, mixed olives and rustic breads slip down easily with a pint of Fuller's London Pride or a glass of wine, while hot dishes are modern British with a Mediterranean slant. On the menu may be baked sea trout; lemon and thyme couscous with chilli oil; pork loin with rhubarb confit, apple and cider jus. Lovely contemporary bedrooms upstairs have large bath and shower rooms and overlook the square, filled on warm summer nights with a merry throng. It's young and fun and conveniently central for Warwick, which has history in spades.

Rooms	5: 2 doubles, 3 triples. £75.
Meals	8am-10pm (9.30pm Sun). Main courses £8.75-£17.50; bar meals £4-£10.50.
Closed	Open all day from 8am.
Directions	In Warwick centre, on market place. Ask about parking.

Jeremy Kynaston
The Rose and Crown,
30 Market Place,
Warwick CV34 4SH
Tel   01926 411117
Web   www.roseandcrownwarwick.co.uk

Entry 714 Map 8

Warwickshire

The Case is Altered
Hatton

No food, no mobiles and a Sopwith Camel propeller suspended from the ceiling. This is a Warwickshire treasure. There's even a vintage bar billiards machine, operated by sixpences from behind the bar. In the main room are stone floors, leather-covered settles and walls covered in yellowing posters offering beverages at a penny a pint. Jackie does not open her arms to children or dogs; this is a place for adult conversation and liquid refreshment. Devotees travel some distance for the pork scratchings and the expertly kept beer. The sign used to show lawyers arguing but the name has nothing to do with the law; it used to be called, simply, 'The Case' and was so small that it was not eligible for a licence. It was made larger, whisky was introduced, the name was changed, and everyone was happy. They've been that way ever since.

Meals	No food served.
Closed	2.30pm-6pm (2pm-7pm Sun).
Directions	Follow Rowington off A4177/A4141 junction, north of Warwick.

Jackie & Charlie Willacy
The Case is Altered,
Case Lane, Five Ways,
Hatton CV35 7JD
Tel 01926 484206

Entry 715 Map 8

Warwickshire

The Orange Tree
Chadwick End

The flagship dining pub of the Classic Country Pubs group has a striking interior. Be seduced by earthy colours, lime-washed low beams, open log fires, big lamps, deep sofas around low tables and chunky lightwood furnishings in airy eating rooms. A gorgeous Italian-style deli counter shows off breads, cheeses and vintage oils. This tastefully rustic-Mediterranean décor with oriental touches is matched by an ambitious, Italian-inspired menu, and diners with deep pockets descend in their droves for authentic wood-fired pizzas and robust, full-flavoured meat dishes cooked on an in-view rotisserie spit. There are also homemade pasta dishes, delicious warm salads and fishy specials. Great wines by the bottle or glass, Greene King ales, a heated patio dotted with stylish teak tables and all-day opening hours.

Meals	12pm-2.30pm (4.30pm Sun); 6pm-9.30pm; no food Sun eve. Main courses £8.95-£18.45.
Closed	Open all day.
Directions	On A4141 between Warwick & Solihull. On edge of village, 5 miles south of M42 junc. 5.

Paul Hales
The Orange Tree, Warwick Road,
Chadwick End B93 0BN
Tel 01564 785364
Web www.theorangetreepub.co.uk

Entry 716 Map 8

Warwickshire

The Boot Inn
Lapworth

The Boot was here long before the canal that runs past the back garden. With its exposed timbers, rug-strewn quarry floors, open fires and daily papers it combines old-fashioned charm with rustic chic. Under the guidance of Paul Salisbury and James Elliot, the down-at-heel boozer became one of the first gastropubs of the Midlands nearly a decade ago, and has been pulling foodies in ever since. Menus have a distinct touch of Mediterranean and Pacific rim: crispy oriental duck salad, Moroccan lamb with red onion and coriander couscous, seared sea bass with peppers, crab and lemon aïoli. Ingredients are as fresh as can be and seafood dishes are a speciality. Eat in the bars or in the stylishly revamped dining room upstairs, and in summer go al fresco: there's a lovely terrace to the side.

Meals	12pm-2.30pm (3pm Sun); 7pm-10pm (9pm Sun). Main courses £9-£18.
Closed	Open all day.
Directions	Off M42 junc. 4 for Hockley Heath; Lapworth signed.

Paul Salisbury & James Elliot
The Boot Inn, Old Warwick Road, Lapworth B94 6JU
Tel   01564 782464
Web   www.thebootinnlovelypubs.co.uk

Entry 717 Map 8

Warwickshire

The Punchbowl
Lapworth

The Punchbowl looks pubby enough from the outside, and functions as such with a big fire and beamed bar dispensing Timothy Taylor Landlord. So it's a surprise to discover that the building is new – the original burnt down 12 years ago. James Feeney has a flair for design, and from simple materials has created a contemporary opulence: candelabra on long wooden tables, modern canvasses and ornate mirrors on bare brick, windows swept by crushed velvet. Food is a strength, menus are printed daily on paper and the cooking embraces many ideas: cumin-crusted tuna with sweet potato purée; spinach and tomato fondue; Thai red prawn curry; classic sirloin of beef with mushroom sauce. There's comfort food, too, in fish and chips and rack of lamb. And the glassed-in patio area has a conservatory feel.

Meals	12pm-2.30pm; 6.30pm-9.30pm (12pm-3.30pm, 6.30pm-9pm Sunday). Main courses £9.95-£16.95.
Closed	Open all day.
Directions	Lapworth off B4439; pub near station.

James Feeney
The Punchbowl,
Mill Lane, Lapworth B94 6HR
Tel   01564 784564
Web   www.thepunchbowllapworth.co.uk

Entry 718 Map 8

West Midlands

The Malt Shovel at Barston
Barston

No surprise that the car park holds some swanky motors. This is a smart, food-driven place that knows its market and caters to it well. Gastropubs may come and go but this is a favourite. Whether you're ensconced in the smart cream-and-green bar, on the trellis-shaded terrace or in the country-rustic restaurant, the food is to savour and the well-kept ales (Tribute, Old Speckled Hen) are matched by some decent wines. The menu covers global as well as pubby treats – Scottish rib-eye steak, tandoori spiced duck, fishcakes, Mexican beef patties – and executes both with aplomb. The culinary innovation extends to the vegetarian options, perhaps a filo tart of crushed carrot topped with a poached egg, courgette strips and rocket pesto. A slick operation out in the country, that's also friendly and relaxed.

Meals	12pm-2.30pm (4pm Sun); 6.30pm-9.30pm; no food Sun eve. Main courses £10.95-£17.95. Set menus £21.50 &£25.50.
Closed	3pm-5.30pm. Open all day Sat & Sun.
Directions	Off A452; 1 mile beyond village.

Helen Somerfield
The Malt Shovel, Barston Lane, Barston, Solihull B92 0JP
Tel   01675 443223
Web   www.themaltshovelatbarston.com

Entry 719 Map 8

Wiltshire

The Wheatsheaf
Oaksey

Ancient on the outside, inglenooked inside – the archetypal English country pub. Local drinkers are welcome, but, with cooking like this, it would be silly to come merely to booze. Peep around the corner from the bar and tradition ends – the dining room has pale wood and sisal floors, cream walls and modern prints, and good-looking food served on big white plates. Chef-patron Tony Robson-Burrell and head chef Guy Opie's imaginative country dishes reflect current trends, so whether you choose a pub classic like Old Spot pork sausages with mash and mustard sauce, or steak and mushroom pudding with bubble and squeak, you'll eat well (while dessert-lovers will relish the baked hot chocolate fondant with rum and raisin ice cream). Real ales include Old Hooky and Sharps Doom Bar, children and dogs are welcome.

Meals	12pm-2pm (12pm-2.30pm Sun); 6.30pm-9pm (6.30pm-9.30pm Fri & Sat); no food Mon. Main courses £5-£16.95; bar meals £5-£10.25.
Closed	3pm-6pm. Open all day Sun.
Directions	Oaksey signed off A429 at Crudwell, 5 miles north of Malmesbury.

Tony Robson-Burrell
The Wheatsheaf,
Oaksey,
Malmesbury SN16 9TB
Tel   01666 577348

Entry 720 Map 3

The Horse & Groom
Charlton

The solidly elegant Cotswold stone house fronted by a tree-sheltered lawn stands well back from the road. Its long history as a coaching inn is documented in the framed prints that hang in rustically atmospheric main bar, all exposed stone, rug-strewn woodblock flooring, assorted scrubbed tables and roaring log fire. Now the dynamic Merchant Inns group has spruced up the dining areas – gleaming tables, polished glasses – and revamped the bedrooms with style and panache. Be charmed by earthy Farrow & Ball colours, Egyptian linen on big wooden beds, flat-screen TVs, claw-foot baths, power showers and tempting toiletries. Back in the bar, former Michelin-star chef Rob Clayton oversees well-priced menus that champion pub classics – homemade beefburger with chips and tomato relish, Wiltshire ham, eggs and chips – alongside more innovative British dishes, perhaps potted liver and honey paté; shoulder of Cotswold lamb with creamy mash, apple fritters and red wine sauce; Pimms jelly with lemon sorbet. And there's a secret walled garden for civilised summer drinking.

Rooms	5 doubles. £69.95-£89.95.
Meals	12pm-9pm (9.30pm Fri & Sat). Main courses £8.95-£15.95; bar meals £4.95-£9.95.
Closed	Open all day.
Directions	Beside B4040 Malmesbury to Cricklade road.

Mark Birchall
The Horse & Groom,
The Street, Charlton,
Malmesbury SN16 9DL
Tel 01666 823904
Web www.horseandgroominn.com

Wiltshire

The Potting Shed Pub
Crudwell

The owners of the hotel across the road have transformed the village inn. As well as the open fireplaces and the kelim sofas, there are – charmingly if eccentrically – a light fitting made from a wheelbarrow, door handles from trowels, hand pumps from fork handles, and old butchers' block tables; a large, airy dining room displays mix 'n' match antiques. Some of the lawns and apple orchard at the back will be turned into an organic vegetable patch, and the food is exuberantly British, from the homemade pork scratchings and rabbit terrine to the Gloucester Old Spot casserole and the whole roasted mallard. Ploughman's and sandwiches further reflect the Potting Shed's focus on real pub values and unpretentious leanings, there's an excellent children's menu, and a hunk of seriously good chocolate if you've no room for pud.

Meals	12pm-2.30pm (4pm Sun); 7pm-9.30pm; no food Sun eve & Mon. Main courses £9.50-£15.50.
Closed	Open all day.
Directions	Village centre on A429 between Cirencester & M4 junc. 17.

Jonathan Barry
The Potting Shed Pub, The Street,
Crudwell, Malmesbury SN16 9EW

Tel	01666 577833
Web	www.therectoryhotel.com

Entry 722 Map 3

Wiltshire

The Vine Tree
Norton

With a fine store of ales and over 30 wines by the glass the old watermill is a watering hole in every sense. It may be hidden away but the faithful return, for the food and the beer. On Sundays, memorable roast sirloin of beef from the neighbour's farm is served with all the trimmings. There's plenty of fresh fish, too, and local game in season, sautéed scallops with wild mushroom risotto, and rack of Cotswold lamb. Service is young and friendly and surroundings are inviting: deep red walls, candlelight and beams, a wood-burning stove; tables in the miniscule upstairs room are super-cosy. In summer, relax and gaze on the immaculate terrace – a delicious spot with urns of flowers and a fountain. This vine tree has a rich harvest for guests – and their dogs – to reap; no wonder Clementine the lab looks so content.

Meals	12pm-2.30pm (3pm Sun); 7pm-9.30pm (10pm Fri & Sat). Main courses £11.90-£16.95; bar meals £6.50-£9.50.
Closed	3pm-6pm. Open all day Sun.
Directions	A429 for Cirencester. After 1.5 miles left for Norton. There, right for Foxley. Follow road; on left.

Charles Walker & Tiggi Wood
The Vine Tree, Foxley Road,
Norton, Malmesbury SN16 0JP

Tel	01666 837654
Web	www.thevinetree.co.uk

Entry 723 Map 3

Wiltshire

The Castle Inn
Castle Combe

After a few thrilling laps on the local racing circuit, slip into a slower gear and head for food and good cheer at the Castle Inn. Sitting centre stage in the old market place, in what is surely one of England's prettiest villages, this famous hostelry has been here since the 12th century. Order a pint of Butcombe out at the front and contemplate the history – the village has barely changed in 400 years. Or retreat to the low-beamed bar with its log fire, stonework and period colours. The food is as civilised as the surroundings: chargrilled swordfish steak with crushed potatoes and tomato salsa, rack of lamb with a mustard crust and port wine sauce. For further celebration there are five champagnes, over 30 bins of wine and heart-warming selections of brandy, cognac and armagnac.

Wiltshire

Quarrymans Arms
Box

Though once a row of simple cottage dwellings, this has been a pub since the 18th century – a friendly, quirky little place. As the name suggests, it once served the stone miners from the local quarry. The mines may be long-gone, but history lingers in the shape of fascinating maps, photos and some lethal-looking stonecutting equipment hanging on the walls. In pride of place near the bar: a framed front page Box quarry story from a 1934 edition of the *Daily Sketch* asks: 'Is this the world's toughest job?'. Food on the changing blackboard menus is more traditional than gastropub, but is straightforward and tasty. Good Wiltshire home-cured ham, steak and ale pie, calves' liver with mustard mash and other staples are perfect fuel for walkers, cyclists and pot-holers intent on visiting the disused mines.

Meals	12pm-3pm; 6pm-9.30pm. Main courses from £15.50; bar meals £8.50-£12.50.	
Closed	Open all day.	
Directions	A350 towards Bath, right onto A420. Right for Yatton Keynell & continue to Castle Combe. Tricky parking.	

Meals	12pm-3pm; 6pm-9pm. Main courses £7.50-£14.50; bar meals £2.50-£7.25.
Closed	3pm-6pm. Open all day Fri-Sun.
Directions	Just off A4, on hillside to right of village; phone for directions.

Bill & Ann Cross
The Castle Inn, Castle Combe,
Chippenham SN14 7HN
Tel   01249 783030
Web   www.castle-inn.info/index.html

John & Ginny Arundel
Quarrymans Arms,
Box Hill, Box, Corsham SN13 8HN
Tel   01225 743569
Web   www.quarrymans.plus.com

Entry 724 Map 3

Entry 725 Map 3

The Pear Tree Inn
Whitley

A cool rustic chic flows effortlessly through the Pear Tree. This is a dreamy blend of French inspiration and English whimsy, a sweep of warm airy interiors that make you feel that you've washed up in dining-pub heaven. Step in under the beams, glide across the flagged floors, dive into an armchair and roast away in front of the fire. Keep going and you come to high-ceiling'd dining rooms where stripped floors are dressed in smart old rugs and old agrarian artefacts hang from the walls. French windows flood the place with light and open up in summer for al fresco suppers (there's a boules piste out there, too). Exquisite bedrooms, up in the eaves or out in the barn, come in lime white and have suede headboards, wonderfully upholstered armchairs, Bang & Olufsen TVs and funky rugs for colour; bathrooms have robes and creamy tiles. As for the food, it's unmissable — the braised beef Jacob's Ladder with buttery mash, the chocolate and hazelnut brownies, the exceptional breakfasts. Locals flock to this rural idyll, and there are wonderful walks from the door. New owners plan to change little.

Rooms	8: 6 doubles, 2 family rooms. £110–£140. Singles £75.
Meals	12pm-2.30pm (3pm Sun); 6.30pm-9.30pm (10pm Fri & Sat, 7pm-9.30pm Sun). Main courses £11.95–£18.50.
Closed	Open all day.
Directions	West from Melksham on A365, then right onto B3353 for Whitley. Through village, then left, signed Purlpit. Pub on right after 400 yards.

Matthew Edwards
The Pear Tree Inn,
Top Lane, Whitley, Melksham SN12 8QX

Tel	01225 709131
Web	www.thepeartreeinn.com

Wiltshire

The Tollgate Inn
Holt

All would pay the toll — were there one — to sample the delights of the Tollgate Inn. In a warm and convivial bar and lounge, lovely leather sofas, a log-burning stove, planked pine tables, newspapers and magazines encourage you to linger over a handpumped pint of Exmoor or a glass of sauvignon. The two dining areas have distinct personalities, the smaller off the bar with a traditional appeal, the upper, in the former chapel of the weavers who worked below, smart with high black rafters, open fire and an eclectic décor. Chef Alexander Venables' pedigree shines through in dishes that make the most of local produce (suppliers are named with the menu) and daily fish from Brixham. Light bites include omelette Arnold Bennett and set lunch is a snip at £10.95; try whole sea bass baked with ginger and fennel or Church Farm sirloin with crayfish and hollandaise. Bedrooms are in excellent order: oak beams, good antiques, smart linen, pretty views, lovely beds. For country views of goats and fields ask for one at the back. Breakfasts are as superb as all the rest.

Rooms	4 doubles. £80–£100. Singles £50–£100.
Meals	12pm–2pm; 7pm–9pm (9.30pm Fri & Sat). Main courses £14.50–£17.50; bar meals £5.50–£8.95; set lunch from £10.95.
Closed	3pm–5.30pm; Sun eve & Mon.
Directions	On B3107 between Bradford-on-Avon & Melksham.

Alison Ward–Baptiste
& Alexander Venables
The Tollgate Inn, Ham Green, Holt,
Bradford on Avon BA14 6PX

Tel	01225 782326
Web	www.tollgateholt.co.uk

Entry 727 Map 3

The Swan
Bradford-on-Avon

This graceful town of honey-coloured stone slips down hill to the river Avon, where a 600-year-old bridge spans the water in sublime style. You can pick up riverside paths and follow them eight miles up to Bath, ride your bike, stop at pubs, then hop on a train and come back for supper. The Swan goes back to the 15th century and stands on the high street. Inside, an easy elegance and relaxed informality go hand in hand. Open-plan interiors fill with light, you get stripped boards, flagged floors, high ceilings and country rugs. There's a small terrace for drinks in the sun, a front bar with an open fire and an airy restaurant that fills with locals, so come for great English food – perhaps Devon crab with toast and lemon, fish pie with cheddar mash, lime cheesecake with fresh raspberries. Uncluttered bedrooms are a treat, supremely comfortable with crisp white linen, padded headboards, delicious fabrics and flat-screen TVs. Those at the back on the upper floors overlook the river. All have bold colours on the walls and super little tongue-and-groove bathrooms.

Rooms	12: 8 doubles, 2 twins/doubles, 2 singles. £95–£140. Singles from £85.
Meals	12pm-2.30pm (3pm Sun); 7pm-9.30pm (10pm Fri & Sat). Main courses £12.50–£15; set lunch £10.50 & £14.
Closed	Open all day.
Directions	M4 junc. 18, then A46 south for Bath. A4 east, then A363 south to Bradford. On right in town, car park behind.

Stephen & Penny Ross
The Swan,
1 Church Street,
Bradford-on-Avon BA15 1LN
Tel   01225 868686

The George & Dragon
Rowde

Behind the unpromising exterior hides a low-ceilinged bar, its stone fireplace ablaze in winter, its half-panelled walls lined with old paintings, its antique clock ticking away the hours. Furnishings are authentically period, there are wooden boards in the dining room, plum-painted walls and plenty of dark timber. The kitchen's chutneys and preserves are for sale, international bottled beers and organic ciders line the shelves and handpumped Butcombe Bitter announces itself on the bar. Experienced owners are maintaining the pub's reputation for fish delivered fresh from Cornwall – with the odd concession to meat eaters. Blackboards list the day's specials such as delectable chargrilled scallops with black pudding brochettes and puddings to diet for. Rooms are charming and individual – Country, Classic or Funky – with wall timbers and wonky floors, contemporary wall coverings, White Company duvets and linen on wooden or brass beds, plasma screens and posh tiled bathrooms. Great value, a treat to come back to after a long walk along the Kennet & Avon Canal.

Rooms	3: 2 doubles, 1 family room. £65–£85.
Meals	12pm-3pm (4pm Sat & Sun), 7pm-10pm (6.30pm-10pm Sat); no food Mon.
	Main courses £9-£17.50; Sunday lunch £15.50.
Closed	3pm-7pm (4pm Sat & Sun); Sun eves & Mon lunch.
Directions	On A342, 2 miles west of Devizes.

Chris Day, Michelle & Philip Hale
The George & Dragon,
High Street, Rowde,
Devizes SN10 2PN
Tel   01380 723053

Entry 729 Map 3

The Lamb on the Strand
Semington

Keep a light foot on the accelerator between Trowbridge and Devizes or you will pass this ivy-clad red brick pub and miss a wonderfully friendly place where staff and locals rub along with easy chat and laughter. Philip and Sue (Cordon Bleu trained) are committed foodies who place an emphasis on honest well-cooked 'cuisine de campagne.' Start with grilled fig and chorizo salad with shaved parmesan before moving on to the heavenly slow-roast belly of pork with braised vegetables. With a wine list "reluctantly sampled" by Philip that covers the entire world you are spoilt for choice. On fine days, step out to the pretty garden and admire the sweeping views, accompanied by a pint of Ringwood, Butcombe or Keystone. Unpretentious with genuine charm is a fair summing up of both pub and landlord.

The Millstream
Marden

A pub-restaurant that opens all day and serves champagne by the glass: not what you'd expect in the Vale of Pewsey? The Millstream has bags of character, a welcome for all and a range of handpumped ales. Pale beams, log-burners and open fires give a fresh appeal to the open-plan space; there's a snug with a leather sofa at one end and a dining area at the other. This picks up the vibe from the bar, but is a gentler place to be, with its upholstered chairs and serene views over the lawn to the river. The chef's modern menu changes daily and the food is divine; much produce is organic, fish comes from Looe and the wine list is long. There's confit of duck on potato gratin; venison loin with fondant potatoes; baked honey and walnut soufflé with brandy brioche. On warm days you may sup on the terrace.

Meals	12pm-2pm; 7pm-9pm.
	Main courses £8.50-£13.50.
Closed	3pm-6.30pm & Sun eve.
Directions	On A361, 3 miles north east of Trowbridge.

Meals	12pm-3pm; 7pm-9.30pm (12pm-4pm; 6.30-9pm Sun); all day bank holidays. Main courses £4-£15.
Closed	Open all day. Closed Mon (except bank hols).
Directions	Off A302 5 miles from Devizes.

	Philip Roose-Francis
	The Lamb on the Strand,
	99 The Strand, Semington,
	Trowbridge BA14 6LL
Tel	01380 870263

	Nicola Notton
	The Millstream,
	Marden, Devizes SN10 3RH
Tel	01380 848308
Web	www.the-millstream.net

Entry 730 Map 3

Entry 731 Map 3

The Angel Inn
Upton Scudamore

A blaze of summer colour on the smart, sheltered decked area that faces south west; beams and a huge log burner in the bare-boarded, terracotta-painted bar; contemporary art and sofas in the split-level restaurant. It's a comfortable and sophisticated environment for Tony and Carol Coates' menu and specials board that delivers straightforward modern food. Informality and decent sized portions are among the attractions, the menu changes frequently and the produce is sourced locally. Fish dishes star, in the form of seared Brixham scallops, whole plaice on the bone, grilled sardines. A surprisingly light sticky toffee pudding makes a satisfying finish. There are Wadworth 6X and Butcombe on tap and several wines of the month chalked up on the board by the bar. Round off the treats with a visit to Longleat.

The Cross Keys
Lyes Green

Two log fires in winter, a landscaped beer garden in summer and ales from Wadworth all year round. The bar is tailor-made for quiet drinking, the front dining room, with its wooden floors and fresh flowers on pine tables, is somewhat posher. This is primarily a dining pub, so there's an intimate restaurant too, inviting with log fire, green dresser, scrubbed oak tables, gleaming glasses and chunky candles. (Booking is advisable at weekends.) Three huge blackboards list the changing menus. Find Wiltshire ham and apple chutney baguettes, baked potatoes with posh fillings, pork, bacon and cider pie and local sausages with onion gravy at lunchtime; on Sundays, fine roasts. Dinner promises asparagus in season, calves' liver with madeira jus and rump steak with peppercorn sauce. There's also a refurbished skittle alley.

Meals	12pm-3pm; 5pm-10pm.
	Main courses £12-£20.
Closed	3pm-6pm.
Directions	Village signed off A350 Warminster-Westbury road & off A36.

Meals	12pm-2pm; 7pm-9.30pm; no food Sun eve.
	Main courses £8.50-£20; bar meals £7.95-£15.95; Sunday roast £9.75-£14.95.
Closed	3pm-6.30pm (7pm Sun).
Directions	Lyes Green is signed off A3098 east of Frome at Chapmanslade.

	Tony & Carol Coates
	The Angel Inn, Upton Scudamore,
	Warminster BA12 0AG
Tel	01985 213225
Web	www.theangelinn.co.uk

	Fraser Carruth & Wayne Carnegie
	The Cross Keys,
	Lyes Green, Corsley BA12 7PB
Tel	01373 832406
Web	www.crosskeyscorsley.co.uk

The Bath Arms
Horningsham

A 17th-century coaching inn on the Longleat estate in a village lost in the country; geese swim in the river, cows munch the fields. At the front, a dozen pollarded lime trees shade a gravelled garden; at the back, two stone terraces soak up the sun. Inside are the best of old and new: flagstones and boarded floors, a stainless steel bar and Farrow & Ball colours. The feel is smart and airy, with a skittle alley that doubles as a sitting room (they show movies here) and shimmering Cole & Son walls in the dining room. Stop for caramelised onion tart, bavette steak with Lyonnaise potatoes, Pimms granita. They grow veg, keep pigs: produce makes its short way to the kitchen, and young guests may be given a small selection of vegetables to take home. Flashman, English Eccentric, Geisha... each of the bedrooms lives up to its name, some in the main house, others in the barn. The Kama Sutra room is heavily influenced by Lord Bath's own series of murals, and there's a spacious lodge overlooking Longleat House, perfectly private for couple or a small family. The walk down to Longleat is majestic.

Rooms	16: 12 doubles, 2 twins, 2 singles. £80–£140.
Meals	12pm-2pm (2.30pm Sat & Sun); 7pm-9pm (9.30pm Fri & Sat); children 6pm-7pm. Main courses £16–£18; bar meals £4.50–£14.95.
Closed	Open all day.
Directions	A303, then A350 north to Longbridge Deverill. Left for Maiden Bradley; right for Horningsham. Through village, on right.

Sara Elston
The Bath Arms,
Longleat Estate, Horningsham,
Warminster BA12 7LY
Tel   01985 844308
Web   www.batharms.co.uk

Entry 734 Map 3

The Bath Arms
Crockerton

The rambling old pub stands on the Longleat Estate, minutes from Shearwater Lake and woodland walks, and draws an eclectic crowd: ramblers, tourists, foodies. With a culinary background that ranges from country-house hotels to The Ivy, Dean Carr presents a pub menu that's a cut above the norm. So expect wild sea bass with chorizo risotto alongside gammon and poached eggs, and rump steak with rocket pesto alongside shepherd's pie, all with a modern twist. There are classy baguettes too, like steak and horseradish, and nursery favourites like sticky toffee pudding. The setting is homely and traditional, the open-plan bar and dining area displaying beams, brasses and plain pine tables; arrive early to bag a bench by the lovely log fire and a pint of local Crockerton Classic. The bedrooms, just two, 'Left' and 'Right', are a big surprise; both are huge with a contemporary yet sumptuous feel. Be cheered by crisp linen on wooden sleigh beds, leather sofas, vast plasma screens, bold modern paintings and bathrooms combining 'wet room' showers with Gilchrist & Soames. Fabulous.

Rooms	2 doubles. £75-£85.
Meals	12pm-2.30pm; 6.30pm-9pm.
	Main courses £10.25-£14.50.
Closed	3pm-6pm.
	Open all day Sat & Sun in summer.
Directions	2 miles south of Warminster off
	A350 towards Shaftesbury.

Dean Carr
The Bath Arms,
Longleat Estate, Crockerton,
Warminster BA12 8AJ
Tel   01985 212262
Web   www.batharmscrockerton.co.uk

Entry 735 Map 3

Wiltshire

George Hotel
Codford

By George! The old roadside inn has been given a new lease of life. Boyd McIntosh and Joanne Fryer used to practise their art at the revered Howard's House in Teffont Evias. Here, Boyd delivers dishes from a compact modern menu: wild sea bass with black olive potato and red pepper fondant, steamed turbot with watercress risotto, corn-fed chicken with mushroom risotto. Joanne is a dab hand at front of house – and her influence is stamped over the understatedly contemporary interiors. Floors are parquet, tiled or pale-carpeted, walls are warmly hued and the furniture is stylishly simple. The bar has a blond-wood counter, there are lush plants, mirrors and a sitting room full of deep sofas. The vase of lilies on the bar adds a civilised touch, as do candles on tables; the winter fires are the icing on the cake.

Meals	12pm-2pm; 7pm-9.30pm. Main courses £8.95-£16.95.
Closed	Tues & Sun eves in winter.
Directions	Off A36 between Salisbury & Warminster.

Boyd McIntosh & Joanne Fryer
George Hotel,
High Street, Codford St Peter,
Warminster BA12 0NG
Tel   01985 850270
Web   www.thegeorgecodford.co.uk

Entry 736 Map 3

Wiltshire

Fox & Hounds
East Knoyle

If you love beech trees and high ridges, make time for a walk with views over the vale before you land at the 17th-century thatched pub on the green. Enter to discover two areas: one bright and conservatory-like, with a great view, the other older and cosier, its fireplace flanked by small red leather sofas. There are warming ales from Youngs and Butcombe, and the inimitable Bishop's Tipple, and a well-presented wine card that tells you exactly what you'll get – which is what you'd expect from a no-nonsense landlord. Being a New Zealander, he cooks in an eclectic, untypical gastro style. Tuck into chorizo, bean and red pepper smoked paprika casserole in red wine with grilled chicken on top and follow that with vanilla cheesecake... you'll stay till the pub closes, no hardship at all!

Meals	12pm-2.30pm; 6.30pm-9.30pm. Main courses £8.50-£16.
Closed	3pm-6pm.
Directions	Off A303 onto A350 to Blandford then follow signs to pub.

Murray Seator
Fox & Hounds, East Knoyle,
Salisbury SP3 6BN
Tel   01747 830573
Web   www.foxandhounds-eastknoyle.co.uk

Entry 737 Map 3

The Lamb at Hindon
Hindon

The Lamb has been serving ale on Hindon's high street for 800 years, give or take a decade. It is a yard of England's finest cloth, a place where shooting parties come for lunch, where farmers meet to chew the cud. They come for huge oak settles, heavy old beams, deep red walls and roaring fires. A clipped Georgian country elegance lingers; you almost expect Mr Darcy to walk in, give a tormented sigh, then turn on his heels and vanish. There are flagstone floors and stripped wooden boards, window seats and gilded mirrors; old oils entwined in willow hang on the walls, a bookshelf is stuffed with aged tomes of poetry. At night, candles come out, as do some serious whiskies and the odd Cuban cigar, and in the restaurant you can feast on game terrine, Angus rump, then local cheeses. Bedrooms come with mahogany furniture, the odd four-poster, perhaps a sofa or a tartan carpet. Fishing can be arranged, or you can shoot off to Stonehenge, Stourhead, Salisbury or Bath. Return for a drink on the terrace and watch village life float by.

Rooms	14: 6 doubles, 6 twins/doubles, 2 singles. £99-£135. Singles £70.
Meals	12.30pm-2.30pm; 6.30pm-9.30pm (7pm-9pm Sun). Main courses £9-£17.95.
Closed	Open all day.
Directions	M3, A303 & signed left at bottom of steep hill two miles east of junction with A350.

Anthony Hughes-Onslow
The Lamb at Hindon,
High Street, Hindon,
Salisbury SP3 6DP
Tel   01747 820573
Web   www.lambathindon.co.uk

Entry 738 Map 3

The Compasses Inn
Lower Chicksgrove

In the middle of a lovely village of thatched and timber-framed cottages, this inn seems so content with its lot it could almost be a figment of your imagination. Over the years, 14th-century foundations have gradually sunk into the ground. Its thatched roof is like a sombrero, shielding bedroom windows that peer sleepily over the lawn. Duck instinctively into the sudden darkness of the bar and experience a wave of nostalgia as your eyes adjust to a long wooden room, with flagstones and cosy booths divided by farmyard salvage: a cartwheel here, some horse tack there; at one end is a piano, at the other, a brick hearth. The pub crackles with Alan's enthusiasm; he's fairly new to the trade, but his genuine hospitality more than compensates. People come for the food as well: figs baked in red wine, topped with goat's cheese and chorizo, or grilled fish from the south coast. Bedrooms are at the top of stone stairs outside the front door and have the same effortless charm; thick walls, wonky windows, new bathrooms. And the sweet serenity of Wiltshire lies just down the lane.

Rooms	4 + 1: 3 doubles, 1 twin/double. Cottage for 4. £85-£140.
Meals	12pm-2pm; 7pm-9pm (9.30pm Sat). Main courses £9-£17; bar meals from £5.
Closed	3pm-6pm (7pm Sun).
Directions	From Salisbury, A30 west, 3rd right after Fovant, signed Lower Chicksgrove, then 1st left down single track lane to village.

Alan & Susie Stoneham
The Compasses Inn,
Lower Chicksgrove,
Tisbury SP3 6NB

Tel	01722 714318
Web	www.thecompassesinn.com

Entry 739 Map 3

Wiltshire

Spread Eagle Inn
Stourhead

While Stourhead Gardens "echo with references to the heroes and gods of ancient Rome", this proper inn with rooms makes more than a passing nod to Bacchus. Mellow and old-fashioned it may appear but peep inside and you find slate or coir floors, Farrow & Ball colours and lovely jugs of garden flowers on old pine tables. In the bar a wood-burning stove is merry and the seats are comfy; you can eat here or in the restaurant that doubles as a sitting room. Red walls, large modern paintings, old prints, the odd game of scrabble create a mood that is cosy and warm. The higgledy-piggledy stairs are great if you're nimble and the bedrooms are peaceful – expect muted colours, white linen, original fireplaces, delightful views. Bathrooms are plain not state-of-the-art, and spotless. Food is English and locally supplied: Wiltshire ham with sweet mustard, west country fish soup, griddled organic salmon salad with anchovy mayonnaise. As for the estate: you can pretend that this stupendous example of a landscape garden with lake and follies is yours when the hoards have gone home (and to residents, entry is free).

Rooms	5: 2 doubles, 3 twins/doubles. £110. Singles £80.
Meals	12pm-9.30pm. Main courses £8.50-£16; bar meals from £5.50.
Closed	Open all day.
Directions	Turn off B3092 signed Stourhead Gardens. Spread Eagle is below main car park on left at entrance to garden. Private car park for Inn.

Andrew & Angela Wilson
Spread Eagle Inn,
Stourton, Warminster BA12 6QE
Tel   01747 840587
Web   www.spreadeagleinn.com

Entry 740 Map 3

Wiltshire

The Malet Arms
Newton Tony

Formerly a bakehouse for a long-lost manor, the old flintstone pub draws walkers from miles around. Expect cracking ales, robust country cooking and a cheerful welcome from Noel and Annie Cardew. The low-beamed bar, cosy with rustic furnishings, blazing logs, old pictures and interesting bits and pieces, would be a nice spot for a pint of Stonehenge Heelstone. Hearty food, listed above the fireplaces, reflects the rural setting, with locally shot game a winter favourite. So fill your boots with a rich stew of pheasant and pigeon in Guinness, venison en croute with mushrooms and fresh herbs or a local beef burger, and follow with Annie's speciality: an old English pudding (Cumbrian tart, Canterbury pie). The pub cricket team play on the playing field opposite and there's live music in the paddock at the back.

Wiltshire

The Forester Inn
Donhead St Andrew

Tiny lanes frothing with cowparsley twist down to this fine little pub in Donhead St Andrew. The revitalised 600-year-old inn sports rustic walls, black beams, a log fire in the inglenook and planked floors; colours are muted, there's not an ounce of flounce and locals still prop up the bar of a late weekday lunchtime. Foodies come from far for chef Tom Shaw's cooking — rib-eye steak with béarnaise, 'a trio of lamb chops' with bubble-and-squeak, goat's cheese omelette, tomato tarte tatin — and fine puddings cooked to order, slowly. Tom uses local Rushmore venison, Old Spot pork and specialises in fresh Cornish seafood — brill with shellfish bisque and mussels, skate wing with brown butter and capers. There's a pretty garden and terrace with views, three ales on tap, cider from Ashton Press and ten gorgeous wines by the glass.

Meals	12pm-2.30pm; 6.30pm-10pm (7pm-9.30pm Sun). Main courses £8.50-£15.
Closed	3pm-6pm (7pm Sun).
Directions	Off A338; 6 miles north of Salisbury.

Meals	12pm-2pm (3pm Sun); 6.30pm-9.30pm. Main courses £10-£25; bar meals £5-£12.
Closed	3pm-6.30pm & Sun from 4pm.
Directions	A30 between Shaftesbury & Salisbury. Through Ludwell then left for Donhead; pub on right in 1.2 miles.

	Noel & Annie Cardew
	The Malet Arms,
	Newton Tony,
	Salisbury SP4 0HF
Tel	01980 629279

Entry 741 Map 3

	Chris & Lizzie Matthews
	The Forester Inn,
	Lower St, Donhead St Andrew,
	Shaftesbury SP7 9EE
Tel	01747 828038

Entry 742 Map 3

Wiltshire

The Horseshoe Inn
Ebbesbourne Wake

The Ebble valley and Ebbesbourne Wake have escaped the intrusions of modern-day life, dozing down tiny lanes close to the Dorset border. A bucolic charm pervades the village inn that has been run as a "proper country pub" by the Bath family for over 30 years. Climbing roses cling to the 17th-century brick façade, while the traditional layout of two bars around a central servery still survives. Old farming implements and country bygones fill every available cranny and a mix of rustic furniture is arranged around the crackling winter fire. Beer is tapped straight from the cask and food is hearty and wholesome, prepared by Pat Bath using local meat and vegetables and game from local shoots. Tuck into steak and kidney pie, fresh fish bake, nursery pud, three roasts on Sundays (do book). Benches and flowers fill the garden.

Pubs are mirroring a laid-back approach to Sundays: a lie-in and a late breakfast, a walk and then lunch. Many now serve roasts up to 4 or 5pm; another trend is to bring the joint to the table.

Meals	12pm-2pm (2.30pm Sun); 7pm-9pm; no food Sun eve or Mon all day. Main courses £9.95-£15; bar meals £4.50-£11.95; Sunday roast £8.50.
Closed	3pm-6.30pm, Mon until 7pm & Sun from 4pm.
Directions	A354 south of Salisbury, right at Coombe Bissett; follow valley road for 8 miles.

Anthony & Patricia Bath
The Horseshoe Inn,
Ebbesbourne Wake,
Salisbury SP5 5JF
Tel   01722 780474

Entry 743 Map 3

The Beckford Arms
Fonthill Gifford

This eighteenth-century inn is quirky and fun, hugely hospitable and deeply comfortable. Enter and be swept up by it all. A huge fire spreads warmth across the main bar; chunky tables support pints of 'Hidden Pleasure', well-worn prints of the area look on, as does a cherub in the corner. Diners are spoilt for places to eat: main bar; conservatory; elegant back room; a garden for summer, and for private parties there's the front room with rollover dining-cum-billiard table. Settle down to roasted partridge with cranberry and chestnut stuffing, accompanied by a glass or two of Château Meunier St Louis from the Corbières region (a mouthful of southern French sun). If simpler fare is your aim then Wiltshire ham with a brace of eggs and chips will hit the spot. Upstairs more fun awaits. The eclectic mix of furniture surprises at every turn: French sleigh beds in many, the odd zebra-print chair or marble-topped table in others, and views to the very pretty garden. You are in ancient territory with much to see and here at the Beckford you have the perfect companion.

Rooms	8: 6 doubles, 2 twin. £80–£90.
Meals	12pm–2.30pm; 6.30pm–9.30pm.
	Main courses £9.95–£13.75.
Closed	Open all day.
Directions	Off B3089 between Hindon & Teffont Magna at Fonthill Bishop.

Feargal Powell
The Beckford Arms,
Fonthill Gifford, Tisbury SP3 6PX
Tel 01747 870385
Web www.beckfordarms.co.uk

Entry 744 Map 3

The Castle Inn
Bradford-on-Avon

On top of the hill that dips down to the mellow heart of Bradford-on-Avon, this impressive renovation of a neglected old inn is the work of pub group Flatcappers. This is their first foray and they have struck gold: the building is splendid inside and out. Enter a warren of rooms in muted greys, reds and greens, lovingly and imaginatively restored. Imagine solid stone walls and polished boards, long farmhouse tables and real fires, leather armchairs and sofas to sink into, books on the shelves, hunting prints on the walls, and portraits of distinguished gentlefolk gazing upon you from a distant past. Six ales from local breweries dominate the bar and muted jazz plays. An all-day menu (sandwiches, salads, brunch dishes) stands alongside British pub classics on the à la carte, while specials include such delights as rabbit ragu with handmade papadelle. Above, four individually designed bedrooms reveal modish wallpapers and stylish hues, wonky door frames and period fireplaces, stunning walk-in bathrooms and wide-reaching views – of the church, or the White Horse on the Wiltshire hills.

Rooms	4: 3 doubles, 1 family room. £90-£140.
Meals	12pm-10pm. Main courses £7.95-£12.95.
Closed	Open all day.
Directions	Entering Bradford-on-Avon on A363, pub is on mini-r'bout before turning for town centre.

	Alex Reilley
	The Castle Inn,
	Mount Pleasant,
	Bradford-on-Avon BA15 1SJ
Tel	01225 865657
Web	www.flatcappers.co.uk

Wiltshire

746 Red Lion Kilmington, Mere BA12 6RP 01985 844263

The four-centuries-old farmhouse has become a quiet, traditional local. Accompany a great value homemade cottage pie with a pint of Merlin's Magic and a fabulous view of the South Wiltshire Downs.

747 Haunch of Venison 1-5 Minster Street, Salisbury SP1 1TB 01722 411313

A tiny, ancient, city-centre pub of great character dating from 1320. A trio of rooms, jammed with shoppers, businessmen and tourists in a bare-boarded, music-free atmosphere, and whiskies galore.

748 The Linnet Great Hinton, Trowbridge BA14 6BU 01380 870354

With enthusiasm, dedication and bags of talent, chef-patron Jonathan Furby has turned the Linnet into a cheerful pub-restaurant. Unusual combinations executed with panache, and great value lunches.

749 The Boot Berwick St James SP3 4TN 01722 790243

Lush gardens, great Wadworth beers and proper pub food (come for Sunday lunch) draw locals and walkers to this ex-cobbler's in the Wylye Valley.

750 The Neeld Arms The Street, Grittleton, Malmesbury SN14 6AP 01249 782470

True country boozer with friendly locals, two glowing inglenooks, fresh tasty food, good beers and drinkable wines. Four-poster beds upstairs, breakfast feasts.

751 The Three Crowns Brinkworth, Swindon SN15 5AF 01666 510366

Intimate, old-style bars and a huge no-smoking conservatory. Real ale, good wine, a garden with views and a large, surprising menu – portions are huge so arrive hungry.

752 Rising Sun Bewley Common, Bowden Hill, Lacock SN15 2PP 01249 730363

Unpretentious stone pub high on a hill above Lacock. Escape the crowds for the terrace and unrivalled views, sup a pint of Moles as hot-air balloons drift across the sky on summer evenings.

753 The Three Tuns High Street, Great Bedwyn, Marlborough SN8 3NU 01672 870280

Bag a table in the bar where original floorboards, hefty oak beams and brick inglenook (ablaze in winter) blend with a miscellany of modern clutter. Walkers and gamekeepers come for great homemade food in whopping portions. New owners – reports please.

Worth a visit

Worcestershire

Butcher's Arms
Eldersfield

A small, two-room pub with a lovely big garden (and a cottage for let in the spacious car park!) the splendid Butchers is still very much a place for regulars popping in for pints of Wye Valley Bitter and Herefordshire cider. It is also fast gaining a reputation for its food, and one of its attractions is a sensibly short menu. James has a hands-on philosophy and cooks single-handedly for just 18 covers a time, while Elizabeth does friendly front of house. He used to work with Alastair Little and his gutsy British dishes use local produce from named suppliers. Be adventurous and tuck into that traditional English delicacy Bath chap, served with potato scone and grain mustard, or loin and shoulder of lamb with braised lentils and leek and bacon mash. A great little place for some 'nose to tail' dining.

Meals	12pm-1.30pm; 7pm-8.45pm; no food Sun eve & Tues lunch. £14.50-£18.50.
Closed	2.30pm-6pm & all day Mon.
Directions	From Tewkesbury, A438 west towards Ledbury; left on B4211 & follow signs for Eldersfield & Lime Street.

James & Elizabeth Winter
Butcher's Arms,
Eldersfield,
Tewkesbury GL19 4NX
Tel   01452 840381

Entry 754 Map 8

Worcestershire

Royal Oak
Kinnersley

It may have housed the laundry for the Croome Park estate but the Royal Oak dazzles these days thanks to the talent of its chef-patron. While business partner Jerry Bedwell creates a friendly front of house, Alistair produces seasonal dishes with big direct flavours – from chicken liver parfait with quince jelly and roast rump of Malvern lamb to Mayhill Green cheese soufflé with homemade piccalilli. Everything is made on the premises – pastas, breads, ice creams – and the value is fantastic. Accompanying it all is an imaginative wine list featuring Malbec and Viognier and well-kept real ales: Hooky, Three Tuns and one guest. The unassuming bar and the pretty little candle-dotted restaurant of this smart yet modest village pub fill up as fast as it takes to say 'last orders please.'

Meals	12pm-2.30pm; 6pm-9pm (12pm-4pm Sun). Main courses £7.25-£13.50.
Closed	3pm-6pm, Sun eve & Mon (except eves in Dec).
Directions	Village signed off A38 3 miles north of Upton-on-Severn

Alistair Forster
Royal Oak, Kinnersley,
Severn Stoke WR8 9JR
Tel   01905 371482
Web   www.royaloakkinnersley.co.uk

Entry 755 Map 8

Worcestershire

Nag's Head
Malvern

No beauty competition winner perhaps, but this low-slung white pub, converted from what was once a row of cottages, and with a timber-clad restaurant that was once a boxing gym, is worth seeking out. Tucked away in the side streets of lovely Malvern is a paradise for fans of whisky or real ale (fans of both tipples may have to be stretcher'd off). There are 25 single malts on offer and 18 beers, three of which are made at the pub's own brewery at Callow End. No wonder the homely bar with its deep-pink walls and living-room feel gets packed. This is a pub's pub. Stick to the bric-a-brac-strewn dining room for food, where ambitious restaurant-style fare (homemade chicken liver pâté, whole lemon sole) is proffered, and let the serious drinkers hog the bar. A great find.

Worcestershire Award winner 2008

The Talbot
Knightwick

It's run by two sisters, Annie and Wiz, chef-owners with a dedication to all things self-sufficient. Hops for their micro-brewed beers are grown here; organic produce comes from the farmers' market they host the second Sunday of every month. Their infectious commitment to using fresh local food pulls a crowd; the crab bisque, raised pies and spotted dick are legendary. Fresh fish comes from Cornwall and scallop beignets are wrapped in nori seaweed (not local, but delicious). The pot-roast lamb recipe is from Alnwick Castle in Northumberland, and the wild duck — drizzled with meat juices, a little grand marnier and served over mashed potato — suggests a touch of genius. Out of the way, on the bank of the Teme (you may fish with a permit): a superb place, well-run, and with a fire in the comfortable bar.

Meals	12pm-2pm; 6.30pm-8.30pm. Main courses £10.50-£17.50.
Closed	Open all day.
Directions	At the bottom of Bank Street

Meals	12-2pm; 6.30-9pm (7-9pm Sun). Main courses £10-£19; bar meals £4.50-£14.
Closed	Open all day.
Directions	From Worcester A44 for Leominster; 8 miles on, through Cotheridge & Broadwas; right on B4197; on left.

SPECIAL AWARD see pages 18-19

Local, Seasonal & Organic Produce

Claire Willetts
Nag's Head,
Bank Street,
Malvern W14 2JG
Tel   01684 574373

Entry 756 Map 3

Annie Clift
The Talbot,
Knightwick, Worcester WR6 5PH
Tel   01886 821235
Web   www.the-talbot.co.uk

Entry 757 Map 8

Worcestershire

The Fleece
Bretforton

"No potato crisps to be sold in the bar." So ordered Lola Taplin when The Fleece was bequeathed to the National Trust after 500 years in her family. It's the sort of tradition that thrives in the Pewter Room where you pitch up for fresh local food, ales from Uley and Weston's Old Rosie cider. Steak and ale casserole with dumplings and locally culled rhubarb in pies and crumbles may tempt you but there is so much more: the Asparagus Festival commences in the courtyard of the Fleece with an auction on the last Sunday in May, summer festivals twirl with Morris dancers and the original farmyard is a gorgeous setting for hog roasts and musical events. The black-and-white timbered building is as stuffed as a museum with historical artefacts, stone flagged floors, big log fires, ancient beams and a wonderful collection of pewter. The timbered bedroom, in the oldest part of the building, is small but perfectly formed, with seagrass flooring and antique mahogany bed. Leave the 21st century behind – by about half a millennium.

Rooms	1 double. £90.
Meals	12pm-2.30pm (4pm Sun); 6.30pm-9pm (6.30pm-8.30pm Sun). Main courses £7-£12; bar meals from £4.50.
Closed	3pm-6pm. Open all day Sat & Sun & every day June-Sep.
Directions	B4035 from Evesham for Chipping Campden. In Bretforton bear right into village. Opp. church in square.

	Nigel Smith
	The Fleece,
	The Cross, Bretforton,
	Evesham WR11 7JE
Tel	01386 831173
Web	www.thefleeceinn.co.uk

Entry 758 Map 8

Worcestershire

The Chequers
Cutnall Green

On the site of an ancient coaching inn, the Chequers was rebuilt 70 years ago. You'd never know: its open fires, comfy sofas and snug little booths have evolved as smoothly as its menu. While the thirsty gather round the church-panel bar with pints of Timothy Taylor's, the hungry head for the dining room – cosy and candlelit with deep red walls, pale exposed beams and a huge display of wines. Make the most of a vibrant 'mod Brit' menu from award-winning chef Roger Narbett: the food bursts with flavour. There's potted duck confit with apricot chutney, roasted Cornish cod with leeks and cheddar mash, and mango syrup and coconut ice pavlova. And if the liqueur coffees catch your fancy, slip off and savour one in the Garden Room, whose sleek, striped, coffee-coloured curtains resemble an upside-down cappuccino.

Meals	12pm-2pm; 6.30pm-9.15pm (9.30pm Fri & Sat); Sun 12pm-2.30pm; 6.30pm-9pm. Main courses £10.25-£13.50; bar meals £4.25-£8.75.
Closed	3pm-6pm (3.30pm-6pm Sun).
Directions	3 miles north of Droitwich Spa on A442 towards Kidderminster. M5 exit 5.

Roger & Jo Narbett
The Chequers, Kidderminster Rd,
Cutnall Green, Droitwich WO9 0PJ
Tel   01299 851292
Web   www.chequerscutnallgreen.co.uk

Entry 759 Map 8

Worth a visit

760 The Swan Hanley Swan, Worcester WR8 0EA
01684 311870
Worth noting if heading for the Malvern Hills – a smartly revamped local overlooking the village green and pond. Contemporary layout and décor, three ales on tap and modern pub food.

761 Plough & Harrow Rhydd Road, Guarlford, Malvern W13 6NY
01684 310453
Nice buzzy atmosphere and impressive upmarket menus with an emphasis on home-grown and local produce, in this rambling 18th-century pub in the wilds outside Malvern.

762 Colliers Arms Tenbury Road, Clows Top, Kidderminster DY14 9HA
01299 832242
Food with a view! A snug little bar, a log fire, a pretty setting, a top quality traditional menu and wine list, and a 'gourmet evening' to tickle foodies' tastebuds.

763 Bell & Cross Inn Holy Cross, Clent, Stourbridge DY9 9QL
01562 730319
A cosy atmosphere with open fires, good pub food (the owner was chef to the English football squad) and a selection of real ales. A surprisingly unspoilt little pub so close to Birmingham. Reports please.

Kings Arms
Heath

Enter Heath and step back years. A string of wool merchants' houses, 100 acres of heathland, a couple of tethered ponies... who'd guess Wakefield was down the road? In the heart of Yorkshire's most unspoilt village is the equally unspoiled King's Arms. In a dark, rich network of tap rooms and snugs, softly hissing gas lamps cast an amber glow on oak-panelled walls, yellowed ceilings and low beams, while a magnificent Yorkshire range is the best of several open coal fires. It's no museum – just a superbly old-fashioned pub that serves Clarks Classic Blond, and Stella for non-believers. Traditional pub grub includes filled Yorkshire puddings and beef and ale pie. Attached is a serviceable restaurant, at the back is a conservatory that breaks the spell. The gardens have gentle moorland views.

Three Acres
Shelley, Huddersfield

A dining pub par excellence where everything ticks over beautifully. The bar is a work of art, brimful of bottles, pumps, flowers and old fishing reels and tackle hanging picturesquely above. Seating is comfy pub style, and there's a large solid fuel stove to warm the central space. Separate areas around the bar have a sea of tables set for dining (white linen, shining glasses); one area specialises in seafood. The overall feel is roomy yet intimate and hugely inviting, with plants, flowers, mirrors, old prints, a baby grand. A sizeable team prepares all the food on site, from potted shrimps to assiette of moorland lamb (rack, stuffed breast, shepherd's pie), and runs the on-site deli. There's also a private dining room. Well-kept beers on pump, scores of fine wines, over 50 whiskies, great sandwiches. Lovely.

Meals	12pm-2pm; 7pm-9pm (12-5pm Sun); no food Sun eve. Main courses £5.95-£9.95.
Closed	3pm-5pm in winter. Open all day weekends and in summer.
Directions	Heath signed off A655.

Meals	12pm-2pm; 6.30pm-9.30pm. Main courses £13.95-£25.95; bar meals from £5.95.
Closed	3pm-6pm.
Directions	5 miles SE of Huddersfield & off A629; signs for Kirburton on B6116; signs for Emley Moor Mast; 0.5 miles south of mast, on minor road above Shelley.

	Andrew Shepherd & Renata Dacosta Kings Arms, Heath Common, Heath, Wakefield WF1 5SL
Tel	01924 377527

	Neil Truelove & Brian Orme Three Acres, Roydhouse, Shelley, Huddersfield HD8 8LR
Tel	01484 602606
Web	www.3acres.com

Entry 764 Map 12

Entry 765 Map 12

Yorkshire

Award winner 2008

The Sair Inn
Linthwaite

Clinging to the side of the valley, the Sair oozes character and a warren of small rooms. Floors of rippling flagstone and scuffed boards carry tables, pews and chairs from The Ark. Massive winter fires ensure that Vulcan would feel at home; Pandora would be delighted by the artefacts and oddments. It's a Yorkshire treasure, enhanced by locals and traditional pub games; the old pub Joanna allows impromptu entertainment, side rooms allow escape from the hubbub. Beers? – to die for, created in the brewhouse near the pub; any or all of a dozen and more. Patrons flock from afar to soak up the atmosphere of this iconic idyll, so concerns about catering are the last thing on anyone's mind. It's uncompromising, not one for shrinking violets, 'grand' in the Wallace and Grommit sense, brilliant value and welcoming to all.

Meals	Sandwiches available Sat & Sun, £1.50.
Closed	Mon-Fri lunch. Open all day Sat & Sun.
Directions	Off A62 in Linthwaite; up Hoyle Ing (past oil tanks painted with sheep; turn opposite); 400 yds up steep hill.

SPECIAL AWARD
see pages 18-19

Authentic pub

Ron Crabtree
The Sair Inn,
Hoyle Ing, Linthwaite,
Huddersfield HD7 5SG
Tel   01484 842370

Entry 766 Map 12

Yorkshire

The Old Bridge Inn
Ripponden

An ancient packhorse bridge and a little low inn… this is the setting. Family involvement over several decades has resulted in a thoroughly civilised, unspoilt little local; a friendly one, too. Three carpeted, oak-panelled, split-level rooms – suitably dimly lit – are furnished with old oak settles and rush-seated chairs. The small, green-walled snug at the top is atmospheric; the bar has a lofty ceiling with exposed timbers and a huge fireplace with log-burning stove; the lower room is good for dining. The buffet lunches are as popular as ever, while the evening menu announces sound English cooking using local produce (try Hubberton rib-eye steak with port and shallot sauce) with a modern slant. The bar is well-used by local folk who come for Timothy Taylor's Best and Black Sheep beers, and wines are good too.

Meals	12pm-2pm; 6.30pm-9.30pm; no food Sat or Sun eve. Main courses £7.50-£10.95.
Closed	3pm-5.30pm (5pm Fri). Open all day Sat & Sun.
Directions	4 miles from junc. 22 M62 in Ripponden.

Tim & Lindsay Eaton Walker
The Old Bridge Inn, Priest Lane,
Ripponden, Sowerby Bridge HX6 4DF
Tel   01422 822595
Web   www.porkpieclub.com

Entry 767 Map 12

Yorkshire

The Alma
Cotton Stones

High on the heather-clad moors this old boozer has a few surprises up its sleeve. The stone paved terrace is large and lovely and the bar is welcoming and warm – all flagged floors, stone walls, glowing fires, pine tables, old settles and gently ticking grandfather clock. Timothy Taylor Golden Best and Landlord are on tap, along with 75 Belgian beers. Most surprising of all: the food is Italian, and fabulous. Vegetables come from the market, local meat is brought in on the bone and every last bit used in stocks and gravy. So tuck into gamberoni all'aglio e burro – that's prawns in garlic butter – or fillet steak, monkfish with pancetta, partridge with Parma ham, and big thin-crust pizzas from a wood-burning oven. Eat in the bar or in the fresh airy dining room, with its chunky chairs and open kitchen.

Meals	12pm-8pm (10pm Fri & Sat). Main courses £7.95-£17.95.
Closed	Open all day.
Directions	A58 from Halifax towards Ripponden, turn right signed Cotton Stones/Millbank; pub 1.5 miles.

David Giffen
The Alma, Cotton Stones,
Sowerby Bridge HX6 4NS
Tel   01422 823334
Web   www.almainn.com

Entry 768 Map 12

Yorkshire

The Old Bore
Rishworth

The Pennines may seem bleak in winter, but drop down to Rishworth and there's a treat in store. Scott Hessel, who has cooked his way from London to West Yorkshire, has warmed a 200-year-old pub, renamed it The Old Bore and claims it is anything but. The carved oak bar is flanked by two dining rooms brimming with antlers, stuffed birds, old prints, gilt mirrors, wine boxes and champagne bottles. The monthly carte has been refined and shows flair – local game and foie gras terrine with spiced damson chutney; monkfish and clam casserole with saffron, tomato and basil; confit of Ryburn lamb shoulder with roast garlic mash, lentils, roast peppers and rosemary – and the two-course menu is a steal. Add a raft of English wines, homemade gins and vodkas and a dining terrace outside and you have a pub that's worth a detour.

Meals	12pm-2.15pm; 6pm-9pm (10pm Sat); 12pm-4pm; 5.30-8pm Sun. Main courses £6.95-£19.95; set menu, 2 courses, £10.
Closed	Mon & Tues.
Directions	M62 junc. 22; A672 for Halifax; 4 miles, then left at lights in Rishworth.

Scott Hessell
The Old Bore, Oldham Road,
Rishworth, Halifax HX6 4QU
Tel   01422 822291
Web   www.oldbore.co.uk

Entry 769 Map 12

Yorkshire

The Millbank
Mill Bank

Savour a pint and a rolling moorland view. The Millbank, clinging to the side of a steep hill, has a stripped-down, architect-scripted interior that combines flagstones and log fires with modern paintings and bold colours. Its friendly, cosmopolitan style is echoed in the food, prepared by Chez Nico-trained Glenn Futter, who creates daily wonders with fresh local produce. There might be beef braised in Guinness with horseradish mash or sea bass with lobster and spinach linguine. And then there are the spoiling puddings, the fine Yorkshire cheeses, the guest beers and the Yorkshire ales (Timothy Taylor's Landlord for one), the excellent wines, the malt whiskies and the first-class snacks in the bar. The steeply terraced garden has lead planters fashionably stuffed with box topiary and bamboo — and those views.

Meals	12pm-2.30pm (12pm-4.30pm Sun); 6-9.30pm (10pm Fri & Sat; 8pm Sun). Main courses £9.95-£18.95; set menu, 2 courses, £11.95; sandwiches from £4.95.
Closed	3pm-5.30pm & Mon lunch. Open all day Sun.
Directions	Off A58 between Sowerby Bridge & Ripponden.

Glenn Futter & Joe McNally
The Millbank, Mill Bank Road,
Mill Bank, Sowerby Bridge HX6 3DY

Tel   01422 825588
Web   www.themillbank.com

Entry 770 Map 12

Yorkshire

Travellers Rest
Sowerby

Caroline Lumley took over this old pub on the moors and started from scratch: she has worked wonders. The inn has kept its big fireplaces and cast-iron stoves, flagged bar, exposed stone and ancient beams, now sanded; Caroline has added atmospheric lighting, background sound, sofas, cushions and throws — and a helipad! It's a great mix of old and new and the result is a pub that appeals both to locals and those from further afield. The pleasant dining room is two archways from the bar, with well-dressed tables and fine valley views. The blackboard menu highlights scrumptious English dishes — chicken and leek pie with homemade chips, lamb shank with redcurrant gravy — while in the stylish bar you can choose between Timothy Taylor's on tap and a champagne cocktail. From the terrace, stunning views over the wild moors.

Meals	5pm-9.30pm Wed-Fri; 12pm-2pm; 5.30-10pm Sat; 12-8.30pm Sun. Main courses £10-£22; bar meals £10.
Closed	Mon & Tues all day, Wed-Fri lunch & 2.30pm-5.30pm Sat. Open all day Sun.
Directions	West of Sowerby Bridge on A672; 5 miles west of Halifax. Signed.

Caroline Lumley
Travellers Rest, Steep Lane,
Sowerby, Halifax HX6 1PE

Tel   01422 832124
Web   www.travellersrestsowerby.co.uk

Entry 771 Map 12

Shibden Mill Inn
Shibden Mill

There's still a pubby feel to this rambling old inn – although it's known for its restaurant. Shibden Bitter, Theakstons and three rotating bitters keep beer drinkers happy in front of several open fires, the deep green valley setting within sound of the mill stream makes for idyllic summer drinking and the wine list continues to win awards. An unstuffy integrity lies behind this venture, from the front-of-house warmth – the staff really are lovely – to the modern British kitchen from which delicious dishes flow: roast pigeon and beetroot risotto; wild turbot with blue cheese soufflé and mussel broth; toffee parfait. (What better to come home to after a brisk valley walk?) There are cosy gate-leg tables and sofas in the bars, crisp white napery and candelabra in the restaurant, and most of the fruit and vegetables come from local Hill Top Farm; this is a special place to which people return. As for the bedrooms, some of which have been recently renovated, they are carpeted, comfortable, individual and equipped with everything, from satellite TV to WiFi. The suite is huge fun.

Rooms	11 doubles/singles/suites. £90–£136.
Meals	12pm–2pm; 6pm–9.30pm (12pm–7.30pm Sun). Main courses £9.95–£17.95; bar meals from £8.95.
Closed	2.30pm–5.30pm. Open all day Sat & Sun.
Directions	Off A58 Halifax–Leeds, near A6036 junction.

Glen Pearson
Shibden Mill Inn,
Shibden, Halifax HX3 7UL
Tel   01422 365840
Web   www.shibdenmillinn.com

Entry 772 Map 12

Yorkshire

The Lord Nelson
Luddenden

Another hidden gem? Sitting squarely opposite a 400-year-old churchyard and a gurgling beck, this curious 17th-century pub was once a meeting place for artists and writers, including Branwell Brönte who worked as a clerk nearby. The interior hasn't changed much since his patronage: thick stone sills and mullion windows, old oak floors, open fire, ancient beams. Timothy Taylor Landlord, Golden Best and IPA Green King are on tap today and there's no food other than snacks (and old-fashioned sweets) though plans are afoot to cater. Outside are two stunning levels of garden with plants spilling from every surface and basket; by the back door is a secluded flagged yard, and a narrow path opening onto a bark-covered area with wooden tables and deckchairs. Views swoop over the village to the hills.

Meals	Snacks only.
Closed	Mon-Fri from 4pm. Open all day Sat & Sun.
Directions	A646 from Halifax towards Hebden Bridge; right signed Booth & Luddenden. Turn right down High Street, then left at fork; pub over bridge on left.

Debbie Collinge
The Lord Nelson,
High Street, Luddenden,
Halifax HX2 6PX
Tel 01422 882176

Entry 773 Map 12

Yorkshire

The Chequers Inn
Ledsham

Fires glow, horse brasses gleam... this honey-stone village inn could be in the Dales. In fact, you're a couple of miles from the A1. The panelled, carpeted rooms radiating off the central bar are cosy with log fires and plush red upholstery; faded sepia photographs are a reminder of an earlier age. Rare handpumped ales from the Brown Cow Brewery at Selby do justice to good English food of Yorkshire proportions: steaming platefuls of lamb shank, cassoulet (duck confit, Toulouse sausage & beans), guinea fowl... and just when you think you're replete, along comes a treacle sponge pudding. The pub has been welcoming travellers since the 18th century and still closes on Sundays; the tradition started in 1832 when the lady of Ledsham Hall, confronting a drunken farmer on her way to church, insisted the pub close on the Sabbath.

Meals	12pm-9pm. Main courses £4.95-£16.95.
Closed	Sun. Open all day Mon-Sat.
Directions	From A1(M) at junc. 42, follow A63 Leeds to Selby road. Turn left & follow signs for Ledsham, 1 mile.

Chris Wraith
The Chequers Inn, Claypit Lane,
Ledsham, South Milford LS25 5LP
Tel 01977 683135
Web www.thechequersinn.f9.co.uk

Entry 774 Map 12

Yorkshire

Whitelocks
Leeds

A gem! Fixtures and fittings have changed little since Victorian times. The long narrow bar is dominated by a tile-fronted counter with its original, marble-topped Luncheon Bar. Fine old button-backed leather banquettes come with panelled, mirrored dividers, while copper-topped tables, stained glass and several grand mirrors add to the 1900s mood. There is no piped music and the place is surprisingly quiet given its city centre position, though it does fill up fast at peak times. Well-kept Deuchars, good wines and a mix of traditional and up-to-date dishes make this a bit of a find. There's also a carpeted dining room with linen-covered tables, and an open fire to add to the atmosphere. Be comforted by sandwiches, steak and ale pie and roast lunches, and avoid busy times – it's seriously small.

What is Slow Food? Slow Food UK is part of a global movement with 80,000 members that urges us, in the words of the 1989 manifesto, to 'discover the flavours and savours of regional cooking and banish the degrading effects of fast food'.

Meals	12pm-9pm (12pm-5pm Sun). Main courses £5.95-£9.95.
Closed	Open all day.
Directions	Next to Marks & Spencer in Central Leeds shopping area.

Charlie Hudson
Whitelocks, Turks Head Yard,
Briggate, Leeds LS1 6HB
Tel   0113 245 3950
Web   www.whitelocks.co.uk

Entry 775 Map 12

The Tempest Arms
Elslack

A 16th-century ale house with great prices, friendly staff and an easy style. Inside you find stone walls and old beams, settles and plump cushions, Yorkshire ales on tap and a smart beamed restaurant. An airy open-plan feel runs throughout with sofas and armchairs strategically placed in front of a fire that burns on both sides. Delicious traditional food is a big draw – the inn was packed for lunch on a Tuesday in April. You can eat wherever you want, so grab a seat and dig into Yorkshire puddings with a rich onion gravy, raised pork pie with homemade piccallili, treacle tart with pink grapefruit sorbet. Bedrooms are just as good. Those in the main house are slightly simpler, but most are ten paces beyond in two newly built stone houses: rather swish with private terraces or balconies overlooking a babbling stream. They have hand-crafted furniture and Molton Brown toiletries, slate bathrooms and flat-screen TVs; a couple have decks with hot tubs to soak in and those at the back have views of the fells. Walkers pile in: the Dales are on the doorstep.

Rooms	21: 9 twins/doubles, 12 suites. £79.95-£200. Singles £59.95-£79.95.	
Meals	12pm-2.30pm; 6pm-9pm (9.30pm Sat); 12pm-7.30pm Sun. Main courses £8.95-£15.95; bar meals from £5.95.	
Closed	Open all day.	
Directions	A56 west from Skipton. Signed left after two miles.	

Martin & Veronica Clarkson
The Tempest Arms,
Elslack, Skipton BD23 3AY
Tel   01282 842450
Web   www.tempestarms.co.uk

Yorkshire

The Pack Horse
Widdop

This old whitewashed inn sags beneath weathered gritstone tiles in a gloriously remote spot. Once, water engineers had a whale of a time constructing reservoirs to slake the thirst of the local textile industry – the pub's stone walls sport old plans and photos of their endeavours. Today's thirsts are those of ramblers on the Pennine Way and riders on the new Pennine Bridleway, which briefly meet right behind the pub. Four or five real ales to enjoy alongside whopping portions of crispy roast duck, rack of lamb and a whole side of grilled plaice ensure this is a popular spot. Two thickly beamed rooms off a passageway bar, with cavernous log fires, horsey ephemera and a comfy rag-tag of furnishings, invite you to unwind over a drink; this is a great pub with grand food, not a dining pub with good beer.

Meals	12pm-2pm (2.30pm Sun); 7pm-9pm (9.30pm Fri; 10pm Sat). Main courses £5.95-£11.95.
Closed	Mon (except bank holidays); weekday lunch Oct-Easter. Open all day Sun.
Directions	From A646 in Hebden Bridge take the road at the Fox & Goose, signed for Heptonstall & Slack. In Slack fork right for Widdop.

Andrew Hollinrake
The Pack Horse,
Widdop,
Hebden Bridge HX7 7AT
Tel   01422 842803

Entry 777 Map 12

Yorkshire

The Fleece
Addingham

A gorgeous place run with flair and passion. The surroundings provide atmosphere, the friendly licensees add something special, and the food's good. Bags of character comes from big open fires, solid tables and old settles, flagged floors, beamed ceilings, exposed stone. It's a big space that at peak times gets busy, but in summer you can spill onto tables on the paved terrace and watch the world go by. Chris Monkman has brought a refreshing enthusiasm for local, seasonal, rustic cuisine: Wharfedale lamb, braised oxtail, ocean-fresh fish. Even the children's menu is brilliant: home-battered fish, omelettes, moules marinières. There's masses of choice and it's pretty good value. Four of Yorkshire's best beers are always available, there's a thoughtful selection of wines, and a number of whiskies, too.

Meals	12pm-2.15pm; 6pm-9.15pm (12pm-8pm Sun). Main courses £7-£17.
Closed	Open all day.
Directions	2 miles north of Ilkley on A65-A650.

Chris Monkman
The Fleece,
Main Street, Addingham,
Ilkley LS29 0LY
Tel   01943 830491

Entry 778 Map 12

Yorkshire

Craven Arms
Appletreewick

Authentically restored by enthusiastic licensees, this ancient rustic, creeper-clad pub (built in 1548) stands among gorgeous hills overlooking Wharfedale. It's a favourite with walkers so you could end up chin-wagging with them alongside the glowing cast-iron range in the classic stone-flagged bar. Just plain settles, panelled walls, thick beams, nothing more; beyond, a snug with simple benches and valley views, and a homely dining room. The final treat are the Wharfedale Ales – Folly Gold, Executioner. Head out back to the loo to take a peek at the amazing function room housed in a replica medieval barn; back in the bar, free of music and flashing games, there are hot sandwiches to be tucked into, and the legendary slow-roasted and minted lamb shoulder. Just the job after a blustery hike or cycle ride across the moors.

Meals	12pm-2pm (2.30pm Fri-Sun); 6.30pm-9pm (8.30pm Sun). Main courses £8.95-£15.25; bar meals £7.50-£10.50.
Closed	3pm-6pm. Open all day Weds-Sun.
Directions	A59 Skipton to Leeds; B6160 at Bolton Abbey towards Grassington; Appletreewick signed right.

Ashley & Hayley Crampton
Craven Arms,
Appletreewick, Skipton BD23 6DA

Tel	01756 720270
Web	www.craven-cruckbarn.co.uk

Entry 779 Map 12

Yorkshire

The Angel Inn
Hetton

The old drovers' inn remains staunchly, reassuringly traditional – but with a stylish restaurant and wines that have come, over the years, to rival the handpumped Yorkshire ales. There's even a 'cave' for private-party tastings. There are nooks, crannies, beams and crackling fires, and thought has gone into every detail, from the antique furniture in the timbered rooms (one with a magnificent oak-panelled bar) to the fabrics and the colours. Menus change with each season and include dishes ranging from filo 'moneybags' of seafood in lobster sauce – the fish comes fresh from Fleetwood – to Yorkshire lamb and rosemary sausage with juniper-scented red wine sauce. Or Goosnargh duck breast with braised red cabbage. The glorious up-hill-and-down-dale drive to get here is part of the charm, and it is best to book.

Meals	12pm-2.15pm (2.30pm Sun); 6pm-9.30pm (10pm Sat, 9pm in winter). Main courses £9.50-£17; bar meals £8.95-£16; Sunday lunch £22.50; Early Bird menus £13.20 & £16.50.
Closed	3pm-6pm.
Directions	North from Skipton on B6265. Left at Rylstone for Hetton. In village.

Juliet Watkins
The Angel Inn,
Hetton, Skipton BD23 6LT

Tel	01756 730263
Web	www.angelhetton.co.uk

Entry 780 Map 12

Yorkshire

The Falcon Inn
Arncliffe

Tucked into the top corner of Littondale, one of the most remote and unspoilt of Yorkshire's dales. Several generations of Millers have been licensees here and they have preserved an inn and a way of life almost lost. The fine bay-windowed and ivy-clad building looks more like a private house than a village local... expect few frills and old-fashioned hospitality. The entrance passageway leads to a small hallway at the foot of the stairs – there's a tiny bar counter facing you, a small, simple lounge, a log fire and sporting prints on the walls. A sunny back room looks out across the garden to open fells. Beer is served, as ever, straight from the cask in a large jug, then dispensed into pint glasses at the bar. At lunchtime, call in for pie and peas, sandwiches and ploughman's lunches.

Meals	12pm–2pm.
	Snacks £2.50–£4.50.
Closed	3pm–7pm. Reduced winter opening times, phone to check.
Directions	Off B6160 16 miles N of Skipton.

Robin Miller
The Falcon Inn,
Arncliffe, Skipton BD23 5QE
Tel   01756 770205
Web   www.thefalconinn.com

Entry 781 Map 12

Yorkshire

The White Lion Inn
Cray

For centuries the White Lion has stood surrounded by moorland high in the Pennines, serving local farmers and cattle drovers. It still does, though walkers have replaced the drovers. In the main bar are wide upholstered settles and dark, plain tables – the ideal backdrop for straightforward soups, ploughman's lunches, pork casseroles, homemade lasagne and steak and mushroom pies, best washed down with a well-kept pint of Taylor's Landlord or Copper Dragon Golden Pippin. At quiet times the crackle of the logs on the fire and the ticking of the clock are all you hear and the owners' relaxed style permeates the place. There are plenty of spots for summer eating outside by the tumbling stream. Some of Wharfedale's footpaths pass by the door, and the views are all you'd hope for, and more.

Meals	12pm–2pm; 5.45pm–8.30pm.
	Main courses £7.50–£15.50.
Closed	Open all day.
Directions	20 miles north of Skipton on B6160.

Phil & Carol Lowther
The White Lion Inn,
Cray, Buckden, Skipton BD23 5JB
Tel   01756 760262
Web   www.whitelioncray.com

Entry 782 Map 12

The Old Hill Inn
Chapel-le-Dale

A proper, wild-country tavern with terrific beer and food. It used to be a farmhouse, then a doss-house for potholers; now it's a comfortable old inn, a warm, safe haven in a countryside of crags, waterfalls, moors and the oddl stone dwelling. Via the porch enter the bar – a large room with open-stone walls, bare boards, old pine tables and big log fire. Six pumps deliver ales in top condition – Black Sheep Bitter, Timothy Taylor, Aviator – while food, served in the candlelit intimacy of the diminutive dining rooms, is well above average pub grub. From Sabena come parsnip and apple soup, pan fried sea bass with warm bean, tomato and olive salad, pheasant casserole in season and homemade bread; from master confectioner Colin, warm chocolate pudding and lemon tart. His sugar sculptures alone are worth the trip.

The Wensleydale Heifer Inn
Leyburn

Be lulled into a false sense of 'leather armchair by the fire' and 'mine's a pint of Black Sheep' security as you step off the street. Enter the Fish Bar and you're met with wall-to-wall seagrass and modish-naff touches. But the welcome is warm, and the food is sensational. Choose dressed crab with potato, capers and chive salad or Cornish fish stew with new potatoes, parsley and olive oil. As for the Whitby cod in crispy Black Sheep Bitter batter with peas and fat chips – it's the best fish and chips this side of Whitby's Magpie Café. Chef David Moss, ex-Crab & Lobster at Asenby, has achieved the impossible: a great fish restaurant as far from the sea as you can get. And there's a shiny, slightly more formal but still kitted-out-with-joke-crockery dining room – guaranteed to put a smile on your face.

Meals	12pm-2.30pm; 6.30pm-8.30pm (6pm-8.30pm Sat). Main courses £9.95-£17.50.
Closed	Monday.
Directions	On the B6255 between Ingleton & Ribblehead.

Meals	12pm-2.30pm; 6pm-9.30pm (12pm-9.30pm Sat & Sun) Main courses £11.50-£22; bar meals (lunch) £4.50-£17; set lunch/early dinner £14.95 & £16.95.
Closed	Open all day.
Directions	On A684 between Leyburn & Hawes.

Sabena Martin
The Old Hill Inn,
Chapel-le-Dale, Ingleton LA6 3AR
Tel   015242 41256
Web   www.oldhillinn.co.uk

David Moss
The Wensleydale Heifer Inn,
West Witton, Leyburn DL8 4LS
Tel   01969 622322
Web   www.wensleydaleheifer.co.uk

Entry 783 Map 12

Entry 784 Map 12

Yorkshire

The Oak Tree Inn
Hutton Magna

A tiny cottage at the end of a row, masquerading as a pub, the Oak Tree was snapped by the Rosses, ready to swap London for the Dales. Alastair trained at the Savoy and together they have created a gem. The front bar has old wooden panelling and whitewashed stone, an attractive medley of tables, chairs and pews, newspapers, fresh flowers and an open fire. The dark green dining area at the back is softly lit, its tables separated by pews. All is delightful and informal. Locally shot game appears on the menu in season and the produce is as fresh as can be, much of it sourced from within a mile of the village. Expect steamed mussels with red onion, chilli, ginger and mint, roast halibut with black pudding and parsley mash, and hot chocolate fondant with pistachio ice cream. Booking is recommended.

The real ale revival
In the 1960s and early 1970s the big breweries flooded the market with keg beers and lager. Then, in 1971, CAMRA (The Campaign for Real Ale) was founded. Their success in inspiring the real ale revival has been a dramatic example of a consumer group in action, forcing the brewing industry to rethink its strategy and produce real ales. The new century has seen a flowering of craft breweries across the country, with beer being brewed on farms, on industrial estates and in sheds behind pubs. The Progressive Beer Duty was introduced in 2002 to give micro-brewers a further boost; now there are over 400 independent breweries in Britain.

Meals	6pm-11pm (5.30pm-10.30pm Sun), booking only. Main courses £14.50-£17.50.
Closed	Mon; Tues-Sun lunch.
Directions	Off A66, 6.5 miles west of Scotch Corner.

Alastair & Claire Ross
The Oak Tree Inn, Hutton Magna,
Richmond DL11 7HH

Tel	01833 627371
Web	www.elevation-it.co.uk/oaktree

Entry 785 Map 12

Sandpiper Inn
Leyburn

Malt whisky lovers will eye the 100 bottles behind the bar appreciatively. In 1999, former Roux Scholar Jonathan Harrison swapped a slick city kitchen for an old stone pub in the Yorkshire Dales. In cosy alcoves beneath low black beams, locals and walkers put the world to rights over pints of Black Sheep and Theakston ale opposite chalkboards listing Jonathan's daily menus: fishcakes with herb sauce, club sandwiches, fish and chips in beer batter, braised beef in Guinness. Cooking moves up a gear in the simple stylish dining room as in-season game, Wensleydale heifer beef and home-grown herbs and veg come into play. Loosen belts before delving into delicious Sunday lunch, which could be roast rib-eye of beef with Yorkshire pudding or Moroccan spiced chicken with couscous. (And a spoiling sticky toffee pudding with butterscotch sauce.) Up a twisting stair at the back, two simple but charming bedrooms lie — fresh, warm and cosy to come back to after you've walked the legs off the dogs. Visit the falls at West Burton — or Middleham for the horses on the gallops.

Rooms	2 doubles. From £75.
Meals	12pm-2.30pm; 6.30pm-9pm (9.30pm Fri & Sat). Main courses £8.95-£13.95 (lunch), £9.95-£18 (dinner); bar meals £4-£6.95.
Closed	3pm-6.30pm (7pm Sun) & Mon all day.
Directions	From A1, A684 for Bedale; on for 12 miles; pub at edge of the Market Place.

Jonathan & Michael Harrison
Sandpiper Inn,
Market Place, Leyburn DL8 5AT
Tel   01969 622206
Web   www.sandpiperinn.co.uk

Entry 786 Map 12

Yorkshire

The Blue Lion
East Witton

The Blue Lion has a big reputation locally; so big it followed our inspector round Yorkshire. Paul and Helen have mixed the traditions of a country pub with the elegance of a country house. This is a bustling place that serves superlative food and no one seems in a hurry to leave. Polished beer taps dispensing Yorkshire ale, stone-flagged floors, open fires, newspapers on poles, big settles, huge bunches of dried flowers hanging from beams, splashes of fresh ones. The two restaurants have boarded floors and shuttered Georgian windows, two coal fires and candles everywhere. Food is robust and heart-warming; local game, chargrilled beef fillet with shiraz sauce, braised Masala mutton with cumin sweet potato. East Witton has an interesting plague tale, Jervaulx Abbey is a mile away and there's an enclosed garden at the back.

Black Sheep Brewery
Masham

Masham is a hugely appealing market town in Wensleydale, and has the added attraction of being the home of the Black Sheep Brewery. The visitor centre and bistro are integral here, at this handsome stone shrine to good ale. The guided tour is fascinating, and you may whet your appetite with a glass or two of bitter before settling down to lunch in the restaurant. Food is straightforward and tasty, perhaps pork medallions with black pudding, or braised lamb shank with root vegetables in Emmerdale beer. The café makes its own cakes, the coffee and snacks are delicious; there's a 'pub', of course, with old oak floors, a wood-burning stove and all your favourite Black Sheep beers on tap. The spacious dining area on its mezzanine level has fabulous far-reaching views over the town to the hills beyond.

Meals	12pm–2pm; 7pm–9.15pm. Main courses £10.50–£25.
Closed	Open all day.
Directions	From Leyburn, A6108 for 3 miles to East Witton.

Meals	10am–4.30pm (6.30pm–9pm Thurs–Sat). Main courses £7.50–£16.95.
Closed	Evenings Sun–Weds.
Directions	Centre of Masham on A6108 between Ripon & Leyburn.

Paul & Helen Klein
The Blue Lion,
East Witton, Leyburn DL8 4SN
Tel   01969 624273
Web   www.thebluelion.co.uk

Entry 787 Map 12

Sue Theakston
Black Sheep Brewery,
Masham, Ripon HG4 4EN
Tel   01765 680101
Web   www.blacksheepbrewery.com

Entry 788 Map 12

Freemason's Arms
Nosterfield

The Freemason's whitewashed exterior may suggest an ordinary village pub but over the years an unusual assemblage of items has been added to the traditional décor: 1900s enamel advertisements, agricultural implements, Union flags, miners' lamps, a piano, and beams littered with old bank notes. It's a low-beamed place with interconnecting rooms, some flagged floors, two open fires, pew seating, soft lighting, candlelight – traditional, unspoilt, cosy and intriguing. It's also a darn good pub, with four local cask ales on offer and a blackboard to tantalise the hungry: partridge in rowan berry sauce, pink liver and onions with bacon. Kris Stephenson enjoys buying locally and delivers with flair. Eat in the bar, or at one of the bigger tables in the far room, perfect for dining. Just the spot after a day at the Ripon races.

Meals	12pm–2pm; 7pm–9pm. Main courses £8–£16.
Closed	3pm–6pm & Mon all day. Open all day Sun.
Directions	On B6267 for Masham, 2 miles off A1.

Kristian Stephenson
Freemason's Arms,
Nosterfield,
Ripon DL8 2QP
Tel 01677 470548

Entry 789 Map 12

The Nags Head
Pickhill

Three racecourses, golf and shooting nearby – sporting guests from all walks of life predominate at this popular country inn. Dark beams, snug fires and polished brass distinguish the tap room, where Black Sheep is on hand pump. Head for the lounge bar or mellow, picture-lined dining room if you wish to eat. If the formula holds few surprises it's because that's what customers have come to expect, and the Boynton family have been here over 30 years. That's not to damn with faint praise, only to acknowledge that generous and unaffected cooking using fresh local produce can be better than high-risk experimentation under the guise of innovation. Tuck into braised squid salad with smoked paprika and chilli, rare breed pork with roasted garlic juice, iced clementine parfait. Courteous staff add to the general sense of well-being.

Meals	12pm–2pm (2.30 Sun); 6pm–9.30pm (9pm Sun). Main courses £8.95–£17.95.
Closed	Open all day.
Directions	4 miles north of A1/A16 junc; 1 mile east of A1.

Edward & Janet Boynton
The Nags Head,
Pickhill, Thirsk YO7 4JG
Tel 01845 567391
Web www.nagsheadpickhill.co.uk

Entry 790 Map 12

Yorkshire

Fox & Hounds
Carthorpe

Part of this 200-year-old pub was once the village blacksmith's, serving the A1; now it draws locals and travellers in search of good food. Vincent and Helen have taken over from her parents, who first put this humble local on the culinary map. The L-shaped bar remains comfortably plush and cosy, with its warm red carpet, soothing classical music and glowing log fires, while the high-raftered dining room displays an interesting array of old smithy implements. Menus champion traditional British dishes cooked with skill and flair, with contemporary touches. There's ham hock terrine with homemade piccalilli, rack of lamb with redcurrant gravy, market-fresh fish… and a sticky ginger pudding served with orange sorbet and sugared nuts. Black Sheep Bitter is on tap and there are decent wines by the glass.

Meals	12pm-2pm; 7pm-9.30pm. Main courses £10-£15; set menu £13.95 & £15.95.
Closed	3pm-7pm & Mon.
Directions	Carthorpe is 4 miles south of Bedale & 1 mile west of the A1.

Vincent & Helen Taylor
Fox & Hounds,
Carthorpe, Bedale DL8 2LG
Tel   01845 567433
Web   www.foxandhoundscarthorpe.co.uk

Entry 791 Map 12

Yorkshire

Carpenter's Arms
Felixkirk

It's warm, cheerful, attractive and fun. Oriental fans by the fire and other oddities are dotted around the heavily beamed interior, along with pictures, books and antique carpentry tools. The panelled, barrel-fronted bar has three sections and bar stools, while rustic tables are cheerful with gingham. Beyond is the dining room, more formal with its white cloths, shining glassware and comfortable period dining chairs. A couple of Yorkshire beers are accompanied by some especially good wines by the glass and the menu is long: homemade Scottish salmon fishcakes with sorrel cream sauce, chicken breast stuffed with goat's cheese wrapped in prosciutto ham, five spice roasted duck – and simple baguettes at lunchtime. This mother and daughter team and their young staff add a bit of spice that makes a visit huge fun.

Meals	12pm-2pm; 6.30pm-9pm. Main courses £10.95-£16.50; bar meals £9.50.
Closed	3pm-6.30pm, Sun eve & Mon all day.
Directions	From Thirsk A170 to Sutton Bank; 1st left for Felixkirk. Pub 2 miles.

Karen & Linda Bumby
Carpenter's Arms,
Felixkirk, Thirsk YO7 2DP
Tel   01845 537369
Web   www.carpentersarmsfelixkirk.co.uk

Entry 792 Map 12

Yorkshire

Fox & Hounds
Goldsborough

Don't be fooled by the swirly carpets and artex walls of this small stone inn in the middle of nowhere. The food served is as delicious as you can be. Jason Davies brings London expertise, Sue Wren adds local charm and together they are producing some of the best pub meals in Yorkshire. Eat cosily by the fire or out in the garden. Wisely, the daily-changing menu restrains itself to half a dozen starters and mains, one pudding and a cheeseboard. Loving care is applied to fresh fish from the Whitby inshore fleet, game from the North York Moors, local meat and organic vegetables. Star turns include slow-roast belly pork and mash, and halibut with fennel. Pudding might be a chocolate terrine; cheese is served with Ampleforth apples and oatcakes. Small being so beautiful, it's wise to book.

Yorkshire

Wheatsheaf Inn
Egton

Unlike many pubs in this area, the friendly family-run Wheatsheaf has shirked expansion and held on to its character. It sits so modestly back from the wide main street you could pass it by; you would miss a good deal. The first entrance brings you into the main bar with low beams and comfy settles, but the main treat is the locals' bar, dominated by its Yorkshire range. This drinkers' den takes 16 at a push and is loved by walkers, fishermen and dogs. A range of cask ales ensures plenty of chatter, while hearty food is a draw, perhaps potted shrimps, fish stew, local partridge in season, sirloin steaks from local farmers. The river Esk at the foot of the steep hill is famous for fly-fishing so there's fishing memorabilia on the walls, and a few angling pictures. Egton is lovely – worth a linger.

Meals	12pm-1pm; 6.30pm-8pm; no food Sun eve. Main courses £9-£18.
Closed	1.30pm-6pm, Mon & Tues all day & Sun eve.
Directions	Village signed off A174 north of Whitby.

Meals	12pm-2pm (2.30pm Sun); 6pm-9pm; no food Sun eve or all day Mon. Main courses £8-£16.95; bar meals £8-£12.50.
Closed	2.30pm-5.30pm & Mon lunch. Open all day Sat & Sun.
Directions	Off A171; 6 miles west of Whitby.

Jason Davies & Sue Wren
Fox & Hounds,
Goldsborough,
Whitby YO21 3RX
Tel 01947 893372

Nigel & Elaine Pulling
Wheatsheaf Inn,
Egton,
Whitby YO21 1TZ
Tel 01947 895271

Entry 793 Map 13

Entry 794 Map 13

Golden Lion
Osmotherley

There's never a dull moment at the old stone inn overlooking the village green and market cross. It is run by young, thoughtful, hands-on owners and a friendly staff, bustles with booted walkers doing the Coast to Coast in the day, and hums with well-dressed diners at night. Arrive early to bag a seat in the brown-wood bar with pew bench seating, raised open fire and flickering candlelight. Nurse a pint of Timothy Taylor's Landlord or a first-class wine as you choose from a refreshingly simple menu. Nothing is over-ambitious: the chef has a modern take on "bourgeois dishes that stand the test of time", as one reviewer phrased it, while more contemporary offerings are free of flourish and fuss. The freshness of approach will have you smiling. Try fish soup or pâté with apricot relish, chicken Kiev or calves' liver with onion mash, perhaps a delectable crumble. If you're staying the night, fresh bedrooms have appealing colours, goose down duvets and super slate-floored showers. As for the village, it's as lovely and unspoilt as any in the North Yorkshire Moors National Park.

Rooms	3 twins/doubles. £80. Singles £60.
Meals	12pm-3pm; 6pm-9pm.
	Main courses £6.50-£14.50.
Closed	3pm-6pm. Open all day Sat & Sun.
Directions	Off A19 10 miles north of Thirsk & Northallerton.

Christie Connelly & Belal Radwan
Golden Lion,
6 West End, Osmotherley DL6 3AA

Tel	01609 883526
Web	www.goldenlionosmotherley.co.uk

Yorkshire

The Birch Hall
Beck Hole

Two small bars with a shop in between, unaltered for 70 years. Steep wooded hillsides and a stone bridge straddling the rushing river and, inside, a glimpse of life before World War II. The Big Bar has been beautifully repapered and has a little open fire, dominoes, darts and service from a hatch; benches come from the station waiting room at Beck Hole. The shop (postcards, traditional sweets) has its original fittings, as does the Little Bar with its handpumps for three cask ales. The original 19th-century enamel sign hangs above the door. Food is simple and authentic: local pies, baked stotties or baps, homemade scones and delicious beer cake. Steep steps take you to the terraced garden that looks over the inn and across the valley. Parking is scarce so show patience and courtesy in this old-fashioned place.

Meals	11am-3pm; 7.30pm-11pm; all day in summer. Sandwiches & pies from £2.
Closed	3pm-7.30pm, Mon eve & Tues in winter. Open all day in summer.
Directions	9 miles from Whitby towards Pickering.

Glenys & Neil Crampton
The Birch Hall,
Beck Hole, Goathland YO22 5LE

Tel	01947 896245
Web	www.beckhole.info

Entry 796 Map 13

Yorkshire

The Anvil Inn
Sawdon

The fact that this village is not on a bus route tells you one of two things; either you're in the back of beyond, or public transport is in a pretty state. Whichever; beat a path to this welcoming door, even if you have to hitch a lift. The Anvil was a working forge until the mid 1980s, the building is over 200 years old and the blacksmith's workshop – now the bar – forms a unusual centrepiece to a great little pub. Partner-chefs Mark and Alexandra have pulled the place up by its bootstraps and have created an environment you'll linger long in. Sit on an old oak pew or lounge in a leather tub chair with a pint of Daleside or Copper Dragon, and scan the tempting menu. Invention without pretension is the philosophy here, and thoughtfully executed, locally sourced food flows from the kitchen. A classic in the making.

Meals	12pm-2pm (3pm Sun); 6.30pm-9pm; no food Sun eve. Main courses £7.50-£9 (lunch), £9-£14.50 (dinner); Sunday lunch £7.75.
Closed	2.30pm-6.30pm & Mon.
Directions	Sawdon is signed north off A170 Thirsk road, 7 miles west of Scarborough.

Mark Wilson & Alexandra Warricker
The Anvil Inn, Main Street, Sawdon,
Scarborough YO13 9DY

Tel	01723 859896
Web	www.theanvilinnsawdon.co.uk

Entry 797 Map 13

Yorkshire

The Coachman Inn
Snainton

It's been an inn since 1776, and was the last staging post for the York mail coach before Scarborough. The bar remains charmingly old-fashioned in an Arts and Crafts way, its solid tables glowing in the firelight. There's warmth in the Irish welcome too, from James, Rita and Kay, and there's nothing dated about the food. Expect modern dishes from a bright young chef; even the breads, chutneys and puddings are homemade and the local ingredients – game in season, fish from Scarborough and Whitby – are impeccable. Dine elegantly on beetroot risotto with crispy parsnip chips, and roast loin of pork with apple, lemon and thyme stuffing. The lovely dining room, running the depth of the building, is broken up by double doors and gingham sofas, its Georgian windows overlooking a pretty side garden.

Meals	12pm-2pm (2.30pm Sun); 6pm-9pm (9.30pm weekends). Main courses £9-£14.50.
Closed	2pm-6pm. Sun eve; Mon & Tues lunch.
Directions	From A170 Pickering-Scarborough road, onto B1258 for Malton.

James & Rita Osbourne
The Coachman Inn,
Snainton, Scarborough YO13 9PL
Tel   01723 859231
Web   www.coachmaninn.co.uk

Entry 798 Map 13

Yorkshire

The Blacksmith's Arms
Lastingham

Low black beams, glowing fires, timeworn saddles, a ghost called Ella and a pint of Daleside Blond. It's a rural dream. You almost slide down to the lovely little village, so deep is it sunk into the valley. The low, rambling, dimly-lit pub has provided shelter and comfort to monks, shepherds and travellers since 1693; now it is visited by gamekeepers, walkers and church enthusiasts; St Mary's (1030) sits next door and, rumour has it, a secret tunnel runs between the two. Once an impoverished priest with 13 children ran both pub and church, to the dismay of his bishop; the current landlord is approved of by all. The little dining rooms are not quite as atmospheric as the bar with its lit range, but this is a great place for a gossip, a pint and hearty traditional food – lamb casserole, Yorkshire hotpot, cod in lager batter.

Meals	12pm-2pm; 7pm-9pm. Main courses £7.95-£12.95.
Closed	In winter, Mon-Thu 2.30pm-6pm & Tues lunch. Open all day Fri, Sat & Sun.
Directions	Left off A170 Kirkbymoorside to Pickering road.

Peter & Hilary Trafford
The Blacksmith's Arms, Front Street,
Lastingham, Pickering YO62 6TL
Tel   01751 417247
Web   www.blacksmithslastingham.co.uk

Entry 799 Map 13

The White Swan Inn
Pickering

Victor swapped the City for the North Yorkshire Moors and this old coaching inn; the place oozes comfort and style. Duck in through the front door to a cosy panelled tap room serving real Yorkshire ales, with smart country furniture, fine wines and eager young staff. Best of all is the dining room and and you'll find heaven on a plate when you dig into supper. Try seared, hand-dived king scallops with air-dried ham, Levisham mutton with Irish cabbage, poached rhubarb on toasted brioche and rhubarb ice cream. Menus change monthly and 80% of the ingredients are locally sourced, with meat coming from Levisham's celebrated Ginger Pig. Breakfast is just as good, and inspired one traveller to write a poem, now framed. Bedrooms — some cool and chic, others traditional — come with pleasing colours, warm radiators, elegant fabrics, antique beds, maybe an armchair and a view of the pretty courtyard. Don't miss the beamed club room for roaring fire, board games and an honesty bar. Castle Howard is nearby, the moors are wild and the steam railway is fun.

Rooms	21: 14 doubles, 4 twins/doubles, 3 suites. £145–£250. Singles from £110.
Meals	12pm-2pm; 6.45pm-9pm. Main courses £11.95–£19.50; Sunday lunch £15.95 & £21.95.
Closed	Open all day.
Directions	From North, A170 to Pickering. Entering town, left at traffic lights, then 1st right, Market Place. On left.

Victor & Marion Buchanan
The White Swan Inn,
Market Place, Pickering YO18 7AA

Tel	01751 472288
Web	www.white-swan.co.uk

Entry 800 Map 13

Yorkshire

The Plough Inn
Fadmoor

It's been a welcoming refuge from the wintry moors for years. Catch sight of it from up high, smoke curling from the stack, and you feel irresistibly drawn. Inside the Plough all is as warm and reassuring as could be; the onetime row of cottage dwellings feels rambling but contained, the several small rooms immaculate with gleaming wood, rosy upholstery and rugs on seagrass floors. The food is a major draw and there are six dining areas in all, the nicest being half-panelled. All have open fires. Dishes range from cod and pancetta fishcakes with sweet chilli and ginger dressing to a mouthwatering steak, kidney and Guinness suet pudding; the soups are very good, and we liked the look of the chocolate and hazelnut terrine. Spill outside to bikes, boots, dogs and a pretty view of the village green in summer.

Meals	12pm-1.45pm; 6.30pm-8.45pm (7pm-8.45pm Sun). Main courses £8.95-£14.95.
Closed	2.30pm-6.30pm (7pm Sun).
Directions	From A170 Helmsley to Kirkbymoorside, left towards Fadmoor.

Neil & Rachael Nicholson
The Plough Inn,
Main Street, Fadmoor,
Kirkbymoorside YO62 7HY
Tel   01751 431515

Entry 801 Map 13

Yorkshire

The Black Swan
Oldstead

In glorious isolation, tucked back from the road, the Black Swan goes back 400 years. The Banks family has farmed for almost as long, now they've transformed the sorry old boozer. Open fires glow, there are stone flags and beams, wooden floors and mix 'n' match furniture; it's a cheerful and comforting space. Knowing a thing or two about food, they source their ingredients locally, the meat coming from nearby farms; bread and puddings are homemade. Old-fashioned salt beef hash with fried egg and homemade brown sauce makes a scrumptious starter; honey roast duck breast with sticky port wine figs, celeriac purée and bobby beans may follow. Take a pint of Copper Dragon to the blossom trees and gaze on the Wolds, then don your boots and stride off from the door. Walking notes are thoughtfully provided.

Meals	12pm-2pm (2.30pm Sun); 6pm-9pm. Main courses £8.50-£14.50.
Closed	3pm-6pm; Mon in winter. Open all day Sat & Sun.
Directions	A19 from Thirsk; left to Thirkleby & Coxwold, then left for Byland Abbey; follow signs left for Oldstead.

Banks Family
The Black Swan,
Oldstead, Coxwold YO61 4BL
Tel   01347 868387
Web   www.blackswanoldstead.co.uk

Entry 802 Map 13

The Abbey Inn
Byland Abbey

Fifty paces from the door, majestic Byland Abbey stands defiant after 900 years. It was one of the first Gothic buildings to rise in the North. Yet in 1536 Henry VIII ordered the dissolution of the monasteries and over the years locals stripped its roof and looted its stone; still it shines. As for the inn, it dates to 1845 and once served as a farmhouse for the monks of Ampleforth. Now run by English Heritage it's a perfect place with interiors that mix tradition, eccentricity and elegance delightfully. Rambling, characterful bars have big fireplaces and carved oak seats on stone flags or polished boards; curtains are drawn across old doorways, and daily papers hang on poles. Food is British-based and interesting: venison with winter berry sauce; griddled, peppered rib-eye steak with potato wedges. Bedrooms upstairs sweep you back to long-lost days: beamed ceilings, panelled windows, fancy beds, a sofa if there's room. Breakfast is cooked to order and brought to your room. Downstairs, doors open onto a terrace that gives way to sprawling lawns. Bring your walking boots: the setting is stunning.

Rooms	3: 2 doubles, 1 suite. From £105.
Meals	12pm-2.30pm (3pm Sun); 6pm-8.30pm. Main courses £9-£15 (lunch), £11-£17 (dinner); Sunday lunch £16.50 & £21.
Closed	3pm-6pm; Sun eve & Mon lunch.
Directions	From A1(M) junc. 49, A168 for Thirsk, then A19 for York. Left for Coxwold after 2 miles. There, left for Byland Abbey. Opposite abbey.

Paul Tatham
The Abbey Inn,
Byland Abbey, Coxwold YO61 4BD

Tel	01347 868204
Web	www.bylandabbeyinn.com

Yorkshire

The Star Inn
Harome

You know you've hit the jackpot as soon as you walk into The Star – low ceilings, flagged floors, gleaming oak, flickering fire, a fat cat patrolling the bar. Andrew and Jacquie arrived in 1996 and the Michelin star in 2002. It's been a formidable turnaround for the 14th-century inn yet the brochure simply says: "He cooks, and she looks after you"... and how! Andrew's food is rooted in Yorkshire tradition, refined with French flair and written in plain English on ever-changing menus that brim with local produce (do book). Risotto of partridge with black trumpet mushrooms, mutton and caper suet pudding, gutsy desserts and a 'cheeseboard of the week'. There's a bar with a Sunday papers-and-pint feel, a coffee loft in the eaves, and their own deli across the road... even the schnapps is homemade. Exceptional.

Yorkshire

The Appletree
Marton

She chooses the wines and he cooks: Melanie and TJ are an unstoppable team. Locals pile in for pints of locally brewed Suddaby's, while the food-conscious seek out the deli counter for its breads, chutneys, chocolates and terrines. TJ's menus reflect the seasons and change every day. Tuck into Yorkshire blue cheese and walnut tart, fillet of black bream with creamed leeks and red pepper oils, steamed orange, apricot and nut pudding. Herbs come from the garden, fruits from the orchard, there are farm-reared meats... expect intense flavours with modern British eclecticism thrown in. Bliss in summer to relax on the orchard patio with a jug of Pimms. In the winter, it's cosy and comforting indoors: a beamed bar with candles and log fires, and a farmhouse-style dining room. At busy times you'd be wise to book.

Meals	11.30pm-2pm; 6.30pm-9.30pm (12pm-6pm Sun). Main courses £13.95-£22.50.
Closed	Monday. Open all day Tue-Sun.
Directions	From Thirsk, A170 towards Scarborough. Through Helmsley, then right, signed Harome. Inn in village.

Meals	12pm-2pm; 6pm-9.30pm (6.30pm-9pm Sun). Main courses £8.50-£17; snacks £3.50-£6.
Closed	2.30pm-6pm (3pm-6.30pm Sun), Mon & Tues all day.
Directions	2 miles from A170 between Kirkbymoorside & Pickering.

Andrew & Jacquie Pern
The Star Inn,
Harome, Helmsley YO62 5JE
Tel 01439 770397
Web www.thestaratharome.co.uk

Trajan & Melanie Drew
The Appletree,
Marton, Kirkbymoorside YO62 6RD
Tel 01751 431457
Web www.appletreeinn.co.uk

Entry 804 Map 13

Entry 805 Map 13

Yorkshire

The Grapes
Great Habton

In an unremarkable Yorkshire Wolds village, an unremarkable pub. Take heart, step inside. Adam and Katie have plans, when cash allows, to spruce up the exterior; in the meantime, enjoy what they've achieved in the short time they've been here. They deserve support in breathing life so beautifully into an old boozer in a sleepy village. Now there's dominoes, cricket, darts, a crackling fire to greet you, and exposed stone walls and fresh flowers to cheer up the old swirly carpets and retro moquette upholstery. And then there's Adam's cooking, which is modern and inventive. Meat, fish and vegetables are regionally sourced, and everything is made from scratch. May breast of pigeon on truffle mash with sloe gin jus inspire you! Add well-kept Bank's Bitter and Jennings Lakeland Ale, and you know you've struck gold.

Meals	12pm-2pm; 6.30pm-8.30pm (12pm-8.30pm Sun). Main courses £8.50-£14.50; Sunday lunch £9.95 & £12.95.
Closed	3pm-6pm & Mon.
Directions	Village signed off B1257 Malton-Helmsley road & A169 between Malton & Pickering.

Adam Myers & Katie Martin
The Grapes,
Great Habton, Malton YO17 6TU

Tel	01653 669166
Web	www.thegrapes-inn.co.uk

Entry 806 Map 13

Yorkshire

The Stone Trough Inn
Kirkham Abbey

A great find: pubby and welcoming, with fabulous food. The bar has low beams, stone walls, roaring log fires and cosy areas for privacy. Much care goes into running this place. The range of beers and wines is excellent, the staff are delightful, and the food people travel for. Adam Richardson is a talented chef, conjuring up platefuls of pressed game and parsnip terrine, halibut on smoked salmon risotto with lemon butter sauce, roast Flaxton lamb with tomatoes and puy lentils, and hot chocolate brownies. You choose from two menus, one for the bar, one for the restaurant. There's also a games room with pool, a fruit machine, dominoes and a TV. On warm days take your pint of Malton Golden Chance onto the front terrace that overlooks the gentle Derwent valley, then stroll down to Kirkham Abbey. The countryside is glorious.

Meals	12pm-2pm; 6.30pm-8.30pm; Restaurant: 6.45pm-9.30pm Tues-Sat; 12pm-2.15 Sun. Main courses £10.95-£18.95; bar meals £7.95-£14.50.
Closed	2.30-6pm & Mon all day. Open all day Sun.
Directions	Between York & Scarborough, 1.5 miles off A64 near Castle Howard.

Adam & Sarah Richardson
The Stone Trough Inn,
Kirkham Abbey,
Whitwell on the Hill, York YO60 7JS

Tel	01653 618713
Web	www.stonetroughinn.co.uk

Entry 807 Map 13

Yorkshire

The Blacksmiths Inn
Westow

All sorts come here: smart young farmers, ladies who lunch, merry families and folk in tweeds. It's on the restaurant side of pub, attractive, understated and buzzy. There's a long, L-shaped bar with the short leg used by local drinkers. The other bit is spacious, flagged to the side, set with big old pine tables, candles and fresh flowers, and a well-fed log burner in a magnificent inglenook. The linked dining rooms are modern Yorkshire-flagged with splashes of red tartan carpet. There's a dedication to serving fresh seasonal food: cream of pumpkin soup with homemade bread and coriander oil, slow cooked honey glazed belly pork with braised savoy cabbage and caramelised apples, garlic confit duck leg with spinach and pickled beetroot, and pan-fried rib-eye steaks with fat chips, field mushrooms and roast tomatoes. A village gem.

Meals	12pm-2pm (4pm Sun); 5.30pm-9pm; no food Sun eve. Main courses £8-£17.95.
Closed	Mon all day, Tues lunch, 2pm-5.30pm. Open all day Sat & Sun.
Directions	A64 for Malton; right for Kirkham Abbey, then Westow; on main street.

Jonathan Cliff
The Blacksmiths Inn,
Westow,
Malton YO60 7NE
Tel   01653 618365

Entry 808 Map 13

Yorkshire

Bay Horse Inn
Burythorpe

Long, low and inviting, the old Bay Horse is the flagship of Real Yorkshire Pubs. With 18 months spent running a French chalet behind her, Claire has swapped a skiing clientele for a horsy one, and visitors and locals come for the food. Simple, flavoursome English dishes are the order of the day, so expect oak-smoked salmon with brown bread, lemon and capers, fillet of beef with creamed leeks, mash and red wine sauce, and bread and butter pudding with roast plums. Meats and cheese are local, fish is from Hartlepool. Warm colours are Farrow & Ball, 'scrubbed' pine tables are matched with comfortable leather dining chairs, and smart light oak floors merge into fine stone flags. A small fire burns in the alcove by the door and there are books and newspapers to browse. It's friendly, young and civilised.

Meals	12pm-2pm; 6.30pm-9.30pm (12pm-8pm Sun). Main courses £7.95-£14.95; sandwiches from £3.95.
Closed	3pm-6pm, Tues lunch & all day Mon. Open all day Sun.
Directions	Kirkham Priory on right, sharp left towards Langton; 3 miles; signs for Burythorpe for 1.25 miles.

Claire Biggs
Bay Horse Inn,
Burythorpe, Malton YO17 9LJ
Tel   01653 658302
Web   www.bayhorseburythorpe.co.uk

Entry 809 Map 13

Yorkshire

Pipe & Glass Inn
South Dalton

In the elegant estate village of Dalton, rejoicing in one of the highest church spires in the Wolds, is this 16th-century inn. The front garden has classic parkland vistas, the back is lushly lawned, the interiors glow with well-being. Turn right for a pubby pint, left to collapse into a leather sofa in front of the fire and plot a meal. Eating and lounging areas are woody and stylish, window seats have chocolate cushions, customers cluck with pleasure as they head to their tables. Kate, front of house, and James, chef, cut their teeth at the Star at Harome, so the food is tuned to the best of local, seasonal and humanely reared. The combinations are adventurous – terrine of hare, 'coq au vin' of guinea fowl with wild garlic mash – the website shares the recipes and the wines come from small producers and are listed by style.

Yorkshire

The White Horse Inn (Nellie's)
Beverley

You could pass the White Horse by: its brick front and old pub sign do not stand out on busy Hengate. Inside is more beguiling – be transported back 200 years. (The building itself is even older.) Known as 'Nellie's', it's a wonderfully atmospheric little place; your eyes will take a while to become accustomed, so dim are the gas-lit passages. Little has changed in these small rooms with their old quarry tiles, bare boards, smoke-stained walls and open fires. Furniture is a mix of high-backed settles, padded benches, marble-topped cast-iron tables, old pictures and a gas-lit, pulley-controlled chandelier. Food is straightforward and good value: sandwiches, bangers and mash, steak and ale pie, spotted dick with custard. The only concession to the modern age is the games room at the back with a pool table and darts.

Meals	12pm-2pm (4pm Sun); 6.30pm-9.30pm; no food Sun eve. Main courses £8.95-£16.95; Sunday roast £10.95.
Closed	3pm-6.30pm & Mon. Open all day Sun.
Directions	Village signed off A164 & B1248, 5 miles north west of Beverley.

Meals	10.30am-5pm; no food Sun. Main courses £4.50-£5.50.
Closed	Open all day.
Directions	Off North Bar, close to St Mary's Church.

James Mackenzie & Kate Boroughs
Pipe & Glass Inn,
West End, South Dalton HU17 7PN
Tel   01430 810246
Web www.pipeandglass.co.uk

Entry 810 Map 13

Anna
The White Horse Inn (Nellie's),
22 Hengate, Beverley HU17 8BN
Tel   01482 861973
Web www.e-hq.co.uk/nellies

Entry 811 Map 13

Yorkshire

St Vincent Arms
Sutton-upon-Derwent

Humming with happy chat, the public bar is the heart of the place, sporting panelled walls lined with brass plates, warm red curtains and tartan carpet. There are up to eight cask beers to choose from and no background music or electronic gadgetry – just an old radiogram. To the left of the lobby is a smaller, snugger bar decorated in pale green with matching tartan carpet; this leads into several attractive small eating areas. Food ranges from sandwiches or smoked haddock risotto to scallops in garlic butter, mussels (recommended), steak au poivre, lobster, roast belly pork with pak choi, and sticky toffee pudding. If you're not into ale there are several wines by the glass. The St Vincent Arms is a great little local and the staff seem to enjoy themselves as much as the customers – you can't ask for more.

Yorkshire

The Blue Bell
York

Unlike most city pubs, the Blue Bell is as it's always been. Its narrow brick frontage on Fossgate, not far from The Shambles and open-air market, is quite easy to miss; once you've found the old pub, you step into a corridor that leads through to the back. On the right, a tiny bar with red-tiled floor and high ceilings, wooden panelling, Edwardian stained glass, cast-iron and tiled fireplace, settle seating on two sides and iron-legged tables. 'Ladies only' used to be confined to the narrow back lounge; now its red carpet is trod on by all. Original fireplaces, polished panelling, interesting old pictures and general clutter… all this and a terrific range of cask beers – at least seven – and wines too. No hot food but hearty sandwiches at lunchtime. Don't miss the annual beer festival in November.

Meals	12pm-2pm; 7pm-9.30pm. Main courses £8-£16.50.
Closed	3pm-6pm (7pm Sun).
Directions	On B1228, 8 miles SE of York.

Meals	11am-2.30pm; 4pm-8pm (11am-8pm Sun). Sandwiches £1.90.
Closed	Open all day.
Directions	In York city centre.

Simon Hopwood
St Vincent Arms, Main Street,
Sutton-upon-Derwent,
York YO41 4BN

Tel	01904 608349
Web	www.stvincentarms.co.uk

Entry 812 Map 13

Jim Hardie
The Blue Bell,
53 Fossgate,
York YO1 9TF

Tel	01904 654904

Entry 813 Map 13

Dawnay Arms
Newton on Ouse

The script on the lintel reads 1778. This stately Georgian building has been rescued from dereliction by Kerry Ward and Martel Smith, who have taken one step sideways from their Leeds brasserie. Now the old boozer in the picture-postcard village is a shrine to modernity. Stone flagged floors and massive fireplaces have been kept, and chunky tables (constructed from timber pilfered from a post office in Durham) and old church pews sit stylishly in a pale palette, broken by splashes of colour from funky cushions and modern art in chubby rococo frames. Faultless food scrupulously sourced flows from a kitchen run by maestro Martel – perhaps steak and kidney pudding with root vegetables and ale sauce, and treacle tart with butterscotch ice cream. There's a glorious riverside garden for lazy summer days.

Fountaine Inn
Linton in Craven

Imagine a village green with a stone bridge and a babbling stream – such is the setting for this 17th-century inn. In spite of some serious sprucing up last year, the Fountaine remains a classic Yorkshire village pub with glowing coal fires, slate floors, curved settles, old beams and cosy corners spread between interconnecting rooms. Weekend walkers arrive in droves for Black Sheep and local Litton ales, all day thick-cut sandwiches and traditional burgers with relish and pickles. Wish to linger longer? Then settle into the dining room for a plateful of Kilnsey smoked trout or brisket beef cooked in port wine gravy. The green is well used in summer; for a seat and shade bag one of the smart benches and brollies out front. Note that the Tempest Arms in Elslack and the Mason Arms in Cumbria are under the same excellent ownership.

Meals	12pm-2.30pm; 6pm-9.30pm (12pm-6pm Sun); no food Sun eve. Main courses £7.95-10.95 (lunch), £9.95-£16.95 (dinner); Sunday lunch £17.95.
Closed	3pm-6pm & Mon. Open all day Sat.
Directions	A19 from York towards Thirsk; left at Shipton following signs to Beningbrough Hall.

Meals	12pm-9pm Main courses £7.50-£13.99; sandwiches from £4.95.
Closed	Open all day.
Directions	Village signed off B6265 south of Grassington.

	Kerry Ward Dawnay Arms, Newton on Ouse, York YO30 2BR
Tel	01347 848345
Web	www.dawnayarms.co.uk

	Chris Gregson Fountaine Inn, Linton in Craven, Grassington BD23 5HJ
Tel	01756 752210
Web	www.fountaineinnatlinton.co.uk

Entry 814 Map 12

Entry 815 Map 12

Yorkshire

Ye Old Sun Inn
Colton

Smack in the centre of a pretty Wolds village stands a spick and span pub. Recently rejuvenated by new young owners, it reveals a refreshing mix of old and new. Eighteenth-century beams and rustic brick fireplaces guarding coal fires combine with more luxurious treats: sumptuous fabrics at leaded windows, tapestry cushions on old oak seats. Relax with the papers and a pint of Timothy Taylor's as you ponder lunch; the menu is dedicated to small producers. Tapas might include two miniature Yorkshire puddings, a slab of ham hock terrine and a pretty pile of black pudding dressed with apples. Haddock comes with fat chips and homemade tartare sauce. There's a tiny deli round the back bursting with local goodies, cookery demos and charity evenings draw the locals and the big garden has long views across fields.

From adventurous gastropubs to village locals, the liveliest pub kitchens are placing an emphasis on British tradition.

Meals	12-2pm (4pm Sun); 6.30-9.30pm. Main courses £5.50-£15.50 (lunch), £11.95-£14.95 (dinner); Sunday lunch £10-£17.
Closed	3pm-6pm, Sun eve & Mon.
Directions	A64 for York; follow signs to Colton.

SPECIAL AWARD
see pages 18-19

Community pub

Ashley & Kelly McCarthy
Ye Old Sun Inn, Main Street,
Colton, Tadcaster LS24 8EP
Tel   01904 744261
Web   www.yeoldsuninn.co.uk

Blackwell Ox Inn
Sutton-on-the-Forest

On the main road that runs through the trim Georgian village of Sutton on the Forest, built in 1823 as a house for a certain Mrs Shepherd, the Blackwell Ox Inn has, in recent years, doubled in stature and size. The interior now is more country hotel than village pub, the walls bedecked with hunting prints and the odd sampler, the dining rooms spruce with cushioned window seats, stiff white napery and soft lights at night. Steven Holding, an enthusiastic young chef of some pedigree, changes the menu daily and is passionate about the rustic flavours of south-western France. Salt cod fritters in beer batter come with aïoli and smoked paprika; monkfish with braised oxtail bourguignon; warm chocolate pudding with clotted cream and salted caramel. The North Yorkshire cheeses are delicious, the bread crusty and homemade, the wines fashionably listed by style. Handsome bedrooms, two with pretty views, sport generous bathrooms and every hotel comfort (Molton Brown toiletries, flat-screen TVs) while breakfasts are as first-class as all the rest.

Rooms	5 twins/doubles. £95-£110. Singles £65-£95.
Meals	12pm-2pm (4pm Sun); 6pm-9.30pm; no food Sun eve. Main courses £8.95-£16.75; bar meals £3.95-£12.95; set menu £10.50 & £13.50.
Closed	2pm-5pm. Open all day Sun.
Directions	Off B1363 7 miles north of York.

	Steven Holding Blackwell Ox Inn, Huby Road, Sutton-on-the-Forest, York YO61 1DT
Tel	01347 810328
Web	www.blackwelloxinn.co.uk

Entry 817 Map 12

The Durham Ox
Crayke

At the picturesque top of the Grand Old Duke of York's hill is an immaculate L-shaped bar of flagstones and rose walls, worn leather armchairs and settles, carved panelling and big fires. There are two more bars to either side, and a dapper, yellow-walled and wine-themed restaurant that draws all and sundry out for lunch. Chalkboards above the stone fireplace and monthly menus list cullen skink with poached egg, chargrilled Mount Grace fillet steak with hand-cut chips, Portobello mushrooms and Yorkshire Blue butter, and treacle tart with egg custard. The Bar Bites menu and the Sunday roasts are inevitably popular. Priced bin-end bottles line the old dresser in the bar, there's a coffee shop serving homemade truffles, a garden with a marquee for summer frivolity, and jazz on Thursdays. Four delightfully quirky rooms in the former farmworkers' cottages have original quarry tile floors, exposed stone and mellow brick walls, beams and brass beds; the far-reaching views across the valley are stunning; in the summer, flowers burst from stone troughs. This is peace and quiet at its best.

Rooms	8 doubles. £100–£140. Singles £70.
Meals	12pm–2.30pm; 6pm–9.30pm (10pm Sat; 8.30pm Sun). Main courses £8.95–£18.95; bar meals from £6.95; Sunday roast from £11.95.
Closed	3pm–6pm. Open all day Sat & Sun.
Directions	Exit right off A19 York–Thirsk. Through Easingwold to Crayke.

Michael Ibbotson
The Durham Ox,
Crayke, York YO61 4TE
Tel   01347 821506
Web   www.thedurhamox.com

Entry 818 Map 12

The General Tarleton

Ferrensby

Chef-patron John Topham and wife Claire run the old coaching inn with an easy charm. The rambling, low-beamed, nooked and crannied brasserie-bar mixes rough stone walls with smooth ones, there are shiny oak tables and a roaring fire. You have Black Sheep Bitter on hand pump, a range of well-chosen wines by the glass and unfussy dishes based on the finest local produce. Here the menu ranges from classic fish soup and ham shank terrine with Cumberland sauce to chargrilled venison with buffalo blue cheese polenta, seafood thermidor and brilliant fish and chips. There's dark chocolate timbale for grown-ups, banana split for children, delightful staff and a great buzz. The cosy-chic dining room, formerly a stables, displays white napery and a grown-up menu to match. For al fresco dining on balmy days there's a new terraced garden. If you are tempted to stay, the comfortable, well-equipped rooms are in a purpose-built extension and flaunt the best of contemporary. And you'll wake to a breakfast as delicious as all the rest.

Rooms	14 twins/doubles. From £120. Singles from £108.
Meals	12pm-2pm; 6pm-9.15pm (9.30pm Sat). Main courses £9.50-£17.95.
Closed	3pm-6pm.
Directions	From A1 junc. 48; A6055 for Knaresborough; pub on right in Ferensby.

John Topham
The General Tarleton,
Boroughbridge Road, Ferrensby,
Knaresborough HG5 0QB

Tel	01423 340284
Web	www.generaltarleton.co.uk

Yorkshire

Worth a visit

820 The Lister Arms Hotel Malham, Skipton BD23 4DB
01729 830330
A jewel in the glorious Dales, with a friendly bar for Thwaites ales and malt whiskies, and hearty home-cooked pub grub. A cobbled terrace for summer, warming wood-burners for winter.

821 Queens Arms Litton, Grassington BD23 5QJ
01756 770208
Glorious walks onto the moors and along the river from this homely 16th-century Dales inn. Head here for warming fires, home-brewed ales, hot food, stunning views.

822 The George Kirk Gill, Hubberholme BD23 5EJ
01756 760223
Sympathetically updated but still fairly basic Dales pub with good beer and traditional pub food. J B Priestley's favourite watering hole – he's buried in the church opposite.

823 The Moorcock Inn Garsdale Head, Hawes LA10 5PU
01969 667488
Wild and remote, crouching in an isolated moorland spot at the top end of Wensleydale. There's a quirky stylishness that is striking in such an unworldly setting; plus local ales and homemade pub grub.

824 Charles Bathurst Inn Arkengarthdale, Langthwaite DL11 6EN
01748 884567
Retreat after a bracing walk to the Codys' wonderful inn tucked high above Swaledale. Rustic pine-furnished interiors; hearty dishes of local produce; pints of Black Sheep.

825 The Red Lion Inn Langthwaite, Arkengarthdale, Richmond DL11 6RE
01748 884218
A cluster of stone dwellings so perfectly huddled that film companies flock. All is carpeted and cosy with wall seats around cast-iron tables and a small snug. Black Sheep and Riggwelter are served in admirable condition, along with pies and sausage rolls.

826 Hack & Spade Whashton, Richmond DL11 7JL
01748 823721
Good seasonal food, Black Sheep beers and bin-end wines at this soft stone pub in an off-the-beaten-track hamlet. Log fires and long views across fertile farming country.

827 Buck Inn Thornton Watlass, Bedale HG4 4AH
01677 422461
Archetypal village pub next to the village green (and perilously close to the cricket pitch). Ever-changing range of local ales and wide ranging menu. Homely, traditional interior, summer barbecues, children's play area.

828 The Fox & Hounds Sinnington, Pickering YO62 6SQ
01751 431577
Old coaching inn in a sleepy backwater below the North York Moors. Expect homely panelled bars with open fires and well-presented modern pub food.

829 The Three Hares Main Street, Bilbrough, York YO23 3PH
01937 832128
16th-Century pub in an unspoilt rural setting (roaming sheep eyeball you as you sip your wine) with a revamped interior and an interesting, balanced menu strong on seasonal produce.

830 The Fat Cat 23 Alma Street, Sheffield S3 8SA
01142 494861
In Sheffield and desperate for a pint? Follow signs to the Kelham Island Museum and this bustling backstreet boozer. Great home-brewed beers and six guest ales await. Good value pub grub.

831 The Cricket Inn Penny Lane, Totley, Sheffield S17 3AZ
0114 236 5256
Smack beside the cricket pitch, down a muddy single-track lane, the old boozer has a new look. A shrine to Farrow & Ball, with stone flags, oak boards, huge fires in the grate and ambitious menus. Reports please.

Worth a visit

Photo: istockphoto.com

Wales

Ship Inn
Red Wharf Bay

The boatmen still walk across from the estuary with their catch. Inside The Ship, fires roar in several fireplaces and bars share nautical bits and bobs. There are pews and benches and bare stone walls, and huge blackboards where the daily specials change almost by the hour. At night, the menu proffers Welsh seafood based on the best the boats have brought in: grilled turbot served with lemon and seasonal vegetables; dressed crab. But the old Ship is so much more – a family-friendly public house where, for 30 years, regulars and visitors have been enjoying great ales and freshly prepared food, from 'brechdanau' – sandwiches – to 'pwdin'. Fine Welsh cheeses, too. These lovely people are as proud of their hospitality as they are of their language – and the vast sea and sand views from the front terraces are inspiring.

Ye Olde Bulls Head
Beaumaris

This was a favourite haunt of Samuel Johnson and Charles Dickens and now attracts drinkers and foodies like bees to clover. In the rambling, snug-alcoved bar there's draught Bass on offer, while in the contemporary brasserie in the stables you have a choice of ten wines by the glass to match your sarnies or Indian-spiced spatchcock poussin. Spot the ancient weaponry and old ducking stool, which contrasts with the sophisticated remodelling of the restaurant upstairs under hammer-beamed eaves. Here, Welsh dishes are designed around seafood from the Menai Strait, and as much beef, lamb and game as the chefs can find on the island. The results: sticky short rib of Welsh black beef, breast of duck with purple figs, and fillets of local brill, seasoned as required with Anglesey sea salt. Service comes with warmth and charm.

Meals	12pm-2.30pm; 6pm-9pm (5-9.30pm Sat; 12pm-9pm Sun). Main courses £7.95-£17.95; bar meals £4.75-£12.95.
Closed	Open all day.
Directions	Off B5025, north of Pentraeth.

Meals	12pm-2pm; 6pm-9pm. Main courses £7.95-£14.80.
Closed	Open all day.
Directions	Castle Street is main street in Beaumaris.

	Neil Kenneally Ship Inn, Red Wharf Bay LL75 8RJ
Tel	01248 852568
Web	www.shipinnredwharfbay.co.uk

	David Robertson Ye Olde Bulls Head, Castle Street, Beaumaris LL58 8AP
Tel	01248 810329
Web	www.bullsheadinn.co.uk

Entry 832 Map 6

Entry 833 Map 6

Carmarthenshire

Angel Inn
Salem

A warm, candlelit, unselfconsciously styled grotto of a place. Former Welsh chef of the year Rod Peterson rules the kitchen, but this isn't one of those restaurants masquerading as a pub; you'd feel as happy sinking into the sofa with a malty pint of Rev James. The bar has a quirky, homely charm — squishy sofas covered in throws, fairylights on corkscrew branches, the odd pot plant or Art Deco mirror — while the dining room is a revelation, its dark glossy floors broken up by lovely antique dressers and carved gothic arches. Staff are smart and attentive and the food divine; in the bar, quiche of duck and lovage with apricot chutney; in the restaurant, braised shoulder of Welsh lamb with a pulse ragout. No designer vegetables here: portions are hearty and satisfying. Enchanting in every way.

Carmarthenshire

The Brunant Arms
Caio

Miles from anywhere, the Vale of Cothi is a place of mystery and legend. In this lovely time-warp village, the pub feels warm, cared-for, cosy and at the community's heart. Owners David and Michael say, modestly, they do "good pub food", but what you get is succulent Welsh black rump steak marinated in red wine and local seasonal game; dive into rabbit stew with herb dumplings or venison steak with pork, peppercorn and chocolate sauce! Expect delightful service, flickering candlelight and proper meals for children; walkers drop by for ploughman's and steaming bowls of cawl. In the bar are traditional tables and chairs, a couple of high-backed settles, logs in the grate, books and bagatelle and five ales on tap, perhaps Caio-brewed Jacobi Red Squirrel. And a lovely little garden with village views.

Meals	12.15pm-2pm; 7pm-9pm; restaurant evenings only. Main courses £9.95-£18.50; bar meals £4.25-£13.95.
Closed	Tues lunch, Mon & Sun all day & 2 weeks early Jan.
Directions	Off the A40 towards Talley, 3 miles north of Llandeilo.

Meals	12pm-2pm; 6pm-9pm. Main courses £7.95-£12.25.
Closed	2.30pm-6pm. Open all day weekends.
Directions	Signed from A482 midway between Lampeter & Llanwrda.

Liz Smith
Angel Inn,
Salem,
Llandeilo SA19 7LY
Tel 01558 823394

David Waterhouse
& Michael Edwards
The Brunant Arms,
Caio, Llanwrda SA19 8RD
Tel 01558 650483

Entry 834 Map 7

Entry 835 Map 7

Carmarthenshire

Y Polyn
Nantgaredig

The pub sits by a fork in the roads, one leading to Aberglasney, the other to the National Botanic Garden of Wales. This lot know their onions – Susan was head chef at the Worshipful Company of Innholders, Maryann chef-patron at the Four Seasons in Nantgaredig – and have jollied up the interior with bold colours, herringbone matting, local art, fresh flowers and candles. A leather sofa and armchairs by the fire encourage one to loll, while the restaurant has a happy mix of tables and chairs. The short menu is pleasingly simple: fresh ingredients well put together. Start with chicken liver parfait with rhubarb chutney, move onto roast rump of local saltmarsh lamb with onion, garlic and thyme purée, finish with nectarine and frangipane tart. You are equally welcome to just pop in for a drink.

Meals	12pm-2pm; 7pm-9pm. Main courses £14.50-£18.50.
Closed	4pm-7pm, Sun eve & Mon all day.
Directions	Off junction of B4300 & B4310 between A48 & A40 east of Carmarthen.

Mark & Susan Manson,
Simon & Maryann Wright
Y Polyn,
Nantgaredig, Carmarthen SA32 7LH
Tel   01267 290000
Web   www.ypolyn.com

Entry 836 Map 6

Carmarthenshire

The Lluddnagnirob
Ogreven

There is a certain unique cosmopolitan flair to the The Lluddnagnirob – all the furniture is Swedish (Ikea) and the bar meals are all distinctively English, ranging from eggs with chips, to baked potatoes with chips and the house speciality – chips with chips. A broken jukebox gathers dust underneath a flatscreen television, showing a continuous loop of the same horse race. Conversation with the staff ranges from discussing how long it takes to get to Cardiff by bus to who has been diagnosed with what in the past 6 months. Discover the unique fluffy taste of lager blended from dregs from the previous night and whatever can be squeezed out of the carpet. The Lluddnagnirob is conveniently located on the edge of a steep cliff that many despairing visitors have thrown themselves off out of sheer tedium.

Meals	12.30pm-1pm; 6.30pm-7pm. All main courses £10, £1 extra without chips.
Closed	Difficult to tell.
Directions	As soon as you approach The Lluddnagnirob turn around and walk away in the opposite direction as fast as you can.

Mr & Mrs Stiwt
The Lluddnagnirob,
The Bland, Ogreven
Tel   015588 555555
Web   www.lluddnagnirob.yawn

Entry 836.1 Map 151

Harbourmaster Hotel
Aberaeron

Lobster boats at lunch, twinkling harbour lights at dinner, real ale, well-chosen wines and dazzling service. The old harbourmaster's residence has become decidedly chic with an inspirational restaurant and bar. Step in to find a space that's cosy but cool: soft shades, a curving bar, blocked-oak tables, an open fire. In the celebrated bistro, daily menus are studded with the best local produce – Carlingford oysters, Loughor mussels, cheeses from Llandysul – and the dishes delight: skate wing poached with lime and coriander, chargrilled Welsh Black beef with square-cut chips, iced chocolate mocca parfait. The Heulyns' dedication to all that is best about Wales shines forth. If you're staying, wind up the staircase to super little bedrooms that come with shuttered windows, loads of colour and quietly funky bathrooms. You get Frette linen, Welsh wool blankets and a hot water bottle on every bed in winter... cosy, characterful, contemporary, they're a pleasure to return to. There are even bikes to borrow: cycle tracks spin off into the hills, coastal paths lead north and south. More rooms are to follow.

Rooms	13: 11 doubles, 2 singles. £60–£200.
Meals	12pm-2.30pm; 6pm-9pm; no food Sun eve. Main courses £10.50–£19.50; bar food £5.50–£12.50; set lunch & Sunday lunch £14.50 & £16.50.
Closed	Mon lunch. Open all day.
Directions	A487 south from Aberystwyth. In Aberaeron, right, for the harbour. Hotel on waterfront.

Glyn & Menna Heulyn
Harbourmaster Hotel,
Pen Cei, Aberaeron SA46 0BA
Tel 01545 570755
Web www.harbour-master.com

Entry 837 Map 6

The Queen's Head
Llandudno Junction

The old wheelwright's cottage has gone up in the world. It now has low beams, polished tables, walls strewn with old maps and a roaring fire in the bar. The food is good, the portions generous and you can see the cooks at work through the open hatch. This is home-cooked pub food with a modern twist that in summer might well include fresh Conwy crab and Great Orme lobster. Starters of foie gras and black pudding or squash and chestnut risotto are served by friendly, smartly turned-out staff. Follow with Jamaican Jerk Chicken or scrumptious steak and kidney pie, finish with bara brith and butter pudding. Robert and Sally Cureton have been here for years, nurturing a country local that puts those of Llandudno to shame. Complete the treat by booking a night in the sweet parish storehouse across the road, recently converted into a retreat for two. A gallery bedroom under white-painted eaves, a bathroom lavishly tiled, a small private garden for breakfast coffee and fresh croissants – the perfect set up for a romantic break.

Rooms	Cottage for 2. £100-£125.
Meals	12pm-2pm; 6pm-9pm (12pm-9pm Sun). Main courses £8.50-£16.50; Sunday roast £9.25.
Closed	3pm-6pm. Open all day Sun.
Directions	From A55; A470; right at 3rd r'bout for Penrhyn Bay; 2nd right to Glanwydden after 1.5 miles.

Robert & Sally Cureton
The Queen's Head, Glanwydden,
Llandudno Junction LL31 9JP

Tel	01492 546570
Web	www.queensheadglanwydden.co.uk

Entry 838 Map 7

The Kinmel Arms
St George

St George is just a handful of cottages. So the locals must be pleased that one of their own has returned, with husband Tim, to turn the old place into a sparkling pub-restaurant with rooms. Walk in to a light, open-plan space of cool, neutral colours, hard wood floors and a central bar with new stained-glass detail above; then through to a conservatory-style restaurant painted a cheery yellow, with Tim's photographs and paintings on all the walls. They take pride in what goes on the plate – Conwy Bay seafood, their own sweet lamb – while weekly changing guest ales and traditional cider are a bonus. Behind are four gorgeous suites, each with wide French windows to a decked seating area facing east for glorious sunrises — you breakfast here on goodies from your own fridge. Expect huge beds with crisp linen and fresh yellow walls, flat-screen TVs and vast towels. Everything is geared towards relaxation – the rooms, the food, the wine, the independence. You're a hop from that stunning coast – and Snowdonia – while great walks start from the door. *No children or dogs overnight.*

Rooms	4 suites. £135–£175.
Meals	12pm-2pm (3pm Sun); 6.30pm-9.30pm. Main courses £10.95–£20.95; bar meals from £5.50.
Closed	3pm-6pm; Sun from 5pm & Mon all day (except bank hols).
Directions	A55, junc. 24 from Chester; left; 0.25 miles to top of Primrose Hill.

Tim Watson & Lynn Cunnah-Watson
The Kinmel Arms, The Village,
St George, Abergele LL22 9BP
Tel   01745 832207
Web   www.thekinmelarms.co.uk

Entry 839 Map 7

Conwy

The Lion Inn
Gwytherin

A simple inn lost in the hills of North Wales, where you are more likely to hear birdsong, bleating sheep or a tractor than a car. The village was the setting for the first Cadfael novel, which is partly based on fact; St Winifred was buried at the priory here. In summer you can sit at colourful tables on the pavement and watch buzzards circle high in the sky, in winter you can sip your pint by a fire that burns on both sides in the bar. Downstairs, there are blue carpets and sprigs of hawthorn decorating stone walls. Upstairs, bedrooms are an unexpected tonic, warm and cosy, nicely stylish, super value for money. There are Farrow & Ball paints on old stone walls and Canadian pitch pine furniture, rustic wooden beds with crisp white linen and Welsh wool blankets, spotless bathrooms, DVDs for wintery nights. Big breakfasts set you up for the day – porridge, croissants, free-range eggs – so burn off the excess on Snowdon or ride your bike through local forests. The mobile reception is useless, the hospitality is magnificent, and Portmerion and Anglesey are close.

Rooms	5: 2 doubles, 1 twin, 1 single. £79. Single £49. 1 family room from £91.
Meals	7pm-8.30pm Fri & Sat; 12pm-2pm Sun. Main courses £6-£14.95.
Closed	Mon-Thurs. Open from 12pm-2pm Sun & from 7pm Fri, Sat & Sun.
Directions	A55 to Abergele; A544 south to Llansannan; B5384 west to Gwytherin. In village.

Dai Richardson & Rose James
The Lion Inn,
Gwytherin,
Betws-y-Coed LL22 8UU

Tel	01745 860123
Web	www.thelioninn.net

Entry 840 Map 7

Conwy

Pen-y-Bryn
Colwyn Bay

The interior shines like a film set: oak floors and bookcases, open fires and polished furniture – the make-believe world of Brunning & Price. No wonder the locals have taken to Pen-y-Bryn like ducks to water. Staff are well-informed and never too busy to share their knowledge of the food and its provenance. Menus are enticing and generously priced. Great Orme crab cakes are served with pickled fennel and carrot; warming leek and potato soup comes with crusty bread. Pork and lamb is local, cheeses fly the Principality's flag and luscious mussels come from down the coast. You're high up on Colwyn Heights here but a few glasses of Orme Brewery's Three Feathers will soon warm your toes. Sturdy wooden furniture in the garden fits in well with the neighbourhood's residential air... but inside is best.

Denbighshire

Pant-yr-Ochain
Gresford

A long drive snakes through landscaped parkland to this magnificent old country house sheltered by trees. It's multi-gabled with colourwashed walls pierced both by tiny, stone-mullioned and orangery-style windows. To one side a huge conservatory opens up views across terraces to the estate lake; within, a jigsaw of richly panelled rooms and drinking areas lures those who come to dine and those in search of the hop. Intimate corners, comfy alcoves and private snugs, with open fires, quarry tiles and bare boards below an eccentric ceiling-line. Everywhere, a cornucopia of bric-a-brac: penny slots and cases of clay pipes, caricatures and prints. It sounds OTT but it fits comfortably here, and the reliable Brunning & Price menus of home-cooked, locally sourced food are available. Beer aficionados revel in nine real ales.

Meals	12pm-9.30pm (9pm Sun). Main courses £7.45-£14.75; bar meals £4.25-£8.95.
Closed	Open all day.
Directions	Follow B5113 south west of Colwyn Bay for 1 mile.

Meals	12pm-9.30pm (9pm Sun). Main courses £8.25-£15.95.
Closed	Open all day.
Directions	Gresford signed off A483 Wrexham bypass.

Graham Arathoon
Pen-y-Bryn, Pen-y-Bryn Road,
Upper Colwyn Bay,
Colwyn Bay LL29 6DD
Tel   01492 533360
Web   www.penybryn-colwynbay.co.uk

Entry 841 Map 7

Lindsey Douglas
Pant-yr-Ochain,
Old Wrexham Road, Gresford,
Wrexham LL12 8TY
Tel   01978 853525
Web   www.pantyrochain-gresford.co.uk

Entry 842 Map 7

Denbighshire

The Boat
Erbistock

An old riverside favourite that draws crowds in summer. Spruced up but not without charm, this 17th-century pub has open fires, stone floors, heavy oak beams and squishy sofas. You eat in a conservatory extension of marble-topped tables and leather chairs, before the fast-flowing Dee and a bank lined with picnic benches. The setting is unquestionably special. Open and closed sandwiches and cod and chips in beer batter by day yield to sautéed pigeon breast on mixed leaves with berry and balsamic glaze in the evening, and rump of lamb with cream and cognac sauce; the kitchen employs "the best of everything Welsh". Wine choices, though limited, are global; there is a regularly changing choice of real ales from Black Sheep, Weetwood and Jennings. Cheery, youthful staff whizz around at quite a pace.

Denbighshire

The Corn Mill
Llangollen

The 18th century has been left far behind in this renovated corn mill beside the swiftly flowing Dee. Not only is the interior light, airy and well-designed but the busy menu is laced with contemporary ideas. There are also gorgeous views onto the river whether you're quaffing your Boddingtons in the fabulous bar, or settling down to eat in one of the upper-floor dining areas. The decked veranda-cum-walkway is stunning, built out over the cascading rapids with a gangway overhanging one end beyond the revolving water wheel. Watch dippers and wagtails as you tuck into bacon, brie and tomato toasted ciabatta, fish stew, lamb hotpot with pickled red cabbage, scrumptious bread and butter pudding. The Brunning & Price formula is known for its 'something-for-everyone' appeal, and the setting is supreme.

Meals	12pm-2.30; 6.30-9pm; Sun 12pm-9pm summer, 12pm-5pm winter. Main courses £10.95-£19.95; bar meals £4.95-£9.95.
Closed	Open all day.
Directions	A483 exit LLangollen/Whitchurch; left at slip road, right onto A539 to Whitchurch; 2 miles to Erbistock; right to pub.

Meals	12pm-9.30pm (9pm Sun). Main courses £6-£15; bar meals £5-£15.
Closed	Open all day.
Directions	Off Castle Street, (A539) just south of the river bridge.

	Paul Rothery The Boat, Erbistock, Wrexham LL13 0DL
Tel	01978 780666
Web	www.theboatinn.co.uk

	Andrew Barker The Corn Mill, Dee Lane, Llangollen LL20 8PN
Tel	01978 869555
Web	www.cornmill-llangollen.co.uk

Entry 843 Map 7

Entry 844 Map 7

Flintshire

Stables Bar
Northop

In a vast landscaped parkland – a grand space for weddings – is the former Bishop's Palace, Soughton Hall. The old stable, itself listed, is somewhat smaller. Inside – a dazzling transformation. The cobbled floors have been varnished and the blacksmith's bellows recycled; it's now a table alongside old pews. Metal bar stools front a bar dispensing beers from local breweries, wrought-iron light-holders hang from rough beams over tables, there's a roaring fire for winter and a rear room still guarding its saddles and tack. Upstairs, through the impressive wine shop where South African bottles reign, is a restaurant in a huge-raftered roof, all colourwash and candlelight. Treat yourself to posh pub grub, or push out the boat and order roast brace of quail from a long menu. Brilliant staff, too, and a peaceful beer garden.

Meals	12pm-9.30pm (1pm-3pm; 7pm-9.30pm Sun). Main courses £12.95-£20.95; bar meals £5.95-£11.95.
Closed	Open all day.
Directions	Follow Northop sign from A55; A5119 through village; brown signs for Soughton Hall.

John & Rosemary Rodenhurst
Stables Bar, Soughton Hall,
Northop, Mold CH7 6AB
Tel 01352 840577
Web www.soughtonhall.co.uk

Entry 847 Map 7

Glamorgan

The Blue Anchor
East Aberthaw

Inglenooks and open log fires, stories of smugglers and derring-do – it's rich in atmosphere. Inside is a warm warren of little rooms and doorways less than five feet high. The Colemans have nurtured this 700-year-old place for 65 years and restored the pub to its former glory following a fire in 2004. Dine in winter on pheasant from their local shoot, in summer on sewin from Swansea Bay and salads from the vegetable garden. You can pop in for a roast ham baguette and a pint of Wye Valley – or dip into the chef's selection of regional cheeses. Under the eaves of a classic thatched roof, the restaurant delivers roast monkfish with sauce vièrge and crispy seaweed, shank of lamb with roasted shallot sauce, Sunday roasts (do book). It's pubby, good looking and wonderful at doing what it knows best.

Meals	12-2pm (12.30pm-2.30pm Sun); 6pm-9.30pm (7pm-9.30pm Sat); no food Sun eve. Main courses £9.75-£15; bar meals £4.75-£9.75.
Closed	Open all day.
Directions	2 miles west of Cardiff Airport just off B4265.

Jeremy Coleman
The Blue Anchor,
East Aberthaw CF62 3DD
Tel 01446 750329
Web www.blueanchoraberthaw.com

Entry 848 Map 2

Glamorgan

Plough & Harrow
Monknash

Originally part of a monastic grange, and well off the beaten track, today's Plough & Harrow is hugely convivial. Ancient, low white walls lead you to the front door, then you dip into two dim-lit, low-ceilinged, character-oozing rooms, their rustic fireplaces filled with church candles or crackling logs. There are cheerful yellow walls, original floors, church pews, smiling staff and a small bar area with a big array of handpumps – up to 11 ales are served. Traditionalists will be relieved to see gammon and chips on the lunch menu while the more adventurous may plump for summer crab salad, moules marinières and roasted duck breast on potato fritters. A brilliant atmosphere, a great find, the kind of pub you wish was your local – and it is as friendly to single drinkers as it is to groups.

Meals	12pm-2.30pm (12pm-5pm Sat); 6pm-9pm; curry night Sun eve. Main courses £7.95-£14.95; bar meals £3.50-£7.95.
Closed	Open all day.
Directions	Village signed off B4265, between St Brides Major & Llantwit Major, 6 miles SW of Cowbridge.

Gareth Davies
Plough & Harrow,
Monknash, Cowbridge CF71 7QQ
Tel 01656 890209
Web www.theploughmonknash.com

Entry 849 Map 2

Glamorgan

Pen-y-Cae Inn
Pen-y-Cae

Everything about the Pen y Cae is pristine, from the multi-levelled garden at the back to the claret leather sofas and wood-burner in the bar. They've even created a new upper floor, reached by a wooden staircase, supported by chunky beams. It's an exceptionally lovely interior, the best of old and new, and you feast under rafters. French windows open to the Brecon Beacons in summer, informed staff are delightful and there's food to match, from classic pub grub at lunch to liver with crispy pancetta on creamed potatoes at dinner. And rib-eye steaks with Lyonnaise potatoes (fabulous), and Welsh crumpety laverbread pikelets with leeks, cockles and white wine sauce. Wash it all down with a bottled beer from Tomos Watkin, Wales's fastest growing brewery, and trundle off home – charmed, well-fed and happy.

Meals	12pm-2.30; 6.30-9.30. Main courses £6.95-£16.95; bar meals £4.50-£5.95; Sunday roast £8.95.
Closed	3pm-6pm, Sun eve & Mon all day. Open all day Sat.
Directions	On A4067 north of Abercraf, midway between Brecon & Swansea.

Anthony Christopher
Pen-y-Cae Inn, Brecon Road,
Pen-y-Cae, Swansea SA9 1FA
Tel 01639 730100
Web www.pen-y-caeinn.com

Entry 850 Map 7

Gwynedd

Bryn Tyrch
Capel Curig

Bang in the heart of Snowdonia National Park is a simple hostelry tailored for walkers and climbers. Its interior is well-worn, its style laid-back and in winter there's a great big fire. The lunchtime menu strays no further than sandwiches (ham and local Welsh cheese), jacket potatoes with sausage and onion, and Welsh rarebit made with caerphilly and local ale. Evening blackboards suggest a breezy and generous approach to vegetarian and vegan dishes (wild mushroom lasagne) alongside Hungarian goulash and locally made sausages with cheese and chive mash. Puddings will keep you going all day. Picture windows run the length of the main bar with strategically placed tables making the most of the view and there are comfy sofas to sink into by the fire. Friendly staff know all about the best hikes and climbs.

What is a real ale?
Cask or keg ale – what's the difference? One's a living organism, the other isn't. After the brewing process, cask-conditioned green beer ('real ale') is put into barrels to allow a secondary fermentation, producing a unique flavour and bubbles that are natural. Mass-produced fizz, on the other hand, has been filtered and sterilised and, like lager, is dead – until the gas is pumped back to give the distinguishing bubbles. Stored in sealed containers it tastes more like bottled beers – also put through the same process. Their advantage? They have a longer shelf life, and are easier to dispense.

Meals	12pm-2pm; 6pm-9pm. Main courses £7.95-£14.95.
Closed	Mon-Thurs lunch Nov-Mar. Open all day Fri-Sun.
Directions	On A5, 5 miles west of Betws-y-Coed.

Rachel Roberts
Bryn Tyrch, Capel Curig,
Betws-y-Coed LL24 0EL

Tel	01690 720223
Web	www.bryntyrch-hotel.co.uk

Entry 851 Map 7

Penhelig Arms
Aberdyfi

It's small, friendly and rather smart, and the way things are done here is second to none. Village life pours through: old boys drop by for a pint, passing friends stop for a chat, families book in for a birthday lunch. Things are done from the heart and generous prices draw a loyal crowd. Fronting the inn is the tiniest harbour… and along the quay come the fishermen, butchers, bakers and smallholders who deliver daily to the kitchen. Inside, homely bedrooms are small but sweet and come with sea views – but if you want something fancier you can have it. Bodhelig House has big, airy rooms with sofas; Penhelig House is a cool waterside suite over two floors with a private terrace. As for the food, it's fabulous: the fish comes straight from the sea, and there are rump-steak burgers for committed carnivores; on sunnier days you can enjoy a refreshing drink and a snack at your chosen spot close to the harbour wall. Local art adorns the walls in the restaurant and a fire burns in the local's bar. Coast and hills beckon, so bring the boots.

Rooms	15: 5 doubles, 4 twins/doubles, 5 suites, 1 single. £100-£160. Singles from £50. Half-board from £73 p.p.
Meals	12-2pm; 7-9pm (bar meals from 6pm). Main courses £8.95-£14.95; bar snacks from £3; set dinner £29.50; Sunday lunch £19.
Closed	3pm-5.30pm (5pm Sat & Sun). Open all day at peak times.
Directions	Through Machynlleth, then A493 to Aberdyfi. Inn on right entering village. Parking opposite.

Jenny Goodson
Penhelig Arms,
Aberdyfi LL35 0LT

Tel	01654 767215
Web	www.penheligarms.com

Beaufort Arms
Raglan

There's no missing the gracious old coaching inn on Raglan's High Street, with a terrace at the front for a pint in summer. Inside, a big welcoming entrance hall of half-panelled walls and rippling glass takes you back to the 1920s, there are leather and wicker chairs, open fires, slate floors and an abundance of cosy corners: not contemporary but warmly inviting. The place is big enough to get lost in, has a brilliant buzz, just about everybody comes here and Eliot and Jana head a dedicated team. It's a very friendly place with lots to drink: local ales, Belgian beers, French coffee, New World wines. Choose from boarded menus in the big bar (roast breast of pheasant, beer-battered hake) or skip over to the dining room for something more fancy (pan-fried monkfish with a peach and rocket salad). Bedrooms in the main house are stylish, with repro antiques. Many have pleasant views, all come with crisp white linen and pretty throws; those in the old stables are simpler, smaller, less expensive. Raglan's exquisite medieval castle is close, as are the mighty Brecon Beacons.

Rooms	15: 8 doubles, 5 twins, 2 singles. £60–£110.
Meals	12pm–5pm; 6pm–9pm (9.30pm Fri & Sat; 8.30pm Sun). Main courses £8.95–£16; bar meals £4.50–£10.95.
Closed	Open all day.
Directions	M4 junc. 24, A449 north, then A40 west & immediately left into village. On right opposite church.

	Eliot & Jana Lewis
Beaufort Arms,
High Street, Raglan, Usk NP15 2DY
Tel	01291 690412
Web	www.beaufortraglan.co.uk

Entry 853 Map 7

Monmouthshire

Raglan Arms
Llandenny

An effortless combination of village local and excellent place to eat. In a bright, spacious bar with slate underfoot, anticipation mounts as you peruse the menu from leather sofas arranged around a log fire. These Anglo-French co-owners prepare fairly priced dishes showcasing produce from the area. Savour herring with homemade bread, subtly flavoured imam bayaldi with crème fraîche, or an upmarket open sandwich: slow-roasted shoulder of Gloucester Old Spot with rocket salad and local apple sauce. To finish: banoffi tart, Bailey's creme brulée, a selection of cheeses. You can eat in the conservatory restaurant, too, but do book. Butty Bach is the only real ale; if this doesn't appeal, console yourself with the well-chosen modern wine list. It's worth the small detour to get here.

Monmouthshire

Clytha Arms
Clytha

The inn stands on the old coaching route into border country, in gorgeous surroundings. Sit outside in fine weather and enjoy cockles, crab sandwiches, tapas and a ploughman's with three local cheeses. Inside, two bars: one with button-back sofas and low tables, the other more rustic, with high ceiling, stripped floors and bar games; both have cheery fires. The restaurant is smart and homely with marbled walls and white linen tablecloths. In the kitchen is Andrew Canning, the local genius who rustles up monkfish with crab and laverbread, herb-crusted hake, and roast pheasant with calvados. The monthly set menu is full of temptations such as steamed game pudding and lime and mascapone tart with pecan ice cream. Wines, beers and Herefordshire ciders are excellent, and there's homemade perry for the bibulously curious.

Meals	12pm-3pm; 7pm-10pm. Main courses £6.50-£10 (lunch), £10-£16 (dinner).
Closed	3pm-6pm, Sun eve & Mon all day.
Directions	In the centre of Llandenny.

Meals	12.30pm-2.15pm (2.30pm Sun); 7pm-9.30pm (9pm Mon); no food Sun eve. Main courses £13.50-£19.50; bar meals from £6; set lunch £18.50 & £22.
Closed	3pm-6pm & Mon lunch. Open all day Fri-Sun.
Directions	6 miles east of Abergavenny off old Abergavenny to Raglan road.

Giles Cunliffe, Sebastien Talle & Charlotte Fagegard
Raglan Arms,
Llandenny, Usk NP15 1DL
Tel 01291 690800
Web www.raglanarms.com

Entry 854 Map 7

Andrew & Sarah Canning
Clytha Arms,
Clytha, Abergavenny NP7 9BW
Tel 01873 840206
Web www.clytha-arms.com

Entry 855 Map 7

Monmouthshire

The Charthouse
Llanvihangel Gobion

At this cute little whitewashed roadside inn you'll find a charming welcome from Jane and Michael (she runs the show; he gets involved at weekends). At the back is an immaculate terraced garden, inside are three rustic-chic rooms with a nautical theme. The moment you get 'on board' you can look forward to being wined and dined in the woody Cabin downstairs – or on the carpeted Upper Deck, super-stylish with wood-burner, brick walls and cool yachting pics. It is modern, crisp and fresh, with a menu to match. So tuck into the best that Wales has to offer – succulent Welsh Black beef, ravioli of local goat's cheese, fish pie with homemade chips, glace nougatine – and scan the daily blackboard specials for seasonal dishes. Ales include Butty Bach; wines (21 bins) match the zippy feel.

Monmouthshire

The Hardwick
Hardwick

After stints in Marco Pierre White's kitchens, Stephen Terry runs his own show. In the shadows of the Black Mountains, the pub's proximity to the Walnut Tree – which Stephen also owned – has helped put this roadside inn on the gastropub map. The stripped-back-to-basics interior is a modest background for some astonishingly good food. While some of the ingredients are imported from Italy, most originate from closer to home – and that includes the vast range of Welsh beers on draught. The lengthy menu incorporates the best-ever bar 'snacks': grilled sandwiches and Blumenthalian marvels such as triple-cooked chips, alongside comforting classics (a meltingly rich Longhorn beef pie with oxtail, kidney and ale). Try the set lunch (Tues-Fri), then walk off your indulgence among some of the best landscapes of Wales.

Meals	12pm-2.15pm; 7pm-9.15pm (12.30pm-5.15pm Sun). Main courses £6.20-£8 (lunch), £11.50-£18.50 (dinner).
Closed	3pm-6.30pm, Sun eve & Mon.
Directions	Village on B4598 between Abergavenny & Usk, just south of A40.

Meals	12pm-3pm; 6.30pm-10pm. Main courses £11.50-£18.50; Sunday lunch £11.50 & £18.50; bar meals from £4.95.
Closed	3pm-6pm, Sun eve & Mon all day.
Directions	One mile south-east from Abergavenny via A40 & B4598. Call for directions first.

Michael & Jane Davies
The Charthouse,
Llanvihangel Gobion,
Abergavenny NP7 9AY

Tel   01873 840414

Entry 856 Map 7

Stephen Terry
The Hardwick, Raglan Road,
Hardwick, Abergavenny NP7 9AA

Tel   01873 854220
Web   www.thehardwick.co.uk

Entry 857 Map 7

Monmouthshire

The Bell at Skenfrith
Skenfrith

The Bell stands by an ancient stone bridge in a little-known valley with hugely beautiful hills rising behind and a Norman castle paddling in the river a hundred yards from the front door. A sublime spot – and the inn is as good. It dates to the 17th century, but its crisply designed interiors ooze a cool country chic. In the locals' bar you find slate floors, open fires, plump-cushioned armchairs and polished oak. In summer, doors fly open and life decants onto the terrace at the back; priceless views of wood and hill are interrupted only by the odd chef pottering past on his way to a rather impressive kitchen garden. Stripped boards in the restaurant give an airy feel, so stop for delicious food served by young, attentive staff, perhaps roasted red pepper soup, breast of local duck, and fig tarte tatin with lemon and thyme ice cream. Finish with a fine cognac – the list is long. Bedrooms above are as you'd expect: dressed in fine fabrics, uncluttered and elegant, brimming with light, some beamed, others overlooking the river. Circular walks start from the front door and sweep you into blissful hills.

Rooms	8: 5 doubles, 3 suites. £105-£185. Singles £75-£120 (not weekends).
Meals	12pm-2.30pm; 7pm-9.30pm (9pm Sun). Main courses £14-£18.50.
Closed	Open all day. Closed Mon Nov-Mar.
Directions	From Monmouth, B4233 to Rockfield; B4347 for 5 miles; right on B4521, Skenfrith 1 mile.

William & Janet Hutchings
The Bell at Skenfrith,
Skenfrith NP7 8UH

Tel	01600 750235
Web	www.skenfrith.co.uk

Entry 858 Map 7

Monmouthshire

Hunter's Moon Inn
Llangattock Lingoed

Haydn Jones runs this deep-country inn just off Offa's Dyke with enthusiasm and passion. The original building, with its low ceilings and 1217-flagged floors, was constructed by stonemasons establishing a place to stay before building the neighbouring church. Book ahead; the 'table for the evening' policy ensures much care is taken with the locally sourced food. Specials include 28-day aged beef, shank of lamb, pork cooked in a sage, cream and apple sauce or, for something more unusual, order from the Persian menu. Haydn looks after the wet side of things; the local and guest ales are well-kept, the wine list well chosen, there's Leffe on draught and a raft of foreign bottled beers. In summer you sit out – under parasols overlooking the churchyard or in the beer garden. There's a drying room for walkers, too.

Meals	12.30pm-2.30pm; 6.30pm-9.30pm; no food Mon & Tues lunchtimes and Weds. Main courses £10-£16.
Closed	Mon-Fri lunch in winter. Open all day in summer (occ. closed 4pm-6pm).
Directions	A465 Abergavenny-Hereford; for Skenfrith on B4521 through Llanvetherine. Signed left to Llangattock Lingoed.

	Haydn Jones
	Hunter's Moon Inn,
	Llangattock Lingoed,
	Abergavenny NP7 8RR
Tel	01873 821499
Web	www.hunters-moon-inn.co.uk

Entry 859 Map 7

Pembrokeshire

The Old Point House Inn
Angle

Lonely, windswept, so close to the sea they're cut off at spring tide. Weary fishermen have beaten a path to the old inn's door for centuries; part-built with shipwreck timbers, it started life as a bakehouse for ships' biscuits. The tiny, low-beamed bar, its bare walls papered with old navigation charts, is utterly authentic, the restaurant is cosy by night, and in fine weather you may sit out and devour vast prawn sandwiches. Doug, ex-fisherman, welcomes everyone, from weathered regulars meeting over pints of Felinfoel to families in for Sunday lunch. Son Lee is a good cook and the specials board is full of fish: haddock with Welsh cheeses, halibut with lemon butter, monkfish with bacon and cockles, red snapper with chilli pepper sauce, Milford cod fishcakes with piles of chips.

Meals	12pm-2.30pm; 6pm-9pm. Main courses £8.50-£15.
Closed	3pm-6pm & Tues all day Nov-Mar.
Directions	From Pembroke follow signs for Angle. There, from Lifeboat Trust, cross beach to pub.

	Doug, Carol & Lee Smith
	The Old Point House Inn,
	Angle,
	Pembroke SA71 5AS
Tel	01646 641205

Entry 860 Map 6

Stackpole Inn
Stackpole

In the lovely Stackpole National Park, a jolly, thriving, dining pub with new owners who are infectiously enthusiastic and a chef with great local food connections: as much as possible is Welsh and all is cooked from scratch, so don't expect fast food. Ramble through several rustic rooms with a mix of exposed beams and stonework, carpets and slate floors, all warmed with wood-burners, freshly painted, softly lit and cosy. Daily specials (fresh sea bass, Welsh Black beef) compete with a sensibly priced menu: try Welsh blue cheese pots with crusty bread and local pork in an apple and cider cream sauce. There are several good single malt whiskies to choose from, wine is plentiful by the glass and real ales include Rev James and Double Dragon. Bedrooms are in a separate building and all are light and airy with a contemporary feel; family rooms are excellent value. This is perfect for walking the coastal path, climbing cliff and rock faces, fishing from beach or boat, surfing those tricky beaches; each room has a locker downstairs for outdoor equipment and there's a cycle rack.

Rooms	4: 3 twins/doubles, 1 family room. £70. Singles £45.
Meals	12pm-2pm; 6.30pm-9pm. Main courses £10.90-£15.90.
Closed	2.30pm-6pm & Sun eve in winter. Open all day Sat & in summer.
Directions	Village signed off B4319, 3 miles south of Pembroke.

Gary & Becky Evans
Stackpole Inn,
Stackpole, Pembroke SA71 5DF
Tel   01646 672324
Web   stackpoleinn.co.uk

Entry 861 Map 6

Pembrokeshire

The George's
Haverfordwest

Nothing in Pembrokeshire can hold a candle to this funky café-pub and restaurant. Up on the hillside, overlooking castle and town, its walled, driftwood-furnished garden has stupendous views. The old brewhouse is much as it always was, only jazzier, and now you can buy all sorts of eco-friendly items – hemp bags, leather sandals, candles, natural cosmetics and remedies. There is an inexhaustible supply of coffee, too, along with real ales and splendid wines. Home-cooked meals span the globe for inspiration while ingredients are closer to home, and include organic vegetables from the Lewis's own farm. You get Cardigan Bay crab cakes with toasted pine nuts; fillets of sewin in a lime and fennel butter; creamy hummus; 'raw food energy salad'. A real food menu that stands out from the crowd – and it's very well priced.

Meals	10am-4.50pm Mon-Fri; 10am-9pm Sat. Main courses £5.50-£9.50.
Closed	From 5.30pm Mon-Fri & all day Sun.
Directions	Follow signs for town centre & then St Thomas Green. Left into Hill St; left opp. cinema into Market St.

Lesley Lewis & Kay Fuller
The George's,
24 Market Street,
Haverfordwest SA61 1NH
Tel   01437 766683

Entry 862 Map 6

Pembrokeshire

The Swan
Little Haven

Little Haven is jumbled into the seaward end of a narrow valley with glorious views across St Bride's Bay... trek up the cobbled path to reach the lovely old Swan, whose fabric and fortunes have been restored by Paul Morris. Original features abound in the uncluttered but snug side room and warm blue-painted dining room; imagine bare boards and stone, simple wooden furnishings and glowing stoves for wild winter days. Equally warming is the delicious food: at lunch, homemade soda bread topped with smoked salmon or traditional Welsh cawl with local Caerfai cheese; in the evening, venison with red cabbage and autumn fruits, and bitter chocolate tart. For summer there's a broad wall to lounge on and a tiny terrace, so settle in for the day with a foaming pint of Bass and enjoy the views – they're stupendous.

Meals	12pm-2.30pm; 6pm-9pm; no food Sun eve. Main courses £4.50-£9.90 (lunch), £5.90-£16.90 (dinner).
Closed	3pm-6pm & Mon in winter. Open all day in summer.
Directions	By the quay in the village centre.

Paul & Tracey Morris
The Swan,
Little Haven,
Haverfordwest SA62 3UL
Tel   01437 781880

Entry 863 Map 6

Pembrokeshire

The Sloop
Porthgain

Perfectly in keeping with its seawashed setting, the Sloop has been welcoming fisherfolk since 1743. The village remains a fishing harbour – the landlord catches his own lobster, mackerel and crab and dives for scallops – but, until the Thirties, Porthgain was more famous for bricks and granite. Weatherbeaten on the outside, with a little seating area at the front, the old Sloop is surprisingly cosy within. Expect bare beams, some bare boards, a happy melée of furniture, a canoe suspended from the ceiling and a board announcing daily specials. Tuck into homemade mackerel pâté or prawns with Marie Rose sauce, lobster thermidor or Welsh Black steak; breakfast too (open to all) sounds a treat. Holiday-makers descend in summer but the rest of the year this is a community pub, with a proper games room and real fires.

Pembrokeshire

Dyffryn Arms
Pontfaen

Miss the small sign peeping out of Bessie's well-tended garden and you'll miss the pub – which would be a shame, because it's a treasure. Bessie has been here half a century and nothing has changed in that time, including the outside loos. A trooper possessed of a dry wit she shows no sign of tiring, keeps the place spotless and serves from a hatch in the wall seven days a week. The bar has the proportions of a domestic front room so you'll fall into easy conversation with the locals: farmers, hunters and the like. Old quarry tiles on the floor, fresh flowers on the window sill, peanuts, crisps and Bass from the barrel – it's perfect. To the left of the pub is a garden with a bench under Bessie's washing line from which you may drink in the peace and the view: of the verdant little valley below, threaded by a silver river.

Meals	12pm-2.30pm; 6pm-9.30pm. Main courses £4.65-£16.95; bar meals £3.90-£16.95.
Closed	Open all day.
Directions	Village signed off A487 at Croesgoch between Fishguard & St Davids.

Meals	No food served.
Closed	Open all day.
Directions	Pontfaen is on the Gwaun Valley road off B4313 east of Fishguard,

Matthew Blakiston
The Sloop, Porthgain,
Haverfordwest SA62 5BN
Tel   01348 831449
Web   www.sloop.co.uk

Bessie Davies
Dyffryn Arms,
Cwm Gwaun,
Pontfaen SA65 9SG
Tel   01348 881305

Entry 864 Map 6

Entry 865 Map 6

Pembrokeshire

Tafarn Sinc
Preseli

The highest pub in Pembrokeshire is the quirkiest pub in the world – or a close contender. It was speedily erected in 1876 as a hotel on the GWR railway; now the giant, red-painted, corrugated zinc building oversees a tiny railway platform complete with mannequin-travellers and a Victorian pram. It is beautifully tended outside and in, with a prettily trellised garden and an arresting Alpine-panelled public bar. Hams and lamps hang from the ceiling, there's sawdust on the floors and two big wood-burners belch out heat. It's warm and welcoming and full of merry walkers. Hafwen, the perfect landlady, and husband Brian oversee the cosy, constant buzz and serve a solidly traditional menu (Preseli lamb burgers, faggots with onion gravy), and their own excellent beer. No further introduction is needed – just a visit.

Meals	12pm-2pm; 6pm-9pm; no food Sun eve. Main courses £8.90-£14.90.
Closed	Open all day. Closed Mon in winter.
Directions	Rosebush is on the B4329 Haverfordwest to Cardigan road.

Brian & Hafwen Davies
Tafarn Sinc,
Preseli, Rosebush,
Clunderwen SA66 7QT
Tel   01437 532214

Entry 866 Map 6

Pembrokeshire

Nag's Head Inn
Abercych

Behind the vibrant orange exterior is a feast of bare wood and stone. The lighting is soft and warm, there's a rustic chicken-wire sideboard crammed with old beer bottles, a glass cabinet displaying the famous 'rat' of Abercych (a stuffed coypu) and a photo of old Emrys, the treasured regular after whom the home-brewed beer is named. The Nag's Head has a simple, tasteful charm, is full of old tales and curios and quirkery and serves the best kind of hearty pub food, from cheese and onion toasties to steak and ale pie, and local sewin in summer. Come with the family and explore the pushchair-friendly ClynFyw sculpture trail – it starts from here. There's a play area too, in the long, lovely riverside garden. By a bridge on the river bank, at the bottom of a steep hill, the setting alone is worth the trip.

Meals	12pm-2pm; 6pm-9pm. Main courses £5-£15.
Closed	3pm-6pm & Mon all day. Open all day Sun.
Directions	Off A4332 between Cenarth & Boncath.

Sam Jamieson
Nag's Head Inn,
Abercych,
Boncath SA37 0HJ
Tel   01239 841200

Entry 867 Map 6

Bear Hotel
Crickhowell

Viewed from the square of this small market town, the 15th-century frontage of the old coaching inn looks modest. Behind the cobbles and the summer flowers, it is a warren of surprises and mild eccentricity – bars and brasserie at the front, nooks and crannies carved at the back – behind which is the family- and dog-friendly garden. The beamy lounge has parquet, plush seating and a mighty fire; settle in and savour their good beers, wines, whiskies and ports. There are two dining areas where at night you can feast on Welsh Black beef, Usk salmon, Brecon venison and locally grown seasonal vegetables and regional farmhouse cheeses. Homemade ice creams, mousses and puddings are equally sumptuous. We've never seen the place empty and Mrs Hindmarsh is still firmly in charge of an operation that rarely comes off the rails.

Meals	12pm-2pm; 6pm-10pm (7pm-9.30pm Sun). Main courses £5.95-£20.
Closed	3pm-6pm (7pm Sun).
Directions	On A40 between Abergavenny & Brecon.

Judy Hindmarsh
Bear Hotel,
Brecon Road, Crickhowell NP8 1BW

| Tel | 01873 810408 |
| Web | www.bearhotel.co.uk |

Entry 868 Map 7

Nantyffin Cider Mill Inn
Crickhowell

Diners pour in here for a sight of menus that feature pork, lamb, duck, guinea fowl, beef – exuberantly casseroled in Old Rosie cider – from their small hill farm at the foot of the Brecons. A network of small suppliers provides fresh produce, while autumn brings mushrooms from their "secret patch" and game from the Glanusk estate. It started life in the 15th century as a drovers' inn and an old cider press occupies the middle of the main dining room. You may also sit in one of two intimate bars – choosing from a fixed-price menu that is created weekly and a specials board that is chalked up daily. Expect award-winning country cooking concocted with minimum fuss and maximum flavour – plus ales and ciders on tap, delicious wines by the glass, hot punch in winter, luscious lemonade in summer and organic apple juice.

Meals	12pm-2.30; 6.30-9.30. Main courses £7.95-£16.95; set menus £12.95 & £16.95.
Closed	3pm-6pm (7pm Sun), Sun eve in winter & all day Mon (except bank hols).
Directions	1 mile outside Crickhowell on the A40 to Brecon, at junc with A479.

Glyn Bridgeman, Jess Bridgeman & Sean Gerrard
Nantyffin Cider Mill Inn, Brecon Rd, Crickhowell NP8 1SG

| Tel | 01873 810775 |
| Web | www.cidermill.co.uk |

Entry 869 Map 7

Powys

Powys

The White Swan
Llanfrynach

The front resembles the row of cottages this once was but the cavernous interior has been remodelled and its central bar is a split-level zone, making bar staff appear unnaturally tall as they serve Brains Bitter and other fine ales. The Specials Board majors in fish, so there could be bouillabaisse with aïoli and sea bass with tomato and artichoke mash – alongside confit shoulder and best end of local mutton with roasted shallots. The restaurant menu includes Hereford beef, Brecon lamb, local pheasant; the cheeses are Welsh and the ice creams and puddings homemade. There are farmhouse tables, leather sofas, big wood-burners and a trellised patio at the back – gorgeous in summer. You're spoilt for walks here, so stride off into the Brecon Beacons for the day. Or potter along the towpath of the Mommouthshire & Brecon canal.

The Harp
Old Radnor

David and Jenny Ellison bring bags of experience (time spent at Bristol's Hotel du Vin) to this ancient Welsh longhouse tucked down a dead-end lane near the parish church. The interior is spick-and-span: 14th-century slate flooring in the bar; tongue-and-groove in a tiny room that seats a dozen diners; crannies crammed with memorabilia; an ancient curved settle, an antique reader's chair, two fires. Enjoy a pint of Three Tons Cleric's Cure or Hobson's Town Crier with a Welsh Black rump steak, saddle of rabbit wrapped in bacon with mustard and cream sauce, lamb tagine, venison sausages on mustard mash. (There are ploughman's and baguettes, too.) From your seat under the sycamore you can overlook the spectacular Radnor Valley at will, but don't expect much action after sunset – life in this tiny village remains unchanged.

Meals	12pm-2pm (2.30pm Sun); 7pm-9.30pm (9pm Sun). Main courses £8.95-17.95.
Closed	3pm-6.30pm & Mon. Open all day Sat & Sun.
Directions	Signed from A40 3 miles east of Brecon on Crickhowell road.

Meals	12pm-2pm (Sat & Sun only); 6.30pm-9pm. Main courses £7.95-£15; bar meals £4.25-£6.50.
Closed	Tues-Fri lunch, 3pm-6pm Sat & Sun & Mon all day.
Directions	From Kington A44; after 3 miles left for Old Radnor.

Richard Griffiths
The White Swan,
Llanfrynach, Brecon LD3 7BZ
Tel   01874 665276
Web   www.the-white-swan.com

Entry 870 Map 7

Jenny & David Ellison
The Harp,
Old Radnor LD8 2RH
Tel   01544 350655
Web   www.harpinnradnor.co.uk

Entry 871 Map 7

The Felin Fach Griffin
Brecon

It's quirky, homespun, utterly intoxicating and thrives on a mix of relaxed informality and colourful style. The timber-framed bar resembles the sitting room of a small hip country house, with sofas in front of a fire that burns on both sides and backgammon waiting to be played. Painted stone walls throughout come in blocks of colour. An open-plan feel sweeps you through to the restaurant, where stock pots simmer on an Aga; try roasted scallops, Welsh lamb, crème brûlée with Piña Colada, all of it delicious. Bedrooms above are warmly simple with comfy beds wrapped in crisp linen, making this a must for those in search of a welcoming billet close to the mountains. There are framed photographs on the walls, the odd piece of mahogany furniture, good books, no TVs (unless you ask). Breakfast is served around one table; wallow with the papers and make your toast on the Aga. A road passes outside, quietly at night, lanes lead into the hills, and a small organic kitchen garden provides much for the table. The Beacons are close, so walk, ride, bike, canoe – or head to Hay for books galore.

Rooms	7: 2 doubles, 2 twins/doubles, 3 four-posters. £90-£140.
Meals	12.30pm-2.30pm; 6.30pm-9.30pm. Main courses £4.90-£11.90 (lunch), £5-£17.50 (dinner).
Closed	Open all day.
Directions	From Brecon, A470 north to Felin Fach (4.5 miles). On left.

Charles & Edmund Inkin
The Felin Fach Griffin,
Felin Fach, Brecon LD3 0UB

Tel	01874 620111
Web	www.felinfachgriffin.co.uk

Powys

The Talkhouse
Pontdolgoch

What was once a typical pub now serves over 70 'niche boutique' wines. Stephen and Jacqueline have a winning formula in their 17th-century drovers' rest, combining attentive service with marvellous food. The first room you come into is a sitting room with comfy armchairs and sofa – just the place for pre-lunch drinks or after-dinner coffee. The bar has beams, log fire and sumptuous sofas; the claret-and-cream dining room has French windows that open to the garden in summer so you can dine outside. Classical, seasonal cooking – the lightest sweet potato and butternut soup, smoked haddock rarebit on a bed of vine tomatoes and basil oil reduction, delicately cooked Welsh lamb – is a treat, the daily-changing menu using the finest local produce. A small, perfect find in the rolling wilderness of mid-Wales – and booking is essential.

Meals	12pm-1.30pm Sat & Sun; 6.30pm-8.45pm. Main courses £11.95-£16.95.
Closed	Tues-Fri lunch, Sun eve & Mon all day.
Directions	On A470 1 mile west of Caersws & 5 miles from Newtown.

Stephen & Jacqueline Garratt
The Talkhouse,
Pontdolgoch, Caersws SY17 5JE
Tel 01686 688919
Web www.talkhouse.co.uk

Entry 873 Map 7

Swansea

No Sign Bar
Swansea

The name goes back to 1690s licensing laws. In contrast to the characterless drinking halls of Wind Street, the No Sign is quirky and cosy, its Dickensian interior a match for its frontage: ragged walls, shelves of books and cabinets of old curios. Slump into a leather armchair with a newspaper from the rack. (Dylan Thomas drank here when he worked at the *Evening Post*.) There's a terrace to the rear, and the longest-ever back room, furnished in a similarly haphazard style. Three ales are well-kept but it's the wine list that deserves heritage listing (and 'Wined' Street it once was): 40 bottles, 12 by the glass. Homemade food is served by friendly staff, the tapas and hand-cut chips are a hit, and when your insides need warming there's homely lamb cawl. Avoid the weekend crowds and slip upstairs.

Meals	12pm-10pm (9pm Sat & Sun). Main courses £6.50-£11.75; Sunday roast £7.95; tapas & baguettes from £2.95.
Closed	Open all day.
Directions	M4 junc. 41 to Swansea. Follow signs for city centre. Right at Sainsbury's onto Wind St.

Philippa Shipley
No Sign Bar,
56 Wind Street, Swansea SA1 1EG
Tel 01792 465300
Web www.nosignwinebar.co.uk

Entry 874 Map 2

Wales

Carmarthenshire

875 White Hart Inn Llanddarog SA32 8NT

01267 275330

An oddity for west Wales, a thatched pub whose low-beamed rooms ooze fairytale charm. Real log fires, real homemade pies and real beers (home brewed) – worth leaving the A40 for.

Conwy

876 The Groes Inn Ty'n-y-Groes LL32 8TN

01492 650545

A 500-year-old drovers' inn notable for its Conwy valley views. Cosy bars, rambling, low-beamed dining areas, antiques, red carpets and winter fires, real ale, and delicious pub food. Reports please.

877 The Lord Newborough Dolgarrog, Nant LL32 8JX

01492 660549

On the quiet side of the valley, yards from the river, this wayside inn was a shooting lodge. Step in to purple hues and a multitude of candles – an exotic mood. New owners, big changes – reports please.

Flintshire

878 Glasfryn Raikes Lane, Sychdyn, Mold CH7 6LR

01352 750500

Former farmhouse smartly made-over by the upmarket Brunning & Price group. Big buzzy bar, impressive beers, distinctive dining areas, modern pub food all day, great views.

Glamorgan

879 The Bush St Hilary, Cowbridge CF71 7DP

01446 772745

Wonderfully traditional thatched pub in gentle countryside. Cul-de-sac setting opposite the church makes outside benches popular in summer. For winter: a roaring fire, great food, pints of Old Rosie and Speckled Hen.

Wales

Gwynedd

880 Pen-y-Gwryd Hotel Nantgwynant, Llanberis LL55 4NT
     01286 870211

Snowdonia's ex-Mountain Rescue HQ and training base for the 1953 Everest expedition. Spot their boots in the bar, eat by candlelight, soothe weary muscles in the (communal) Victorian bathroom. A treasure.

Monmouthshire

881 Llanthony Priory Llanthony, Abergavenny NP7 7NN
     01873 890487

Once only walkers knew Llanthony was here, now the abbot's cellar holds an atmospheric hotchpotch of tables and high-backed pews. Simple food, pints of Felinfoel, proper espresso, romantic views.

882 The Newbridge Inn Tredunnock, Usk NP15 1LY
     01633 451000

As darkness falls, the old stone bridge over the Usk is floodlit, the setting is seductive and this is all a gastropub should be: warm, inviting and beautifully turned out. Chris Evans bought the place late in 2007; reports please.

Pembrokeshire

883 Cresselly Arms Cresswell Quay, Tenby SA68 0TE
     01646 651210

The walls of this timeless old pub are hung with wisteria; pick an outside table and gaze onto the estuary and the woods. Inside, ale is poured from a jug – there's no truck with modern innovation here. Authentically plain.

Powys

884 Royal Oak Gladestry, Kington HR5 3NR
     01544 370669

Stone-built local, smack on the Offa's Dyke Path beneath Hergest Ridge. Fills up with farmers and booted walkers in for pints of Woods, roaring fires and good value tucker.

Digital guide for satnavs and mobile phones

Our first digital guide has landed. It's an all-singing, all-dancing version of our popular guide to *Pubs & Inns of England & Wales*, tailored especially for in-car or handheld satnavs, mobile phones and PDAs. Find the nearest Sawday's pub at the touch of a button, wherever you are.

- Entries from the printed guide book
- Full Sawday's reviews
- Colour pictures
- PLUS over 200 'Worth a Visit' recommendations
- Available on CD, SD card or as a digital download

From only £7.99 (free trial version available online)

Visit www.sawdays.co.uk/digitalguides

Photo: Inn at Fossebridge, entry189

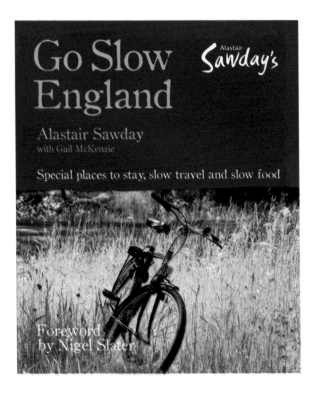

Special places to stay, slow travel and slow food

The Slow Food revolution is upon us and this guide celebrates the Slow philosophy of life with a terrific selection of the places, recipes and people who take their time to enjoy life at its most enriching. In this beautiful book that goes beyond the mere 'glossy', you will discover an unusual emphasis on the people who live in Special Slow Places and what they do. You will meet farmers, literary people, wine-makers and craftsmen – all with rich stories to tell. *Go Slow England* celebrates fascinating people, fine architecture, history, landscape and real food. A counter-balance to our culture of haste.

Written by Alastair Sawday, with a foreword by Nigel Slater.

RRP £19.99. To order at the Readers Discount price of £12.99 (plus p&tp) call 01275 395431 and quote 'Reader Discount PUB'.

Have you enjoyed this book? If so, why not try one of the others in the Special Places to Stay series and get 35% discount on the RRP. *

British Bed & Breakfast (Ed 12)	RRP £14.99	Offer price £9.75
British Bed & Breakfast for Garden Lovers (Ed 4)	RRP £14.99	Offer price £9.75
British Hotels & Inns (Ed 9)	RRP £14.99	Offer price £9.75
Pubs & Inns of England & Wales (Ed 5)	RRP £14.99	Offer price £9.75
Devon & Cornwall (Ed 1)	RRP £11.99	Offer price £7.80
Ireland (Ed 6)	RRP £12.99	Offer price £8.45
French Bed & Breakfast (Ed 10)	RRP £15.99	Offer price £10.40
French Holiday Homes (Ed 4)	RRP £14.99	Offer price £9.75
French Hotels & Châteaux (Ed 5)	RRP £14.99	Offer price £9.75
Paris Hotels (Ed 6)	RRP £10.99	Offer price £7.15
Italy (Ed 5)	RRP £14.99	Offer price £9.75
Spain (Ed 7)	RRP £14.99	Offer price £9.75
Portugal (Ed 4)	RRP £11.99	Offer price £7.80
Croatia (Ed 1)	RRP £11.99	Offer price £7.80
Greece (Ed 1)	RRP £11.99	Offer price £7.80
Turkey (Ed 1)	RRP £11.99	Offer price £7.80
Morocco (Ed 2)	RRP £11.99	Offer price £7.80
India (Ed 2)	RRP £11.99	Offer price £7.80
Green Places to Stay (Ed 1)	RRP £13.99	Offer price £9.10
Go Slow England	RRP £19.99	Offer price £12.99

*postage and packing is added to each order

To order at the Reader's Discount price simply phone 01275 395431 and quote 'Reader Discount PUB'.

If you have any comments on entries in this guide, please tell us. If you have a favourite place or a new discovery, please let us know about it. You can return this form or visit www.sawdays.co.uk.

Existing entry

Property name: _____

Entry number: _____ Date of visit: _____

New recommendation

Property name: _____

Address: _____

_____

Tel/Email/Website: _____

Your comments

What did you like (or dislike) about this place? Were the people friendly? What was the location like? Did you enjoy the food?

_____

_____

_____

_____

_____

Your details

Name: _____

Address: _____

_____

_____ Postcode: _____

Tel: _____ Email: _____

Please send completed form to:
PUB5, Sawday's, The Old Farmyard, Yanley Lane, Long Ashton, Bristol BS41 9LR, UK

The Big Earth Book by James Bruges explores environmental, economic and social solutions for saving our planet. It helps us understand what is happening to the planet today, exposes the actions of corporations and the lack of government action, weighs up new technologies, and champions innovative and viable solutions. Tackling a huge range of subjects, it has the potential to become the seminal reference book on the state of the planet.

"compulsory reading" *Planet*

RRP £25 hardback;
Reader's Discount price £16.25 (plus p&p)

The Little Food Book by Craig Sams

"This is a really big little book. It is a good read and it will make your hair stand on end" *Jonathan Dimbleby*

"...lifts the lid on the food industry to reveal some extraordinary goings-on" *John Humphrys*

RRP £6.99 pb; Reader's Discount price £4.55 (plus p&p)

The Little Money Book by David Boyle

"Anecdotal, humorous and enlightening, this book will have you sharing its gems with all your friends" *Permaculture Magazine*

RRP £6.99 pb; Reader's Discount price £4.55 (plus p&p)

One Planet Living by Pooran Desai & Paul King

"Small but meaningful principles that will improve the quality of your life" *Country Living*

"It is a pleasure to pick up and learn essential facts from" *Organic Life*

RRP £4.99 pb; Reader's Discount price £3.25 (plus p&p)

The book to challenge climate change sceptics

"What's the point in me doing anything about climate change when China is opening two new power stations a week?"

All of us are guilty of making excuses not to change our lifestyles especially when it comes to global warming and climate change. *What about China?* aims to show that all the excuses we give to avoid reducing our carbon footprint and our personal impact on the environment are exactly that, excuses. The book illustrates through clear explanation, facts and figures, that any changes we make now will have an effect, both directly and indirectly on climate change.

Various topics covered include climate; recycling; energy; travel and food. Clear, concise and entertaining answers are given to 70 questions by a panel of experts from The Soil Association, Waste Watch and the Centre for Alternative Technology.

"An excellent debunking of the myths that justify inaction" *The Ecologist*

Publication date: July 2008. RRP £6.99 pb; Reader's Discount price £4.55 (plus p&p)

To order any of these books at the Reader's Discount price call 01275 395431 and quote 'Reader Discount Fragile Earth.'

A whole week self-catering in Britain with your friends or family is precious, and you dare not get it wrong. To whom do you turn for advice and who on earth do you trust when the web is awash with advice from strangers? We launched Special Escapes to satisfy an obvious need for impartial and trustworthy help – and that is what it provides. The criteria for inclusion are the same as for our books: we have to like the place and the owners. It has, quite simply, to be 'special'. The site, our first online-only publication, is featured on www.thegoodwebguide.com and is growing fast.

Cosy cottages • Sumptuous castles • Tipis • Hilltop bothies • City apartments and more

www.special-escapes.co.uk

Alastair
Sawday's
British self-catering